Perceiving Reality

Perceiving Reality

Consciousness, Intentionality, and Cognition in Buddhist Philosophy

Christian Coseru

OXFORD
UNIVERSITY PRESS

OXFORD
UNIVERSITY PRESS

Oxford University Press is a department of the University of Oxford.
It furthers the University's objective of excellence in research, scholarship, and education by publishing worldwide.

Oxford New York
Auckland Cape Town Dar es Salaam Hong Kong Karachi
Kuala Lumpur Madrid Melbourne Mexico City Nairobi
New Delhi Shanghai Taipei Toronto

With offices in
Argentina Austria Brazil Chile Czech Republic France Greece
Guatemala Hungary Italy Japan Poland Portugal Singapore
South Korea Switzerland Thailand Turkey Ukraine Vietnam

Oxford is a registered trademark of Oxford University Press
in the UK and certain other countries.

Published in the United States of America by
Oxford University Press
198 Madison Avenue, New York, NY 10016

First issued as an Oxford University Press paperback, 2015.

Library of Congress Cataloging-in-Publication Data
Coseru, Christian.
Perceiving reality : consciousness, intentionality, and cognition in
Buddhist philosophy / Christian Coseru.
pages cm
Includes bibliographical references and index.
ISBN 978-0-19-984338-1 (hardcover: alk. paper); 978-0-19-025311-0 (paperback: alk. paper)
1. Knowledge, Theory of (Buddhism) 2. Consciousness—Religious aspects—Buddhism.
3. Buddhist philosophy. 4. Phenomenology. I. Title.
BQ4440.C68 2012
121′.340882943—dc23
2011049529

For Sheridan

CONTENTS

Acknowledgments ix
Abbreviations xv

1. Introduction: Taking the Structure of Awareness Seriously 1
2. Naturalizing Buddhist Epistemology 17
    2.1. Doctrine and Argument 18
    2.2. Reason and Conceptual Analysis 22
    2.3. Interpretation and Discourse Analysis 30
    2.4. Logic and the Subjectivity of Thought 40
    2.5. Cognition as Enactive Transformation 43
    2.6. Phenomenological Epistemology and the Project of Naturalism 50
3. Sensation and the Empirical Consciousness 57
    3.1. No-self and the Domains of Experience 58
    3.2. Two Dimensions of Mind: Consciousness as Discernment and Sentience 68
    3.3. Attention and Mental Proliferation 71
    3.4. Cognitive Awareness and Its Object 75
4. Perception, Conception, and Language 86
    4.1. Shared Notions about Perceptual Knowledge 90
    4.2. Debating the Criteria for Reliable Cognition 97
    4.3. Cognitive Aspects and Linguistic Conventions 102
    4.4. Epistemology as Cognitive Event Theory 109
5. An Encyclopedic and Compassionate Setting for Buddhist Epistemology 124
    5.1. Dependent Arising and Compassion 125
    5.2. Mapping the Ontological and Epistemological Domains 135
    5.3. Perception and the Principle of Clarity 139
6. Perception as an Epistemic Modality 141
    6.1. The Conditions for "Perceptual Knowledge" 142
    6.2. Perception, Conception, and the Problem of Naming 154

6.3. Phenomenal Content, Phenomenal Character, and the Problem of Reference 167
6.4. Cognitive Errors and Perceptual Illusions 182
7. Foundationalism and the Phenomenology of Perception 192
7.1. Intrinsic Ascertainment and the "Given" 195
7.2. Particulars and Phenomenal Objects 198
7.3. Foundationalism and Its Malcontents 213
7.4. Naturalism and Its Discontents 222
7.5. Beyond Representation: An Enactive Perception Theory 226
8. Perception, Self-Awareness, and Intentionality 235
8.1. Reflexivity and the Aspectual Nature of Intentional Reference 236
8.2. Phenomenal Objects and the Cognitive Subconscious 250
8.3. The Intentional Structure of Awareness 255
8.4. An Epistemological Conundrum: Explaining the Subject-Object Relation 263
9. In Defense of Epistemological Optimism 274
9.1. A Moving Horizon 276
9.2. Embodied Consciousness: Beyond "Seeing" and "Seeing As" 280
9.3. Epistemic Authority Without Manifest Truth 297

Bibliography 305
Index 345

ACKNOWLEDGMENTS

One incurs a significant amount of debt in writing a book. Many people have provided support and assistance through comments and conversations along the way as I undertook this work, and I am extremely grateful to them all. This book is the fruit of a philosophical journey that spans four continents. In Australia, where this project began a little over a decade ago, I benefited greatly from regular discussions with Dirk Baltzly, Richard Barz, Ben Dorman, Jeremy Evans, Pamela Lyon, Chris Mortensen, Roy Perrett, Graham Priest, McComas Taylor, Sonam Thakchöe, Aat Vervoorn, and Greg Young. Special thanks are due to Royce Wiles for his nimble proofreading, often on very short notice, and for extending his hospitality in a most generous fashion. I am particularly indebted to the outstanding philosophical community at the Australian National University, which provided a richly stimulating environment in which to pursue one's philosophical passions. Special thanks go to Daniel Stoljar and Frank Jackson for patiently indulging my questions and for allowing me to participate in the life of the philosophy program at the Research School of Social Sciences.

In Calcutta, my first teacher and mentor, the late Sibajiban Bhattacharyya, introduced me to the rigors of Indian logic nearly two decades ago and got me thinking about the centuries-old Buddhist-Nyāya debate, which in turn prompted me to consider the foundational role of perception for knowledge, which then motivated me to think about the structure of awareness. The germ of this book lies in an extensive conversation we had during my last visit to his house in the spring of 2001, when he persuaded me that if I wanted to understand why Indian and Buddhist philosophers have spent so much time problematizing consciousness I should look no further than at the character of experience itself. Of the many other Indian scholars and pandits who deserve recognition, special thanks go to Asim Kumar Datta who secured a fellowship for me at the Asiatic Society and thus gave me the freedom to pursue my research interests at leisure; to Pandit Dinesh Shastri Bhattacharyya who, despite old age and ill health, was always very enthusiastic in sharing his encyclopedic knowledge of the *śāstras*; to Rita Gupta for her generous advice when this project was just beginning to take shape; to V. N. Jha for urging me read Bhartṛhari before delving deeper into the texts of the

Buddhist epistemologists; but most of all to Prabal Kumar Sen, a true *kalyāṇa-mitra*, who never tired of reminding me to read Sanskrit philosophical literature in the original whenever possible, and when I expressed my interest in reading the *Pramāṇavārttika*, made sure I did not forget that Dharmakīrti was also a poet.

A generous grant from the Australian National University allowed me to spend six months conducting research at libraries in Cambridge, Paris, Rome, Calcutta and Sarnath. I am especially thankful to Craig Jamieson, curator for the South Asia manuscript collection at the University of Cambridge, who assisted me in locating valuable research materials and, as fellow of Queens' College, introduced me to the many pleasures of High Table dining. In Rome, courtesy of an old friend, Liviu Bordas, I also had the pleasure of a long evening of spirited conversation about Dharmakīrti and, of course, Dante with Raffaele Torella in his attic atop Rocca Priora.

Closer to home, I am also indebted to my colleagues in the philosophy department at the College of Charleston who have nurtured an environment of free and open exchange of ideas, no matter their source, and to the many visiting speakers in our colloquium series who over the last six years have helped me, often inadvertently, to find better ways of explaining what exactly goes on in the name of Buddhist philosophy. Of those many visitors, special thanks go to David Chalmers for his inspiration and prodigious philosophical curiosity, to Phillip Kitcher for reminding me that the best philosophy is never divorced from its history, and to Anne Jacobson for some helpful tips on how to integrate classical and contemporary sources in the philosophy of mind. My determination to complete this book also owes a great deal to Glenn Lesses, whose undoubtedly sage advice (as department chair) against undertaking book-length projects before getting tenure strengthened my foolish resolve to do otherwise.

This book is an outgrowth of my doctoral dissertation, though perhaps scarcely recognizable to those who counseled me on that project. John Powers supervised the dissertation out of which this book developed and has continued to encourage me at a distance in many ways. Our regular and often lengthy conversations proved invaluable in helping me to navigate the arcane world of Buddhological scholarship. Without his unwavering support this project could not have taken shape. Three dissertation examiners served that particular ritual function of providing methodic and insightful criticism: Purushottama Bilimoria read through what is now a very distant cousin of this book, and survived; Georges Dreyfus gave me the benefit of his fine critical eye and masterful expertise, and unwittingly helped me to find a more profitable direction in which to develop my project (he remains a constant source of inspiration); Mark Siderits offered his very thorough and apt comments on many ideas that eventually found their way into this book, all the while continuing to provide one of the best examples of how one may do work in Buddhist philosophy from an analytic philosophy perspective.

Many other members of the academic community have contributed to this project in more ways than I can possibly acknowledge. Richard Hayes, in his characteristically spry and witty style, provided some timely and helpful criticism on material that is now part of chapter 8; Parimal Patil gently nudged me some years ago when this project was languishing; Matthew MacKenzie engaged me in an afternoon of spirited conversation about why everything, but especially consciousness, is illuminated on a glorious (and luminous) spring day in Vancouver during the Pacific APA; Wolfgang Fasching sought to persuade me two years ago, at that wonderful biennial gathering of consciousness researchers in the Sonoran desert, that phenomenological approaches to consciousness are impervious to naturalization; Bill Waldron has over the years pointed me in some helpful directions and has taught me much by his generous correspondence and sharing of ideas; Jonathan Gold invited me to present some material from this book at the Columbia Society for Comparative Philosophy and very graciously agreed to comment. I also thank the members of the audience there, especially Jake Davis, Tao Jiang, and Graham Priest, for many helpful comments.

I am also thankful to Mario D'Amato, Dan Arnold, Stephen Collins, Hubert Dreyfus, John Dunne, M. David Eckel, Vincent Eltschinger, Charles Goodman, the late Wilhelm Halbfass, Pascale Hugon, Birgit Kellner, Dan Lusthaus, Sara McClintock, Eleanor Rosch, Charles Siewert, Evan Thompson, Tom Tillemans, Jan Westerhoff, Paul Williams, and many others too numerous to mention for so generously sharing their work, and for helping to clear the way for this project. Its rather imperfect execution is entirely my fault. Thanks are also due to two anonymous referees from OUP for providing detailed and immensely helpful comments on my manuscript. I also wish to thank Cynthia Read and Lisbeth Redfield at Oxford University Press for their guidance in seeing this book through to the final stages of production, and to Lynn Childress for her very thorough copyediting job. Lisbeth deserves additional thanks for picking the fine art that graces the cover of this book, thus ending an agonizingly long search for an aesthetic representation of that most elusive and seemingly transparent of all activities: perceiving.

There are a few people to whom I owe a special debt of gratitude. Jonardon Ganeri read through what was still an unpolished draft of the entire book and provided many helpful comments and suggestions, all of which prompted significant improvements. The final chapter of the book owes much to his recent work on emergentism. Jay Garfield, who has seen this project take shape over the years, deserves special credit on a number of levels: first, for encouraging me to participate in the Australasian Association of Philosophy annual conferences and to try out my ideas by giving papers; second, for helping to steer this book onto a philosophical course closely aligned with contemporary debates in that discipline; and third, for urging me to pursue its publication when I was most in need of encouragement. Not only did he read the entire manuscript twice and supply copious and thorough comments but also taught me to be skeptical of claims against reason. Both as mentor and as a dear friend, he continues to be a tremendous source of inspiration and to provide one of the best and most influential models for how one may pursue this cross-cultural philosophical conversation. Along with his wonderful wife, Blaine Garson, he has also extended his legendary hospitality on many occasions at their charming retreat in the woods of Amherst.

I must also thank my mother, Veronica, and my sister, Camelia, for their love and trust, but above all for indulging my peripatetic existence for the past two decades, and my wonderful in-laws, Phyllis and Vernon, for their love and unsurpassed generosity.

My deepest thanks go to Sheridan Hough, my colleague, spouse, and fellow philosopher. To have one's best, most critical and most supportive reader as one's life companion is truly an enviable condition. Fortunately for those who know Sheridan (but perhaps unfortunately for her!) she combines her philosophical and literary erudition with an unmatched skill as a proofreader. She has not only helped bring clarity to many parts of this book, but has saved me the embarrassment of countless stylistic imperfections. Many more flaws might have been eliminated had I resisted the urge to craft some of my own idioms. Most of the phenomenological material that made its way into this book stems from our ongoing conversations about the importance, and indeed the inescapability, of Husserl's work for any descriptive account of experience (though I will grant her that of the two, Virginia Woolf is perhaps a better phenomenologist). Scarcely a page in this book has been left untouched by her masterful editorial work and it is to her that I dedicate this volume with all my love.

Lastly, a pat of thanks goes to a dear furry friend, who woke me up at all hours of the night and, when sleep wore away, provided warmth, comfort, and companionship over a period of six months as I completed work on this book. B.B.F.C., our big black and fluffy Maine Coon cat, passed away not long after I got news that Oxford was to accept my manuscript for publication. This book bears the stamp of his discerning paw.

C.C.

Some of the material in this book has been presented at, and appeared in, other venues. An early version of chapter 7 was published as the article "Buddhist 'Foundationalism' and the Phenomenology of Perception," *Philosophy East and West* 59 (4): 409–439. Chapter 8 includes revised material from "Naturalism and Intentionality: A Buddhist Epistemological Approach," *Asian Philosophy* 19 (3): 239–264, and from "Taking the Intentionality of Perception Seriously: Why Phenomenology is Inescapable," *Philosophy East and West* (65 (3)). Chapter 3 includes material that was summarized in "Mind in Indian Buddhist Philosophy," *The Stanford Encyclopedia of Philosophy* (Winter 2009 Edition), edited by Edward N. Zalta. http://plato.stanford.edu/entries/mind-indian-buddhism/. I am grateful to the editor of these publications for permissions to use this material in revised form here. Parts of chapter 4 were presented in a panel entitled "Buddhism Naturalized?" at the XVIth Congress of the International Association of Buddhist Studies in New Taipei City, Taiwan, June 2011. I am grateful to Mark Siderits for organizing that panel and to the audiences there for their helpful comments and suggestions.

ABBREVIATIONS

AK	Abhidharmakośa of Vasubandhu (in Pradhan 1975)
AKBh	Abhidharmakośabhāṣya of Vasubandhu (in Pradhan 1975)
AKVy	Abhidharmakośavyākhyā (Sputhārthā) of Yaśomitra (in Shastri 1970–1973)
AN	Aṅguttara Nikāya attributed to Śākyamuni Buddha (in Morris 1989–1995; Hardy 1979)
AS	Abhidharmasamuccaya of Asaṅga (in Tatia 1976)
ASBh	Abhidharmasamuccayabhāṣya of Asaṅga (in Tatia 1976)
CS	Caraka Saṃhita of Agniveśa (in Sharma and Dash 1976)
D	sDe dge Tibetan Tripiṭaka
DĀ	Dhvanyāloka of Ānandavardhana (in Shastri 1940)
DN	Dīgha Nikāya attributed to Śākyamuni Buddha (in Rhys Davids and Carpenter 1995–2007)
HB	Hetubindu of Dharmakīrti (in Steinkellner 1967)
HBṬ	Hetubinduṭīka of Arcaṭa (in Sanghavi 1949)
KSP	Karmasiddhiprakaraṇa of Vasubandhu (in Lamotte 1936)
L	Locana of Abhinavagupta (in Shastri 1940)
MĀ	Madhyamakāloka of Kamalaśīla (D3887)
MAK	Madhyamakālaṃkārakārikā of Śāntarakṣita (D3884)
MAP	Madhyamakālaṃkārapañjikā of Kamalaśīla (D3886)
MAV	Madhyamakāvatāra of Candrakīrti (in La Vallée Poussin 1970)
MBh	Mahābhāṣya of Patañjali (in Kielhorn 1962–1972)
MMK	Mūlamadhyamakakārikā of Nāgārjuna (in De Jong 1977)
MN	Majjhima Nikāya attributed to Śākyamuni Buddha (in Trenchner 1993; Chalmers 1993–1994)
MS	Mīmāṃsāsūtra of Jaimini (in Frauwallner 1968)
NB	Nyāyabindu of Dharmakīrti (Malvania 1955)
NBṬ[d]	Nyāyabinduṭīkā of Dharmottara (in Malvania 1955)

NBṬⱽ	Nyāyabinduṭīkā of Vinītadeva (in Gangopadhyaya 1971)
NM	Nyāyamukha of Dignāga (in Tucci 1930)
NP	Nyāyapraveśa of Śaṅkarasvāmin (in Tachikawa 1971)
NS	Nyāyasūtra of Akṣapāda Gautama (in Tarānātha, Amarendramohan, and Hemantakumar 1985)
NSBh	Nyāyasūtrabhāṣya of Vātsyāyana (in Tarānātha, Amarendramohan, and Hemantakumar 1985)
NV	Nyāyabhāṣyavārttika of Uddyotakara (in Tarānātha, Amarendramohan, and Hemantakumar 1985)
NVTṬ	Nyāyavārttikatātparyaṭīkā of Uddyotakara (in Tarānātha, Amarendramohan, and Hemantakumar 1985)
PDS	Padārthadharmasaṃgraha of Praśastapāda (in Jetly 1971)
PrasP	Prasannapadā of Candrakīrti (in La Vallée Poussin 1903–1913/1970; May 1959)
PS	Pramāṇasamuccaya of Dignāga (in Steinkellner, Krasser, and Lasic 2005)
PSV	Pramāṇasamuccayavṛtti of Dignāga (in Steinkellner, Krasser, and Lasic 2005)
PSṬ	Pramāṇasamuccayaṭīkā Viśālāmalavatī of Jinendrabuddhi (in Steinkellner, Krasser, and Lasic 2005)
PV	Pramāṇavārttika of Dharmakīrti (Chapter 1 in Gnoli 1960; Chapters 2, 3, 4 in Miyasaka 1971–1972; Tillemans 2000)
PVĀ	Pramāṇavārttikālaṃkāra of Prajñākaragupta (in Sāṅkṛtyāyana 1953)
PVin	Pramāṇaviniścaya of Dharmakīrti (in Vetter 1966; Steinkellner 1973)
PVinṬ	Pramāṇaviniścayaṭīkā of Dharmottara (in Krasser and Steinkellner 1989)
PVSV	Pramāṇavārttikasvavṛtti of Dharmakīrti (in Gnoli 1960)
PVV	Pramāṇavārttikavṛtti of Manorathanandin (in Sāṅkṛtyāyana 1938–1940)
SN	Saṃyutta Nikāya attributed to Śākyamuni Buddha (in Feer 1975–2006)
Sn	Sutta Nipātta attributed to Śākyamuni Buddha (in Andersen and Smith 1990)
SP	Sambandhaparīkṣā of Dharmakīrti (in Frauwallner 1934)
SSV	Sāṃkhyasūtravṛtti of Aniruddha (in Garbe 1888)
ŚV	Ślokavārttika of Kumārila (in Shastri 1978)

TBh	Tarkabhāṣā of Mokṣākaragupta (in Iyengar 1952)
TS	Tattvasaṃgraha of Śāntarakṣita (in Shastri 1968)
TSP	Tattvasaṃgrahapañjikā of Kamalaśīla (in Shastri 1968)
TS/P	TS and TSP referenced together
VB	Vibhaṅga (in Rhys Davids 1904)
ViṃŚ	Viṃśatikā of Vasubandhu (in Lévi 1925)
ViṃŚV	Viṃśatikāvṛtti of Vasubandhu (in Lévi 1925)
VN	Vādanyāya of Dharmakīrti (in Much 1991)
VM	Visuddhimagga of Buddhaghosa (in Shukla 1984)
VP	Vākyapadīya of Bhartṛhari (in Rau 1977)

Perceiving Reality

CHAPTER 1

Introduction: Taking the Structure of Awareness Seriously

If one is impressed by the irreducible uniqueness of mental life, and yet happens to be a naturalist, or even a physicalist, one would want to carve out a niche within the heart of one's naturalism in order to find a place secure enough for the intentional.

(Mohanty 1986: 505)

"The mind," Hume once argued, "can never exert itself in any action, which we may not comprehend under the term of perception."[1] Hume was right, and in that sense he comes very close to a position that Buddhist philosophers have advocated for two and a half millennia: perceptual awareness in its multifaceted forms is the beginning and end of our conscious lives. This book is about the structure of that perceptual awareness, its contents and character, and about what we stand to learn when we realize that the world we inhabit is inseparable from our perception of it.

A distinctive and influential philosophy of perception emerges in the Buddhist tradition from the analyses of consciousness and cognition associated with that system of thought and method of descriptive analysis known as the Abhidharma.[2] With Dignāga and Dharmakīrti, the initiators of a Buddhist school of epistemology, this systematic inquiry into the

1. Hume (2000: 291).

2. Lit. "concerning" (*abhi*) "the teachings" (*dharma*), usually translated as "higher doctrine"—the systematic scholastic analysis of the Buddha's teachings as contained in the eponymous genre of philosophical literature. See Frauwallner (1995) and Willemen, Dessein, and Cox (1998) for detailed discussions of the origins and scope of this literature, which develops over a period of several centuries beginning around 300 B.C.E.

philosophical foundations of empirical knowledge plays a formative role in shaping what would eventually become the dominant approach to Buddhist philosophy of mind at such well-established universities as Nālandā and Vikramaśīla. According to this approach, a philosopher's views on perception are central to his or her epistemological and metaphysical commitments. Thus, questions about what there is and how we come to know it, become questions about the nature of awareness itself, its modes of disclosure, and its contents. And here the Buddhist comes surprisingly close to a position that is widespread among Western phenomenologists: to say about something that it exists is not primarily to make an ontological assertion but to provide a descriptive account of experience. On this view of perception, empirical awareness is intrinsically perspectival: it does not simply manifest a given object, a particular, but it is also in some sense self-manifesting, self-given. To perceive is to occupy a specific vantage point. This dual aspect view of awareness, whose origins may be traced to early Abhidharma accounts of cognition in terms of luminosity (viz., the lamp that makes itself manifest while illuminating others),[3] becomes an axiomatic principle of Buddhist epistemology and a subject of debate between the Buddhists[4] and their principal opponents, the Naiyāyikas ("philosophical logicians") and the Mīmāṃsakas ("hermeneuticians").

The central concern of this book is a range of arguments advanced by two prominent philosophers at the university of Nālandā, Śāntarakṣita and Kamalaśīla,[5] in support of the role that a particular understanding of the structure of awareness must play in settling epistemological disputes. What is significant about these arguments is that they provide a model for integrating the phenomenological and cognitive psychological concerns of Abhidharma traditions within the dialogical-disputational context of Buddhist epistemology. In unpacking the central arguments of Buddhist epistemology I am not simply pursuing a project in the history of philosophy, much less in the history of Buddhist thought alone. Rather, I am committed to the view that both the specific style of these broadly Sanskritic

3. The Mahāsāṃghika ("Great[er] Community") view of self-cognition found in *Mahāvibhāṣā* ("Great Commentary") articulates precisely such an account. See Yao (2005: 15).

4. The "Buddhists" stand here for those who adopt the epistemological concerns of Dignāga and Dharmakīrti. These authors' views on mind and cognition differ significantly from those advanced by Mādhyamika philosophers who follow Candrakīrti's (fl. 640) critique of reflexive awareness (for which, see chapter 8.1). Unless otherwise noted, all unspecified uses of "Buddhist" (or its plural form) refer to the former group.

5. The dates for Śāntarakṣita (c. 725–788) and Kamalaśīla (740–795) are those given by Frauwallner (1961: 141–143), based on textual references and historical records, including their visits to Tibet at the invitation of king Khri srong lde btsan (c. 740–798).

argumentative strategies and the universality of the metaphysical and epistemological theses under dispute are better showcased (and understood) if made continuous with contemporary philosophical concerns. The principal methodological reason for emphasizing *continuity* over *comparison* reflects a specific intuition about the scope of philosophical inquiry: one which says that its problems, though often couched in historically and culturally contingent terms, are nonetheless grounded in all aspects of conscious experience for a person at any given time.[6] To the extent that contemporary philosophical debates—and the theoretical advances and empirical findings that inform them—provide clear accounts of a wider range of conscious experience, they can be profitably used in probing the Buddhist epistemological project such that the implications of its theses (as well as their strengths and limitations) are fully borne out.

A central argument of this book is that epistemological inquiries in India, particularly with regard to examining the sources of reliable cognition, have never displayed the sort of non-naturalism characteristic of the Cartesian and Kantian traditions in Western philosophy. Thus, with the return to naturalism in epistemology and phenomenology, hence to understanding cognition in embodied and causal terms,[7] we are now in a better position to appreciate the contributions of Buddhist philosophers to epistemology.

Let me clarify from the outset that I take naturalism to be a commitment to considering the empirical evidence from the sciences of cognition in settling questions about the acquisition of beliefs. More broadly, naturalism refers to the notion that reality is exhausted by nature, though there is no agreement among contemporary philosophers on exactly what counts as "nature." Indeed, philosophers with weak commitments to naturalism operate with a rather unrestricted notion of nature, whereas stronger adherents to naturalism define it more stringently.[8] Eliminativist positions, which seek to reduce mental content to, say, neurophysiological processes do not, I think, do justice to the phenomenal or qualitative aspects of experience, and provide little or no support for the framework of a phenomenological epistemology. My position on naturalism, which I shall henceforth refer to as *phenomenological naturalism*, closely aligns with the enactive and embodied

6. A similar approach is at work in Ganeri (2012). Note that Ganeri does not label his analysis of the philosophical literature of classical India, which he considers neither comparative nor historical in scope.

7. For one of the earliest accounts of causal theories of knowledge, see Goldman (1967). A causal account of knowledge simply states that a person's belief that *p*, say that it is raining, is true *iff* it is the case that *p* (that is, if it is *actually* raining). For a review of various causal theories of mental content, principally those advanced by Fred Dretske, Jerry Fodor, Ruth Garrett Millikan, David Papineau, Dennis Stampe, and Dan Ryder, see Rupert (2008).

8. See Papineau (2007) for an extensive survey of various positions on naturalism.

approach to cognition: cognitive awareness is to be thought not as an internal state of mind or brain locked into linear causal chains of sensory input and behavioral output. Rather, it is to be understood as a structure of comportment, an intentional orientation and attunement to a world of actions, objects, and meaning.[9] The enactive approach to cognition, as championed by its proponents, is non-reductionist because it relies primarily on dynamic systems theory, whose working premise is that in order to understand complex systems such as sentient beings, we must pay close attention not only to their constitutive elements but also to their organization.[10] As such, it allows for cognition to be understood in causal terms without reducing the contents of awareness to noncognitive elements.

A focus on causal accounts of cognition is shared by all Indian epistemological theories, Buddhist or otherwise. It is with Dharmakīrti, however, that an examination of the underlying processes of cognition becomes instrumental in determining which epistemic practices are conducive to effective action, captured by the well-known theory of the pragmatic efficacy of cognitions. By contrast, modern Western philosophers, beginning with Descartes, argue that justification, specifically the justification of reasons for why certain beliefs ought to be classified as knowledge, is the main focus of epistemic inquiry. What sets the two traditions apart seems to be the fact that, as Jitendranath Mohanty pointed out some time ago, "the distinction, common in Western thought, between the causal question and the question of justification was not made by the Indian theories."[11]

While Mohanty is right about the absence of this distinction in Indian and indeed Buddhist epistemology, this should not necessarily be seen as an unfortunate oversight. Rather, the absence of a distinction between the causal question and the question of justification is indicative of the fact that epistemic inquiry in India is primarily driven by pragmatic rather than normative concerns (that is, by concerns about how we come to believe something rather than why might we be justified in believing it). Indeed, if Indian epistemologies treat as warranted only that cognition which corresponds to its object and

9. I follow Thompson's (2007b: 38–43) account of the relevance of dynamic systems theory in bridging human experience and cognitive science. This conception of enactive and embodied cognition finds its roots in Husserl's notion of the life-world (*Lebenswelt*). The paradigm of embodied and enactive cognition is explored at length in Dreyfus (1979), Hutchins (1995), Clark (1997), Hurley (1998), Lakoff and Johnson (1999), Noë (2004), Gallagher (2005), and Thompson (2007b).

10. This account of the relevance of dynamic systems theory to understanding cognition in causal terms follows closely Varela (1999) and Thompson (2007a). As Thompson notes, "because dynamic systems theory is concerned with geometrical and topographical forms of activity, it possesses an ideality that makes it neutral with respect to the distinction between the physical and the phenomenal, but also applicable to both" (2007a: 357).

11. Mohanty (2000: 149).

is produced in the right way, it seems to me, they have a way of explaining epistemic dispositions as resulting from our embodied condition (rather than as attitudes of a disembodied cogito serving the justification of its beliefs).[12]

This book should be of interest both to philosophers looking for non-Western approaches to consciousness and cognition, and to scholars of Indian and Buddhist philosophy primarily interested in various aspects of the Buddhist epistemological tradition. For the benefit of readers with little or no background in Indian and Buddhist philosophy I have adopted throughout English equivalents of technical philosophical terms, providing the original Sanskrit term in parentheses where necessary. In order to capture the polysemy of Sanskrit philosophical concepts and show sensitivity to context, occasionally a key technical term would have more than one English equivalent. For instance, *vijñāna* is translated both as "consciousness" and as "cognitive awareness," since it designates both a basic form of sentience and a discerning type of awareness. Likewise, *pramāṇa*,[13] which I will translate as "source of knowledge" or "reliable cognition," could be rendered as "epistemic warrant" (since it also refers to the specific aspect or quality of a cognition that makes it an instance of knowledge[14]). Brief explanations for the choice of English equivalents of Sanskrit philosophical concepts are provided in

12. As it turns out, recent research programs in cognitive psychology have not validated the distinction between causal and normative account of our epistemic intuitions. Indeed, traditional normative accounts of epistemic intuitions have been challenged in recent years by a substantive body of empirical research, which shows that there are significant variances across cultural subgroups in the way the objects of experience are described and categorized. These studies appear to confirm Alvin Goldman's (1992: 160) point that the perceived uniformity of our epistemic intuitions is most likely attributable to the "fairly homogeneous subculture" to which philosophers belong. See Nisbett and Ross (1980), Haidt, Koller, and Dias (1993), Weinberg, Nichols, and Stitch (2001), and especially Nichols, Stich, and Weinberg (2001) (the last two studies for an interesting take on epistemology as ethnography). I thank my colleague Sheridan Hough for bringing to my attention the relevant work of Nichols to the empirical investigation of our epistemic intuitions.

13. This key term is variously translated as "true cognition" or even "truth," and more literally as "means of knowledge," though the sense of the term varies significantly depending on the context. For instance, Matilal (1985: 203) takes *pramātva*, usually translated as "truth," to be just one of meanings of *prāmāṇya*, the theory of the means for the apprehension of truth. Following his brief survey of various translations in French and German for *pramāṇa*, Ruegg (1994b: 403–404) observes that although we do not yet have a satisfactory translation, "means" or "instrument of knowledge (or cognition)" captures the sense of the term in its technical use. At least in the Buddhist context, a *pramāṇa* is primarily concerned with, and oriented toward, achieving pragmatic aims, and thus bears on objects capable of bringing about intended results. See also Hugon (2011).

14. The notion of "epistemic warrant" I have in mind here is as developed by Alvin Plantinga who extends the traditional notion of epistemic justification (of true beliefs) also to include as a necessary condition for the warrant the optimal functioning of one's cognitive systems in the production of the respective belief. See Plantinga (1986, 1993).

the footnotes, where the reader will also come across modern philosophical glosses on different concepts and theories.

Now, let me briefly explain why I am situating my project at the intersection of phenomenology and analytic philosophy of mind. First, in the giving and defending of "reasons" Nyāya and Buddhist epistemologists operate on similar principles to those found in the tradition of analytic epistemology. Drawing from contemporary debates in epistemology between, for instance, internalists and externalists, or foundationalists and coherentists, becomes an essential and indispensable step in assessing the positions of the Buddhist epistemologists on such topics as the nature of evidence.[15] But it also guarantees an innovative treatment of these South Asian philosophical materials: the goal is to go beyond the task of historical reconstruction and endeavor to propose novel solutions to enduring and genuinely universal philosophical problems.[16] Second, the Abhidharma traditions with their phenomenological approach to investigating the elements of existence and/or experience provide the basis on which Dignāga, Dharmakīrti, and their followers deliberate on such topics as the ontological status of external objects and the epistemic import of perceptual and intentional states of cognitive awareness. Finally, approaching historical authors that belong to a different cultural and philosophical horizon than that of the modern West also demands that hermeneutical considerations come into play.

In framing the approach of this book in philosophical terms I do not mean to downplay alternative methodologies, principally those concerned with text-critical (that is, philological) issues pertaining to editing and translating Buddhist philosophical texts.[17] Nor do I want to imply that such studies fail in some significant way to capture the scope of the Buddhist epistemological enterprise. My contention is simply that our understanding of, and engagement with, the Buddhist epistemological project is better served by the methodologies and conceptual resources of philosophy. The real challenge, as I see it, is devising the best possible approach to integrating such complex and diverse epistemological canons as those of classical India and the West.[18]

15. For an Indian philosophical account of evidence, see Matilal (2002b). For a contemporary philosophical account of evidence, see Achinstein (2001).

16. For an encouraging recognition of the universality of some of our philosophical problems, and the ways in which comparative philosophy can make a compelling case for integrative solutions that bridge the cultural and historical divides between Western and non-Western philosophy, see Strawson (1998: 327).

17. Detailed discussions pertaining to the translation and interpretation of Buddhist philosophical literature are found in Lopez (1988), Powers (1993), Ruegg (1995), and Tillemans (1997). I address some of these interpretive issues in chapter 2.

18. Significant contributions in this direction are found in Matilal (1971, 1986), Mohanty (1992b), Dreyfus (1997), Ganeri (1999a, 2001), Siderits (2003), and Arnold (2005a).

The working assumption of this book is that the tradition of epistemological inquiry within Buddhism could be seen as advocating a form of naturalism that links it strongly to the Sautrāntika and Yogācāra[19] formulations of Abhidharma reductionism. Although epistemological theories in Buddhism ultimately attempt to justify a core set of Buddhist principles, and thus reflect specific doctrinal concerns, questions regarding the *foundation* of these principles are addressed on both metaphysical and empirical grounds. I will argue that naturalized epistemology (and phenomenology) and the cognitive sciences which inform it share with the Buddhist epistemological tradition of Dignāga and Dharmakīrti a common concern: developing a theory of knowledge that does not divorce logical arguments from descriptive accounts of cognition. For the Buddhist, the ultimate source of these descriptive accounts is the Abhidharma, in its specifically Sautrāntika-Yogācāra synthesis of thinkers like Vasubandhu (c. 350 C.E.).[20]

We must be careful, however, not to read too much into a philosophical program whose roots are historically and culturally different that those of the modern West. At the same time we can (and indeed should) profitably engage the thought of historical Buddhist thinkers when such thought addresses perennial philosophical problems. Such investigations, of course, must be mindful of Hans-Georg Gadamer's caveat about the objectivist claim that it is possible to interpret the thought of a historical author in such a way as to suggest that the interpreter does not enter in the event.[21]

One of the most enduring themes of the Sanskritic philosophical tradition is the debate over the number and nature of reliable means of belief formation (although, this tradition is principally concerned with cognitive "events" or states of "cognition" (*jñāna*) that are epistemically warranted

---

19. Sautrāntika and Yogācāra stand respectively for "Follower of [Canonical] Discourse School" and "Practice of Yoga School."

20. Vasubandhu is generally thought to have written his earlier works, in particular the *Abhidharmakośa*, from a Sautrāntika perspective, while most of his later treatises are expositions of various aspects of Yogācāra philosophy. This claim is based on the assumption that there is only one Vasubandhu. On the hypothesis of two Vasubandhus, proposed because of discrepancies in matters of style and doctrine in the works that are attributed to him, see Frauwallner (1951).

21. Gadamer (1975) argues for the well-known "pluralist" or "anti-objectivist" view, according to which understanding a text, historical event, or cultural phenomenon is a complex process in which there is a "fusion of horizons," such that the object of interpretation and the interpreter's perspective are not easily distinguished. Gadamer's insistence on there being a plurality of views does not mean that he endorses a type of relativism (he does acknowledge that there are criteria for distinguishing between right and wrong interpretations). Rather, he simply insists that an interpreter's prejudices and prejudgments (*Vorurteile*) are not only inescapable but also indispensable, for no interpreter stands outside the horizon of history. For a critical defense of Gadamer's view that objectivism is not possible because the object of understanding is always constituted anew in each act of understanding, see Weberman (2000).

(*pramā*), rather than with "beliefs" proper[22]). Much of this debate centers on an examination of our cognitive capacities and on issues pertaining to the structure and function of Sanskrit grammatical thought. While controversies are at the heart of any tradition of epistemological inquiry, in India they most often reflect (and are enforcing of) scholastic and doctrinal affiliation: philosophical views are framed within a specific scholastic paradigm which is in turn expanded within a genre of commentarial literature that seeks to explain and facilitate access to the original insight. When innovation occurs, as it often does, it is presented as statements or modes of reasoning that make explicit what might have only been alluded to in a canonical or foundational text of that particular school of thought.

Dignāga's *Pramāṇasamuccaya* ("Collection on the Sources of Knowledge," hereinafter the *Collection*) is generally recognized as the first systematic treatment of the sources of knowledge from a Buddhist perspective. Indeed, Dignāga (c. 480–540) is rightly credited with having inaugurated a new era in Indian thought with his synthesis of epistemological, grammatical, and psychological theories.[23] This new model of epistemological inquiry, which is expanded in great detail less than a century later by Dharmakīrti (c. 600–660)[24] (and significantly altered in certain respects) rests on two sets of premises: first, it adopts a specific view of language as a means of reasoning and deliberation first articulated in the Sanskrit grammatical tradition but also formalized by the early Naiyāyikas; second, it incorporates insights from the Abhidharma traditions concerning the phenomenology of perception and conceptual cognition.

The specifics of these two sets of premises, their formative influence, and the manner in which they contributed to the development of a Buddhist epistemology of perception, in particular as reflected in the encyclopedic work of Śāntarakṣita and Kamalaśīla—the *Tattvasaṃgraha* ("Compendium of True Principles") and its *Pañjikā* ("Commentary"),[25] hereinafter the *Compendium* and its *Commentary*—form the major coordinates of this book. These two sets of premises are instrumental in the adoption by the Buddhist epistemologists of a phenomenological perspective in describing the role of perception for knowledge. Key to this phenomenological account of perception is the notion that self-awareness is constitutive of perception.

22. For discussions of the difference between cognitive "events" and states of "belief," see Matilal (1986: 101ff.), Mohanty (1992b: 134–135), and Patil (2009: 42–43). For an account of "belief" that captures both its dispositional (or occurrent) and phenomenal (or experiential) aspects, see Schwitzgebel (2002).

23. Dignāga's contribution to the development of Indian logic and epistemology is treated at length in Vidyābhuṣaṇa (1921), Mookerjee (1935), Frauwallner (1959), Hattori (1968), Hayes (1988), Matilal (1998), and Pind (2009).

24. For a review of the debate about Dharmakīrti's dates, see Lindtner (1980).

25. For recent reviews of the scholarly literature on the TS/P, see Funayama (1992), Steinkellner and Much (1995), and McClintock (2010).

I will argue that—in conceiving of self-awareness as constitutive of perception— Śāntarakṣita and Kamalaśīla, like other successors of Dignāga and Dharmakīrti, share a common ground with phenomenologists in the tradition of Edmund Husserl and Maurice Merleau-Ponty,[26] and with analytic philosophers of mind interested in phenomenal consciousness,[27] all of whom contend that perception is best understood as bearing intentional content. I refer here primarily to the notion of "intentionality" as initially developed by Brentano and (following him) by Husserl and Merleau-Ponty. On this phenomenological account of intentionality, to perceive an object (or to have a perceptual experience) is to apprehend an intentional relation: whether the object intended in perception (the one the perception is *of*) is real is less important than how it is intended or that it is intended. Indeed, one of the features of intentionality is that it reveals the co-constitutive nature of perception and that which is perceived; as such, it *discloses* the world rather than attempting to establish a relationship to a discrete, "external" world. I shall argue that the Buddhist epistemologists' treatment of self-awareness (*svasaṃvedana*) displays similar features.

Can knowledge be established on a foundation of phenomenal or conscious experience, specifically on a type of cognitive awareness that is nonconceptual and inerrant, as the Buddhist epistemologists claim? Isn't this type of foundationalism, like the sort one associates with the sense data theorists, a discredited philosophical program (as Wilfrid Sellars and all critics of the "Myth of Given" have argued)? Can the Buddhist epistemologists' definition of perception be justified in terms of our understanding of the phenomenology of perception? Is it correct to assume that what turns the continuous flow of experience into perceptually distinct objects are the conceptual and categorizing tendencies of an embodied mind? Finally, how might we reason on the basis of such empirical testimony? These questions are at the heart of a lengthy philosophical dispute between the Buddhist epistemologists and their opponents, chiefly the Naiyāyikas and the Mīmāṃsakas. Insofar as this dispute can be integrated into contemporary philosophical debates, it ought to invite the same sort of scrutiny one would expect of all enduring philosophical problems, regardless of their historical origin. If philosophical issues raised by the Buddhist epistemologists can be shown to have any

26. Note that philosophical phenomenology as currently understood is a heterogeneous discipline, including, but not limited to, such subfields as *transcendental phenomenology* (concerned with how objects are constituted in pure awareness), *naturalistic phenomenology* (concerned with how consciousness presents the natural things), *existential phenomenology* (concerned with the experience of choice and action in concrete situations), and *hermeneutical phenomenology* (concerned with the interpretive structure of experience). For a detailed survey of the various subfields of phenomenology, see Embree et al. (1997).

27. Including such representative accounts as one finds in Siewert (1998), Kriegel (2009), Chalmers (2010), Bayne (2010), and Schwitzgebel (2011).

relevance beyond the confines of the history of Indian and Buddhist thought, the need to engage them from the perspective of our expanded understanding of the nature of consciousness and cognition (as exhibited, for instance, in the sciences of the mind) becomes imperative. I spell out the reasons for such an engagement, while addressing a broad set of methodological and metatheoretical issues, in chapter 2.

The Buddhist epistemologists advance what might initially look like a representationalist theory of knowledge. On closer scrutiny, this apparent "representationalism" in effect masks a complex phenomenalism that ascribes nonconceptual cognitive content to direct experience, as well as a causal theory of cognition that aims to explain the relation between varying modes of awareness and their corresponding constitutive elements. In order to fully unpack this Buddhist theory of knowledge I shall draw from the internalism vs. externalism debate in analytic epistemology,[28] and the critique of that debate from the standpoint of philosophical phenomenology.[29] The guiding methodological insight at work in this book is that a phenomenological account of perception on models first provided by Husserl and Merleau-Ponty best serves to translate the intuitions of the Buddhist epistemologists about the cognitive function of perception. Given the immediacy and directness of sense experience, as defined by Dignāga, Dharmakīrti, and their successors, the sense-object relation is an issue of continuous concern (just as for Husserl perception and that which is perceived is ultimately constituted by intentional content). The Buddhist epistemologist thus insists on treating each cognitive event as a new introduction to an object. Furthermore—as I will demonstrate—this continuing concern for the sense-object relation also explains why the Buddhist epistemologist treats cognition as bearing the characteristic marks of embodiment: it is the dynamic of the five aggregates[30] that ultimately gives the cognitive event its expression.

The theory of knowledge advanced by Śāntarakṣita and Kamalaśīla resembles Western variants of representationalism as proposed by, among others, Descartes and Locke. These similarities, however, extend only as far as the

28. Following Kornblith (2001: 4ff.), I understand this debate as an outcome of the dilemmas faced by the Cartesian epistemologist, whose internalist perspective on the justification of belief must confront the possibility that such internal belief could be dubitable, and thus be constrained to find a way to coordinate internal belief with external reality.

29. Such a critique is advanced by, among others, Carman (1999, 2007), Siewert (2005), Thompson (2007a), and Zahavi (2004a, 2009).

30. The Buddhist answer to the problem of personal identity stands in contradistinction to most classical philosophical attempts to reduce the individual, or his or her mind, to some metaphysical core such as a "soul" or "self." Instead, the individual personality is regarded as the dynamic product of the five aggregates of grasping: form or body, sensations, apperception, volition or dispositional formations, and consciousness. See chapter 3 for a detailed analysis of the five aggregates.

general view of representationalists who admit that while perception may provide immediate access to the domain of phenomenal experience, we come to apprehend it as a realm of discrete entities only as a result of categorical and conceptual discriminations. These conceptual discriminations (or representations) are in fact the cognitive counterparts of empirical objects, although the precise ontological status of empirical objects is a matter of dispute among representationalists. Indeed, it is hard to find a general definition of representationalism in Western (or for that matter South Asian) philosophy of mind that adequately covers the various theories subsumed under it. Although most proponents of representationalism agree on the existence of different "mediums" of representation (e.g., ideas, images, language, symbols, etc.), there is significant debate concerning the content and nature of these representations and the causal relations that obtain between that content and its referent (viz., the empirical reality).[31] This explains in part why representationalists can hold both internalist and externalist positions.[32] Seeking to reconcile nominalist views of concepts (which regard concepts as abstract objects) with realist views of mental content, some have proposed that we treat mental content as a mode of presentation that views concepts as psychological properties of mental representations.[33]

For Śāntarakṣita and Kamalaśīla, as for all Buddhist epistemologists, the apprehension of a resemblance (*sādṛśya*) between different objects, which marks the transition from an indistinct perceptual experience to a distinct cognitive event, is in itself a form of conceptual apprehension. It should be noted that unlike, say, Locke's attempt to solve the problem of representationalism by dissociating between two types of ideas (viz., sensible and intelligible), Śāntarakṣita and Kamalaśīla regard any cognitive event that involves discerning or discrimination as bearing the characteristic of conceptuality. While this position implies that resemblance relations should be taken as unreal—and here Śāntarakṣita and Kamalaśīla are in agreement

31. The dominant view, known as the representational theory of mind, is that the internal systems of representations have clear structure and a language-like syntax. This view has also come to be known, after Fodor (1975), as the *language of thought hypothesis*.

32. An example of a realist form of representationalism is articulated by the psychologist Max Velmans who argues for a distinction between *descriptions* of phenomena (which represent the phenomena themselves) and *theories about* phenomena (which represent their causes and several other inferred patterns). For Velmans, even appeal to such categories as "universals" to describe the phenomena or their causal relations suggest that "there is a 'reality' which is like something" (Velmans 2000: 163). For a general overview of representationalism in Western philosophy from Plato and Descartes to contemporary cognitive philosophers, see Watson (1995). A detailed survey of representational theories of consciousness is found in Lycan (2006).

33. This is particularly the case with the unified theory of concepts advanced by Laurence and Margolis (2003, 2007).

with Dharmakīrti's critique of relations—this does not necessarily invalidate representationalism. For Śāntarakṣita and Kamalaśīla, representationalism reflects an understanding of the nature of epistemic practices rather than commitment to a certain ontology. What we perceive is mediated by our internal expectations, propensities, as well as the range of our sensory systems.[34] How we identify and conceive of what is perceptually apprehended, however, depends on our linguistic and conceptual practices.[35]

This approach to cognition represents an important aspect of Buddhist epistemology and demands a closer and more detailed scrutiny than this introduction can provide. For the moment, let me clearly emphasize its significance for one of the premises outlined above, namely, that conceptual analysis is a reliable source of knowledge only to the extent that it is grounded in nondeceptive and inerrant experiences. As I shall argue at length in chapter 6, the observation of similarity between objects is not the direct cause of internally apprehended relations of resemblance. Instead, the representational content is generated following a process of aspectual rendering, which is in keeping with the reflexive nature of cognitive events. The cognitive model which Śāntarakṣita and Kamalaśīla develop—primarily in their discussion of the characteristics of external objects—centers on the theory of cognitive aspects (*ākāravāda*), more specifically on the notion that in cognizing we are directly acquainted both with the phenomenal content (*viṣaya-ākāra*) and the phenomenal character (*jñāna-ākāra*) of experience. While this model finds parallels in the sense data theories advanced by Bertrand Russell and George E. Moore, I will argue that Husserl's phenomenological account of intentional objects offers a more viable alternative.

Like many of their predecessors, Śāntarakṣita and Kamalaśīla are preoccupied with explaining what exactly lies at the juncture of perception and conception. As in many other instances, Dharmakīrti provides the standard answer. For him, conceptual cognitions arise from grasping an object by means of an act of recognition (*pratyabhijñāna*) that brings it under a certain concept. However, the concept by means of which an object is grasped as such, say as a "blue lotus," does not entirely correspond to the perceptual aspect of the object as phenomenally given. Rather, how the object is conceived also depends upon the evocative capacity of language, as the medium of conceptual apprehension, to represent the object.[36] For Śāntarakṣita and Kamalaśīla,

---

34. Whether the appearance of an object in cognition is due to the apprehension of a sensory object (*viśaya*) or merely to the presence of an internal object (*ālambana*) is a complex issue that calls into question the ontological positions of the Buddhist epistemologists. This issue is addressed below (chapter 4.4).

35. See, for example, TS 1214–1217 and TSP, *loc. cit.*

36. Dharmakīrti defines a concept as "a cognition with a phenomenal appearance that is capable of being conjoined with linguistic expression" (NB I, 5: *abhilāpasaṃsargayogyapratibhāsā pratītiḥ kalpanā*).

this argument provides sufficient ground for claiming that conceptions have the capacity to capture the contents of experience only to the extent that we bracket common assumptions about the function of linguistic reference, a position that finds full expression in the semantic theory of exclusion (*apoha*). For example, the category of distinction (*vyavaccheda*), which can be universally applied to all objects of experience, is not an intrinsic feature of the object, but of the cognitive process that entails the recognition of contrasting features in the apprehension of objects.

It is perhaps safe to assume that the origins and development of Buddhist epistemology as a distinct type of discourse mark the gradual acceptance of certain canons of logic and argumentation by those Buddhist philosophers who regarded polemical engagement with their Brahmanical opponents as vital to influencing their standing in the wider philosophical community. A good reason for this engagement might have been an eagerness on the part of the Buddhists to guarantee that their mode of argumentation is commensurable with the methods of reasoning formulated by the Naiyāyikas. Perhaps the most important concern of the Buddhist epistemologists, one that finds a clear articulation in the *Compendium* and its *Commentary*, is the need to withstand the criticism that core doctrinal principles such as those of momentariness and dependent arising cannot be defended on rational grounds (or, as the case may be, lack empirical support).

As Buddhist philosophers would argue, our cognitive propensities are beginningless, each thought being merely the continuation of an endless series of previous thoughts, which constantly inform, influence, and direct our intentional acts.[37] These cognitive propensities manifest most vividly as traces of memory and conceptual elaborations. The Buddhist epistemologists came to reject memory as a reliable source of knowledge and to regard conception as completely dissociated from perception. While an exploration of the historical context in which this dissociation occurred is beyond the scope of this book, in chapter 3 I offer a speculative reconstruction of the sort of empirical reasons that might warrant limiting perception (as a source of knowledge) to nonconceptual states of cognitive awareness.

In this regard, it ought to be noted that—for the Buddhist epistemologists—perception is not only an epistemic modality for establishing which cognitive event (or what aspect of it, and under which circumstances) counts as knowledge but also a cognitive process to be understood within the framework of classical Abhidharma psychology. Indeed, Nyāya and Buddhist philosophers did not make a radical distinction between epistemological and psychological accounts of cognition (at least not in the way that dominant currents in modern Western philosophy drifted away from naturalist explanations

37. See AKBh *ad* AK III, 19d.

after Kant).[38] It is precisely the practice of translating logical arguments back to their perceptual source that resulted in Indian theories of inference being branded as forms of psychologism, a derogatory label for the seeming conflation of logical reasoning with the psychology of perception mainly associated with Gottlob Frege and the tradition of logical positivism. That exclusionary branding no longer holds true. As Francis Pelletier, Renée Elio, and Philip Hanson[39] argue in their examination of what Willard Van Orman Quine called "the old anti-psychologistic days,"[40] the newly expanded understanding of our cognitive architecture provided by the sciences of the mind makes it possible to be psychologistic about logic, albeit in a novel way. I shall explore the implication of this resurgent psychologism for our evaluation of the Indian theories of inference in my brief treatment of the semantic theory of exclusion in chapter 4.

In this book I am primarily concerned with the analysis of perception, although an account of the relation between perception and conception will also be provided. The analysis of perception provides the empirical foundation that gives Buddhist epistemology its pragmatic anchorage. The precise definition of perceptual knowledge (an important subject of dispute among the Indian epistemologists) led to several interpretive solutions, the details of which form the primary contents of my analysis. Dharmakīrti's overarching influence on subsequent generations of Buddhist and Brahmanical philosophers meant that his ideas took on the appearance of a standard account of the Buddhist epistemological standpoint. While no one disputes the paramount importance of Dharmakīrti, both Śāntarakṣita and Kamalaśīla display a sufficient degree of originality in espousing their views to warrant an independent consideration.[41] Our main source, the *Compendium* and its *Commentary*, is not only a vast collection of Buddhist doctrines recorded in the second half of the eighth century C.E. but also a highly polemical work bearing testimony to the sustained disputes between Buddhist and Brahmanical philosophers during what is perhaps the golden era of Indian philosophy. The polemical nature of the *Compendium* and its *Commentary* is further evinced by the importance that Śāntarakṣita and Kamalaśīla accord to issues of metaphysics and epistemology in their attempt to refute a multitude of views and establish their own perspective on the nature of reality. This Buddhist perspective on the nature of reality is anchored in a thorough defense of the principle of dependent arising. The aim of chapter 5 is to examine the

38. See Mohanty (1992b: 130).
39. Pelletier, Elio, and Hanson (2008: 9ff.).
40. Quine (1969: 84).
41. Unless, of course, one is specifically concerned with the various ramifications of Dharmakīrti's epistemological innovations as reflected in the work of his immediate commentators, as is the case in Dunne (2004), or in the works of his Tibetan interpreters, as is the case in Dreyfus (1997).

context and scope of Śāntarakṣita and Kamalaśīla's encyclopedic work and map out its epistemological and ontological concerns, with a focus on the tension between epistemic dispositions and altruistic concerns.

More immediately, the three principal points of debate that form the subject of the present investigation concern: (1) whether a perception that is "devoid of conception" (*kalpanāpoḍha*) can be said to be cognitive, and if so in what sense; (2) what is the precise relation between language and conceptual analysis, and what sort of causal conditions, if any, are at work in the generation of meaning from verbal content; and (3) in what ways do the Abhidharma analyses of consciousness and cognition constrain the Buddhist epistemologist's understanding of the epistemic role of perception. Chapter 6 and parts of chapter 4 deal with these three principal points of debate.

Adequately addressing these issues demands that the views of Śāntarakṣita and Kamalaśīla are separately treated, taking into account their individual styles of argumentation and their specific audiences. However, while seeking to locate differences in their approaches, one should not overlook the fact that in the *Compendium* and its *Commentary*, Śāntarakṣita and Kamalaśīla concern themselves with answering questions that form an integral part of the Buddhist epistemological enterprise, and their solutions to these questions are to a large extent contingent on its conceptual and theoretical resources.[42] This enterprise is concerned, *inter alia*, with answering the following questions: What forms the proper basis of a knowledge event? What sort of objects do perceptual cognitions ultimately intend? Is perceptual knowledge representational in character or should it rather be understood as a type of embodied action? What sort of phenomenological account of perception does the Buddhist epistemological tradition advance? These questions are taken up in chapter 7, which addresses the wider philosophical implications of the Buddhist analysis of particulars in the context of contemporary debates about foundationalism in epistemology and phenomenology.

In the end, no discussion about perception and its mode of presentation can take place outside the horizon of consciousness. It is consciousness that ultimately provides the evidential ground for all modes of inquiry. For the Buddhist epistemologists consciousness, as reflexive awareness, is not just another event in the chain of dependently arisen phenomena but its disclosing medium. The precise nature of this reflexive awareness is the subject of chapter 8, in which I argue for the possibility of an intentional but

42. For several arguments about why the TS/P might be regarded as an epistemological (that is, as a *pramāṇa*) work, primarily on account of its structure and scope, see Blumenthal (2004: 30ff.) and McClintock (2010: 61–62). Indeed, the emphasis on reasoning (*yukti*), and on a specific audience composed primarily of so-called "proponents of reasoning" (*nyāyavādins*), is a clear indication to this effect. It is generally assumed that Śāntarakṣita and Kamalaśīla adopt mainly a Madhyamaka position in their later works.

nonrepresentational form of consciousness. I conclude in chapter 9 with some reflections on the promise of cross-cultural approaches to Buddhist philosophy of mind, with hopes of tackling, among other issues, the old dilemma of the distinction between seeing and seeing as from the perspective of an enactive approach to cognition. For the Buddhist, thus, perceiving reality ultimately marks an intentional orientation in a world that is experientially constituted. Examining the nature of this distinctive perceptual orientation in the arena of current philosophical debates is the main concern of this book.

CHAPTER 2

Naturalizing Buddhist Epistemology

There are several ways of approaching the Buddhist epistemological tradition, as our brief introductory survey of the context and scope of this enterprise demonstrates. In addressing the issue of methodology I also wish to make clear that much as we may strive for a philosophically illuminating and textually accurate account, certain presuppositions remain implicit in any theoretical endeavor. These presuppositions primarily, but not exclusively, concern the method and style of argumentation, and the theoretical intuitions that inform one's argumentative strategies. In approaching the Buddhist epistemological tradition from the perspective of phenomenological naturalism I regard its arguments as articulating a specific type of discourse, in which descriptive accounts of experience and rational justification are locked into a twin concern. At the same time I am aware that we need to engage the arguments of the Buddhist epistemologists in ways that make their thought relevant to contemporary philosophical debates. This necessity is both historical and theoretical; however, it is impeded by hermeneutical difficulties arising from the intimate connection in India between philosophical reflection and the language in which it was conducted, namely Sanskrit. Hence, a detour through the linguistic theories of the Sanskrit grammarians is an almost unavoidable hurdle in getting the right spin on the Buddhist wheel of reasoning.

The Buddhist epistemologist's broadly empirical approach to knowledge means that reasons, though articulated in the language of Sanskrit grammatical thought, are also meant to provide an account of how things are before we set out to theorize about them. For the Buddhist, this theorizing accords with the phenomenological stance that perception represents a form of implicit knowing that cannot be improved upon by conceptualization. The Buddhist response to how language and conceptual analysis can operate as reliable cognitions is captured by the well-known semantic theory of exclusion (*apoha*), whose operating premise is that "exclusion" and "negation" serve as the only effective ways of using linguistic signifiers without subscribing to a correspondence theory of truth. Although a full account of the *apoha* theory falls outside the scope of this book, the Buddhist account of perception I offer here raises some important issues for conceptual analysis and has a number of consequences for our understanding of the role and function of linguistic reference that are worth further investigation. In what follows, I address a broader set of methodological and metatheoretical concerns that, I hope, will showcase the importance of empirical research and theoretical intuitions in advancing the study of Indian and Buddhist philosophy.

2.1 DOCTRINE AND ARGUMENT

Let us begin, first, by clarifying the scope of Buddhist philosophy by addressing the idiosyncratic and nonspecific use of "philosophy" in the study of Indian and Buddhist traditions. Most often such use pertains simply to historical treatments of philosophical ideas rather than philosophy proper, and thus reflects certain disciplinary biases characteristic of modern Indological and Buddhological research. Can we develop a genuinely philosophical approach to Buddhist thought? William Edelglass and Jay Garfield have recently claimed that we can if we proceed to explain that, like their Western counterparts, Buddhist philosophical concerns too can be classified along metaphysical, epistemological, ethical, and hermeneutical lines.[1] If the goal of Buddhist metaphysics is to explain the nature of reality such that gaining insight into this nature eliminates confusion, Buddhist epistemology lays the methodological foundation for achieving this goal. Likewise, ethical and hermeneutical considerations come into play when the goals are establishing the appropriate rules of moral conduct or resolving doctrinal disputes. Correctly identifying and categorizing not just texts and authors, but their respective views and arguments, is a first step in framing a genuinely philosophical approach to Buddhist thought.[2] Thus, rather than seeking to find out whether the various schools of Buddhism have any parallels in Western thought, a more productive attempt is to work out a broad consensus about the nature and scope of philosophical inquiry.

1. Edelglass and Garfield (2009: 4).
2. Similar efforts to frame a genuine philosophical approach, in this case for Indian philosophy more generally, are found in Matilal (1986), Bilimoria (1988), Mohanty (1992b), Bhattacharyya (1993), Chakrabarti (1999), and Ganeri (2001, 2011b, 2012). Addressing the so-called dogmas of Orientalism, Matilal also takes issue with the "pop mysticism" that is characteristic of vulgarizing presentations of Indian philosophy, in particular of Advaita Vedānta and Madhyamaka Buddhism (Matilal 2002a: 370–376).

In his comprehensive discussion of lexical equivalents of "philosophy" in Indian languages, Wilhelm Halbfass noted that while parallels with what is commonly designated as "philosophy" in the West are clearly to be found in the Indian and Buddhist doxographical literatures, this is philosophy as defined by tradition, that is, as "a spectrum of firmly established, fully developed doctrinal structures" and not as "as an open-ended process of asking questions and pursuing knowledge."[3] While I agree with Halbfass that the presence of an "open-ended" process of philosophical inquiry is precisely why Western philosophy has undergone such dramatic changes in modern history[4]—such that many of its traditional inquiries are no longer regarded as being within its purview—this is by no means an exclusive feature of Western thought, but it is also true of philosophical movements in India, as evinced by the tradition of philosophical debate (*vivāda*).

Modern definitions of philosophy restrict its domain of activity only to that type of thinking which operates as a rational and critical appraisal of all modes of knowledge, including knowledge itself. It is largely this definition that is partly responsible for the false dichotomy between rational or argumentative and interpretive or speculative that has often been used to dissociate analytic from phenomenological and hermeneutical philosophy, and more generally Western from non-Western philosophy (the same fault line is often seen as separating modern philosophy from medieval scholasticism). An often cited example of this dichotomy is Anthony Flew's uncharitable remark: "Philosophy, as the word is understood here, is concerned first, last and all the time with argument. It is, incidentally, because most of what is labeled *Eastern Philosophy* is not so concerned—rather than any reason of European parochialism—that this book draws no material from any source east of Suez."[5]

The past three decades have seen numerous examples—besides efforts to bridge analytic and phenomenological traditions[6]—of work in Indian and Buddhist philosophy that are rigorously argumentative in precisely the sense that Flew reserved for Western philosophy.[7] For the most part these studies

3. Halbfass (1988: 273).

4. As the authors of the *Oxford Companion to Philosophy* remind us: "[m]ost definitions of philosophy are fairly controversial... because what is called philosophy has changed radically in scope in the course of history, with many inquiries that were originally part of it having detached themselves from it" (Honderich 1995: 666). This is also true to a certain extent of philosophical movements in India, although the effort to preserve continuity with the past remains a defining characteristic of the Indian style of philosophical inquiry.

5. Flew (1971: 36).

6. See, for instance, Petitot et al. (1999), Smith and Jokic (2003), Smith and Thomasson (2005), and Christensen (2008).

7. See, especially, Matilal (1986), Ganeri (1999a, 2001), Garfield (2002), Siderits (2003), Arnold (2005a), Patil (2009), and D'Amato, Garfield, and Tillemans (2009).

focus primarily on those traditions of argumentative philosophy, chiefly the Nyāya, Madhyamaka, and Buddhist epistemology, where the giving and examination of reasons takes center stage.[8] There is, however, a plurality of views regarding the scope of these argumentative practices, an issue I will explore at length in chapter 4. A central point of controversy concerns the authority of verbal or scriptural testimony, so that affirming or denying it operates as a criterion for doxographical classification. For instance, while the Naiyāyikas include verbal testimony (which refers specifically to the words of the Vedas) in their list of epistemic warrants, they do not regard it as intrinsically ascertained, as do the Mīmāṃsakas (for whom the Vedas are authorless (*apauruṣeya*) and thus infallible). The Nyāya position is summed up well by Satischandra Chatterjee who notes that, "while the validity of verbal testimony depends on its being based on the statement of a trustworthy person, its possibility is conditional on the understanding of the meaning of that statement."[9] Thus, whereas the Naiyāyikas regard investigation by means of reasoning (*ānvīkṣīkī*) as an appropriate description of their philosophical practices,[10] Mīmāṃsā philosophers have tended to rebuke its excessive use.[11] A similar difference in attitudes toward the role of rational inquiry is at work within the Buddhist tradition: indeed, the adoption of certain canons of positive argumentation by Dignāga, Dharmakīrti, and their successors would encounter strong opposition from antirealist Mādhyamika philosophers like Candrakīrti (c. 600–650).

Tillemans (2008a) does a wonderful job of laying out the scope and range of both Buddhist and Brahmanical concerns with matters of argumentation. These concerns include, but are not limited to, such issues as establishing canons of right thinking and rules of debate, articulating the difference between arguments for oneself and for the other, addressing the problem of universals and the relation between language and conceptual thought, critically evaluating the role of scripture and scholastic affiliation in debate, and deciding the number and nature of epistemic warrants, as well as the criteria under which logical reasons can be warranted. See also contributions by Arnold (2008b), Dreyfus (2008), McClintock (2008), Siderits (2008), and Tillemans (2008b) to the same volume.

8. The Sanskrit term commonly employed to refer to this form of argumentative philosophy is *ānvīkṣikī* (lit. "investigating by means of reasoning"). On the appropriateness of using *ānvīkṣīkī* as an equivalent for "philosophy," including other Sanskrit cognates such as *tarkavidyā* ("science of logic") and *hetuśāstra* ("theory of reasoning"), see Hacker (1958: 54–83), Halbfass (1988: 263–286), and Matilal (2002a: 358–369).

9. Chatterjee (1950: 317).

10. First employed by Kauṭilya in his *Arthaśāstra* I.2. 1–12.

11. Considering the adoption of *ānvīkṣikī* as a defining term for "philosophy" Matilal remarks: ". . . at some point in history there was not much difference between the use of the term '*ṣaṭ-tarkī*' and *ṣaḍ-darśana*,' and hence the equation *ānvīkṣikī* = *darśana* (a *rūdra śabda*) = philosophy was possible" (2002a: 365). Regardless of whether such an equation was possible, it is safe to say that this debate is indicative of the presence in Sanskrit philosophical literature of a plurality of attitudes regarding the proper nature of philosophical inquiry.

It is this varying attitude toward the role of rational inquiry that is ultimately instrumental in differentiating between philosophy as a quest for reasons (*hetuvidyā*) and philosophy as a path (*darśanamārga*), even though this differentiation does not necessarily point to separate domains of activity but rather to separate stages in the pursuit of a common goal. Karl Potter is perhaps the first to have coined the term "path philosophy"[12] to account for the common preoccupation among Indian philosophers with finding a path to complete freedom (*mokṣa*) and the means for achieving it. Some of the greatest Indian philosophers (e.g., Nāgārjuna, Śaṅkara, Rāmānuja, etc.) count as path philosophers, precisely for the fact that they provide a role model for those who seek such freedom, however it may be defined.[13] And there are few traditions of reflection in which the concept of path (*mārga*) is more central than Buddhism. To help us distinguish between various aspects of what may be properly called "path theory," Robert Buswell and Robert Gimello have proposed the following taxonomy: (i) the relationship between the path and the ideal person (i.e., the Buddha); (ii) the path in relation to its obstacles; (iii) the difference between the path of knowledge (*jñāna-mārga*) and the path of purification (*visuddhi-mārga*); (iv) the tension between path-oriented goals and scholasticism; and (v) the position of "path-theory" vis-à-vis hermeneutics, religion, and culture.[14] The concept of "path" acts as a central interpretive category due to the manner "in which it incorporates, underlies, or presupposes everything else in Buddhism, from the simplest act of charity to the most refined meditative experience and the most rigorous philosophical argument."[15] From a traditional point of view, the common goal of this "path" philosophy is emancipation from cyclic existence (*saṃsāra*), regardless of the manner in which this goal is defined and pursued by each school.[16] Something like a path-oriented attitude toward the scope of philosophical inquiry is at work in most Indian schools of thought, except perhaps for the Cārvāka physicalists, whose secular and skeptical agenda sets

12. This coinage is reminiscent of the classical Hellenistic sense of *philia sophia* (lit. "love of wisdom"), since, on the whole, Indian and Buddhist philosophers seem to address the same broad metaphysical and moral concerns that preoccupy Platonist and Stoic philosophers. The historian of philosophy Pierre Hadot is perhaps the strongest advocate of such a definition of philosophy. Hadot insists that classical philosophers viewed their professional pursuits as "an effort to live and think according to the norms of wisdom" (Hadot 1995: 59).

13. As Potter noted, "a person who is ready to get on a path is sometimes called an *adhikārin* by Indian path philosophers. The *adhikārin* must have considerable experience in getting to know himself, for he has come a long way in the search for freedom" (1963: 37).

14. Buswell and Gimello (1992: 2–36).

15. Buswell and Gimello (1992: 6).

16. The Buddhists refer to it as cessation (*nirvāṇa*), indicating a state that marks the end of cyclical existence (*saṃsāra*), while all Brahmanical schools refer to this final goal as liberation (*mokṣa*).

them apart from this general path orientation. For the most part the modern Western understanding of the goal of philosophical inquiry is devoid of any reference to the need for overcoming the limitations of the human condition. Where such references are encountered, as in the case of existential phenomenology, the goal is most often defined in secular terms.[17]

2.2 REASON AND CONCEPTUAL ANALYSIS

If engaging the arguments of the Buddhist epistemologists in ways that make their thought relevant to contemporary philosophical debates is the goal, then adopting some of the principles, positions, and strategies that inform these debates becomes inevitable. Buddhist epistemology done in an analytical or phenomenological mode is no longer traditional Buddhist *pramāṇavāda* ("doctrine of epistemic warrants") but a new type of philosophical discourse informed by, and reflecting, contemporary philosophical concerns. In that regard, some of the methodological principles characteristic of the contemporary philosophy of discourse,[18] in which the views of historical authors and those of modern interpreters are made to enhance each other, also become relevant. This discursive approach raises the issue of the relationship between epistemology and hermeneutics, even though the Buddhist epistemologists are not necessarily preoccupied with problems of interpretation (although some of those traditions which they critique, principally the Mīmāṃsā, do have these concerns), but rather with establishing the grounds for knowledge.

A good example of how the philosophy of discourse can be applied to the Buddhist tradition, albeit in a different context, is found in Bernard Faure's epistemological critique of Chan Buddhism. Tracing the varied contours of

17. One of the most influential examples of "secular" existentialism is Heidegger's definition of the human condition in terms of *Dasein*. Heidegger conceives of the *Dasein* as a particular way of being-in-the-world rather than a mode of existence that is defined by the attempt to transcend the limitations of the human condition (1986: 321ff.). However, given their predominantly religious and soteriological concerns, nineteenth-century precursors to existentialism like Kierkegaard may be viewed as sharing some of the same concerns as these Indian "path" philosophers.

18. By "philosophy of discourse" I mean specifically the rhetorical turn in twentieth-century Western philosophy, characterized primarily as an attempt to distance philosophical arguments from a pretense of methodological neutrality. This is by no means a unitary movement, but encompasses the works of major thinkers such as Heidegger, Habermas, Bakhtin, Foucault, and Derrida. Derrida, for instance, has consistently argued that philosophy, despite all its attempts to reorganize itself as a form of meta-discourse, is bound to remain permanently subjected to the uses of metaphor: "Présence disparissant dans son propre rayonnement, source cachée de la lumière, de la verité et du sens, effacement du visage de l'être, tel serait le *retour* insistant de ce qui assujettit la métaphysique à la métaphore" (Derrida 1972: 320).

comparison, counterpoint, and intertwining that hermeneutical philosophy engenders, Faure not only champions the case for using modern theoretical frameworks, but explains why certain methodological assumptions underpinning the interpretation of classical non-Western traditions need to be called into question:

> [E]ach methodological approach creates its own object and must in turn be questioned, on not only methodological grounds but also hermeneutical and epistemological grounds. Above all, we must always keep in mind that each approach, however "objective" it claims to be, has certain ideological implications and fulfills specific functions within the academic field. Even if Pierre Bourdieu rightly urges us to "objectify the objectification itself" and to clarify the position of the writer, this does not entail, as he seems to believe, that doing so will secure a much-vaunted "scientificity."[19]

Faure calls attention to the obvious fact that humanistic disciplines are primarily concerned with the analysis and interpretation of cultural artifacts, and as such are shaped by trends and mentalities specific to a given culture or epoch and its intellectual critics. Unless philosophical inquiry is regarded as (or simply reduced to) theorizing on the basis of the empirical results of natural science, it cannot be said to operate on a scientific model. Rather, it too depends upon a communicative model, which cannot achieve objectivity simply by bringing one's own methodological and critical thinking principles in line with established canons of scholarly analysis and rational inquiry. Of course, one could go as far as to claim that even theorizing on the basis of empirical data involves interpretation and carries in its wake the prospect of ambiguity and difference: the lesson of naturalized epistemology, as Quine argued in his now classic essay "Two Dogmas of Empiricism,"[20] is that theories are underdetermined even by the best observational data, given the latter's episodic, fragmentary, and limited reach.[21] Furthermore, the persistence of performative traits, as well as the inescapability of the first-person

19. Faure (1993: 4). A similar approach is adopted by Gómez (1995: 206), who suggests that "we will be well advised.... to open the field [i.e., Buddhist studies] to alternative models"; he gives several examples of attempts already undertaken in this direction, including Gudmunsen's (1977) contrasting of Buddhist and post-structuralist theories of language, and Tuck's (1990) hermeneutics of comparative philosophy approach. For a different perspective on the uses (and abuses) of theory in the field of Buddhist studies, see Cabezón (1995) and Tillemans (1995).

20. Quine (1951).

21. In naturalized epistemology, the view that theories are underdetermined by empirical data is sometimes invoked as providing a ground for fallibilism, and for asserting that our knowledge claims are at most derived from inferences to the best explanation. Fallibilism is more problematic for normative epistemology than for intentionalist and causal accounts of knowledge such as those advanced by Indian and Buddhist philosophers. Indeed, the Buddhist epistemologist would favor the

perspective, are central to any type of philosophical discourse, for no philosophical argument obtains outside the horizon of a person's consciousness in which a given tradition of reflection becomes operational.

In the case of engaging the arguments and argumentative strategies of classical Buddhist and Indian philosophers there is the additional discursive layer of the commentarial tradition, in which every major work is embedded. Although a commentary may enjoy a certain autonomy, it most often remains inextricably tied to the original text in terms of its topic and stated purpose.[22] It is a well-known feature of Indian philosophical writing that it often operates on a synchronic model. As a consequence historical considerations are not given precedence over philosophical ones in comparing and contrasting the views of authors from different historical periods. The tradition is treated as a chorus of several voices operating on different scales but nevertheless in synchrony.

This absence of historical referentiality in Indian philosophical literature has been attributed in part to the preeminence of ritual and the ritual hermeneutics developed in the Mīmāṃsā tradition, which interpreted the Vedic rituals as a form of participation in a constant renewal of past events that effectively telescoped the historical dimension.[23] That even the Buddhists, who rejected the authority of the Vedas and disengaged from participation in Vedic rituals, nonetheless retained this ahistorical model clearly suggests that this pervasive absence of historical referentiality in classical India is a vexing problem. An interesting outcome of this lack of historical referentiality is the fact that India developed some of most complex doxographies to be found in any classical philosophical tradition.[24] This preference for doxographical argumentation also explains why South Asian philosophers do not usually claim to be innovators, even when they do improve upon or substantively alter doctrinal positions held as authoritative within a particular school.

As is often the case, a commentator that flourished at a much later period would analyze a text for a completely different audience than the one intended

---

view that our knowledge claims align closely with practical interests. For a discussion of fallibilism and its implications for normative epistemology, see Stanley (2005).

22. On rare occasions a commentary may become a self-standing work. In our case, one example is Dharmakīrti's *Pramāṇavārttika* ("Commentary on the Sources of Knowledge," hereinafter the *Commentary*), which although conceived as a commentary on Dignāga's *Collection*, eventually came to replace it and became the root text for nearly all subsequent treatments of topics that Dignāga had dealt with in his original work.

23. See Pollock (1989: 607).

24. Typically, authors are classified either according to scholastic affiliation, that is, as a Naiyāyika ("reasoner"), Mīmāṃsaka ("investigator of the profound [meaning]"), Pramāṇika ("epistemologist"), or doctrinally, as a "propounder of duality" (*dvaitavādin*), a "propounder of emptiness" (*śūnyavādin*), "propounder of aspectual cognition" (*sākāravādin*), etc. Cf. Houben (2002: 473).

by its original author. That means we, as modern readers of these texts, tread on fewer certainties (*niścaya*) than might otherwise be assumed. In order to compensate for this lack of certainty, it becomes necessary to reconstruct philosophical arguments and to find adequate interpretive strategies, while at the same time keeping in mind that one writes for a modern audience that often shares different concerns than those envisaged by traditional authors. I am well aware that such "reconstructions" play at most a heuristic function, facilitating our understanding of distant philosophical ideas, so that we may reclaim them for ongoing philosophical debates. To claim otherwise would be akin to recreating the past to suit modern sensibilities. In effect, arguing against the alleged scientificity of text-based scholarship in the study of Buddhist philosophy, some interpreters have claimed that a translation that presents the original text accurately is in fact impossible. Thus, Luis Gómez: "With de Man, I believe translation is impossible, and with Foucault I regard interpretation as the insertion into a text of a new and foreign voice—hence, a 'displacement of authority'."[25] Insofar as philosophical progress is made by building on previous arguments, such "displacement of authority" is in effect unavoidable.

Whether one strives for a base line account of the thought of a seminal Buddhist author[26] or for the sort of philosophical reconstruction that brings such an author in conversation with modern philosophers, interpreting the "original" intent remains an issue of continuing concern. It is a given that both Śāntarakṣita and Kamalaśīla are syncretic thinkers and, as such, adopt different perspectives depending on the types of arguments and audience they engage with. Consensus on how best to understand the philosophical position of a historical author in this case is perhaps a nonissue given that interpreters participate in what Paul Ricoeur calls a "conflict of interpretation" (on account of the fact that, as the medium of symbolic expression, linguistic and theoretical constructs are susceptible to continuing exegesis).[27]

---

25. Gómez (1995: 208). Gómez reacts against what he calls the "fundamentalism" of text-based Buddhist scholarship: "When I say that translation is impossible and interpretation is fraudulent, I refer to certain ideas of translation and interpretation. That is to say, a translation that represents the original accurately is impossible. The only perfect translation that can be is the original itself.... A 'critical apparatus' that gives us the true and original social and psychological reality of the text's meaning is absurd, by virtue of the gulf to which the 'apparatus' bears witness, and by virtue of the fact that no one can represent accurately and thoroughly the social and psychological reality of anything—not even his or her own reality" (1995: 208–209).

26. Such is the case, for instance, with Dunne's (2004) presentation of Dharmakīrti's philosophy as articulated in his principal work and the earliest available commentaries, chiefly those of Devendrabuddhi and Śākyabuddhi.

27. Even though Ricoeur (1969) admits that language, as the field of symbolic expression, and the interpretive strategies deployed in order to explicate it, are mutually constituted, this does not mean that interpretations are not relative to the

Furthermore, even in epistemology arguments and theories are part of a discourse of interpretation and reinterpretation, one that often poses as many new problems as it solves. By engaging the works of Buddhist and Brahmanical philosophers not merely as historical materials (presumably, documenting a mode of thinking that belongs exclusively to a particular philosophical culture and epoch) but rather as different modes of philosophical inquiry, we are challenged to revisit and reconceive philosophical problems of enduring value. In his landmark study of Dharmakīrti's philosophy as reflected in Tibetan sources—*Recognizing Reality*[28]—Georges Dreyfus offers an elaborate treatment of the problem of universals, a major topic of Dharmakīrti's discourse, and a classic example of an enduring theme of scholastic philosophy.[29] In concluding his analysis, Dreyfus admits that neither antirealist nor realist solutions are in the end satisfactory. The issue is not whether universals are real, but whether they are effective as philosophical categories, and whether or not Dharmakīrti's mode of discourse is sufficiently ambiguous to accommodate opposing interpretations:

The problem of universals has been raised again and again and alternative solutions proposed. None of them, however, has been considered completely satisfactory, although each can be defended.... The repetition of this scenario across cultures suggests that problems such as these are of a peculiar nature. The problem of universals

---

theoretical structures of various hermeneutical protocols (e.g., semantic, ontological, exegetical, historical, etc.).

28. The title of this book is in many respects a "homage" to the sort of critical engagement with the Buddhist epistemological tradition that Dreyfus advances in his book.

29. Treating Buddhist philosophy as a form of scholasticism, similar to medieval European scholastics, has received a mixed response in Buddhist studies circles. Cabezón, who adopts the term and pleads in favor of its usage in Buddhist studies, suggests that there is nothing to fear in scholasticism per se or its ideological implications. Seeking to emancipate it from its medieval European origins, Cabezón proposes that we adopt a more benign view of scholasticism and regard it as an indispensable method for historical analysis: "Any project that seeks to examine an issue such as language in a scholastic philosophical tradition must, it seems to me, describe the views of that particular school, discuss the sources upon which such a system is based, but more important it must explain why particular sources were relied upon and why those sources were read in the way they were" (Cabezón 1994: 10). In a different take on the relevance of scholasticism as a methodological category in Buddhist studies (which is also a critical review of Cabezón's proposal) van der Kuijp does not view scholasticism as an idiosyncratic feature of medieval European attempts to appropriate Aristotle. Van der Kuijp suggests, on the contrary, that scholasticism could also be viewed as characteristic of traditional monastic Buddhism. For example, the study and transmission of the works of Dharmakīrti follow a specific scholastic pattern: "unlike the temporary proscription of some of Aristotle's works from the Parisian academic scene in the early thirteenth century, Dharmakīrti's writings enjoyed fairly continuous study, first in India until at least the fifteenth century and, with a minimum of friction, in translation in the Tibetan cultural area from the eleventh century to the present" (van der Kuijp 1998: 563).

is not empirical. Appealing to some hitherto unknown facts or a new theory is of little help. Defensible solutions are proposed but philosophers keep arguing, for the conflict is not just about finding a solution but also about what would a solution look like if it were found.[30]

This notion that the problem of universals is not empirical reflects, however, a tacit commitment to a version of the classical theory of concepts. Recently, Dreyfus has revised his earlier view by advancing a naturalized account of concept formation that is "causally constrained."[31] On this new interpretation of Dharmakīrti's understanding of the cognitive function of conception, language is anchored in concrete and pragmatic (rather than merely epistemic) situations. Citing the pre-reflective cognitive aspect of color perception, Dreyfus sees categorization practices as subservient to the "dictates of our perceptual apparatus,"[32] concluding that our judgments of similarity (and/or difference) result simply from the fact that we are "naturally" disposed, perhaps for evolutionary purposes, to apprehend similarity and/or difference in the empirical domain. Dreyfus's conclusion, that "for Dharmakīrti this is all there is to say,"[33] seems to suggest that he now favors an empirical approach to the problem of universals, even as he interprets the function of conceptual cognition in the Buddhist epistemological context in antirealist terms. As I will argue later on, a naturalized approach to epistemology has the added advantage of opening the discussion about universals also to input from the sciences of cognition, which provide not only new ways of mapping our cognitive architecture but also new insights about the nature, acquisition, and function of concepts. Does that make the problem of universals an empirical one? Perhaps. But it does not make a naturalized account of universals less susceptible to interpretation.

Let me briefly note that the so-called *classical theory of concepts*, which has dominated philosophical and grammatical accounts of concepts in both India and the West from ancient times to the middle of the twentieth century, has been supplanted by several new theories.[34] The classical theory (also known

30. Dreyfus (1997: 447–448).
31. Dreyfus (2011: 210). Note that, against strong conceptualist readings of Dharmakīrti's nominalism as advanced, for instance, by Siderits (1999), Dreyfus now proposes a low-level "embodied" account of concept acquisition and use based on our direct experience of difference and similarity.
32. Dreyfus (2011: 220).
33. Dreyfus (2011: 220).
34. I follow the comprehensive survey of theories of concepts in Laurence and Margolis (1999). Chakrabarti and Siderits (2011: 15–24) also offer a very useful review of Western theories of concepts, highlighting both similarities and differences mainly with Nyāya, Vaiśeṣika, and Buddhist theories, though they do not seem to address the issue of whether Indian theories fall under the classical view of concepts.

as the *definition view*) takes concepts (primarily those that correspond to the lexical items of natural languages) to be structured mental representations that possess within themselves the necessary and sufficient conditions for their application, and are ultimately reducible to features that express sensory or perceptual properties. But this theory (and its variants) cannot adequately answer a series of crucial problems: (i) there are few, if any, cases of well-defined concepts; (ii) naturalized epistemological arguments against analyticity challenge the notion that concepts have definitions; (iii) one can be erroneously in the possession of a concept, so its use cannot be traced back to its definition; (iv) both concepts and categorizations admit of a certain degree of indeterminacy, further undermining the view that determinate answers can always be obtained from set definitions; and (v) concepts and categorizations admit of a certain degree of typicality, which means that not all instances of categorizing something under a certain concept are on par.[35]

While most new theories of concepts[36] set out to answer the challenges posed by these problems, few depart from the notion that, as fundamental constructs in any theory of mind, concepts must necessarily be understood in terms of their structure. The *prototype theory of concepts*, for instance, states that concepts or words are not governed by definitions but by open-ended sets of properties, which are context specific and can occur in different arrangements. To use an example, the word "tree" (*vṛkṣa*), which encodes the notion of a flowering plant with leaves and branches, can, on this theory, be extended to accommodate nonflowering plants (mosses), plants with needles instead of leaves (conifers), and plants with leaves but not branches (ferns). This theory avoids some of the difficulties posed by the classical account of concepts: specifically the problem of analyticity, which stipulates that concepts must encode the necessary conditions for their application.

The only theory of concepts that regards their representational or semantic content as having no structure is *conceptual atomism*. Conceived primarily as a reaction to descriptivist theories of meaning (as advanced, among others, by Saul Kripke and Hilary Putnam), conceptual atomist takes the view

35. This last problem is first documented in Rosch and Mervis (1975). When presented with the task of categorizing entities such as fruit types or bird species under the category of how "good they are" or how "typical they are," Rosch and Mervis discovered that subjects have no problem ranking the members of various categories (apples, pears, pomegranates, etc.) in ways that cannot be accounted for by appealing to the definitional view of concepts, since the features picked by these concepts ("fruit" or "bird") were not shared by the individual members in the group. For example, Laurence and Margolis (1999: 25) cite a study in which robins were identified as highly "typical" birds because they have most of the features commonly identified with birds, whereas chickens and vultures, judged to have fewer bird features, were classed as less typical.

36. Laurence and Margolis identify at least four new theories of concepts: (1) the prototypical; (2) theory-theory; (3) neoclassical; and (4) conceptual atomism.

that a concept's content is determined not by its structure or definition but by its "standing in an appropriate causal relation to things in the world."[37] As its most influential proponent, Jerry Fodor explain conceptual atomism in terms of information processing models that account for the reliable correlations that can be established between two types of events in a causal chain. On this account, the mental content expressed by a given concept, say that of "cow," conveys information about the thing it designates when it reliably correlates with its establishing causal factors. Thus the concept of "cow" is a negative one in that it does not correlate with universal concepts such as "animal" or defining characteristics such as "dewlap." Rather, it performs its indexical or semantic function insofar as there is a causal relation such that some individual cow comes under the concept "cow" just in case it instantiates the property of being a cow. Fodor explains instances of erroneous uses of the concept (as when, for example, "cow" is used for a misidentified horse) as being asymmetrically dependent on the lawful relations that establish concepts as the designators of certain properties.[38] The aspect of this theory that interests us as having potential relevance for interpreting the semantic theory of exclusion (*apoha*) is that relations among concepts are not constitutive of their content. The advantage of this theory is that it takes structure and reference to be merely associated with the concept rather than being constitutive of its nature.

As these new theories suggest, a naturalized account of concepts offers new ways of examining the traditional issues of definition, categorization, and reference, such that questions about the effectiveness of universals as categories of thought are not divorced from questions about their acquisition and pragmatic function. The naturalized approach itself is not, however, unproblematic: although the sciences of cognition make claims of objectivity, empirical results acquire the status of knowledge only insofar as they are interpreted in light of a given hypothesis, and, as we noted above, theories are in general underdetermined by the empirical data. Indeed, some critics of the explanatory gap between physical processes and consciousness have proposed that we think of this gap in epistemological rather than ontological terms. This proposal locates the gap in the different ways in which the discourse of the physical and the discourse of the mental actually proceed. The gap, it is claimed, is between two sets of concepts rather than between mind and world or, in Buddhist terms, between the domain of conceptual construction and a direct (perceptual) openness to what is given.[39] But this

---

37. Laurence and Margolis (1999: 60). As we will see below (chapter 4), this seems to be precisely the kind of account of linguistic reference that Dharmakīrti's relation of causal generation (*tadutpatti*) implies.

38. Fodor (1987) calls his theory the *asymmetric dependence theory*.

39. Stoljar (2005) calls this the "phenomenal concept strategy."

view, which reflects a commitment to reductive physicalism (that is, to the notion that even phenomenal concepts can be explained in physical terms), runs counter to the conceivability thesis: it is plausible that phenomenal concepts are either explainable in physical terms (in which case, they do not capture our epistemic situation) or they are not (in which case, they do have the capacity to describe the character of phenomenal knowledge).[40]

2.3 INTERPRETATION AND DISCOURSE ANALYSIS

Let's return for now to the question of interpreting Śāntarakṣita and Kamalaśīla's texts, specifically to their defense of a specific account of perceptual knowledge. Is this account empirically and/or phenomenologically anchored? Or is it a purely speculative account? And does it bear any resemblance to similar accounts in Western philosophy? As these questions indirectly suggest, the problem of interpretation is also one of methodology. Nevertheless, one must remain open to the possibility that the results of interpretation might not always fit within existing theoretical frameworks. One option, perhaps the most common, is to continue redefining (and refining) the less controversial aspects of doctrine and seek new texts and contexts in an ever-growing web of interstitial discourse.[41] An alternative option, the one adopted in this book, is to blur the boundary between theory and method and pursue a model of analysis that allows modern philosophical perspective to play a role in the analysis and transmission of Indian and Buddhist philosophy. The result is an open attitude toward exegesis that does not sacrifice the tension between textual analysis and representation, between traditional perspectives and modern philosophical interpretations.[42]

This method of mediating between the discourses of Buddhist and Western philosophers is sufficiently flexible to allow both analytic epistemology and phenomenology to play a role in the process of analysis and interpretation. The relevance of theoretical and methodological discussions in both analytic

40. See Chalmers (2006) for a detailed defense of the view that accounts of phenomenal concepts derive either from an epistemic relation of acquaintance or from demonstrative or indexical accounts of reference.

41. The "interstice" is one of the preferred organic metaphors of the French post-structuralist tradition. Blanchot, Foucault, Derrida, and Deleuze, among others, make ample use of it. The interstice offers an epistemological model of fluidity, indeterminacy, and decentered intertextuality. It can also signify spaces (or discontinuities) between the text and the apparatus of references and cross-references that are the necessary ingredient of any work of scholastic philosophy.

42. Faure defines his epistemological critique of Chan not as a comparative enterprise "on the basis of superficial terminological resemblances" but rather as an effort "to intertwine and cross-graft these various types of discourse, in the hope that they might enhance each other" (1993: 11).

epistemology and phenomenology to specialized fields such as Buddhist philosophy cannot be overestimated. Ever since Theodore Stcherbatsky's influential neo-Kantian reading of Dharmakīrti, following his translation and analysis of Dharmottara's *Nyāyabinduṭīkā* ("Commentary on a Drop of Reasoning"), philosophers and Buddhologists have pondered the implications of such highly interpretive approaches to the history of Buddhist thought.[43] Some have taken issue with the fact that Stcherbatsky interpreted Dignāga's semantic theory of exclusion through Dharmakīrti's lenses and viewed all intellectual movements in India as "systematic reactions to trends within immediately preceding intellectual movements."[44] Others have faulted Stcherbatsky for his Kantian inspired a priori framework in his interpretation of Dharmakīrti's reason of essential nature (*svabhāvahetu*).[45] But even critics admit that Stcherbatsky viewed the Buddhist epistemologists as active participants in the pan-Indian disputes concerning various epistemological concepts and theories, and as such worthy of a thorough philosophical approach.[46]

Stcherbatsky appears to have favored a thematic approach to the study of Buddhist epistemological literature, as well as a willingness to engage the Buddhist philosophers not only as a Buddhologist and historian of ideas but also as a Western philosopher well acquainted with the dominant philosophical currents of his time. Stcherbatsky also realized that literal translations of Buddhist technical terms faced the risk of philosophical opacity and insisted on the importance of finding points of convergence between Western and Buddhist philosophical theories: "When the subject of discourse consists in a deduction of one proposition from two or several others...we have no doubt that it is a syllogism. But when we are faced by the necessity of deciding whether a characteristic act of our understanding is to be rendered as judgment, we must know what a judgment is."[47] Despite Stcherbatsky's insistence on the importance of being philosophically sensitive as a translator and interpreter of Buddhist philosophical texts, philology continues to command the study of Buddhist philosophy. The philological approach relies on the principle that texts can (be made to) speak for themselves. A widely shared assumption is that taking a neutral stand is not only desirable but also possible, and that the text-critical methodology can effectively retrieve the *mens auctoris*.

43. Cf. Steinkellner (1973: 120–124), van der Kuijp (1979: 6–8), Herzberger (1986: 219–223), and Hayes (1988: 11–16).

44. See Hayes (1988: 12).

45. See Steinkellner (1973).

46. Indeed, Stcherbatsky's extensive appendices to his *Buddhist Logic* include translations and discussions of relevant parts of Vācaspati Miśra's *Nyāyavārttikatātparyaṭīkā* and *Nyāyakaṇikā*, as well as a detailed overview of the dispute surrounding the Buddhist theory of perception, from Vasubandhu and Dignāga to Dharmakīrti, Vinītadeva, Jinendrabuddhi, and Dharmottara.

47. Stcherbatsky (1930: I, 226–227).

For instance, in his discussion of the merits of the philological method in comparison with other approaches, Tom Tillemans notes that most philologists labor under "the conviction that by understanding in real depth the Buddhist languages, and the history, institutions, context and preoccupations of an author and his milieu, progress can be made toward understanding that author's thought."[48] Although most philologists work primarily with texts and historical records, the shift from textual exegesis to making claims about understanding the actual thought of an author comes rather naturally to a philologist. The successful deployment of the philological method by scholars such as Ernst Steinkellner in understanding "the mind" of a historical figure like Dharmakīrti is often invoked to remind philosophers just how much progress can be make in understanding historical authors by delving into their texts. But showcasing the merits of the philological approach need not imply that scholars should forgo philosophical analysis altogether. Indeed, as some of the most valuable contributions to the study of Buddhist philosophy have shown, one can draw extensively from Western philosophical sources and remain faithful to a historical author without couching one's interpretations, as Tillemans puts it, "in the same problematic or obscure language that is the author's."[49] At the same time, Tillemans indicates that he is only going part of the way in his philosophical appraisal of Buddhist thought: "using philosophical tools is not, however, an attempt at appropriating Dharmakīrti so that he might somehow become relevant to a contemporary Buddhist philosophy."[50] Contemporary philosophy, it is claimed, has moved beyond the concerns of seventh-century philosophers such as Dharmakīrti, whose thought has little relevance beyond what some would call Buddhist "theology" or "soteriology."

This claim that Dharmakīrti's philosophical system, with its reductionism, its strict mind–body dualism, and its highly fragmented ontology of partless atoms, should prove less appealing to modern philosophers is, however, unwarranted. There are many aspects of Dharmakīrti's philosophy, and indeed of the Buddhist epistemological enterprise as a whole, that are dated; there is also, however, much that has both enduring appeal and modern relevance. Dharmakīrti's causal account of knowledge, the practice of bracketing ontological commitments while examining mental content, and a systematic and rigorous first-person perspective are good examples of these.[51]

In bridging Western and Buddhist philosophical traditions significant progress has been made in the nearly three quarters of a century since

48. Tillemans (1995: 269).
49. Tillemans (1999: 4).
50. Tillemans (1999: 5).
51. If Dan Arnold's recent attempt to interpret Dignāga's and Dharmakīrti's notion that reflexive awareness (*svasaṃvedana*) is ultimately the only warranted cognition as some sort of commitment to a version of Kantian metaphysical idealism is any indication, the Buddhist epistemological tradition continues to invite novel philosophical reassessment. See especially Arnold (2005a, 2009).

Stcherbatsky's pioneering work.[52] Although today we are in a better position to assess the scope of the Buddhist epistemological tradition, agreement about how best to translate its arguments using the vocabulary and methods of Western philosophy is yet to be reached. Given the radical diversification of logic and epistemology in the past century, the nonspecific use of Buddhist "logic" or "epistemology" can be problematic. An unavoidable consequence of using "logic" or "epistemology" in a transcultural sense is that it can easily obscure the fact that the Indian theory of inference (*anumāna*), although neither a type of Aristotelian syllogistic logic nor something similar to modern predicate calculus, nevertheless has its internal order and coherence. As Mohanty pointed out some time ago, what we have here is a "striking combination of cognitive psychology" with the "needs of a dialogical-disputational context and the strictly logical demand of validating a belief."[53] Moreover, the recognition that conventional syllogistic logic covers just first-order logic and that there are a wide variety of "logics" (modal, temporal, counterfactual, many-valued, probabilistic, non-monotonic, fuzzy, etc.), makes it possible to assume that the Indian theory of inference can either be assimilated to one (or several) of these new logics or accommodated as a new type of logic.

Of course, the proposal that we altogether abandon the concept of syllogism as an accurate description of the "inference for the other" (*parārthānumāna*) in Buddhist "logic" as employed by early generations of scholars is not new. Reacting against the superficial similarity and trivial uses of the Aristotelian syllogism, Tillemans claims that such uses "blur the philosophically interesting points where Buddhist logic is *sui generis*."[54] This argument rests on the notion that in the inference for the other the thesis statement (*pakṣavacana*) is not derived, as in the syllogism, from two premises, in this case from the necessary presence of the similar (*sapakṣa*) and dissimilar (*vipakṣa*) examples. Rather, the inference for the other is concerned with the validity of the reason on which the inference is based and with the relationship of pervasion (*vyāpti*) that obtains between the corresponding terms. Nonetheless, some critics have argued against this narrow definition of the syllogism as a system of formal logic and also against the notion that the absence of probandum (*sādhyanirdeśa*) is a specific characteristic of the argument for the other.[55]

52. Among the most recent contributions to this growing and increasingly sophisticated rapprochement of Buddhist and Western debates in metaphysics, epistemology, and philosophy of language are Tillemans (1999), Garfield (2002), Siderits (2003), D'Amato, Garfield, and Tillemans (2009), and Siderits, Tillemans, and Chakrabarti (2011).

53. Mohanty (1992b: 105).

54. Tillemans (1991: 81) See also Tillemans (1984) for an earlier presentation of the same critique.

55. See especially van Bijlert (1989: 88–90). For a detailed discussion of various positions modern scholars have adopted on the nature of *parārthānumāna* and the

I want to claim that, in light of our consideration so far of the argumentative strategies of the Buddhist epistemologists, the so-called Buddhist "logic" or "epistemology" may be best described as a system of pragmatic or context-dependent reasoning. Unlike the deductive systems of semantic reasoning, which are context-free, pragmatic reasoning is largely inductive and encompasses the types of logic (non-monotonic and paraconsistent) that represent reasoning from premises that are context specific. On this model of pragmatic reasoning, while a sentence φ may be a pragmatic consequence of a set of premises ϕ it need not be a pragmatic consequence of a larger set of premises $\varphi \cup \Psi$.[56] Indeed, following Dignāga's inductive model of reasoning, we reason by first observing the occurrence of certain properties in an object or class of objects and the nonoccurrence of those same properties when the object is absent. We establish that in order for a linguistic utterance to acquire the status of logical proof, the reason (*hetu*) must be present in the thesis (that is, in the position that is stated), be also present in similar positions, and be absent from all dissimilar positions. This is Dignāga's well-known model of the triple inferential mark (*trairūpya*), which operates by deriving hypothetical statements from past observations of the inductive domain. Take the example of empirical objects: experience reveals that all objects which come into existence due to causes and conditions are impermanent, for whatever is produced must necessarily cease. Conversely, a permanent object cannot be produced. Thus, a proposition of the type "Sound is impermanent, because it is a product," is true so long as we do not encounter an example of permanent (or indestructible) sounds. Were we to come across such a counterexample, the proposition will be falsified. Shoryu Katsura has defined this type of logic as "hypothetical reasoning based on induction."[57] To the extent that this system of reasoning, which is based on the observation and nonobservation of evidence, is open to revision so as to accommodate cases where there is a violation of the linguistic convention, we may describe it as a system of pragmatic reasoning. Dharmakīrti's attempt to ground reasoning on a stronger principle than mere observation and nonobservation of the evidence would lead him to postulate that there must be some "essential connection" (*svabhāvapratibandha*) between the thesis and what is to be demonstrated in order to provide a stronger basis for reasoning. But even though this essential connection is meant to overcome the challenge posed by reliance on hypothetical reasoning, it is not pragmatically neutral, since Dharmakīrti's ultimate criterion for truth is the causal efficacy of cognitions.

---

function of the thesis (*pakṣa*) in the reasoning model of the triple inferential mark (*trairūpya*), see Oetke (1994: 27ff.).

56. For an account of pragmatic reasoning, see Bell (2001: 46ff.).
57. Katsura (2007: 76).

It should be possible, therefore, to make the Buddhist epistemological program of Dignāga and Dharmakīrti, particularly as adopted by Śāntarakṣita and Kamalaśīla, relevant to contemporary philosophical debates if we adopt a broader view of the scope of "Buddhist philosophy." It has been claimed that any attempt to define "Buddhist philosophy"—as encapsulated in the works of such classical philosophers as Nāgārjuna, Vasubandhu, Dharmakīrti, and Śāntarakṣita—in contemporary terms is inevitably bound to reflect the intellectual proclivities of the interpreters themselves.[58] Typical examples, for instance, include viewing Nāgārjuna as a proto Wittgenstein or Dharmakīrti as an earlier version of Husserl. While such highly interpretive approaches to Buddhist thought may prove problematic, no approach, insofar as it operates within the horizon of contemporary philosophical concerns, can escape this unavoidable predicament. As Matthew Kapstein puts it, rightly in my view:

> Our problem is not to discover, *per impossibile*, how to think Buddhism while eliminating all reference to Western ways of thought; it is, rather, to determine an approach, given our field of reflection, whereby our encounter with Buddhist traditions may open a clearing in which those traditions begin in some measure to disclose themselves, not just ourselves.[59]

Such an approach can indeed be devised if one engages Buddhist thinkers like Dharmakīrti or Śāntarakṣita *philosophically*, that is, in the same way one reads Descartes or Kant as informers of contemporary philosophical debates. This engagement, however, is not free of interpretive concerns, specifically when the intention of the originator of a specific idea is not obvious. Although Buddhist hermeneutical theories distinguish between the intentional (*ābhiprāyika*) and implied (*neyārtha*) uses of the meaning of a given text, they do not dissociate between the *meaning* (or the objective sense) of a text in its own historical context (conceived as a true reflection of the author's intention) and its *significance*, that is, whatever an interpreter makes of the respective text in his or her own context.[60] As Gadamer has convincingly demonstrated, it is impossible to ascertain the intention of the author while also claiming that meaning is intrinsic to the text itself. Rather, interpretation works by effecting a "fusion of horizons":

---

58. See Tuck (1990). Reflecting on the attempt to make Buddhist philosophers relevant to contemporary debates in Western philosophy, by looking for theoretical and conceptual affinities, Conze (1967: 226) claimed that such efforts were not only "objectively unsound" but in fact had not been successful in interesting "Western philosophers in the philosophies of the East." Conze's skepticism about the efficacy of the comparative method has had a significant impact in certain quarters of the Buddhist studies field, where a lack of philosophical expertise in the translation and interpretation of Buddhist philosophical literature continues to be easily tolerated.
59. Kapstein (2001: 3).
60. As proposed by, among others, Hirsch (1976, 1984).

> Every age has to understand a transmitted text in its own way, for the text is part of the whole of the tradition in which the age takes an objective interest and in which it seeks to understand itself. The real meaning of a text, as it speaks to the interpreter, does not depend on the contingencies of the author and whom he originally wrote for. It certainly is not identical with them, for it is always partly determined also by the historical situation of the interpreter and hence by the totality of the objective course of history.[61]

Understanding the meaning of a text and, by implication, inferring the intention of the author, is therefore inextricably linked to the interpreter's own intentionality and self-understanding.[62] If the meaning of a text is historically contingent, it cannot form an object of methodological analysis, for the analysis in turn depends upon whatever significance an interpreter attributes to the original text in the first place. Indeed, the distinction between *meaning* and *significance* cannot be upheld if one is committed to the notion that uncovering the "original" meaning of a text is part of an interpreter's self-understanding.

If Gadamer is right (and we have good reasons to believe that he is), then an "objectivist" and "historicist" paradigm of interpretation, such as one often finds in text-critical studies of Buddhist epistemology, is problematic. While few scholars dispute the effectiveness of text-critical approaches in recovering the works of classical Buddhist authors, weighing in the philosophical import of their ideas demands a certain degree of philosophical expertise.[63] Of course, the question of how to approach a philosopher from a former age and/or a different culture does not invite a straightforward answer. In a study of the overall scope of Dignāga's philosophy, Richard Hayes draws a similar distinction between philosophically and historically oriented approaches to Indian and Buddhist philosophy, highlighting both

---

61. Gadamer (1975: 261–262).

62. As Gadamer states, for example, in his discussion of the hermeneutical implications of biblical exegesis, "the texts of the New Testament are themselves already interpretations of the Christian message; they do not wish to call attention to themselves, but rather to be mediators of this message" (1976: 58). By analogy, we could assert that the texts of the Buddhist epistemological tradition do not wish to draw attention to them as textual materials fit for exegesis but rather to mediate our understanding of various logical and epistemological arguments in relation to a specific topic.

63. Referring to the authority that dictionaries and other lexical tools have enjoyed in the translation and interpretation of Buddhist philosophical works, Ruegg (1995: 146–147) points out that the philological method, quite apart from whatever one may claim in its name, is not immune to "lexical incoherence." One example of such incoherence that is pertinent to our study is the translation of *saṃjñā/sañña* and of *pratyakṣa* by the same English word "perception." As Ruegg notes, "[I]f in a well thought-out and coherent terminology *saṃjñā* is to be translated by 'perception', *pratyakṣa* could not be, and conversely" (1995: 146).

differences and points of convergences. Although he regards both philosophical and historical approaches as legitimate, Hayes seems to suggest that the historical model is preferable owing to its more intimate connection with the task at hand: elucidating the thought of the traditional author.[64] In the majority of cases, however, a historical approach to classical Indian and Buddhist philosophy is likely to uphold the distinction between the meaning of a text and its significance and to regard contemporary philosophical concerns as being at variance with those of premodern philosophical traditions.

Neither approach, however, falls entirely outside the scope of comparative philosophy. But the practice of comparative philosophy, where typically the methods, theories, and conceptual resources of one tradition are used for solving problems in the other, all too often ends up with asymmetric and incongruous conceptual schemes. The typical response to the conundrums of comparative philosophy has been to eschew it altogether in favor of new forms of scholasticism almost exclusively concerned with text-critical issues and intradoctrinal disputes specific to any of the major Asian philosophical traditions. A more interesting response has come recently from Mark Siderits in the form of a new style of philosophical inquiry he calls "fusion philosophy."[65] Simply put, fusion philosophy is the counterpoising of distinct philosophical traditions for the purpose of solving problems that are central to philosophy.

Whether or nor fusion philosophy holds the promise of making philosophy a truly global and cross-cultural enterprise, the possibilities that it opens up, not just for solving problems but also methodological dilemmas that are central to philosophy, are numerous. Such possibilities are already apparent in works that adopt a constructivist and cosmopolitan[66] rather than purely exegetical approach to the study of premodern philosophical traditions. Various obstacles, however, still stand in the way of such an enterprise given that, as Garfield reminds us, "we operate in the shadow of colonialism and its intellectual wing, orientalism."[67] It is not the legitimacy, let alone the absence of works dedicated to translating and commenting on Asian texts for Euro-American audiences, or vice versa, that is at stake, but the deeply problematic nature of these intercultural philosophical ventures. The problematic nature

64. Hayes (1988: 2ff.).
65. Siderits (2003: 1).
66. Flanagan (2011: 2), who introduces the term, defines the "cosmopolitan" style of doing philosophy as the "exercise of reading and living and speaking across different traditions as open, non-committal, energized by an ironic or skeptical attitude about all the forms of life being expressed, embodied, and discussed, including one's own." The cosmopolitan philosopher is thus both a listener and a speaker for the philosophical traditions (and currents) he or she engages with, and lives "at the intersection of multiple spaces of meaning."
67. Garfield (2002: 230).

concerns the types of inquiries that must accompany such enterprises, without which we cannot begin to talk about a single truly intercultural tradition. Garfield's list includes inquiries into:

> the historical conditions under which it takes place; into the respective characters of each of the textual traditions brought thereby into contact; into the relations they bear to one another; into the nature and the very possibility of the linguistic and cultural translation such interchange involves; and finally into the very possibility of reading a text into a tradition that is not one's own.[68]

While I agree that such inquiries are a valuable and perhaps indispensable component of any cross-cultural philosophical enterprise, they can become overly restrictive when it comes to pursuing questions that are central to philosophy. If the Buddhist epistemological program is to be made continuous with contemporary philosophical concerns, then, we may legitimately ask whether it is to be treated as a system of formal logic, as a type of cognitivism, or, as I claimed above, a system of context-dependent reasoning.

Furthermore, a text-critical approach to Indian philosophical literature has no equivalent in the Indian doxographical traditions, where authors are principally concerned with philosophical problems per se (rather than with influences and historical considerations), in much the same way modern philosophers address certain problems as not necessarily contingent upon the historical and sociocultural contexts in which they are formulated.[69] The method of discourse analysis does create, however, a different sort of tension between, on the one hand, the claim that interpretation is never final—because each act of interpretation displaces auctorial intent and makes a new claim of authority—and on the other, the insistence that certain philosophical problems (if not necessarily the solutions to these problems) have a perennial status. A topical or tenet-based approach[70] to addressing—in the hope

---

68. Garfield (2002: 231).

69. Eltschinger (2008: 532) makes a similar point when he argues that Buddhist philosophical texts, specifically those that reflect the concerns of Mādhyamikas and the Buddhist epistemologists (and employ their discursive strategies), insofar as they focus on issues of logic and argumentation, are not easily (if at all) reducible to the historical circumstances of their production (or localizable in terms of socioreligious concerns).

70. Tenet systems, which are philosophical summaries (*siddhānta* lit. "demonstration") of the viewpoints of different schools and subdivisions of those schools, developed into an extensive literary genre in the Buddhist monastic institutions, first in India and subsequently in Tibet. Playing in some regards the same role as technical manuals do today, they centered on core Buddhist doctrines and aimed to give a clear exposition of each philosophical viewpoint that could then be criticized or defended in philosophical debate. Among the most significant contributions made by Tibetan authors to the tenet literature, two works deserve mention:

of solving—philosophical problems, no matter what their original source, is precisely what Śāntarakṣita and Kamalaśīla adopt in the *Compendium* and its *Commentary*.

The methodology of discourse analysis aims to interrogate the Buddhist philosophical texts, to force them outside of their traditional context and to ask of them questions that could not otherwise be asked. In this process of decontextualization one cannot claim a neutral standpoint. Rather, each operation of decontextualization creates in turn its own context, perhaps that of a contemporary Buddhist philosophy or simply of a philosophical discourse in which the arguments and argumentative strategies of Buddhist philosophers are at least worthy (if not yet equal) contributors. But in order to succeed, this methodology of discourse analysis must show tolerance for discontinuity, difference, and ambiguity. I want to claim that classical thinkers like Śāntarakṣita and Kamalaśīla, whose interests were sufficiently broad, may be found to entertain, without losing consistency altogether, views that vary on several counts, as suggested in the hyphenated doxographical designation of their philosophical positions as Svātantrika-Mādhyamika or Yogācāra-Mādhyamika. This situation is not specific to Śāntarakṣita and Kamalaśīla alone, but can also be found in Dharmakīrti (and many of his commentators), on whose views they rely to a great extent. In Dharmakīrti's case, a good example of such discontinuity is found in his attitude toward the ontological status of external objects, which is at best ambiguous and at worst contradictory.[71] Thus, when Śāntarakṣita and Kamalaśīla attempt to clarify their own position regarding the reality of external objects in the *Bāhyāthaparīkṣā* ("Examination of External Objects"), they seem to advocate a natural progression from a Sautrāntika realist position to an idealist (or perhaps phenomenalist) Yogācāra position, although this latter position creates certain tensions in their attempt to demonstrate, elsewhere in the *Compendium* and its *Commentary*, that it is real objects or particulars that are apprehended in perception.[72]

Jam-dbyangs-bzhad-pa's (1648–1721) *Great Exposition of Tenets* (*Grub mtha' chen mo*) and Lcang-skya-rol-pa'i-rdo-rje's (1717–1786) *Presentation of Tenets* (*Grub pa'i mtha'i rnam par bzhag pa*).

71. See, for example, PV III, 194–224 and 333–341, where there is no clear indication as to whether Dharmakīrti adopts the view of those who hold objects of perception to be internal (*antarjñeyavādin*) or of those who consider them to be external (*bāhyārthavādin*).

72. In this chapter of the TS/P, the authors appear to advocate the notion that external objects (*bāhyārtha*) are illusory constructs on the grounds that "grossness" (*sthulatva*) does not really exist and that what is termed grossness is merely a conceptual construct resulting from the perception of aggregated entities. This chapter contains a detailed defense of atomism and of the possibility of ascertaining the veridical nature of cognition without appealing to the principle of correspondence (*sadṛśya*). See especially TS 1972–1978 and TSP *loc. cit.*

2.4 LOGIC AND THE SUBJECTIVITY OF THOUGHT

Acknowledging the possibility that Śāntarakṣita and Kamalaśīla adopt different viewpoints depending on whether they discuss the nature of external objects or the character of internal states of cognitive awareness is therefore crucial to explaining these apparent inconsistencies. Any attempt to abstract the complex and often contradictory contents of experience (i.e., to make sense of what is going on) sooner of later must confront the limits of thought. The assumption that Śāntarakṣīta and Kamalaśīla (like any other Buddhist philosopher before or after them) cannot hold contradictory viewpoints because of a well-established prohibition against "contradiction" (*virodha*) in Indian philosophy is thus unwarranted.[73] Such prohibition does not necessarily imply that Indian philosophers cannot be found to contradict themselves. Even when Buddhist philosophers invoke the schema of two truths to explain how a proposition can be affirmed from one perspective and denied from another, contradictions can persist. Logical reasoning, after all, is also a matter of conjecture.[74] Indeed, any philosophical view may be deemed false or even incoherent if it is not supported by an empirical account (and/or rationally justified in light of some plausible hypothesis) or lacks an orderly continuity with previously stated positions.

As the eloquent and sometimes playful critique of a skeptic such as Jayarāśi (fl. c. 800) shows, epistemologists (whether Buddhist or Brahmanical) get themselves into all sorts of contradictory situations by trying to uphold various logical positions. One of Jayarāśi's strategies, as Eli Franco has clearly shown, "is to take a Buddhist argument, originally formulated against the Naiyāyikas or the Mīmāṃsakas, and to apply it against the Buddhists themselves."[75] One such example, for instance, is Jayarāśi's use of a Buddhist argument against the idea that the universal resides entirely in the particular or in part of it, to refute the Buddhist's own claim about the production of cognition (which, the Buddhist asserts, has no parts).[76]

---

73. In a discussion of the significance of Nāgārjuna's tetralemma (*catuṣkoṭi*), Tillemans (1992: 195) makes a broad assumption that is somewhat relevant to my discussion: "The prohibition against 'contradiction' (*virodha*) is accepted by all schools of Indian philosophy, including the Buddhist schools. It would thus be surprising if a treatise by a great Buddhist philosopher were to go against such a key principle."

74. Incidentally, *tarka*, the technical term for "logic" or the "science of logic," also means "conjecture" or "supposition" from √*tark*, "to suppose," "suspect," or "conjecture."

75. Franco (1994: 475).

76. Franco summarizes Jayarāśi's position as follows "if a cognition is produced completely by its object, it cannot be produced by other causal factors; if it is partly produced by the object, it would have parts and lose its unity. . . . If the causal efficiency of an object is exhausted in producing its cognition, it cannot produce the object in the next moment. Nor can it produce the object with only part of itself, because it has no parts" (1994: 477).

It is partly on the basis of a perceived discrepancy between logic and phenomenal experience that Mādhyamikas like Candrakīrti launch a critique of the Buddhist epistemological program.[77] This book preempts such unwarranted criticism by adopting a different theoretical perspective, one that does not aim to solve inconsistencies when and where found, but rather asks whether such inconsistencies reflect an the inherently contradictory nature of the subjective domain when confronted with the objective order of logical truths. In Western philosophy, this resistance to reconciling such inconsistencies would eventually lead, through the genesis of Husserl's work—from *Experience and Judgment* to *Ideas I*—to the birth of phenomenology. To the young Husserl it was obvious that even though true and false judgments "contain no subjective words such as 'evidence'... they derive their sense and legitimacy from evidence."[78] Husserl would eventually reject the empiricism of his teacher Franz Brentano and come to embrace the idealism of his mathematician friend Georg Cantor.[79] Even so, in *Logic and Transcendence* Husserl recognizes that logic turns both toward ideal objects and toward the subjective modes of reasoning that ground our thought. When a proposition is judged true "in the evidence of a fulfilling adequation,"[80] it becomes true *once and for all* so that its contradictory opposite is false. The problem, however, as Husserl himself was forced to admit, is that "once and for all" is a subjective locution that belongs to the subjective experience of temporality. Logical reasoning takes place in a horizon of experience that is inherently subjective and temporal.

Now, unlike the deductive system of Aristotelian syllogistic logic (or modern predicate calculus), Indian logic is grounded in a concern with specifying the criteria of empirical knowledge. Claims, including claims that are rooted in relations of logical entailment, do not just present us with facts about the respective subject matter. How might we distinguish, then, between the way logical subjects and logical predicates function, and the subjective aspects of thought? On the standard answer, we might follow the model offered by Frege or Strawson, and distinguish between meaning and reference. All we have to do then is cast a given sentence in a canonical form of *S* is *p*. Following this formal procedure, the meaning of the predicate term becomes a concept which has the capacity to sort through the various objects of experience. But this process of formalization takes place within a horizon of reflection where predicates (*exist*, *believe*) are turned into concepts, which eventually

77. See PrasP II, 58–77, and translation in May (1959). For detailed treatments of the main issues that Candrakīrti addresses in his critique of Dignāga's definition of perception, see Siderits (1981), Sprung (1979), and Arnold (2005a).
78. Husserl (1969: 194).
79. See Hill (2009) for a presentation of the crises and theoretical conflicts that mark the genesis of Husserl's phenomenology.
80. Husserl (1969: 194).

acquire the status of ideal entities (rendered in standard notations such as *b* (*X*, *p*) or "*x* believes that *p*"). With a system of ideal entities and operators in place, it becomes possible to engage in different types of knowledge enterprises (inferring general statements from particular premises) in different domains (philosophy, sociology, biology), where various forms of entailment control how concepts operate and claims to knowledge are advanced. What this sort of analysis masks is the fact that such claims to knowledge are not primitive. Rather, they derive from implicitly pragmatic contexts where our dialogical exchanges might have the form *b* (*X*, *p*) or *S* is *p*, but in reality are concerned not with representing facts or establishing logical truths, but with acquiring, perfecting, and transmitting practical knowledge and skills.[81]

As Bimal Krishna Matilal noted, while dispelling some of the misunderstandings of early interpreters of Indian logic, no system of logic operates outside the domain of pragmatic or evidence-based reasoning:

> [I]n spite of the neatness, elegance, and precision of a deductive system like that of Aristotle, it is undeniable that a good deal of our actual reasonings may not follow the deductive pattern. The reasoning of an experimental scientist, a historian or an ordinary man trying to ascertain the truth of a particular matter, is a reasoning from what may be called "evidence" to what we can call "conclusion." Even most of our philosophical arguments, where we try to depend more or less upon empirical evidence, belong to this type of inference.[82]

A system of logical reasoning necessarily presupposes that the validity of an argument is not contingent on the truth of its premises but simply on the argument's logical structure. Matilal simply makes the case that whether we are dealing with deductive or inductive arguments we invariably find ourselves having to turn away from the actual structure of the argument and appeal to experience or to a coherent system of beliefs when trying to establish the truth of a proposition. But experience is no less contradictory. Indeed, Dharmakīrti was among the first to consider factual contradictions, which he traced to cognitions apprehending a change in the causal series affecting both perceiver and object perceived, as when a sensation of hot is replaced by a sensation of cold in the same locus.[83] Arguably most contradictions, not just

81. Discussing Husserl's conception of world as horizon, Welton (2003: 226ff.) notes that in expressing our practical involvement with situations and things our language is descriptive rather than representational. Our pragmatic uses of language and reasoning in these situations (building a house, fixing a car) function as tools that enable us to work with others, rather than "mirrors that reflect the world."

82. Matilal (1985: 89). Indeed, for Dharmakīrti, evidence of an empirical (*read* perceptual) kind is actually necessary for the justification of certain inferential procedures. Cf. McClintock (2010: 71).

83. See NB III, 75–76. For a very informative discussion of the concept of contradiction in Indian philosophy, see Bandyopadhyay (1988).

those of the factual type, have their basis in experience, for our descriptions of reality are ultimately anchored in the life-world.

Alternatively, following Dreyfus's proposal for regarding Dharmakīrti's pragmatic approach toward ontological questions as operating on an "ascending" or "sliding" scale of analysis, we may also assume that different descriptions of reality, though mutually contradictory, are meant to be hierarchically structured.[84] Dharmakīrti's (and, following him, Śāntarakṣita and Kamalaśīla's) adoption of seemingly contradictory viewpoints is not, as Dreyfus notes, "an example of confusion or a deviant logic, for Dharmakīrti sees these propositions as logically contradictory, but he also sees them as complementary or at least pragmatically compatible."[85] We may view this operational pragmatism, therefore, as an example of the common Buddhist trope of expedient means (*upāyakauśalya*) since these different descriptions of reality are not logically equivalent but rather hierarchical.[86]

2.5 COGNITION AS ENACTIVE TRANSFORMATION

It is a common feature of Indian philosophical systems to argue for preserving the tradition—or more specifically the words of the tradition (*śruti* or *āgama*)—as conveying a vision of reality that is not apparent, but requires constant actualization through a dynamic praxis of interpretation. This praxis, which involves listening to a set of axiomatic statements (*śrutamayī*), reflecting upon their intended meaning (*cintāmayī*), and actualizing their significance in an enactive manner (*bhāvanāmayī*), is essentially an epistemic practice.[87] Its foundation is to be found in various types

84. See Dreyfus (1997: 83, 99, 104), where he refers to Dharmakīrti's adoption of different perspectives regarding the nature of reality as an "ascending scale of analysis." Dreyfus identifies in total four positions from which Dharmakīrti appears to operate, in which "three assume the existence of external objects while the fourth one rejects this presupposition." The fourth position is that of Yogācāra, which rejects the reality of external objects. See also Dunne (2004: 65–79), who calls the fourth and highest level of analysis at which Dharmakīrti presumably operates "epistemic idealism," a position which differs from that of "external realism"—the ontological standpoint from which Dharmakīrti defends most of his philosophical positions. Kellner (2010) has recently called into question the "sliding" scale of analysis model on account of the complexity of Dignāga and Dharmakīrti's account of the epistemic function of self-awareness. See also chapter 7, below.

85. Dreyfus (1997: 99).

86. See also Dunne (2004: 83ff.) and McClintock (2010: 86–87). The notion of different levels of analysis is in fact an integral part of Buddhist hermeneutics, finding full exposition in texts such as the *Saṃdhinirmocana-sūtra* ("Examination of the Profound Meaning"), whose composition answers the demand for accommodating seemingly conflicting statements found in the *Nikāyas* ("discourses").

87. See, for example, Vasubandhu's discussion of this progression toward the contemplative realization of wisdom in AKBh *ad* AK VI, 5cd: *nāmālambanā kila śrutamayī*

of meditative attainments that are discussed at length in the vast corpus of Abhidharma literature, specifically in the main texts of the Sautrāntika and Yogācāra Abhidharma schools. In its advocacy of disciplined observation and mental training, the Yogācāra school in particular provides the pragmatic and phenomenological tools that Buddhist epistemologists require in order to map out the cognitive domain.[88] It is this praxis, which leads Buddhist epistemologists to claim that the Buddha, whose views they propound, is a true embodiment of the sources of knowledge (*pramāṇabhūta*).[89]

But the Buddhist epistemologist's appeal to the Buddha as an enlightened knower to justify his or her claim that perception and inference are trustworthy sources of knowledge—because the Buddha declares them to be so—involves a certain circularity. Steinkellner explains this circularity rather well:

> (1) Our ordinary valid cognitions (*pramāṇa*) establish the authority of the Buddha's teaching (*buddha-vacana*); (2) the validity of our cognitions (*prāmāṇya*) is understood as their reliability (*avisaṃvaditva*); (3) reliability depends on successful activity (*puruṣārtha-siddhi*); (4) all human goals are determined by the "ultimate goal" (*nirvāṇa*); the "ultimate goal" is indicated in the Buddha's teaching (*buddha-vacana*).[90]

---

prajña/nāmārthālambanā cintāmayī/kadācidvyañjanenārthamākarṣati kadācid arthena vyañjanam/arthālambana eva bhāvanāmayī.

88. Critics of the revealing capacity of meditative practices (for instance, Franco 2009), just like critics of the efficacy of the phenomenological method, often claim that the insights thus gained at best give us another theoretical perspective rather than pre-theoretical access to experience itself. For a synthetic overview of the evidence and arguments in support of the efficacy of meditative practices to regulate attentional and affective processes, see Lutz, Dunne, and Davidson (2007). For a phenomenological account of the pragmatics of experience, see Depraz, Varela, and Vermersch (2003). I discuss this issue below (chapters 7 and 8).

89. The idea of embodying the sources of cognition is a translation of the Sanskrit concept of *pramāṇabhūta*. The first attested use of "*pramāṇabhūta*" is found in Patañjali's *Mahābhāṣya* on Pāṇini I.1.1, *vārttika* 7: *pramāṇabhūta ācāryo darbhapavitrapāṇiḥ śucāv avakāśe prāṅmukha upaviśya mahatā prayatnena sūtrāṇi pranayati sma*. In his translation of this *vārttika*, Filliozat (1975: 376) adopts the meaning "le Maître qui possède l'autorité" on the basis of the common commentarial definition of *pramāṇabhūta* as *pramāṇyam prāptaḥ*. For the occurrence and meaning of this key concept in grammatical and philosophical texts, see the detailed treatment in Ruegg (1994b). For a discussion of Dharmakīrti's gloss on this term in his *Commentary* (PV II, 7a: *tadvat pramāṇaṃ bhagavān*) and the interpretation of "*tadvat*," see Krasser (2001). A general discussion of the use of epithets and arguments in the Buddhist epistemological tradition is found in Jackson (1988). Further analyses of *pramāṇabhūta* are found in and Vetter (1964), van Bijlert (1989), Steinkellner (1983, 1994), Tillemans (1993), Franco (1997), and van der Kuijp (1999), and Dunne (2004).

90. Steinkellner (2003: 328).

This circularity refers to the fact that perception and inference are taken to be instrumentally capable of demonstrating that the Buddha is a trustworthy teacher. Because of his trustworthiness, his teachings are valid and provide further proof that only perception and inference qualify as sources of knowledge (again, to come full circle, because the Buddha has established that to be the case).[91] Does appeal to the authority of the Buddha as a true embodiment of the sources of knowledge undermine the Buddhist epistemological stance? Not necessarily. Indeed, as Franco notes in his detailed treatment of Dharmakīrti's appeal to the Buddha as the embodiment of reliable cognition, "Dharmakīrti argues here... that the Buddha used perception and inference, not that they are valid because of him."[92] Precisely what it means to "embody" the sources of reliable cognition remains an open question, regardless of whether Dharmakīrti's argument is found to be circular or not. It is not enough to say that the Buddha is a true embodiment of reliable cognition: one must also specify how. Dharmakīrti's answer to the "how" invokes three elements: the Buddha embodies the sources of knowledge by means of his compassion and knowledge, and by means of the actions that bear testimony to his knowledge and compassion.[93] But neither listing the Buddha's attributes nor the fact that he reasons and acts on the basis of compassion and knowledge justify the veracity of *our* cognitions (and the sources thereof).

This appeal to authority and particularly to the Buddha's extraordinary cognitive abilities raises another important question: do Buddhists regard epistemological reasoning as in some sense having a soteriological dimension? After all, the Buddha is no ordinary thinker, since he presumably reasons (at all times) from the perspective of an enlightened being. Then, should Dignāga and Dharmakīrti's epistemological method, much like Nāgārjuna's dialectics, be seen as having a special kind of critical or even therapeutic function: perspicacious reasoning in the first case and the relinquishing of all views in the latter?

It has been argued that the tradition of reflection inaugurated by Dignāga and Dharmakīrti does not have as its sole concern the establishment of stringent rules of debate.[94] For instance, in addressing Dharmakīrti's specific use of inference of the cause from the effect (*karyānumāna*), Steinkellner has argued on more than one occasion that it is reasonable to assume that

91. Various formulations of this argument, first proposed by Nagatomi (1959) and Vetter (1964), are also found in Franco (1997, 1999) and Dunne (2004).

92. Franco (1999: 65).

93. Cf. PV II, 282, and its translation and discussion in Franco (1997: 21).

94. Arguments in favor of viewing Buddhist epistemology as having a soteriological function are found in Steinkellner (1982), van Bijlert (1989), Hayes (1984), and Jackson (1993). These authors usually criticize earlier treatments by Stcherbatsky (1930: 37) and Conze (1962: 264), who regarded *hetuvidyā* as a secular activity.

Dharmakīrti's motive is ultimately soteriological in that "he wants to investigate whether a kind of 'progressive, proleptic causality,' necessarily to be acknowledged as a real soteriological fact in the conception of progress toward Buddhahood" has a rational basis.[95] Progress toward Buddhahood depends on the possibility of effecting some radical change in the mental continuum, the ultimate result of which is a transformation of the basis (*āśrayaḥ parivartate*), that is, effectively a transformation of the constitutive elements of existence and/or experience. But is this cognitive and affective transformation possible, as it is claimed in the contemplative and ethical literature? And if it is possible, can a descriptive account of its underlying causal mechanism, one that is sufficiently compelling, be offered? However we may answer these questions, it is worth noting that Dharmakīrti's position toward the natural efficacy (*bhāvaśakti*) of certain forms of meditation indicates that he was indeed familiar with the literature on meditation and ritual practice.[96] It is most likely under the influence of such literature that he developed his proof for taking yogic perception (*yogipratyakṣa*) as a source of reliable cognition. Dharmakīrti's acknowledgment of the possibility and indeed efficacy of supernormal vision (*atīndriyadarśana*) and supernormal knowledge (*atīndriyajñāna*) may indeed have had a definitive impact on his epistemological theories.[97]

For Śāntarakṣita and Kamalaśīla perception, specifically a disciplined mode of perceptual attentiveness, becomes essentially the enactive awareness that allows for the contents of experience to be transformatively understood (and realized). Such proof of the efficacy of yogic perception is advanced in defense of the notion that one can attain a vision of selflessness through cultivation (*abhyāsa*), though this so-called proof is merely pointed at rather than rationally justified.[98] As the author of an important text on medita-

95. Steinkellner (1999: 35).

96. Eltschinger (2001: 8) has adduced significant evidence that Dharmakīrti refers to certain Tantric texts such as the *Kādambarī* and *Megha Sūtra* verbatim and thus appears to endorse the efficacy of certain meditative practices.

97. Dunne (2006) takes the view that Dharmakīrti's epistemological account of perception discounts any appeal to the notion that special forms of cognitive awareness such as yogic perception represent a full-blown encounter with the real. Taking the exact opposite view, Eltschinger (2009) has recently marshaled copious evidence (both textual and analytical) for taking Dharmakīrti's account of yogic perception as epistemically warranted. I discuss the issue of yogic perception below (see chapters 6 and 8).

98. See TSP *ad* TS 1360, and discussion in McClintock (2011: 200). As McClintock notes, in what appears to be the final proof of the Buddha's omniscience (see TS 2048–2049), Śāntarakṣita describes omniscience by pointing to the specific character of his enlightened state, rather than to a particular vision, since omniscience is said to be nonperceptual in character. Omniscience is a state of effortless (*anābhoga*) knowledge of all things (*sarvajña*), though it is debatable whether Śāntarakṣita and Kamalaśīla understand omniscience to lack any phenomenal character.

tive cultivation, Kamalaśīla makes clear that even a state of non-ordinary or supramundane cognition, though nonconceptual in character, is not to be understood as lacking any mentation (*manasikāra*). Such a state of cognitive awareness is typically a form of insight (*prajñayā*) by means of which one gains direct knowledge of various phenomena.[99] What Kamalaśīla argues against is the mistaken view that meditative cultivation essentially amounts to casting aside all mental activity and achieving a state of unconscious concentration (*asaṃjñīsamāpatti*).[100] Like Śāntarakṣita, Kamalaśīla clearly emphasizes that meditative practice should not be regarded as antithetical to philosophical inquiry and debate, but rather as an extension of it.

It has also been argued that with Dignāga and Dharmakīrti there is an important shift in Buddhist attitudes toward the role of philosophical debate: it is the soundness of arguments rather than winning a dispute that becomes the defining characteristic of Buddhist epistemology.[101] Philosophical debates in classical India (as elsewhere) were elaborate staged confrontations that often impacted a scholar's reputation and academic career. That tradition of debate, which continues to this day in the Tibetan monastic communities, is understood to have a threefold aim: (1) help the opponent overcome his wrong views, rather than embarrass him; (2) posit the right view by clearing whatever uncertainties arise due to mistaken beliefs; and (3) resolve whatever inconsistencies and criticism might arise from one's position. It is this final need to remove misconceptions and philosophical biases often stemming from commonsense assumptions that could provide a justification for treating epistemic inquiry as an essential preparatory step for further training involving contemplative practices.[102]

It remains, however, a matter of conjecture just how far we can advance the claim that the arguments of the Buddhist epistemologists are entirely circumscribed by a soteriological *telos*—that of developing an enlightened perspective on the nature of things (and not simply that of winning debates and vanquishing opponents). As will be argued in chapter 5 despite the fact that ethical and religious concerns are not altogether absent, Śāntarakṣita and Kamalaśīla clearly state that the nature of their project is primarily epis-

---

99. *Bhāvanākrama* I, 212.

100. Note that Kamalaśīla composed the *Bhāvanākrama* ("Stages of Meditation"), essentially a philosophical manifesto for the gradualist path of cultivation, in response to the Great Debate of Lhasa (c. 792) between the Chinese and Korean Ho-shangs Chan teachers and the highly scholastic Indian tradition that he and Śāntarakṣita represent. See Demiéville (1947, 1952), Gómez (1987), McRae (1987), and Ruegg (1989a) for an account of this debate.

101. Dharmakīrti makes this argument in VN XXII, 15–20, where he differentiates between the debate strategies of those seeking victory (*vijigīṣuvāda*) and those who adhere to the methods of reasoning (*nyāyānusaraṇam*) simply in order to help others reach the correct view. Cf. Jackson (1987: 5).

102. Cf. Perdue (1992: 8–13)

temological. As an encyclopedic work composed with the explicit purpose of teaching the fundamental principles of Buddhist philosophy, the *Compendium* and its *Commentary* are both complex and far-ranging in scope. It is essentially a syncretic work addressing a large and diverse philosophical audience. It is conceivable, therefore, that in adopting this syncretic approach, Śāntarakṣita and Kamalaśīla embrace all the pragmatic aspects of their discursive enterprise, including the need to persuade their audience that the sort of philosophical progress in understanding they argue for reflects an implicit hierarchy of knowledge.

This notion that philosophical arguments bear an undisclosed rhetorical residue is not an alien concept for our Buddhist authors. Indeed, Indian philosophers, even when they rejected the suggestive power of words (*dhvani*) (as did the Naiyāyikas and the Mīmāṃsakas),[103] were aware that words have both literal and intended meanings, and that telling the difference between the two depends on more than stating the intention. Words are suggestive in ways that transcend individual usage. Theories of rhetoric like that developed by Ānandavardhana (fl. c. 860 C.E.) in his *Dhvanyāloka* ("Illumination of the Suggestive Power of Words") argue that in order to deliver an effective discourse and capture the audience, the suggestive meaning (*vyañjanā*) must dominate the literal sense (*vācyārtha*).[104] In his elaborate commentary on Ānandavardhana's theory of suggestion, Abhinavagupta (c. 975–1025) makes a compelling case for treating even philosophical arguments as rhetorical constructs. When philosophical disputation is carried on in a public setting, arguments have pragmatic effects: they inspire in an audience certain emotive states (*bhāva*) and can engender sympathetic feelings toward the cause or object of those emotive states, that is, the meaning, purpose, or aesthetic form of the discourse. In an argument aimed primarily at the Mīmāṃsakas, who regard the apprehension of aesthetic sentiments (*rasa*) as nothing more than ascertaining another person's mental state (*paracittavṛttimātra*), Abhinavagupta defends the view, common among the Ālaṃkārikas ("aestheticians"), that the power of suggestivity (*vyañjakatva*) goes well beyond inferential comprehension:

---

103. The dispute between the philosophers and the Ālaṃkārikas centers on the various attempts on the part of philosophers to explain or assimilate suggestion (*dhvani*) into inference (*anumāna*), implication (*arthāpati*), metaphor (*lakṣaṇa*), etc. The reader is directed here to consult Amaladass's (1984) excellent exploration of the philosophical implications of *dhvani*. For a discussion of the parallels between the hermeneutical use of intentional (*ābhiprāyika*) and implied (*neyārtha*) meanings in Buddhist literature, and the use of suggestive and resonant meanings by the Ālaṃkārikas, see Ruegg (1989b).

104. See DĀ, k.13: *yatrārthaḥ śabdo vā tam artham upasarjanīkṛtasvārthai/vyaṅktaḥ kāvyaviśeṣaḥ sa dhvanir iti sūribhiḥ kathitaḥ//* "Poetry as a distinctive literary form which the wise call *dhvani*, is that [type of discourse] in which the [literal] sense or the word, subordinates its own meaning, [and] suggest that [nonliteral, for example, poetic] meaning."

The Mīmāṃsaka, who are aware of our own manner of cognizing, should be asked this question: Is it the case that becoming aware of the aesthetic sentiment is merely the apprehension of another mental state? [We urge you:] Do not commit the error [of thinking so]. What aesthetic sentiment can one experience by inferring mental states that reflect worldly matters? The experience of aesthetic sentiment is a supramundane delight, truly an enjoyment of the emotive factors (*vibhāvas*), etc., which are the soul of poetry. One should not reduce it to memory, inference and the like. Rather, the aesthete, whose mind has reached perfection in the ability to make inferences of the cause from the effect, cognizes the emotive factors, etc., not in a detached manner, but by becoming sensitive to their delight or, in other words, by developing sympathy towards them. This [sympathetic attitude] is the source that nurtures the full enjoyment of the aesthetic sentiment which arises from it. The nature of this cognitive state is pure enjoyment of the emotive factors, which arise from one's own identification with them. [This is] an experience that reaches out to a different state than [what can be achieved through] recollection and inference. This enjoyment has not arisen as a result of having used some source of knowledge, so that it might qualify as memory.[105]

For Abhinavagupta it is this sympathetic attitude that creates in an aesthetically sensitive audience the disposition to act in an involved manner. His claim is that what one apprehends in a discourse is not merely due to the types of arguments and argumentative strategies employed but also to the power of suggestion to induce certain dispositions and emotional responses that go beyond mere verbal comprehension. I think a similar suggestive purposefulness is also apparent (though not explicitly stated) in the manner in which Śāntarakṣita and Kamalaśīla present their arguments in the *Compendium* and its *Commentary*.[106] To give but one example of such a discur-

105. DĀ, 1.18: *idaṃ tāvadayaṃ pratītisvarūpajñe mīmāṃsakaḥ: kimtra paracittavṛttimātre pratipattir eva rasapratipattir abhimatā bhavataḥ? na caivaṃ bhramtavyaṃ; evam hi lokagatacittevṛttyanumānamātram iti kā rasatā? yas tva laukikacamatkārātmā rasāsvādaḥ kāvyagatavibhāvādicarvaṇaprāṇe nāsau smaraṇānumānādisābhyena khilīkārapātrīkartavyaḥ/kiṃ tu laukikena kāryakāraṇānumānādinā saṃskṛtahṛdaye vibhāvādikaṃ pratipadyamāna eva na tāṭasthyena pratipadyate api tu hṛdayasaṃvādādāparaparyāya sahṛdayatvāparavaśikṛtatayā pūrṇībhaviṣyad rasāsvādāṅkurī bhāvenānumānasmaraṇādisaraṇimanāruh yaiva tanmayī bhavanocitacarvaṇaprāṇa tayā/na cāsau carvaṇā pramāṇāntarato jātā pūrvaṃ, yenedānīṃ smṛtiḥ syāt/.* Translation, slightly adjusted for consistency, per Ingalls, Masson, and Patwardhan (1990: 162).

106. McClintock (2010) offers a detailed reconstruction of the "rhetoric of reason" in the TS/P. Her main focus is the concept of omniscience (*sarvajñā*) as presented in the final chapter. McClintock makes extensive use of Perelman and Olbrechts-Tyteca's (1969: 45) notion that "the goal of argumentation . . . is to create or increase the adherence of minds to the theses presented for their assent." A rhetoric based on the idea that argumentation operates as principal motivator for undertaking specific actions nicely complements the traditional theories of suggestion (*vyañjanā*, *dhvani*) (as the main motivator for undertaking specific actions) developed by the Indian

sive strategy, Kamalaśīla declares that in Śāntarakṣita's presentation of the Buddha's teachings, an intelligent reader will find a goal that is worth pursuing and the means for accomplishing it:

> Considering the stated purpose [of this work], an intelligent reader would actively engage in studying the teachings [contained therein], having heard [the author] assert their intended purpose, specially [having taken into consideration] that there is nothing that could invalidate such an assertion. Only by means of an impending cause does a person resort to any action. Regarding the question under consideration, apart from our assertion [viz., statement of purpose] no other impending cause can be found; [indeed] no action would take place prior to stating the significance of this work.[107]

This argument—which states that for any intelligent person the Buddha's teachings would prove not only reasonable but sufficiently appealing to compel such a person to actively study them—is but one of the (rhetorical) strategies that Śāntarakṣita and Kamalaśīla employ. Whereas such a strategy, which aims to give reasonable assertions enough suggestive power to impend action, may prove effective in drawing the attention of a disinterested reader, it is not enough to persuade many of those whose views are debated at great length in the *Compendium* and its *Commentary*. In order to achieve their goal of persuading an educated audience that there is great merit in undertaking the study of Buddhist philosophy, Śāntarakṣita and Kamalaśīla make use of a wide range of arguments, including their appeal to the extraordinary cognitive capacities of the Buddha.

2.6 PHENOMENOLOGICAL EPISTEMOLOGY AND THE PROJECT OF NATURALISM

In approaching the arguments of the Buddhist epistemologists from the methodological standpoint of phenomenological naturalism I will draw freely from current debates in analytic epistemology and phenomenology,[108] particularly in relation to the project of naturalism.

Ālaṃkārikas, with which both Śāntarakṣita and Kamalaśīla would have been acquainted. See, for example, TS 911–913, 1011–1017 and TSP *loc. cit.*, where Śāntarakṣita discusses Bhāmaha's theory of the suggestivity of words and responds to his criticism of *apoha* as found in his *Kāvyālaṃkāra* ("Ornament of Poetry") 6, 16–19.

107. TSP *ad* TS 1–6: *tadvadihāpi avyāhataprayojanādivākyaśravaṇācchāstreṣu pravarttamānāḥ prekṣāpūrvakāriṇo bhaviṣyanti; upāyenaiva pravṛtteḥ/na hy atrāpi pravṛttā vabhyupāyāntaramasti; śāstrārthasya prākpravṛtteratyantaparokṣatvāt/.*

108. Henry Pietersma's discussion of the nature and scope of phenomenological epistemology is helpful and relevant here. See Pietersma (2000: 8–11). For a

The naturalistic turn in contemporary epistemology represents an indirect response to a growing body of scientific data pointing to the fact that ordinary sensory experience is not a trustworthy source of knowledge. More specifically, naturalism represents an attempt to integrate the evidence from psychology (more specifically from cognitive psychology and cognitive neuroscience) in settling questions about how we acquire our beliefs. I have already noted that the tradition of epistemological inquiry within Buddhism, insofar as it addresses questions regarding the foundation of knowledge not only on logical but also on empirical and phenomenological grounds, could be seen as advocating a form of naturalism that links it strongly to psychology, in this case to Abhidharma reductionist accounts of experience. The question now before us is whether extending the Abhidharma analyses of consciousness and cognition to take into account the findings of cognitive science alters in a fundamental way the scope of Buddhist epistemology, and whether phenomenological naturalism offers a viable way of making the Buddhist project continuous with contemporary philosophical concerns.[109]

Insofar as epistemological inquiries in both India and the West are seen as traditionally operating with the presupposition that (at least under certain conditions) perception is a reliable cognition, and opens up to a domain of external objects, they fall under what Husserl calls the "natural attitude." Against this widespread orientation, Husserl proposed that epistemology adopt a transcendental orientation and concern itself not with the objects of perception (or conception) but with the intentional acts themselves. As a constitutive aspect of consciousness, intentionality thus captures the specific *orientation* that marks the character of different states of cognitive awareness. Given their commitment to reflexivity, the Buddhist epistemologists in effect approach experience as a phenomenological epistemologist would, that is, by cultivating a reflective perspective on the act of cognizing itself. This is evident, for instance, in the dual-aspect theory of cognition advanced by the Yogācāra, which is integral to the Buddhist epistemological enterprise. Unlike the Nyāya external realist, the Buddhist epistemologist does not describe cognitive experience from a third-person perspective, that is, in terms of a natural relation between what Armstrong calls the "belief state" and "the situation which makes the belief true."[110] Rather, as we shall see in

comprehensive treatment of phenomenology and the project of naturalism, see Petitot et al. (1999).

109. Garfield (2012) makes a compelling case for why recent advances, for instance, in the phenomenology and cognitive science of attention, perception and memory are much more likely to tells us just how well grounded (empirically rather than metaphysically), if at all, these Abhidharma analyses of consciousness and cognition really are, rather than provide justification for the truths of classical Buddhist metaphysics.

110. Armstrong (1973: 157).

our discussion of Śāntarakṣita and Kamalaśīla's examination of perception, a pre-reflective first-person orientation is always implicit in the Buddhist epistemological account of cognition.

Now, the Abhidharma philosophical project is also reductionist in that it analyses phenomena by reducing them to their constitutive elements, which alone are taken to be ultimately real. In the case of its analysis of persons or selves, the Abhidharma reduces the individual to an impersonal and impermanent stream of psychophysical elements in a causal series.[111] But as we shall see in the next chapter, the Buddhist is not an eliminativist. Although persons may be reduced to their more basic constitutive elements, cognitive awareness itself, insofar as it functions as an explanatory principle, is irreducible. Phenomenological naturalism thus offers a promising way to retain the horizon of experience provided by what Husserl calls the life-world (*Lebenswelt*), which scientific naturalism must presuppose, and at the same time recognize that science too "streams into" this horizon of experience.[112]

Quine's influential analysis of the failure of traditional epistemology to answer the problem of the foundation of our beliefs ended with a proposal that we abandon a priori reasoning and devote ourselves instead simply to studying the psychological processes by which we form beliefs. Quine's proposal did not go unchallenged,[113] and so in response to many of his critics Quine would subsequently reformulate some of his earlier views by allowing epistemology to play its traditional normative functions in addressing questions of value and moral judgment.[114] Nevertheless, he has helped inaugurate a new movement in epistemology where stronger forms of naturalism now exist side by side with other, more moderate forms,[115] which allow for evaluative questions about rationality, justification, and knowledge to be pursued in a traditional manner.[116] But even advocates of this weaker form of naturalism agree that the sciences of cognition have much to contribute in resolving epistemological problems.

111. Mark Siderits offers what is perhaps the most thorough and philosophically interesting account of Buddhist Reductionism. Drawing from analytic philosophy of mind, Siderits proposes something analogous to the notion that persons nonreductively supervene on the aggregates. See Siderits (2003: 89–96).

112. See Husserl (1970a: 113) and discussion in Thompson (2007a: 83).

113. See Kim (1988), BonJour (1994), Foley (1994), Fumerton (1994), and Almeder (1998) for various critiques of Quine's arguments and attempts to reinstate traditional epistemology as a first science.

114. See, for example, Quine (1981).

115. Kornblith (1997, 1999) and Stich (1990) have argued against rationality as a foundational principle for traditional epistemology.

116. See Goldman (1992a) for a critique of the notion of justified belief in epistemology. The mutual relevance of epistemology and cognitive science is addressed in Goldman (1992b, 1993).

The methodological strategy I pursue here is largely indebted to an emerging consensus that philosophical inquiry as currently understood must take the empirical and cognitive sciences seriously. Epistemology, and Buddhist epistemology in particular, has always had close ties to the philosophy of perception. But the philosophical questions about perception that Buddhist and Western philosophers have traditionally pursued—What is the difference between perception and conception? What is the difference between sensation and perception? What is the difference between perception and action? In what sense is perception a source of knowledge?—are now part of a wider research program that addresses questions that could not have been raised but for advances in the empirical study of cognition.[117] If philosophers both East and West have traditionally regarded perception as an essential but perhaps not central component of any theory of knowledge, the notion that perception may actually play a larger role than hitherto thought is relatively new. The findings of both phenomenology and embodied cognitive science suggest that perception is in effect normative: how an object appears depends in large measure on there being an optimal context for its apprehension.[118] In examining the Buddhist epistemological account of perception, I adopt (and adapt) this important (phenomenological) notion, first articulated by Merleau-Ponty, that in perceiving we naturally tend toward clarity, and toward reaching a maximal grip of apprehensibility. Perception in effect is a type of embodied action, an engagement and entanglement with situations and things. Of course, the Buddhist is not a stranger to the principle of clarity, since she too understands the veridicality and efficacy of cognitions in terms of their degree of clarity, distinctness, or vividness (*spaṣṭa*).

For instance, research on imagery over the past three decades has revealed that our thinking and discursive capacities, including the use of words and abstract concepts, engage a series of imagery processes associating each sensory stimulus with symbolic structures that manifest internally as mental images.[119] The specific nature of these internal images is still a subject of dispute. Proposals range from Kosslyn's early pictorial framework of analysis, in which images are treated as mental depictions of cognitive processes, to descriptive theories based on semantic models, advocated mainly by Pylyshyn.[120] A third proposal, which has received significant attention in recent years, centers on the notion that perception does not operate as a pas-

117. A similar view with respect to the centrality of perception theories for contemporary philosophy of mind is articulated in Nanay (2010: 3).

118. For a recent philosophical treatment that explores and expands Merleau-Ponty's account of the normativity of perceptual experience, see Kelly (2010). The normative representation of objects and evidence for ecological bias in object recognition are explored at length in Konkle and Oliva (2006).

119. See, for example, Kosslyn (1980, 1994).

120. See, for example, Pylyshyn (1981, 1999).

sive faculty that merely relays information from the sensory domain to the mind, but rather that it plays an active role in constructing its apprehended objects. Known as the perceptual activity theory, this new proposal blurs the boundary between indirect perception and imagination and suggests that imagery should in fact be viewed as a process of perceptual projection.[121] This process of perceptual projection, however, does not involve the experience of internal mental images. Rather, on a phenomenological account of imagination such as we find, for instance, in Husserl's analysis of imagination, in visualizing an object we mentally enact or embody a possible perceptual experience.[122]

This research has significant implications for those seeking to translate and interpret non-Western contributions to philosophy of mind. By providing more adequate empirical knowledge concerning the nature and function of human cognition, the sciences of the mind open up new possibilities for understanding the various factors that inform, condition, and constrain our reasons, motivations, and experiences. While any attempt to do justice to the complex ramifications of modern research on perception and imagery is far beyond the scope of this book, where appropriate I shall seek to explore the implication that such research might have for our understanding of the Buddhist epistemological perspective on the interplay between perception and conception. Indeed, to the extent that Buddhist epistemology is anchored in the reductionist accounts of Abhidharma traditions, it already understands cognition in terms of a complex nexus of psychophysical causes and conditions. For the Buddhist, the cognitive process cannot be explained outside this nexus of apparent and less apparent (in the case of memories and impressions resulting from past actions) causal and conditioning factors. In adopting the approach of phenomenological naturalism, I want to emphasize the pragmatic character of epistemic inquiry in the Buddhist tradition and, at the same time, suggest that ongoing debates in the interdisciplinary field of cognitive science concerning the mind–body problem, the cognitive functions of perception, concept formation, and the nature of illusions, are not irrelevant to the translator and interpreter of Buddhist philosophical texts.

Take for instance the mind–body problem, generally associated with the Cartesian legacy of postulating a radical chasm between the physical and the mental domains. The mind–body problem, then, becomes the problem of how a nonphysical thing can interact with or otherwise receive input from the physical domain. Reactions to this problem in contemporary philosophy of mind and cognitive science range from the utterly dismissive (there is no mind–body

---

121. Among its main proponents are Ellis (1995), Ramachandran and Hirstein (1997), Noë (2004), and Thompson (2007a).

122. See Husserl (2006). For a phenomenological critique of the mental imagery debate, see Thompson (2007a).

problem, because what we call "mind" is just a folk-psychological notion for a wide range of cognitive states that can be understood in terms of underlying neuro-physiological processes)[123] to the downright skeptical (it can never be resolved, a position also known as mysterianism).[124] For eliminativists, who adopt a reductive physicalist position, mind and cognition are merely emergent properties of complex neural assemblies in the brain.[125] Harder to classify, and considered by their proponents as lying outside the divide between dualism and physicalism, are supervenient theories, which claim that mind supervenes over the physical domain but is not reducible to it.[126] Sharing some common positions with the supervenient theories, dual-aspect theories of mind argue that while experience requires a complex neural architecture for its realization it must nonetheless be treated as a fundamental non-supervenient property of the natural world.[127] Finally, there are the less common, but well articulated, reflexive models of consciousness, which postulate that mind and matter are part of the continuum of existence, co-originate and are codependent in their manifestations—a complex position with several variants (sometimes associated with certain forms of panpsychism).[128]

Now, the Buddhist epistemologist's answer to the mind–body problem is framed both by discussions about the basis or support of cognition (that is, by questions which ask what causes the arising of cognition given her metaphysical commitment to the momentary nature of all phenomena) as well as by a commitment to reflexivity. Awareness is thus constitutive of a constant and continuous stream of discrete cognitive events (including, but not limited to, various conditioning and dispositional factors). For the Buddhist epistemologist, then, the mind–body problem is not the problem of how cognition can arise from, or otherwise relate to, the causal order of the

---

123. A view advocated by, among others, Hardcastle (1995), Flanagan (1992), Churchland (1986), and Churchland (2002).

124. For a detailed working out of this position, see McGinn (1991).

125. A now classical eliminativist position on the mind is found in Dennett (1991).

126. The supervenience thesis can be summed up as follows: if *y* is supervenient on *x*, then for any *x*-type phenomenon there must be a *y*-type phenomenon. In the language of emergence, mental characteristics are dependent, or supervene on physical characteristics in that the mental cannot undergo an alteration in some respect that is not reflected in an alteration of the physical. As Kim notes, the supervenience thesis is to be understood as a conjunction of two claims: "*the covariance claim*, that there is a certain specified pattern of property covariation between the mental and the physical, and the *dependence claim*, that the mental depends on the physical" (Kim 1993: 165, emphasis in original). For an early treatment of supervenience in philosophy of mind, see Horgan (1982, 1984).

127. Such a theory is advanced by Chalmers (1996).

128. For a well-articulated reflexive theory of mind, see Velmans (2000). The Husserlian phenomenological tradition takes consciousness to be inherently reflexive. For a recent reworking of the reflexive nature of consciousness, see Janzen (2008) and Kriegel (2009). I discuss the reflexivity thesis below (chapter 8).

physical domain but of how this causal order, which also includes irreducible cognitive elements, conditions the arising of specific cognitive events. For instance, while taking up the issue of the relation between cognition and the body Dharmakīrti is clear that cognition cannot arise from something non-cognitive, that is, it cannot arise from the body to the extent that the body is taken to be merely the material substrate of being. Against the challenge of the Cārvāka physicalist, who claims that cognition finds its ultimate source in the physical body, Dharmakīrti invokes the principle of "unwarranted consequences" (*atiprasaṅgāt*):[129] there must be limits to what can cause what. Otherwise, any causal chain could give rise to anything: yogurt could be produced as easily from clay as from milk, a dog could give birth to a pig, and so on. Dharmakīrti seems to be advancing here something like an argument to the best explanation: "let only what is observed as the cause always be considered the cause."[130] That is, like causes like, except when intervening factors bring about a transformation at the basis (as in the caterpillar's metamorphosis into a butterfly). Such appeal to natural causation makes the Buddhist epistemologist who follows Dharmakīrti's account of the relation between cognition and the body a sort of naturalist, even though, in the end, Dharmakīrti takes a non-reductionist stance on consciousness.

Leaving aside exegetical concerns about working out the best possible reconstruction of the Buddhist epistemological project (one that is both historically and textually accurate) critics might still point out that Buddhist epistemology operates on soteriological rather than naturalist grounds: its ultimate aim is demonstrating the validity of the Buddhist path and its corresponding metaphysical doctrines. Of course, on a purely doctrinal reading of the Buddhist epistemological enterprise, soteriological concerns might not resonate well within the generally secular framework of modern scientific and philosophical inquiry. This book, however, advances a different claim: namely, that the Buddhist epistemologist's reliance on a version of empiricism and on certain widely shared canons of positive argumentation, seems to disqualify, at least in principle, any appeal to religious authority.

---

129. See PV II, 35–36ab.
130. PV II, 44cd. Cf. Taber (2003: 492). See also Franco (1997: 105ff.).

CHAPTER 3

Sensation and the Empirical Consciousness

At its foundation, the Buddhist epistemology of perception rests on the descriptive accounts of consciousness and cognition advanced by the Abhidharma scholars. These accounts constitute the starting point for a series of complex arguments that Śāntarakṣita and Kamalaśīla present in supporting their own analysis and interpretation of key doctrinal aspects in Dignāga and Dharmakīrti's definitions of perception. Although it can be assumed that Śāntarakṣita and Kamalaśīla have in mind primarily a Buddhist audience, it is also evident from their elaborate criticism of rival theories—in particular those of Uddyotakara and Kumārila Bhaṭṭa—that they take a strong polemical stand within the wider Indian philosophical context.

It is proper, therefore, that we begin our analysis with a review of canonical[1] and Abhidharma sources on the specific characteristics of the sensory systems as instruments of perception. For the Buddhist epistemologists, it is largely Vasubandhu's works[2] that constitute the main source for their

1. By "canonical" I mean here the corpus of texts that are usually considered authoritative by the Buddhist epistemologists. These include texts associated with both the Sautrāntikas and the Yogācāras, as well as those that are part of the Theravāda tradition. The difference between the Sautrāntika and the Theravāda canon is minor. The Sautrāntikas accept the four *āgamas* ("collections") that correspond to the four *nikāyas* ("baskets") of the Theravādins, viz., the *Dīrghāgama*, the *Madhyamāgama*, the *Saṃyuktāgama*, and the *Ekottarāgama*. While the second usage of "canon" applies exclusively to the texts considered as authoritative by the Theravādins, in the broader sense it applies to what may be termed "canonical" by later Ābhidharmikas such as the Sarvāstivādins, the Vaibhāṣikas, and the Yogācārins. Cf. Collins (1982: 90f).

2. Principally the *Abhidharmakośabhāṣya* ("Commentary on the Treasury of Higher Knowledge") but also his Yogācāra works. On Vasubandhu's sources for his AKBh, see Frauwallner (1995). According to Frauwallner, Vasubandhu seems to have relied mainly on three Abhidharma texts: Dharmaśri's *Abhidharmasāra*, Ghoṣaka's

theories of perception. Indeed, insofar as the *Compendium* and its *Commentary* are classifiable as epistemological works, Śāntarakṣita and Kamalaśīla would be regarded as proponents of that model of philosophical inquiry advanced by Dignāga and Dharmakīrti, which itself shares many of the metaphysical positions of the Yogācāra tradition. Indian doxographers usually distinguish between early Yogācāra-Vijñānavādins such as Asaṅga and Vasubandhu, who rely on canonical sources (*āgamānusāriṇo*) and the latter Yogācāra-Vijñānavādins, mainly the epistemologists, who rely on the authority of logic and reason (*nyāyānusāriṇo*). As we saw in the last chapter, the Buddhist epistemologists in general discount appeal to scriptural authority in their effort to settle doctrinal disputes. Although the Buddha's teachings often serve as a point of reference for elaborating on various aspects of Buddhist doctrine, in general arguments consider not the authority of the Buddha as such, but his own appeal to empirical evidence and sound reasoning.[3] In other words, the Buddha's teachings are authoritative because he relies on empirical experience and sound reasoning, not because he declares them to be so. Of course, given the progression of knowledge, the question arises as to whether the Buddha's teachings could be considered fallible if they do not accord with, say, the findings of modern science. This issue is particularly pertinent, as we shall see below, when we consider the no-self doctrine. Its reductionist account of human agency does not sit well with a theory of knowledge such as the Buddhist epistemologists advance, which takes the reflexive aspect of cognitive awareness to be irreducible. The brief review of canonical and Abhidharma sources that follows is mainly aimed at identifying the doctrinal principles that underpin the Buddhist epistemological account of perception.

3.1 NO-SELF AND THE DOMAINS OF EXPERIENCE

Speculations on the nature of the sensory systems and the manner in which they construct a sense of being in the world as an individual, cognizing agent have a long and complex history in India. A full account of this history with reference to each philosophical school is beyond the scope of this book.[4] Here

---

Abhidharmāmṛtaśāstra, and Kātyāyanīputra's *Jñānaprasthāna*. From these last three works, Vasubandhu adopted his categorical classification of Abhidharma topics according to the five aggregates (*pañcaskandha*). Vasubandhu's model of systematic treatment of Abhidharma topics finds a distant echo in the TS/P, particularly in the *Sthirabhāvaparīkṛa* and the *Traikālyaparīkṣā*, where the views of the Sarvāstivādins and the Vaibhāṣikas are debated at length.

3. See Obermiller (1931: 99) and Hattori (1968: 73). For an analysis of the importance of scriptural-based inferences (*āgamāśritānumāna*) for epistemologists, with particular focus on Dharmakīrti, see Tillemans (1999).

4. The reader may consult the comprehensive, albeit dated, coverage of Indian psychological theories in Sinha (1958).

I offer only a cursory treatment of those Abhidharma theories of consciousness and cognition that were adopted by the Buddhist epistemologists.[5] Within the wider philosophical context of preoccupations with knowledge and its sources, the Buddhist authors encountered the Brahmanical theories of perception and conception as articulated primarily in the Sāṃkhya, Nyāya-Vaiśeṣika, and Mīmāṃsā schools. Buddhist speculations on the nature of perceptual phenomena are found throughout the Nikāya ("Collections of Discourses," hereinafter *Discourses*),[6] although it is only in the Abhidharma literature that we encounter various attempts to formulate a systematic psychology of perception. I shall begin first with a summary of canonical references to perception and related phenomena, followed by a brief account of Abhidharma perspectives on consciousness and cognition as articulated mainly in Vasubandhu's work.

The term most commonly associated with sensory activity, "sense power" (*indriya*),[7] is found in the *Ṛg Veda*, a collection of hymns dealing with various religio-philosophical topics central to the Brahmanical tradition. Here the senses are likened to lesser deities who act as Indra's messengers to the lower realms. The senses are regarded as manifestations of Indra's specific powers and correspond to his capacity for knowledge (*buddhīndriya*) and action (*karmendriya*).[8] This early mythological narrative in which lesser deities are the agencies of sensory activity in humans bears some structural similarity to Descartes's account, in his *Treatise of Man* and *Passions of the Soul*, of the animal spirits which, flowing from the pineal gland, control the activity of sensation and imagination, as well as bodily movements. In the Upaniṣads, this mythological account gives way to a philosophically nuanced view of sensory activity as the direct result of contact between the self and the world.[9]

---

5. The work that constitutes the most authoritative source of Abhidharma theories for the Buddhist epistemologists is Vasubandhu's AKBh. Direct references to the AKBh are found in nearly every epistemological treatise from Dignāga and Dharmakīrti to later commentators such as Vinītadeva, Dharmottara, and Jinendrabuddhi. References to the AKBh are found also throughout the TS/P.

6. See, for example, MN I, 111–112.

7. I have adopted "sensory" as a definition of *indriya* (lit. "belonging to Indra," "power"), following Vasubandhu's definition in AKBh (Pradhan 1975: 38): *kaḥ punarindriyārthaḥ/"iti paramaiśvarye"/tasya indranti iti indrayāṇi/ata ādhipatyārtha indriyārthaḥ/* ("Once again, what is the meaning of *indriya*? *Iti* means the supreme power (*paramaiśvarye*); [*Indriyas*] refer to the powers of Indra. *Indriya* refers thus to that which is sovereign (*ādhipati*)").

8. See, for example, ṚgV IX, 107; also *indriyaṃ* is used generically in reference to Indra's powers (ṚgV I, 55,103; II, 16).

9. On the Upaniṣadic understanding of perception, the senses (*indriyas*) are created from the substance of sense-objects (*arthāḥ*) and with the specific purpose of revealing the latter. However, the revealing agent is the self (*ātman*). See, for example, *Kaṭ ha Upaniṣad*, I, iii, 4 (*indriyāṇi hayānāhurviṣayāṃs teṣu gocarān/ātmendriyamanoyuktaṃ bhektetyāhurmanīṣiṇaḥ*) and I, iii, 10 (*indriyebhyaḥ parā hyarthā arthebhyaśca paraṃ manaḥ/manasastu parā buddhirbuddherātmā mahānparaḥ*).

For the early Buddhists the rejection of a permanent self as the agent of sensory activity posed a significant challenge. Indeed, if there is no agent (*kartṛ*), and if actions (*karman*) are merely transient events arising within a continuum of causally interconnected states, how, then, is the efficacy of karmic processes to be explained? Disagreement among modern interpreters of the no-self doctrine attests to the difficulty of providing a definitive account of this core aspect of Buddhist philosophy. Thus, early interpreters such as Caroline Rhys Davids and Isaline Horner thought that the way Buddhists understood and used the term "consciousness" was not very different from the way Upaniṣadic philosophers talked about the self.[10] Perhaps the most detailed attempt to support a two-tier understanding of the doctrine of no-self comes from Kamaleswar Bhattacharya, who has forcibly argued that the denial of self in Buddhism most often targets common views such as those that associate the self with the psychophysical aggregates, and not the metaphysical notion of self.[11]

But as Michel Hulin has demonstrated in his comprehensive study of classical Indian speculations on the principle of ego (*ahaṃkāra*), the early Buddhist tradition is characterized primarily by an attempt to break free from both a speculative notion of an ultimate immutable and eternal self and, at the same time, from the more concrete psychological ego that is responsible for the imputation of such a false sense of self.[12] Indeed, later Buddhist traditions develop specific notions, such as that of mind-stream, life-continuum mind, and repository consciousness (*citta-santāna*, *bhavaṅga-citta*, and *ālaya-vijñāna*, respectively) precisely in order to avoid the metaphysical trappings of the traditional notion of self.[13]

Thus, Peter Harvey argues that the notion of a "self which witnesses" most probably refers to deeper aspects of consciousness acting as "conscience."[14] In a similar vein, Steven Collins delineates several points supporting the

---

10. See Rhys Davids (1924: 75) and Horner (1936: 145). Horner claimed that some canonical passages (e.g., *Anguttara Nikāya* I, 149–150) actually provided support for the notion of self as an "unchanging witness" (*sākṣin*). A similar view has been defended in a recent philosophical reworking of the notion of "witness consciousness" by Albahari (2006).

11. Bhattacharya (1973: 64).

12. Hulin (1978: 43–44): "Le bouddhisme ne manquera d'ailleurs pas . . . d'identifier l'*ātman* 'speculative' à l'ego psychologique indûment hypostasié. Dans ce circle vicieux d'une illusion psychologique et d'une construction spéculative reposant l'une sur l'autre on reconnaîtra sans peine le cycle même de la transmigration, de la servitude."

13. Extensive critiques of the attempt to find support in the canonical literature for the existence of a higher self, perhaps equated with consciousness, are found in Warder (1970), Collins (1982), Kalupahana (1987), Harvey (1995), and De Silva (2005). Vasubandhu's *Pudgala-pratiṣedha-prakaraṇa* ("Treatise on the Negation of the Person") provides one of most detailed critiques of the personalist view.

14. Harvey (1995: 22).

no-self view as the correct account: (1) the metaphysical notion of self as eternal and unchanging is actually just plain erroneous (a defect of speculative opinion); (2) taking the body to be the self is a mistaken view; (3) consciousness itself is not the self; (4) it is impossible to speak of a self apart from experience; (5) a false sense of self may be acquired from the habitual use of pronominal forms such as "I" and "mine."[15] The denial of a permanent self, as well as the refusal to treat persons as referring to anything real and permanent, forms an integral part of the Buddhist analysis of consciousness. The frequent use of indexicals such as "I" (*ahaṃ*) and "mine" (*mama*) does not indicate that the Buddha accepts the conventional reality of persons either. Rather, as Collins suggests, a good way to avoid such misapprehensions is to offer more elegant translations of Pāli and Sanskrit compounds in which the term "self" appears: for instance, translating "master of himself" (*attādhīna*) as "free" or "independent," "at peace with himself" (*khematta*) as "tranquil," or "self-guarded" (*rakkhitatta*) simply as "prudent."[16]

The centrality of the no-self doctrine in Buddhist thought is explained on the basis of its pragmatic role in guiding the adept on the path to enlightenment. Furthermore, the no-self doctrine provides a justification for treating endurance, independence, and self-subsistence as neither desirable nor attainable, but rather as what they are: mistaken notions resulting from the habitual tendency to construct a substantive identity from a stream of psychophysical phenomena. The Buddhist claims that our sense of self as an autonomous being is imputed and our attribution of inherent existence to it habitually acquired,[17] just as Hume claims that a self is never apprehended in the series of perceptions that are characteristic of the mental domain.[18] This routine misapprehension of the discrete phenomena of experience as a self leads to a dualistic perspective: things appear and are categorized as either objective (thus external, but empirically accessible) or as subjective (thus internal, and immediately accessible to consciousness). Puzzled by this dualistic outlook, we cope by constructing an imaginary self as the permanent locus of experience.

This imaginary self, usually conceived in substantial terms as an unchanging reality behind the changing phenomenal world, is in effect the root cause of the pervasive ignorance that afflicts the human condition. From a

15. See Collins (1982: 87–115). See also Oetke (1988), who interprets the no-self doctrine as reflective of a "revisionary" metaphysics that denies not a self as such but rather the self as something qualified by the property of being the subject of experience or as the referent of such subjective experience.

16. Collins (1982: 72).

17. Cf. SN IV, 102; MN I, 130.

18. The parallelism between the Buddhist and Humean reductive analyses of the self is explored at some length in Giles (1993), Tillemans (1996), and Kapstein (2001).

metaphysical point of view, however, the no-self doctrine extends beyond the domain of subjective experience, to characterize all phenomena. Indeed, it is not just persons that are said to be selfless but all the elements of existence as well. To appreciate the uniqueness of the Buddhist no-self doctrine one has to contrast it with the two most common alternatives: eternalism and annihilationism (or physicalism). The eternalist, usually the Upaniṣadic philosopher, claims that the innermost part of ourselves, the subtle and abiding self, sometimes equated with pure consciousness, exists for all eternity even as the ordinary person undergoes constant change, ultimately resulting in his or her demise. At the opposite end of the spectrum we find the physicalist who sees human agency as contingent and finite. The Buddhist perspective, called the "middle path between extremes" or simply the "middle way" (*madhyamā-pratipad*) offers a very different account of human existence: what we routinely call ego, self, soul, or individual personality, are merely conventional terms that do not apply to anything real.

Along with the rejection of a permanent agent, the Buddhist authors make a clear distinction between the sensory faculty and the sensory organ—as in, for instance, the distinction between the faculty of vision (*cakṣurvijñāna*) and the organ of sight (*cakṣurdhātu*)[19]—and conceive of the senses as receptacles (*adhiṣṭhāna*) of experience rather than physical organs interacting with empirical objects. Unlike the Brahmanical view of the senses as the faculties of an internal agent, the Buddhists regard the senses as links or mediators joining together the external spheres of sensory activity (*bāhirāyatana*) with the internal spheres of perception (*ādhyātmikāyatana*).[20] The development of a complex vocabulary of psychological concepts—in which the self is understood in terms of a collection of conditioned (*saṃskṛta*)[21] personality constituents (the five aggregates), acting and being acted upon following the principle of dependent arising—is the direct result of this need to account for sensory activity and cognition without reference to an enduring metaphysical self. It is important to clarify at this stage that the rejection of an enduring self did not undermine the common use of pronominal

19. I use "sensory faculty" as a translation of *indriyagocara*, following the Abhidharma distinction between the sensory process (as in the case of, say, vision) and the sensory organ (the eye and visual system). See AKBh *ad* AK I, 9cd.

20. See, for example, ASBh II, 90 (Tatia 1976: 85): *adhyātmabahirddhā kāyaḥ katamaḥ / ādhyātmikāyatana saṁbaddhāni bāhyānyāyatanāni/ indriyādhiṣṭhānāni pārasāṃ tānikāni cādhyātmikāni rūpīṇyāyatayāni.* "What is the internal-external body? It is the external spheres, which form the bases of sensory activity, and which are connected with the internal spheres; they are also the inner material spheres pertaining of others [e.g., eye, ear, etc.]."

21. The etymology of *saṃskṛta* is derived from *kṛta*, "fashioned," and *sametya*, *saṃbhūya*, "union," "combination" or "collection," meaning thus something which is made by the collective combination of causes and conditions. See AKBh *ad* AK I, 7ab: *sametya saṃbhūya pratyayaiḥ kṛtāḥ.*

terms designating the activities of individual agents. Rather, such uses were restricted to the analyses of selflessness as a philosophical doctrine. As for the question of what holds these aggregates together, the Buddhist canonical literature is quite clear—the proliferating tendencies (*prapañca*) of the reasoning and deliberating (*vitarka-vicāra*) mind:

> Dependent on the eye and forms, visual-consciousness arises. The meeting of the three is contact. With contact as condition there is feeling. What one feels, that one perceives. What one perceives, that one thinks about. What one thinks about, that one mentally proliferates (*papañceti*). With what one has mentally proliferated as the source, perception and notions resulting from mental proliferation beset a man with respect to past, future, and present forms cognizable through the eye.[22]

Although this passage clearly illustrates that a discerning type of consciousness[23] accompanies each of the sensory modalities, in this case the visual-consciousness, what causes these associations between perception and conception are the habitual mental proliferations. As we read elsewhere: "Ordinary people are endowed with a perception that proliferates. Possessed of a perceiving consciousness, they apprehend things through mental proliferation. Dispelling the mind-made [perceptual] states that belong to the lay life, one engages on the path to liberation."[24]

This notion that the ordinary mind is characterized by a habitual tendency toward the proliferation of ideas, thoughts, images, etc. would become crucial in the Abhidharma analyses of consciousness and cognition. In the *Discourses*, this tendency toward the proliferation of ideas is more closely associated with sensation and is connected with consciousness only insofar as perception is considered to be proliferating and constructive in its character, that is, insofar as perception is taken to primarily refer to perceptual judgments.[25] Because this tendency toward proliferation of ideas depends on the activities of the six spheres of contact, its dynamics are sustained by the constant flow of sensory impressions generated through contact

22. MN I, 111–112: *cakkhuñ c'āvuso paṭicca rūpe ca uppajjati cakkhuviññāṇaṃ, tiṇṇaṃ saṅgati phasso, phassapaccayā vedanā, yaṃ vedeti taṃ sañjānāti, yaṃ sañjānāti taṃ vitakketi, yaṃ vitakketi taṃ papañceti, taṃ papañceti tato nidānaṃ purisaṃ papañcasaṅkhā samudācaranti atītānāgatapaccuppannesu cakkhuviññeyesu rūpesu.* This formula occurs in a slightly modified form in several other places in the Nikāyas. See, for example, MN I, 259; SN IV, 67ff., 86.

23. In the Nikāyas, *vijñāna* (Pāli = *viññāṇa*) translates most commonly as "discerning awareness," whereas in the Abhidharma the term acquires the meaning of "witnessing consciousness." See SN II, 95; III, 87, MN I, 292.

24. SN IV, 72: *papañcasaññā itarītarā narā/papañcayatanā upayanti saññino/manomayam gehasitañca sabbaṃ/panujja nekkhammasitaṃ irīyati.*

25. See MN I, 65; SN I, 100 and IV, 52, 71; AN II, 161 and III, 393; Sn 530.

between perceiver and perceived. Ordinarily, one is constantly assailed by these proliferating tendencies, so that the capacity for having veridical perceptual experiences is seriously compromised. The psychological impact of this proliferating tendency on perception is significant: due to the spontaneous proliferation of mental imagery, perceptual objects are apprehended only as grasped by conceptual and linguistic conventions.[26]

Thus, what is meant by perception in the *Discourses* is simply a cognition (*saṃjñā*) that bears on the contents of sense experience.[27] This awareness of the constant flow of sensory impressions suggests that cognition in its perceptual aspect has a dual aspect: from a subjective perspective, it is the bare consciousness that attends to the flow of sensations, whereas from an objective perspective, it corresponds to the spheres of the sensory domain (*saṃjñāyatana*) and their respective objects. The implication of this chain of causal relations that string together perception, object perceived, and perceiving consciousness is that external objects cannot be apprehended in the absence of empirical awareness, or indeed that empirical awareness, by its very nature, discloses experience as the ultimate ground of being and becoming. This dual-aspect view of empirical awareness inevitably leads to the conclusion that the diversity and manifoldness of the perceived world,[28] rather than revealing a profuse ontology, instead discloses the proliferating tendencies of perceptual representations.[29] Moreover, this dual aspect view of awareness already foreshadows the dissociation between the subjective (*grāhaka*) and the objective (*grāhya*) aspects of conscious apprehension that play an essential role in later Buddhist thought, particularly in the Yogācāra tradition.

Thus, in the *Discourses*, mental proliferation (*prapañca*) appears to function primarily as a synonym for ignorance (*avidyā*). In that sense, the Buddhist use of "ignorance" bears resemblance to the use of "illusion" (*māyā*) in the Upaniṣads,

26. Cf. De Silva (2005: 244).

27. See AN II, 162–163. A separation between perception and higher cognitive activities that are associated with conception is already foreshadowed in these early canonical accounts of the cognitive process.

28. Pāli dictionaries derive the etymology of *papañca* from √ *pra* + *pañc*, meaning "diversity," "manifoldness," or "expansiveness."

29. See Sn 876, 878: *nāmañca rūpañca paṭicca phassā/icchānidānanī pariggahanī/icchāya'santyā na mamatta matthi/rūpe vibhute na phusanti phassā* [876]. *na saññasaññi na visaññasaññi/nopi asaññi na vibhūtasaññi/evaṃsametassa vibhoti rūpaṃ/saññanidānā hi papañcasaṅkhā* [878]. ("Contacts are dependent upon name and form. Possessions have their origin in longing. When longing does not exist, possessiveness does not exist. When form has disappeared, contacts do not make contact [876]. . . . He has no common perceptual cognition of perceptions, he has no defective cognitive perception of perceptions, he is not without perceptual cognition, he has no perceptual cognition of what has disappeared. For one who has attained such a state, form disappears (*vibhoti rūpaṃ*), for that which is named diversification (*papañcasaṅkhā*) has its origin in perception" [878]).

both notions capturing the common idea that empirical awareness, as understood from the perspective of common sense, presents us an image of the world that is not entirely free from our own propensities.[30] It is primarily this projective capacity of the mind that superimposes upon the constant flow of phenomena notions such as self and other, which in turn create the conditions for grasping and attachment. One of the outcomes of grasping is the imputation of individual existence upon the activity of the empirical consciousness. In the chain of causation of the twelve factors of existence, the individual personality (i.e., *nāmā-rūpa* or the psycho-physical aggregate) is considered to be a product of consciousness.[31] Due to the tendency to proliferate ideas, what is perceived is grasped after; thus one develops notions such as existence (*sat*) and nonexistence (*asat*), myself (*svayam*) and other (*anya*). On this account of mentation, conceptual grasp of the constant flow of phenomena, while seemingly dependent upon the presence or absence of stimuli at the sense-doors, in fact results directly from the sensations caused by these stimuli. Thus, although the sensory systems appear to present the world in its immediacy, what an individual perceives also depends upon the capacity of his or her internal mental processes to represent the contents of experience. In the constantly changing domain of sensory phenomena, there are no independent entities, but only textures or clusters of sensory impressions that come into existence and go out of existence depending upon the activity of an apprehending consciousness.[32] This view is clearly illustrated in the *Lokantagamaṇasuttaṃ* ("Concise Statements on Going beyond the [Material] World"), in which we read:

30. The term *prapānca* (the Sanskrit equivalent of the Pāli *papañca*) does not appear in pre-Buddhist Brahmanical literature. With the exception of later Upaniṣads, the first systematic use of the term is found in Gauḍapāda's *Āgama-śāstra* ("Collection of Doctrines"). The term appears in the expression *prapañcaopaśama* and designates the "cessation of the manifestation of the world" as seen by the wise one. See, for example, AS II, 35: *vītarāgabhayakrodhair munibhir vedapāragaiḥ/nirvikalpo hy ayaṃ dṛṣṭaḥ prapañcopaśamo'dvayaḥ*. ("The cessation of the manifestation of the world, which is devoid of duality and imagination, is seen by the wise ones who, having reached the other shore of the Vedas, are free from attachment, fear and anger"). The expression *ayaṃ dṛṣṭaḥ prapañcopaśama* in the above *kārikā* is almost synonymous with the use of *svapnamāye yathā dṛṣṭe* ("as dream and illusion are seen") in a previous *kārikā*, which states that the wise ones see the manifestation of the world as a dream and an illusion. See, for example, AS II, 31: *svapnamāye yathā dṛṣṭe gandharvanagaraṃ yathā/tathā viśvam idaṃ dṛṣṭaṃ vedānteṣu vicakṣaṇaiḥ*. For a detailed study that traces Gauḍapāda's indebtedness to the Buddhists, in particular to Nāgārjuna's MMK, see Bhattacharya (1943).

31. See SN III, 90 [*Channasuttaṃ*]: *avijjāpaccayā saṃkārā, saṃkārāpaccayā viññāṇaṃ, viññāṇaṃpaccayā nāmarūpaṃ*.

32. See SN IV, 88 [*Lokasamudayasuttaṃ*]: *cakkhuñca paṭiccā rūpe vuppajjati cakkhuviññāṇaṃ, tiṇṇaṃ saṅgati phasso, phassapaccayā vedanā*; SN IV, 40 [*Samiddhilokapañhasuttaṃ*]: *yattha kho samiddhi atthi cakkhu atthi rūpā atthi cakkhuviññāṇaṃ atthi cakkhuviññaṇa viññātabbā dhammā, atthi tattha loko vā lokapaññātti vā*.

In the world by which one is a perceiver of the world, a conceiver of the world—this is called the world of the Noble One's Discipline. And what... is that in the world by which one is a perceiver of the world? The eye is that in the world by which one is a perceiver of the world. The ear... The nose... The tongue... The body... The mind is that in the world by which one is a perceiver of the world, a conceiver of the world.[33]

What we learn here is that in the fluctuating world of bare sensory awareness, cognitions (and the entities they disclose) exist only as aggregated phenomena of experience. However, these elements that are constitutive of experience are not simply the counterparts of corresponding physical objects, since what lies outside the sphere of perception is always already constituted by the dynamic structures of our cognitive architecture.[34] The world *as perceived* is brought into existence through the activity of the senses and goes out of existence with the cessation of sensory activity. This phenomenal realm is not an objective world that exists over and above its collective or intersubjective apprehension, for such a world is not within the purview of empirical awareness. The *Discourses*, thus, present us with a picture of the "world" (*loka*) as representing the diversity and manifoldness of perceptual phenomena that finds its ultimate source in the activity of the conscious mind.[35]

It ought to be made clear that the notion of a mind-dependent world—or simply a world *as experienced*—should not be taken as indicative of covert idealism. The *Discourses* do not deny the reality of the elements of existence and/or experience (*dharma*). Rather, they simply suggest that we cannot properly discern the phenomenal character and content of experience in the absence of any reference to the specific aggregates of consciousness. From a first-person perspective, the body, as an instrument (*karaṇa*) of sensory activity, is both the medium of contact with the world and the world with which it comes in contact.

Such a view finds an interesting parallel in Husserl's account of the paradoxical nature of the body as revealed through phenomenological reduction. For Husserl, phenomenological reduction (*epoché*)—essentially a method of bracketing ontological assumptions about the natural world in order to

33. SN IV, 96: *yena kho āvuso lokasmiṃ lokasaññi hoti lokamanī, ayaṃ vuccati ariyassa vinaye loko. kena cāvusso lokasmiṃ lokassanī hoti lokamānī? cakkhunā kho āvuso lokasmiṃ lokasaññi hoti lokamānī, sotena kho āvuso... ghānena kho āvuso... jivhāya kho āvuso... kāyena kho āvuso, manena kho āvuso lokasmiṃ lokasaññi hoti lokamānī.*

34. It is this analysis of the content of experience that leads the Ābhidharmikas to the notion of "cognitive aspects" (*ākāra*), which represent the particular mode of presentation of the contents of one's experience. For an account of aspectual nature of cognition, specifically of perception, in the Abhidharma literature, see Dhammajoti (2007).

35. SN I, 40 [*Cittasuttaṃ*]: *cittena nīyati loko cittena parikassati, cittassa ekadhammassa sabbeva vasamanvagūti.*

examine the intentional structures of consciousness—reveals the twofold appearance of the body, first as a biological entity (*Körper*) connected to the continuum of life, and second as a medium for the expression of life (*Leib*). The body is thus the locus of lived experience and, as such, has the capacity for both exploration and receptivity. It is this intuition about the dual nature of sensation, in its transitive and intransitive aspects, which led Husserl to the concept of the life-world (*die Lebenswelt*): a world of lived experience whose boundaries are not fixed but constantly shifting in relation to the desires, actions, and attitudes of an agent.[36] As Merleau-Ponty, who appropriates Husserl's notion of the life-world as the lived-world (*le monde vécu*) clearly suggests, "I cannot understand the function of living body except by enacting it myself,"[37] for "my body appears to me as an attitude with a view to a certain actual or possible task."[38] For Merleau-Ponty, the world or, better still, the environment, is not just a structured domain of causally nested objects and relations but a meaningful realm of experience. This world *qua world*, as Taylor Carman (echoing Merleau-Ponty) has recently argued, "affords, invites, and facilitates, just as it obtrudes, resists, thwarts, eludes, and coerces."[39] It would appear thus that the model of empirical consciousness advanced in the *Discourses* roughly corresponds to what some contemporary philosophers have termed non-reductive "one-level theories of consciousness": that is, theories which propose that consciousness is essentially a matter of having or being an awareness of a world that does not require a prior (representational) awareness of our own mental states.[40]

Something analogous to a notion of the lived world is at work in the Buddhist view that body, mind, and world arise in dependence upon each other. However, the origin and cessation of the body as a medium of experience is outside the horizon of empirical awareness, for what resides at the limits of our manifested world cannot be known through perception. The notion that the origin and cessation of empirical reality is not itself perceptible is clearly stated in the *Rohitassasuttaṃ* ("Concise Statements [Addressed] to Rohitassa"):

> As to that end of the world, friend, where one is not born, does not age, does not die, does not pass away, and is not reborn—I say that it cannot be known, seen or reached by traveling...I say that without having reached the end of the world there is no

36. For an account of the phenomenology of the life-world, see in particular Husserl (1970a: Part III, A).
37. Merleau-Ponty (2002: 87).
38. Merleau-Ponty (2002: 114).
39. Carman (2005: 86).
40. See Thomasson (2008). One level theories of consciousness stand in opposition to higher order thought theories, which postulate that conscious or phenomenal states are essentially those states of which we are immediately aware.

making an end to suffering. It is, friend, in just this body endowed with perception and mind that I make known the world, the origin of the world and the cessation of the world.[41]

In these early strata of the *Discourses*, we come across a model of cognition as dependent on the coming together of three factors: an object, a moment of conscious awareness, and the apprehension that ensues when the first two factors come into contact. A clear distinction is thus made between the world, its apprehension, and the consciousness that apprehends it. What is meant by "world" in this context, however, is not an independent domain of physical entities and relations, but the "phenomenal world of perception" (*lokasaṃjñā*) that depends on the conceptual and proliferating activities of the mind. The notion that consciousness acts as a causal condition for the appearance of objects, while not a direct rejection of external realism, prefigures the phenomenalism of later Abhidharma schools, principally the Sautrāntika and Yogācāra, where consciousness, treated either as a mental continuum or as a receptacle of awareness, becomes an irreducible fundamental reality.

3.2 TWO DIMENSIONS OF MIND: CONSCIOUSNESS AS DISCERNMENT AND SENTIENCE

One of the problems that modern interpreters confront when attempting to establish the nature of "consciousness" as a *dharma*, that is, as a factor of existence and/or experience is the ambiguity of this concept in the canonical literature and the diversity of interpretations found in the Abhidharma traditions. Despite significant recent progress in this area, we still need a comprehensive survey of the semantic evolution of the notion of "consciousness" across the Nikāya and the Abhidharma literature.[42] For instance, addressing the issues of what accounts for the continuity of life in the absence of an enduring self, Collins has pointed out that both the "mental faculty" (*manas*) and the "mind" (*citta*) are treated in the canonical literature as constructs (*abhisaṃkhāra*) and thus not as occurrent unchangeable entities. Whether consciousness too is constructed or constructive (reflecting the active and passive senses of *abhisaṃkhāra*) remains an issue of debate. Collins claims

41. SN I, 63 [*Rohitassasuttaṃ*]: *yattha kho āvuso na jāyati, na jīyati, nā mīyati, na cavati, na uppajjati, nāhaṃ taṃ gamanena lokassa antaṃ ñāteyaṃ dattheyyaṃ patteyyanti vadāmīti . . . na kho panāhaṃ āvuso, appatvā lokassa antaṃ dukkhassa antakiriyaṃ vadāmi. api cāhaṃ avusso imasmiññeva byāmamatte sasaññimhi samanake lokañca paññāpemi. lokasamudayañca lokanirodhañca lokanirodhagāminiñca paṭipadanti.*

42. A detailed and philosophically relevant survey of the notion of self-awareness (*svasaṃvedana*) in the Abhidharma literature up to Dignāga and Dharmakīrti can be found in Yao (2005).

that upon attaining cessation (*nirvāṇa*), it is the *constructive* consciousness that ceases, not the *constructed* consciousness, which must exist "as a 'karmically-resultant-consciousness' (*vipāka-viññāṇa*)."[43] In his own comprehensive analysis of the nature of consciousness as reflected in the *Discourses* and the Abhidharma, Harvey translates *viññāṇa* as "discernment" based on the etymological derivation of the term from "*vi*" + "*ñāṇa*," meaning a "kind of knowledge (*ñāṇa*) which separates (*vi*)."[44] As the verbal form *vijānati* indicates, *viññāṇa* is that which "discerns," "discriminates," and "distinguishes."[45]

The Buddhist philosophical vocabulary thus comprises at least three terms for what we ordinarily designated as "mind": *manas* ("mental power" or "mental faculty"), *vijñāna* ("discernment" or "consciousness"), and *citta* ("mind" or "thought"). The term that most generally translates as "mind" in the Abhidharma traditions—that is, *citta*—also denotes thought and it is usually used in conjunction with the "mental constituents" (*caitta*) with which it stands in a reciprocal relation. Thus, whereas *citta* ("mind") denotes the subjective aspect of the mental domain (e.g., a state of reflexive awareness), *caitta* ("mental constituents") refers to specific cognitive states, such as sensations, perceptions, feelings, and volitions. These mental constituents are understood specifically as cognitive domains or as sensed textures that mold our experience and give it its qualitative aspects—the phenomenal character of "what it is like."[46]

I have already indicated above that in the *Connected* and *Middle Length Discourses* "consciousness" is often treated as a synonym of "apperception" (*saṃjñā*). This lack of clear dissociation between perceptual cognition, understood here as empirical awareness, and consciousness, as the apprehending and discerning faculty, is made clear by frequent references to perceptual cognition as the cause of attachment to the contents of sense experience. Furthermore, perceptual cognition is often contrasted with wisdom (*prajñā*) indicating that what is meant by it is not sensory activity proper but rather the consciousness that bears upon it.[47] But this is

43. Collins (1982: 207).

44. Harvey (1995: 143).

45. See, for example, SN III, 87 and MN I, 292.

46. Note that in works such as Buddhaghosa's *Visuddhimagga* ("Path to Purity") and Vasubandhu's AKBh, *manas*, *vijñāna*, and *citta* are used more or less synonymously as designating the same mental reality. However, in the *Mahāyānasaṃgraha* (MSG I, 6), Asaṅga takes the three terms as designating different realities: *citta* is said to stand for the Yogācāra notion of receptacle consciousness (*ālayavijñāna*), *manas* refers to the mental domain and its afflictive tendencies, and *vijñāna* to the six types of cognitive awareness (bodily, sensory, apperceptive, etc). Cf. Lamotte (1938: 15).

47. See, for example, Sn 538: *saññaṃ tividhaṃ panujja saṅkaṃ kappanaṃ neti tamahāu ariyoti*. ("Having thrust away the triple perception, the mud, he is not subject to illusion and they call him an *ariya*"). Sn 806: *tasiddha diṭṭhe vā sute mute vā pakkapitā natthi aṇupi saññā*. ("By him not even an insignificant notion has been formed here in respect of what is seen, heard, or thought").

not "consciousness" as an autonomous cognitive awareness. Rather, it is the consciousness of a specific sense modality: visual-consciousness, auditory-consciousness, etc. Because the mental faculty is also regarded as a sensory system, the consciousness that reflects upon its activity is termed "introspective consciousness" (*manovijñāna*). Consciousness, in this sense, requires perceptual cognition or, more specifically, requires attention (*āvartana*),[48] given that the activity of the sense alone does not give rise to perception. The latter requires attending to the stimuli, and it is this latter form of cognitive awareness that transforms the amorphous mass of sensory input into a percept. In the formula of dependent arising that we encounter at several places within the *Discourses*, consciousness is said to arise in dependence upon the sensory organ and the physical object. However, the mode of presentation of this world of phenomenal experience, and its continuing existence depend in their turn upon the activity of empirical consciousness:

> Mind and body condition contact... By whatever properties, characteristics, signs or indications the mind factor is to be conceived, in the absence of such properties... would any grasping at the idea of the body factor be manifest? No, Sir... Or in the absence of any such properties by which the body factor is designated,... would any grasping at the notion of sensory reaction be manifest? No, Sir... By whatever properties, characteristics, signs or indications the mind factor is conceived, in their absence is there any contact to be found? No, Sir. Then, Ānanda, just this, namely mind and body, is the root, the cause, the origin, [and] the condition for all contact. I have said: "Consciousness conditions mind and body."[49]

Passages such as this present a metaphysical picture of mental and psychological individuation as arising in dependence upon the activity of empirical consciousness.[50] Moreover, the sense of individuation is dependent upon the activity of empirical consciousness not only for its coming into being but

48. The nominal form *āvartana* derives from *ā* + √ *vṛt* "to turn towards," "to avert." The Pāli form is *āvajjana* (with the synonymous form *āvaṭṭanā*), meaning "turning to," "paying attention," "apprehending," "adverting the mind."

49. DN II 2, 20–21: *nāmarūpapaccayā phasso'ti... yehi... ākārehi yehi liṅgehi yehi nimittehi yehi uddesehi nāmakāyassa paññatti hoti, tesu ākāresu tesu liṅgesu tesu nimittesu tesu uddesesu asati api nu kho rūpakāye adhivacanasamphasso paññāyethāti. no hetaṃ bhante... yehi... ākārehi yehi liṅgehi yehi nimittehi yehi uddesehi nāmakāyassa ca rūpakāyassa ca paññāti hoti, tesu ākāresu tesu liṅgesu tesu nimittesu tesu uddesesu asati api nu kho adivacanasamphasso vā paṭighasamphasso vā paññāyethā? no hetaṃ bhante... yehi... ākārehi yehi liṅgehi yehi nimittehi yehi uddesehi nāmarūpassa paññāti hoti, tesu ākāresu tesu liṅgesu tesu nimittesu tesu uddesesu asati api nu kho phasso paññāyethā? no hetaṃ bhante. tasmātihānanda eseva hetu etaṃ nidānaṃ esa samudayo esa paccayo phassassa yadidaṃ nāmarūpaṃ... yathā viññāṇapaccayā nāmarūpaṃ* [63].

50. See SN II, 10: *viññāṇe kho sati nāmarūpaṃ hoti. viññāṇapaccayā nāmarūpa'ti.*

also for its cessation.[51] Consciousness, however, is not treated as the direct cause for the manifestation of body, feelings, and perceptions. Rather, the Buddhist tradition assigns this causal role to the four elements.[52] The structure is one of mutual formation: on the one hand, feelings, perceptions, and volitions are caused by contact resulting from intentional states of cognitive awareness; on the other hand, the psycho-physical aggregates in turn condition the manifestation of consciousness.[53] Indeed, the *Discourses* do not offer a comprehensive picture of consciousness as a distinct phenomenon, but only as something that arises and passes away as a result of the activity of all the other psychophysical elements. Its characteristic aspect is determined by the sensory system with which it happens to be associated. Thus, the distinctive aspect of visual consciousness is determined by the makeup of the visual system and not by any intrinsic properties of its own.

The rejection of an immutable self, abiding in each individual, seems to have undermined all attempts to analyze consciousness on its own terms. Even though the Buddhists adopt the Sanskrit term "*vijñāna*" as an appropriate designation for consciousness, the interpretations found in the *Discourses* and the early Abhidharma deny its immutability and instead regard it as indistinct from perceptual cognition. At this early stage in the development of a Buddhist theory of mind, *vijñāna* still retains its double meaning: (1) that of "consciousness" as a factor in the chain of dependently arisen phenomena that is essential for the continuity of the karmic process; and (2) that of "cognition," a faculty that is associated with each of the five sensory modalities and with the mind.[54] In later Abhidharma textual traditions, such as those of the Sautrāntika and Yogācāra Schools, consciousness is discussed mainly in relation to the aggregates of cognition, which comprise the five senses and the mental faculty of discernment.[55]

3.3 ATTENTION AND MENTAL PROLIFERATION

The circularity that is apparent in nearly all discussions of the role of consciousness as a causal principle (in which consciousness acts both as sentience

51. See SN II, 12: *viññāṇe kho asati nāmarūpaṃ na hoti. viññāṇanirodhā nāmarūpanirodho'ti.*

52. See SN III, 102: *mahābhūtapaccayo rūpakkhanddassa paññāpanāya.*

53. See SN III, 102: *phasso hetu phasso paccayo vedanākkhandassa paññāpanāya. phasso hetu phasso paccayo saññākkhandassa paññāpanāya.*

54. See SN III, 87; MN I, 292.

55. See AK I, 16a and AKBh *loc. cit.*: [verse] "Cognition is the impression relative to each object. [commentary] The aggregate of cognition (*vijñānaskandha*) constitutes the impression (*vijñapti*) relative to (*prati*) each object and the direct apprehension (*upalabdhi*) of each object." ([verse]: *vijñānaṃ prativijñaptiḥ*; [commentary]: *viṣa-yaṃ viṣ ayaṃ prati vijñāptir-upalabdhir-vijñāna skandha ityucyate*).

and discerning awareness) can, at least in part, be traced to the semantic fluidity of technical terms in the early canonical literature and the proliferation of descriptive accounts of experience. It is perhaps safe to assume that the task of establishing coherent typologies for consciousness and cognition was left to Abhidharma scholars, whose solutions, as we shall see, are not free of inconsistencies.[56] One example that is relevant to our discussion is the later Abhidharma reinterpretation of the notion of "contact" as a causal condition for the occurrence of a perceptual event. Thus, whereas in the *Discourses* "contact" (*sparśa*) has a causal function, in the Abhidharma it becomes a derivative aspect of empirical consciousness.[57]

As I noted above, "attention" (*āvartana*)[58] is not a key term in the canonical literature, where various cognitive functions are treated as distinct forms of consciousness. The term becomes significant in the Abhidharma, where the generality of consciousness is replaced with more concrete mental functions that perform specific tasks. Thus, the mere coming together of object, sense organ, and consciousness is not sufficient for a knowledge event (*prāmāṇya-jñapti*) to arise. What is needed is a consciousness that attends to its object. Under normal circumstances, the senses are always open and continuously receive sensory impressions. However, we become aware of their presence as objects of perception only when we direct our attention to a specific element within our perceptual field. While a discrepancy between what is meant by "contact" in the *Discourses* and the Abhidharma is indeed apparent, this does

---

56. On more general discrepancies between the canonical literature and the Abhidharma, see Gombrich (1990: 11). In Gombrich's view the Abhidharma interpretation of canonical literature ought to be favored, even if its perspectives do not appear to be entirely accurate from an historical perspective: "some of my colleagues are finding inconsistencies in the canonical texts which they assert to be such without telling us how the Buddhist tradition itself regards the texts as consistent—as if that were not important. My own view is not, I repeat, that we have to accept the Buddhist tradition uncritically, but that if it interprets texts as coherent, that interpretation deserves the most serious attention." See also Gethin (2001: 18–19) for a similar view that emphasizes the need to consider the discussion of core Buddhist doctrines in the context of Buddhist practice, rather than as metaphysical reflections on par with comparable movements in Western philosophy: "[I]n the Buddhist thought discussion of *paṭicca-samuppāda*, *anattā*, and *nibbāna* is not pursued as an end in itself but subordinated to the notion of the spiritual path, which is hardly true of the discussion of causality, change and metaphysics in western thought."

57. For instance, Sarathchandra (1958: 28) notes that "contact" (*sparśa*, Pāli = *phassa*) describes "the relationship between sense organ, object, and sensation. In the Abhidharma, however, contact is described as the effect of the coming together of these three, and as actually taking place after consciousness is brought to bear on the contents of experience, that is, after the act of attention."

58. The term *āvartana* is used here to refer to the mind turning toward or paying attention to a certain object, coming closer to what is commonly understood by attention: a consciousness that reflects upon or takes notice of the four types of objects: body (*kāya*), feeling (*vedanā*), mind (*citta*), and the elements of existence and/or experience or phenomena (*dharma*) broadly understood.

not necessarily imply that Abhidharma scholars are responsible for altering the original canonical meaning (assuming an "original" meaning is at all discernible). Rather, it may be reasonable to assume that this novel interpretation reflects a shift of perspective in the more general analysis of the chain of causation of the twelve causes (*nidānas*). The Ābhidharmikas focus primarily on understanding causation from the perspective of consciousness because consciousness is central to effecting the changes that are necessary for an individual engaged on the noble eightfold path to make any real progress. Thus, while contact cannot be prevented so long as consciousness inhabits, and is conditioned by, the psychophysical aggregates, feelings and perceptions that result from contact are within the purview of consciousness. The importance accorded to attention in the Abhidharma is directly related to the fact that it has the capacity to bring an object into focus, thus enabling various forms of mindfulness meditation (*bhāvāna-smṛti*).[59]

In recent years, modern experimental psychology has come to a similar conclusion: attention operates as a causal condition for perception, for without attending to what the senses present to us, no information is consciously registered. As the phenomenon of inattentional blindness demonstrates, if it is not consciously attended to, a stimulus cannot cause a perceptual event to arise, despite the tight correlation between the intensity of the stimulus and the degree of perceptual acuity.[60] This analogy is not simply intended as a vindication of the Buddhist analysis of perception. Rather, my aim here is to emphasize the gradual shift from the empirical accounts of perception found in the *Discourses* to its psychological reevaluation in Abhidharma as a more plausible explanation for this apparent inconsistency.

As will be argued in the next chapter, for perception to acquire epistemic status, sensory apprehension and sense impressions, perceiving and object perceived must be dissociated. The problematic nature of this dissociation is

---

59. These are the four stations or foundations of mindfulness (*smṛty-upasthāna*): perceiving the body (*kāyānupaśyanā*), perceiving the feeling (*vedanānupaśyanā*), perceiving the mind (*cittānupaśyanā*), and perceiving dharmas (*dharmānupaśyanā*). One of the earliest accounts of these four forms of perception in the Buddhist Sanskrit literature is found in the *Mahāparinirvāṇa-sūtra* of the Mūlasarvāstivāda school. See, for example, *Mahāparinirvāṇa-sūtra* 200. This fourfold formula of the *smṛ-ty-upasthānas* (Pāli = *satipaṭṭhānā*) is found throughout the Nikāyas. See, for example, DN II, 90; III, 58, 141, 221, 276; MN I, 339–340; SN V, 141–192, 294–306. Cf. Gethin (2001).

60. See in particular the recent experiments conducted by Arien Mack and Irvin Rock, which demonstrate the phenomenon of inattentional blindness. As a cognitive phenomenon, inattentional blindness occurs when an individual fails to notice an obvious object in the perceptual field due to lack of attention or due to focusing on another, secondary, object. As Mack and Rock note, "the discovery of inattentional blindness raised serious questions about whether in fact anything at all is perceived without attention and ultimately led us to adopt the working hypothesis that *there is no perception without attention*" (1998: 14).

partly responsible for the disputes that arose in later Abhidharma literature concerning the meaning and function of key terms such as "contact" (*sparśa*), "apperception" (*saṃjñā*), and "cognitive awareness" (*vijñāna*). Thus, whereas sensory impressions result from contact with an object, the subjective aspect of perceptual experience requires the presence of an attentive instance of consciousness for its actualization. Although contact acts as a causal condition for perception (albeit an indirect one: contact causes feeling, which in turn gives rise to perception), it is the presence of a discerning awareness that ultimately defines sensory activity as perceptual. However, the relationship between sense and object remains as problematic (and as elusive) for contemporary researchers as it was for the early Buddhists, since the sensory systems do not appear to enjoy a uniform relationship with their specific objects.[61] I shall return to this point below when I examine the role of object apprehension in the occasioning of a perceptual event.

In their efforts to explain the relationship between sense and object, the Ābhidharmikas turn toward attention (*āvartana*)[62] and wonder whether attention should be taken as an aspect of consciousness or as yet another type of consciousness similar to the consciousness accompanying sensory and mental activity. For instance, in the *Vibhaṅga* ("Book of Analysis," hereinafter *Book of Analysis*) we read that the five types of consciousness do not arise without attention and advertence, thus suggesting that empirical consciousness requires attention for its objects to come into focus.[63] Moreover, the preeminent role accorded to attention in the Abhidharma analyses of cognition anticipates the complex debates surrounding the ontological status and cognitive role of consciousness in the Yogācāra tradition. Indeed, the Yogācāra analysis of consciousness and cognition is particularly significant in view of the fact that its philosophical presuppositions inform nearly all aspects of the Buddhist epistemological account of perception.[64]

61. The sensory systems are divided usually in two groups, depending on whether they come into contact with their objects (*prāpyakāri*), such as touch, taste, and smell, or not (*aprāpyakāri*), such as sight, hearing, and mind.

62. As we have already noted, in the Pāli Abhidhamma the term most commonly used to convey the sense of attentive awareness is *āvajjana* (lit. "paying attention," "adverting the mind"). Other synonyms for "attention" include *samannāhāra* (lit. "concentration," "bringing together") and *manasikāra* (lit. "attention," "pondering," "fixed thought"). In Buddhist Hybrid Sanskrit literature, the term *āvartana* acquires a rather negative connotation signifying, according to Edgerton (1953: 107), "wandering, straying about" and also "devious winding, with implication of deceptive, wily movements."

63. See VB, *Ñāṇavibhaṅgo*, 321: *na asamannāhārā uppajjantī'ti: samammāharantassa uppajjanti. na amanasikārā uppajjantī'ti: manasikarontassa uppajjanti.*

64. In tracing the origins and development of Buddhist thought in India, the usual casting of Dignāga, Dharmakīrti, and their commentators as representing a Sautrāntika-Yogācāra synthesis, more commonly referred to as the school of rea-

Furthermore, in the *Book of Analysis* we also encounter explicit statements to the effect that the five types of empirical consciousness (viz., visual, auditory, etc.), which arise following contact between the sense and the object, lack attentive orientation toward an object, as well as any discriminative capacity.[65] Only a fully formed consciousness can give rise to the voluntary act of attention. Attention, in other words, is dependent upon the activity of consciousness. At the same time, a form of attentive alertness (*cittānupassana*) operates at the conscious level, directing the senses toward a specific object within their field of activity. This orientation toward the object is partly caused by the intensity of the stimulus and partly by the attentive presence of a pre-reflective cognitive awareness. The first stage of attention acts by bringing the object into focus (*ārammaṇa-paṭipādaka*). This stage is largely involuntary. Once the object appears at the threshold of awareness, a second stage of attention develops, which helps sustain interest in the object by ensuring its continuous presentation (*vīthipaṭipādaka*). Finally, once the object is continuously available to the senses, there arises an attention, which in turn gives rise to, and provides full support for, perceptual cognition. At this stage, the object is essentially present in its specific mode of givenness.

3.4 COGNITIVE AWARENESS AND ITS OBJECT

The Ābhidharmikas are not alone in trying to understand the relationship between the sensory systems and their objects. Most other Indian philosophers engage in similar attempts, although they do not always arrive at the same conclusions. As I have indicated above, one of the most problematic aspects of this type of inquiry is the classification of the sensory systems depending upon whether they are considered to be interacting or not with their specific objects. Thus, the senses of smell, taste, and touch are classified in the Abhidharma as directly interacting (*prāpyakāri*),[66] in view of the fact that they appear to reach out and come in direct contact with their objects. By contrast, sight and hearing do not directly interact with their objects and are thus categorized as unattainable (*aprāpyakāri*). The classification of the sensory systems into attainable and unattainable is not, however, universally shared by all schools of Indian philosophy. In general, the Nyāya-Vaiśeṣika, Mīmāṃsaka, Sāṃkhya, and Vedānta agree that by virtue of their empirical

soning (Skt. *nyāyānusāriṇo*), reflects later attempts to construct a comprehensive taxonomy of early Buddhist scholastic affiliations.

65. See VB, *Ñāṇavibhaṅgo* 322: *pañca viññāṇa anābhogāti: pañcannaṃ viññāṇaṃ natthi āvajjanā vā ābogovā samannāhāro vā manasikāro vi. pañcahi viññāṇehi na kañcī dhammaṃ paṭivijānātīti: pañcahi viññāṇehi na kañci dhammaṃ paṭivijānāti.*

66. From *prāpya*, *prāptavya* + *kārin*, meaning "attainable through touching," or "effective when touched."

nature all five senses are in immediate contact with their objects.[67] At the same time a distinction is made between the senses as perceptual systems and their anatomic and physiological basis (*adhiṣṭhāna*).[68]

Indian philosophers generally dispute the process or the causal mechanism by which distant objects act or are acted upon by the senses. In its own analysis of perceptual objects, the Buddhist tradition adopts an empirical standpoint. The notion that perception is caused by modifications that are internal to the cognitive systems (*buddhīndriya*), as proposed for instance by the Sāṃkhyas, or by alterations in the degree of attentiveness of each instance of cognitive awareness (*jñānapariṇāma*), as advocated by the Mīmāṃsakas, is rejected in favor of an account of the direct causal relations that obtain between the sensory systems and their specific domains of activity. The senses are treated neither as physical organs nor as immaterial cognitive systems. Rather, they are considered as part of a totality of elements operating within a specific sphere of activity.[69] There are altogether twelve spheres or bases for the manifestation of empirical consciousness, divided into six cognitive faculties and six classes of corresponding domains of activity. The *Discourses*, as we saw earlier, contain multiple and often contradictory accounts concerning the causal relationships that obtain between the spheres of activity and the different modes of empirical consciousness that correspond to each form of cognitive activity.

The model of the twelve spheres of perception and the eighteen elements offers a schematic representation of the interdependent arising of each manifested consciousness. For instance, Vasubandhu defines the perceptual systems and their empirical domains as faculties that extend the activity of consciousness into the physical world. There are six external spheres (*bāhyāyatana*) and six internal spheres (*adhyātmāyatana*), each corresponding

67. Sinha (1958: 4–5, 21–25).

68. This distinction is usually associated with the Sāṃkhyas, who explain the contact between the senses and their objects as resulting from the ability of the sense to adopt the form (*vṛtti*) of the object. See, for example, Aniruddha's *Commentary on Enumeration* (*Sāṃkhyasūtravṛtti*), SSV II, 23. For the Buddhists, the senses, while not directly confined to their anatomic basis, are nevertheless supported by their physiological organs. See, for example, *The Book of Causation* (*Nidānavagga*) (SN II, 3–4).

69. Vasubandhu's interpretation of *āyatana* is found in the AKBh *ad* AK I, 20a: *cittacaittāyadvārārtha āyatanārthaḥ/nirvacanaṃ tu cittacaittānāmāyaṃ tanvantīti āyatanāni.* ("*Āyatana* means 'entrance' (*ayādvāra*) or place of origin for [the manifestation of] mind and mental constituents. Etymologically, the term *āyatana* signifies that which brings forth the mind and the mental constituents"). The etymology proposed here suggests that while empirical consciousness arises in dependence upon the coming together of two factors, i.e., the cognitive function (sight, hearing, etc.) and its corresponding domain of activity (e.g., visible forms, etc.), its manifestation is not caused by the sensory systems. Rather, the spheres of sensory activity (*indriyāyatana*) are doorways through which consciousness emerges or is brought forth into the world of sensible forms (*rūpāyatana*).

to a sensory system and its specific domain of activity.[70] The only exception to this symmetric correspondence between senses and their objects is the mind or, more specifically, the mental cognitive awareness (*manovijñāna*). Despite its characterization as a cognitive faculty that acts upon nonempirical objects, the mind is always conceived as arising from its own preceding moment or, in other words, from a previous instance of introspective awareness. Vasubandhu makes this point explicit in response to the Vaibhāṣika objection that introspective awareness cannot be considered as the basis for the manifestation of a new instance of conscious apprehension because, for the liberated, the last moment of consciousness does not have its preceding moment as a cause:

The first five conscious apprehensions arise on the basis of their [corresponding] sensory systems, the sense of vision, etc.; the sixth conscious apprehension, mind, does not have a similar [empirical] basis. It is called mind or mind-element (*manodhātu*) because any of the six conscious apprehensions can serve as its basis of manifestation...

Objection: If the term mind signifies conscious apprehension or thinking, which upon its cessation [serves as] the basis for [the manifestation of] another instance of conscious apprehension, then the last thought of a liberated person (*arhat*) cannot become mind, because it is neither an immediately preceding cause for thinking nor a basis for its manifestation.

Response: On the contrary, this last thought does serve as a basis [for successive thoughts] and has the characteristic of mind. [In the case of the *arhat*] the absence of a successive cognition in consciousness (*uttaravijñānasaṃbhūtiḥ*), such as the conceptualization of a new [moment of] existence, is due to the absence of other [necessary] causes, activities, and desires that condition [the manifestation of a] new thought, not to its intrinsic characteristics.[71]

The main point that Vasubandhu seems to be arguing for is that in itself (that is, as pure awareness or reflexivity) the mind is not causally related to the production of new thoughts; instead, these result from factors that condition thinking (in particular, the thinking of deluded thoughts, such as the attribution of independent existence to what in reality is only a stream of phenomena). In their analysis of the conditioned elements of existence

70. The classification given in the AKBh only counts the sensory systems and their corresponding domains of activity as *āyatanas*, although mind is also treated as a sense. See, for example, AKBh *ad* AK I, 14b: *āyatanavyavasthāyāṃ daśayatanāni/cakṣur-āyatanaṃ rūpāyatanaṃ yāvat kāyāyatanaṃ spraṣṭavyāyatanam iti.*

71. AKBh *ad* AK I, 17cd: *pañcānāṃ vijñānadhātūnāṃ cakṣurdhātv-āyatanādayaḥ pañcāaśrayāḥ/ṣaṣṭhāsya manovijñānadhātorāśrayo'nyo nāsti/atastadāśrayaprasiddhyarthaṃ manodhāturūpadiṣṭaḥ/...arhatastarhi caramaṃ cittaṃ na mano bhaviṣyati/nahi tadasti yasya tatsamanantarātīti syād-iti/na/tasyāpi manobhāvenāvasthitattvāt anyakāraṇavaikalpyāttu nottaravijñānasaṃbhūtiḥ.*

(*saṃskṛtadharma*), the Abhidharma traditions single out contact between sense and object, as well as the ensuing perception, as the main factors contributing to the process of conceptual proliferation. The dissociation between the sphere of apperception (*saṃjñāyatana*) and the transformation of consciousness (*vijñānaparināma*) also marks a distinction between the physical and immaterial domains. However, consciousness is not treated as an enduring, abiding function of the self (or, indeed, as the essential attribute of the self), but rather as a stream of momentary events of cognitive awareness. Thus, the separation between the stream of consciousness (*citta-saṃtana*) and the forms of cognitive awareness (*vijñāna-dhātu*) that result from the operations of the cognitive systems within their specific domains of activity can be interpreted to mean at least two things. First, consciousness is not *produced* through contact between the sense and its object; rather, the coming together of sense and object *extends* a particular aspect of consciousness, such as visual consciousness. Second, the stream of mental events continues beyond the physical realm (or at least beyond the realm of form), where the gradual dissolution of empirical awareness gives rise to supra-mundane cognitions (*lokottarajñāna*), the unique property of which is the non-sensory apprehension of mental content (*caittadharma*). This (intuitive) mode of apprehension, however, is still perceptual in character, in the sense that it presupposes a direct and non-mediated mode of givenness of the mental content.

In addition to the classification of the elements of existence in accordance with the twelve spheres of activity and the six forms of consciousness, the Abhidharma traditions conceive of the human individual as consisting of five types of aggregates that serve as the bases of what we ordinarily designate as persons: (1) material form or body; (2) sensations; (3) apperception; (4) volition or dispositional formations; and (5) consciousness.[72] This aggregated view of persons informs all aspects of Buddhist thought and is indispensable to any account of cognition. Thus, in replacing the agent or cognizing "I" with a play of causal factors resulting in momentary cognitive events, the Buddhist tradition treats the cognizing agent as merely another way of referring to the embodied and dynamic functioning of the five aggregates. But, of course, it is not enough to acknowledge that the Buddhist tradition regards cognition as embodied. Rather, it is legitimate to ask how exactly do the aggregates embody and enact a (sense of) self, even as Buddhism denies the ultimate existence of such a self.[73]

72. See AKBh *ad* AK I, 7ab: *rūpaskandhevedanāskandhaḥ saṃjñskandho vijñānaskandhaścetyete saṃskṛtādharmāḥ.*

73. With the exception of the Buddhist Pudgalavādin sect, all other Buddhist schools reject the notion of a self as an appropriate description of the five aggregates. For a detailed account of the Pudgalavādins' personalist view, and Vasubandhu's critique of it, see Duerlinger (2003).

In this classification, the first collection of aggregates, form or materiality, stands for objects regarded as compounded entities.[74] Form is understood to be "compounded" in only one of the two senses in which compoundedness can be interpreted: that of being the product of causes and conditions (the other refers to entities that are produced by putting parts together). The category of form also includes the sensory systems, which from an anatomical and physiological point of view are material forms. Unlike the Sāṃkhyas, the Buddhists do not regard the activity of the sensory systems as resulting from contact with an immaterial soul or intellect, but rather view them as resulting from causes and conditions that operate in the natural world. The empirical approach of Abhidharma, particularly in its analysis of the elements of existence, does not imply physicalism, at least not in the modern sense of that term.[75] Rather, materiality is analyzed from the perspective of an individual's experience of sensations that reveal physical objects as having specific properties such as resistance, transformation, or destruction. In analyzing the views of the Vaibhāṣikas and other Abhidharma philosophers regarding the nature of materiality (*rūpa*), Vasubandhu clarifies that "form" is to be understood as something that is either disrupted as a result of impact with an agent or as something that opposes resistance (*pratighāta*). However, these properties do not extend to the atoms, which, according to Abhidharma, form the building blocks of materiality. Although as monadic units the atoms are seen as devoid of any formal properties (*rūpaṇa*), as atomic compounds (*saṃ ghātastha*, *saṃcita*) the atoms are subject to the same properties of resistance and destruction as any other material entities, which can be apprehended by the senses.[76] Thus, "form" refers to the phenomenal properties of an entity as they are perceptually apprehended. The difficulty of reconciling atomism, a fundamental tenet of the Buddhist ontology, with the phenomenology of perception is apparent in early Abhidharma debates between the Vaibhāṣikas and the Sautrāntikas on the issue of whether the sensible qualities of objects (e.g., color, shape, etc.) supervene on the atoms. For the Vaibhāṣikas, secondary properties such as color are in fact substances (*dravya*) similar to the four great elements. For the Sautrāntikas, color is a derived property that

74. I take the aggregates of form (*rūpa-skandha*) to be "compounded" in only one of the two senses in which *saṃskṛta* can be interpreted: that of being the product of causes and conditions (the other refers to entities that are produced by putting parts together). A *dharma* is never a compounded entity in the second sense of the term.

75. Stoljar (2010: 5) defines physicalism as the thesis "that everything is physical" with the caveat that "most physicalists do not mean that absolutely everything is physical or that every particular is physical or even that every property is physical." Rather, physicalism should be taken to mean simply that "every instantiated property is necessitated by some physical property."

76. See AKBh *ad* AK I, 13d: *pratighāto rūpeṇetyapare/paramāṇurūpaṃ tarhi rūpaṃ na prāpnotyarūpaṇāt/na vai paramāṇurūpam ekaṃ pṛthag bhūtam asti/saṃghātasthaṃ tu tad rūpyata eva/atītānāgataṃ tarhi rūpaṃ na prāpnoti?*

is not elemental like the primary elements of fire, water, etc. Rather, secondary properties are treated by the Sautrāntikas as the potentialities (*śakti*) of an aggregate of elements. Similarly, the Sautrāntikas conceive the atom (*paramāṇu*) not as a substantial impartite entity, but rather as the subtlest collection of material elements (*rupasaṃghāta*).[77] For Vasubandhu, who adopts the Sautrāntika view, the material properties grasped by the senses (the *upādāya rūpa*) are in fact emergent properties of subtle collections of elements whose phenomenal properties reflect the constitution and function of the perceptual systems. For instance, fluidity in the case of water is not a primary property of water atoms but a secondary property reflecting a specific configuration of water element atoms. A different configuration of the same atoms of the water element may produce the sensation of hardness and coldness, as in the case of ice.

An object *as perceived* is such that it makes its causal efficacy present by occasioning different types of experience. For example, water causes the experience of wetness and fluidity, rocks the experience of resistance or hardness, and irregular surfaces the experience of roughness. The materiality of the object of experience, which is embedded within the perceptual sphere of each sense, at the same time obstructs and limits these sensory modalities (e.g., a wall limits movement, night restricts vision). In discussing the characteristics of the senses as opening up or disclosing specific perceptual spheres, I noted that form, as a physical quality, is not a property of the external object but rather *a modality of its perceptual apprehension*. We see a blue sky (*nīlākāśam*), not because there is a determinate object "sky" (*ākāśa*) having the property of "blueness" (*nīlatva*), but rather because our visual system has adapted to seeing certain frequencies of light as blue. As color qualia "blue" can only be apprehended as such by a visual system directed by visual awareness.

The second collection of aggregates, sensations or feelings (*vedanāskandha*), defines the quality of the impressions that result from contact between the sense and its object. Sensations have a tripartite nature (pleasant, unpleasant, and neutral) and differ depending on the sensory modality in which they originate. Thus, what is pleasant to the eye may not be pleasant to taste or touch, and what is pleasant to taste may not be pleasant to the eye or to touch. Sensations are associated with each of the five corresponding sensory modalities and with the mind. In the case where the experience is not physiological but mental, we may experience certain mental states as relaxing, stressful, or indifferent. How we respond to these feelings (typically, if pleasant with grasping, if unpleasant with avoidance) conditions our acquisition and reinforcement of habits and coping skills. Moreover, while sensations vary in their degree of intensity, until one effects an alteration of the habitual response, they continue to elicit the same sort of reactions.

---

77. See AKBh *ad* AK II, 22ab.

The third collection of aggregates comprises apperception and refers to the capacity to comprehend the specific marks (*nimitta*) of experienced phenomena.[78] Apperception (*saṃjñā*) refers to the generic modality in which we experience phenomena as the result of a multiplicity of factors including memories, expectations, dispositions, feelings, and conceptualizations. This apperceptive cognitive event encompasses the sense of knowing something in its totality of aspects. Thus, perceiving a tree is apprehending it as such by virtue of the fact that one has had previous experience of the same or similar objects, and thus has the notion of "tree" as a botanical species with a certain configuration (roots, trunk, branches, leaves, color and texture of bark and leaves, etc.). But one does not see the tree merely as a botanical species. Rather, the tree is also apprehended as a source of food, medicine, timber, oxygen, or as shelter. However, as we shall discuss later on, this apperceptive cognition, which joins together sensory and mental cognitive events, and thus presumably gives us an image of the object as such (as it is presented to awareness) differs from the pure nonconceptual perception, which the Buddhist epistemologists regard as the only warranted mode of cognitive apprehension.

The fourth collection of aggregates includes all conditioned phenomena (*saṃskṛta*).[79] The conditioned phenomena included in this category of aggregates comprise dispositional formations most often referred to as volitions (*cetanā*). Although treated as separate from the other four aggregates, dispositional formations include all the conditioned factors that are intrinsic to consciousness (*saṃprayuktasaṃskāra*), as well as factors that are dissociated from consciousness (*viprayuktasaṃskāra*).[80] Dispositional formations are habitual latencies that predispose and motivate an individual to have certain

78. See AK I, 14: *saṃjñā nimittodgrahaṇātmikā*. The mark or characteristic of a phenomenon is its distinctive quality. Etymologically, *saṃjñā* (Pāli = *saññā*) derives from *saṃ* + √*jñā*, meaning "to know," "to understand," "to be aware of," but more appropriately in a philosophical context "to make intelligible" or "cause to be understood," thus indicating the causative function of perception predicates. The term is more commonly translated in Buddhist literature as "discernment," "conceptualization," or "discrimination."

79. See AKBh *ad* AK I, 15: *saṃkārāḥ saṃskāraskandhaḥ*. Vasubandhu emphasizes that although the other collections of aggregates (e.g., *rūpa*, *vedanā*, *saṃjñā*, and *vijñāna*) are also conditioned phenomena, the *saṃskāra-skandhas* refer specifically to volitions (*cetanā*) as the preeminent factor in bringing forth (*abhisaṃskar*) the future existence of an individual. Here, I translate *saṃskāra* (Pāli = *saṅkhāra*) as "dispositional formations." Other common translations include "mental constructions," "motivations," "conditioning factors," and "embodied conditioning."

80. Vasubandhu finds support in the *Connected Discourses* (*Saṃyukta-Nikāya*) for including the mental constituents and the factors that are dissociated from thought in the category of *saṃskāra-skandha* (SN V, 450): *te jātisaṃvattanikepi saṅkhare abhisaṅ karitvā jarāsaṃvattanikepi saṅkhāre abhisaṅkaritvā maraṇasaṃvattanikepi sāṅ-khāre abhisaṅkharitvā sokaparidevadukkhadomanassupāyāsasaṃvattanikepi saṅkhāre abhisaṅ khāritvā*. "Delighting in such volitional formations, they generate volitional formations that lead to birth, generate volitional formations that lead to aging, generate

types of experience while at the same time determining to a large extent the manner of his or her response to those experiences.

The fifth and last collection includes the aggregates of consciousness (*vijñāna-skandha*). In contrast to perceptual cognition, consciousness is defined as the direct apprehension (*upalabdhi*) of an object in the form of impressions (*vijñapti*) or traces (*vāsanā*) left by the object in consciousness.[81] Consciousness is what ensures that all other aggregates operate together as a cognizing subject. Thus conceived, consciousness manifests as a dual apprehension of the activities of all the other four aggregates coupled with self-consciousness, even though the issue of whether consciousness is reflexive is a subject of debate within the Buddhist tradition and between various Buddhist and Brahmanical schools. It suffices to mention here that the Buddhist epistemologists take consciousness as being inherently reflexive and describe it not with the aid of mirror metaphors—that is, the mind as mirror reflecting back the perceived phenomena—but rather with plastic metaphors: consciousness is said to assume the form of whatever object it cognizes. As we shall see, not only is consciousness inherently reflexive for the Buddhist epistemologists, it is also intentional, such that each instance of cognitive awareness already discloses a subject-object relation.

In the schematic analysis of the five aggregates only form is a physical aggregate *stricto sensu*. While sensations, apperception, and volitions can acquire an objectual aspect, they are not empirical objects proper. Thus, a sensation such as pain is not reducible to the physical substrate, say, a finger, in which it is instantiated. Rather, as object-oriented cognitive aspects, sensations, apperception, and volitions are included in the broader Abhidharma category of mental factors (*caitasika*). On the issue of whether consciousness itself can acquire an objectual aspect, there is disagreement among the various Buddhist schools and between Buddhist and Brahmanical traditions. This disagreement centers on whether consciousness is a knowable object (*jñeya*) or an intrinsically ascertaining awareness, in other words whether consciousness (understood here as pre-reflexive awareness) is a precondition for knowledge. In true phenomenological fashion, the Ābhidharmikas are specifically concerned with how things show up to us, with the phenomena

---

volitional formations that lead to death, generate volitional formations that lead to sorrow, lamentation, pain, displeasure, and despair."

81. See AKBh *ad* AK I, 16a: *viṣayaṃ viṣayaṃ prati vijñāptir upalambdhir vijñāna skandha ityucyate*. In his commentary on this verse, Yaśomitra expands this definition to mean that consciousness or mind grasps the object only (*vastumātra*). In contrast, the mental factors, which are associated with the cognitive processes such as sensation or apperception, apprehend the specific characteristics of objects (*svalakṣaṇa, nimitta*). See AKVy *ad* AK I, 16a: *pratir vīpsārthaḥ/viṣayaṃviṣayaṃ pratīty arthaḥ/upalabdhir vastumātragrahaṇaṃ/vedanādayas tu caitasā viśeṣā viśeṣagrahaṇarūpaḥ.*

of experience just as they appear to us before we set out to reflect and theorize about them.

On one account of experience—which, as we shall see later (chapter 8), becomes normative for the Buddhist epistemologists— each cognitive event arises in the form of a dual-aspect cognition: self-awareness coupled with object awareness. Without reflexivity, our (reliable) cognitions would lack the immediacy, vividness, and clarity upon which the Buddhist epistemologists rest their knowledge claims. Without this primordial reflexivity—the argument goes—we could not tell the difference between perception, memory, and imagination, or discriminate between erroneous and nonerroneous cognitions.

To conclude our discussion of the Abhidharma analysis of consciousness and cognition, we may briefly refer to Vasubandhu's discussion of the various types of limitations imposed upon the senses in virtue of their natural constitution and the natural constitution of their apprehended objects. Vasubandhu mainly describes three types of resistance (*pratigha = pratighāta*) by which objects limit the activity of the sense: (1) resistance pertaining to obstructions (*āvaraṇapratighāta*), exemplified by the fact that a body, or any of its anatomical parts, obstruct the manifestation of a similar body in that very location; (2) resistance pertaining to the object (*viṣayapratighāta*), exemplified in the case of vision by fact that its activity is impeded by the absence of light (as when night restricts vision);[82] and (3) resistance pertaining to the causal support (*ālambanapratighāta*), exemplified by the fact that mind and mental states are restricted by their objects (more appropriately, this refers to the fact that the mind can only apprehend abstract mental objects, not empirical entities).[83] Vasubandhu also clearly distinguishes between the object (*viṣaya*) as the entity toward which the sense extends its activity and the object as the causal support (*ālambana*) for the apprehension of its likeness in thought:

What is the difference between the [empirical] object and the [object as a cognitive] support? "Object" refers to that [entity] toward which the sense organ directs its activity. What is meant by "support" is that which is grasped by the mind and the mental constituents (*cittacaittairgṛhyate*). Why, again, is it said that [cognition] is

82. Interestingly, in his example, Vasubandhu refers to the supposed difference between the human and the bat eye: the absence of light might obstruct vision for humans, but it facilitates vision for bats. Obviously, Vasubandhu could not have been aware that bats navigate by means of a sonar system rather than some special type of night vision.

83. See AKBh *ad* AK I, 28ab: *pratigho nāma pratighātaḥ sa ca trividhaḥ/āvaraṇaviṣayā-lambanapratighātaḥ/tatrāvaraṇapratighātaḥ svadeśe parasya uttpattipratibandhaḥ/yathā hasto hastenāhataḥ upale vā/upalo'pi tayoḥ/viṣayapratighātaś cakṣurādīnāṃ viṣayiṇāṃ rūpādiṣu viṣayeṣu/...ālambanapratighātaś cittacvaittānāṃ sveṣvālambaneṣu.*

resistant either in respect to its object or its support? [That is] because there is no sensory activity on account of another [object]. Furthermore, "resistance" can also refer to the activity of falling upon or resisting (*pratighāto*) in relation to its own object.[84]

Regarding the issue of what constitutes the basis for cognition, the Ābhidharmikas seem unambiguous: the basis of cognition is to be found in the sensory system itself, because cognitions change mainly following modifications at the level of sensory apprehension rather than in the mental stream.[85] Even when a change in the mental stream appears to precede or take place in the absence of any sensory stimulus, it is largely the result of unconscious traces (*vāsanā*) of previous experience. By their nature, the senses respond to the presence or absence of any stimuli: it is this responsiveness that largely determines how an object enters the domain of empirical awareness. At the same time, a change in the stream of impression at the sense "doors" becomes an object of perceptual awareness only when additional factors intervene to focus the attention upon the content of a given individual sense sphere. For instance, changes in the degree of illumination of a particular room become part of one's awareness and thus acquire the status of a percept only when they are intended as such, that is, only when they enter the horizon of awareness. This model of cognitive dynamics raises a problem: does the arising of cognition follow the sense or the object? For the Buddhist epistemologists, who in general follow Vasubandhu's account of the psychology of perception, perception follows the sense rather than the object. This is primarily the reason why, when consciousness accompanies seeing, it is designated as "visual consciousness" (*cakṣurvijñāna*) rather than "consciousness of the visible" (*rūpavijñāna*). This particular mode of conceptualizing the nature of empirical awareness clearly indicates that cognition ultimately rests (or finds its support) on the sensory system, not on the object. This insight is also borne by empirical research on the perspectival nature of perceptual apprehension: indeed, in looking at the same object, different individuals apprehend it differently owing to their unique disposition and other conditioning factors, including their psychological constitutiveness (adults see it differently than children, whose cognitive systems are not fully developed, and those with optimally functioning cognitive systems see it differently than those with various types of cognitive impairment).

---

84. AKBh *ad* AK I, 29bc: *kaḥ punarviṣayālambanayor viśeṣaḥ?/yasmin yasya kāritraṃ sa tasya viṣayaḥ/yac cittacaittairgṛhyate tad ālambanam/kaḥ punaḥ svasminviṣaye pravarttamānamālambane vā pratihanyata ityucyate?/tasmāt pareṇāpravṛttāḥ/nipāto vā'tra pratighāto yā svaviṣaye pravṛttiḥ/.*

85. See AK I, 45ab: *tad vikāravikāritvādāśrayāś cakṣurādayaḥ* ("The basis for cognition is [to be found in] the sensory system, for cognition changes depending on whichever sensory system [it is associated with]").

Neither the canonical literature nor the early Abhidharma schools provide detailed accounts of the means by which we may discriminate between veridical and non-veridical states of cognitive awareness. Works such as the *Kathāvatthu* ("Points of Controversy") do concern themselves with the rules, and the various types, of debate and consider a wide range of views, but there is no systematic account of the criteria that ensure certainty. For systematic treatments of the epistemological import of various states of cognitive awareness we must turn to the Buddhist epistemological tradition initiated by Dignāga and Dharmakīrti. It is generally agreed that this tradition sprang out of a growing preoccupation with issues of logic and language among those Buddhists who regarded polemical engagement with their Brahmanical opponents as vital to their philosophical enterprise and scholarly standing. In spearheading a new model of epistemological inquiry, Dignāga and Dharmakīrti significantly changed the course of Buddhist philosophy in India. In order to see how this new model of inquiry is adopted and adapted by Śāntarakṣita and Kamalaśīla in their defense of core Buddhist principles, let us first examine the wider philosophical context of preoccupation with knowledge and its sources in which the Buddhists and their Brahmanical opponents carry their debates.

CHAPTER 4

Perception, Conception, and Language

Debates about the proper way to conduct epistemic inquiries, and about the kind of sources that can provide evidential ground for knowledge, form an integral part of the Indian philosophical tradition. Although attempts to reconcile various perspectives are not unknown, there is generally no universal agreement concerning the number, nature, object, and result of what might be properly termed an "accredited" source of knowledge. An exception is made, however, in the case of perception: most philosophers agree that the testimony of direct experience ought to play a central role in any theory of knowledge. As early Naiyāyikas make obvious, without accurate perceptions inference and verbal testimony would lack the sort of epistemological relevance that is typically attributed to them. Indeed, what use would inference have if, in trying to infer the presence of fire from an observation of smoke, one were to mistake dust (or mist) for smoke? And how could verbal testimony be reliable for the hearing impaired? But grounding knowledge on a foundation of empirical experience is not without its challenge: perceptual ambiguities are often experienced even under the best conditions of observation, and there is always the possibility of less than optimal perceptual functioning.

The systematic investigation of the epistemic function of perception that Śāntarakṣita and Kamalaśīla undertake in their encyclopedic work is exemplary both as a critique of rival views, and as a systematic presentation of the Buddhist standpoint. In their attempt to critically investigate (and refute) what other philosophers establish as an evidential ground for knowledge, Śāntarakṣita and Kamalaśīla spend a great deal of time contrasting perception with other cognitive modalities. We may regard this contrastive analysis as an attempt to specify the characteristics of the phenomena under investigation for the sake of reaching greater clarity about the issues under dispute. It is proper therefore that we begin with a brief overview of the historical context of this pan-Indian philosophical debate, and first identify the main characters, works, and issues under dispute.

The first systematic inquiry into the sources of knowledge in the Buddhist context is associated with Dignāga's magnum opus, the *Collection*.[1] Earlier texts such as Nāgārjuna's *Vigrahavyāvartanī* ("Dispelling of Disputes") and Āryadeva's *Śataśāstra* ("One Hundred Verses Treatise") seem to have been primarily concerned with establishing the proper rules of debate (*vivāda*) and did not display the full range of epistemological concerns that is found in the works of Dignāga. It is with Dignāga's principal work that for the first time we come across a thoroughly critical appraisal of the dominant theories of the day,[2] and a new model of epistemological inquiry.[3] This model, which is further expanded less than a century later by Dharmakīrti, rests on two major premises: (i) on the one hand, it adopts a specific view on the identity of language and conceptual thought, principally advocated by grammarian-philosophers such as Bhartṛhari[4] (c. 4th century C.E.); (ii) on the other hand, it incorporates insights from the Abhidharma traditions concerning the phenomenology of perception and conceptual apprehension. These two sets of premises become instrumental in the adoption by the Buddhist epistemologists after Dignāga of an intentional account of perception, which, as we shall see, is restricted to certain types of cognitive awareness, only.

The most systematic, although not the earliest,[5] exposition of the sources of knowledge in Indian philosophy is found in the Nyāya-Vaiśeṣika tradition,

1. See Vidyābhuṣaṇa (1921: 270). See also Tucci (1928, 1929) for an early exploration of logical texts from the pre-Dignāga period, including his Sanskrit reconstruction of *Tarkaśāstra* and *Upāyahṛdaya*. Matilal likewise notes, "although there were some so-called logical texts written by the Buddhists in the pre-Dignāga period... we must recognize that the Buddhist contribution to the development of logic in India actually began with Dignāga" (Matilal 1998: 88).

2. With the exception of Vedānta (or Uttara Mīmāṃsā), which had not received a systematic formulation by the sixth century C.E. to which Dignāga's dates are usually assigned.

3. The importance of Dignāga as an innovator in logic and epistemology is explored at length in Frauwallner (1959), Hattori (1968), and Hayes (1988). Extensive treatments of Dignāga's *apoha* theory are found in Herzberger (1986), Katsura (1991), Siderits (1985, 1986, 1999), and Pind (2009).

4. The influence of Bhartṛhari's ideas of language on Dignāga's thought was first noted in Iyengar (1950). For subsequent treatments of the impact of the grammarians on Dignāga's thought, see Frauwallner (1959), Hattori (1968, 1980, 1993), Herzberger (1986), Lindtner (1993), and Kelly (1993).

5. The credit for being the earliest doctrinal system concerned with interpreting the corpus of religio-philosophical writings of ancient India, i.e., the Vedas, goes to Mīmāṃsā, the first school to have pondered the issue of apprehending the truth of cognitions arising from various sources. The Mīmāṃsakas found that of all the sources of cognition, speech (*śabda*) seemed to enjoy a privileged role in its capacity to generate cognitions about nearly all aspects of phenomenal experience, whether present, past, or future, near or far, subtle or gross, etc. See, for example, MS 1.1.2. Cf. Matilal (1985: 203).

which also provides much of the technical vocabulary for subsequent treatments of logico-epistemological topics. As a method of inquiry, *nyāya* (commonly translated in English as "reasoning") is universally adopted by most Indian philosophers, regardless of their doctrinal affiliations. The specific meaning of the term "*nyāya*" itself is subject to interpretation among the Naiyāyikas. For instance, Vātsyāyana defines "*nyāya*" as the examination of an object with the aid of reliable cognitions.[6] In the *Nyāyavārttika* ("Commentary on Reason"), Uddyotakara adds that this sentence should be understood to mean that "reasoning" stands for all the "reliable cognitions," for in the absence of an apprehension of the object collectively by all cognitive modalities, reasoning is incomplete and does not qualify as a source of knowledge.[7] This definition anticipates a series of long discussions in which notions such as "source of knowledge" (*pramāṇa*) and "object of knowledge" (*prameya*) are examined with reference to each of the four cognitive modalities admitted by the Naiyāyikas—perception, inference, verbal testimony, and comparison—and to the function each of these modalities plays in the overall economy of cognition. The universal currency that *nyāya* enjoys in the Sanskrit philosophical literature is primarily due to its role as a systematic method of inferential reasoning. As Surendra Barlingay notes with respect to philosophers not sharing the doctrinal standpoint of Nyāya:

> Though they reject the metaphysical tenets, they accept the general methodology of the Nyāya-Vaiśeṣika school and soon, thanks to their efforts, instead of remaining a mere school of philosophy, it attained the position of pre-eminence in the science of methodology. Thus in ancient India a pupil was first required to learn grammar and then Nyāya or logic. Unless a student took lessons in Nyāya he was not supposed to be competent to study Pūrva Mīmāṃsā or Vedānta.[8]

In their epistemological debates, the Buddhists primarily engage with the Nyāya tradition, whose origins go back to the *Nyāyasūtra* ("Treatise on Reason," hereinafter *Treatise on Reason*) of Akṣapāda Gautama (c. 150 C.E.) and the two early commentaries by Vātsyāyana (c. 350–450) and Uddyotakara (c. 540 C.E.) (the *Nyāyasūtrabhāṣya* and the *Nyāyavārttika*, respectively). Along with later commentators such as Jayanta Bhaṭṭa (c. 840–900), author of the *Nyāyamañjarī* ("A Blossoming of Reason"), and the Kashmiri Naiyāyika Bhāsarvajña (c. 860–920), author of the *Nyāyabhūṣaṇa* ("Ornament of Reason"),

6. See NSBh *ad* NS 1, 1.1: *kaḥ punarayaṃ nyāyaḥ? pramāṇairarthaparīkṣaṇaṃ nyāyaḥ/.* "What does *nyāya* mean? It means the investigation of things with the aid of *pramāṇas*."
7. See NV *ad* NS 1, 1.1: *naikaikaṃ pramāṇamarthaparicchedahetubhāvena vyavatiṣṭamānaṃ nyāya ityucyate, kintu samasthāni.*
8. Barlingay (1975: 5).

these works are representative of what doxographers refer to as the old school of Nyāya. These early Naiyāyikas together with the Vaiśeṣika philosopher Praśastapāda, author of the *Padārthadharmasaṃgraha* ("Compendium of Categories"), represent the main protagonists in the Buddhist-Nyāya debate, which reaches its climax between the eighth and the eleventh centuries, and ceases with the disappearance of Buddhism from India.

From the perspective of the Nyāya tradition, the *terminus post quem* of its engagement with the Buddhist epistemologists is marked by the refutation of various Buddhist doctrines, chiefly that of momentariness, by Udayana (c. 1050–1100) in his celebrated work, the *Ātmatattvaviveka* ("On Discriminating the Reality of the Self").[9] Whether or not Udayana's work offers the final and definitive refutation of Buddhist epistemological theories—and whether the dialogue between these two archrival traditions would have continued had Buddhism endured in India after the twelfth century—is a matter of speculation. What is certain is that post-Udayana Naiyāyikas ceased to engage with the various arguments of later Buddhist epistemologists such as Jñānaśrīmitra (c. 1010–1060) and Ratnakīrti (c. 1020–1070) (elder contemporaries of Udayana).[10] In Tibet, where the Buddhist epistemological tradition continued to evolve in isolation from the Indian philosophical context, debates shifted to intra-doctrinal disputes between various factions of the two main philosophical schools of Madhyamaka and Yogācāra.[11]

On their part, Nyāya authors did not completely cease to address certain aspects of Buddhist epistemology, in particular relating to various implications of Dharmakīrti's arguments about the role of such key categories as "essential nature," "effect," and "non-perception" (*svabhāva-*, *kārya-*, and *anupalabdhi-hetu*, respectively). Of all the works written by the Buddhist epistemologists, it seems that it is mostly Dharmakīrti's *Vādanyāya* ("Discourse on Reasoning") that continued to exercise an influence upon subsequent generations of Nyāya and Jaina logicians.[12] Indeed, its mention in a late Nyāya work

9. See Laine (1998) for a translation and discussion of Udayana's work.

10. Patil (2009: 35ff.) makes a compelling case that in his debate with the Naiyāyikas, particularly in his *Īśvarasādhanadūṣaṇa* ("Refutation of Arguments for Establishing Īśvara"), Ratnakīrti already addresses what might be called a generic and reconstructed Nyāya position rather than target specific authors and their arguments. This, of course, mirrors the similar generic Buddhist position that Udayana confronts.

11. Assessing the evolution of Buddhist epistemology in Tibet, Ruegg notes that Tibetan interpreters did not lack familiarity with the main doctrinal positions of the Brahmanical schools, if the Tibetan doxographical (*grub mtha'*) literature is any indication. But they did evolve a tendency to synthesize and universalize these doctrinal positions into something like "transhistorical philosophical positions and views that continue to possess an abiding significance within much later Buddhist thought" (Ruegg 2004: 336).

12. See especially Much (1991: xvii). For a brief survey of post-Udayana Nyāya reactions to Buddhist epistemology with a focus on Dharmakīrti's *Vādanyāya*, see also Chinchore (1991).

such as Mathurānātha's (1600–1675) *Tarkarahasya* ("Subtle Points on Logic") is a clear indication of its authoritative status in Nyāya circles.

4.1 SHARED NOTIONS ABOUT PERCEPTUAL KNOWLEDGE

For the Buddhist epistemologists, perception necessarily involves contact between the sense and the object, which is explained in terms of certain causal chains that mediate the relation between the perceptual occasion and its constitutive factors.[13] On this account, the type of discriminating cognition (*vikalpakajñāna*) that apprehends objects as possessors of both generality (*jāti*) and individuality (*vyakti*) cannot be treated as perception. Unlike the Naiyāyikas and the Mīmāṃsakas, who regard perceptual judgments as an essential step of the cognitive process leading up to conception, Dignāga and all subsequent Buddhist epistemologists reject the notion that perception can apprehend anything other than unique particulars. On this view, universals cannot form the object of perceptual apprehension.

Recall that the Buddhist is a sort of process thinker who classifies mind and mental phenomena principally in terms of the specific activities they perform. Thus, the mental activity that corresponds to cognizing the immediate impressions of the senses is treated as a sort of introspective apprehension of mental content. The reliability of this introspective cognition is ascertained on the evidential basis that non-sensory realities such as ideas, dreams, and memories can be held before the mind's eye, so to speak, before they become objects of reflective analysis. Similarly, the possibility of self-awareness, the mind's directedness upon itself, is ascertained on what is taken to be the qualitative and perspectival character of conscious apprehension. Note that the emergence of the subject-object relation is a function of the perceptual occasion rather than an outcome of higher order, metacognitive states. As we shall see in chapter 8, the dual-aspect nature of cognition is in effect characteristic of all cognitive events insofar as they arise bearing an intentional relation. Indeed, Dignāga seems to suggest that the self-cognition—this inherently intentional aspect of cognition—is an irreducible, factive element of our cognitive architecture.[14] We may regard these two modes

13. See NV *ad* NS 1, 1.4 and ŚV, *Pratyakṣa*, 38–39. Both Dignāga and Dharmakīrti follow Vasubandhu on the issue of contact between the object and the sense. Vasubandhu's account can be found in AK III, 30 and AKBh *loc. cit.* Dignāga considers the notion that perception involves contact between the sense and the object when he advances the view that perception (*pratyakṣa*) is named after the sense rather than after the object (see PS I, k4ab). For Dharmakīrti's discussion of this issue, see PV III, 194 and discussion in Dunne (2004: 23–25).

14. See PSV 95b.2: *de yul la ni 'dod chags la sogs pa nyid bzhin du mngon sum ma yin yang, rang rig pa la ni ma yin pa'i phyir skyon med do.* PS I, k9a: *rang rig la yang 'dir 'bras bu.*

of apprehension—self-awareness and introspective awareness—as broadly corresponding to what modern philosophers call "reflexivity."[15]

There is some fundamental disagreement among these early Indian philosophers about whether it is proper to talk about internal mental processes using the language of sense perception. Gautama[16] and Kumārila[17] clearly resist this move, while Uddyotakara[18] and nearly all subsequent Naiyāyikas grant that at least some aspects of thought could be understood in minimally apperceptive terms. As the first Buddhist to wrestle with the manner in which the Naiyāyikas construe the epistemic function of sense perception, Dignāga articulates what would become the standard Buddhist epistemological position: insofar as we are talking about apprehending objects as belonging to specific classes and categories we are not talking about perception.[19]

Disagreements do not stop at the examination of the character of cognition but also extend to its contents. There are philosophical differences, for instance, regarding the causes of perceptual error and the experience of illusory perceptions. There is also significant disagreement regarding whether illusions are perceptual or conceptual, which feed into a long dispute about whether perception can ever be defective. For Dignāga, the source of perceptual error is located in the mind, particularly the ordinary, untrained mind whose projective tendencies tend to obscure and distort the contents of awareness.[20] Insofar as perception represents a direct and unmediated

15. In general terms, "reflexivity" refers to the capacity of mental operations to turn or be directed back upon the mind itself. In a philosophical sense, "reflexive consciousness" denotes a range of cognitive events including self-reference, self-description, self-ascription, etc. but more generally refers to our awareness of being the subject of a particular type of experience.

16. See NS 1, 1.14: *gandharasarūpasparśaśabdāḥ pṛthivyādiguṇāḥ tadarthāḥ*.

17. See ŚV, *Pratyakṣa*, 169: *cakṣūrūpādibhedasthu pañcadhaiva vyavasthitaḥ/tena nīlādibhede'pi nendriyānantyakalpanā*. "The division of the eye, etc. and of visible color, etc. are settled as being limited to only five. Thus, although other colors such as blue, red, etc. are included in this division, no separate organs should be conceived [as corresponding to the perception of each of these colors]."

18. See, for example, NV *ad* NS 1, 1.4: *indriyārtha-sannikarṣa-grahaṇene-indriyamanaḥsaṃyoga ukto veditavyaḥ/kiṃ kāraṇam? ubhayorasādhāraṇatvāt/na ca yāvadasādharaṇaṃ kāraṇaṃ tāvat sarvamabhidhātavyamityarthaḥ*. "The purpose that would be served by the mention of the contact of the sense with the mind is already accomplished by the mention of that between the sense organ and the object. How so? For the simple reason that both these contacts are peculiar to perception; and it is not intended [by the *sūtra* to supply an exhaustive enumeration of] all the specific causes that bring about perception; [the *sūtra* mentions] only one specific causes (*asādharaṇaṃ kāraṇaṃ*), as the mention of any one specific cause suffices to differentiate perception from the other forms of knowledge."

19. Dignāga's discussion and criticism of the Nyāya account of perception is found in the PS (P 97b.8–99b.6). See Hattori (1968: 36–41; 190–199).

20. See PS I, 7cd–8ab: *'khrul dang kun rdzob shes pa dang, rjes dpag rjes su dpag las byung, dran dang mngon 'dod ces bya ba'o, mngon sum ltar snang rab rib bcas*. "Erroneous cognition, cognition of empirical reality, inference, its result, recollection, and desire

mode of acquaintance with the bare phenomenon it cannot—according to Dignāga—be considered a source of illusions or errors, for that requires at a minimum a conceptual schema and the deployment of logical predicates such as "true" and "false." The assumption here is that ordinarily, perception involves some element of discernment and recollection, and is coupled with dispositional reactions to its contents. But this assumption is predicated on the notion that it is possible for the mind to be stabilized in meditative equipoise, and for its constructing and confabulating tendencies to be brought under voluntary control. An important phenomenological criterion for identifying states of meditative equipoise as such is that of vividness (*spaṣṭa*). Of course, this sort of exclusive evidence is not ordinarily accessible, and thus not open to precisely the kind of scrutiny the Buddhist wishes to submit those other sources of knowledge that she deems unreliable (for instance, verbal testimony).

Perhaps the most significant point of disagreement among Indian philosophers has to do with whether perception is instrumental in the determination of physical properties. For Dignāga, who takes the distinction between direct and indirect modes of cognizing as normative, only a direct acquaintance with the contents of experience counts a reliable source of knowledge.[21] Naiyāyikas like Vātsyāyana and Uddyotakara take the exact opposite view: in perception all the intrinsic characteristics of an object are directly known (*jijñāsā*).[22] But it is Kumārila in particular who takes issue with the notion that vividness, particularly in the case of yogic perception, is a true indicator of nondeceptiveness. Such a notion, as he explains, would suggest that perception is a more authentic source of knowledge than revelation (*śruti*):

The perception of a past or future, small or hindered, object is said to be possible for yogins and the liberated. For these [yogins], the claim that perception is the apprehension of what is presently manifest is not proven. Otherwise, the reason of Dharma being a future occurring object remains unresolved, on account of objects that are allegedly apprehended by yogis and enlightened beings. In order to avoid these defects, we state what is commonly recognized, namely that [connection of

---

are not true perceptions and are accompanied by obscurity (*sataimira*)." In his autocommentary, Dignāga further explains that erroneous cognition (*bhrānti-jñāna*) is not a perceptual but a conceptual event. See PSV *ad* PS 94b.4: *re zhig 'khrul pa'i shes pa ni smig rgyu la sogs pa la chu la sogs par rtog pa'i.* "Erroneous cognition (*bhrānti-jñāna*) is not a true perception because it arises conceptually constructing, for example, water, etc. out of such things as vapor floating over sand" (translation *per* Hattori 1968: 28).

21. It is Dharmakīrti who stipulates this criterion in order for perception to be counted as an authentic source of knowledge (i.e., a *pramāṇa*). See PV II, 283ab: *na vikalpānubaddhasyāsti sphuṭārthāvabhāsitā.*

22. By intrinsic characteristic, the Naiyāyikas mean that objects possess both particularity (*vyakti*) as well as generality (*jāti-sāmānya*). See, for example, NSBh *ad* NS 1, 1.4.

sense and object must be ascertained as] "existing." Indeed, there is no yogic perception apart from sense perception. Since it [viz., yogic perception] is also [a mode of] perception, it must be apprehending something present or else, like our [notion of] perception it must arise from an existing connection [between sense and object]. The cognition of an object that is not present, which arises for yogins and the liberated, is not perception, [just] like desire, memory, and so forth [which also arise without an external object]. It is not [an instance of] perception because it is not established as a source of knowledge, like direct apprehension. The absence of these two characteristics is indicated by the term "existing."[23]

The objections raised here do call into question things like the possibility of apprehending nonexistent past and future objects, or the notion that the range of perceptual awareness extends beyond the existing connection of sense and object. But Kumārila's main concern is the very notion that perception—because it is involved even in apprehending the words of the Vedas (more specifically because it precedes inference by means of which the words of the Vedas are apprehended)—could have a causal role in generating verbal knowledge (*śabdapramāṇa*).[24] Such a position would, of course, be seen as undermining the very foundation of the Mīmāṃsā epistemological system, even though Kumārila has to admit that all sound inferences must in turn be preceded by reliable perceptions.[25]

---

23. ŚV, *Pratyakṣa*, 26–31: *atītānāgate'pyarthe sūkṣme vyavahite'pi ca/pratyakṣaṃ yogināmiṣṭaṃ kaiścinmuktātmanām api//vidyamānopalambhatvamasiddhaṃ tatra tān prati/bhaviṣyattvasya vā hetostadgrāhyairvyabhicārita//mā bhūtām iti tenāha lokasiddhaṃ sadityayam/na lokavyatiriktaṃ hi pratyakṣaṃ yoginām api//pratyakṣatvena tasyāpi vidyamānopalambhanam/satsamprayogajatvaṃ vāpyasmatpratyakṣavad bhavet// teṣām avartamāne'rthe vā nāmotpadyate matiḥ/pratyakṣaṃ sā tatastveva nābhilāṣa-smṛtādivat//lokecāpyaprasiddhatvāt pratyakṣatvapramāṇataḥ/pratibhāvad dvayāsattvaṃ sadityetena kathyate*. Translation, slightly altered for consistency, per Taber (2005: 54ff.).

24. ŚV, *Pratyakṣa*, 94–95: *pratyakṣeṇa gṛhītvā ca varṇān vede'pi gṛhyate/prameyamiti so'pi syāt tatpūrvatvādakāraṇam//tatpūrvakatvād yat tāvat prāmāṇyaṃ tadasambhavaḥ/pratyakṣeṇa gṛhītvā ca, liṅgādyanyatamaṃ dhruvam*. "Also [asserts the opponent] it is only after the letters have been recognized through perception that the object of the Vedas is apprehended. Therefore, being preceded by perception the Vedas could not be the means of knowing *karma*. [We reply]: Some hold that the precedence of perception is not the cause [of inference]; [the opponent's statement is interpreted to] mean that the authority of perception, due to its precedence, does not apply [in the case of the words of the Vedās]."

25. ŚV, *Pratyakṣa*, 96–97: *pratyakṣeṇa gṛhītvāt ca, liṅgādyanyatamaṃ dhruvam/ pravṛttiranumānāderna ca dharme'sti tādṛśam//anumānānumānāder na cāpyastīha sambhavaḥ/sambandhaliṅgiliṅgānāṃpurvasiddherasambhavāt*. "Also, inference and the rest can function (*pravṛttiranumānā*) only when the sign (*liṅga*) has been apprehended in perception, and in the case of [knowledge of the] *dharma* no such [apprehension] is observed. Nor is it possible to have an inference of inference, because any prior ascertainment of the relationship between the premises and the terms involved [in the inference] is impossible."

This trenchant dispute about the right definition of perception raises both epistemological and ontological questions. Indeed, questions about the nature of things cannot ultimately be settled without some kind of account about how we come to ascertain their existence. If the nature of reality is such that it can become an object of empirical scrutiny, then scripture cannot count as a source of knowledge. On the other hand, if knowledge of temporally and spatially distant things can only be had by means of revelation (or verbal testimony), then our most common intuitions cannot provide more than a basic guidance for what is immediately available to empirical awareness. For the Buddhist who follows Dignāga's account of perception, yogic perception possesses this special capacity to apprehend things as they truly are, that is, as part of a causal continuum of manifest phenomena. Whether this peculiar type of empiricism commits the Buddhist to foundationalism is, however, an issue of debate (see chapter 7).

Of course, there is a natural progression from questions about the type of epistemic activities perception intends to issues about the ontological status of its contents. The Buddhist epistemologist would eventually come to regard only objects that are causally effective as physically real. As Dharmakīrti—the initiator of this theory—notes, "only an entity capable of producing an effect is ultimately existent,"[26] because, as he further clarifies, "the capability and incapability to produce an effect are essentially the [distinguishing] characteristics of the real and the unreal entity."[27] Stock examples of unreal objects in the Sanskrit philosophical literature include such things as the horns of a hare, crow's teeth, or the son of a barren woman. These objects are taken to be mere conceptual fictions that possess only a nominal existence.[28]

Ordinarily we would grant that the dissociation between empirical and mental objects (or in Lockean terms, between simple and complex ideas) is simply a matter of specifying their mode of apprehension. But this is not always the case. Perceptual illusions generate sensory impressions that seem identical to those caused by real perceptual stimuli, despite the fact that they lack causal efficacy. And given that most illusions persist after disambiguation, the possibility that error is an integral part of the perceptual mechanism itself, rather than an outcome of the apperceptive and categorizing aspects of thought, cannot be ruled out. On what basis, then, do we ascertain that certain classes of abstract mental objects such as essential natures (*svabhāva*)—which are twice removed from the empirical domain—are real?

26. PV I, 166abc: *sa pāramārthiko bhāvo ya evārthakriyākṣamaḥ*.

27. PVSV 84, 5f *ad* PV I, 166: *idam eva hi vastvavastunor lakṣaṇaṃ yad arthakriyāyogyatā'yogyatā ca*.

28. Nonexistent objects should, however, be distinguished from empty subjective terms, which play a role in discussions related to the intentional character of consciousness. See discussion of this problem in McDermott (1970), Shaw (1974, 1978), and Matilal (1971: 123–144; 1985: 76–85).

In the case of perception, knowledge of the illusory nature of an object is gained as a result of its (i.e., the object's) failure to fulfill a practical goal. Although an illusory object retains the appearance of a real object, it lacks the latter's material and functional properties (e.g., illusory water cannot quench thirst, apparent motion fails to indicate the direction of movement). The bifurcation of reality into what has and does not have the capacity to achieve an intended aim reflects an understanding of phenomena that takes causality rather than justification as the main criterion for dissociating between true and false beliefs, between veridical and deceptive cognitions.

In their definition and analysis of perception, the Naiyāyikas adopt the realist perspective of the Vaiśeṣika ontology. Objects of sense are treated as substantial entities that exist and have real properties, which can be empirically apprehended. According to this perspective, the senses reach out and apprehend the specific characteristics of objects. These characteristics, although disclosed as such by the cognitive process, are in fact treated as intrinsic properties of the things themselves. For example, the apprehension of the color of a jar is due to inherence (*samavāya*) of the color property in the jar and to contact between the eye and the jar:

> In the perception of the color [of the jar] the contact of the eye with the color, the latter not being a substance, is [of the nature] of inherence in that which is in conjunction; because the color [which is in contact] subsists in the jar which is in conjunction with the eye, this "subsistence" being of the nature of inherence. In the perception of the genus subsisting in the color, the "contact" is of the form of inherence in that which inheres in that which is in conjunction [the genus inhering in the color, which inheres in the jar, which is in conjunction with the eye].[29]

For the Naiyāyikas, it is chiefly Uddyotakara who sets the epistemological program (for how the content of empirical awareness is to be ascertained) by being the first to adopt the Vaiśeṣika list of categories.[30] In addition, we also need to be aware of semantic differences in the use of terms such as *padārtha*

29. NV *ad* NS 1, 1.4: *adravyeṇa ca tadgatarūpādinā saṃyuktasamavāyaḥ; yasmāccakṣuṣā saṃyukte dravye rūpādi varttata iti/vṛttistu samavāyaḥ/rūpādivṛttinā sāmānyena saṃyuktasamavetasamavāyaḥ/sannikarṣaḥ*.

30. See Halbfass (1992: 73) for an analysis of this aspect of Uddyotakara's ontology. On this issue, see also Potter (1977: 144) and Dunne (2004: 27–28). The translation of *guṇa* as "quality" does not convey the sense of inherence (*samavāya*) that this term has in Indian epistemology. In Nyāya epistemology specifically, objects are not spoken as having similar qualities. Rather, it is the quality-universal (*guṇa-jāti*) that is responsible for their qualitative resemblance. Although the Buddhist epistemologists do not accept the Vaiśeṣika list of categories, it is an interesting speculative question whether their own analysis of the constituent elements of existence and/or experience (*dharmas*), as adopted mainly from Vasubandhu, displays any formal similarity to the manner in which the categories are discussed by Praśastapāda or Vātsyāyana.

to denote both a "category" in the classical sense as referring to the Vaiśeṣika list of categories, and in the more specific sense of "a topic of discussion" as it is commonly employed in Sanskrit philosophical literature.[31] The Nyāya-Vaiśeṣika tradition for the most part adopts a realist position: categories such as substance, quality, and motion are considered to be within the purview of sense-experience. They exist independently as empirical entities (or aspects thereof). The Nyāya-Vaiśeṣika position is similar to that adopted by the Sarvāstivāda Ābhidharmikas, who claim that the elements of existence and/or experience, as generic categories, do have a physical substrate.

These early deliberations about the function and character of perception anticipate one of the most fundamental problems in Indian epistemology: is consciousness aspectual in character or should it rather be understood as mere witnessing? If perception can only apprehend particulars, notions such as "universal" (*jāti*) can only arise at the conceptual level, thus suggesting that thought naturally adopts the form of the object it cognizes (and subsequently universalizes it). Although the Buddhist epistemologists do not accept the reality of resemblance relations, they agree that intentional objects are cognitively efficacious. A difficulty presents itself when one attempts to explain how the spatio-temporal properties of empirical objects can be apprehended by means of internal representations. This difficulty is usually overcome by adopting a perspective that most closely aligns to Yogācāra phenomenology. On this account, external objects exist only as perceived. As Dharmakīrti observes, "the existence of objects that are different [from consciousness] depends on their appearance as such [i.e., as different from consciousness]."[32] The conception of an "appearance as such," that is, as different from consciousness, implies a form of representationalism in which cognition copies the form of the object. Whether this copying mechanism also implies realism about universals, or at least about universal relations, depends on how the representationalist mechanism is understood to operate. If resemblance relations are constructed rather than perceived, then consciousness is "aspectual" in character. But realism about universals is possible only if perception is understood as having the capacity to apprehend generic features as, in some sense, mind-independent. Thus, we must allow for perceptual judgments to be treated as effective modes of empirical apprehension, in which case consciousness merely mirrors the object without adopting its form. This mirroring consciousness lacks any projective capacity and thus can neither mediate nor discern any form of conceptual elaboration.

31. This issue is addressed at length by Halbfass, who notes that even when *padārtha* is taken in the literal sense of "meaning" or "object of word", it still retains a notion of linguistic reference. As such, "*padārtha* is, indeed, a key word of semantic reflection in the Nyāya and other traditions. However it is also used in a less literal and more causal sense, as 'basic issue' or 'topic of discourse'" (Halbfass 1992: 77).

32. PV III, 214cd: *tadupaplavabhāve ca teṣāṃ bhedo 'py upaplavaḥ*.

The Buddhists are not alone in pondering the question of whether consciousness is aspectual or non-aspectual in character. Indeed, answers to this question cut across doctrinal and scholastic lines.[33] Whether the aspectual (*sākāra*) and non-aspectual (*nirākāra*) terminology is a useful criterion for dissociating different positions about the intentional structure of consciousness is, indeed, debatable.[34] The common use of the notion of cognitive "aspects" in Buddhist metaphysical and epistemological texts for describing the nature of awareness suggest not only that it has large applicability but also that it is an indispensable category for describing the mechanism of perceptual knowledge. Furthermore, as Śāntarakṣita and Kamalaśīla seem to argue, if the cognition of an object were in some sense taken to be formless, it would no longer be proper to talk about cognition at all.[35] Thus, understanding the nature of consciousness and, by extension, inferring its cognitive capacities is seen by the Buddhist epistemologists as tantamount to resolving the issue of the possibility of direct perception (in all its aspects).[36]

4.2 DEBATING THE CRITERIA FOR RELIABLE COGNITION

The analyses of consciousness and cognition that we sketched in the previous chapter provide a window into the growing concern with epistemological topics that came to dominate later Abhidharma debates. A key feature of these debates is the sense that a resolution of how best to defend core Buddhist metaphysical principles like dependent arising and momentariness depends on a particular understanding of the constitution of our cognitive systems. Unlike the largely phenomenological framing of consciousness and cognition in the Abhidharma, the Buddhist epistemologists develop

33. See Kajiyama (1965), Moriyama (1984), and Tillemans (1990: 41–42; 51 n. 113) for general discussions of the difference between the aspectualist (*sākāravādin*) and the non-aspectualist (*niākāravādin*) with particular reference to the Yogācāra tradition.

34. McClintock, for instance, argues that the controversial issue is not whether awareness is formless or not, but whether the representational content of an ordinary cognizer is real or not: "If it is judged to be unreal (*alīka*), then images will not occur in the awareness of awakened beings; if, however, images are real (*satya*), then there will be nothing to prevent them from arising in the awareness of buddhas and so on" (McClintock 2003: 165 n. 70). A phenomenological take of this controversy, such as I am advancing here, places the emphasis not on the ontological status of various "aspects" of awareness, but on their function in dissociating the phenomenal content from the phenomenal character of experience.

35. See, for example, TS 1998–2018 and TSP *loc. cit.*

36. These are, usually, sensory perception (*indriyapratyakṣa*), mental perception (*mānasapratyakṣa*), self-awareness (*svasaṃvedana*), and perception of the yogi (*yogipratyakṣa*), although there is some debate about whether mental perception and self-awareness are two different types of perception or two aspects of the same mode of perceptual apprehension.

their theories in *epistemological* terms: that is, they are less concerned with providing descriptive accounts of how cognition operates and more with the epistemic status of those cognitions, their truth bearing relations, and the different modes of ascertainment. But phenomenological concerns are not altogether absent; rather, they operate as background assumptions that inform and guide their epistemic practice. The Buddhist epistemologist approaches reflective inquiry and debate as a cognitive theorist might, that is, with the intent of settling epistemological disputes by providing detailed, descriptive, and functional accounts of our cognitive architecture. As I have already argued, one way to conceive of the difference between a theory of reasoning (*nyāyavāda*) and a theory of reliable cognition (*pramāṇavāda*) is to think of the former simply as a system of formal rules of reasoning and of the latter as an enterprise concerned with knowledge and its sources or modes of acquisition.[37]

This effort to find common ground by agreeing on the nature, number, and function of epistemic warrants might seem like a persuasive strategy. It is nevertheless conceivable that in singling out perception and inference—and indirectly rejecting revelation, comparison, non-apprehension, memory, and so on—as the only reliable sources of knowledge the Buddhist epistemologists are genuinely concerned with the possibility of establishing a thoroughly humanistic epistemology, in the pragmatic sense of that term. I refer here in particular to William James's notion of a "humanistic" or "voluntaristic" epistemology.[38] On this view, epistemic dispositions, as experiences of truth making, stem from both our experience and our beliefs, such that truths are neither independent of human experience nor conceived *ex nihilo*. Such "pragmatic" truths are, at least in principle, constantly in the making.[39]

This effort to find an epistemological common ground is also motivated by the general preoccupation among Indian philosophers with establishing

---

37. As Kamalaśīla explains, a "philosophical logician" (*nyāyavādin*) is simply someone who has mastery over the art of argumentation. An "epistemologist," that is, someone preoccupied with the sources of knowledge (*pramāṇa*), must by contrast argue, at least in principle, from an "enlightened" perspective, which is best understood as a perspective that takes into account the pragmatic aspects of knowledge acquisition (see TSP *ad* TS 3605).

38. James (1907: 251ff.).

39. James (1907: 252). To the extent that Buddhist epistemologists are preoccupied with establishing the sources of knowledge on epistemologically neutral grounds, their approach resembles that of Western pragmatists. Attempts to find points of convergence between pragmatism and Buddhism are found in Kumari (1987) and Powers (1994). Those critical of such a rapprochement, notably Hayes (1993), have argued that pragmatism, at least in its original Peircean formulation, displays certain features, such as amorality, interest in knowledge for knowledge's sake, fallibilism, etc., that are quite contrary to the pursuit of certainty, ethical conduct, and liberating knowledge characteristic of the Buddhist epistemologist's "pragmatic" approach.

the appropriate rules of debate. Philosophical debates are a time-honored tradition in India. The earliest reference points to the royal patronage of philosophical debate (*vāda* or *kathā*) and the incentives and prestige that it afforded its winners.[40] The rules of debate were, however, formalized much later. In the Buddhist context, the earliest attempt to codify rules of debate is found in the *Katthāvatthu* ("Points of Controversy"). For the Brahmanical tradition, the earliest records that have survived are the *Caraka-Saṃhitā* ("Medical Works of Caraka") and the *Treatise on Reason*.[41] The development of the Buddhist epistemological tradition appears thus to be circumscribed to the more specific goals of the Nyāya tradition, in which the rules of debate are framed within an epistemological rather than doxographical context.[42] In the *Treatise on Reason*, Gautama distinguishes three types of debate: (i) an honest debate (*vāda*) in which both parties engage in a spirit of fairness to establish the truth about a specific topic; (ii) a competitive debate (*jalpa*) in which the goal is winning by whatever means; and (iii) a deleterious debate (*vitaṇḍa*) in which the aim is to defeat the opponent by whatever means. Beginning with Dharmakīrti, the Buddhists admit only *vāda* as a legitimate form of debate, arguing that the goal of philosophical disputation is to help others adhere to the methods of good reasoning by correcting their misunderstandings, not to win a debate.[43] Sanctioning only perception and inference as epistemic warrants along with an insistence on using the appropriate rules of debate suggests that, in addition to their adherence to certain canons of rationality, the Buddhist epistemologists also seek to demonstrate the reasonableness of those principles whose reality they ascertain on empirical or experiential grounds.

Since reliable perceptions are seen as foundational for inferential reasoning, the validity or invalidity of inferences is not simply a matter of reasoning

40. See *Bṛhadāraṇyaka Upaniṣad* IV, 1.

41. See, for instance, CS 2, 8.31 and NS 1, 1.32.

42. Prior to Dignāga, such attempts include mainly manuals: *Upāhṛdaya* ("The Essential Auxiliary"), *Tarkaśāstra* ("The Manual of Reason"), and Vasubandhu's *Vādavidhi* ("Rules of Debate"). With Dignāga's *Nyāyamukha* ("Introduction to Reasoning") and *Hetucakraḍamaru* ("Drum of the Wheel of Reasons"), and especially with Dharmakīrti's *Nyāyabindu* ("Drop of Reasoning") and *Vādanyāya* ("Discourse on Reasoning"), the Buddhists find themselves as active contributors to the logico-epistemological literature. For the pre-Dignāga period, see Tucci (1929), Randle (1930) and Wayman (1958). For Dignāga, Dharmakīrti, and their commentators, see Steinkellner and Much (1995). On the rules of debate, Śāntarakṣita follows Dharmakīrti's *Discourse on Reasoning*, on which he also wrote a commentary (viz., the *Vipañcitārthā*). For a detailed overview of the history of dialectics and debate in India, see Oberhammer (1963) and Matilal (1998).

43. See VN (XXII, 15–21): *tasman na yogavihitaḥ kaścid vijigīṣuvādo nāma/ parānugrahapravṛttās tu santo vipratiprannaṃ pratipādayanto nyāyam anusareyuḥ satsādanābhidhānena bhūtadoṣodbhāvanena vā, sākṣipratyakṣaṃ tasyaivānuprabodhāya/ tad eva nyāyanusaraṇaṃ satāṃ vādaḥ, ukte nyāye tattvārthī cet pratipadyeta.*

within the bounds of certain canons of rationality; instead, the truth-value of inferential reasons also depends on what is deemed to be perceptually attainable. Although the Buddhist epistemologists reject "analogy" (*upamāna*) as an epistemic warrant, they nevertheless contend that logical reasoning depends both on adhering to certain inferential rules and procedures, and on reliable beliefs. It is this reliance on empirical evidence in establishing the soundness of inferences that has suggested the label of psychologism to Indian logic.[44]

The close integration of psychological considerations about the function of our cognitive systems with logical arguments is a peculiar feature of Indian philosophy in general, but it occupies center stage in the Buddhist epistemological tradition. This naturalistic account of cognition is specifically at work in Dharmakīrti, who claims that a trustworthy cognition (*avisaṃvāda*) must also be causally effective. Note, however, that Dharmakīrti's criterion of trustworthiness applies not only to perceptual cognitions but to conceptual cognitions as well. Unlike perception, whose trustworthiness is a function of its immediate apprehension of particulars, conceptions represent indirect modes of apprehension, and are trustworthy only insofar as they reflect the distinctive qualities of real particulars, thus ensuing in purposive action.[45] As we shall see later on, Śāntarakṣita and Kamalaśīla (following Dharmakīrti) contend that a real entity (*vastu*) is not established on metaphysical grounds but on the basis of its capacity for bringing about an effect.[46]

Now, for the Buddhist epistemologists, error is not something that is in the purview of empirical awareness. Indeed, Dignāga adopts the idea of inerrancy (*aviabhicāra*) from the Nyāya definition of perception: "Perception is a cognition generated through the contact between the object and the sensory faculty, which is inexpressible, inerrant and definitive."[47] But whereas the Naiyāyikas use the qualifier "inerrant" to exclude perceptions caused by defective sensory faculties, for Dignāga the source of error is entirely in the

44. Indian philosophers did not make a radical distinction between formal arguments and the psychological and empirical processes by means of which one construes a formal argument. See Mohanty (1992b: 106–113) and Matilal (1998: 104) for a brief discussion of the issue of psychologism in the context of Indian logic.

45. See PVSV *ad* PV I, 75d: . . . *iti tatpratibanddhajanmanāṃ vikalpānām atapratibhāsitve 'pi vastuny avisaṃvādo maṇiprabhāyām iva maṇibhrānteḥ nānyeṣām tadbhedaprabhave saty api yathādṛṣṭaviśeṣānusaraṇam*. On the interpretation of causal efficacy as a criterion for reality, see Dreyfus (1997: 65–67), Dunne (2004: 84–85), Katsura (1984), Mikogami (1979), Nagatomi (1967–68), and Steinkellner (1971).

46. See PVSV *ad* PV I, 172: *yad arthakriyākāri tad eva vastv ity uktam*. Śāntarakṣita and Kamalaśīla adopt the same definition throughout the TS/P. See, for example, TSP *ad* TS 415–416: *idam eva hi vastulakṣaṇam yad arthakriyāsāmarthyaṃ*. Similarly, unreal things are specifically defined as lacking in causal efficiency. See, for example, TSP *ad* TS 417: *tathā hi śaśaviṣāṇādau yad avastutvam iṣṭaṃ tatrārthakriyāsāmarthyaviraha eva nibandhanam*.

47. NS 1, 1.4: *indriyārthasannikarṣotpannaṃ jñānamavyapadeśyamavyabhicāri vyavasāyātmakaṃ pratyakṣam*.

mind, since he refuses to admit defective sensory input as perceptually warranted. It is Dharmakīrti who adds the qualifier "nonerroneous" (*abhrānta*) to Dignāga's definition of perception, thus acknowledging that not all perceptual errors are the result of conceptual or higher order thought processes.[48] Dharmakīrti's addition of the qualifier "nonerroneous," of course, is not new, but corresponds to the Nyāya definition of perception as inerrant, and can be also found in Asaṅga's use of inerrancy to exclude from perception such erroneous cognitions as the illusory circle of a firebrand, mirages, and phantoms.[49]

The interpretation of nonerroneous as nondeceptive, as well as the complex issue of whether Dignāga denied the possibility of perceptual illusions, attributing all instances of perceptual error to conceptual cognitions, is an important topic of debate among Dharmakīrti's commentators. For the purpose of this study, I am only concerned with what seem to be the two main contentious issues of this debate: (i) whether Dignāga's definition of perception is incomplete without the addition of "nonerroneous," because it fails to account for cases of perceptual illusions;[50] and (ii) whether "nonerroneous" can be taken to mean "nondeceptive,"[51] which would entail that under no circumstance can an instance of perceptual awareness be deceptive. Implicit in these two issues of the debate is a series of considerations regarding the interpretation of a key passage from Dignāga's *Collection* in which the exact significance of "erroneous cognition" remains ambiguous.[52] This dispute, which we shall examine at length in chapter 6, centers on an interpretation of the notion of "obscurity" (*sataimira*), which is contrasted with

48. Dignāga's definition is found in the PS 3c: *pratyakṣaṃ kalpanāpoḍham*. "Perception is [that cognition which is] devoid of conceptual construction." In the PV, Dharmakīrti follows Dignāga's definition of perception without any modifications. His addition of *abhrānta* is found for the first time in PVin 252b.3: *pratyakṣa kalpanāpoḍham abhrāntam*. "Perception is [that cognition which is] devoid of conceptual construction and nonerroneous."

49. See AS (Tatia 1976: 152): *pratyakṣaṃ svasatprakāśābhrānto'rthaḥ/... abhrāntagrahaṇam alātacakramāyāmarīcikādivyudāsārthm iti*. "Perception is [that cognition which] in itself [is] clear and nonerroneous... 'Nonerroneous' is used for [the purpose of] excluding [erroneous cognitions] such as the illusory circle of a fire-brand, a mirage, a phantom."

50. On this issue Jinendrabuddhi (fl. c. 680 C.E.) and Dharmottara (fl. c. 800 C.E.) appear to take Dignāga's side against Dharmakīrti and nearly all his commentators, including Śāntarakṣita and Kamalaśīla.

51. On this issue Dignāga and Dharmottara appear to diverge from Dharmakīrti and his immediate commentators, Devendrabuddhi (fl. c. 675 C.E.) and Śākyabuddhi (fl. c. 700 C.E.), as well as Śāntarakṣita and Kamalaśīla. See Steinkellner (1994) and Dunne (2004).

52. See PS I, 7cd–8ab: *bhrāntisaṃvṛttisajjñānam anumānānumānikaṃ/smartābhilāṣikaṃ ceti pratyakṣābhaṃ sataimiraṃ*. Hattori (1968: 28) translates the verse as: "[E]rroneous cognition, cognition of empirical reality, inference, its result, recollection, and desire are not true perceptions and are accompanied by obscurity (*sataimira*)."

"vividness" (*spaṣṭa*), raising the philosophically interesting issue of whether obscurity indicates an exception (*apavāda*) from veridical perceptions (a cognitive event that is not an instance of perception, though it may seem so), an impaired perception (as in the case of individuals afflicted with such conditions as jaundice), or an instance of deceptive cognition (as in the case of actual perceptual illusions).[53]

These considerations about the proper way of distinguishing erroneous from nonerroneous states of cognitive awareness concern primarily three things: (i) the nature of the perceptual object (*arthasvabhāva*), (ii) the effectiveness of perceptual cognitions apprehending the object (*arthakriyāśakti*), and (iii) the resulting internal representation (*vikalpakajñāna*) of that object, which is cognized by means of an association with a word or an mental object. As far as the nature of the perceptual object is concerned, this is nothing but the unique particular (for instance, a patch of color). A cognition is effective in apprehending its object when it stands in a direct causal relation to that object: in this case, when it can be ascertained that the perceived object as perceived (that is, as appearing in perception) is not due to some incongruous factors such as memory or hallucination. Finally, the internal representation of the object refers to the content of that awareness by which the object is apprehended as such, which in Husserlian terms may be referred to as its noematic content.

4.3 COGNITIVE ASPECTS AND LINGUISTIC CONVENTIONS

In articulating their epistemology of perception Śāntarakṣita and Kamalaśīla adopt Dharmakīrti's seemingly representationalist theory, but not without some qualifications: a domain of cognitive or phenomenal "aspects" (*ākāra*)[54] is posited in order to account for the specific mode of presentation of both perceptual and inferential cognitions. The cognitive aspects are taken here as referring not to pictures in the mind but to the phenomenal content and

53. For modern discussions of this dispute, see Stcherbatsky (1930: 155), Hattori (1968: 97), Franco (1994: 445–446), Krasser (1991: II, 73), Funayama (1999: 84–90), and Dunne (2006). See also chapter 7.2.

54. The translation of *ākāra* (lit. figure, aspect, appearance, or disposition) as "phenomenal aspect" seeks to enlarge its meaning to refer to other common translations that render it as "sign" or "token." The use of 'aspects' to refer to various modalities of cognitive apprehension may be traced back to Asaṅga (c. 350 C.E.). For example, in the *Mahāyānasaṃgraha* (2, 16), Asaṅga interprets *ākāra* as the "mode" under which we imagine the dependent nature (*paratantra-svabhāva*). Lamotte translates this passage as follows: "Il faut une imagination (*parikalpa*) et un imaginé (*parikalpya*) pour faire une nature imaginaire (*parikalpitasvabhāva*)... L'imaginé, c'est la nature dépendante (*paratantrasvabhāva*). La nature imaginaire, c'est l'aspect (*ākāra*) sous lequel on imagine la nature dépendante. L' "aspect," c'est-à -dire la manière (*katham*)" (1938: 108–109).

character of experience. For instance, there is a specific qualitative aspect to perceiving color: the phenomenal character of the experience of seeing blue is rather different than, say, that of seeing orange or red. Similarly, pains too have specific phenomenal character. The phenomenal character of a stomachache is quite different than that of anxiety or boredom. I take the Buddhist to be operating here with the notion that the aspectual theory of cognition is suggestive of a phenomenological account of intentionality. For instance, epistemic feelings such as calm, surprise or concern appear as signs that indicate (or represent) the perceptual object just as it is intended (e.g., calm in the face of impending danger, surprise at the electoral outcome, etc.). Attempts to define the nature of these phenomenal aspects, which refer to the specific mode of presentation characteristic of each cognitive event, are the origin of a lengthy dispute in Indian philosophy that cuts across doctrinal and scholastic boundaries. Thus, some philosophers[55] maintain that consciousness is inherently intentional—in other words, that consciousness takes the form of whatever objects it cognizes, a position known as aspectualism (*sākāravāda*).[56] Others[57] consider consciousness to be mirrorlike in its nature, reflecting an object without being modified by it. In other words, for these philosophers—generally classified as proponents of non-aspectualism (*nirākāravāda*)—consciousness is devoid of any internal representations.[58] Thus, the theory of "phenomenal aspects" (*ākāravāda*) represents a third dimension of the Buddhist epistemological project, providing an explanatory bridge between empirical and phenomenological accounts of cognition. The aspect of this theory that interests us here is the dissociation between the intentional object (*viṣayākāra*) and its mode of presentation (*pratibhāsa*).

55. These are philosophers who mainly self-identify as Sāṃkhya, Advaita Vedāntins, Sautrāntika, and Yogācāra Buddhists.

56. In his discussion of the ontological characteristics of two main Indian philosophical systems, the Nyāya-Vaiśeṣika and Advaita Vedānta, Mohanty draws some parallels between the Buddhist Yogācāra perspective on knowledge and that of the Advaita Vedānta, noting the centrality of the issue of self-knowledge in these systems: "the Buddhist Vijñānavādin . . . holds that knowledge is self-manifesting and also that it has its forms" (Mohanty 1980: 208). Mohanty's observation suggests that for Vedāntins and Yogācāra Buddhists, the "aspectual knowledge" (*sākāravāda*) perspective embodies the quintessential definition of any form of cognitive activity.

57. These are philosophers who mainly self-identify as Naiyāyikas, Mīmāṃsakas, Jainas, Vaibhāṣika, and some Mādhyamikas.

58. In his brief overview of the dispute between the aspectualists and the non-aspectualists, Kajiyama (1965: 428) argues that all the four schools of Buddhism [i.e., Vaibhāṣika, Sautrāntika, Madhyamaka, and Yogācāra] could in effect be classified from the standpoint of *ākāravāda*. Kajiyama lists a number of sources for this classification, including Guṇaratna's *Tarkarahasyadīpikā*, 47 and Mādhava's *Sarvadarśanasaṃgraha*, 46. Śāntarakṣita and Kamalaśīla address this dispute in the *Bahirarthaparīkṣā* ("Examination of External Objects").

Let me explain this seemingly representationalist stance of the Buddhist epistemologists in Husserlian phenomenological terms. In introducing the notion of "noema" Husserl meant to account for the precise way in which consciousness comes to apprehend what is outside itself, and thus become an instance of veridical cognitive awareness. First, a clarification of the meaning of "noema" itself is in order, given the controversies that surround its wide usage and the extensive literature on the topic.[59] In phenomenological reflection, we apprehend a relation between the *object-as-intended* (that is, the noema) and the *object-that-is-intended* (the object itself)—the lotus flower as perceived (as seen and smelled) and the lotus flower itself. The controversy concerns the precise status of the noema: is it an internal representational aspect, an ideal sense or image that mediates the intentional relation between the intentional act and the object intended, between the cognition apprehending the object and the object itself? Or rather, is the noema the object itself as apprehended in phenomenological reflection: the object as experienced, the lotus flower just as it is perceived?

The representationalist interpretation of the noema asserts that consciousness opens up to the world of objects (both physical and mental) only by means of the noema, which acts as an intermediary realm of sense or ideal types.[60] One consequence of the representationalist interpretation is that it takes intentionality away from consciousness. The second interpretation, which I adopt here, asserts that the object and the noema (i.e., the object as perceived) are two aspects of the same cognitive event, since what we are aware of is inextricably bound up with how our awareness discloses it, with how the object appears to us.[61] This is precisely the view I take the Buddhist epistemologists to be advancing when they propose the two-aspectual theory of cognition: that is, each instance of cognitive awareness arises in its dual form as cognition of the object coupled with self-cognition.

The implication of Śāntarakṣita and Kamalaśīla's representationalist stance is that the mind comes to know that its ideas conform to the real objects only when ideas appear as aspects of perceptual objects rather than aspects of propositional attitudes. For the Buddhist epistemologist, then, the apprehension of a resemblance between different objects is the result of conceptual thought, given that its operations depend on categorical use (apprehending objects as belonging to different classes: genus, species, etc.). This apprehension of resemblances goes beyond the immediate perceptual experience, insofar as it is constitutive of conceptual and categorical thought. As with Locke's empiricist account of mental representation, the mind knows

59. See Drummond (2003) for an overview of the relevant literature. See also *infra* chapter 7.

60. See, for example, Smith and McIntyre (1982: 87).

61. See Gallagher and Zahavi (2008: 119ff.).

that its ideas agree with real objects only when these ideas resemble the contents of the perceptual occasion. When these ideas do not have an empirical basis, they cannot be seen as true representations of real phenomena.

As I shall argue later on, the observation of a similarity between objects is not the direct cause of internal representations. Instead, representational content is generated following a process of conceptual construction that operates on latent habitual tendencies. However, language is essential, because discursive thought apprehends objects only as represented in language, and not as given in perception. In other words, verbal expressions provide access only to nominal forms, and never, at least in the opinion of the Buddhist epistemologists who follow Dignāga's semantic theory of exclusion, to particulars, because words do not indicate their objects directly.[62]

Early in his discussion of the epistemic function of perception, Śāntarakṣita rejects the view that taking language as the essential medium in which thoughts are represented necessarily implies that qualitative experiences of color and odor, which are empirically disclosed, are purely conceptual phenomena:

> Even though [the activity of perceiving] is described with the aid of words such as "perceptible" and the like, there is no inconsistency in admitting that perception lacks conceptual content; indeed, "conceptual content" does not imply "expressed by words." Otherwise, colors, odors, etc. would qualify as conceptual constructs. Thus, despite what some misguided individuals assert, [namely that "perception" actually means *sensory awareness*], how, then, can it be asserted that "free from conceptual content" can be cognized, even without a referent?[63]

All of Śāntarakṣita and Kamalaśīla's predecessors had been preoccupied with explaining the epistemic gap between perceptual and conceptual states of cognitive awareness. With Dignāga the dissociation between veridical and non-veridical perceptions provides an additional epistemic gap between what seems to be the case and what is actually the case.[64] Dharmakīrti provides

---

62. This view is first stated in an often quoted verse from one of Dignāga's lost works, the *Sāmānyaparīkṣā*: *nārthaśabdaviśeṣasya vācyavācakateṣyate/tasya pūrvam adṛṣṭatvāt; sāmānyaṃ tūpadekṣyate*. See *Nyāyāgamānusāriṇi Nayacakravṛtti*, 615, 12–13. See also TSP *ad* TS 961, which quotes ŚV, *Apohavāda*, 102. For a detailed analysis of Dignāga's semantics of word universals (*śabdasāmānya*) and meaning universals (*arthasāmānya*), see Pind (1991).

63. TS 1238cd–1240: *tādātmyapratiṣedhaś ca pratyakṣasyopavarṇyate//tadādhyakṣādiśabdena vācyatve 'pi na bādhyate/kalpanāviraho 'dhyakṣe na hi sā śabdavācyatā// anyathā rūpagandhādeḥ savikalpakatā bhavet/ato nāspadam evedaṃ yad āhuḥ kudhiyaḥ pare*.

64. This knowledge gap does suggest a form of disjunctivism about perceptual knowledge (roughly, the thesis that veridical and non-veridical states of cognitive awareness do not share relevant epistemic features). The Buddhist, of course, is concerned with how cognitive awareness can be constitutive of a certain openness to the

the standard solutions to bridging these gaps. First, veridical perceptions are judged as such by virtue of their capacity to bring about the fulfillment of a certain purpose. Secondly, conceptualizations are warranted when they appropriately disclose the intentional order of the cognitive domain. The intentional object, however, does not entirely correspond to its perceptual appearance (that is, to the object as perceived). Rather, how we conceive of an object also depends on the evocative capacity of language. It is thus that Dharmakīrti identifies four types of erroneous perceptions:

> A cognition that apprehends an object by means of a linguistic sign is a conceptual cognition of that [object]. In its nature [that particular type of cognitive awareness] is not a linguistic sign; hence, any type of [cognition as reflective awareness] is non-mediated [by conceptuality]. There are four types of perceptual error: three types which have their basis in conceptual awareness and one that is rooted in nonconceptuality.[65]

For Śāntarakṣita and Kamalaśīla, this argument provides sufficient ground for claiming that concept mastery and categorizing skills do not necessarily translate into the capacity to discern the specific characteristics of perceptual objects. For example, the concept of "resemblance" or "identity of appearance" (*sārūpya*),[66] which picks out certain characteristics that objects of experience apparently share, is not an intrinsic feature of the perceptual occasion, but a case of conceptual positing of resemblance relations. We shall examine in detail Śāntarakṣita and Kamalaśīla's understanding of the psychological processes that underlie this cognitive propensity toward conceptualization when we address in detail the implication of the semantic theory of exclusion—the Buddhist epistemological attempt to formulate a theory of meaning that rejects realism about universals—for the analysis of perception.

For now, let me simply introduce the most basic elements of the semantic theory of exclusion: in Dignāga's formulation, words do not designate their object directly but rather by an exclusion of all other possibilities. For instance, the word "cow" designates the class of entities that are not non-cow. The basic intuition behind this theory is that every concept or linguistic

---

world such that practical aims can actually be achieved, rather than with justifying any internal beliefs about perception in the absence of warrant.

65. PV III, 287–288: *śabdārthagrāhi yad yatra tajjñānaṃ tatra kalpanā/svarūpaṃ ca na śabdārthastatrādhyakṣamato 'khilaṃ//trividhaṃ kalpanājñānamāśrayopaplavodbhavaṃ/avikalpakamekaṃ ca pratyakṣābhaṃ caturvidhaṃ.*

66. Of course, the "aspect" under which an object is apprehended does not mirror the object, for its phenomenal characteristics are dependent on several additional factors, including the constitution and function of the perceptual systems, various cognitive and affective dispositions, and external conditions. For a somewhat similar view, see Dunne (2011: 87) and Dreyfus (2011: 215).

symbol cleaves the universe into two mutually exclusive classes: the class of entities that come under the respective concept and class of entities that do not (which includes practically everything else).[67] The question of linguistic reference becomes then a question of conceptual determinacy that avoids the pitfalls of correspondence theories of truth (and their word-to-world relations). Thus, in the case of concepts such as "cow" and "brindled" we have a hierarchy of conceptual determinacy: the former excludes all entities that do not fall under it, while the latter exclude those plus all the other non-brindled cows. With reference to cows, "brindled" possesses a higher degree of determination, the function of which is to exclude a progressively higher domain of entities, while its own scope is further constrained by immediately superordinate categories such as "brindled dairy cow." In this ascending hierarchy of increased generality, "cow" represents the most general but least determinate concept in its class, whereas "Elsie," the Jersey cow used in American advertising, or "Nandini," the Hindu cow of plenty, represent the least general but most determinate concepts.[68]

The Buddhist thus restricts word-meaning relations to an internal semantics (that is, to the symbolic structures that govern the operations of mind[69]): the application of the word "cow" is simply all that cognitive processes that originate in the apprehension of actual cows have in common. But the causal condition on the basis of which words are applied to things, while intrinsic to thought (and linguistic conventions), is also conditioned by experience. While the Buddhist epistemologist rejects the reality of universals, she accepts the natural substratum on the basis of which words are capable of designating not just *a* particular but also a class of objects. In rejecting the reality of universals, the Buddhist nominalist denies that this natural substratum, which prompts language use, actually inheres in the particular. In other words, the Buddhist rejects the Naiyāyika's view that the word "cow" actually designates "cow universal," which, like all universals, is presumably the proper basis for the application of names to things.

Of course, the semantic theory of exclusion is meant to address the very possibility of linguistic reference. In Sellarsian terms, "the real test of a theory of language" is to account not for exclusions or "thinking in absence" but for positive determination, for "thinking in presence," in other words,

67. For similar discussions of this aspect of *apoha*, see Hayes (1988: 211), Dreyfus (1997: 210), and Arnold (2006: 421).

68. For Dignāga's account of a hierarchy of concepts, see PS V, 35, and translation and discussion in Katsura (1979: 17) and Hayes (1988: 298–299).

69. The direction of development for the Buddhist semantic account seems to point toward an understanding of the operation of exclusion (*apoha*) mainly as a theory of mental content. Patil (2009: 198) thinks that the theory of exclusion may be better understood as a theory about the intentional content of thought and action, even though on the surface it works as a theory of semantic value.

for "those occasions on which the fundamental connection of language with non-linguistic fact is exhibited."[70]

Indeed, what should count as a proper cause of the application of names to things is a vexed question in Indian philosophy. Its roots are usually traced back to the debates among the Sanskrit grammarians about word-meaning relations. But it is the grammarian-philosopher Bhartṛhari who is credited for the view that the capacity of a word to signify a class of objects stems from its double identification, first with the natural substratum (*adhikaraṇa*) of a particular object, and second with the different substratum (*vyadhikaraṇa*) of objects in the same class.[71] The notion that a word signifies its object through a double identification of that word—first with the natural substratum of a particular entity and second with the different substratum of other entities—is also at work in Abhidharma definitions of the particular as a thing that bears its own characteristic mark. Thus Vasubandhu indicates that a "particular" refers to the unique features of a given element of existence and/or experience or rather to that specific element itself.[72] However, the Buddhist epistemologists, beginning with Dignāga, depart from this specifically Ābhidharmika use of the notion of particular (*svalakṣaṇa*). Whereas Vasubandhu regards particulars as real properties of objects or mental states, Dignāga understands them to be the irreducible real individuals that are directly apprehended in perception. In Dignāga's system, the particular, as conceived by thinkers like Vasubandhu, more adequately designates universals rather than particulars (these issues are addressed at length in chapter 8).[73]

The theoretical implications of this semantic transition from the Ābhidharmika's to the Buddhist epistemologists' account of particulars are significant: they inform the Buddhist nominalist stance and a particular type of epistemic phenomenalism centered on the descriptive analysis of cognitive aspects. With Dharmakīrti, this epistemic phenomenalism becomes the preferred philosophical approach to bridging the gap between perception and conception, and has a lasting impact on the subsequent development of Buddhist epistemology. What is peculiar about Śāntarakṣita and Kamalaśīla's contributions to the Buddhist epistemological enterprise, however, is their effort to integrate the psychological and phenomenological perspectives of the Sautrāntika and Yogācāra Abhidharma within this

70. Sellars (1997: 65 §30).

71. See VP, *Vṛttisamuddeśa*, 347: "The word which signifies a genus is applied [to an object] in the same manner as the word 'swing' [in the expression 'the swings are crying'] signifies indeed that which lies in the swing [i.e., the crying babies], and refers to a swing [as 'swing'] only [in its primary sense]." (*mañcaśabdo yathādheyaṃ mañceṣv eva vyavasthitaḥ/tattvenāha tathā jātiśabdo dravyeṣu vartate).*

72. See AKBh *ad* AK VI, 14cd.

73. On this semantic transition, see Katsura (1991: 137ff.), Dunne (2004: 81–84), and Arnold (2005a: 18–34).

enterprise. Whether their syncretic approach is simply a consequence of the encyclopedic scope of the *Compendium* and its *Commentary* or can be attributed to a deliberate philosophical commitment on the part of Śāntarakṣita and Kamalaśīla (as key figures in the dissemination of Buddhism to Tibet) to present a unified vision of Buddhist doctrine, is an open question. While seeking an answer to this question falls outside the scope of this book, my analysis of some key aspects of Śāntarakṣita and Kamalaśīla's epistemology is not without its hermeneutical constraints: the historical distance cannot be bridged without an active participation in, and sharing of, the concerns and presuppositions that inform the Buddhist epistemological tradition or a particular philosophical reconstruction thereof.

4.4 EPISTEMOLOGY AS COGNITIVE EVENT THEORY

The Buddhist epistemological account of perception represents an important chapter in the development of Indian Buddhist philosophy. Although the *Compendium* and its *Commentary* are independent works and not commentaries on either Dignāga or Dharmakīrti's works, the exposition of their views occupies a substantial portion of it, as do the views of several other Buddhist and Brahmanical authors. Indeed, Śāntarakṣita and Kamalaśīla are indebted not only to Dharmakīrti himself but also to his commentators, in particular Devendrabuddhi and Śākyabuddhi.[74] In all, more than twenty authors are directly mentioned by name in the *Compendium* and its *Commentary*. Of these, the views of Uddyotakara and Kumārila occupy center stage.[75] What justifies taking these works as a representative account of the Buddhist epistemology of perception is primarily their encyclopedic perspective, in which Dharmakīrti's alleged improvements upon Dignāga's views on perception, as well as the criticism of Uddyotakara and Kumārila, are clearly discernible.[76]

Any project of philosophical reconstruction, which seeks to make the thought of historical authors relevant to contemporary philosophical audiences, is challenging at best. Tacit assumptions about the role of historical circumstances in constraining philosophical reflection and analysis are always at work, for one can only interpret a tradition from one's own historical perspective and never, as Gadamer reminds us, *sub specie aeternitatis*. Any

74. See Dunne (2004: 9 n. 16).

75. As Bhattacharrya (1926: lx) notes in his preface to the first edition of the TS/P: "it seems probable that the *Tattvasamgraha* was written mainly to refute the arguments and theories of Kumārila and Uddyotakara."

76. Besides Devendrabuddhi and Śākyabuddhi, Śāntarakṣita and Kamalaśīla also quote extensively from Vinītadeva. For attempts to place the dates of Śāntarakṣita and Kamalaśīla in relation to those of Dharmottara and Jinendrabuddhi, see Funayama (1992, 1999) and Krasser (1992). A complete chronological list of authors that are directly mentioned in the TS/P is found in Bhattacharyya (1926: lxix–lxxi).

attempt at making Buddhist epistemology a legitimate contributor to modern philosophical debates must be both historically anchored and philosophically edifying. Hermeneutical concerns are therefore unavoidable, if only because we are seeking to interpret a tradition of inquiry that was itself preoccupied with interpreting its own past and reevaluating its own standing in a constantly evolving philosophical culture. Thus, beyond the laborious task of establishing textual traditions, as well as problems of composition and authorship, rests an important philosophical concern: how do certain ideas come to dominate particular philosophical traditions and to what particular event do we trace their origin?[77]

More specifically for our inquiry: why did Dignāga and Dharmakīrti adopt and adapt the methods of reasoning formulated by the Naiyāyikas, whereas Nāgārjuna and some of his successors did not? In the introduction I argued that this shift in attitude toward epistemology resulted from a willingness on the part of some Buddhists to ensure that their argumentative methods were aligned with those formulated by the Naiyāyikas. I also surmised that one key motivating factor in this enterprise might simply be to answer the criticism that the central doctrines of Buddhism[78] could not be defended on logical grounds, complicated by Nāgārjuna's skeptical stand on the role of positive argumentation. Indeed, whether Nāgārjuna's preferred style of argumentation—known in Nyāya as "destructive debate" (*vitaṇḍā*), and consisting in a refutation of an opponent's thesis without proposing a thesis of one's own—is a legitimate enterprise remains a subject of ongoing debate. Furthermore, Nāgārjuna's use of the tetralemma (*catuṣkoṭi*) has been both vigorously defended and faulted for its apparently inconsistent use of logic. The defenders regard it as proposing a range of views, including rational mysticism,[79] pragmatic empiricism,[80] conceptual holism,[81]

77. See Powers (1993: 11ff.), Lopez (1988), and Tillemans (1997) for the hermeneutical implications at work in text-critical approaches to Buddhist philosophical literature. As we saw above (chapter 2), Tillemans, for instance, make a good case for interpreting classical Buddhist texts and authors without disregarding concepts that are relevant to contemporary philosophical debates: "La méthode philologique, conçue à la manière étroite des *Geisteswissenschaften* du XIXe siècle, est donc souvent critiquée, à juste title, parce qu'elle ne répond pas d'un façon adéquate à notre besoin de savoir ce que veut dire les textes. It est inévitable, dans cette quête de sens, que nous interprétions les textes dans des termes et schémas quit sont d'une importance fondamentale dans la pensée actuelle. Autrement dit, nous ferons des interprétations que nous soutiendrons comme correctes, parce que rigoureusement justifiées par l'évidence textuelle—tout en admettant que les termes seraient parfaitement inconnus aux auteurs historique eux-mêmes" (1997: 13).

78. E.g., momentariness (*kṣaṇikavāda*), absence of an enduring self (*anātma*), conditioned entities as lacking inherent existence (*dharmanairātmya*).

79. See Stcherbatsky (1927) and Murti (1960).

80. See Warder (1970) and Kalupahana (1986).

81. See Gudmunsen (1977) and Thurman (1980).

deconstructionism,[82] and more recently, paraconsistent logic.[83] Critics have been less susceptible to giving credit to these claims.[84]

As Buddhist philosophers typically argue, our cognitive propensities are part of a continuing chain of events and relations. Each thought arises as part of an endless series of previous thoughts, and in turn informs, conditions, and directs our intentional acts.[85] The most obvious manifestations of this continuing chain of cognitive events are traces of memory, coping skills, and specific conceptual schema. For the Buddhist epistemologists memory, by virtue of its episodic and fragmentary character, never acquired the status of a reliable source of knowledge. Likewise conception, given its association with propositional and imagistic thought[86] came to be regarded as a secondary and somewhat imperfect cognitive modality. This dissociation between conceptual thought and direct perception may actually have an experiential basis, and reflect the proclivity of Abhidharma philosophers for fine-grained analyses of mental content. While exploring the historical context in which this dissociation occurred is not within the purview of our inquiry, explaining the role of this distinction between conceptual and nonconceptual cognitive states for the Buddhist epistemologists is.

It is a trivial observation that for the Buddhist epistemologist perception is not only a psychological process to be understood within the framework of classical Abhidharma psychology, but an epistemic modality for establishing a cognitive event as an instance of knowledge. It has been argued that Buddhist philosophers did not make a radical distinction between epistemology and the psychological processes of cognition, at least not in the Western sense in which modern philosophy had drifted away from naturalist explanations after Descartes.[87] This understanding of epistemology as cognitive theory is most clearly illustrated in Dignāga's formulation of the method of reasoning known as the triple inferential mark (*trairūpya*),[88] which relies on empirical observation as the most authentic criterion of establishing the validity of inferential cognitions. According to Dignāga, in order to yield

82. See Magliola (1984).
83. Garfield and Priest (2003, 2009).
84. See Robinson (1957, 1972), Matilal (1971, 1985), Tillemans (1992), Hayes (1994), and Huntington (2007).
85. See AKBh III, 19: *etena prakāreṇa kleśakarmahetukaṃ janma taddhetukāni punaḥ kleśakarmāṇi tebhyaḥ punarjanma ityanādi bhavacakrakaṃ veditavyaṃ.*
86. "*kalpanā*" literally means "fancy," "imagination," or "invention," from √*kḷp*- "to form, frame, imagine, invent." However, throughout this book I will be translating *kalpanā* as "conception" and occasionally as "imagery."
87. Given the types of activities subsumed under *pramāṇavāda*, a more apt translation of this knowledge enterprise would be something like "cognitive theory." The Buddhist "pramāṇavādin" is thus a "cognitive theorist" rather than a mere logician in the traditional sense of that term.
88. This is the peculiar way of grounding the logical reason initiated by Dignāga and is given systematic treatment in his *Hetucakranirṇaya* ("Demonstration of the Wheel of Reason").

knowledge, the logical proof (*hetu*) should (i) be present in the thesis (*pakṣa*), i.e., in the position that is stated; (ii) be also present in similar positions (*sapakṣa*); and (iii) be absent from dissimilar positions (*vipakṣa*).[89] In practical terms, this means that to prove a thesis, for example, that sound is impermanent, what is needed is a thesis and its contrary:

A: Sound is impermanent because of being produced (*pakṣa, hetu, sādhya-dharma*) = (sound, impermanence, being produced).

~A: No instance of eternal non-produced sounds can be found (*vipakṣa*).

On the limits of Dignāga's inductive method[90] and its criticism by the Brahmanical philosophers more will be said later. For now, let's consider Dharmakīrti's solution to the problem of induction. As is well known, it is largely in response to Dignāga's (allegedly) failed attempt to solve the problem of induction by means of the triple inferential method, that Dharmakīrti formulates his well-known principle that reasoning from the empirical data must be grounded on more than the simple observation and nonobservation of occurring associations and dissociations. Of course, this is the well-known method of *anvaya* (association of the evidence with the property to be established through it) and *vyatireka* (dissociation of the evidence with the property to be established), which, as Cardona and others[91] have demonstrated, Dignāga borrowed from the grammarians. Dharmakīrti would expand this method to include also a discussion of the evidence-subject relation (*pakṣadharmatā*), by means of which the trustworthiness of the former is established.

Thus, Dharmakīrti postulates that for a sound argument to obtain two natural relations between the evidence and what is to be established thereby must be present: the relation of identity (*tādātmya*) and that of causal generation (*tadutpatti*). Dharmakīrti's answer to the question of how these two natural relations are to be ascertained is framed by his defense of core Buddhist

89. For a detailed treatment of the relationships that obtain between these three conditions, see Herzberger (1986:174–182), Hayes (1988: 154ff.), and Matilal (1998: 90–100). A comprehensive analysis that traces the evolution of the triple inferential mark across several sources and authors, including Vasubandhu's *Vādavidhi*, Śaṅkarasvāmin's *Nyāyapraveśa*, Uddyotakara's *Nyāyavārttika*, Dignāga's *Nyāyamukha*, and Dharmakīrti's *Pramāṇavārttika* and *Nyāyabindu* is found in Oetke (1994).

90. Dignāga's formulation of the triple inferential mark is found, *inter alia*, in PS II, 5cd: *anumeye 'tha tattulye sadbhāvo nāsti tāsti* (translation and discussion in Hayes (1980: 253–254). See also PSV 29a: *de la mngon sum mam rjes su dpag pas mthong gi rjes la de'i rigs dang mthun pa la yang spui'i tshul gis phyogs thams cad dam phyogs gcig la yod par grub pa'o//ci'i phyir zhe na/de dang mthun pa kho na la yod ces nges par gzung ba'i phyir ro//de dang mthun pa la yod pa kho na'o zhes ni brjod par mi bya ba'i phyir ro* (cf. Katsura 1983: 545).

91. See Cardona (1967–68: 337), Hayes (1988), Katsura (2004).

metaphysical principles (principally that of momentariness). It is here that Dharmakīrti's text raises three important issues concerning the nature of evidence and the role of perception in disclosing something essential about the order of the causal domain.[92] First, what is the nature of evidence or, more specifically, of the evidential property (*hetu*) for the thesis, or that which is to be established (*sādhya*)? Second, what would be the implication of asserting that the truth of the major premise can be known by perception? And finally, can a careful inspection of the effect, in the case of Dharmakīrti's *kāryānumāna* argument—that is, the argument that an inference is sound only when one infers from the effect to the cause and not vice versa—be conducive to ascertaining the unique causal totality that is its source?

The answer to the first question is clear: only the two natural relations of identity and causal generation can serve as evidential property for the thesis. I will turn to these in a moment. The second question does not invite a straightforward answer. As Hayes and Gillon have recently argued, to claim that one can know the truth of the major premise by perception amounts to saying that whatever conclusion one may arrive at through inferential reasoning can also be known by perception.[93] That possibility, presumably, would make inferential reasoning a redundant source of knowledge. But it need not be so, and this is where I think a naturalized account of reasons can cast new light on this epistemological conundrum: for inferential reasoning, as we have argued,[94] turns both toward ideal objects and toward the subjective modes of apprehension that ground our thought. Take the example just used: experience, the Buddhist claims, reveals that all objects which come into existence due to causes and conditions are impermanent, for whatever is produced exists by virtue of its supporting causal chains and ceases when that causal support ends. Conversely, a permanent object cannot be produced. That is how we arrive at a logical reason. Thus, a proposition of the type "Sound is impermanent, because it results from effort" is true so long as we do not encounter an example of permanent (hence unproduced) sounds. Were we to come across such a counterexample, the proposition will be falsified. But appealing to empirical observation as a premise ties logical reasoning to the ability to establish causal connections between the things

92. In Dharmakīrti's technical vocabulary, the notions of identity (*tādātmya*) and causal generation (*tadutpatti*) represent two essential conditions on the basis of which we distinguish between theories of meaning and theories of reference. The truth of the former is contingent upon the semantic content of the sentence, whereas the truth of the latter requires additional empirical knowledge of the causal relation that obtains between the designated objects. See also Hayes (1988: 254) and Arnold (2006: 421), both of whom suggest that whereas Dignāga's account of the operation of exclusion (*apoha*) should be understood as concerning the relation of identity, Dharmakīrti is mainly interested in the causal relation.

93. Hayes and Gillon (2008: 362).

94. See *supra* 2.3.

we directly experience. And exploring the limits of our ability to establish various causal connections between the elements of experience is more readily associated with psychological inquiries into the nature of our perceptual and cognitive systems.

Let's take a closer look at Dharmakīrti's descriptive analysis of the role of causation for inference.[95] First, in order to establish the sort of evidence that can serve as a warrant for sound inference and, at the same time, to rule out those instances of erratic attribution of a connection between evidence and the property to be proven, Dharmakīrti avails himself of various examples of things that are ordinarily thought of in conjunction: the act of speaking and passion, rice and cooking, a living body and breathing, perceptual awareness and the senses, and, of course, the stock example of fire and smoke.

The question is: what sort of properties, whether observed or unobserved, in similar or dissimilar cases, can be counted as evidence for asserting a given thesis? And how are such properties ascertained? That is, how does one come to know the truth of the major premise? Dharmakīrti uses the first two examples to argue against the principle that mere observation and nonobservation of occurring associations and dissociations is a sufficient ground for sound inferential reasoning. In the case of the act of speaking and passion, observation of their occurring association is just a case of erratic evidence, for at most the act of speaking can serve as ground for inferring the presence of a speech organ and a capacity to communicate, not of passion.[96] Of course, here he is indirectly rejecting the notion that speech requires passion—seen as an affliction—for its cause, since Buddhas, who are certainly observed to speak, cannot do so on account of something that they have presumably overcome. In the case of rice and cooking, nonobservation in dissimilar cases does not provide sufficient grounds for sound inference either: even though one may observe grains of rice cooking in a cauldron, one cannot thereby infer that all grains of rice are cooked simply because they are in the cauldron. Indeed, some may be uncooked.[97]

How, then, can one escape the risk that there may be unobserved instances to the contrary, given that observation of a relation between things at a given place and time does not necessarily guarantee that the same relation will obtain in other places and at other times? For Dharmakīrti the solution to this conundrum is appeal to rules of reasoning that best reflect the nature of causally efficient entities: that is, to the so-called natural relation (*svabhāvapratibandha*) between the properties of an inference. As Dharmakīrti makes clear, one cannot infer from a cause to its effect, or from a causal totality (*kāraṇasāmagrī*) to an effect, because there is always the

95. As found in PV II, 11–38, and its auto-commentary.
96. See PVSV II, 12.3.
97. See PVSV *ad* PV II, 13.1.

chance of impending factors preventing the arising of the given effect (as when, for instance, some of the rice in cauldron is clumped). But Dharmakīrti does admit that one can infer from the effect to the cause, though only in a restricted case. As he writes: "Therefore, only an immediate effect enables the inference of a cause, because it is dependent on it."[98] The Sanskrit here for "immediate" is *nāntarīyakam*, which can also be translated as "inseparable" or "without interval," conveying the sense of tight proximity that is associated with causal-cognitive chains.

For Dharmakīrti, thus, an awareness of the causal totality can serve as a legitimate basis only for asserting that effects arise due to a variety of causes and conditions, not for which specific effect(s) arises due to which specific set of causes. Much like Dignāga before him, Dharmakīrti too is concerned with maximizing our predictive capacity to make sound inferences, the ultimate goal of which is achieving desired ends.[99] Dharmakīrti's view of the role of causality for reasoning may be, then, summarized as follows: one can only legitimately infer from the effect to the cause, and only in the case of an immediately arising effect, since even knowing the causal totality for a given effect, does not guarantee that impending factors would not preempt its arising.

Now, a naturalized account of the *kāryānumāna* argument would have to take into account at least two things:

a. Any empirical evidence that the reason, or that which is to be proven, acquires its evidential status as a result of factors that are inherent to our cognitive architecture, specifically to information processing systems that translate perceptual content into action;
b. Any theoretically robust account of how intentional content, as the subjective basis for reasoning, can in turn play a causal role in explaining how acting toward some desired end is successfully accomplished.

Let me make clear that there are different strategies of naturalization, and that some may prove more effective than others. The one that I favor here takes the view that reasons can be naturalized both by bridging the gap between phenomenology and natural science, and by extending the concept of what counts as natural to include also the mental.[100] The general idea is

98. PVSV *ad* PV II, 12.4: *tasmān nāntarīyakam eva kāryaṃ kāraṇam anumāpayati, tatpratibandhāt*. Translation *per* Hayes and Gillon (2008: 340).

99. Answering the question of whether Dharmakīrti's motive is ultimately soteriological when he frames the *kāryānumīna* argument the way he does is less relevant in this context.

100. This model is favored by Barry Smith (1995) and David W. Smith (1999), both of whom take their inspiration from Gibson's (1979) ecological approach to perception.

that perceptual and higher order cognitive processes have evolved to provide *effective* and *meaningful* interaction with the environment, and thus to maximize both our observational and predictive skills. Of course, these are, at best, working hypotheses and play, at most, a heuristic role: but they do provide an account of reasons that is both scientifically informed and phenomenologically constraining.

Let us return to our second leading issue: to say that the truth of the major premise can be known by perception is to put forth a particular view of perception; one which views perceptual awareness as a form of embodied action. On this view, perceptual awareness does require input stimuli for its activation but the resulting perceptual occasion derives from a set of preconscious or preattentive processes of selection and grouping operating on the input data. These processes are generally thought to be representational: they *re-present* schematic components of perceptual experience following sensory-motor modalities. Perceptual awareness is thus inherently projective (or predictive) with the object (or content) of perception being the result of interactions between the input stimuli and dynamic information processes that are part of the architecture of sensory systems.

To take just one example, evidence from neuroscience relating to cases of blindsight and visual form agnosia indicates that achieving a desired end, say, navigating objects in an environment without seeing them, can be achieved in the absence any direct perceptual awareness of the object, so long as the largely unconscious causal mechanisms that regulate sensorimotor intentionality remain functional.[101] The philosophical upshot of this sort of phenomena is that there might be additional perceptual cues that enable such individuals to make accurate judgments, and thus successfully attain an object even without being directly aware of its spatiotemporal coordinates or form. Such cues regulate the sensorimotor contingencies of perception and enable the sort of pragmatic reasoning that undergirds the successful accomplishment of that given task even for the blindsighted person. The phenomena of blindsight and visual form agnosia, to take but these two examples, present us with a different understanding of cognition, one that views it not

101. For a now classical account of the phenomenon of blindsight, see Weiskrantz (1998). While there is no consensus about how blindsighted patients actually succeed in detecting, localizing, and discriminating visual objects despite lacking visual awareness, most favor the explanations advanced by Milner and Goodale (1995) and Carey, Harvey, and Milner (1996), who propose that blindsighted patients are instead guided by subtle behavioral and sensorimotor cues. As a normal condition of the visual system (according to Binsted et al. 2007), blindsight shares some characteristics with *visual form agnosia*, which typically results from damage to both temporal lobes, though the part of the visual cortex that controls motion perception remains intact. In visual form agnosia one cannot recognize shapes, despite having some minimal conscious visual experience, but retains sensorimotor abilities.

as a faculty of some kind of internal agent but as a reflexive process that is embodied and embedded within the environment of which it is a part.

On this account of cognition, direct perceptual awareness, as conceived by the Buddhist, is an effective source of knowledge precisely because it is a form of embodied action. For to perceive is to understand how we cope with the environment we inhabit. We cannot cope very well if we take the world to be constituted of entities, the spatio-temporal location and characteristics of which lack any reference to subjects of experience. This observation brings us to our third and final issue: can a careful inspection of the effect be conducive to ascertaining the unique causal totality that is its source?

Dharmakīrti argues that an inference from the cause to the effect is unsound. Now, what about inference from the effect to the cause? Consider the typical example of a park ranger: in spotting a column of fire rising above a mountain top, she can legitimately infer that there is a fire, but not whether the fire is fuelled by redwoods or by eucalypts. On closer inspection, the park ranger may detect from the peculiar color and odor of the smoke that it is eucalypts that fuel the fire, but still not know whether the fire was started by lightning or by ambers drifting from a campsite. Closer inspection still may reveal that an arsonist in fact started the fire.

But this example, which is adapted here from Hayes and Gillon,[102] overlooks an important fact: the park ranger's experience. For unless this is her first day on the job, ideally she already has the sort of requisite knowledge and embodied skill demanded by the task at hand: ascertaining the unique causal totality of a given column of smoke. Her perception of smoke happens within a certain horizon of background intuitions about the height and distance of the smoke column, the time of day, current weather conditions, whereabouts of campsites, the conditions of flammability for various tree species, and a recent history of arsonist attacks. It is this horizon of background intuitions that, on a model of embodied cognition, accounts for the efficacy of the inferential process (from the effect to the cause).

A central principle of the embodied and enactive cognition paradigm is that at least a subset of our cognitive processes are not entirely internal but rather are co-constituted by external processes. It is for this reason, I think, that Dharmakīrti's *kāryānumāna* argument could be interpreted as a species of what Fred Keijzer and Maurice Schouten describe as *process externalism*: the view that (inferential) cognition and mental processes in general depend on, or are continuous with, bodily processes that extend into the environment by virtue of the tight relations between perception and action.[103] Such an account, if I may venture to add, steers clear of the typical conundrum of metaphysical interpretations: trying to square how someone like Dharmakīrti

102. Hayes and Gillon (2008: 366).
103. Keijzer and Schouten (2007: 114).

can argue for both external realism (the view that there is a way that things are that is independent from our cognitions) and what John Dunne and others call "epistemic idealism"[104] (namely, the view that all entities that are present to awareness, including those that are seemingly extra-mental, are nothing but aspects of cognition). Process externalism (or what Andy Clark and David Chalmers call "active externalism"[105]) also goes against supervenient and eliminativist theories, both of which claim that first-person, psychological accounts of cognition are a matter for neuroscience alone to solve. Taking Dharmakīrti's argument about inferring from the effect to the cause as a species of process externalism, is just one of the many ways in which a naturalist account of cognition that is non-reductive or eliminativist can advance our understanding of key aspects of the Buddhist epistemological enterprise.

In addressing epistemic questions by appealing to the mechanism of knowledge acquisition (and not simply by stating the formal aspects of inference), Buddhist and Nyāya logicians appeared—at least to early generations of scholars who came under the influence of logical positivism—suspiciously guilty of psychologizing tendencies (a rebuttal associated in Western philosophy with the Fregean legacy). The roots of this rebuttal lay in the birth of psychology as a scientific discipline in the nineteenth-century, and the subsequent antipathy of many philosophers toward its claims of being a science of the mind and of cognition. This antipathy is evinced first in Kant's outright dismissal of the possibility of measuring psychological phenomena and subsequently in the gradual move toward mathematics and logic following the efforts of Neo-Kantians like Frege and Russell to ground philosophical certainty on logical and mathematical reasoning alone. Frege admits no confusion between the psychological process of thinking and pure thought, which he sees as something that is common to all humankind irrespective of language or cultural differences. In the tradition of logical positivism that he helped inaugurate, psychological states have nothing to do with logic and philosophy and are thus irrelevant in terms of exploring the realm of meaning and their cognates, i.e., mathematical objects. Moreover, Frege thinks that the sense/meaning and its reference are irreconcilable with the subjective ideas of each individual. As he puts it: "one man's idea is not that of another; while the sign's sense may be the common property of many and therefore is not a part or a mode of the individual mind."[106] In light of significant recent progress in the scientific understanding of the nature and dynamics of cognition, antipsychologism is no longer tenable as a philosophical attitude.[107]

---

104. See Dunne (2004: 70).
105. Clark and Chalmers (1998).
106. Frege (1960: 59).
107. See especially Grzegorczyk (1999). Earlier defences of psychologism in epistemology are found in Haack (1975) and Block (1981). The issue of psychologism in the context of Western critiques of Indian logic from the perspective of logical

In the Indian philosophical context the separation between epistemology and psychology has been less apparent, since arguments require both formal consistency and an external method of verification in the form of analogies to a known fact of experience. For the Buddhist epistemologists, however, the latter does not count as a source for knowledge. The preeminent role assigned to perception by Dignāga and all subsequent Buddhist epistemologists runs counter to the reliance on verbal testimony, and hence language, as the most effective source of knowledge, typical of orthodox Brahmanical thought. In India, linguistic considerations have been at the heart of much philosophical reflection. Indeed, for a philosopher-grammarian like Bhartṛhari they form the quintessential topic of his philosophical speculations. With Dignāga, these linguistic considerations become central to the Buddhist epistemological enterprise. As it has been convincingly argued, Bhartṛhari had indeed influenced Dignāga in formulating his own views on the relation between language and conceptual thought.[108] For instance, in the *Saṃbandhasamuddeśa* ("Exposition on Relations") section of the *Vākyapadīya* ("Of Sentences and Words"), Bhartṛhari writes: "A word is based on a cognition which does not reflect its object in its entirety. It expresses the object, without ascertaining its own [perceived] form, in another form [as represented in language]."[109] Based on ideas expressed here and elsewhere in this section of *Vākyapadīya*,[110] Dignāga appears to have concluded that words did not relate to objects directly, but only through an intermediary process of conceptualization.[111]

The notion that the domains of language and conceptual thought are mutually entailing is common among the Sanskrit grammarians, a notion that Dignāga seems to have adopted largely under the influence of Bhartṛhari. In reducing verbal testimony to a type of inferential cognition, Dignāga appears to have modeled his theory of reasoning on Bhartṛhari's position concerning the dependence of inferential arguments on the grammatical rules of language comprehension. Indeed, attempts to systematize and justify the scriptural tradition as a source of knowledge are central to all Brahmanical schools, with Pūrva and Uttara Mīmāṃsā placing special emphasis on ver-

positivism is also examined at length in Mohanty (1985), Phillips (1995), Matilal (1998), Chakrabarti (1999), and Ganeri (1999a). Note that these studies also propose a broader notion of epistemic logic based especially on developments of the Navya-Nyāya school.

108. Cf. Frauwallner (1959), Hattori (1968), Herzberger (1986), and Hayes (1988).

109. See VP III, 54: *akṛtsnaviṣayābhāsaṃ śabdaḥ pratyayam āśritaḥ/artham āhānyarūpeṇa svarūpeṇānirūpitam* (translation *per* Houben, 1995: 393).

110. Dignāga wrote a commentary on this section of VP, preserved now only in Tibetan as *Traikālyaparīkṣā* (*Dus gsum brtag pa shes bya ba*).

111. In the *Dvādaśāranayacakra*, Mallavādin quotes a second line of this paraphrase as "between these [the mental construct and the word] there is a mutual relation; that word does not touch the object." Cf. Ganguli (1963: 232) for a discussion of this verse.

bal testimony, which is usually ranked higher than perceptual knowledge. Purushottama Bilimoria sums up rather well the significance of verbal testimony (*śabdapramāṇa*) for Indian epistemologists:

> The uniqueness of *śabda* as a means of knowing, lay in its having the capacity to be a special instrument among an aggregate of conditions. In particular, it seemed that *śabda* has the capacity to elicit knowledge in contexts and conditions where the other means of knowing seemed to fall short or proved to be less adequate and not very informative. The possibilities of communication that words open up . . . and their encapsulating power, were also reckoned to present certain advantages that most of the other sources clearly lacked.[112]

This unique capacity that words have—not simply in yielding knowledge where other sources of cognition fall short but also in interpreting and transmitting it—is not limited to propositional logic and philosophical grammar. Rather, a theory of verbal comprehension must also take into consideration the principles of Sanskrit poetics, with its three different levels of comprehension: (i) verbal, which results from the capacity of articulate sounds to generate meaning; (ii) conceptual, which results from abstracting the contents of the sounds uttered (or heard); and (iii) intuitive, which denotes the comprehension in a flash, which is taken to be the true source of verbal testimony. Summarizing Bhartṛhari's doctrine of "intuitive meaning" (*sphoṭa*), Kunjunni Raja writes:

> First, we have the actual sounds of the words uttered; this is the *vaikṛta-dhvani*. These sounds reveal the permanent *prākṛta-dhvani* which is an abstraction from the various *vaikṛta-dhvani*-s. . . . The third stage is the *sphoṭa* which is the whole utterance considered as an integral unit and as an indivisible language-symbol.[113]

For Bhartṛhari, therefore, it is the intuitive meaning, rather than purely conceptual or phonetic representations, that is realized through verbal comprehension.[114] The Buddhist epistemologist's attempt to construe verbal comprehension as a particular case of inferential reasoning thus marks a radical departure from the theories of the Sanskrit grammarians as articulated by Bhartṛhari. It also parts way with the Mīmāṃsakas, for whom Vedic utterances afford a specific type of comprehension that cannot be reduced to inferences about ordinary states of affairs.

---

112. Bilimoria (1988: 9).
113. Kunjuni Raja (1963: 14–15).
114. See, for example, VP II.1, 76, 78, 83: *sphotasyābhinnakālasya dhvanikālānupātinaḥ/grahaṇopādhibhedena vṛttibhedaṃ pracakṣate* [76]. *śabdasya grahaṇe hetuḥ prākṛto dhvanir iṣyate/sthitibhedanimittatvaṃ vaikṛtaḥ pratipadyate* [78]. *sphoṭarūpāvibhāgena dhvaner grahanaṃ iṣyate/kaiś cit dhvanir asaṃvedyaḥ svatantro'nyaiḥ prakalpitaḥ* [83].

But there is another reason why the Buddhist epistemologist reduces verbal testimony to inferential reasoning and accords perception a privileged epistemic status. For the Buddhist, perception provides the empirical foundation and thus a neutral ground upon which questions of both verbal testimony and logical fitness are to be addressed. Perception is thus discussed in its double aspect: (i) as evidential ground for knowledge; and (ii) as an instrument of direct apprehension. In that respect, the Buddhist epistemologist regards the source of knowledge (*pramāṇa*) as in some sense identical with its outcome (*pramāṇaphala*): the knowledge event (*pramā*). Knowledge, it is claimed, has an instrumental or embodied aspect: I can only know what I am constitutionally (that is, biologically or physiologically) capable of attaining by means of a given cognitive capacity in all its sensorimotor aspects. But what I see (or, rather, the event of seeing) cannot be properly dissociated from the act itself, for each cognitive event is inherently intentional. This aspect is clearly articulated by Dharmakīrti, who extends the common usage of *that which is a source of knowledge* to include knowledge itself or its result. This knowledge is not the sort of insight characteristic of highly realized bodhisattvas, generally associated with yogic perception,[115] but primarily knowledge of empirical facts.[116] Knowledge of empirical facts depends on the possibility of having veridical cognitions, and on the capacity to recognize that erroneous cognition can take many forms, including, but not limited to, entertaining false notions, being subject to perceptual illusions, and engaging in defective modes of reasoning.

Of course, the conditions under which cognition is classed as erroneous (*bhrānti*) are the focus of all post-Dharmakīrtian accounts of perception. Detailed expositions of erroneous cognition identify at least five such kinds of cognition:

i. error of apperception (*saṃjñābhrānti*), as in the case of seeing water in a mirage of water;
ii. error pertaining to number (*saṃkhyābhrānti*), when a person is afflicted with diplopia;
iii. error pertaining to shape (*saṃsthānabhrānti*), when seeing a circle of fire in a whirling fire-brand;

115. For the importance of yogic perception (*yogi-pratyakṣa*) in Dharmakīrti's formulation of his epistemological theories, see Dunne (2006) (who downplays its role) and Franco (1993, 1997), Yao (2005), and Eltschinger (2009), who argue that Dharmakīrti did not completely disregard the implications of yogic perception in formulating his theories. I think Eltschinger has made a sufficiently compelling case for taking the testimony of yogic perception as relevant to Dharmakīrti's epistemology.

116. In his summary of Dharmakīrti's theory of truth, Katsura (1984: 215) notes that "Indian theories of truth (*prāmāṇya-vāda*) deal with empirical knowledge alone and Dharmakīrti in his preserved treatises is primarily concerned with the epistemological and logical problems of our worldly existence." Katsura seems to oppose here the view that Dharmakīrti's epistemological concerns are in the service of a soteriological telos.

iv error pertaining to color (*varṇabhrānti*), when a non-yellow object is seen as yellow by a jaundiced person;
v. error pertaining to movement (*karmabhrānti*), as in the case of seeing moving trees when running through a forest.[117]

Recall that Dignāga omits references to erroneous cognition in his definition of perception. Whether correcting this omission, as Dharmakīrti does, represents an improvement on Dignāga's definition of perception is a subject of debate among Dharmakīrti's historical commentators. Given Dharmakīrti's commanding influence as an authoritative interpreter of Dignāga's thought, it comes as no surprise that Śāntarakṣita and Kamalaśīla follow his example: they concede that Dharmakīrti not only effectively addresses the criticism leveled against Dignāga by his Brahmanical critics, but that he also corrects his views where they seem to lead to unwarranted conclusions.

Dharmakīrti's profound impact on subsequent generations of Buddhist and Brahmanical philosophers is particularly evident in the epistemology of perception. In justifying Dharmakīrti's alteration of Dignāga's definition of perception, and the implication this alteration had in the overall economy of his system, Śāntarakṣita appears to have taken Dharmakīrti's side, while Kamalaśīla seems more intent on accommodating the two perspectives. Understanding their position adequately demands that the views of Śāntarakṣita and Kamalaśīla must be teased out by paying close attention both to their individual styles of argumentation and to their respective philosophical commitments. While seeking to locate potential differences in their approaches, however, one must not overlook the main concern at work in the *Compendium* and its *Commentary*: here Śāntarakṣita and Kamalaśīla set out to investigate problems that form an integral part of the Buddhist epistemological enterprise, and their solutions to these problems are, to a large extent, contingent on the conceptual and theoretical resources of that enterprise. The Buddhist epistemological enterprise is concerned, *inter alia*, with answering a set of questions, chief among which are those pertaining to the epistemic character of perceptual states of cognitive awareness.

While no one disputes the paramount importance of Dharmakīrti, both Śāntarakṣita and Kamalaśīla display a sufficient degree of independence in their epistemological views to warrant an independent consideration.[118] In

117. Cf. ASBh IV, 2, 193: *bhrantirgrāhyagrāhakābhiniveśaḥ/bhrāntyāśrayo yasmin nāryjñānagocare saṃskāranimittamātre'bhūtaparikalpātmake sati bālānāṃ so 'bhiniveśaḥ pravartate/abhrāntyāśrayas tathatā, nirvikalpasya jñānasya tadadhiṣṭhānatvāt/ bhrāntyabhrāntilokottarajñānānu kūlāḥ śrūtamayyādayaḥ kuśalā dharmāḥ/ abhrāntinirvikalpajñānaṃ/abhrāntiniṣyanda āryamārgapṛpṭhalabdhāḥ kuśalā dharmāḥ*. See also Funayama (1999: 75) for a detailed discussion of this passage.

118. Unless, of course, one is specifically concerned with the various ramifications of Dharmakīrti's innovations as reflected in the work of his immediate or distant commentators.

the remainder of this book, I will focus on unpacking the arguments that Śāntarakṣita and Kamalaśīla advance in supporting a certain definition of perception—which, while retaining the gist of Dignāga's intention, bears the mark of his great commentator, Dharmakīrti. More specifically, I shall attempt to show that although Śāntarakṣita and Kamalaśīla mount a general defense of the Buddhist definition of perception against its critics, mainly the Naiyāyikas and the Mīmāṃsakas, their defense is secondary to what I take to be the broader scope of the *Compendium* and its *Commentary*: a synthesis of Buddhist principles that is phenomenologically constrained and epistemologically defensible.

As our cursory analysis of the content and scope of the *Compendium* and its *Commentary* in the next chapter will reveal, Śāntarakṣita and Kamalaśīla set out to argue that *it is* possible to attain a greater degree of certainty about the true nature of things through careful observation, and a sustained effort of reasoning and deliberation. It is precisely through such sustained effort—and a methodical reliance on what are taken to be the right sources of knowledge—that a true philosophical illumination of the highest human goal may be pursued.

CHAPTER 5

An Encyclopedic and Compassionate Setting for Buddhist Epistemology

The examination of perception that Śāntarakṣita and Kamalaśīla undertake in the *Compendium* and its *Commentary* draws from a long and rich history of philosophical debates that reach back several centuries. These debates are mimetically present throughout their work: the authors often quote verbatim from a large number of works as they attempt to engage with this tradition not simply as doxographers but also as creative contributors. In outlining the contents, Kamalaśīla in particular considers the whole range of philosophical views that were current during his (and Śāntarakṣita's) time, but focuses his attention primarily on the main protagonists in this wider pan-Indian philosophical conversation: the grammarian Bhartṛhari, the Ālaṃkārika ("aesthetician") Bhāmaha, the Mīmāṃsaka Kumārila Bhaṭṭa, the Naiyāyika Uddyotakara, as well as Dignāga and Dharmakīrti. Of these, Kumārila and Uddyotakara are given special attention. Indeed, entire chapters of the *Compendium* and its *Commentary* are devoted to a refutation of the views of these two authors.[1]

The *Compendium* and its *Commentary* are thus not only a vast collection of philosophical doctrines recorded in the second half of the eighth century C.E. but also a highly polemical work that bears testimony to the sustained disputes between Buddhist and Brahmanical philosophers during this golden era of Indian philosophy. The polemical nature of the *Compendium* and its *Commentary* is further evinced by the importance accorded to problems of

1. For instance, chapters II, X–XV, XVIII are almost exclusively devoted to refuting the theories of the Naiyāyikas. Chapter XVI targets the views on language advanced by Akṣapāda Gautama, Bhartṛhari, and the Ālaṃkārika Bhāmaha, as well as those of Uddyotakara and Kumārila, while chapters XIX, XXIV, XXV are devoted to refuting various Mīmāṃsā theories.

logic and epistemology,[2] the ultimate aim of which is to provide a sound epistemological foundation for such core Buddhist principles as that of dependent arising (*pratītyasamutpāda*). Śāntarakṣita's philosophical acumen is obvious in the careful and considered manner in which he proceeds with his arguments, drawing examples from both Buddhist and non-Buddhist sources, and anticipating possible objections at every step of the way. In Śāntarakṣita we also come across an erudite and insightful thinker who, it seems, is not without a sense of humor.[3]

In the *Examination of the Characteristics of Perception* (*Pratyakṣalakṣaṇaparikṣā*, hereinafter the *Examination of Perception*), which will be discussed at length in the next chapter, Śāntarakṣita and Kamalaśīla are in dialogue mainly with Uddyotakara and Kumārila.[4] The complexity of the issues debated in this community of discourse demands that we first identify the overall scope of Śāntarakṣita and Kamalaśīla's project before we set out to examine their contributions to the Buddhist epistemology of perception.

5.1 DEPENDENT ARISING AND COMPASSION

There is little doubt that Śāntarakṣita composed the *Compendium* as an independent work. This is evident both in the statement of purpose and in the structure of the work, which represents a unique synthesis of philosophical disputes from what may be best described as a broadly phenomenological perspective (typically associated with Sautrāntika-Yogācāra synthesis). Śāntarakṣita lays out the whole contents of his work in an ingenious set of opening statements, which form the object of a lengthy analysis by Kamalaśīla. While it is customary for Buddhist philosophers to begin their work by praising the Buddha, their ultimate source of inspiration, the opening stanzas of the *Compendium* are reminiscent of Nāgārjuna's statement of deference to the Buddha, which serves as a pretext for uncovering the agenda of his main work, the *Mūlamadhyamakakārikā* ("Stanzas of

2. Works of a purely epistemological nature are attributed to both authors. Śāntarakṣita is the author of a commentary on Dharmakīrti's *Vādanyāya* ("Discourse on Reasoning"), the *Vādanyāyavīpañcitārtha* ("Complete Unfolding of the Meaning of the Discourse on Reasoning"), which is lost in original Sanskrit and preserved now only in Tibetan translation (*Rtsod pa'i rigs pa'i 'grel pa don rnam par 'byed pa shes bya ba*, D3192). Kamalaśīla, on the other hand, wrote a commentary on Dharmakīrti's *Nyāyabindu* ("Drop of Reasoning"), the *Nyāyabindupūrvapakṣasaṃkṣipti* ("Exposure on the Opponents of the Drop of Reasoning"), also preserved now only in Tibetan (*Rigs pa'i thigs pa'i phyogs snga ma mdor bsdus pa*, D 4232).

3. As Bhattacharyya notes in reviewing the contents of the TS/P, Śāntarakṣita's humour "is seen very frequently when his opponent is reduced by his arguments to a theory which is also an accepted fact in Buddhism" (Bhattacharyya 1926: xiv).

4. They also consider the views of two less known Naiyāyikas, Bhāvivikta and Śaṅkarasvāmin.

the Middle Way"), and its philosophical presuppositions.[5] Nāgārjuna, for instance, refers to the Buddha as the "best of speakers," and the one who taught the doctrine of dependent arising as the ultimate truth pertaining to the nature of causality.[6] Similarly, Śāntarakṣita declares in the opening stanzas of the *Compendium*:

This *Compendium of True Principles* is composed after having bowed to that all-knowing one, who is the best of speakers, who does not rely on an independent scripture, who, in wishing for the welfare of the world, developed great compassion over innumerable eons, [and] proposed the doctrine of dependent arising, which is difficult to understand, in that it bears no relation to causes such as primordial nature, the divine, both [the divine and primordial nature], the self, and other entities; which is transitory; which is the ground on the basis of which actions, their results, and the connection between the two is postulated; which is devoid of superimposed attributes such as quality, substance, action, genus, inherence, and so forth; which is the object of words and cognitions only [insofar as they operate] as superimposed attributes; which is cognized by the two clearly defined sources of knowledge; whose nature is not mixed with anything else in the slightest degree; which is not intercalated; which has no beginning and no end; which is like a reflected image and other similar things; [and] which is free from conceptual elaborations.[7]

As these introductory stanzas clearly illustrate, the central topic of the *Compendium* is the causal principle of dependent arising. Its exposition is given in the form of a list of attributes that exemplify other aspects of Buddhist doctrine. In Kamalaśīla's commentary, each of these attributes becomes the subject of a separate examination. Śāntarakṣita's statement of purpose is much more extensive than is Nāgārjuna's, as is his proposed method of demonstration. Unlike Nāgārjuna's preferred style of argumentation, which

5. See McClintock (2010: 95), who identifies a parallelism in terms of both language and structure between the two sets of opening verses.

6. MMK 1–2: *anirodham anutpādam anucchedam aśāśvatam/anekārtham anānārtham anāgatam anirgamaṃ//yaḥ pratītyasamutpādaṃ prapañcopaśamaṃ śivaṃ/deśayāmāsa saṃbuddhas taṃ vande vadatāṃ varaṃ.* "I praise him, the fully enlightened one, the best of speakers, who taught dependent arising, which is auspicious, [which represents] the appeasement of mental proliferations, [and which is] non-ceasing, non-arising, non-annihilation, non-permanence, non-unitary, non-plural, non-manifesting, and non-disappearing."

7. TS 1–6: *prakṛtīśobhāmādivyāpārarahitāṃ calam/karmatatphalasambandhavyavasthādisamāśrayam//guṇadravyakrīyājātisamavāyādyupādhibhiḥ/śūnyam āropitākāraśabdapratyayagocaram//spaṣṭalakṣaṇasaṃyuktapramādvitayaniścitam/anīyasāpi nāṃśena miśrībhūtāparātmakam//asaṃkrāntim anādhyantaṃ pratibimbādisannibham//sarvaprapañcasandohaninirmuktam agataṃ paraiḥ//svatantraśrutinissaṅgo jagaddhitavidhitsayā/analpakalpāsaṅkhyeyasātmībhūtamahādayaḥ//yaḥ pratītyasamutpādaṃ jagāda gadatāṃ varaḥ/taṃ sarvajñāṃ praṇamyāyaṃ kriyate tattvasaṃgrahaḥ.*

relies on the tetralemma,[8] Śāntarakṣita adopts the argumentative strategies of the Buddhist epistemologists. Another distinguishing feature that sets the two works apart is their underlying ontological presupposition. As I hope shall become clear from a cursory analysis of its contents, the authors of the *Compendium* and the *Commentary* operate mainly with a phenomenalist perspective, while the antirealist (Madhyamaka) view remains a marginal point of reference.[9] Given the encyclopedic nature of the *Compendium* and its *Commentary*, Śāntarakṣita and Kamalaśīla cite a great many authorities and, like many of their predecessors, take up different positions as they set out to examine a whole range of topics.

We have already established that this perceived lack of ontological commitment stems mainly from what I take to be a genuinely phenomenological stance at work in the *Compendium* and its *Commentary*; this lack of ontological commitment, however, may also be regarded simply as a consequence of the ubiquitous Buddhist practice of expedient means (*upāyakauśalya*)—the pragmatic need, encountered in nearly all Buddhist thinkers of the Mahāyāna ("great vehicle") tradition, of distancing their views from those of early Buddhists by incorporating the latter as provisional stages on the path to higher understanding.

The pragmatic function of expedient means is made explicit in lengthy declarations of purpose and careful analyses of the subject matter that usually accompany all major philosophical works. Kamalaśīla's analytic description of purpose is instructive in the way it links the definition of purpose to the compassionate aim of Buddhist teachings, namely, bringing an end

---

8. Unlike the use of positive argumentation in the Dignāga-Dharmakīrti school to establish the validity of Buddhist principles, Nāgārjuna's dialectics aim to prove, on the contrary, that the sources of knowledge and their objects are mutually dependent and cannot establish the reality of entities as self-characterized. See, for example, *Vigrahavyāvartanī* ("Dispeller of Disputes"), 31–35, and discussion in Westerhoff (2009: 183–188).

9. Wood (1991: 219ff.) has argued against treating the TS/P as a Madhyamaka work on four counts: (i) the Yogācāra perspective is presented as the correct view (*siddhānta*) throughout; (ii) Śānkarakṣita and Kamalaśīla rely mostly on the authority of Dignāga and Dharmakīrti in crafting their arguments; (iii) despite occasional references to Madhyamaka works, neither Śāntarakṣita nor Kamalaśīla appear to endorse Madhyamaka views; and (iv) the TS/P appears to advocate throughout views that conflict with Madhyamaka. Wood certainly makes a good case for treating the authors of the TS/P as Buddhist epistemologists, though his conclusion is not necessarily warranted. I agree with McClintock (2010: 37–38) that even though in the TS/P Śāntarakṣita and Kamalaśīla on occasion seem to reject the reality of external objects, they do not explicitly argue from a Madhyamaka perspective. Furthermore, we must keep in mind that both Śāntarakṣita and Kamalaśīla are also the authors of Madhyamaka works, in which they appear to advocate the Madhyamaka perspective as ultimate (see *Madhyamakālaṃkāra* and its *Vṛtti* and Kamalaśīla's *Madhyamakālaṃkārapañjikā*). Likewise, Keira (2004: 21) argues that even in strictly Madhyamaka works like MĀ, Kamalaśīla does not forgo the methods and argumentative strategies of the Dharmakīrtian epistemological tradition.

to human suffering (even though this is decidedly not an ethical work). Throughout this work, the authors are at pain to stress that sloppy reasoning and adherence to unwarranted beliefs cannot be conducive to acquiring an enlightened perspective on the nature of things. It is for this reason that Kamalaśīla advances his meticulous presentation of the work's aim: unsuspecting minds, he reasons, might fail to recognize its usefulness and perhaps ignore it altogether, were it not for a careful and detailed presentation of its contents. But outlining its contents alone is not sufficient. One must also declare its ultimate purpose, since a prospective inquirer would surely undertake to follow the teachings contained therein with the assurance that such undertaking would bring about the desired result.[10] Furthermore, Kamalaśīla is keen to emphasize that the goal of the proposed teachings (an enlightened perspective on the nature of things) is within reach and can be accomplished by suitable means.

What if a prospective reader fails to be impressed by declarations of purpose or detailed descriptions of thematic contents? Such a reader, then, must be reminded that the quest for knowledge is an enterprise whose ultimate aims are pragmatic, and that right knowledge is a necessary precondition for the success of such pragmatic undertakings.[11] In other words, no reader can deny that knowledge gathered from reliable sources can serve as a genuine motivator for action, and as a guarantor that one's goal is within reach, a view typically associated with Dharmakīrti. Glossing on this view, Dharmottara (c. 740–800) identifies the need to teach critical thinking as the principal motivation for composing epistemological works, which serve as the best and most effective guide to purposeful action.[12] Like Dharmottara, Kamalaśīla too is not content merely to reiterate Dharmakīrti's position on the scope of epistemology. Rather he provides a detailed analysis of the relationship between aims and motivations that showcases the pragmatic aspects of epistemic inquiry. For opponents of this approach, the claim that there is an immutable relationship between the declaration of purpose and the domain

---

10. See TSP *ad* TS, 1–4: *prāghānyena tu prayojanameva pravṛtyaṅgam; tatarthitayaiva śāstreṣu śrotṛjanasya pravṛtteḥ . . . tacca prayojanamanuguṇopāyamupadarśanīyam, na punaraśakyatatsādhānānuṣṭānam.*

11. Here, Kamalaśīla appears to simply follow Dharmakīrti's declaration in the opening stanza of his *Nyāyabindu* ("Drop of Reasoning"): "The accomplishment of all human aims is preceded by right knowledge, therefore, the latter is here explained" (NB I, 1: *samyagjñānapūrvikā sarvapuruṣārthasiddhir iti tad vayutpādyate*).

12. See NBṬ[d] III, 23: "[Sentient beings] strive for desired ends seeking after [that] knowledge which is conducive to obtaining the objects that bear the characteristic of purposeful action (*artha-kriyā-samartha*). The knowledge that is sought after is [that] examined in [epistemological] treatise(s). Thus, right cognition (*samyagjñānam*) is that cognition which indicates reality as an entity endowed with the capacity for purposive action" (*arthakriyārthabhiś ca arthakriyāsamarthārthapráp tinimittaṃ jñānaṃ mṛgyate/yacca tairmṛjyate tadeva tena śāstre vicāryate/tato'rthakriyā samarthavastugraharśakaṃ samyagjñānam*).

of experience is unfounded; the intelligent act only on the basis of assumptions derived from the judicious deployment of reason: "The conduct of intelligent seekers is based on ascertainment and ascertainment derives only from reliable cognitions; the statement of purpose is not a source of knowledge in relation to such external things as the contents [of a treatise]."[13]

A yet further objection concerns the treatise's thematic contents: these contents and whatever can be achieved by undertaking its study are two completely different things that should not be understood in terms of a relation between producer and produced.[14] The reason adduced here to justify this difference is that there always seems to be a discrepancy between verbal intention and its corresponding action. Finally, an assertion of purpose for those who already know it (that is, for the Buddhists) is futile, for they already act in accordance with its stated purpose. These are serious objections that challenge the received view that Buddhists engage epistemological problems with the aim of enlightening their audience rather than vanquishing their opponents in debate. Now, Kamalaśīla does admit that false and doubtful beliefs are no deterrent to acting, and that the ignorant are just as driven to act as the learned (and perhaps even more so). Indeed, inasmuch as there always are unforeseen obstacles and other intervening factors, the course of an action cannot always be ascertained on the basis of sound inference. But he is quite cautious about the implications of complexity for any theory of causation. This prompts Kamalaśīla to declare: "[Such things as] continuity [with the cause], the [anticipated] result or the efficacy [of the cause] are not trustworthy [sources] in the case of uncertain effects, because obstacles and other impediments are always likely to occur."[15]

In addition to obstacles and other external impediments, a significant contributing factor to perpetuating uncertainty about the consequences of actions is the desire for particular outcomes. When actions are driven by a desires for specific outcomes rather than any sort of reasoned deliberation, it is only natural to entertain the possibility that such desire-driven actions may fail to achieve their goals.[16] Indeed, a possible objector may regard uncertainty about the outcome of even a perfectly intended action as highly plausible given that not all philosophical works are composed with the aim of engendering an enlightened attitude.[17] Kamalaśīla rejects such

13. TSP *ad* TS, 1–4: *nanu prekṣāvatāṃ pravṛttirniścayādeva, niścayaśca pramāṇādeva, na cāsya prayojanavākyasyātrābhidheyādau bāhye'rthe prāmāṇyamasti; tatrāsya pratibandhābhāvāt.*

14. See, for example, TSP *ad* TS 1–4. This refers to the relations identity (*tādātmya*) and causal generation (*tadutpatti*) discussed above (see chapter 3).

15. TSP *ad* TS, 1–6: *sāmagrīphalaśaktīnāṃ pariṇāmānubandhini/anaikāntikatā pratibandhādisambhavāt.*

16. See TSP *ad* TS, 1–6: *nanu prayojanaviśeṣārthitaiva puṃsaḥ prayojana-viśeṣasaṃśayotpattihetuḥ prāgvidyata eva.*

17. Cf. TSP *ad* TS, 1–6: *prayojanaviśeṣapratipādakaśāstrāntaropalabdheśca.*

claims on the ground that only the ignorant can be prevented by desires and various dispositional factors from viewing emancipation as the highest goal of humankind.[18] The learned presumably act in accordance with what is reasonable, and it is primarily to an intelligent audience that Śāntarakṣita and Kamalaśīla direct their arguments.

Having thus demonstrated why it is necessary to declare one's intentions forthright, Kamalaśīla sets out to describe the aims of this work as threefold: (i) pertaining to the action (*kriyā*), (ii) pertaining to results of that action (*kriyāphala*), and (iii) pertaining to the subsequent result of the first action (*kriyāphalasya phala*).[19] Implicit in this threefold description of purpose is the agent (in this case, Śāntarakṣita, but also Kamalaśīla himself), for the treatise is nothing but the object or end result of the agent's action. Challenging the standard Sanskritic model of action-object-agent (*pramātṛ-prameya-pramiti*), Kamalaśīla explains intentionality in a manner that occludes the agent and instead places emphasis on action itself and its results as the guiding principles of cognition.[20] This accords with the no-self view, and indirectly aims to stress the paramount importance of a work that, as the title suggests, is conceived as a synthesis of true (metaphysical) principles. And since it is typical of the Sanskritic philosophical genre that a statement of allegiance to a founding figure prefaces works, the *Compendium* and its *Commentary* are thus assumed to be seamlessly continuous with the words of the Buddha himself, the actual originator of the teachings.

Expanding upon his definition of purpose, Kamalaśīla distinguishes primarily between its instrumental and semiotic (*lakṣaṇa*)[21] aspects. Its instru-

---

18. See TSP *ad* TS, 1–6: *tathāpi na sā sarveṣāṃ sammukhībhavati; avyutpannapuruṣārthānāṃ muḍhadhiyāṃ keṣāñcidasammukhībhāvāt.*

19. TSP *ad* TS 1–6: *tac ca prayojanaṃ śāstrasya trividhaṃ kriyārūpaṃ kriyāphalaṃ kriyāphalasya phalam.*

20. Notwithstanding their epistemological differences, all schools of Indian philosophy treat cognition as a form of internal activity resulting from modifications (*vṛtti*) of the cognitive faculty (*buddhi*). Although the Buddhists reject this model, the interdependent arising of consciousness and cognition is nevertheless treated as a series of discrete cognitive events (*jñeya-vṛtta*). Given their rich metaphorical content, action verbs are extensively used to describe cognitive functioning in Indian philosophical literature. Indeed, as Matilal notes, "the Sanskrit grammatical tradition extends the metaphor of movement to mental events such as knowing, cognizing, being certain, etc. The root "*gam*" means primarily to go, but when suitably prefixed, it means knowing ('*ava-gam*', '*adi-gam*', etc.)" (Matilal 1986: 115–116).

21. In Indian philosophy and grammar, *lakṣaṇa* (lit. "sign," "distinctive mark," "token," or "characteristic") is a technical term with rich and varied connotations. The term is a nominal derivative from √*lakṣ*- meaning "to define," "to characterize," "to mark," or "to sign." Following Pierce's trichotomic model of semiosis, which has been adopted in some form or another by nearly all contemporary writers on semiotics, D'Amato (2003: 191) treats the Sanskrit terms *lakṣya*, *lakṣaṇa*, and *lakṣaṇā* as corresponding to the distinction between the signified, the signifier, and signification. Thus, *lakṣya* is translated as the signified or the object, *lakṣaṇa* as the sign or the signifier, and *lakṣaṇā* as the process of reference or signification by means of which

mental aspect is obvious in the fact that a philosophical work is primarily conceived as a medium for expounding certain views to others, being thus either an instrument (for the author) or an agent (for the reader).[22] The instrumental aspect covers the purpose in terms of the form of the action—its contents, structure, argumentative procedures, etc. On the other hand, the semiotic aspect of the purpose resides in the fact that a work signifies its meaning to another and, assuming this other comprehends its meaning, the work has the capacity to change her mind. This change (in the mind of the reader) is precisely the purpose in terms of the result of the action. For Kamalaśīla, it is this result that constitutes the primary purpose of a work, and the reason for undertaking the action of composing it.[23] Kamalaśīla treats the third aspect of the purpose, which pertains to the work as a semiotic object,[24] as too obvious to require further examination. The assumption here is that the work itself is a sign for what it attempts to convey. As we shall briefly see, only in relation to an interpreter does the *Compendium* and its *Commentary*, as a collection of written utterances, become a semiotic object.[25]

The prerequisite of an interpreter seems to underscore the centrality of the action-oriented model of intentionality proposed by Kamalaśīla, unless we admit that the work itself is an accurate and truthful rendition of the Buddha's teachings. Kamalaśīla does hint at the possibility that doubt may be entertained about whether their work offers a true perspective on the nature of reality, as suggested by its title, but dismisses it as inconsequen-

---

the sign indicates its object. The Sanskrit vocabulary contains several other terms for "sign," including *liṅga*, *nimitta*, and *saṃjñā*. While *lakṣya* corresponds unambiguously to the notion of referent or object (i.e., that which is signified), *lakṣaṇa* and *lakṣaṇā* are subject to complex analyses in the Sanskrit philosophical and grammatical literature. For instance, *lakṣaṇa* corresponds also to the Nyāya concept of "definition," while *lakṣaṇā* refers to the secondary or "metaphorical" meaning of a word. The usage of *lakṣaṇā* as "metaphorical sense," goes back to Patañjali's *Great Commentary* (*Mahābhāṣya*), (vārttika 14) and is commonly employed as such in Nyāya, Mīmāṃsā, and Ālaṃkāra texts.

22. See TSP *ad* TS 1–6: *śāstrasya parapratipādanāyā 'rabhyamāṇasya kāraṇatvaṃ vā bhavet, kartṛtvaṃ vā.*

23. TSP *ad* TS 1–6: *phalākhyaṃ tu prayojanaṃ pradhānaṃ, tadarthatvāt kriyārambhasya.*

24. The TS/P can be treated as a semiotic object insofar as it functions as a sign for a specific reality, in this case, the reality of the causal principle of dependent arising. Drawing on Charles Morris's (1971) distinction between pure and descriptive semiotics (the former dealing with the "formative discourse of semiotics" and the latter with its "designative discourse"), D'Amato (2003: 186) proposes a study of Buddhist semiotics along the same distinctive lines: (i) an analysis of Buddhist semiotics (the interpretation of signs from a Buddhist doctrinal position), and (ii) a semiotic analysis of Buddhist cultural forms. Although the TS/P could be analyzed from a semiotic point of view as a Buddhist cultural form, our study will focus on the interpretive strategies that are constitutive of its own semiotics.

25. The role of the interpreter is essential, since in the Buddhist context there is no direct correspondence between words and what they designate.

tial.[26] In view of the synchronic model of presentation that is characteristic of Indian philosophical writings, we are invited to suspend judgment and take it on good faith that the authors are reliable exponents of the Buddha's teachings.

Simply stated, the purpose of this encyclopedic work is encapsulated in its title: this is a "compendium of true principles" (*tattvasaṃgraha*),[27] the principal aim of which is to facilitate easy comprehension. But, as Kamalaśīla explains, the ultimate motivation for undertaking such a monumental task is really compassion for all who seek understanding:

> The reason for [undertaking to write] this treatise is [so] that those true principles that lay scattered here and there are compiled and rendered intelligible. Hence, the action bears the characteristic of *compilation*. The result of this act of compiling the true doctrines consists in facilitating their comprehension by generations of learned persons, as made manifest by [the use of] the word "*compilation*." It is easier for the learned to understand them, if the true principles are [presented] in a compiled form. The work [of compilation] has been undertaken for the purpose of facilitating comprehension, because it is difficult to comprehend such principles when they lie scattered. For this reason the author has used the word "*compilation*" in the sense of an easily comprehensible compendium of true principles. Comprehension of these principles alone, however, is not the [only] purpose [in undertaking this task]. Insofar as other scholars have accomplished the exposition of true principles in the past, such an attempt would be worthless. Hence, the ulterior motive of the present treatise is that of helping others, since the composition of this work has been undertaken for the benefit of others.[28]

Of particular significance in this passage is Kamalaśīla's exposition of the ultimate motive of helping others, which is said to be central to Śāntarakṣita's and his own philosophical endeavors. As he further clarifies, those of lesser

---

26. See TSP *ad* TS 1–6: *anabhidheyatvāśaṅkāvyudāsārthamupadarśanīyeti cet? na; abhideyakathanādeva tadāśaṅkāyā vyudasthatvāt.*

27. Note that *tattva* is an important Sanskrit philosophical term that in both form and meaning resembles the Latin scholastic term *quidditas*, usually translated as the "essence" or "true nature of the thing itself." Kapstein (2001: 10), for instance, translates "*Tattvasaṃgraha*" as the "*Gathering of Tattvas.*" I shall be using *tattva* in the sense of "principle" or "tenet" rather than in the essentialist sense implied by the Latin *quidditas*. "Tenet" is more appropriate given the contents of the TS/P and its polemical stance.

28. TSP *ad* TS 1–6: *yato'nena śāstreṇa teṣāṃ tattvānāmitastato viprakīrṇānāmekatra buddhau viniveśalakṣaṇaḥ saṃgrahaḥ kriyate; atastāmeva saṃgrahaśabdena darśatavān/ asyāśca tattvāsaṃgrahakriyāyāḥ pratipādyasantānagatastattvāsukhāvabodhaḥ phalam/ tadapi saṃgrahaśabdena prakāśitameva/ekatra hi saṃkṣiptasya tattvasya pratipattuḥ sukhenodgraho jāyete, duḥkhena tu viprakīrṇasyati kṛtvā sukhodgrahakāraṇaṃ saṃgrahaṃ saṃgrahaśabdena pratipādayaṃstattvāsukhāvabodhārthamidamārabhyata iti prakāśayati/na tu tattvābodhamātramasya phalam; evaṃ hi śāstrasya praṇayanavaiyarthyaṃ syāt, purvācāryairva tattvaniścayasya kṛtatvāt/ato viśeṣataḥ parānugrahasyāpi bhāvāt, parārthatvācca śāstrasya.*

intellect may find it difficult to grasp important philosophical ideas if they are not systematically presented. Presumably, it is out of concern for these individuals that works such as this one may be composed. The rhetorical implication of this statement is obvious in the iterative manner in which the argument stresses the sincerity of the goal and the selfless and compassionate motives of its authors. By defining the aim of the work as *ease* of comprehension,[29] the authors attribute any perceived lack of clarity or confusion not on any presumed dullness on the part of their readership, but rather to extrinsic factors such as the dispersed state in which the Buddhist doctrines are found. Any hint that unintelligibility or confusion might actually be attributable to internal inconsistencies in the Buddhist doctrine itself is overlooked. The authors appear to have an unwavering confidence both in the Buddha's teachings and in the effectiveness of their undertaking.

In concluding his demonstration of purpose, Kamalaśīla explains the meaning of the expression "wishing for the welfare of world" (*jagaddhitavidhitsayā*), which Śāntarakṣita employs in his introductory verses, as corresponding to the action of compiling these Buddhist philosophical doctrines.[30] In other words, the welfare of the world becomes the true motive for undertaking to compose a work of this magnitude and scope, and as such is to be understood both as the action itself and its result. Wishing for the welfare of the world is thus both a motivating factor and the result of becoming acquainted with these core Buddhist principles, the systematic exposition and defense of which is explicitly stated to bring about the said welfare. Kamalaśīla also indicates that the purpose is such that the means by which it can be accomplished are suitable;[31] it is only with the aid of certain suitable means that an intelligent seeker may fully comprehend the meaning of the these true principles, which is nonerroneous (*aviparyāsa*) and edifying (*prakāśāka*). As he writes:

Absence of error consists in realizing the true connection between an action and its result, and comprehending the doctrine of the selflessness of persons and things. And this absence of error derives from this work, which clearly espouses the principle

29. The use of a polysemic adjective such as *sukhā*, meaning "easy," "facile" but also "joyful" or "pleasant" to convey what the treatise seeks to achieve carries a strong rhetorical charge. The implied meaning (*vyañjana*, *arthapatti*) is that facilitating comprehension is bound to generate pleasant feelings of satisfaction in the learner. Thus, whereas the immediate aim of the TS/P is to enable an intelligent seeker to grasp the meaning of the true doctrines with ease, ultimately what is sought is a joyful state of realization. This rhetorical strategy is further accentuated by the use of terms such as *duḥkha* (lit. "suffering" or "discontent") to convey the sense of difficulty, relying again on the polysemic valence of the term, which has both cognitive and affective aspects.

30. TSP *ad* TS 1–6: *jagaddhitavidhānārthaṃ tattvasaṃgrahaḥ kriyate*.

31. See TSP *ad* TS 1–6: *etaccānuguṇopāyameva prayojanamupadarśitam*.

of dependent arising, by means of a gradual process of listening, thinking, and meditating [on its significance]. Thus, it is understood that "wishing for the welfare of the world" is accomplished through the action of compiling the true doctrines.[32]

As this statement makes amply obvious, the *Compendium* and its *Commentary* do more than offer a synthesis of Buddhist metaphysical and epistemological principles: in this synthesis one also finds an exposition of the means by which one can accomplish what the treatise claims to be the highest goal of humankind: the welfare of the world. The means consist in a gradual process of listening, thinking, and meditating; this process is instrumental in removing erroneous cognitions and facilitating clear understanding of what is perhaps the central thesis of the entire work: *that interdependent arising underscores the manifestation of all phenomena*. It is worth recalling that the gradual path to higher understanding—which in Śāntarakṣita and Kamalaśīla finds some of its strongest proponents—represents a synthesis of pragmatic and epistemic goals. Indeed, the exalted state in which all energies are expended for the welfare of the world is achieved only when both afflictive and cognitive obscurations have been removed. Through this double emphasis on pragmatic and epistemic goals, Kamalaśīla aims to convince his audience that the *Compendium* and his own *Commentary* serve not merely as collections of epistemological tenets but as primers of practical philosophy that instruct in the right manner of acquiring and perfecting such critical thinking skills.

Before we attempt briefly to review the contents of the *Compendium*, we may also note that Kamalaśīla, prior to his summary of the subject matter, gives a précis of the relation between the purpose already stated and the contents of the work. This is especially significant to our inquiry, as here Kamalaśīla, following Śāntarakṣita's opening stanza, links the doctrine of dependent arising to the Buddha's omniscience and asserts its infallibility on the basis of a demonstration of the validity of omniscient cognition. This demonstration is presented in the final chapter, which, as we shall see, is treated as the logical conclusion of the entire work.[33]

---

32. TSP *ad* TS 1–6: *aviparyāsaś ca yathāvat karmaphalasambandhābhisampratyayaḥ, aviparīta pudgaladharmanairātmyāvabodhaś ca/sa cāsmād aviparītapratītyasamutpāda samprakāśākāc chāstrāc chravaṇacintābhāvanākrameṇopajāyata ity ato 'vagamyata eva tattvasaṃgrahakriyāto jagaddhitam api sampadyate iti.*

33. In her detailed analysis of the discourse of omniscience in the TS/P, McClintock (2010) regards the final chapter on omniscient cognition (*sarvajña*) (along with the two preceding chapters) as primarily concerned with issues of religious authority (the Mīmāṃsaka defense of the intrinsic validity of the Vedas being the main target). Given its distinctly religious orientation, the final chapter appears to go beyond the overall scope of the work: namely, a clear and methodical exposition of various metaphysical and epistemological topics from a Buddhist standpoint.

While the argument from omniscience is significant, what preoccupies Kamalaśīla in particular is countering the view, shared by some non-Buddhists, that the principle of dependent arising is contrary to reason or that it lacks the requisite categorical normative force. To this end he argues for viewing the *Compendium* as an extensive defense against the criticism of those philosophers who regard such core Buddhist principles as the result of sloppy reasoning (*viṣamahetu*) and confusion (*vyāhata*) about the proper mode of conducting epistemological inquiries.[34] That neither he nor Śāntarakṣita are content to rely on the Buddha's omniscience to prove the reliability of what are taken to be fundamental principles of the nature of reality (and of the structure of cognition)[35] is made amply obvious by fact that the bulk of their work is dedicated to a thorough and methodical examination of a whole range of epistemological and metaphysical topics.

5.2 MAPPING THE ONTOLOGICAL AND EPISTEMOLOGICAL DOMAINS

As we saw above, Śāntarakṣita's introductory stanzas provide a succinct overview of the entire contents of the *Compendium*. From the outset we learn that its central topic is the principle of dependent arising, and that its presentation is given in the form of a comprehensive list of defining characteristics. Śāntarakṣita lists transitoriness[36] and the basis for ascertaining the true

34. See TSP *ad* TS 1–6: *sa ca ayaṃ pratītyasamutpādaḥ parairviṣamahetuḥ pramāṇavyāhatapadārthādhikaraṇaścesyate*. "[The doctrine of] dependent arising should be treated has been regarded by other philosophers as [a sign of] sloppy reasoning and confusion about the topic of the categories of valid cognition." For an interesting discussion about whether Buddhist principles such as momentariness and dependent arising should be treated as categorically normative for all rational agents, see Griffiths (1999), who calls into question the practice, and McClintock (2010: 53ff.) and Patil (2009: 360), who take Buddhist authors like Śāntarakṣita, Kamalaśīla, and Ratnakīrti to be judicious rational agents intent on advancing persuasive arguments.

35. It is obvious that neither Śāntarakṣita nor Kamalaśīla consider appeal to an authoritative person (*pratyayaitapuruṣa*) as a necessary condition for epistemic reliability. The two sources of reliable cognition, perception and inference, ought to be sufficient for establishing the grounds of reliability. The authors are sensitive to the fact that appealing to the Buddha's authority or grounding their arguments on Buddhist scripture is not an acceptable proof for their Brahmanical critics. Unlike Dharmakīrti, Śāntarakṣita and Kamalaśīla offer a less restrictive demonstration of proof for inaccessible matters (*atyantaparokṣa*), since they do not appear to predicate the reliability of those principles declared universal by the Buddha on his omniscience. See Tillemans (1993) and McClintock (2010: 318ff.) for an extensive discussion of this issue.

36. This characteristic is the subject of the eighth chapter, the *Examination of Time* (*Sthirabhāvaparīkṣā*), in which Śāntarakṣita offers a defense of the doctrine of momentariness (*kṣaṇikabhaṅga*) and its causal efficacy (*arthakriyā*) by demonstrating the produced (*kāraka*) nature of phenomena. Most of Śāntarakṣita's arguments

connection between actions and their results as the sole characteristics of the principle of dependent arising.[37] The main point of this succinct taxonomical exercise is to exclude dependent arising from being associated with such categories as primordial nature,[38] the divine,[39] the self,[40] essence, primordial sound, and the universal spirit.[41] The ultimate aim of these investigations, however, is to demonstrate that supernatural agencies are mere conceptual fabrications that have neither causal efficacy nor explanatory force. Unlike such fixed and immutable principles as "primordial nature" or "universal spirit," the principle of dependent arising alone captures the nature of phenomena, seen as essentially transitory and as arising due to a multiplicity of causes and conditions, none of which can be taken to stand outside the order of the causal domain.

The Buddhist metaphysical position on the transitory nature of phenomena is centered on the principle of momentariness, which postulates that things exist only as series of discrete moments of existence. On metaphysical grounds, the principle of momentariness offers an effective refutation of the permanence of things: permanence implies immutability, and immutability is incompatible with the fact that perception reveals change, not immutability, to be the pervasive characteristic of all phenomena. As Kamalaśīla notes in his commentary, the doctrine of momentariness affords a one-stroke refutation of the idea of eternal primordial causes, regardless of whether these are taken to be external realities or constitutive principles of cognition (such as, for instance, the eternal self).[42]

---

form a direct criticism of the Nyāya perspective on the production and destruction of things as presented by Uddyotakara.

37. This is the ninth chapter, the *Examination of the Relation between Action and Result* (*Karmaphalasambandhaparīkṣā*), which addresses the implication of the doctrine of momentariness for understanding the relationship between actions and their results.

38. This corresponds to the first chapter of the TS/P, the *Examination of Nature* (*Prakṛti-parīkṣā*), which explores in detail the Sāṃkhya concept of primordial nature (*prakṛti*). The main argument here is that an uncaused cause, which is taken to be formless and immutable, cannot explain the causal complexity of physical phenomena.

39. The second chapter, the *Examination of God* (*Īśvaraparīkṣā*), addresses Nyāya and other theistic systems, which postulate God as the ultimate cause for the production of things on account of the fact that inanimate things have no causal efficacy.

40. This corresponds to the six subsections of the seventh chapter, the *Examination of the Self* (*Ātmaparīkṣā*), which provides a critical assessment of the notion that a metaphysical self can have causal powers (a view endorsed in schools as diverse as the Nyāya-Vaiśeṣika, Mīmāṃsā, Sāṃkhya, Digambara Jaina, Advaita Vedānta, and the Buddhist Vātsīputriyas).

41. These comprise respectively the fourth, fifth, and sixth chapters of the TS/P: the *Examination of the Doctrine of Intrinsic Nature of the World* (*Svābhāvikajagadvādaparīkṣā*), the *Examination of Primordial Sound* (*Śabdabrahmaparīkṣā*), and the *Examination of the Person* (*Puruṣaparīkṣā*).

42. See TSP *ad* TS 350–351: *"calam" ityetad viśeṣaṇa samarthanārthamāha—atha vetyādi/niravaśeṣapadārthavyā pinaḥ kṣaṇabhaṅgasya prasādhanādeva prakṛtīśvarādeḥ paraparikalpitasya sakalapadārtharāśerekaprahāreṇaiva.*

In addition to rejecting the causal efficacy of supernatural agencies, Śāntarakṣita and Kamalaśīla offer a critique of the six categories of the Nyāya-Vaiśeṣika tradition, dedicating a separate chapter each to substance, quality, action, universals, particulars, and inherence.[43] Implicit in this sixfold classification of categories are the characteristics of "existence" and of being "apprehensible." Existence is treated as a distinct category on account of the fact that it is a characteristic common to all produced things.[44]

One investigation in which the methodological separation between ontological and epistemological issues is not strictly observed is the examination of external objects.[45] Here the externalist perspective of the Sautrāntikas, which has been employed to reject the reality of the Nyāya-Vaiśeṣika categories,[46] is replaced with the internalist perspective of Yogācāra, as Śāntarakṣita and Kamalaśīla prepare to argue that the phenomenal content of awareness depends not on the impressions left by external objects but on residual traces stemming from the receptacle consciousness.[47] Furthermore, Śāntarakṣita and Kamalaśīla address a series of mereological questions which, as we shall see later on, have important consequences for the Buddhist account of perception: does perception grasp an object as (i) nondistinct from the atoms, (ii) in the form of an aggregate of atoms, or (iii) as an organic whole?[48] The examination of external objects leads to the epistemological core of the *Compendium*: a critical account of the nature of our cognitive capacities the principal focus of which is a defense of Dignāga and Dharmakīrti's account of epistemic warrants.[49]

Of equal epistemological significance is the examination of the Jaina doctrine of the multifarious nature of things, which centers on the notion that, as categories of thought, "universal" and "particular" are not mutually exclusive; rather, they capture the different aspects of a given phenomenon.[50] In

---

43. These correspond respectively to the tenth through to the fifteen chapters.

44. See TSP *ad* TS 1–6: *ye ca dharmivyatirekiṇo dharmāḥ kaiścidupavarṇyante, yathā–'ṣṇṇāmapi padārthānāmastitvaṃ sadupalambhakapramāṇaviṣayatva' ityevamādayaḥ, teṣ āṃ grahaṇam.*

45. The *Examination of External Objects* (*Bahirarthaparīkṣā*) comprises the twenty-third investigation of TS/P.

46. According to this perspective, an external object is real only in so far as it provides causal support for the emergence of a cognitive aspect (*ākāra*) that bears its resemblance.

47. See TS 1308–1310 and TSP *loc. cit.*

48. See TSP *ad* TS 1966–1968: *tatra pratyakṣasiddho'rtho bāhyo bhavannaneko vā paramāṇuto'bhinno bhavet, eko vā tairārabdho'vayavī, sthūlo'nārabdho vā--iti pakṣā.*

49. This comprises the seventeenth and eighteenth examinations (of perception and inference, respectively). The examination of perception and inference together with the examination of the sources of knowledge form the epistemological core of the TS/P.

50. See the *Examination of the Multifarious Nature of Things* (*Syādvādaparīkṣā*).

refuting the Jaina perspective, Śāntarakṣita adopts the phenomenologist's stance that apprehending an entity as possessing different aspects is a consequence of the availability of different epistemological protocols. While he does not seem to deny the diversity and richness of the external phenomena, the pluralist account of causation (that is, the view that there can be different accounts of phenomena that are mutually entailing) is deemed logically indefensible. Finally, there is the examination of the trans-temporal theory of the elements of existence and/or experience (*dharmas*) advanced by the influential Abhidharma School of the Vaibhāṣikas,[51] and the skepticism of the Lokāyata physicalists, who raise a series of important objections regarding the consistency of certain Buddhist claims (in particular, the apparent incompatibility between the doctrine of the impermanence of things and the persistence of cognition).[52]

In concluding their philosophical *tour de force*, Śāntarakṣita and Kamalaśīla undertake an extensive refutation of the Mīmāṃsā epistemological position on the authority of scriptural revelation and intrinsic ascertainment,[53] which also serves as the basis for their demonstration of the possibility of omniscient cognition. The necessity of demonstrating omniscience may be taken as indicating that Śāntarakṣita and Kamalaśīla, like all Buddhist epistemologists before them, do not regard ordinary cognitions (that is, merely doxastic modes of apprehension[54]) as epistemically warranted.[55] For Śāntarakṣita, the assumption that intrinsic and/or extrinsic ascertainment is a defining characteristic of all cognitive events would make it impossible to discriminate

51. See the *Examination of the Trans-temporal Existence of Things* (*Traikālyaparīkṣā*), which aims to demonstrate that the principle of dependent arising is non-diachronic (*asaṃkrānti*).

52. This comprises the twenty-second examination of the TS/P, which aims to demonstrate that dependent arising "has no beginning and no end" (*anādyantam*).

53. This comprises the twenty-fourth and the twenty-fifth examinations. According to Kamalaśīla, the *Examination of Revelation* (*Śrutiparīkṣa*) sets out to prove that, in espousing dependent arising, the Buddha does not appeal to any autonomous scripture, while the *Examination of Intrinsic Ascertainment* (*Svataḥprāmāṇyaparīkṣā*) aims to demonstrate that whatever truth such autonomous scripture might contain cannot be intrinsically ascertained. These two demonstrations specifically target the Mīmāṃsā endorsement of the scriptural authority of the Vedas, primarily as defended by Kumārila.

54. "Ordinary cognitions" is what Śāntarakṣita and Kamalaśīla call those cognitive states that do not count as epistemic warrants. One such example would be the apprehension of phenomenal realities as permanent and unchanging.

55. The basis upon which a cognitive event is ascertained as epistemically warranted can be both intrinsic and extrinsic to the event: intrinsic ascertainment (*svataḥ-prāmāṇya*) is typical of inferential reasoning, whereas perception is externally ascertained (*arataḥ-prāmāṇya*). It should be noted that Śāntarakṣita and Kamalaśīla do not adopt Dharmakīrti's radical stance that only inference is intrinsically ascertained. Like some of Dharmakīrti's earlier commentators (Śākyabuddhi in particular), Śāntarakṣita and Kamalaśīla contend that a perception that apprehends an object as capable of fulfilling a specific purpose can be intrinsically ascertained.

between true and false cognitions. Only direct and unmediated modes of apprehension (such as yogic or trained perception) can grasp the true nature of things.

5.3 PERCEPTION AND THE PRINCIPLE OF CLARITY

As this succinct overview of the contents of the *Compendium* makes clear, the need to identify reliable cognitions is essential if one is to prove that the principle of dependent arising is neither a mere verbal invention, nor simply the unsubstantiated postulation of an unobserved phenomenon. Following Dharmakīrti, Kamalaśīla invokes the principle of clarity, claiming that there are good reasons for accepting dependent arising—the causal nexus underlying the manifestation of all phenomena—as a true principle on account of the fact that it is clearly perceived. Furthermore, dependent arising is also taken to be free of the three types of defects the Naiyāyikas attribute to a misunderstanding of the concept of definition, particularly when attempting to define an entity by indicating what it excludes. These are the defects of impossibility (*asaṃbhava*), over-applicability (*ativyāpti*), and under-applicability (*avyāpti*).[56] The defect of over-applicability refers to a definition that includes—besides the characteristics that are proper to the respective entity—some other accidental characteristics. The defect of under-applicability calls attention to situations when some of the characteristics of an entity are not specified. Finally, the defect of impossibility applies to definitions which include characteristics that are totally nonspecific to the entity defined.[57] This appeal to the principle of clarity in an examination of perception and inferential reasoning ensures that one does not attribute to these sources of cognition capacities that are beyond their reach. After all, it is because of a misapprehension of what perception can actually deliver that the Naiyāyika thinks inherence relations are within the purview of empirical awareness. Likewise, it is because of a misapprehension of the role and function of conceptual analysis that names are taken to refer to things on the basis of some intrinsic property to the thing itself. To say, as Śāntarakṣita does, that dependent arising "is cognized by the two clearly defined sources of cognition,"[58]

56. Cf. TSP *ad* TS 2: *spaṣṭatvaṃ ca lakṣaṇasyāsambhāvyāptyativyāptidoṣarahitatvāt.*

57. For the Naiyāyikas *asambhava* is but an extreme case of *avyāpti*, which occurs mostly when the definiendum (*lakṣya*) and the definiens (*lakṣaṇa*) are not coextensive (*samanyatva*), that is, when the definition fails to specify all the characteristics of the given entity. See, for example, NS I, 1.3 and NV *loc. cit.* Extensive discussions of the concept of definition (*lakṣaṇa*) in Indian philosophy, with particular focus on Nyāya, are found in Biardeau (1957), Staal (1961), and Matilal (1985: 164–176).

58. TS 3: *spaṣṭalakṣaṇasaṃyuktapramādvitayaniścitam.*

is thus to assert a tight coupling between cognition, its operations, and its contents.

This notion that one can directly apprehend the true nature of reality reflects a true optimism about the possibility of knowledge. An adequate account of the function and scope of our cognitive faculties is therefore paramount in settling ontological disputes: any definitive pronouncement about the (ultimate) nature of things must take into account not only what it is (and is like) to cognize but also what is thus apprehended and what a given object indirectly reveals about our constitution as cognitive agents. Anticipating the detailed analysis of perception in the seventeenth chapter of the *Compendium*, Kamalaśīla gives a cursory indication of how it may be understood:

> Concerning perception, its specific characteristic is that of being free from conceptual construction and nonerroneous. This is exactly as declared by the Master (i.e., Dignāga). As [the Master] said—"One who possesses visual cognition cognizes the blue [color], but not as [an object having the] blue [color]." The expression "cognizes the blue" means that the cognition [of blue] does not apprehend an object contrary to itself, indicating thus that it is nonerroneous; the expression "not as blue" indicates on the other hand that no connection between the name "blue" and the cognition [of blue] is found, meaning thus that [the respective cognition] is non-conceptual [in character].[59]

From this brief definition of perception we learn that only non-mediated (by explicit conceptual structures) and inerrant states of cognitive awareness qualify as perception. As we noted in the previous chapter, Dignāga's definition of perception includes only the qualifier "devoid of conception." Dharmakīrti's addition of the qualifier "nonerroneous" comes in response to the criticisms of Uddyotakara[60] and Kumārila,[61] both of whom fault Dignāga's definition for its failure to account for cases of perceptual illusion. Thus, the examination of perception that Śāntarakṣita and Kamalaśīla undertake in the *Compendium* and its *Commentary* can be seen as an attempt to address these criticisms and advance the conversation in this key area of epistemological inquiry. In the next chapter, we turn to consider the various arguments, criticisms, and rejoinders that inform the Buddhist epistemological account of perception.

---

59. TSP *ad* TS 3: *tatra pratyakṣasya lakṣaṇam—bhrāntikalpanābhyāṃ rahitatvam/ tacca bhagavatoktameva/yadāha—'cakṣurvijñānasamaṅgī nīlaṃ vijñānāti, no tu nīlam' iti/tathā hi 'nīlaṃ vijñānāti ityanenāviparītaviṣayatvākhyāpanādabhrāntatvamuktam, "no tu nīla" ityanena nāmānuviddhārthagrahaṇapratikṣepāt kalpanārahitatvam.*

60. See NV 41.22–43.5.

61. See ŚV, *Pratyakṣa*, 51–84.

CHAPTER 6

Perception as an Epistemic Modality

The foregoing analysis has identified the intellectual and theoretical context in which the Buddhist epistemological enterprise develops and flourishes. At the core of this enterprise are two specific notions that are central to our investigation. First, the notion that the domains of verbal expression and conceptual thought are coextensive; and secondly, the view that perception discloses not only a domain of unique particulars but also their mode of givenness. We now turn to see how these two notions play out in Śāntarakṣita and Kamalaśīla's defense of the standard Buddhist epistemological account of perception. The analysis that follows is thematically structured and focuses on three main issues that should preoccupy the perception theorist: (1) what is the cognitive function of perception as an epistemic warrant; (2) what is the ontological status of perceptual objects; and (3) what specifically is the relation between perception and conception. It should be noted from the outset that, as elsewhere in the *Compendium* and its *Commentary*, Śāntarakṣita and Kamalaśīla adopt a polemical stance, establishing their views largely as critical reactions to rival theories of perception. We are thus presented with a picture of cognitive awareness as possessing a dual capacity: it reveals its contents and its own specific character at once.

For these two thinkers momentariness—and all that it entails—is not a conceptual construct: rather, it is perceptually disclosed as a fundamental principle governing the nature of phenomena. Perception (specifically, direct perception) is said to be capable of uncovering a domain of discrete events[1] undergoing constant transformation. For this reason, a definition of perception such as the Nyāya realist provides—that is, perception as the apprehension of real spatio-temporal entities possessed of intrinsic

1. Insofar as change and motion (or the objects undergoing them) are observable phenomena we may talk about perception possessing this discerning capacity.

characteristics—is rejected on the grounds that it attributes to perception capacities that are beyond its reach. It is this erroneous construal of perception (and of its capacities) that leads, according to the Buddhist, to the mistaken view that universals are perceptually apprehensible as relations of inherence. The purpose of Śāntarakṣita and Kamalaśīla's critique of the definitions of perception (advanced by their opponents) is twofold: first, they reject the notion that perception apprehends entities as being qualified by real universals; second, they argue that perception, as a direct mode of cognitive apprehension, reveals dependent arising as the only veridical account of causality, and thus as the fundamental law governing the manifestation of phenomena. On this view, aggregation (essentially the characteristic of all objects in the class of what J. L. Austin calls "medium-sized dry goods") and its emergent properties are merely conceptually attributed. In effect, by stating that perception apprehends an interdependent nexus of causes and conditions (*hetusāmagrī*) rather than physical objects and their specific properties, Śāntarakṣita and Kamalaśīla, like Dignāga and Dharmakīrti before them, propose new standards of common sense.

I use "common sense" here neither in its Aristotelian acceptation of *sensus communis*, the faculty that fuses all sensory impressions into one singular percept, nor in the Kantian sense of natural intelligence. Rather, by common sense (at least in this context) I mean ordinary, untutored perception. I take it that the naïve realist relies on the notion that common sense stands mainly for habitual sense perception. However, "naïve realism," as Matilal (echoing Sellars and Armstrong, two staunch defenders of realism) reminds us, "is not really naïve."[2] A better and widely used descriptive concept for referring to a philosophy of the common sense would be "direct realism." It is precisely this type of direct realism that constitutes the main target of Buddhist epistemological critiques, which rest on the notion that a proper analysis of the sources of belief formation must take into account the phenomenology of first-person experience. As will become clear from the analysis that follows, the Buddhist advances neither indirect realism (or representationalism) nor idealism, but rather a peculiar type of active perception phenomenalism that is essentially nonrepresentational in character.

6.1 THE CONDITIONS FOR "PERCEPTUAL KNOWLEDGE"

It may be proper to begin by acknowledging that certain differences are apparent between Dignāga's understanding of the meaning and function of conception (*kalpanā*) and its interpretation by Dharmakīrti and his immediate commentators, as well as by Śāntarakṣita and Kamalaśīla. For instance,

2. Matilal (1986: 1).

Dignāga uses "conception" to refer to the process by which things, which are essentially inexpressible, are indirectly referred to through an association with a word or verbal expression.[3] The defining characteristic of conception is its capacity to associate the contents of experience with words. Dignāga gives several examples of such associations: arbitrary names, genus nouns, quality-nouns, action nouns (i.e., verbs), substance nouns, and so on. All these nouns, including those that denote no real entity (*artha-śūnya-śabda*), represent various instances of conceptual thought and are thus excluded from the sphere of the perceptual. The notion that conception stands for a thought process (viz., reference) the primary function of which is the categorization of the elements of existence and/or experience underscores the centrality of perception. Indeed, in order to be able to provide accurate descriptions of the phenomenal contents of experience, there must be a lower level of non-conceptual but cognitive sensing that grounds our linguistic and categorizing practices. Otherwise, concepts would apply to phenomena in a totally arbitrary manner, something that not even the Naiyāyika is willing to concede. Support for this dissociation between the intentionality of perception and the self-referentiality of conception is found in a well-known example given by Vasubandhu: there is a distinction between the apprehension of something blue and the conception that follows that direct apprehension, namely "this is blue."[4] Conception thus encodes not only the naming of what in effect is taken to be inexpressible but also, and more importantly, the specific association between words and things that makes possible this ostensive denotation.

Following Dignāga's example, Kamalaśīla cites the divergent opinions of different authors concerning the nature, result, object, and number of the sources of cognition, as one of the main topics of epistemological inquiry.[5] These divergent opinions are particularly informative in that they reveal the various criteria that Indian philosophers employ to distinguish reliable cognitions from ordinary, folk beliefs. One such criterion is that of reliability,

3. By conceptual construction Dignāga means "the association of name (*nāman*), genus (*jāti*) etc. with a thing perceived," which for him "results in the verbal designation of the [respective] thing." See PSV *ad* PS (K 3d): *ming gang rigs sogs su sbyor ba'o* (*nāmajātyādiyojanā*) as quoted in TSP *ad* TS 1221.

4. The distinction is marked here by the use of the particle *iti*. See PSV *ad* PS I, 4ab: *chos mngon pa las kyang "mig gi rnam par shes pa dang ldan pas sngon po shes kyi sngon po'o snyam du ni ma yin no," "don la don du 'du shes kyi don la chos su 'du shes pa ni ma yin no" zhes gsungs so.*

5. In the PSV, Dignāga does not explicitly mention the fourfold objection concerning the sources of knowledge. This reference is found in Jinendrabuddhi's PSṬ 11b.1: *'gal ba'i rtogs pa ni log par rtogs pa rnams te, phan tsun 'gal ba'i mtsan nyid byed pa'i phyir ro*; and 11b.7: *de la 'bras bu dang rang gi ngo bo dang yul dang grangs la log par rtogs pa bzhi rnams te, da rnams las grangs la log par rtogs pa bsal ba'i don du gsungs pa, mngon sum dang ni rjes su dpag, mngon sum dang ni rjes su dpag, ces pa la sogs pa'o.* See also TSP *ad* TS: *tatra pramāṇe svarūpaphalagocarasaṅkhyāstu pareṣāṃ viprattiś caturvidhā.*

which is primarily conceived in terms of the distinctive characteristics of the sources of knowledge. In general, Indian philosophers agree that perception and inference[6] are the principal sources of knowledge. A dispute arises, however, when it comes to identifying the constraints that must be applied to these cognitive modalities in order to ensure that the outcome is knowledge rather than mere unwarranted belief. Thus, when Śāntarakṣita deems unacceptable the definitions of perception and inference proposed by the Naiyāyikas, he simply reacts to their epistemological commitment to direct realism, specifically to the notion that perception picks out not only real particulars but also the universals that inhere in them.

The claim that perception apprehends phenomena as rigidly categorized by the realist forms the main target of their criticism. For Śāntarakṣita and Kamalaśīla, as for all Buddhist epistemologists, perception can only establish that things are impermanent and momentary. A misunderstanding of the capacity and function of this mode of cognitive apprehension can result in a failure to grasp the full implications of the causal principle of dependent arising. Therefore, at least from a Buddhist standpoint, any attempt to define perception as the activity of forming perceptual judgments, the result of which is the apprehension of external objects as characterized by stable physical properties, runs counter to the view (taken to be axiomatic by the Buddhist), that things and the cognitive events that instantiate them are episodic and relational.

Furthermore, Kamalaśīla also rebuffs the Vaiśeṣika assumption that perception effectively refers either to perceptual judgments or to the sense organs. In doing so, he simply follows the Abhidharma view that the sensory organs are in fact noncognitive by nature,[7] for sensory input without conscious apprehension cannot give rise to a perceptual occasion. Here, Kamalaśīla specifically refers to the opinions of the Naiyāyikas and the Vaiśeṣikas for whom perception reaches out to the object and apprehends it either by means of some kind of direct contact or simply by an apprehension at a distance.[8] On this account, perception operates either by effecting an immediate contact with the object, or by providing a ground for perceptual judgment. Kamalaśīla's critique also implicitly targets the view of Kumārila, who admits as warranted both determinate and indeterminate modes of

6. The Naiyāyikas, as we saw above, add to this list of epistemic warrants analogy and verbal testimony.

7. See TSP *ad* TS 1212: *tatra savikalpakam ajñānasvabhāvaṃ vā cakṣurādikaṃ pratyakṣaṃ pramāṇam iti pratyakṣasvarūpavipratipattiḥ*.

8. For instance, Vātsyāyana defines perception as the "functioning or action of each sense toward an object, the action having the form either of contact or of cognition" (NSBh I, 1.3: *akṣasyā'kṣasya prativiṣayaṃ vṛttiḥ pratyakṣam/vṛttistu—sannikarṣaḥ, jñānaṃ vā*). In addition, Uddyotakara states that universals and particulars can be both perceptually and verbally apprehended. See *Nyāyavārttika ad* NS I, 1.3: *pratyakṣeṇāpi sāmānyaviśeṣatadvatāṃ grahaṇam, śabdenāpi*.

cognitive awareness. Unlike the Naiyāyikas, Kumārila concedes that in perception there is a gradual transition from an indeterminate stage, in which neither the particular nor the universal are apprehended as such, to a stage where the object appears as being qualified by genus, class, etc.[9]

Having identified what he takes to be his opponents' mistaken views regarding the nature of perception, Śāntarakṣita proceeds to give his own definition of perception: "Perception is free from conceptual construction and nonerroneous. Conceptual construction is a cognition that is associated with verbal expression. However, it is not [considered as] the cause of verbal expression."[10] To this definition Kamalaśīla adds the following gloss:

In this case, direct perception is that cognition which [the master] has declared as free from conception and nonerroneous, for in every case, it is the subject of definition that is thus defined, as in expressions such as "that which tremors is the fig tree." Here, the subject of definition is "perception," for it is the significance of this [perception as a cognitive faculty] that forms the subject [of investigation]; it is not the significance of "free from conceptual construction" and "nonerroneous" that is the subject; if that were the case, the latter would take on [the role of what is thus signified] . . . [Seeking to clarify] what [type of] conception is designated here as that [conceptual content] which is absent in [the cognition designated as] perception, [the master] declares that "Conceptual construction is a cognition that is associated with verbal expression." [Question:] Is that [conceptual construction], which Śaṅkarasvāmin and others have refuted in detail as being the cause of verbal expression, also implied? [To this question the master] answers: "No, it is not [implied as] the cause of verbal expression, and the like." [The word] "implied" [is] considered [necessary in this context] . . . Verbal expression signifies verbal designation, and the cause of [verbal] expression is the genus, name, etc. for verbal designation is not possible in the absence of qualifiers such as genus, etc. The term "and the like" in this context refers to notions such as reasoning and deliberation [which act as] causes for the gross and subtle [aspects of the] mind that are associated with words, and likewise, the assumption of grasping and the grasped. [The term] "verbal expression" signifies a word [as a verbal signifier], and it is a generic form (i.e. a universal). That aspect [of cognition], which appears as associated with that word, is called an expression.[11]

---

9. See ŚV, *Pratyakṣa*, 112–113: *asti hyālocanā jñānaṃ prathaṃ nirvikalpakam/ bālamūkādivijñānasadṛśaṃśuddhavastujam//naviśeṣonasāmānyaṃtadānīmanubhūyate/ tayorādhārabhūtāttu vyaktarevāvasīyate*.

10. TS 1213: *pratyakṣaṃ kalpanāpoḍham-abhrāntaṃ abhilāpinī/pratītiḥ kalpanā klṛptihetutvādyātmikā na tu*. Śāntarakṣita's definition of perception closely follows Dharmakīrti's account in PVin I, 4, in particular the *pāda* ac: *pratyakṣaṃ kalpanāpoḍham abhrāntam abhilāpinī/pratītiḥ kalpāna* (154a6–154b1): *mngon sum rtog bral ma 'khrul ba/ . . . rtog pa mngon par brjod can gyi//shes pa*). Cf. Funayama (1992: 61 n. 43).

11. TSP *ad* TS 1213: *tatra jñānasya kalpanāpoḍhatvamabhrāntvaṃ ca anūdya pratyakṣatvaṃ vidhīyate, sarvatraiva lakṣyasya vidhīyamānatvāt/yathā—yaḥ kampte*

Kamalaśīla's explanation, it seems, aims to clarify three main points: (i) the difference between the word "perception," the actual subject of definition, and its referent (in other words, the difference between language and non-linguistic phenomena); (ii) what is meant by conception and by the absence of conceptual content in perception; and (iii) whether the use of words such as "perception" and "conception" can meaningfully (and ostensibly) articulate the difference between their referents. First, Kamalaśīla explains that this definition of perception is intended as a phenomenological description of a certain type of experience (viz., direct perception), and not as a semantic account of action predicates. Second, he identifies the Buddhist position on the relation between language and conceptual thought: thought has a quintessentially discursive character and is dependent on the structure of language (as its medium of expression), that is, principally on an account of meaning (rather than reference). Lastly, Kamalaśīla endorses the Buddhist epistemological view, that the debate over the meaning of action predicates and their nominal forms cannot be settled on semantic grounds alone. We have already noted that in his criticism of Dignāga's definition of perception, Uddyotakara rejects what he sees as an inappropriate use of definitional terms. For Uddyotakara "perception" cannot denote that which is inexpressible for it is already expressed. If the referent of what it means to perceive were inexpressible it would admittedly remain unnamed (and thus unknown). But we do *meaningfully* use the term "perception" and its cognates, so it cannot be that perception designates that which is inexpressible. Thus, for Uddyotakara such allegedly sloppy use of language displays ignorance on the part of the Buddhist of the proper import of philosophical terminology. Moreover, it also shows disregard for the concept of definition (*lakṣaṇa*), which assigns determinate meanings to words.[12] For Uddyotakara

---

so'śvattha iti/lakṣyamatra pratyakṣam; tallakṣaṇasyaiva prastutatvāt/na tu kalpanāpoḍhābhrāntalakṣaṇaṃ, yena tadvidhīyata iti syāt/... ka punaratra kalpanā'abhipretā, yadapoḍhaṃ jñānaṃ pratyakṣam? ityāha—abhilāpinī pratītiḥ kalpana iti/atha yasyāṃ klṛptihetutvādyātmikāyāṃ śaṅkarasvāmiprabhṛtaye vistareṇa doṣamuktavantaḥ; sa api kiṃ gṛhītavyā? uta na? ityāha—klṛptihetutvādyātmikā na tviti/gṛhyata iti śeṣaḥ/... klṛptiḥ—vyapadeśaḥ, taddhotutvaṃ jātyādīnāmiti boddhavyam; yato jātyādiviśeṣam antareṇa na vyapadeśo'asti/ādiśabdena śabdasaṃsargacittaudārikasūkṣmatāhetū vitarkavicārau, tathā grāgyagrāhakakalpanetyevamādi grahītavyam/abhilāpaḥ—vācakaḥ śabdaḥ, sa ca sāmānyākāraḥ, sa vidyate yasyāḥ pratibhāsataḥ stathoktā.

12. The concept of definition (*lakṣaṇa*) is a very important concept in Sanskrit philosophical literature. It is one of the three elements on the basis of which topics are to be classified and discussed in a philosophical treatise: (i) *uddeśa* (an enunciation of philosophical categories); (ii) *lakṣaṇa* (the definition); and (iii) *parīkṣā* (the investigation of those categories) (see NSBh *ad* NS I, 1.3 (introduction): *trividhā cā'sya śāstrasya pravṛttiḥ;—uddeśo lakṣaṇaṃ parīkṣā ceti*). According to Vātsyāyana, the purpose of definition is to differentiate an entity from whatever does not possess the nature (*tattva* = essence) of that entity (See NSBh *ad* NS I, 1.3 (introduction): *tatra uddiśtasya tattvavyavacchedako dharmmo lakṣaṇam*). For modern discussions of the Nyāya concept of definition, see Staal (1961), Biardeau (1957), and Matilal (1985:

perception, as an epistemic category, requires some positive determination. Hence, to regard it as devoid of any conceptual content is effectively to render the word "perception" meaningless (*avācaka*).[13]

It is tempting to see this debate between the Buddhist epistemologists and their opponents as a mere verbal disagreement that could easily be settled by giving an account of linguistic reference. But I think there is more at stake here than meets the eye. Although most philosophers would disagree, as David Chalmers has recently argued, that there is a distinction between "questions of fact and questions of language," it is nonetheless the case that intuitions about a particular state of affairs and varied uses of categorical terms seem to suggest otherwise.[14] A mere verbal disagreement does not (and should not) call into question facts about a certain domain, only their description. But in most domains of knowledge, and especially in philosophy, verbal disagreement can often reflect a different way of conceiving of a particular idea (or state of affairs) that tells us something significant about the author's theoretical viewpoint. And if conceivability is justifiably admitted as a fundamental mode of cognizing, then disagreements about such notions as "perception" must run deeper than negotiating the best account of what is agreed to be factually the case.

The disagreement between the Buddhist epistemologists and the Naiyāyikas on the proper definition of perception is as much a disagreement about matters of fact (what exactly constitutes the domain of direct experience) as it is about what we can reasonably conceive to be the function of action predicates or of causally indexical notions. Thus, in accusing the Buddhist for being something like an epistemic theorist of vagueness, we see in Uddyotakara the Naiyāyika's mistrust of causal theories of reference: if experiential content is not straightforwardly captured by linguistic and inferential relations, then the realist's methodological reliance on the testimony of common sense experience is seriously compromised.

164–202). The Nyāya definition statement (*lakṣaṇavākya*) contains both a signifier (*lakṣaṇa*) and a signified (*lakṣya*), the two terms being treated as coextensive. Classical Nyāya appears to advocate an extensional semantics, where the signifier acts as a distinguishing feature of external objects. As Matilal (1985: 178) observes, "a philosopher [i.e., a Naiyāyika] gives a definition by assigning to the object . . . the defining property (*lakṣaṇa*) and by his act of definition he intends to produce some effect or consequence, i.e., an awareness in his students or readers so that they would be able to recognize or identify the object or objects defined as *distinct* from other."

13. See NV *ad* NS I, 1.4: *atha na pratyakṣam? avācakastarhi pratyakṣaśabdaḥ*.

14. Chalmers (2011). Although he thinks that all disputes in some sense retain an element of verbal disagreement, Chalmers nonetheless thinks a case could be made that there are some primitive concepts, call them "bedrock concepts," that anchor our conceptual practices. If we were to accept that "there is a privileged nondefective bedrock concept of existence," then we would have to concede the effectiveness of such concepts as descriptive categories of experience.

Responding to this objection, Śāntarakṣita starts with the observation that objects cannot always be cognized as distinct entities in the absence of linguistic reference: "The cognition that is capable of connecting a word and an object, even when words such as "tree" and the like are not actually applied, appears as being associated with verbal expression."[15] For example, when I cognize something as a leafy green branching expansion, even though I have not brought it under the category of "tree" or "live oak," I am not (or not only) perceptually attending to the object. What Śāntarakṣita is effectively saying here is that when we undergo the kind of cognitive experiences that are primarily characterized by the association of names and things, we are operating in the domain of discursive or conceptual thought. The conceptual content of discursive thought is, of course, intended by means of propositional attitudes. Regardless of whether one makes use of one word or another, discursive thought is qualitatively distinct from the direct modes of apprehension one associates with perceptual experience.

Elaborating on this point, Kamalaśīla explains that here we have a clear case of conceptual content being in fact perceptually apprehended or, more specifically, of perception having the capacity to establish not only (as we shall briefly see) the contents of awareness but also the character of this content and its associations.[16] In other words, it is only because I am immediately acquainted with the specific content and character of my mental states that I can discriminate between seeing an object and thinking about it. Although we are not explicitly told at this stage which specific mode of perception is capable of performing this function, it is reasonable to suspect that Śāntarakṣita makes an implicit allusion to self-awareness (*svasaṃvedana*) as an intrinsic aspect of all conscious cognitive events. But here Śāntarakṣita also clearly demonstrates the Buddhist epistemologist's indebtedness to Bhartṛhari, the first thinker to have systematically argued that the domains of language and conceptual thought are coextensive.[17] Bhartṛ hari plays a key role as an interpreter of the old debate, familiar to Indian grammarians, between Vājapyāyana and Vyāḍi concerning the proper basis for naming. That debate, as we saw earlier, centers on an old question that had preoccupied most grammarians after Pāṇini, namely, what is it that is primarily signified by words: universals or particulars? The debate's origins may be traced to Katyāyana's well-known aphorism on names, which Patañjali quotes in his *Mahābhāṣya* ("Great Commentary"): "The occasioning basis for the use of a name is that

15. TS 1214: *śabdārthaghaṭanāyogyā vṛkṣa ityādirūpataḥ yā vācāmaprayoge 'pi sābhilāpeva jāyate.*

16. See TSP *ad* TS 1214: *anena pratyakṣata eva kalpanāyāḥ siddhimādarśayati; sarvaprāṇābhṛtāmanu[bhava]siddhatvād vikalpasya.*

17. See VP I, 1.129: *itikartavyatā loke sarvā śabdavyapāśrayā/yāṃ pūrvāhitasaṃskāro bālo'pi pratipadyate.*

quality on whose presence a name is applied to a thing."[18] In other words, names are given to things on the basis of a quality which belongs to them (that is, to the things themselves) and not in an arbitrary manner. I will not examine in detail the complex ramification that Katyāyana's aphorism has elicited in successive generation of grammarians.[19] Recall from our earlier discussion[20] that Bhartṛhari had taken a different stand from the early grammarians on the relation between words and the things they designate. As Bhartṛhari states in the *Sambandhasamuddeśa* ("Exposition on Relation"): "Whether the object to be signified is eternal or non-eternal, a person cannot establish in any way a relation of objects with words, in the absence of a relation already created."[21] For Bhartṛhari the object is eternally connected with a word and as such is qualified by the respective word type (*śabdajāti*) but also by substance (*dravya*) and gender (*liṅga*). Moreover, all the properties of an object are simultaneously grasped in a single instance of cognition. Thus, the relation of the term to its referent in a cognitive episode in which reference is grasped is the same as that between a transitive cognitive aspect and that which it intends. Bhartṛhari takes perceptual cognition to be effectively transparent to its mode of realization: that is, the means by which perception effects its operations are not subjectively available. Bhartṛhari also contends that, just as the internal representation is causally related to the apprehended object, so too are words in a causal relationship to their imagistic representation: "The word is thus causally [related] to the object, because it (i.e., the object) becomes apparent as a result of [the word being uttered]. Similarly, the comprehension of the word [by a listener] is due to the object being an object of cognition (*buddhiviśaya*)."[22] In support

18. *Mahābhāṣya Vārttika* 5 on Pāṇini 5.1.1.19: *siddhaṃ tu yasya guṇasya bhāvād dravye śabdaniveśas tadabhidhāne*. Translation per Herzberger (1986: 26).

19. For such a detailed treatment the reader may turn to Radhika Herzberger's (1986: 9–70) excellent study, which examines Bhartṛhari's position within the Sanskrit grammarian tradition vis-à-vis Dignāga and Dharmakīrti.

20. See above chapter 3.3.

21. VP, 3III, 3.38: *nitye 'nitye 'pi vācye 'arthe puruṣeṇa kathaṃ ca na, saṃbandho'kṛtasaṃbandhaiḥ śakyate*. For a detailed discussion of this verse, see Houben (1995: 253–256). See also Biardeau (1964: 425–426) for a translation and discussion of the entire context of this stanza. As Biardeau observes, for Bhartṛhari there is a permanence that characterizes the relationship between words and objects even on the phenomenological level, though this permanence is not tied to the ontological status of the object: "Sur un plan encore 'phenomenologique', Bhartṛhari insiste d'abord sur la permanence qui caractérise les rapports de la parole et de l'objet, permanence qui est indépendante de la nature réelle et de l'existence ou de l'inexistence actuelle de l'objet externe: l'accent est mis encore une fois sur l'autonomie de la parole et sur le caractère propre de l'univers du discours" (Biardeau 1964: 425).

22. VP III, 3.32: *śabdaḥ kāraṇaṃ arthasya sa hi tenopajanyate/tathā ca buddhiviṣayād arthāc chabdaḥ pratīyate*. In his discussion of this stanza in relation to Bhartṛhari's representational theory of knowledge, Houben (1995: 246) takes the "object" (*artha*)

of the notion that conception is always associated with verbal expression, Śāntarakṣita and Kamalaśīla invoke the Abhidharma account of intentional acts. Following Vasubandhu's Abhidharmic account, an action may be defined as comprising volition (*cetanā*) and its ensuing result.[23] However, the action in fact involves two distinct types of activity: the volition itself and the intentional act (*cetayitvā*) by means of which it is realized. As Vasubandhu explains, the action itself, although conceived of as a dual process of volition and its result, in fact consists of three discrete stages: bodily, verbal, and mental action (*kāyavāṅmanaskarmāṇi*). These respectively correspond to the basis, the intrinsic nature, and the original cause of the action. These three actions, although apparently separate, in reality represent the same action viewed from three different perspectives. From the perspective of its basis, the action is grounded in the body, which serves as its instrumental basis. From the perspective of its own nature, the action consists in verbal expression. Finally, from the perspective of its originating principle, the action finds its ultimate cause in the realm of the mental.[24] Although Śāntarakṣita and Kamalaśīla do not make any explicit reference to this Abhidharma definition of intentional acts, it is plausible that Vasubandhu's conflation of verbal action with internal representation serves as a basis for the adoption by the Buddhist epistemologists of the idea that discursiveness is indissociable from conception. But Śāntarakṣita and Kamalaśīla also take into account the theories of the Sanskrit grammarians, principally the notion that language is instrumental for the development of conscious activity.[25] Of particular philosophical interest in this context is the theory of the "evocative power of words" (*dhvani*). According to this theory, words have the capacity to convey a certain image of reality, in this case, the reality of a perceptual object that is conceptually apprehended. Thus Kamalaśīla:

---

as indicating the referent (that is, the actual object) rather than the meaning. However, Ogawa (1999: 271) has proposed that the object in this stanza should be regarded as referring to the object of cognition. Note that this verse is also quoted by Śāntarakṣita in the *Śabdārthaparīkṣā*, TS 890. In his commentary on TS 891, Kamalaśīla sums up Bhartṛhari's view as endorsing a version of the correspondence theory of truth: the object's image or representation arises in the mind as corresponding to an external entity and is grasped as such—as an external entity (TSP *ad* TS 891: *anye to buddhyārūdham evākāraṃ bāhyavastuviṣayaṃ bāhyavastutayā gṛhītaṃ buddhirūpatvenāvirbhāvitam śabdārtham ahuḥ*).

23. AK 1b: *cetanā tatkṛtaṃ ca tat.*

24. See AKBh *ad* AK 1b: *kimāśrayataḥ āhosvit svabhāvataḥ samutthānato vā/ āśrayataścedekaṃ kāyakarma prāpnoti/sarveṣāṃ kāyāśritatvāt svabhāvataś cet vākkarmaikaṃ prāpnoti/vacasaḥ karmasvabhāvatvāt/samutthānataś cenmanaskarmaikaṃ prāpnoti/sarveṣāṃ manaḥ samutthitatvāt.*

25. In his commentary Kamalaśīla adds an interesting quotation from Bhartṛhari that expresses the view that activities are based on words or the ability to use language toward a certain end. See TSP *ad* TS 1215: *yathoktam—"itikarttavyatā loke sarvāśabdavyapāśrayā/yāṃ purvāhitasaṃskāro bālo'api pratipadyate."* This corresponds to *Vākyapadīya* I, 1.129.

[Conception] manifests in these [infants] also by presenting the object, which is evoked by suggestive sounds (*dhvani*) through the medium of vague syllables and existing only as internal "magic words" [that draw the attention] as if it were [something] external, [and] by virtue of this [conception] later in their life they become capable of apprehending the relevant conventions (*saṃketa*).[26]

Following the standard Sautrāntika Abhidharma account that Śāntarakṣita and Kamalaśīla appear to embrace, conception and verbal expression represent forms of activity that manifest an individual's intention to express certain ideas or engage with certain objects of experience. This intentionality springs from the continuous residual impressions (*vāsanā*) of past associations between things and names.[27] In the *Karmasiddhiprakaraṇa* ("Treatise on Action"), Vasubandhu, for instance, had expanded on the idea that impressions from past experience are instrumental in effecting the activities of the karmic continuum that are constitutive of the individual personality.[28] The difference between the Yogācāra notion of receptacle consciousness and the Brahmanical view of self is explained thus: the receptacle consciousness can provide a basis for the reception of consciousness traces (*vijñānavāsanā*), whereas a self, if conceived as singular and immutable, is incapable of providing such a support.[29] Śāntarakṣita's summary of this Abhidharma perspective on the structure of cognitive awareness is useful in framing his argument that the connection between language and conceptual thought is not a matter of conjecture but can in fact be perceptually apprehended: "As a result of the continuity of residual impressions due to the constant co-evolving of word and object (*nāmārthabhāvanā*) in his former existence, even the newly born child is capable of activity, in view of his connection with this conceptual content."[30] Elaborating on this statement, Kamalaśīla argues that direct experience

26. TSP *ad* TS 1215: *sā pūnaḥ sanmūcchitākṣarākāradhvaniviśiṣṭam antarmātrāviparivarttinamarthaṃbahirivādarśayantī teṣāṃ samupajāyate, yathā paścāt saṅketagrahaṇakuśalā bhavanti.*

27. In his exposition of the Sautrāntika perspective on the relationship between volition and action, Vasubandhu uses the example of the traces of volitional acts to suggest that the intention to engage in a certain action is not entirely determined by the present volition but also stems from the traces left by past volitional actions. An action—such as, for instance, the intention of a breaking rules—is guided by volition and by the traces left by this volitional act. See, for example, AKBh *ad* AK IV, 27d: *avijñaptivadasaṃvaro'pi nāsti dravyata iti sautrāntikāḥ/sa eva tu pāpakriyābhisaṃdhir saṃvaraḥ/sānubandhe yataḥ kuśalacitto'pi tadvānucyate.*

28. See KSP III, 2, 40.

29. Cf. Lamotte (1936: 70). As Lamotte notes in relation to the function of the receptacle of consciousness, "the mechanism of the ripening of action is to be sought in the internal evolution of the mental series. The action, which is a thought associated with a special volition, is momentary: it perishes immediately upon arising. But it 'perfumes' (*vāsanā*) the mental series (*cittasaṃtana*), which is its point of departure; it creates in it a special potentiality (*śaktiviseṣa*)" (1936: 28).

30. TS 1215: *atītabhavanāmārthabhāvanāvāsanānvayāt/sadyojāto 'pi yadyogād iti karttavyatāpaṭūḥ.*

establishes, as a matter of fact, that conceptual thought *is* associated with verbal expression, that is, that thought has an essentially discursive character.[31] For Kamalaśīla, it is direct perception that ultimately establishes the character of conception. Moreover, we can also discern in his argument both a developmental and an evolutionary perspective on consciousness, which locates the cause for the capacity to be reflexively aware in past experiences.[32] Indeed, Buddhist philosophers argue that conscious activity would be impossible without the continuum of cognitive activity from previous experience and the force of beginningless traces (*anādivāsanā*) left by these past cognitions. I shall return to this complex dispute concerning the basis of consciousness and cognition below when I examine Śāntarakṣita's notion that warranted cognitions must bring about effects that are different from their sources.

Śāntarakṣita—in seeking to demonstrate that these theories accord with the received view of the role of natural language as the medium of conceptual thought—appeals to the authority of the grammarians, in particular to Bhartṛhari's views on the identity between language and conceptual thought. As Śāntarakṣita declares, conception arises as a result of an internal desire to express oneself: "That [conception] which is clearly cognized in a moment of thinking or imagination, as if it were pervaded by words, cannot be ignored."[33] And again: "The relation between words and objects, obtained by means of conception, is erroneously superimposed. If this conception were inexistent, the said relation, even if it were of such a nature (e.g., erroneous), would not be possible, because other things, such as external objects, cannot support this relation."[34]

In arguing that conception is indistinguishable from verbal content and that discursive thinking (as opposed to, say, intuitive thinking) is driven by the rules of language comprehension, Śāntarakṣita is simply expressing a view that becomes common in the Sanskrit grammarian tradition after Bhartṛhari. Note, however, that Bhartṛhari had taken an absolute idealistic stand on the question of naming, which Śāntarakṣita and Kamalaśīla (like other Buddhist epistemologists before and indeed after them) in fact reject.

31. See TSP *ad* TS 1215: *pratyakṣata eva kalpanāyāḥ siddhimādarśayati; sarvaprāṇabhṛtāmanu[bhava]siddhatvād vikalpasya.*

32. A detailed exposition of this view is found in the *Lokāyataparīkṣa* (TS chapter X), where Śāntarakṣita and Kamalaśīla defend the notion of a continuum of consciousness against the view that consciousness arises from the elements or from a certain transformation of the elements. See TS 1885 and TSP *loc. cit.* Dharmakīrti's refutation of the same Lokāyata perspective on the bodily basis of cognition is found in PV II, 378.

33. TS 1216: *cintotprekṣādikāle ca vispaṣṭe yā pravedyate/anuviddheva sā sabdair pahnotuṃ na śakyate.*

34. TS 1217: *tasyāś cādhyavasāyena bhrāntā śabdārthayoḥ sthitiḥ/anyāyogād asattve 'syāḥ sadṛśya api na sambhavet.*

By attributing logical primacy to word universals (*śabdajāti*), Bhartṛhari maintains that external objects are named on the basis of word universals, thus indirectly suggesting that the perceptual event which occasioned the encounter with such objects does not play an indexical function in the naming process. Dignāga, as is well known, rejects Bhartṛhari's idealist stance on the application of names to things: "Although that which is expressed by a word has many properties, it is not cognized in its entirety through a word. The word performs the task of isolating its referents according to its intrinsic relations to what it expresses."[35] In what is still a disputed issue, Herzberger interprets Dignāga's statement that words cannot convey the diverse nature of objects to mean that he opposes "Bhartṛhari's doctrine that the object, 'qualified by all its qualifiers' (*sarvaviśeṣaṇaviśiṣṭaṃ*) is simultaneously given (*yugapat*) in a single utterance (*sakṛd uccāraṇa*) of a word," an opposition which ultimately reflects "Dignāga's intention of coming to terms with problems which surrounded Kātyāyana's aphorism, namely the condition that names are unrelated before they enter descriptive (*karmadhāraya*) compounds."[36]

Expanding on Śāntarakṣita's view that conception arises from some sort of inner verbal impulse, Kamalaśīla explains that the constructive aspect of language comprehension is also revealed through effective signs (*kāryaliṅga*) in the form of linguistic conventions (*śābdavyavahāra*). This means that linguistic conventions concerning the relationship between words and things provide enough evidence to conclude that conception arises from conventional language use.[37] We acquire the capacity to associate words and things as a consequence of conceptual constructive habits inherited as conditioning factors of past experience. This capacity to make associations does not in any way reflect a real correspondence between words and the objects they designate. Neither does it mean that the objects of verbal designation are nonexistent, or that no correspondence between words and things can ever be established. Rather, Kamalaśīla simply reinforces the Buddhist claim that our capacity to establish connections between words and things is a conventional, conceptual habit. The capacity to apprehend relations or establish various correspondences between words and things, name them, and infer their nomological properties[38] is a projective mental capacity.

---

35. PSV, 12: *bahudhāpyabhidheyasyanaśabdātsarvathāgatiḥ/svasambandhānurūpyeṇa vyavacchedārthakāry asau*. Translation *per* Hayes (1988: 277).

36. Herzberger (1986: 111). For detailed treatments of this issue, see Ho (1996), Hattori (1980), Katsura (1991), Pind (1991, 2009), and Siderits (1999).

37. See TSP *ad* TS 1216: *tasyāś ca ityādinā śābdavyavahārākhyakāryaliṅgato'pi siddhimāha*.

38. I take "nomological" in this context to mean something that is essentially necessary as opposed to something that is merely contingent. Examples of essentially necessary things are natural laws, such as the laws of physics. By contrast, contin-

In other words, there is no real connection between words and things, as words are mere conventional designations. In the absence of conception it is not possible to establish any connections at all, for perception can apprehend only unique particulars (not relations). Although Śāntarakṣita and Kamalaśīla regard the interpenetration of language and conceptual thought as real, they reject the notion that words designate metaphysically real universals or that there is a real relationship between words and objects. This point is made clear by Kamalaśīla, when he states that in the absence of conception, not even an illusory connection between words and things is possible:

> In such circumstances, if this conception were absent, then this connection between words and objects would not be possible even as such, that is, even as an erroneous cognition, because that [*tasyā* = connection between word and object] rests upon the intentional [aspect of conception], and because it has been already demonstrated that external things such as the particular and the like lack fitness as word objects.[39]

The denial of a real connection between words and things is also the hallmark of the Sautrāntika and the Yogācāra Abhidharma traditions whose views Śāntarakṣita and Kamalaśīla appear to endorse, though in a modified version. It is largely on the model provided by the Sautrāntikas and the Yogācāras that Śāntarakṣita and Kamalaśīla dismiss the reality of universals, reducing them to mere conceptual constructs.

6.2 PERCEPTION, CONCEPTION, AND THE PROBLEM OF NAMING

Nyāya philosophers have invoked the manifold aspects of perceptual awareness as proof that perception is capable of apprehending both real particulars and the universals that inhere in them. It is a fundamental tenet of Nyāya metaphysics that universals are not mere conceptual constructions. In evaluating the manner in which Śāntarakṣita and Kamalaśīla reject the Nyāya perspective on universals, we can begin by first identifying the context of their critique of universals as effective categories of cognition. While the Buddhist epistemologists make extensive use of the notions of "particular" and "universal," and regard them as effective semantic categories, they reject the notion (advanced chiefly by the Vaiśeṣikas) that such categories are ontic realities. Following Dignāga, the Buddhist epistemologists take cognition to

---

gency is a property of logical necessity as in the case of a disjunction whose disjuncts are contrary (either it is a sunny or it is a cloudy day).

39. TSP *ad* TS 1217: *yadi cāsyāḥ kalpanāyā asattvaṃ syāt, tadā sā—śabdārthavyavasthā, idṛśyapi—bhrāntāpi, na sambhavet; tadabhiprāyavaśāt tasyāvyayasthānāt, anyeṣāṃ ca svalakṣaṇādīnāṃ bāhyānāṃ vācyatvenāyogasya pratipāditatvāt.*

be operating in two distinct domains: that of particulars, which can only be perceptually apprehended, and that of universals, which can be apprehended by means of inferential reasoning only:

> The sources of knowledge are perception and inference because the object of cognition has only two characteristics. There is no object of cognition other than the particular characteristic and the universal characteristic because perception has as its object the particular and inference the universal characteristic of the thing.[40]

Dignāga's definition of conception, however, would prove challenging to succeeding generations of Buddhist epistemologists. As we have already noted, his definition of conception as the connection with a name or a universal retains a certain degree of ambiguity: first, about the epistemic function of conception itself, and secondly about the ontological status of conceptual objects. This ambiguity is largely responsible for subsequent attempts (by Dharmakīrti and his successors) to interpret Dignāga's stance on the relationship between language and thought as an oblique endorsement of the reality of universals—albeit understood not as shared properties, but in terms of the exclusion of the other (the "other" being the class of all homogeneous and heterogeneous objects). Dignāga's theory of semantic exclusion, as is well know, is adopted and adapted by all Buddhist epistemologists. Śāntarakṣita and Kamalaśīla's discussion of this theory is likewise primarily concerned with rejecting the reality of universals as substantive categories, and with refuting some aspects of Bhartṛhari's view on language. But Śāntarakṣita offers a novel interpretation of *apoha*: for him the "exclusion of the other" *operation* is to be understood in psychological rather than logical terms. For Śāntarakṣita, thus, a concept is associated with a specific entity on the basis of its (that is, the entity's) mode of appearance in cognition.[41]

---

40. PS I, 1: *pratyakṣam anumānam ca pramāṇea yasmād lakṣaṇadvayaṃ/prameyaṃ na hi svasāmānyalakṣaṇabhyām anyat prameyam asti/svalakṣaṇaviśayaṃ hi pratyakṣaṃ sāmānyalakṣṣaṇaviṣayaṃ anumānam iti pratipādayiṣyāmaḥ*. On this passage, I follow Herzberger (1986: 14) and van Bijlert (1989: 15) in translating *hi* in *na hi svasāmānyalakṣaṇabhyām* as "for" or "because" and not as "only" as Hattori (1968: 24) does. Although linguistically possible, accepting Hattori's translation would amount to conceding that there is a complete and unbridgeable gap between the perceptual and the conceptual domains, which I think is not tenable (considering Dignāga's overall view on names and naming). I agree with Herzberger that although the "meaning universal" (*arthasāmānya*) may be viewed as residing in its bearer (viz., "word universal" (*śabdasāmānya*)), it is not completely dissociated from its support (viz., the perceptual).

41. See, for example, TS 1005: *tān upāśritya yaj jñāne bhātyartha pratibimbakam/ kalpake'rthātmatā'bhāve'pyarthā iti eva niścitam*. For an extensive discussion of Śāntarakṣita's interpretation of *apoha*, see Hattori (1980). Hattori shows Śāntarakṣita's indebtedness to Bhartṛhari's concept of a "sudden flash of intuition" (*pratibhā*) as an example of how the meaning of words is instantly produced from both words and

In his examination of the discursive nature of conception, Śāntarakṣita appeals to the stock example of the admixture of milk and water: once completed, this process renders the two substances indistinguishable. But a Nyāya realist would admittedly claim that conception cannot be regarded as a faculty that effects connections between universals and particulars because no such connections are ever perceived: "Some consider that conceptual content is whatever enables a connection with the genus and the other categories. However, such an argument is not demonstrably valid on account of the fact that the genus, etc. have been rejected, and also because it [i.e., the universal] is never perceived."[42] In an ironic quip, Śāntarakṣita proclaims that it is precisely the non-perception of a connection between name, universal, object and so on, which proves that such a connection is unreal:[43] "Insofar as the genus and the rest are never perceived, their connection is not manifest—as in the case of an admixture of milk and water—how can their connection with an object be possible?"[44]

The point made here is obvious enough: universals are not the sort of thing that can be perceptually apprehended. The concept of height or circularity is not something I am perceptually acquainted with. Rather, such categories of thought depend on our capacity to generalize and form

sentences (see TS 1027: *pratibimbātmako'pohaḥ padādapyupajāyate/pratibhākhyo jhāṭ ity eva padārtho'pyayam eva*). Reflecting on Śāntarakṣita's use of "reflection" (*pratibimba*) as a synonym of *pratibhā*, Hattori notes, "both the sentence and the word function to produce immediately in the mind of the listener a positive image, which is expressed by the term '*pratibhā*' or '*pratibimba*.' The image is also named '*apoha*,' since it is differentiated from the image generated by the other sentences or words" (Hattori 1980: 69). As is well known, Śāntarakṣita and Kamalaśīla were criticized for this positive interpretation of *apoha*. Siderits sums up quite well the implications of Śāntarakṣita's innovative interpretation of *anyāpoha* as involving a double negation (a *prasajya* and a *paryudasa*): "The issue of psychological feel of verbal comprehension is something of a red herring for the Apohavādin, since the *apoha* account is meant to explain the causal processes involved in using kind terms, and not how those processes will feel to the cognizer" (Siderits 1999: 348). But as I argued above, the causal account and the first-person account of conceptual apprehension are not easily unhinged.

42. TS 1218: *jātyādiyojanāyogyām api anye kalpanāṃ viduḥ/sā jātyāder apāstatvād adṛṣṭeś ca na saṅgatā*.

43. It should be noted that this non-perception, is not a positive perception of an absence (*anupalabdhi*), which is a different cognitive capacity, but simply the absence of any perceivable or conceivable connection between words and things. Śāntarakṣita and Kamalaśīla discuss the concept of negative perception or perception of negative facts in their refutation of various other sources of knowledge in the *Pramāṇāntarabhāvaparīkṣā*. See also Kellner (1997) and Taber (2003) for recent discussions of the notion of negative cognition in Indian philosophy.

44. TS 1219: *jātyādīnāmadṛṣṭa tvāt tadyogāpratubhāsanāt/kṣīrodakādivac cārthe ghaṭā ghaṭate katham*. As Funayama (1992: 71 n. 87) notes, this is an allusion to an example used by Dharmakīrti in his PVin I, 44, 11–14. See also Franco (1997: 499 n. 298) for an alternative translation of this verse, which emphasizes the notion that universals lack the pragmatic power to effect connections with their substratum.

abstractions. Adopting a typical conceptualist stance, Śāntarakṣita takes the imperceptibility of universals as proof that any connection between universals and particulars—the presumed pervasion of the object by a universal that is a central tenet of Nyāya epistemology—is at best apparent, nothing but the product of imagination, for universals can never be empirically established:

In order to specify which one is to be accepted and which one to be rejected, two kinds of conceptual content have been ascertained [to exist by Dignāga] (i.e., that which establishes a relation between names and objects (viz., reference) and that which establishes a relation between words and their meanings), corresponding to views held by our own party and by the opponents.[45]

The "connection with a name, etc." persists in one's mind after it has indicated the immediate cause of this conception itself. Hence, the assertion [made by Dignāga] is not irrelevant.[46]

Thus, in response to the opponent's rejection of conceptualism (that is, of the notion that a connection between universals and objects can be effected only by means of conception), Śāntarakṣita (following Dignāga) claims that the non-perception of universals provides sufficient grounds for treating all so-called connections between universals and particulars as fictitious. Words and descriptive categories are applied to things not in virtue of any real principle of reference but merely on the basis of conceptual conventions that reflect established practice. Examples such as that of the homogeneous mixture of milk and water are cited as illustrations for the conceptualist position: in thinking about a particular object or state of affairs we are effectively bringing them under a given concept or category, which can act as a placeholder. In reality, however, such taxonomic sorting through the elements of experience leaves no trace or imprimatur. Commenting on this example, Kamalaśīla explains that the absence of a connection with universals, whether in thought or in language, is postulated by virtue of the fact that universals are never perceived as separate from their substratum:

Like in [a mixture of] milk and water, etc., [means]: When milk and water, having been mixed up, do not appear as separate, it is not possible to connect them. Similarly, even if the universal and the rest did exist, they are never distinguished from their

---

45. TS 1220: *heyopādeyaviṣayakathanāya dvayoktitaḥ/parāparaprasiddheyaṃ kalpanā dvividhoditā.*

46. TS 1221: *nāmādiyojanā ceyaṃ svanimittam anantaraṃ/ākṣipya varttate yena tena nāprastutābhidhā.* In the above verse *aprastuta* is rendered usually as "irrelevant" or "not to the point." In this context the case concerns something that is viewed as a general assertion by stating only a particular instance.

substratum; hence it is impossible for them (i.e., the universal and the rest) [to be connected] with their substratum.[47]

In other words, we observe that in nature some substances mix in such a way that the resulting product is not a conglomerate of parts but an organic whole. As an emergent property of the physical domain, wholeness is not a product of parts being assembled together as they are brought under a specific category (as is the case for chairs and tables). Kamalaśīla's appeal to empirical observation extends to the domain of the mental: our categorizing practices must, by virtue of our participation in the order of the causal domain, reflect the dynamic, self-organizing, and emergent nature of agency. Entities are categorized as belonging in certain classes not by virtue of there being a natural connection between universals and particulars, but simply because they form an object of categorization. Is Dignāga's definition of conception (as a cognition that is associated with both propositions and words designating universals) thus misguided? Such, at least, is the opponent's claim: "In this case, if conception, as a cognition that is associated with the universal and the rest, cannot be defined in this way, why did the author of the definition (i.e., Dignāga) assert that conception consists in the connection with a name, universal and so on?"[48]

Note that this criticism is coming from a Naiyāyika and, in framing their responses, Śāntarakṣita and Kamalaśīla are careful to avoid the notion of inherence (*samavāya*). Their reasoning in this context is apparently quite straightforward: whatever does not appear as separate from its substratum cannot be separated from it, since any thought of separation *is* a case of conceptual elaboration and thus cannot be a proof for the existence of universals.[49]

However, a more important objection raised against the view that universals are mere conceptual fictions concerns the fact that they are nevertheless postulated (at least by Dignāga) as resulting from the association of various classes of words such as names, verbs, and so on, with perceived things, by virtue of which the latter are expressed. If, as the Buddhist claims, perception lacks the sort of determination that elicits appropriate conceptualization with regard to an object's spatio-temporal location and properties—assuming that conceptual elaboration is a property of cognition (*jñānadharma*)—then

47. TSP *ad* TS 1219: *kṣīrodakādivacceti/yathā kṣīrodakādermiśrībhūtasya vivekenāpratibhāsanān na ghaṭanā śakyate kartum, tadvajjātyadīnāṃ sattve'pi vivekenāśrayādapratibhāsanānna śakyate tadāśrayeṇa sahetyarthaḥ*.

48. TSP *ad* TS 1220: *yadi tarhi jātyādiyojanā kalpanā na yuktaiva, tat kathaṃ lakṣaṇakāreṇoktam—"nāmajātyādiyojanā kalpanā" iti?*

49. See TSP *ad* TS 1219: *kṣīrodakādivacceti/yathā kṣīrodakādermiśrībhūtasya vivekenāpratibhāsanānna ghaṭanā śakyate kartum, tadvajjātyādīnāṃ sattve'pi vivekenā'rayādapratibhāsanānna sakyate tadāśrayeṇa sahetyarthaḥ*.

the Buddhist must account for our apparent ability to discriminate objects as individuals belonging to different classes and genres. Such discrimination, argues the Naiyāyika, is only possible if the association of name, universal, and so on, is a perceptual rather than a conceptual event.

This debate, which covers an important chapter in the early development of Indian epistemology, originates in the literature of the Sanskrit grammarians. Like Dignāga, Dharmakīrti, and their Nyāya and Mīmāṃsā opponents, the grammarians held divergent views concerning the basis for naming and reference. I have already provided a summary of this debate in chapter 4 where we concluded that Dignāga's semantic theory of exclusion is partly conceived as a reaction against Bhartṛhari's strongly nominalist stance. But while he accepts Dignāga's theory of semantic exclusion, Dharmakīrti finds it insufficient for establishing the truth of universal sentences. That insufficiency, as we saw, would eventually lead him to formulate his doctrine of the two natural relations between the evidence and what is to be established thereby: identity (*tādātmya*) and causal generation (*tadutpatti*).[50] Although largely faithful to Dharmakīrti's position vis-à-vis the "natural relation" (*svabhāvapratibandha*)[51] between abstract terms, Śāntarakṣita and Kamalaśīla seem to adopt a reconciliatory position. The conundrum faced here is whether conceptual cognitions are mediated by reference to real universals—ones inherent in the substratum of objects—or simply to different classes of names that belong exclusively in language. Their solution is simply to split the "*nāmajātyādiyojanā*" compound (that is, the possessive compound "the connection with a name, universal, and so on"), and state that the connection with the universal is to be rejected, while the connection with the name is to be preserved as the correct view: "Here, what is to be rejected refers to conceptual content as the connection with a universal, which is the view held by the opponents; and what is to be accepted refers to conceptual content as connection with a name, which is the view held by our own party."[52] In support of this view they quote Dharmakīrti's unambiguous statement that conception is essentially that cognition which is associated with a verbal expression.[53] Glossing on this statement, Kamalaśīla identifies "the

50. A first formulation of this doctrine is found in PV I, 40–42: *sarve bhāvāḥ svabhāvena svasvabhāvavyavasthiteḥ/svabhāvaparabhāvābhyāṃ yasmād vyāvṛttibhāginaḥ//tasmād yato yato 'rthānāṃ vyāvṛttis tannibandhanāḥ/jātibhedāḥ prakalpyante tadviśeṣāvagāhinaḥ//tasmād yo yena dharmeṇa viśeṣaḥ sampratīyate/na sa śakyas tato 'nyena tena bhinnā byavasthitiḥ.*

51. For discussions of Dharmakīrti's reason concerning essential nature (*svabhāvapratibandha*), see Steinkellner (1973, 1991a), Oetke (1991), Hayes (1987), Iwata (1991), and Dunne (2004: 145–222).

52. TSP *ad* TS 1220: *tatra heyā jātyādiyojanā paraprasiddhā kalpanā, upādeyā svaprasiddhā nāmayojanākalpanā.*

53. See PVin as quoted in TS 1222: *nāmajātyādayaḥ sarve yojyante vānayeti sā/ tathoktā kalpanā proktā pratītir abhilāpini.*

connection with a name, universal, and so on" compound as a *bahuvrīhi*,[54] that is, as a nominal compound in which the two terms involved, "name" and "universal," are not related. What this compound names is not directly designated by either term:

> The indication of that immediate cause is achieved in two ways. "That [conception] by means of which the connection between the two [i.e., name and universal] is brought about" is how the compound "the connection of name, universal, and so on" is explained. This is a nominal compound, even when the substratum of name and universal are not the same, because the compound indicates conceptual elaboration or [also] because the effect is attributed to the cause in a figurative way.[55]

It is not exactly clear why Śāntarakṣita interprets Dignāga's use of this compound the way he does. Reflecting on this issue, Eli Franco takes the view that by splitting the compound as such the Buddhist is simply restating his commitment to rejecting the reality of universals. Franco takes Śāntarakṣita's reluctance to read Dignāga as endorsing the reality of universals as suggestive of a misattribution and invites us to consider that perhaps that portion of the text might in fact "express the thought of an opponent."[56] In other words, just because some object distinguished by a universal is designated by a word or a verbal compound does not mean that this sort of propositional content renders the universal a mere linguistic or conceptual fiction. Thus, Franco: "If we say that a thing qualified by a quality such as white is expressed by the word 'white', do we imply that the quality white does not exist? Certainly not."[57] The problem, as I see it, is not whether words lack a connection to the things they designate, but whether we should conclude that an account of the effectiveness of linguistic practices actually necessitates any real connection of words with universals. As I will argue at length in the next chapter, phenomenal concepts operate such that their extensional properties (viz., reference, truth-conditions, etc.) are always implicit. For instance color terms, as phenomenal concepts, become effective as taxonomic categories only when instantiated by phenomenal experiences of color.

---

54. In Sanskrit grammar a *bahuvrīhi* (lit. "much rice") is an exocentric or attributive compound whose function is to characterize an entity without either its constituent terms directly naming it. The compound describes "he whose rice is abundant," in other words, a "rich person." Other examples include such compounds as *kṛtakārya* ("he by whom his purpose is achieved" = a facilitator) and *cintāpara* ("he for whom thought is the highest" = lost in thought). In English we may cite such common examples as *loudmouth*, *highbrow*, *half-wit*, etc.

55. See TSP *ad* TS 1221: *tasyākṣepo dvābhyāṃ prakārābhyām/nāmādīnāṃ yojanā yato bhavati sā rathoktā/gamakatvād vaiyadhikaraṇye'pi ca bahuvrīhiḥ*.

56. Franco (1984: 394).

57. Franco (1984: 394)

Given that all nouns in the compound are in the instrumental case, they play the role of instruments (*karaṇabhūta*): that is, universals are simply conceptual devices by means of which things are discerned as such, even if ultimately it is words that afford that discerning—in the form of verbal reports of the contents of experience. That universals are merely instrumental is true, regardless of whether one adopts a Fodorian language of thought model (a mentalese)[58] or simply contends that thought is intrinsically verbal in character. Whether Śāntarakṣita's interpretation of the "connection of name, universal, and so on" compound is meant to bring Dignāga's definition of conception closer to that of Dharmakīrti is a matter of conjecture. Śāntarakṣita's main concern may simply be to defend the notion that universals are unreal, even though Dignāga's statement could also suggest the contrary.[59] At least for now, how it is that linguistic conventions and conceptual habits translate into effective actions must remain an open question.

The notion that we refer to things simply as a result of establishing a connection between the thing and its corresponding name, and not in virtue of any relation of inherence between word and object, is at the core of the semantic theory of the Buddhist epistemologists. Śāntarakṣita and Kamalaśīla are not particularly original in assuming that universals must play an instrumental role in any theory of meaning. The usefulness of categories such as proper names, verbs, adjectives, and arbitrary words is made obvious by the fact that they provide a systematic and effective way of describing experience without thereby implying that as signifiers of conceptual content they have more than a nominal existence. This observation is especially pertinent to the issue of how classes of words such as proper names are applied to persons. While assuming that the definition of conception as the connection of names with things, in virtue of which the latter are designated, may hold true for natural kinds, the opponent regards such a definition as too narrow (*avyāpin*) to serve as a proper basis for the application of proper names to persons, since proper names, unlike words designating qualities and actions, do not perform the same instrumental function. In other words, the arbitrary name Ḍittha contains no description of the character of the person bearing that name other than as a generic indication of class or cast provenance. Proper names are convenient designations the purpose of which is to foster a sense of identity and facilitate interpersonal relations in the social sphere. For Kamalaśīla, as for all Buddhist philosophers, there is an added dimension to the arbitrariness of proper names: they cannot convey the sense of

58. See Fodor (1975).

59. In his translation of the relevant paragraph of PSV, Franco proposes that we take *viśiṣta* to be a predicate rather than an attribute of the object, as Śāntarakṣita does (Franco 1984: 396–397). On Franco's reading of this compound, genus-words (*jātiśabda*) are distinguished by a genus (*jāti*), quality-words (*guṇaśabda*) by a quality (*guṇa*), and so on.

change, transformation, and becoming that is in keeping with the Buddhist metaphysical principle of momentariness. As he notes:

> Words such as "Ḍittha," which are known as proper names, cannot denote that entity whose unique characteristics are marked by momentary variations; they denote the universal as inherent in that entity only insofar as that universal inheres in an entity within the bounds of a certain timeframe. For otherwise, how could a proper name, without [also] denoting a universal, having been applied to an individual at a certain stage [of her life] such as childhood, can also denote the same individual in old age? Even those who hold the opinion that the body is not momentary, but endures through different stages [of life] have to admit that in the course of time an ever different biological nature (*anyadravyam*) manifests, in virtue of whose manifestation, and the aging of its component parts, the body at a later stage of life is different from that at an earlier stage. Even on the view that it is the same body which undergoes transformation [through aging], the name associated with the body at a certain stage of its development cannot denote the same body at a further stage of development. [For example, just as] the word "milk," which has the capacity to denote milk in its fresh stage, is not applicable to curd, so also in the case of the body, names [applied to it in childhood] cannot be applied [to it] in youth or old age.[60]

Kamalaśīla uses this example to suggest that proper names do not naturally pick out individual persons, nor do they entail descriptions that count as the meaning of the name. Dignāga's view that names only apply to unique particulars (in this case, to unique persons) still holds true (assuming, of course, that persons can be understood as unitary or singular entities). Whether universals exist or not has no bearing, for this reason, on the operations of cognition at the conceptual level. In effect, conceptual elaborations do not depend upon the reality of universals or their inherence in real particulars. Rather, they depend upon practical conventions derived from observations of the manner in which phenomenal entities are perceptually disclosed.

Summing up his defense of the notion that words—which refer to natural kinds such as cows—denote both universals and unique particulars, the opponent's criticism is that without a proper rule for distinguishing natural kinds from linguistic conventions, there is no proper base for the applications

60. TSP *ad* TS 1225: *etad uktaṃ bhavati—ye'pyete ḍitthādayaḥ śabdā yadṛcchāśabdatvena pratītāḥ, te'pi janmanaḥ prabhṛtyāmaraṇakṣaṇad anuvarttamānāḥ pratikṣaṇabhed abhinnamasādhāraṇabhedena vastu gamayitumaśaktāḥ kālaprakarṣam aryādāvacchinna vastusamavetāṃ jātimabhidheyatveno pādadate, anyathā hi bālādya vasthābheda paricchinnavastu bhagavaṣayatayā nirūḍhāḥ kathaṃ vṛddhādya vasthopahitabhedamapi vastu pratipādayeyuḥ/yeṣāmapi "na kṣaṇiko dehaḥ, kiṃ tarhi? kālāntarāvasthāyī" iti darśanam, teṣamapi yathākālamapacīyamānāvayasambandhād, avayavāpacayādvā, anyad dravyamavasthābhedeṣviti siddham.*

of names to things.[61] This criticism primarily targets Dignāga's semantic theory of exclusion, namely the view that words apply to things through exclusion of all other possibilities, rather than by virtue of any relation of inherence. Neither Śāntarakṣita nor Kamalaśīla expand on this issue here,[62] having already offered a critical investigation of various views on universals, primarily those of Uddyotakara, Bhāvivikta, and Kumārila elsewhere in the *Compendium* and its *Commentary*.[63] Here, they simply contend that naming reflects actual popular usage, rather than any intrinsic relationship between names and the specific objects that they purportedly pick.

Having so far considered the manner in which words relate to things and having defended the notion that common names rather than real universals are apprehended in conception, Śāntarakṣita turns to a passage from Dignāga's *Nyāyamukha* ("Introduction to Reasoning"), which defines cognition as an apprehension associated with words: "Thus, the passage from the *Introduction to Reasoning* should be explained in the same manner. The use of the form "cognition" is meant to indicate that what is apprehended is a conception associated with verbal expression."[64] Kamalaśīla interprets this notion as implying that perception is that cognition of the form of things which lacks the conceptual propensity toward attributing determination based on qualifying and denotative adjuncts (*viśeṣaṇa-abhidhāyaka-abhedaupacāreṇa*). In other words, perception lacks the capacity to apprehend qualifying and denotative adjuncts, which serve as the basis for categorizing entities under the token-type distinction. This capacity, like the ability to apprehend differences, is conceptual in character and reflects not the natural order of things but the logical order in which things are categorized by a mind engaged in conceptualization.[65] Kamalaśīla offers the following argument summing up Dignāga's view on the distinction between the two fundamental modes of knowing, perception and conception:

The following view is thus stated: When [Dignāga] mentions that a cognition is "sensory perception" in contradistinction to conception, he clearly indicates that conception is (also) a property of cognition. What is meant by this passage is that "that cognition which is devoid of conception in terms of a false imposition of identity in relation to a name is sensory perception." On the other hand, that cognition which is determinate and of the nature of conception is not sensory perception. The semantic

61. See TS 715–719 and TSP *loc. cit.*
62. A detailed defense of the Dignāga's theory of semantic exclusion is offered in chapter XVI, where Śāntarakṣita and Kamalaśīla examine and criticize Kumārila's views on language.
63. See TS 707–821 and TSP *loc. cit.*
64. TS 1236: *evam Nyāyamukhagrantho vyākhyātavyo diśānayā/jñānam ity abhisambandhāt pratītis tatra coditā.*
65. See TSP *ad* TS 1236.

implication [of these statements] is that conception, in contrast to sensory perception, consists in the [cognitive] association with a verbal expression.[66]

Kamalaśīla thus proposes that determination (*vikalpakatva*) be taken as the criterion for distinguishing perception from conception.[67] This proposal is in keeping with Śāntarakṣita's view that the qualifying property (*viśeṣaṇa*), which may also refer to differentiation, is indicative of conceptual cognitions. Indeed, it is precisely through the exclusion of other possibilities (*anyāpoha*) that words effect the differentiating operation and not by recourse to universals.[68] Kamalaśīla elaborates this point further when he explains that it is by means of word particulars (rather than universals) that differentiation occurs. Word particulars indicate their objects directly by excluding all other possibilities, for words acquire their signifying capacity from conventional usage and not through any property that inheres in the designated thing.

Moreover, as we saw earlier, Śāntarakṣita rejects the notion that "conception" and "being expressed by words" are in any way identical. Thought depends on language for some of its operations, but it is not confined to it. Imagistic and symbolic processes, though also conceptual in character, are not however verbally realized. The thrust of this argument is that certain phenomenal concepts pick out entities and properties that are not determined by their verbal form. Otherwise, as Śāntarakṣita quips, even sensory experiences of colors and odors would be treated as linguistic constructs. This observation comes in the context of his rejection of the notion that an object of perceptual awareness acquires determination by means of verbal indexicality:

> Even if that [sensory perception] is expressed with the aid of words such as "*adhyakṣa*" and similar words, it is not inconsistent with the fact that in sense-perception conceptual content is absent, the reason being that "conceptual content" does not

66. TSP *ad* TS 1236: *etaduktaṃ bhavati—kalpanāvaiparītyena jñānameva pratyakṣatvena darśayatā jñānadharmatvaṃ kalpanāyā darśitam/tathā cāyamartho bhavati—yajjñāṃ nāmādyabhedopacāreṇāvikalpakam, tat pratyakṣam; yattu jñānaṃ tathāvikalpakaṃ tat kalpanātmakatvān na pratyakṣam iti sāmarthyādabhilāpinī pratītiḥ kalpaneti pratyakṣavaiparītyena sidhyati.*

67. Note that the Sanskrit word for designating something "determinate," *vikalpa*, is a cognate of *kalpanā*, which in this context stands for conception or conceptual cognition. In addition, *vikalpa* can also mean doubt, uncertainly, or error, thus implying that the capacity for error, in an epistemic sense, is primarily characteristic of conceptual cognitions. If perception is defined as free of conception, then it is also, by definition, free from error. We will return to the issue of mistaken cognitions below as we examine Kamalaśīla's analysis of illusory cognitions.

68. See TS 1237: *yadvā viśeṣaṇā medo yenānyāpohakṛcśrutiḥ/jātyādīnāṃ vyavacchedamanena ca karotyayam.*

imply "expressed by words." Otherwise, colors, odors and the rest would appear as conceptual constructions.[69]

In other words, even though sensory perception is expressed with the aid of phenomenal concepts, and phenomenal concepts can be abstracted from experience and used as a basis for conceptual meaning, this does not mean that perception *qua* sensory awareness is thereby conceptually constrained by the referents of action verbs such as *seeing* or *hearing*.[70] Different languages have different words and expressions for phenomenal concepts that are deployed to describe the phenomenal content and character of experience, but these terms are not constitutive of perception *qua* direct sensory apprehension.

Besides emphasizing the difference between the nonspecific use of phenomenal concepts and perceptual apprehension, this passage also implies that perception and conception are distinct modes of cognition: as a direct mode of apprehension, perception gives us the particular as perceived, that is, as an entity within the horizon of awareness, whose appearance does not entirely depend upon its actual properties (and any additional factors), but is also determined by its mode of givenness; conception, by contrast, apprehends an object as falling under a specific category (genus, species, and so on). But the Naiyāyikas are not entirely unjustified in taking issue with Dignāga's view that the cognitive content of direct perception is inexpressible. It is obvious that we *do* have the capacity to report the contents of empirical awareness. In seeing a white lotus I see an object pervaded by a certain color, evenly spread across a specific lotuslike volume, and positioned within a determined region of my perceptual horizon. What is less obvious, however, is whether our verbal reports capture the implicit, immediate, and multifaceted character of our perceptual experience. The Nyāya argument, first articulated by Uddyotakara, runs as follows:

Others [i.e., Dignāga] have offered another definition of perception: Perception is that [cognition] which is free from conceptual elaboration.... It [i.e. perception] means the connection with name and universal.... These authors should be asked the following question: First, what is denoted by the word "direct perception" [in Dignāga's definition]? If it is direct perception [that is thus denoted], then why is it

69. TS 1238–1240: *evaṃ pratītirūpā ca yadaivaṃ kalpanā matā/tādātmyapratiṣedhaś ca pratyakṣasyopavarṇyate//tadādhyakṣādiśabdena vācyatve 'pi na bādhyate/kalpanāviraho 'dhyakṣe na hi sā śabdavācyatā//anyathā rūpagandhādeḥ savikalpakatā bhavet/ato nāspadam evedaṃ yad āhuḥ kudhiyaḥ pare.*

70. Indeed, the Sanskrit word *pratyakṣa* (lit. "that which is before (*prati-*) the eye (*akṣa*)") does not determine the experience of what it is like to see, hear, or feel, anymore than the Latin verb *percipere* (lit. "to seize, obtain, or understand," from *per* + *capere*) or its English form *perception*, have a fixed set of referents.

considered as inexpressible? If, on the other hand, it is not direct perception [that is thus meant], then, the word "direct perception" becomes meaningless (*avācaka*). Furthermore, if it is held that direct perception denotes a generic thing, we ask: [First,] is this generic thing something other than, or identical to, direct perception?... Second, if the expression "free from conception" denotes direct perception, then this definition is contradictory; and if, on the contrary, it is not denoted [by that expression], then the expression "free from conception," even in that instance, is meaningless. Third, [the definition] "perception is that [cognition] which is free from conception" is a sentence. What does this sentence refer to? If it refers to direct perception [as a determined cognition, then] it is contradictory. Why? Because direct perception is actually denoted by the sentence "direct perception is free from conception" and yet [according to this definition] it is referred to as inexpressible.... If, on the other hand, it is not direct perception that is [thus] denoted, then the statement "direct perception is that [cognition] which is free from conception" is just meaningless words.[71]

As we saw above, Kamalaśīla counters the Naiyāyika's criticism that language determines the content of experience by reinforcing the separation between two different cognitive modalities (perception and conception) created by the different kinds of objects that they intend. Kamalaśīla thus defends Dignāga's view that only nonconceptual modes of cognitive awareness warrant the label "perception." In other words, whether we use the Sanskrit term *pratyakṣa* or its English cognate *perception*, we must not lose sight of the fact that as a phenomenal concept "perception" is the intentional object of a specific mode of cognitive awareness. It is not (or not only) a descriptive category whose meaning can be established by definition. Phenomenal concepts that include action verbs such as "seeing" or "looking up" have their reference determined by phenomenal descriptions. The Buddhist position is that as

71. NV *ad* NS I, 1.4: *apare tu manyante pratyakṣaṃ kalpanāpoḍham iti/... nāmajātiyojaneti/... te idaṃ praṣṭavyāḥ—atha pratyakṣaśabdena ko'rtho'bhidhīyate iti? yadi pratyakṣam? kathamavācyam/atha na pratyakṣam? avācakastarhi pratyakṣaśabdaḥ/atha pratyakṣaśabdena sāmānyamucyata iti, etadapi sāmānyaṃ kim pratyakṣavyatirekyāhros vadavyatirekīti?/... atha nocyate, tathāpi kalpanāpoḍhavacanaṃ vyartham, pratyakṣaṃ kalpanāpoḍham iti ca vākyam/athāsya vākyasya ko'rthaḥ? yadi pratyakṣam? vyāghāptaḥ/ katham? pratyakṣaṃ kalpanāpoḍham iti cānena vākyenābhidhīyate/.../atha na pratyakṣamasyārthaḥ, varṇeccāraṇamātraṃ tarhyetadvākyaṃ pratyakṣaṃ kalpanāpoḍham iti.* Echoing this classical debate between the Naiyāyikas and the Buddhists on the status of perceptual knowledge, Matilal asks the same question with a modern audience in mind: "Does the mere ability to put things into words involve inference, but not necessarily an awareness of what they express? If our answer is affirmative, do we have to accept the consequence that the mute can only see and never infer? Is every case of seeing a case of inference? Is it only a matter of variation in the degree, to which our seeings are 'recognized' as inference? Does cognition necessarily involve some minimal processing of information? Can there be pure sensations which are cognitive but not necessarily interpretative?" (Matilal 1986: 256).

recognitory notions, phenomenal concepts are conceptually irreducible: one cannot acquire the notion of "that which is before the eye" (the literal meaning of *pratyakṣa*) by a priori postulation and definition, for it is not possible to provide an account of phenomenal concepts in non-phenomenal terms.[72]

6.3 PHENOMENAL CONTENT, PHENOMENAL CHARACTER, AND THE PROBLEM OF REFERENCE

Simply pointing to the constitutive difference between what it is like to perceive and any descriptive account thereof is not, however, sufficient to persuade the Naiyāyikas that their epistemology is grounded in a specific notion of what perception can and should disclose. Whether perceiving entails any determination or, on the contrary, represents a direct and unmediated horizon of givenness, cannot be decided by rigorous conceptual analysis. It is the experience of perception itself, rather than any theoretical assumptions about it, which must serve as the referent for our use of the term "perception."[73] It is largely this debate about whether descriptive uses of language and conceptual analysis should be tied to experience that is at the heart of the dispute between the Buddhists and their opponents. Indeed, without agreement about the extension, content, and character of perceptual experience, and about its relation to other cognitive modalities, philosophical disagreements about the meaning and proper use of epistemic categories become merely verbal disputes.[74]

In common usage, "perception" is often substituted for any of its sensory modalities. For instance, in the expression "I feel he must be right because his argument makes sense," "feeling" picks out the notion that one perceives

72. For an account of phenomenal concepts as descriptive categories of experience, see Papineau (1993), Perry (2001), and Tye (1995, 2000).

73. Although this may seem to be just another issue of terminology, in reality it reflects the divide between the Sanskrit grammarians on the proper status of the linguistic sign (*liṅga*). As we saw above, the Buddhist epistemologists ground their semantic theories on Dignāga's theory of semantic exclusion. Whether words designate real particulars or merely constitute a verbal indication (*vāgvijnapti*) of the speaker's intention (*buddhirūpa*) is a debated issue. Unlike Dignāga, Dharmakīrti rejects the notion that the theory of semantic exclusion also holds for word universals (*śabdasāmānya*), limiting its application only to word particulars (*śabdaviśeṣa*). In Dignāga's case, the operation of exclusion of the other (*anyāpoha*) applies both to word particulars and word universals, in large measure because Dignāga opposes Bhartṛhari's distinction between nouns (which share an invariable relation (*avinābhāva*) with the meaning they convey) and merely articulated sounds (*dhvani*). By reinstating the view that the operation of exclusion applies to both word particulars and word types, Śāntarakṣita and Kamalaśīla, it seems, follow Dignāga rather than Dharmakīrti. See TS 1085–1086 and TSP *loc. cit.*

74. For a detailed discussion of the difference between merely verbal and presumably substantive philosophical disputes, including the issue of whether such a distinction is even tenable, see Chalmers (2011).

a reason for why a certain state of affairs is the case. Similarly, one may say, "I can now see why he left the party," after being given some explanation about the political views of its new leader. These cases of perception are different from those in which seeing refers to the direct apprehension of an object, as in "I see the sky is clearing." Matilal, in discussing the ambiguities inherent in the common use of words denoting direct perception, makes an interesting observation that is quite relevant to my interpretation of how the Buddhist epistemologists explain the role of perception:

> Consider the following. I see the new edition of the Encyclopedia at the corner of the bookcase from this chair. My daughter presumably sitting in the same chair sees the Encyclopedia (or, probably, those books her Daddy calls the Encyclopedia). A Sherlock Holmes would see not only the new edition, but probably, also the Oxford shop from which the volumes were purchased and perhaps even that they had not been used by me for the last six months![75]

The implication, as Matilal aims to illustrate in his example, is that "seeing" or "perceiving" in this common nonphilosophical sense "involves varying degrees of inference."[76] This position, which has been advocated by Naiyāyikas from Uddyotakara to its modern exponents, is given a new twist by Matilal, who suggests that even direct perception is in some way mediated by inferential and conceptual processes that are not noticeable in the first instance:

> Whenever I look in that direction, I almost instantaneously see that there is the new edition [i.e., of the Encyclopedia]. Arguably, I do not now even have to "notice" the particular color-tint (*rūpa*) of those volumes in order to see that there are those volumes. How about my nine-year-old daughter's perception? Is it not easily decidable as an inference... How about a baby, who has just learned to speak a few words among which the word encyclopedia is not included? In such cases, we would be reluctant to impute inference.

Matilal's contention is that the difference between perception and conception may be one of degree rather than kind, for if inference were confined to discursive thought alone, then persons with underdeveloped linguistic or inferential cognitive capacities would not be able to form perceptual judgments. Recent studies of the interplay between perception and conception seem to suggest that this intuition is unfounded in at least one aspect: the dependency relation between perception and conception, though mutually constraining, seem to be grounded in perceptual rather than conceptual processes.[77] Although abstract and modality-free conceptual use is central to inferential reasoning, it depends on perceptual representations, since it is the

75. Matilal (1986: 255).
76. Matilal (1986: 255).
77. See Barsalou (1999, 2005, 2009) and Goldstone and Barsalou (1998).

latter that guide conceptualization and constrain its use. As proponents of perception-based theories of concepts argue, the radical separation between similarity-based systems (which ground conception in perceptual similarities) and rule-based systems (which anchor conceptual cognitions in abstract reasoning) is based on a reading of the empirical data that is strongly biased by intuitions about the autonomy of higher forms of abstract thought.[78]

The evidence from cognitive neuroscience and experimental philosophy is that perceptual processes play a far greater role in abstract reasoning than hitherto thought.[79] The *perceptual symbols systems* theory of cognition,[80] for instance, advances the view that perceptual representations, which are to be understood as subconscious and subpersonal, thus implicit, are constitutive of all forms of knowledge, not just of perceptual modes of cognitive awareness. Human knowledge, on this model, "contains no non-perceptual representations."[81] Goldstone and Barsalow's brief summary of this model of cognition is worth citing in full:

> These perceptual representations are not necessarily holistic. Instead, a perceptual representation can be a schematic aspect of a perceptual state extracted with selective attention and stored in long-term memory. For example, selective attention might focus on the form of an object, storing only its shape in memory and not its color, texture, position, size and so forth. This schematic extraction process not only operates on sensory states, it also operates on internal mental events, extracting aspects of representational states, cognitive operations, motivational states and emotions. Once these schematic perceptual representations become established in memory, they can function as symbols. They can refer to entities in the world, they can combine productively using combinatoric and recursive mechanisms and they can implement propositional construal of situations.[82]

Although we may disagree, on phenomenological grounds, with Goldstone and Barsalow's view that perceptual cognitions are not holistic, the notion

78. For a review of review of the evidence in support of this distinction, see Shanks and St. John (1994), and Sloman (1996).

79. See contributions on a variety of central issues such as moral and abstract reasoning, in Knobe and Nichols (2008). Experimental philosophy is just another extension of the enterprise of naturalizing epistemology by uncovering the psychological processes that underlie everyday judgments about a variety of epistemic norms.

80. See, especially, Barsalou (1999).

81. Goldstone and Barsalou (1998: 234).

82. Goldstone and Barsalou (1998: 235). Drawing primarily from research on the cognitive neuroscience of perception, Prinz (2002, 2007) has been one of the most influential proponents of the view that all mentality (including all conceptual modes of apprehension) is perceptually based. Recently, Prinz has gone as far as to defend the view that "all consciousness is perceptual consciousness, and hence located at the intermediate level of our perceptual systems" (2011: 178). It is a similar sort of view that I take the Buddhist epistemologists to be advocating in their defense of the primacy of our perceptual modes of cognitive awareness.

that attentional and motivational factors play an essential role in perception deserves serious consideration. As we saw in our analysis of the Abhidharma account of perception, sensory activity requires attention for a cognitive event to become an instance of perceptual apprehension. A later discussion of the dual-aspect nature of cognition advanced by the Buddhist epistemologists will make clear the intuition that perceptual awareness is inherently reflexive; an insight that suggests an interesting correspondence with the view that conceptual thought is grounded in symbolic schemas that encode perceptual information. By taking perception to be a warranted cognition only insofar as it operates in a nonconstructive mode, the Buddhist assumes that perceiving is a form of implicit knowing. Conceptual cognition may extend this knowing to classes of objects that fall outside the domain of immediate apprehension, but this indirect, inferential mode of knowing is pragmatic and context-based.

The more relevant question, for now, concerns not whether perception and conception are constitutively different (something which, at least from the point of view of the Buddhist epistemologists, is settled in the affirmative), but rather the ways in which they differ. We might ask: on what basis are Dignāga, Dharmakīrti, and their interpreters justified in asserting that perception does not involve any interpretive processes? To answer this question, Śāntarakṣita and Kamalaśīla appeal to the phenomenal aspects of direct experience, namely to the fact that perception and conceptual discrimination are not always coupled. To illustrate this point they cite the common experience of mind wandering while still maintaining interest in a given perceptual object: "Sensory perception is clearly cognized to be 'free from conceptual content,' because even when one's mind is interested in other [objects], one perceives the blue color and other phenomena through his [other] sensory organs."[83] What we have here is a standard example of cognitive decoupling, namely, the notion that one's train of thought need not, and indeed often does not, align with the content of one's perceptions. It is only to the extent that perception and conception intend the same object that these two distinct cognitive modalities can be aligned at all. The intended object in this case is the object *as perceived* or *as conceived*. The proof that cognition has this intentional character—that is, that it always manifests in the form of a subjective aspect intending an objective aspect—is advanced on the basis of evidence from introspective modes of cognizing such as yogic perception. Introspective awareness reveals that there are states of mind in which there can be a direct apprehension of phenomena without any conceptual activity. Dharmakīrti puts forward precisely such a view:

The proof that perception is devoid of conceptual elaborations is to be found in perception itself. Conceptualizations are grounded in names and are individually established in themselves. By withdrawing one's mind from the [external] objects

83. TS 1242: *pratyakṣam kalpanāpoḍhaṃ vedyate 'tiparisphuṭam/ anyatrāsaktamanasāpy akṣair nīlādivedanāt.*

> one abides calmly in oneself. In this state, a cognition is born from the senses [and] is seen by the mind as form. [When] thoughts gradually return, one [is capable] of identifying one's own conceptual elaborations [and recognize] that the previous conceptual state did not come from the senses.[84]

Dharmakīrti argues for the existence of nonconceptual states on phenomenological rather than logical grounds. He defends the notion that perception is a form of nonconceptual sensing in which there is cognitive awareness but no interpretation of, or judgment based on, the contents of this awareness. Through a process similar to the Husserlian *epoché*, perceptual judgments and conceptualizations are apprehended as constituting an overlapping cognitive layer that obscures the contents of the perceptual awareness.

It should be noted, however, that ordinary experience is not transparent with regard to the content of awareness and thus cannot serve as evidential ground for establishing the disjunction of perception and conception. Just as the phenomenological bracketing affords an awareness of the interdependent nature of object apprehension (in other words, an awareness that cognition reveals an intentional relation to the object rather than establishes a connection with a putatively external or internal object), so also in the Buddhist tradition the detached awareness by means of which one attends to phenomena directly and without any mediation reveals the secondary order character of conceptual elaborations. Citing Dharmakīrti's argument that meditative states of cognitive awareness provide evidence for direct perception, Dreyfus suggests that taking into account the deep phenomenology of meditation may in fact be the only way in which we can grasp what Dignāga, Dharmakīrti, and their successors have in mind when they define perception as free from conception:

> Due to the speed of the mental process, the untrained person usually cannot differentiate conceptual from non-conceptual cognition. Only on special occasions, such as in some form of meditation, can a clear differentiation be made. There, the flow of thought gradually subsides, and we reach a state in which there is a bare sensing of things. In this state, shapes and colors are seen just barely; that is, they are seen as delivered through our senses without the adjunctions of conceptual interpretations. When one gradually emerges from such a non-conceptual state, the flow of thoughts gradually reappears, and we are able to make judgments about what we saw during our meditation. One is then also able to make a clear differentiation between the products of thoughts and the bare delivery of the senses.[85]

---

84. PV III, 123–125: *pratyakṣaṃ kalpanāpodhaṃ pratyakṣeṇaiva sidhyati/ pratyātmavedyaḥ sarveṣāṃ vikalpo nāmasaṃśrayaḥ//saṃhṛtya sarvataścintām□ stimitenāntarātmanā/sthito'pi cakṣuṣā rūpam īkṣate sākṣajā matiḥ//punarvikalpayan kiñcadāsīnme kalpanedṛśī/vetti ceti na pūrvoktāvasthāyāmindriyād gatau.*

85. Dreyfus (1997: 351). Drawing from Husserl's account of intentionality, Dreyfus has recently argued for the notion that perception displays something like a phenomenal type of intentionality only in certain meditative states (2007: 109). I

As we saw earlier on in our discussion of the distinguishing marks of perceptual cognition, perception is characterized by clarity or vividness (*spaṣṭa*), whereas conception, due to its discursive character, is presumably unclear (or at least less clear). Although clarity and vividness are the primary attributes of perception, they can also be applied, as descriptive or phenomenal categories of experience, to conception (a mathematician's solution to a given problem, say, the Poincaré conjecture, may actually appear move vivid than his or her perceptual surroundings). Again, the difference between perception and conception is not simply one of degree[86] but of modality, since the clarity of perception depends on the presence of the object within the range of the sensory apprehension, whereas the clarity of conception (though not entirely amodal) depends on correct reasoning and the effective use of language.

Although Śāntarakṣita and Kamalaśīla do not refer directly to meditative states in their assertion that perception is clearly apprehended as devoid of conception, they nevertheless invoke the same argument as Dharmakīrti, namely that our senses continue to attend to their objects even when the mind is directed toward something else. Their argument answers the opponent's query about why it is that one cannot have two simultaneous conceptions, one that attends to something other than the sensory object and one that attends to the sensory object itself. The problem here concerns the possibility that awareness can accommodate both a perceptual apprehension of one object and the conceptualization of another object:

> At that particular time, there is no further conceptual content which is connected with the name of that object [such as blue, etc.], because no such conceptual content is perceptible, and because the simultaneous presence of both [conceptual content of blue, etc. and other objects] cannot be maintained.[87]

Expanding on this argument, Kamalaśīla notes that the possibility of two conceptions occurring simultaneously is contradicted both by (the testimony of) perception (*pratyakṣavirodha*) and from the point of view of the meaning of the assertion (*abhyupāgamavirodha*). Here again, Kamalaśīla expands upon Dharmakīrti's view that it is impossible to hold conceptions about dissimilar

---

address this issue below (chapter 8.3), where I take a strongly intentionalist stance that regards intentionality or directedness as an essential features of all perceptual states.

86. Dreyfus too appears to suggest that in terms of clarity the difference between the two is simply one of degree rather than kind: "Dharmakīrti's argument does not exclude the existence of degrees of clarity between conceptions, some of which may be clearer than others. Nevertheless, they are all unclear in comparison to perception" (1997: 351).

87. TS 1244: *tadā tannāmasaṃsargī vikalpo 'sty aparo na ca/dṛśyasyāpratisaṃvitter anīṣṭeś ca dvayoḥ sakṛt.*

phenomena concomitantly. As Dharmakīrti declares in his own rejection of the notion that two conceptions can be simultaneously held: "When [cognition and its form] are directly experienced by that [cognition of the form] itself the assumption of two simultaneous cognitions, as asserted [by the opponent] is not experienced."[88]

In other words, the structure of cognitive awareness is such that one cannot think about two different things at the same time, but that one can think of something while perceptually attending to something else. Cognitive events can only be cross-modally simultaneous. Common examples include reading while listening to music, or thinking about one's dinner guests while preparing dinner. One of the classical examples found in the Sanskrit philosophical literature is that of thinking of offering gifts to a dancer while immersed in the perceptually saturated experience of watching her perform to the rhythms of accompanying music:

When watching a female dancer, all sensations are simultaneously apprehended, although [as the opponent might argue] there are numerous intervening [sensory] conditions. However, if this [simultaneous cognition] were regarded as erroneous, due to the rapid succession of the perceptual input, then [one can further argue that] there is rapid succession in cognitions of words such as *latā* and *tāla*, etc. when uttered together. Why is it that a misconception of simultaneity is not evident in this case?— Also, in the case of the occurrence of mental activity alone, no succession should be apparent, because all mental cognitions occur in rapid succession and do not last for any length of time. [This means that] in all these instances [where rapid succession occurs], no sequential order can be perceived in relation to any object. However, [any object] is apprehended in a simultaneous cognition, just as in the case of the perception of sound, etc. [in relation to the direct perception of the female dancer].[89]

88. PV I, 178ab: *tayaivānubhave dṛṣṭaṃ na vikalpadvayaṃ sakṛt*. This passage is interpreted by Manorathanandin as follows: "If a form and its own nature (as conceptually grasped) are assumed to be the object of direct experience of that cognition of form, that implies the existence of two different conceptions (*vikalpadvayaṃ*), namely "this is a form," and "this is the apprehension of a form." However, these [two different conceptions] are not possible, because they are invalidated by experience" (PVV *ad* PV III 178: *tayaiva rūpabuddhayā rūpasya svātmanaś ca anubhave'bhyupagamyamāne—rūpam iti rūpānubhava iti ca vikalpadvayaṃ sakṛt syāt, tacca nāsti, anubhavabādhitatvāt*).

89. TS 1249–1252: *nartakīdṛṣṭyavasthādāv akhilaṃ vedyate sakṛt/bahubhir vyavadhāne 'pi bhrāntiḥ sā cāśuvṛttitaḥ//latātālādibhuddhīnām atyarthaṃ laghuvartanam/sakṛdbhāvā bhimāno 'taḥ kim atrāpi na vartate//śuddhe ca mānase kalpe vyavasīyeta na kramaḥ/tulyā ca sarvabhuddhīnām āśuvṛttiś cirāsthiteḥ//ataḥ sarvatra viṣaye na kramagrahaṇam bhavet/sakṛdgrahaṇabhāsas tu bhavecchabdādibodhavat*. Funayama (1992: 102 n. 241) proposes that TS 1249ab ("numerous intervening [sensory] conditions" (*bahubhir vyavadhāne 'pi*)) could be read as espousing the view of the opponent, although that is not explicitly stated. Śāntarakṣita does not endorse this idea, as it is made clear by Kamalaśīla in his commentary on these verses. However, the idea of simultaneous apprehension (*vedyate sakṛt*) may on the whole be attributed to the opponent.

Elaborating on the opponent's contention that in watching a dancer one simultaneously apprehends a cluster of sensations, Kamalaśīla argues that to assume such simultaneity is actually the case leads to an unwarranted conclusion: namely, that cognitive states are indistinct with regard to their knowledge source.

While watching the female dancer, although five other kinds of sensations interfere with each individual sensation, it [i.e., each sensation] appears as if adjacent or contiguous with the other [sensations]. For instance, when one sees the female dancer one also hears the tunes of a song, tastes the camphor and other spices, smells the fragrance of flowers in front of the nose, feels the air blowing from the fan, and thinks of giving the female dancer presents of dress and ornaments. Thus, if despite numerous intervening [sensory] conditions, the illusion of the simultaneity of sensory cognition becomes manifest due to the quick succession in which cognitions arise; then, in the case of syllables heard in rapid succession as, for instance, when one hears the words *latā* and *tāla* or *sara* and *rāsa* [together] as [though] resulting from [rapidly] intervening cognitions, the two words *sara-rāsa* simultaneously appear when heard. [Thus,] there should be neither an auditory recognition of two separate words nor an apprehension of the two different objects they denote. Furthermore, when there arises only pure conceptual content in the form of pondering over various philosophical issues, without any intervention from different cognitions such as visual perception, their [viz., these ponderings'] appearance happens in quick succession, and it is impossible to determine their sequentiality. In addition, as all cognitions are momentary, because they occur in quick succession, they cannot endure for any length of time, so that no cognition of succession for any object is [ever] apprehended; "just as in the case of apprehending sound" means just as in the case of the perception of sound, taste, etc., while watching the female dancer.[90]

By rejecting the notion that simultaneity is a condition of phenomenal experience in the case of having multiple rapidly succeeding sensations, Kamalaśīla raises some important issues regarding what vision science describes as the phenomenon of "perceptual binding."[91] Perceptual binding

---

90. TSP *ad* TS 1249–1252: *ekaikā dhīḥ pañcabhirdhībhirvyavadhīyamānā'pi nartakīdarśanāvasthāyāmavyavahit eva pratibhāti/tathā hi—yadaiva nartakīmutpaśyati tadaiva gītādiśabdaṃ śṛṇoti, karpūrādirasamāsvāyati, nāsikāpuṭavinyastakusumāmedaṃ jighrati, vyajanāniládisparśaṃ ca spṛśati, vastrābhāranādidānādi ca cintayati; tataś ca yadi bahubhirvyavadhāne'pi buddhīnāṃ sakṛd bhāvabhrāntirāś ūtpattibalādupajāyate, tadā latā tālaḥ, saro rasaḥ—ityevamādavekaikajñānavyavadhānād varṇaśrutīnāmatyarthaṃ laghuvarttanamastī sakṛdvarṇapratibhedaś ca nasyāt/kiñca—buddher vijātīya cakṣurādi vijñānāvyavahite nānāvidyārthacintārūpe vikalpe samutpadyamāne; sīghravṛttirasti iti na kramavyavasāyaḥ prāpnoti/sarvāsāṃ ca buddhīnāṃ kṣaṇikatvena cirānavasthānādāśuvṛttirastīti kasyacidarśasya na kramavati pratītiḥ syāt/śabdādibodhavaditi/nartikīprekṣāvasthāyāṃ śabdādisaṃvedanavat.*

91. On the neuroanatomy of vision, see Zeki (1993), and Zeki and Bartels (1999).

describes the process by which sensory input is aggregated through a process of selection and grouping in the somatosensory cortex, which in turn gives rise to the distinct objects of subjective awareness. In the case of hearing, simultaneity occurs when a sequence of two acoustic cues, such as two syllables above a certain threshold, are perceived not as separate but as a single phonetic event.[92] I think it is possible to interpret Kamalaśīla's rejection of the notion that we can actually perceive simultaneity in a series of succeeding sounds as resulting from his commitment to something like a sensorimotor account of phenomenal experience.[93] Perception is not a passive relay of sensory input, not even the apprehension of an internal representation of external reality. It is not something that happens to us; rather it is something we do.[94] Objects are apprehended depending on the perceiver's spatio-temporal orientation and situatedness, and their constancy is an illusory construct based on the fact that ordinarily perceivers only attend to a narrow region of their visual field. It is this dependency of the perceived on the perceiver's orientation and disposition that Kamalaśīla perhaps has in mind when he claims that an illusion of simultaneity is only possible if one ignores "the numerous intervening sensory conditions."

Kamalaśīla here defends the Buddhist notion that simultaneity is not a characteristic of the perceptual event; rather, it is a conceptual construct, superimposed upon what in effect is an experience of sequentiality. The fact that one *does* distinctly hear the words *latā* and *tāla* or *sara* and *rāsa* indicates that they are perceptually apprehended as separate. Indeed, they are discerned as different auditory events and, as such, have different phonetic markers. If that were not the case and simultaneity were admitted, it would lead to the undesirable consequence of admitting the sameness of all apprehended phenomena, something that not even the Naiyāyika wishes to admit.[95]

The purported simultaneity of pure conceptual content is rejected on similar grounds, for propositional attitudes are not entirely devoid of any phenomenal character or aspect of their own. The thought "Paris is the capital of France" may not differ from one moment to the next in terms of

92. On the phenomena of boundary recognition, and modal and amodal completion, see Pessoa, Thompson, and Noë (1998).

93. For a sensorimotor approach to perception, in particular to visual perception, see O'Regan and Noë (2001, 2002), Noë (2002c), and Noë and O'Regan (2002). Noë and O'Regan argue that seeing is not the result of information processing of visual input in the brain (visual cortex) coupled with visual awareness, but rather "depends on patterns of interaction between the perceiver and the environment" (2002: 567).

94. Cf. Noë and O'Regan (2002: 567).

95. The opponent's argument that conjoined words such as *latā* and *tāla* or *sara* and *rāsa* are simultaneously apprehended is disproved by experience. The fact that one can discriminate these words as such—as distinct phonemes—is a proof of their successive occurrence, even if they seem contiguous.

being held as a propositional attitude with intentional content, but it does in terms of its phenomenal character. For the thought to be epistemically warranted, at a minimum I must have mastery of the concept of "capital" and a basic knowledge of political geography. But how this thought is entertained depends also on its mode of presentation, on what John Searle calls its *aspectual shape*.[96] The general idea is that whenever a certain thought, perception, or desire becomes the object of awareness, it is invariably presented in a specific way or under a certain aspect. Kamalaśīla here endorses a view that many phenomenologists and analytic philosophers of mind share. As Tim Crane sums it up: "there is no such thing as simply thinking about an object, as opposed to thinking about it (say) as *a present from one's mother*, or as *one's most precious possession*."[97] The important point to make here is that *phenomenal character* (that is, how things show up to discerning awareness) is not a theoretical construct, but the pre-theoretical givenness that any theory of cognition must explain (or, at the very least, take into account).

Now, given that Buddhists endorse the view of momentariness, how can the conjoined sounds in our example be apprehended as occurring in succession rather than simultaneously? The idea that momentariness implies simultaneity—on account of the fact that no cognition of succession can ever arise if everything is momentary—is rejected on empirical grounds: it is precisely the perception of things arising in quick succession (that is, of both the manifest object and the transitional process) that makes it possible to apprehend their differentiating aspects (tonal frequency, hues, etc.). Furthermore, as the text (and the example) makes clear, the perceptual mode of "seeing" the dancer is expressed using not just generic verbal forms such as "seeing" (*darśana*) but also forms such as "looking up" (*utpaśya*) that capture the sensorimotor aspect of vision. As a form of embodied action, the experience of seeing is itself constitutive of the sequential flow of experience.

Another stock example in the Sanskrit philosophical literature that illustrates the conceptual superimposition of simultaneity on a set of perceptions (that in fact is sequential) is that of the whirling firebrand. When it is twirled rapidly, the firebrand produces the illusion of a circle. The opponent argues that the circle of fire is clearly perceived and that this perception is not due to a conceptual superimposition but to the remembrance of the preceding moment of perception or rather to the simultaneity of adjoining perceptions:

In the case of the whirling firebrand, the illusion of simultaneous cognition appears in the form of a [fire] wheel; this illusion does not arise on account of a connection of [successive] perceptions of the rotating firebrand, since the [continuous] circular form is vividly perceived. This means that the connection [of successive perceptual

96. Searle (1992: 155).
97. Crane (2003: 38).

stimuli] is achieved only through recollection and not as the result of the sensory perception [of a wheel of fire]; past objects cannot be apprehended in perception, and the object of this recollection is not vividly perceived, as it has already vanished [at the next moment of recollection]. For this reason [as the opponent would assume] the appearance [in cognition] of this wheel [of fire] could not be vivid.[98]

The opponent argues that perceptual vividness in the case of the whirling firebrand is due to recollection and not to actually seeing a circle, since past events cannot constitute an object of perceptual awareness. Moreover, vividness, which is the main characteristic of visual perception, depends on the object being present within the threshold of this sense modality. For Kamalaśīla, the circle, while seemingly vivid, is not perceptually apprehended as such; rather, its seeming circularity is simply the result of processes that are constitutive of the structure of perceptual awareness. The illusion, in this case, does have its source in the perceptual domain, but it is not an instance of perceptual cognition, since what appears in the form of a circle cannot be the result of successive perceptions:

The appearance of this illusion is not due to the connection of successive visual perceptions. Then what [kind of illusion] is it? It [is an error which] originates simultaneously and at once from the sensory systems in the form of a circle, [and] as the result of specific causal conditions.[99] [This is the case] because [the error] appears clearly in perception, for [as Dharmakīrti has said] a cognition connected with conception lacks vividness.[100] [And] also because the connection with perception is achieved through recollection, not by means of perception, as that cognition which arises due to the proximity of an object [at the sense doors] is devoid of the capacity to apprehend past objects. [Also] the object of such [past] recollections lacks vividness—why?—because it has already vanished [by the time a perceptual awareness arises]. Hence, because the perception of a rotating firebrand would be indistinct, it is not a mental illusion. As a matter of fact, it is [an illusion] arising from sense perception. Therefore, the example cited by the opponent lacks a probandum.[101]

---

98. TS 1253–1255: *alāte 'pi sakṛd bhrāntiś cakrābhāsā pravartate/na dṛśyāṃ pratisaṃdhānād vispaṣṭaṃ pratibhāsanāt//tathā hi pratisaṃdhānaṃ smṛtyaiva kriyate na tu/ darśanenavyatītasyaviṣayasyānavagrahāt//yaścāsyāviṣayonāsauvinaṣṭatvātparisphuṭaḥ/ tataḥ parisphuṭo nāyaṃ cakrābhāsaḥ prasajyate.*

99. The arising of a conscious cognitive event depends, as we saw earlier in our discussion of the Abhidharma view on perception, upon the presence of the object, the sensory organ, and attention. For instance, in order to cognize a form (*rūpavijñāna*, i.e., have the cognition of a form), four factors are necessary: the visual sense (*cakṣurindriya*), the visible object (*viṣaya*, *artha*), ambient light (*āloka*) (in the case of visual objects), and thinking (*manaskāra*).

100. The verse that Kamalaśīla paraphrases here is found in PV I, 283: *na vikalpānubaddhasyāsti sphuṭārthāvābhāsitā/svapne'pi smaryate smārta na ca tat tādṛ. garthavat.*

101. TSP *ad* TS 1253–1255: *yato netaṃ mānasī bhrāntiḥ kramavarttinī darśanāni ghaṭ ayantī samupajāyate, kiṃ tarhi? sakṛdekaivendriyajā cakrākārā bhrāntiḥ sāmagrīviśeṣa-*

The main contentious issue in this debate is whether illusions occur at the level of sensory awareness, or are instead the result of higher order interpretive processes that engage conceptual thought. The Naiyāyika contends that a circle of fire is vividly perceived and that the illusion is "real" in the sense that the visual system grasps an actual circle, even though upon subsequent analysis one knows that there is no tangible circle in the whirling firebrand (but at best a circular movement). The Buddhist position (articulated here by Śāntarakṣita and Kamalaśīla) is that cognitions of the sort that result in apprehending something as a circle of fire cannot be perceptual in character, because apprehending an object as defined by such properties as circularity or circular movement depends on recollection. Therefore, the circle in the whirling firebrand is only a superimposed image, and in fact lacks the vividness attributed to it by the opponent. Perception, as Kamalaśīla's argument goes, can only grasp unique particulars, and the circle caused by the whirling firebrand is not a unique particular but a construct that bears all the characteristics of (top-down) conceptual cognitive processes: at best it is a phenomenal aspect of a specific mental state. Kamalaśīla's appeal to the phenomenology of perception is not very explicit here, but an investigation of the actual cause of perceptual illusions is carried out in more detail later in the chapter when he analyzes erroneous cognitions.[102]

So far Śāntarakṣita and Kamalaśīla have been attempting to justify Dignāga's definition of perception by recourse to the phenomenology of perception. Next they attempt to justify the same definition inferentially:

Moreover, when a thing provides no causal basis for ascertaining a certain form (*rūpasthitikāraṇam*), that thing is not cognized as real by the wise. For example, a white horse, because of the absence of dewlap and other features, is not established to be a cow. [Similarly] in sensory perception, there is no causal support for the cognition of an object as having conceptuality as a determining character, which would result in apprehending a thing and its properties simultaneously. Brindled cows are contrary examples [to this thesis]. Otherwise, this would lead to undesirable conclusions. Thus, the reason put forward is not inadmissible because qualifiers such as genus and the rest have been rejected by us and because these properties are not cognized as different from the substratum. [Even if such properties as genus, etc. were admitted], as such qualifiers of this type do not [really] exist.[103]

---

balādutpadyate; vispaṣṭapratibhāsatvāt/na hi vikalpānubaddhasya spaṣṭapratibhāsitvaṃ yuktam/tathā hi—ghaṭanā kriyamāṇā smṛtyava kriyate, nendriyajñānena; tasya vastu sannidhānabalabhāvino 'tītārthagrahaṇāsāmarthyām/yaś cāsyāḥ smṛteviṣayaḥ, nāsau parisphuṭaḥ; kasmāt? vinaṣṭatvāt/tasmādaspaṣṭābhatvaprasaṅganneyaṃ mānasī bhrāntiḥ, kiṃ tarhi? indriyajā—iti sādyavikalpo dṛṣṭāntaḥ.

102. See TS 1311–1328 and TSP *loc. cit.*

103. TS 1256–1259: *yadi cāpyasya bhāvasya yadrūpasthitikāraṇam/na vidyate na tattvena sa vyavasthāpyate buddhaiḥ//avidyamānasāsnādir yathā karto gavātmanā/viśe-*

Śāntarakṣita here returns to consider the causal aspect of perceptual objects. Unlike conceptual objects, which depend on thought alone, perceptual objects and the cognitions that instantiate them do not arise in the absence of external stimuli. The form of an external object is ascertained on the basis of its efficient cause. In addition, as Kamalaśīla explains, non-perception can also act as a cause in establishing the basis for the application of names to things:

> The argument goes as follows: If the causal basis for ascertaining a certain form in an entity is absent, [that entity] is not ascertained as having that form by the wise; for instance, a white horse is not ascertained as having the form of a cow, where the causal basis for designating it [as] a cow, such as [the presence of] a dewlap, etc. is absent in the horse. In the case of direct perception, which is produced as a result of the presence of an object such as blue, the causal basis for its connection with conception in the form of the apprehension of the object as qualified by its qualifiers is absent; thus the cause [as the connection with conception] is not apprehended.[104]

If one rejects the view that perception apprehends an object based on conditions that serve as a causal basis for the appearance of the object in perception, rather than as a result of (perceptual) judgments that apprehend the object as qualified by certain qualifiers, then, argues Kamalaśīla, one runs the risk of committing oneself to the absurd view that all entities are uniformly ascertained in all forms (*sarvathā sarvasya*).[105]

Having demonstrated that perception is never associated with conception, Śāntarakṣita concludes his discussion by stating that names which express word particulars do not have the capacity to act as signifiers because the specific individual does not function as a referent for a word-meaning relation. In other words, objects do not imply their names. There is no object-to-word ontology that can explain how names end up being associated with the things they designate on the basis of some property that is intrinsic to the object. Śāntarakṣita's position here is not unlike that which Quine puts forth in his seminal essay "On What There Is."[106] That is, in using a name, one need not be committed to there being a specific referent for that term, nor should

---

ṣaṇaviśiṣṭārthagrahaṇam na ca vidyate//savikalpakabhāvasya sthiter ākṣe nibandhanam/ vipakṣaḥ śābaleyādir anyathātiprasajyate//na cāprasiddhatā hetor jātyādeḥ pratiṣedhataḥ/bhedena cāparicchedān na cāsty evaṃ viśeṣaṇam.

104. TSP *ad* TS 1256–1259: *prayogaḥ—yasya yadrūpaṃ vyavasthitau nimittaṃ nāsti, na tat tathā prekṣāvadbhirvyavahartṛbhirvyavasthāpyate, tadyathā—avidyamā najoprajñnaptinimittabhūtakakudādisamudāyaḥ karko gotvena/nāsti ca pratyakṣasya nīlādyasādhāraṇaviṣayabalenotpadyamānasya savikalpakabhāvavyavasthitau viśeṣaṇaviśiṣṭārthagrahanaṃ nimittam iti kāraṇānupalabdhiḥ.*

105. TSP *ad* TS 1256–1259: *sarvathā sarvasya vyavasthānaprasaṅgo vyavasthāpayituś cāprekṣāpūrvakāritāprasaṅgo bādhakaṃ.*

106. Quine (1948).

one commit to there being an entity that stands as its meaning if one uses a meaningful term. In effect, Śāntarakṣita, much like Quine, argues against substantive theoretical positions that assert that words are meaningful (or can be meaningfully used) only if there are entities that they can mean.[107] The silvery astral body that waxes and wanes as it orbits the Earth is picked by a heterogeneous class of names: *moon* in English, *lune* in French, *chandra* in Sanskrit, and *tsuki* in Japanese. As a phenomenal concept that captures the experience of seeing a certain astral body, however, "moon" can acquire a categorical function for a theory of planetary motion. Semiosis thus operates only within the domain of conceptual thought and, although the object can function as the referent that provides a causal basis for inferential judgments, ultimately the basis of naming is entirely conceptual:

> Also, the name, which is [considered to be] the specific characteristic of the word, cannot be a signifier since the notion of specific characteristic as [an object] signified and that [of the specific characteristic] as a word signifier have both been rejected. For this reason, the relation between word and referent has been regarded as something that is superimposed [upon things which actually do not display such relations]. On the other hand, sensory perception cognizes an object only [in respect to its specific characteristics], which are not falsely superimposed, and only when those specific characteristics are present—and insofar as some intervening factor is present, the specific characteristic is not present.[108]

To illustrate this point, Śāntarakṣita once again cites the example of the perception of blue, which is apprehended directly and without any connection with the word "blue": "[Concerning] the nature of blue and other things, in view of being different from other [colors], it is not possible to agree on its [specific verbal designation]; therefore the perception of things [such as blue, etc] is not associated with verbal expression."[109] Śāntarakṣita here lays claim to the phenomenalist view that we can have color experiences even in the absence of color concepts. Indeed, our experience of color is more fine-grained than our capacity to conceptually articulate it with the aid of color

---

107. Indeed, Quine's parsimonious ontology—which allows him to commit to the *possibility* of "things that are F" without thereby endorsing the *existence* of "things that are F"—is not unlike that of the Buddhist epistemologist whose ontology of point instant particulars commits her to using language non-referentially. See Soames (2007), for an account of the debate between Quine and Carnap on ontology, analyticity, and meaning.

108. TS 1260–1262: *nāmāpi vācakaṃ naiva yacchabdasya svalakṣaṇam/svalakṣaṇasya vācyatvavācakatve hi dūṣite//adhyāropitam evāto vācyavācakam iṣyte/anāropitam arthaṃ ca pratyakṣaṃ pratipadhyate//svalakṣaṇasya sadbhāve sadbhāvāt tadabhāvataḥ/vyavadhānādibhāve ca tasyāpi vyatirekataḥ.*

109. TS 1263: *aśakyasamayo hy ātmā nīlādīnām ananyabhāk/teṣām ataś ca saṃvittir nābhijalpānuṣaṅginī.*

categories (that is, we typically perceive more shades of color than we can name or indeed have names for). Vision opens up a domain of experience whose richness and detail far outstrips the capacity for conceptual apprehension. That is, one can never fully possess all the concepts necessary for giving a full account of the phenomenal content (and character) of experience at any given time. One may not possess color concepts for all the range of colors in the spectrum of visible light, yet it is obvious that one can nonetheless have rich color experiences. Similarly, one can very well imagine not knowing what a platypus is—not having ever seen either a live specimen or a picture of it— and in seeing one for the first time, have a perceptual experience of an organism unlike anything one has seen before.[110] Assuming that it is possible to understand "organism" not merely as a demonstrative concept, but as an innate cognitive response to entities with behavioral abilities, at the very least one perceives something that does not fall under any concept. This immediate mode of acquaintance not only suggests a certain decoupling of perception from conception but also confirms the intuition of the Sautrāntika Ābhidharmikas that language functions as a system of conventions (against the view of orthodox Brahmanical thought, which postulates an intrinsic connection between language and reality). Although the Buddhist epistemologist admits that there are different kinds of concepts, and that phenomenal concepts do not have their reference fixed by descriptions of the contents of experience, it is still the case that concepts (and conceptual thought) do not exhaust our experience.[111]

It should be noted in this context that the Ābhidharmikas were not unified in their view of language. The Buddhist epistemologist, for the most part, follows the Sautrāntikas for whom word meaning depends upon agreement within a specific community of speakers about the word's denotative capacity. For the Sautrāntikas, thus, word types, phrases, and phonemes are forms of speech and thus qualify as "words capable of generating meaning." The Sautrāntikas also insist that speech should be taken in the sense of a verbal utterance that calls a certain object to attention—more specifically, in a sense that it is agreed upon by a community of speakers. On the other hand, the Sarvastivādins contend that word types are not speech because speech is merely articulated sounds and, by themselves, articulated sounds

110. It is interesting to note that when news of the discovery of a strange quadruped mammal with birdlike features (it has a beak, hence the Latin name *ornithorhynchus anatinus* "birdlike snout ducklike") reached Europe for the first time, zoologists doubted its existence, with some even dubbing it a hoax. The implication here is that conceptual cognition often constrains perception to what is deemed rationally possible on the basis of certain assumptions about natural laws.

111. For a defense of the view that we perceive far more shades of color than we have color concepts for, see Evans (1982) and Peacocke (1986).

(e.g., a yell) do not make their meaning or referent comprehensible.[112] Finally, the Vaibhāṣikas regard word types as "conditioned factors dissociated from thought" (*cittaviprayuktasaṃskāras*). For the Vaibhāṣikas, speech is nothing but vocal articulation, and meaning is not conveyed by vocal articulation alone. Rather, only a specific type of vocal articulation can manifest a name, and only that name can then be an indicator of meaning.[113]

6.3 COGNITIVE ERRORS AND PERCEPTUAL ILLUSIONS

Having examined the arguments that Śāntarakṣita and Kamalaśīla adduce in support of the Buddhist definition of perception (as formulated by Dignāga and further expanded by Dharmakīrti), let us now turn to the issue of cognitive errors and perceptual illusions. As we saw earlier, Dignāga's definition of perception does not mention the qualifier "nonerroneous" (*abhrānta*) as a condition for the reliability of perceptual cognitions nor the equivalent term "non-deviating" (*avyabhicārin*).[114] Rather, it is Dharmakīrti who for the first time adds the qualifier "nonerroneous" to the definition of perception.[115] All subsequent commentators, including Śāntarakṣita and Kamalaśīla, thus follow Dharmakīrti's definition of perception rather than Dignāga's. However, unlike Śāntarakṣita, who retains Dharmakīrti's definition unaltered, Kamalaśīla seems to be interpreting nonerroneous as "nondeceptive" (*avisam□vādaka*), thus adding a new dimension to understanding what causes a cognition to deviate (*vyabhicār*) from the contents of awareness as immediately given.

Śāntarakṣita and Kamalaśīla, in defending the notion that the definition of perception must necessarily include the qualifier "nonerroneous" in order to exclude illusory perceptions and perceptions caused by a defective sense, pursue three main goals:

- a general explanation of the mandatory use of "nonerroneous" and Kamalaśīla's explanation of nonerroneous as nondeceptive;
- a refutation of those Buddhists who hold the view that all perceptual errors are in fact cases of conceptual misidentification;

112. See AKBh *ad* AK II, 46cd.

113. See AKBh *ad* AK II, 47ab. Of these three positions, it is that of the Vaibhāṣikas that resembles the grammarians' understanding of the word-meaning relation, particularly as articulated by Bhartṛhari in his doctrine of *spoṭa*. Cf. Pind (1991: 278–279).

114. See NS I, 1.4.

115. The term appears for the first time not in the *Pramāṇavārttika* but in his later work, the *Pramāṇaviniścaya* (PVin 252b.3: *pratyakṣa kalpanāpoḍham abhrāntam*. "Perception is [that cognition which is] devoid of conceptual construction and nonerroneous."

- a criticism of those Buddhist authors who contend that the definition of perception is sufficient without the addition of "nonerroneous."

The Buddhist epistemological literature contains several other examples of erroneous cognitions, including the classic rope-snake, although these examples are in fact pan-Indian. For instance, the multiple or double moon illusion is said to occur in both normal persons as well as in those affected by the "cloudy vision" (*timira*) disease.[116] Given that Dharmakīrti and his successors distinguish between perceptual errors that are caused by an impaired sense organ (*indriyabhrānti*) and errors of discernment (or delusions) that are caused by the mind (*manobhrānti*), it becomes easier to understand why Kamalaśīla treats "erroneous" as a synonym of "deceptive" in his definition of perception. Perception, while not infallible, is nevertheless a nonerroneous cognition. The sensory systems do not have the capacity to effect epistemic discriminations in terms of true or false, since we are warranted in accepting the contents of experience *qua* objects of sensory apprehension (hence the old adage: "seeing is believing"). The circle of fire that is perceived in a rapidly rotating firebrand is a seeming object of perceptual awareness, though no actual circular object is thus perceived.

Recall that Dignāga distinguishes between perceptual judgments (*savikalpa pratyakṣa*) and pseudo-perceptions (*pratyakṣābhasa*), a distinction that after him becomes normative for the Buddhist epistemologists. Among Dignāga's examples of pseudo-perceptions are erroneous cognitions (for instance, the illusory motion of the river bank when floating down a river), conventional cognitions of empirical reality (the naïve realist perception of objects as immediately given to sensory awareness), inference, the result of inferential reasoning, memory, and cognitions that take the form of wishing for something to happen. While Dignāga does not state explicitly whether these pseudo-perceptions include also cognitions caused by impaired sense organs, Dharmakīrti is less ambiguous, contending that *sataimira* should indeed be interpreted to mean "together with *timira*," that is, together with cognitions resulting from impaired sense organs.

Śāntarakṣita begins his discussion by noting that the qualifier "nonerroneous" is essential to the definition of perception in order to exclude from it various types of visual impairment, such as those resulting in the visual

116. This eye disease is known in the medical literature as *myodespopsia* or *vitreous floaters* and refers to a condition in which a patient sees small, thread-like fragments floating in the visual field. This condition arises when the gel-like vitreous humor that fills the eyeball breaks down into fibrils, the actual floaters that the patient sees. Vitreous floaters are made visible by the refracted light that passes through them or by the shadows they cast on the retina. Their threadlike nature explains the perceptual phenomenon of seeing strands of hairs or a hair-mesh in patients affected by "cloudy vision." See Solso (1994: 15) for a basic account of this particular condition and its implications for vision.

experience of "hair-mesh" (*keśoṇḍraka*) and similar types of illusion: "The term 'nonerroneous' [in the definition of perception] is understood as excluding [from perception] a cognition of "hair-mesh" and so on. These [viz., cognitions of hair-mesh and so on], being erroneous, are not regarded as [conducive to] knowledge."[117] Kamalaśīla adds the following commentary:

Here, the term "nonerroneous" should be taken to mean "nondeceptive," and not "having for its basis the form of the object [as it appears in cognition]." Otherwise, the definition of perception, which ought to accord with both theories (those of the Yogācāra and the Sautrāntika), would be incomplete because the Yogācāras do not admit an [external] object for cognition. "Being nondeceptive" [in this context] refers to the causal efficacy to achieve the attainment of an object that is capable of fulfilling a desired purpose; [it does] not [refer to] its own attainment, because it is possible that an impending cause [to its attainment] may become manifest. [Opponent:] If that is so, [only] "nonerroneous" should be employed [in the definition of perception]. What is the purpose of mentioning "free from conceptual construction"? [Response:] Not so, because in that case inference, which [essentially] is a [type of] conceptual cognition, would also be considered [an aspect of] direct perception.[118]

Cognitions such as those caused by scarred retinas are considered by Śāntarakṣita to be cases of defective perception that have their cause in the sensory, rather than the mental, domain. While Śāntarakṣita's definition of "perceptual error" is not different from Dharmakīrti's, Kamalaśīla's commentary provides an innovative and more informative gloss. Kamalaśīla interprets "nonerroneous" as "nondeceptive," and thus leaves open the possibility that cases of nonconceptual cognitions may nevertheless be deceptive. The example adduced to illustrate this point is that of dream cognitions, for dreams are precisely the types of experiences that lack both conceptual content and the purely sensory character of perceptual apprehension. Kamalaśīla appears to be claiming that the qualifier "nonerroneous" is necessary in order to exclude from the class of veridical perceptions, which alone qualify as a reliable source of knowledge, dreams and various forms of illusory apprehension:

It is not true, as some philosophers claim, that erroneous cognition is purely mental, for [perceptual error] appears only when the sense is present and disappears when that (i.e., sense) is destroyed. Like the snake-rope illusion, if [the cognitive] error

117. TS 1211: *keśoṇḍrukādivijñānanivṛttyarthamidaṃ kṛtam/abhāntagrahaṇaṃ taddha bhrāntatvānneṣyate pramā.*

118. TSP *ad* TS 1311: *abhrāntamatra avisaṃvāditvena draṣṭavyam, na tu yathā'-vasthitālambanākāratayā/anyathā hi yogācāramatenālambanāsiddher ubhayanayasamāśrayoṇeṣṭasya pratyakṣalakṣaṇasyāvyāpitā syāt/avisaṃvāditvāṃ cābhimatārthakriy āsamarthārthaprāpaṇaśaktiḥ, na tu prāpaṇameva; pratibandhādisambhavāt/yadyevam, abhrāntagrahaṇamevāstu, kiṃ kalpanāpoḍhagrahaṇeneti? na; anumāna vikalpasyāpi pratyakṣatvaprasaṅgāt.*

were mental, it should disappear when the sense [apprehension] disappears even if the error of the sense has not disappeared. But that does not appear to be the case because it continues to be clearly perceived.[119]

In his commentary, Kamalaśīla reiterates the need to retain the qualifier "nonerroneous" in the definition of perception for the purpose of accommodating other types of perceptual apprehension such as the perception of the yogi, which fall under the rubric of "introspective" modes of cognitive awareness (the content and phenomenal character of which is markedly different from, say, hearing specific sounds or seeing particular shapes). Yet these internal or self-reflective modes of cognitive awareness are nonetheless nonconceptual and nonerroneous. Kamalaśīla is simply advancing something like the Cartesian view of the cogito: I may be wrong about the content of my visual, auditory, or introspective experience, but not about its occurrence. This fine-grained discrimination of different levels of perceptual awareness, Śāntarakṣita and Kamalaśīla claim, provides sufficient ground for rejecting the notion that cognitive errors only belong in the domain of conceptual thought (given the evidence from defective sensory apprehensions).

In citing the examples given by the other party (possibly a group of Buddhists who upheld Dignāga's view that perception can never be mistaken),[120] Kamalaśīla could indeed be referring to Jinendrabuddhi and other critics of Dharmakīrti, who thought that so long as an object's configuration, mass, and spatio-temporal coordinates are properly apprehended it is inessential that its color be also correctly perceived. Current theories of color perception would categorize this instance simply as an example of surface or object recognition, which depends on several factors such as depth, illumination, and edge detection. The opponent here seems to be suggesting that color blindness does not represent a major handicap for perceptual cognition, and that it does not provide sufficient grounds for dismissing an instance of perceptual awareness as erroneous. Otherwise, one would have to dismiss direct perceptions in colorblind individuals as pseudo-perceptions and make color apprehension a necessary condition for veridical perception.

---

119. TS 1312–1313: *mānasaṃ tadapītyeke naitadindriyabhāvataḥ/bhāvāt tadvikṛ tāvasya vikṛteś copalambhataḥ//sarpādibhāntivaccedamanaṣṭe'pyakṣaviplave/nivartteta manobhrānteḥ spaṣṭaṃ ca pratibhāsanāt.*

120. In the *Pramāṇasamuccayaṭīkā*, after having examined the causes that give rise to the erroneous cognition of a yellow conch, Jinendrabuddhi concludes: "It is established to be true that deceptive cognition is pseudo-perception, and hence even a (cognition) which is erroneous and free from conception is direct perception of (a thing) inasmuch as it is nondeceptive concerning that thing; and that (a cognition which is) deceptive concerning (a thing) is pseudo perception." PSṬ 34b4: *bslu ba'i shes pa ni mngon sum ltar smnag ba'o zhes pa ste/de lta na 'khrul pa rnam par rtog pa med payang gang la mi bslu ba der mngon sum nyid yin la/gang la bslu ba der ni de ltar snang ba nyid do zhes pa 'di grub par 'gyur ro.* Cf. Funayama (1999: 89).

Rather, the implication is that all cases of deception are the result of inferential cognitions, and hence are conceptual rather than perceptual in character. Provided one is aware of being color blind, one learns to navigate one's environment in ways that take into account the limitations imposed on visual perception by that specific condition.[121] For these authors, mistaking a yellow conch for a white conch due to color blindness is not an instance of perceptual error: that is, the perception of the conch is veridical, for color is only a secondary property of the object. The object's spatio-temporal features are correctly apprehended, though its apprehension *as a yellow* conch is an actual instance of deceptive cognition (indeed, one sees objects as wholes and not just their surface or reflectance properties). Against this view, Śāntarakṣita makes a very important empirical observation: "there can be no separate [apprehension of] form apart from color."[122] In other words, he takes the view that color is a salient cue in object recognition.[123] Whether Śāntarakṣita takes memory of an object's color as assisting in the recognition of the object, even in the absence of an apprehension of color, is not clear. What is obvious is that two conditions must be satisfied for a cognition to be warranted: it must be compatible both with the appearance of the object and with its mode of apprehension.

Although the dispute over the nature of those cognitions that deserve the label "erroneous" is not clearly spelled out, it is suggestive of an important distinction: that between perceptual illusions and mental delusions. Kamalaśīla's solution to this dispute is to focus not on the content (or object) of perceptual illusions and mental delusions, but on the causal factors

121. The debate on the cognitive status of color perception in modern philosophy and cognitive science is complex and far-ranging. A major divide exists between those who regard colors as perceiver-dependent (that is, dependent on the dispositioanal properties to affect light) and those who regard them as objective properties of objects. Among the latter group, some take the properties of colors (hue, saturation, and luminance) as reducible to physical microstructures, while others take them to be irreducible properties of physical bodies. Furthermore, there are those who deny the existence of colors altogether, for color properties do not have a place in the picture of the universe painted by modern physics. Most current debates on colors center either on what are taken to be their unknown properties (for those subscribing to some form of physicalism) or on their complex dispositional properties (for those adopting a phenomenological stance). For a comprehensive account of the philosophical debate on color perception, see Maund (1995). See also McLaughlin (2003) for a version of the dispositional account of color perception.

122. TS 1328ab: *na varṇavyatiriktaṃ ca saṃsthānam upapadyate.*

123. The issue of whether surface color apprehension in a visual display contributes to object recognition is still controversial. Edge-based theories argue that objects are recognized mainly on the basis of their shape, whereas surface-based theories argue that the apprehension of color plays a significant, if minimal, role in aiding object recognition. Recent studies, however, seem to suggest that long-term color memory does function as a top-down mechanism of object-recognition. See Mapelli and Behrmann (1997), Tanaka, Weiskopf, and Williams (2001), and Bramão et al. (2011) for general surveys of the literature.

underlying these erroneous cognitions. Of the two classes of cognitive error, only mental delusions can be dispelled by further reflection. Perceptual illusions cannot be eliminated through critical reflection, for the contents of perceptual awareness cannot be altered at will. This dissociation between perceptual illusions and mental delusions thus justifies Kamalaśīla's use of "nondeceptive" as a proper synonym for "nonerroneous."[124]

In order more clearly to articulate the difference between the mental and sensory bases of erroneous cognitions Śāntarakṣita points to the seeming cognitive impenetrability of perceptual illusions: even without diverting one's attention from the object of perception (that is, even without being inattentive or presumptive in one's perceptual appraisals), one still continues to experience illusory cognitions (for instance, the illusion of a double moon):

The notion that erroneous cognition occurs when the sense is present, because no veridical cognition intervening [to disprove that] is ever apprehended, cannot be said to be unproven. Even when the mind is not directed toward other objects, one has the uninterrupted perception of the double moon, etc., which indicates that the generation of [the erroneous cognition of the double moon] is not inherited (that is, not indirectly caused by introspective awareness).[125]

Commenting on this point, Kamalaśīla explains the difference between perceptual illusions and mental delusions in terms of the capacity to have volitional control over their appearance. Thus, whereas mental delusions may be eliminated simply by an act of will or through sustained critical reflection, visual illusions are beyond one's capacity of voluntary control. Furthermore, as Kamalaśīla explains, a cognition is to be ascertained as nonerroneous on two grounds: (i) compatibility with the appearance of the object (that is, its appearance should be nondeceptive (*pratibhāsam avisaṃvāda*); and (ii) compatibility with the form of the object as being conducive to effective action (*rūpārthakriyāprapti*). On this two-tier mode of ascertainment, erroneous cognition, such as that of a yellow conch for those affected with jaundice, fails both the appearance and the practical efficacy test:

On the other hand, certain Buddhists do not wish to employ the qualifier nonerroneous [in the definition of sensory perception] because [they claim that] even an erroneous cognition of a yellow conch [for what in reality is a white conch] is sense perception. [That is established] on account of the fact that it cannot be inference as

124. See TSP *ad* TS 1314–1319: *"mānasī ca bhrāntirvicārānivartate" ityatrāpyanaikāntikatvaṃ bhāvasāmānyabuddhibhiḥ*.

125. TS 1320–1321: *tadbhāvabhāvatā sākṣanna siddhā'bhrātacetasā/vyavadhānaṃ na siddhaṃ hi na hi tad vedyate'ntarā//anyārthāsaktacitto'pi dvicandrādi samīkṣate/avicchinnamato nāsti pāramparyasamudbhavā.*

it is not generated from an inferential mark. [The fact] that it (i.e., sense perception) is warranted is evinced by its nondeceptiveness. This is the reason why Dignāga did not employ [the qualifier] nonerroneous in his definition of perception. On account of the fact that "erroneous cognition, cognition of empirical reality, inference, and the rest" are mentioned as resembling perception, "nondeceptive" and "devoid of conception" [come to convey what actually] is indicated in the master's definition. Also, he (i.e., Dignāga) mentions *sataimira*, which can be interpreted as follows: *timira* ["obscurity"] signifies ignorance—as exemplified by expressions such as "dispelling the obscurity of the dull"—which should be understood to mean "deceptive cognition."[126]

It is possible that Kamalaśīla might be referring here to Jinendrabuddhi's own extensive discussion of the controversy surrounding the interpretation of "obscurity" (*timira*).[127] Indeed, in a long passage from his commentary on Dignāga's *Collection*, Jinendrabuddhi appears to be criticizing Dharmakīrti and some of his followers for denying that instances of illusory experience should be regarded as having a basis in direct perception:

In that case, by means of this word for an exception, [namely] "*sataimira*," the cognition whose sensory system is impaired through external or internal causes, though free from conception, should not be treated as a perceptual appearance; and in the word "*sataimira*," obscurity (*timira*) merely indicates [those] causes of impairment [that are present] in the sensory systems because even cognitions of impaired sensory systems qualify as [instances of] perception. Thus, the qualifier "nonerroneous" [added by Dharmakīrti][128] should not be used [in the definition of perception], because it is [an] accepted [fact] that even certain erroneous [cognitions caused by impaired sensory systems] still qualify as [instances of] perception in certain [aspects].[129]

It is obvious that Jinendrabuddhi follows Dignāga's view that "nonerroneous" is an unnecessary qualifier for those types of cognition (viz.,

126. TSP *ad* TS 1323: *kecittu svayūthyā evābhrāntagrahaṇaṃ necchanti; bhrāntasyāpi pītaśaṅkhādijñānasya pratyakṣatvāt/tathā hi—na tad anumānam; aliṅgajatvāt/pramāṇaṃ ca; avisaṃvāditvāt/ata eva ācāryadiṅnāgena lakṣaṇe na kṛtamabhrāntagrahaṇam/ "bhrāntiḥ saṃvṛttiḥ sā jñānam anumānam" ityādinā pratyakṣābhāsanirdeśād avisaṃvādi kalpanāpoḍham iti evaṃ vidhamiṣṭamācāryasya lakṣaṇam/sataimiram iti tu timiraśabdo'yamajñānaparyāyaḥ/"timiraghnaṃ ca mandānām" iti yathā/timire bhavaṃ taimiram, visaṃvādakamityarthaḥ.*

127. As found in Dignāga's PS I, 8ab.

128. See PVin 1.4b.

129. PSṬ 8a1–3: *na tarhi sataimiram ity anenāpavādapadena bāhyābhyantaropaghātapratyayopahatendriyajñānaṃ kalpanāpoḍhatve 'pi pratyakṣābham uktam. kevalaṃ tatra sataimiravacane timiraṃ sarvendriyapaghātapratyayopalakṣaṇamātram ity evaṃ vyākhyeyam, upahatendriyajñānasyāpi kasyacit pratyakṣatvāt. nāpy abhrantam iti viśeṣaṇaṃ kartavyam, bhrāntasyāpi kasyacit kvacit pratyakṣatveneṣṭatvāt.* Cf. Krasser (1991: I, 73–74), Funayama (1999: 88), and Chu (2004: 116–117).

inference, memory) that operate outside the perceptual domain. The problematic issue, however, concerns whether cases of illusory perception should be excluded from the domain of warranted empirical awareness. Could it be the case that Jinendrabuddhi is here simply defending some kind of Husserlian intentional stance that all our perceptual experiences, including the illusory ones, are experiences of something? Is he saying that we may be wrong about the content of a given instance of cognitive awareness but not about its type? That is, is Jinendrabuddhi advancing the view that I can never be mistaken about the character of my perceptual experience even when a specific type of impairment prevents me from having, say, optimal color vision? It is difficult to gauge Jinendrabuddhi's intention in this context. It may be true that perceptual illusions are warranted cognitions insofar as they indirectly reveal the limitations of our cognitive systems. But the illusory or erroneous character of the respective perception becomes apparent only after the event. The colorblind person does not know she has this perceptual defect until she undergoes testing. We are generally not aware of our blindspot until it is revealed to us by experiment. Since illusory perceptions lack pragmatic efficacy, they cannot serve as reliable instances of cognition, though they are nonetheless forms of direct apprehension. Specifying the criterion of "nonerroneousness" as a necessary condition for warranted empirical awareness is then necessary if perception is to have the epistemic status the Buddhist attributes to it. It remains, however, an open question whether the criteria of erroneousness and nonerroneousness are appropriate in the case of perception, whose operations (at least for the Buddhist) fall outside our discriminating and valuing judgments.

Indeed, cognizing something as erroneous requires discrimination and identification, which Kamalaśīla (following Dignāga) regards as inferential in nature: to state that cognition is erroneous is to bring it in the space of logical reasons. It is perhaps this higher order categorical use that those successors of Dignāga, to whom Kamalaśīla alludes, have in mind when they assert that even for those with different types of sensory impairment (for instance, the jaundiced) perception still operates in direct, nonconceptual mode. That a person affected with jaundice apprehends a white conch as yellow does not mean that apprehending its true color (viz., white) is due to some inferential process. The same could be said about the person with normal vision, for the whiteness of the conch is something that is given in perception, and explainable in terms of an individual's sensitivity to light and not in terms of his or her possession of the appropriate color concept.

Although he does not entirely reject Dharmakīrti's emendations—namely, his addition of "nonerroneous" as a necessary qualifier for perception (for it to count as an epistemic warrant)—Kamalaśīla does, however, recognize the need for interpreting the qualifier "nonerroneous" as a signifier for "nondeceptive."[130] His rationale for preferring this interpretation seems rather straightforward: perceptual illusions (and defective perceptions) do not really qualify as cognitive errors but rather as cases of deceptiveness. Thus, "deceptiveness" is a useful but limited qualifier and should be restricted to indicating that common sense perception is not a trustworthy source of knowledge because, as material aggregates, the sensory systems are subject to certain limits and limitations (due to their natural constitution and the constitution of their domains of apprehension). The first type of restriction is internal: we are physiologically limited to perceiving only a narrow range of light frequencies (a range that, as we now know, varies across species). The second type of restriction is external, and covers various types of obstacles such as motion (in the case of motion induced blindness), the composition and temperature of fluid mediums such as air and water (ground heat waves, for instance, cause straight lines to appear curved), and the absence of light (night restricts vision).

I gather that Kamalaśīla has in mind these limits and limitations when he interprets the meaning of nondeceptiveness. Under these limiting conditions, the senses either cannot clearly apprehend their objects or apprehend objects that do not exist as perceived. Mirages are a good example of deceptive but nonerroneous perceptions. Kamalaśīla's use of the qualifier "nondeceptive" in the definition of perception may be suggestive of the need to acknowledge the natural limits and limitations imposed upon the senses in virtue of their constitution and the constitution of their corresponding spheres of activity. In this case, a jaundiced perception is simply a species of perceptual limitation just as a mirage is a case of perceptual limit, since factors that are external to the function of the visual system are actually involved in generating the respective illusion. Neither case, however, is an instance of erroneous cognition, since the latter, like recollection, needs to contain an inferential component. Cognizing mirages *as* mirages is thus an instance of warranted perception.

In his concluding summary to the *Examination of Perception*, Kamalaśīla once again returns to consider the issue of why the qualifier "nonerroneous"—used by the Buddhist to define perception—should be retained. The reason put forward here is that without it the definition of perception would suffer

130. It should be noted here that there is an intra-doctrinal dispute between those who, like Vinītadeva, interpreted "nonerroneous" (*abhrānta*) as a case of "nondeceptive" (*avisaṃvādin/avisaṃvādaka*), and those who took Dharmottara's example that "nonerroneous" refers to the form of an entity (*vasturūpa*) and not to the cognition itself. For Dharmottara, the qualifier "nonerroneous" refers to the nature of the object that is apprehended and not to the manner of its apprehension (see NBṬ[d] VIII, 21: *abhrāntam arthakriyākṣame vasturūpe'viparyastam ucyate/arthakriyākṣamaṃ vasturūpaṃ saṃnivedaśopādhidharmātmakam*. Cf. Funayama (1999: 80–81).

from the defect of over applicability (*ativyāpti*): that is, perception would include not just instances of reliable empirical cognition, but other types of apprehension that, while seemingly perceptual in character, lack practical efficacy.[131]

By establishing that perception, in order to count as a source of knowledge, must necessarily be devoid of conception and nondeceptive, Śāntarakṣita and Kamalaśīla's ultimate aim is to provide a basis for effective action. But they also seek to justify their claim that the principles they propound are in accordance with the nature of things and not the product of conceptual elaborations. In the next chapter we turn to examining the wider philosophical implications of this Buddhist claim about perception, specifically to the notion that some kind of direct, non-mediated awareness is attainable and as such can provide an experiential basis for phenomenological descriptions that avoid the pitfalls of empiricist foundationalism.

---

131. See TSP: *tathā hi—kośoṇḍrakādibuddhīnā api prāmāṇyaprasaṅgānmā bhudativyāptitā lakṣaṇadoṣaḥ—ityato 'vaśyakaraṇīyamabhrāntagrahaṇam ityuktam.*

CHAPTER 7

Foundationalism and the Phenomenology of Perception

The persistence of perceptual ambiguities, even under the best observational conditions, always challenges an attempt to ground knowledge on a foundation of empirical experience. Few philosophers, however, would argue that the reliability of perception is a nontrivial issue for epistemology. If anything, reasoning from experience would be compromised, as in the classical example of trying to infer the presence of fire from an observation of smoke, while mistaking dust for smoke. For the Buddhist epistemologists, the problem of the reliability of perception is central to their knowledge project. Indeed, they argue that empirical awareness, when properly deployed, can and does reveal the nature of reality at its most fundamental level: a causally interdependent nexus of psycho-physical phenomena in a constant state of flux. As we saw above, this non-ordinary form of empiricism is precisely what Śāntarakṣita and Kamalaśīla appeal to in their defense of the principle of dependent arising.

This Buddhist epistemological claim about perception is, of course, strongly counterintuitive: ordinarily our experience opens up to a world populated with autonomous, enduring entities (and selves) that do not change from moment to moment. It is this basic intuition about continuance that allows us to recognize previously encountered entities and make predictions about their future. From a phenomenological point of view, however, what we take to be "selves" and "entities" are disclosed as series of discrete cognitive episodes and aggregated phenomena of experience. Moreover, an intentional consciousness is always co-present in each instance of perception, manifest in the fact that there is *something it is like* to be apprehending an object, to use Thomas Nagel's well-worn formula. Here "intentionality" captures not only the mind's directedness toward an object but also the mind's own open awareness.

This transitory nature of the perceived *as perceived* is one of the main reasons why a phenomenological account of perception best serves to translate the intuitions of the Buddhist epistemologists about the cognitive function of perception. Indeed, just as Husserl regards intentionality as constitutive of perception and that which is perceived, so also the Buddhist epistemologist takes the sense-object relation as an issue of continuing concern; hence, the Buddhist's insistence that each cognitive event represents a new acquaintance with the object. This continuing concern for the sense-object relation explains why the Buddhist treats cognition as bearing the characteristic marks of embodiment: it is the dynamics of the five aggregates that gives the cognitive event its expression. It also explains why the pursuit of reliable cognitions, contrary to what one might expect, does not automatically qualify Buddhist epistemology as a type of foundationalism.

Let me begin, first, by calling into question the assumption that the epistemological concerns of Dignāga, Dharmakīrti, and their successors reflect a commitment to foundationalism. First, if there is a "founding givenness" that direct perception provides, it cannot be constituted by ontologically distinct particulars, be they unique "properties" or "property bearers." Instead, direct perception captures the co-presence of sense and object characteristic of the "raw" phenomena of experience. The main point of the Buddhist epistemological project is, thus, to build on insights about the structure of experience (making it pragmatic in scope): in Dharmakīrti's celebrated formulation, it is because all successful human actions are preceded by right knowledge that epistemology, understood as an inquiry into the sources of reliable cognition, is a worthwhile enterprise.[1]

Teasing out the "founding givenness" of perception in a way that lays no recognizable claim to foundationalism is precisely how a phenomenological approach to perception proceeds: after all, our *reflection* on the contents of experience, unlike direct perception itself, is not perspectival. In other words, whereas no single instance of perception can ever exhaust the object, perceptual judgments always apprehend the object exhaustively, by laying out certain claims about its nature and properties. It is a difference in their conception of the operations of thought that explains why the Buddhists and their principal opponents, the Naiyāyikas, take such opposite stances on what perception can and does apprehend.

Consider the different positions that Buddhists and Naiyāyikas adopt vis-à-vis perceptual ambiguities. For instance, when the early Naiyāyika philosopher Vātsyāyana gives the example of a person unable to decide whether

1. NB I, 1: "Right knowledge precedes the attainment of all successful human action, [and] this [is the reason for] giving an exposition of it." (*samyagjñānapūrvikā sarvapuruṣārthasiddhir iti tad vyutpādyate*).

what is seen rising in the distance are (columns of) dust or smoke,[2] he touches upon one of the most complex questions in the phenomenology of perception: what turns the continuous flow of sense experience into perceptually distinct objects? Vātsyāyana is mainly concerned with the consequences of this indecisiveness for perception, precisely by noting the fact that one could easily mistake such cognitions resulting from contact between the sense and the object for perception (that is, for indirect perception, which alone can serve as a basis for certainty). But he is also preoccupied with meeting the Nyāya epistemological demand that a causal account of perception include both indeterminate and determinate types of cognitive awareness. The first is resolved by adding to perception the qualifier "nondeceptive" (*avyabhicāri*) (thus eliminating perceptual illusions) and the latter simply by adding the qualifier "determined" (*vyavasāya*) (thus eliminating ambiguity).

It is with similar sorts of demands for defining the boundary conditions of empirical knowledge, I claim, that the Buddhist epistemologists define perception as a cognition entirely free of conceptual content. In doing so, they reject the intuitively more plausible account that perception starts with the indiscriminate sense data and ends up with something like a set of shared properties. Much of the dispute between the Buddhists and the Naiyāyikas on precisely what sort of cognitive capacities perception has, in fact, is directed at solving the ambiguity dilemma.

The placing of logical constraints to insure that perception discloses precisely the categories of a realist ontology, it seems, does not fully address the issue of perceptual indecisiveness. For the Naiyāyika, thus, the idea that the sense-object relation sometimes reveals ambiguities and illusions is a problem rather than a topic of study. Indeed, the Buddhist–Nyāya debate reveals an asymmetrical engagement in the epistemological project: the Buddhist epistemological account, informed by Abhidharma psychology, regards conceptual proliferation as the cause rather than the solution to the persistence of ambiguity; for Nyāya, on the other hand, perceptual judgments are the key, since perception is also defined as having the capacity to pick out universals.

In what follows, I defend a central thesis of the phenomenology of perception that I believe the Buddhist epistemologists would support: our cognitive faculties are embodied and embedded within the environment of which we are a part. I also argue that this intuition, which informs recent efforts within the Western philosophical tradition to overcome the legacy of the disembodied Cartesian cogito, seems to be at work, albeit in a modified form, in the Buddhist epistemological project. A central premise of the embodied cognition thesis, in the words of cognitive scientist Francisco Varela, philosopher Evan Thompson, and psychologist Eleanor Rosch, is that "first,

2. See NSBh *ad* NS I, 1.4.

cognition depends upon the kinds of experience that come from having a body with various sensorimotor capacities, and second, that these individual sensorimotor capacities are themselves embedded in the more encompassing biological, psychological, and cultural contexts."[3]

It is this covariance between our sensorimotor capacities and the phenomenal contingencies in which they are embedded that explains, for instance, why perceptual constancy forms the backbone of successful experience and insures that, to give an example, red apples remain red under all natural conditions of luminance, and people appear to retain their size even as they are about to disappear from view. The embodiment thesis, then, leaves the question of epistemic foundations open to negotiation, as first-person phenomenological perspectives gather to unravel the "raw" data of experience: the unique particulars that constitute the objects of experience become, as proposed by Varela et al., the "paradigm of a cognitive domain that is neither pre-given nor represented but rather experiential and enacted."[4] The subject-object relation thus extends beyond the cognitive to the experiential domains: "perception is not simply embedded within and constrained by the surrounding world; it also contributes to the enactment of this surrounding world."[5]

On the view advanced here, the particulars apprehended in perception are neither independent spatio-temporal entities nor purely intentional objects. Rather, they correspond to the dynamic co-determination of sense-consciousness and object characteristic of each cognitive event. The naturalist perspective informing the embodied cognition thesis is also an invitation to explore the role of perception pragmatically. The epistemic question of discerning the truth value of our cognitive states becomes, then, a subject for pragmatics. Indeed, the view that perceptual awareness has a pragmatic character resonates rather well with the Buddhist notion that any theory of reliable cognition ultimately depends on the purposeful efficacy of cognitions.

7.1 INTRINSIC ASCERTAINMENT AND THE "GIVEN"

It is commonly assumed that Buddhist philosophers of the Dignāga-Dharmakīrti tradition pursue a foundationalist agenda. This assumption is based on the requirement that at least some perceptions must be treated as intrinsically ascertained (*svataḥ prāmāṇya*). The project of the Buddhist epistemologists is thus framed in ways that resonate with the sort of foundationalism one finds criticized, for instance, in Sellars. This criticism centers

3. Varela, Thompson, and Rosch (1991: 172–173).
4. Varela, Thompson, and Rosch (1991: 171).
5. Varela, Thompson, and Rosch (1991: 171).

on the so-called "Myth of the Given," the idea that all knowledge ultimately rests on a foundation of non-inferential, belief-based knowledge.

Epistemological foundationalism is primarily concerned with the justification of knowledge which—of course—should be the main concern of any critique of Buddhist foundationalism. The basic view, as articulated by Tillemans, for instance, is that Buddhist philosophers adopt a position rather common among philosophers both East and West: that is, while conception might not accurately capture the contents of our experience, at least the *data* of experience, in itself, "must be real and unassailable."[6] We are thus told that the Buddhist preoccupation with defining what counts and what does not count as a source of knowledge—one that insures unmistakable access to the Given—is precisely that of traditional epistemology. But, the story goes, traditional epistemology contains irreconcilable tensions.

Of course, if we interpret epistemic foundationalism as grounding all knowledge in intrinsically ascertained cognitions, then, the key initiators of the Buddhist epistemological project, Dignāga and Dharmakīrti, *do* appear to be pursuing a foundationalist agenda (even though the issue of epistemic foundations is only explicitly treated in the commentarial literature on Dharmakīrti). But Dignāga does not address the issue of the intrinsic ascertainment of cognitions, and Dharmakīrti only frames it terms of their practical efficacy. For Devendrabuddhi (an early commentator of Dharmakīrti), who distinguishes between intrinsic and extrinsic ascertainment (*svataḥ-* and *parataḥ prāmāṇya*), perceptions are generally not intrinsically ascertained, except when related to the accomplishment of a human goal.[7] Śākyabuddhi (another early interpreter of Dharmakīrti's work) adds to the above the requirement that the causes of error be absent for perception to be intrinsically ascertained.[8] Dharmottara is the first to give a more nuanced account of the difference between intrinsic and extrinsic modes of ascertainment in the case of perceptual cognitions: "trained perception" (*abhyāsavat pratyakṣa*) and the perception associated with the fulfillment of a purpose may be intrinsically ascertained, whereas a perception in which the connection with an object is uncertain is not. To use an example, the way I grasp an entity by apprehending its general characteristics may be intrinsically ascertained—I apprehend an entity as having branches and leaves, that is, I apprehend a "treelike" entity—but its specific characteristics, that is, whether it is a Dhava (*anogeissus latifolia*) or a Palāśa (*butea frondosa*) tree are extrinsically ascertained.[9] On this account, closer scrutiny is actually required for

6. Tillemans (1990: 37–38).
7. See *Pramāṇavārttika-pañjikā* (D5a6–7), and translation and discussion in Dunne (2004: 376).
8. See *Pramāṇavārttika-ṭīkā* (D72a4-b1) and translation and discussion in Dunne (2004: 375 n. 4).
9. See PVinṬ 13.1–2.

apprehending those specific characteristics, uncertainty about which may impede placing the respective entity under the right category of, say, flowering plants. In his own comprehensive treatment of the nature of cognitions in the *Commentary*, Kamalaśīla identifies tree principal forms of perceptual apprehension as intrinsically ascertained: self-awareness, yogic perception, and "trained" or repeated perception.[10] The concern of the Buddhist epistemologists, however, is a different sort of concern than, for instance, that of modern empiricists targeted by anti-foundationalists. Here I want to make a heuristic suggestion. Perhaps we ought to frame the question of what motivates these Buddhists to accord perception a preeminent status over any other source of knowledge as two separate issues: first, the issues of whether the reliability of perception must be intrinsically ascertained, except for those instances where the connection with the object is uncertain (in which case, its reliability is extrinsically ascertained); second, the issue of whether the intrinsic ascertainment clause reflects a logical concern with avoiding infinite regress or an epistemic concern with how best to secure an indubitable status for perceptual cognitions. Thus, for example, I know that I am seeing a fire when my apprehension of fire also leads to ascertaining it as something that has the capacity to burn, radiate heat, or cook meals.[11]

The *locus classicus* of anti-foundationalism—at least within the tradition of analytic philosophy—is Sellars's critique of the sense-datum theorists: the criticism targets the distinction between the act of awareness, which is purported to give access to a phenomenologically simple, further irreducible, "Given," and the object, the pure sense datum of experience (for instance, a patch of color). While acknowledging various disagreements among sense-datum theorists about whether or not these acts of pure sensing are further analyzable, Sellars is keen to point out that the sensum itself is, ultimately, a relational property, since we cannot refer to a sensed something without reference to a *subject* of experience. Even alternative notions, such as *sensibles* or *sense properties*, still give the impression that "sensed items could exist without being sensed"[12]—a presupposition that Sellars and all critics of sense-datum theories find problematic.

But there is another reason why the epistemological category of the "Given" is regarded by Sellars as problematic: for sense-datum theorists the

10. For Kamalaśīla's comprehensive treatment of the difference between intrinsic and extrinsic ascertainment, see TSP *ad* TS 2944. For a detailed treatment of the status of intrinsic and extrinsic cognitions in the Buddhist epistemological literature, see also Steinkellner (1992: 259) and Krasser (2003).

11. For a discussion of the difference between intrinsic and extrinsic ascertainment with regards to Devendrabuddhi and Śakyabuddhi, see Dunne (2004: 294–297). In the TSP *ad* TS 2944, however, Kamalaśīla clearly demonstrates that cognitions are only intrinsically ascertained in some limited cases, while in most other cases they depend upon external conditions.

12. Sellars (1997: 15.).

given is neither the subject-object relation nor the phenomenally simple act of sensing, but the particular itself. In other words, the sense-datum theorist is confronted with a dilemma: either we sense particulars, in which case sensing is not epistemically warranted, or sensing is epistemically warranted, and what is thus sensed are facts, that is, states of affairs, rather than particulars. Either way, the presumption of some special epistemic access to non-inferential knowledge is ruled out: sensed colors, for instance, are not phenomenal data but epistemic facts about the content of experience.

Indeed, on Sellars's reading of the empiricist program, the Buddhist epistemologist, insofar as he or she grants perception cognitive status, is a foundationalist. But the Buddhist is not simply ascertaining the cognitive status of elemental sensing (the sort one associates with "raw" or primitive phenomenal experience). Rather, she stipulates that perceptual cognition needs two further constraints for its reliability: first, the requirement that only a restricted class of nondeceptive and non-inferential cognitions be counted as perception and, second, the demand that perception be understood as constituted by intentional content. It is the conflation of these two constraints that blurs the philosophically interesting consideration of whether or not the Buddhist epistemologists pursue a foundationalist agenda. Matilal was right, I think, to point out that the Buddhist argument—that perceptual awareness must necessarily be free of conception—is quite compelling if we take the view that perceptual cognitions reflect the causal power of the apprehended object: "if a perceptual awareness . . . can represent things that are in no way connected with the perceptual occasion, then one can be perceptually aware of anything and everything at any occasion since there would be no restriction on what the awareness could and would represent."[13] Any attempt to expand the range of perception beyond what is empirically given must necessarily confront the restriction problem: perception, then, becomes more like imagination in its (unrestricted) capacity to represent anything and everything.

7.2 PARTICULARS AND PHENOMENAL OBJECTS

The question of the epistemic status of perceptual cognitions is not the only problem with a foundationalist reading of the Buddhist epistemological project. I want to suggest a model that will seem, hopefully, a more suitable alternative: while it may be true that Buddhist epistemologists are preoccupied with establishing reliable grounds for knowledge, their program resembles that of the Husserlian phenomenologist rather than that of the modern empiricist or rationalist. Buddhist epistemology, at least in

13. Matilal (1986: 319).

the main tradition of Dignāga and Dharmakīrti, has a phenomenological orientation.

First of all, for the Buddhist epistemologist the nondeceptiveness of perception (i.e., its epistemically warranted status) does not imply, *pace* Tillemans, that its contents are factual *qua* objects extrinsic to awareness. Rather, perception is epistemically warranted because of, and only when, its content (that is, the object as perceived), is reflective of the causal cognitive web experience: only when I bracket ontological assumptions about a given object of experience, say a lotus flower, can I attend to its mode of presentation (as something of a particular size, color, degree of bloom, and intensity of fragrance). Second, this notion of perception as a cognition that is free of conception and capable of direct and unmistakable access to what is phenomenally given already represents an evolved stage in the formation of a cohesive theory of perceptual knowledge (*pratyakṣajñāna*) within the Buddhist tradition. Dignāga, as we saw above, does not view error as something that is within the purview of perception,[14] but rather as a consequence of conceptual discriminations. Unlike the Naiyāyikas, who use the qualifier "nonerroneous" to exclude perceptions caused by some kind of sensory impairment (e.g., color blindness, astigmatism, etc.), Dignāga treats perceptual illusions as a type of mental delusion. In the end, however, Dharmakīrti's recognition that distorted perceptions may in fact be caused by defective sense organs becomes the dominant Buddhist epistemological position. It is the pragmatic efficacy of the given object as directly encountered, then, that acts as a corrective, excluding from perception ambiguities and illusions.

Because the Buddhist conceives of perception as a constantly new introduction to an object, what is phenomenally given occurs within a wider horizon of the givenness of experience itself and is constituted not as a structurally unique entity but as change or, rather, as the principles underlying change: dependent arising and momentariness. But, we may ask, how can perception effectively cognize aggregated phenomena in constant motion as enduring, unitary, objects without the aid of concepts and higher order thought processes? After all, the (Sautrāntika) Abhidharma is clear that the object of perceptual awareness is the particular only as cognizable *sensibilia*. For example, only what is audible can be heard and only what is visible can be seen, and what is thus heard and seen depends on its phenomenal mode of

14. Dignāga treats perception (*pratyakṣa*) as an inerrant (*aviabhicārin*) cognition, an idea he adopts from the Nyāya definition of perception as found in the NS I, 1.4: "Perception is a cognition generated through the contact between the object and the sensory faculty, [and] which is inexpressible, inerrant and definitive" (*indriyārthasannikarṣotpannaṃ jñānamavyapadeśyam avyabhicāri vyavasāyātmakaṃ pratyakṣam*).

presentation. Dignāga's response to the above question invokes the "holistic" character of perceptual cognition:

> It is mentioned [in the Abhidharma treatise] that "these [sense-cognitions] take a unique particular (*svalakṣaṇa*) as their object insofar as it is the particular in the form of a [cognizable] sense-sphere (*āyatana-svalakṣaṇa*) and not in the form of a [constituent] substance [viz. an atom] (*dravya-svalakṣaṇa*)." How is this to be understood? There [in the Abhidharma passages cited above], that [perception], being caused by [the sense-organ through its contact with] many [aggregated] objects, takes the whole (*sāmānya*) as the object of its sphere of operation. Since it [viz., perception] is caused by [the sense-organ through its contact with] many substances [viz., aggregates of atoms], it is said, in respect to its sphere of operation, that it takes the whole as its object; but [it does] not [mean that it operates] by conceptually integrating that which is many and separate.[15]

Dignāga seems to be suggesting here that, in perception, the fragmentary and discrete elements of experience are apprehended as a unitary whole. It does not mean, however, that we perceive an object in its entirety, as though all its aspects were available at once: it only means that each instance of perception has a horizon structure that discloses both the particular aspect of the object *as experienced* and the perceiver's intentional stance. Thus, to use an example, perceiving color means having the visual experience of a specific shade, say, of cherry red or lime green. It is not as though perception acquaints us with varying shades of red or green as universal color categories, over and above the cognitive events in which they are instantiated. Rather, color qualia is just that: the qualitative experience of unique shades, which is the product of particular circumstances of luminance, the physiology of light perception, and self-awareness. If the appearance of a patch of blue in perception as a unitary, structureless whole is not the result of a subsequent process of conceptual construction, how, then, do we recognize it as such? We do, says Dignāga, because every instance of perceptual awareness is accompanied by self-awareness (*svasaṃvedana*). We do not simply perceive color: we have the experience of what it is like to be perceiving color.

This observation is interesting, I think, because it highlights the mutual tripartite constitutiveness of object intended, the intentional act, and the structureless given. It is here that the Buddhist epistemologist parts with traditional epistemology both East and West. Like a Husserlian

15. PSV *ad* PS I, 4ab: *rdas kyi rang gi mtshad nyid la ni ma yin no zhes kyang ji ltar gsungs she na, der don du mas bskyed pa'i phyir/rang don spyi yi spyod yul can/de rdas du mas bskyed par bya ba'i phyir na rang gi skye mched la sphyi'i spyod yul can zhes brjod kyi, tha dad pa la tha mi dad par rtogs pa las ni ma yin no*. Translation, slightly adjusted, *per* Hattori (1968: 26–27).

phenomenologist, he contends that experience extends the boundaries of the given, constraining "our reason to go beyond intuitionally given physical things."[16] These physical "things" are either the natural kinds of the realist or the sense-datum of the empiricist. In either case, the Buddhist agrees with Husserl that "whatever physical things there are," and whatever their ontological status, "they are as experienceable physical things."[17] In Buddhist terms, these discrete entities that bear their own distinctive mark (*svalakṣaṇa*) are particulars only *qua* phenomena of experience.

Phenomenologically, then, the "Given" is a non-inferential cognitive *event* that cuts through the dilemma of the sense-datum theorist: sensing *just is* the sort of perceptual awareness best suited to apprehend the constitutive elements of experience; it is not knowledge of "facts." This phenomenological sensing is, I think, fittingly captured by Merleau-Ponty's notion that reflection bears upon and discloses an unreflected experience. As a reflection, however, it depends upon, and has to acknowledge, the primacy of the world over its own operations: not of an abstract or putatively independent world, but of a world that is "given to the subject because the subject is given to himself."[18]

But does this "unreflected experience" have any cognitive content? Hubert Dreyfus has argued, I think convincingly, that this pure phenomenological sensing does have, indeed, "a kind of *intentional* content: it just isn't conceptual content."[19] Taking as an example master level chess, specifically lightning chess, Dreyfus suggests that at the speed it takes to play a game in less than two minutes, players must necessarily rely "entirely on perception and not at all on analysis and comparison of alternatives."[20] The master chess player's knowledge is thus embodied (that is, it cannot be analytic). The main target of Dreyfus' criticism is McDowell's conceptualism (as developed at length in his *Mind and World*[21]). In rejecting the possibility of nonconceptual cognitive states, and in advancing an intellectualist view—best captured by Merleau-Ponty's observation that for the intellectualist "judgment is everywhere pure sensation is not, which is to say everywhere"[22]—McDowell, like Sellars, joins Kant by endorsing what Dreyfus calls "the Myth of the Mental."[23] Phenomenology, thus, opens up a third alternative beyond the "bare Given" and the "mere conceptual"; hence, the invitation to "accept the possibility

16. Husserl (1983: 105).
17. Husserl (1983: 105).
18. Merleau-Ponty (2002: xi).
19. Dreyfus (2006: 11).
20. Dreyfus (2006: 8).
21. McDowell (1994).
22. Merleau-Ponty (2002: 39).
23. Dreyfus (2006: 17).

that our ground-level coping opens up the world by opening us to a *meaningful* Given—a Given that is *non-conceptual* but not bare."[24]

Similarly, drawing primarily from James Gibson's (1979) ecological approach to perception, José Bermúdez has argued for the possibility of developing a nonconceptual point of view, one that goes beyond both the empiricist distinction between sensation and belief, and the rationalist view that a representation of the world can only be had by means of conception.[25] However paradoxical it may sound, we must concur with Bermúdez that "there are forms of non-conceptual self-consciousness that are both logically and ontologically more primitive than the higher forms of self-consciousness."[26] Indeed, the complex and multilayered structure of self-awareness can be easily overlooked if one ignores the phenomenology of perception.[27]

Despite the ambiguities in Husserl's statement that there is a direct correspondence between an inherently noetic content and a noematic content,[28] such that each perception "has its noema" or the "perceived as such," there is little doubt that Husserl conceives of the phenomenological reduction (*epoché*) as precisely the instrument by which we can describe the data of perception *as perceived*: "What is this perceived as such? . . . We can obtain the answer to the above question by pure openness to what is essentially given; we can describe 'what appears as such' in complete evidence."[29]

But there is more to being (phenomenologically) aware of the perceived as such than seizing upon the noema of what is essentially given: we only apprehend it (viz., the Given) one aspect at a time, and this apprehension of the discrete elements of experience creates a certain allure for what, indeed, is yet to be given. Commenting on what the infinite potentialities of experience hold for our apprehension of the given, Husserl writes:

> The division applying to what is genuinely perceived and what is only co-present entails a distinction between determinations with respect to the content of the object that are actually there, appearing in the flesh, and those that are still ambiguously

24. Dreyfus (2006: 12).
25. See Bermúdez (1995, 2000).
26. Bermúdez (1998: 294).
27. For an account of direct perception that regards it as in some sense always connected with imagery and higher order thought processes, see Fodor and Pylyshyn (1981).
28. This ambiguity was first noted by Dreyfus (1982: 98) while exploring the different interpretations of the meaning of Husserl's perceptual noema (the intentional correlate of perceptual consciousness). The two dominant interpretations are those of Gurwitsch (1967) and Føllesdal (1969). Føllesdal proposes a Fregean model of the noema as a concept, while the latter argues that the noema best fits the Gestalt theory description of a percept. For a recent review of the (continuing) debate on the meaning of Husserl's noema, see Zahavi (2004a: 42–66).
29. Husserl (1983: 128).

prefigured in full emptiness. Let us also note that what actually appears, is, in itself, also laden with a similar distinction. Indeed, the call resounds as well with respect to the side that is already actually seen: "Draw closer, closer still; now fix your eyes upon me, changing your place, changing the position of your eyes, etc. You will get to see even more of me that is new, ever new partial colorings etc. You will get to see structures of the wood that were not visible just a moment ago, structures that were formerly only viewed indeterminately and generally," etc. Thus, even what is already seen is laden with an anticipatory intention. It—what is already seen—is constantly there as a framework prefiguring something new.[30]

Thus, each instance of perception reveals a new aspect of an object, making accessible what was hitherto unknown (but brimming with potentiality). There is more, for instance, to visual consciousness than what is immediately apprehended, namely, the prefiguration of what is yet to be seen or of what might be seen. This distinction between what is genuinely perceived and what is merely co-present in the perceptual event becomes clear only after the *epoché*: it is only the *genuinely perceived*, then, that counts as nonconceptual noematic content.

I want to claim that the Buddhist epistemological account of perception is phenomenological in a sense that captures the intent of Husserl's method of *epoché*: its aim is to convey that particulars are defined in relation to some kind of unique nonconceptual noematic content. It seems that Husserl quite clearly distinguishes between the data of the inherent noetic content or *hyle* (the *qualia* of experience, e.g., redness, hardness) and the data of the noematic content (the thing perceived *as perceived*, e.g., the round plate, which seems oval from one's specific vantage point sitting at the table): "Corresponding in every case to the multiplicity of Data pertaining to the really inherent noetic content, there is a multiplicity of Data, demonstrable in actual pure intuition, in a correlative '*noematic content*.' This noema, or perceptual sense (*Sinn*) is nothing but the *perceived as perceived*."[31] This epistemologically relevant nonconceptual noematic content (e.g., that specific apple-like-shade-of-red by which something is apprehended as a red apple) cuts through the dilemma of choosing, on the one hand, between a coherence theory of justification (in which beliefs are justified because they belong to a coherent system of beliefs) and a (presumably bare) perceptual "Given."

A case for the epistemic relevance of nonconceptual noematic content has been made recently by Michael Shim, who argues that Husserl's noema, contrary to Dagfinn Føllesdal's Fregean interpretation, also admits, besides internal representational content, noemata of the perceptual sort that are nonconceptual. If indeed, as Shim suggests, Husserl allows for the noematic

30. Husserl (1952: 183; 1989: 216).
31. Husserl (1983: 214).

nonconceptual content to be perceived, then solving the problem of the veridicality and reliability of perceptual cognitions demands not simply an abandonment of the natural attitude but also effecting the *epoché*. Without the phenomenological reduction, conceptualization easily reduces the contents of perception to a theoretically coherent system of beliefs about experience, thus forcing a conclusion that coherentists, for instance, share with Naiyāyikas: *the content of experience is conceptual*.[32]

Furthermore, I want to suggest another reason why the "Myth of the Given" (so-called by Sellars) and the "doctrine of the Naturally Given" (Rorty's terminology)[33]—namely, that knowledge essentially stands for any cognitive apprehension of entities immediately present to consciousness—do not capture the intent of the Buddhist epistemological program.

Before we take a more in-depth look at these Buddhist thinkers, let's consider two of the most robust responses to current debates about foundationalism: phenomenological philosophy and naturalized epistemology. For its part, phenomenology relies on a methodology of bracketing the natural attitude, and thus resists the tendency to rest arguments about foundationalism on a naïve acceptance of the world and of our common experience of it. On the other hand, naturalized epistemology diverts the discussion about foundationalism in the direction of the sciences of cognition, where investigations into the structure and dynamics of cognition take precedence over issues of justification and a priori reasoning.

Phenomenology starts with the premise that any critique of foundationalism, which neither brackets nor examines the natural attitude, is essentially limited to logical reductions only: at best it can shift the attention from inquiring about the epistemic nature of statements, insofar as they reflect facts about the world, to analyzing their logical content and their propositional meaning. Consider, for instance, John Drummond's claim that phenomenology, albeit apodictic and transcendental, is effectively a "nonfoundationalist discipline."[34] Responses to foundationalism, then, may be sorted along three main critical attitudes: (i) logical (the Fregean tradition), (ii) epistemological (the Kantian tradition), and (iii) phenomenological (the Husserlian tradition). For the logical attitude, the concern is mainly confined to the distinction between valid and sound arguments. To this logical distinction, the epistemological attitude adds concerns about the formal content of a statement and the experienced objectivity. It is only in the phenomenological attitude, however, that we attend to intentional consciousness, which

32. Shim (2005: 209–229).

33. Rorty (1980: 104). Note that Rorty understands the doctrine of the "naturally given" to encompass both the Cartesian and behaviorist accounts of the "perceptually given."

34. Drummond (1991: 45).

means that any phenomenological account of knowledge must take into account *three* things: (i) the knowing or experiencing subject, (ii) the experienced object itself, and (iii) the experienced object *as experienced*.

It is precisely to the extent that we go beyond the interplay between "sense" and "object," and seek to account for the structure of the intentional act, that we operate within the phenomenological attitude. The anti-foundationalism that drives most debates in epistemology testifies to this oversight, since it largely lacks an account of intentional consciousness. Until recently, most discussions in analytic epistemology either neglected intentionality or reduced it to analyses of perceptual content.[35] Furthermore, attempts to naturalize intentionality have concentrated largely on the so-called "tracking approach"—an effort to understand intentionality in terms of tracking relations between physical items.[36] While phenomenological analyses of intentionality have shifted the attention in most analytic epistemology away from reductive explanations of experiential content,[37] much remains to be done.[38]

It is well known that both Frege and Husserl conceived of their projects as reactions to psychologism. But their conceptions of what should count as foundational for knowledge are substantially different. For his part, Frege's reduction of the experienced content to a third realm of logical sense effectively collapses the experienced content into a realm of self-evident and self-justifying statements about relations between subject and object, the inner and the outer. This relation is conceived either externally, that is, as causation, presentation, representation, etc., or, most often, left unexplained. The contrast with the phenomenological attitude could not be more obvious: subject and object are not externally correlated "wholes" but parts of the all-encompassing intentional act. The object is the intentional object as intended, which is why, as Drummond maintains in his critique of the foundationalism debate, "the experienced or the intentional content of experience

35. As Drummond claims, such reductive treatments "reduce the immediate object of our experience from the object itself to the perceptual content, thus subjectifying the objective content, and they conceive this content as a psychic content" (1991: 49).

36. See, especially Kriegel (2011: 68ff.). Kriegel (2011) offers a critique of the naturalizing intentionality program in analytic philosophy of mind, while at the same time advancing a robust new framework for naturalizing all intentionality by integrating naturalized non-experiential intentionality (as captured by the tracking model) within naturalized experiential intentionality (or phenomenal intentionality). It is this experiential intentionality, as captured by the character of conscious experiences (a character that conscious experience has by virtue of being conscious) that resists naturalization.

37. See Strawson (2005) for a critical survey of the current discussion of intentionality in analytic philosophy.

38. I sketch such an account, with reference to perception, below (see chapter 8).

is not 'psychologized' or 'logicized'."[39] "Experience," "experienced object," and "experienced object as experienced" are all defining events within the same *experienced objectivity*. Indeed, Drummond brings out quite clearly the sense of the intentional correlation between the (intentional) act and the (intended) object when he argues that the phenomenologist studies not consciousness in a world that is pre-consciously given and already constituted, but "consciousness *of* the world . . . as that which makes possible the world as such, not in the sense that it makes possible the *existence* of the world, but in the sense that it makes possible a *significant* world."[40]

Now: let's see whether these arguments in favor of a non-foundationalist phenomenological reflection, and of the inherent intentionality of consciousness, serve better to illustrate the Buddhist philosophical program of Dignāga and Dharmakīrti (and whether the Buddhist philosophical program might, despite its apparently foundationalist stance, share a common ground with phenomenology and its method). The question before us, then, is whether the Buddhist epistemological commitment to knowledge of the "Given" is suggestive of a foundationalist project.

Let's begin, first, with the Buddhist Abhidharma notion that only partless entities count as (ultimately) real. This point is demonstrated by Vasubandhu, who differentiates things such as pots and clothes, which exist only conventionally, from what is ultimately real. The argument at play here is that entities which can be physically fragmented or dissolved in conceptual analysis are not ultimately real, unlike the elements of existence and/or experience (*dharmas*) which are:

> When the apprehension of an entity persists after that entity has been reduced through conceptual analysis, that entity exists ultimately, e.g., *form*: while form may be reduced to atoms, and while we may exclude from it through cognitive analysis other qualia (such as taste, etc.), the apprehension of the proper nature of *form* persists. Feelings too are to be understood [as ultimately true]. As this [empirical awareness] exists ultimately, it is [also] ultimately true. As declared by older authorities: the manner in which entities are perceived, either by means of a supra-mundane cognition or by means of a subsequently acquired mundane cognition, is how they ultimately exist.[41]

---

39. Drummond (1991: 49).

40. Drummond (2007: 61).

41. AKBh *ad* AK VI, 4: *anyadharmāpohe'pi buddhayā tat paramārthasat/tadyatha rūpam/tatra hi paramāṇuśe bhinne vastuni rasārhānapi ca dharmānapohya budhayā rūpasya svabhāvabuddhirbhaktyeva/evaṃ vedanādayo'pi dṛṣṭvyāḥ/etat paramārthan bhāvāt paramārthasatyam iti/yathā lokotareṇa jñānena gṛhyate tat pṛṣṭhalabdhena vā laukikena tatha paramārthasatyam/ . . . pūrvācāryāḥ/.*

Several arguments are put forward here: first, that only entities which persists after physical fragmentation and conceptual analysis count as ultimately real; second, that our sense experiences (feelings, vision, etc.) are real by virtue of our condition of embodiment, and that what they disclose is also real; and finally, that the manner in which entities are apprehended is precisely how they ordinarily exist—keeping in mind that the unique particular is here understood to refer to an entity within the sphere of perception (*āyatana-svalakṣaṇa*), thus to the perceived *as perceived*, not to the properties of a substantive entity (*dravya-svalakṣaṇa*). The arguments adduced in support of the view that the ultimately real is irreducible take into account the doctrine of momentariness: what we apprehend as distinct spatio-temporal entities are, in fact, discrete series of phenomena[42] undergoing constant change. In equating reality with momentariness, the Buddhist epistemologist adheres to the atomism, which is a common characteristic of all Abhidharma schools.

There is, however, an important shift in emphasis from ontological to epistemological concerns within those schools of Ābhidharmic thought, the Sautrāntika and Yogācāra, with which the concerns of the Buddhist epistemologists are most often aligned. The "real" is described in pragmatic rather than ontological terms. If the phenomenal reality were made up of changeless and enduring entities, the effects produced by such entities would be equally changeless and enduring, giving rise to a logical impossibility: what does not change cannot produce any effect, for its effect would either be identical with the generating cause or would consist in a perpetual iteration of itself. Such is, then, the conclusion that Dharmakīrti draws following his appraisal of Vasubandhu's notion that only partless entities are ultimately real. For Dharmakīrti, *causal efficacy*, or the ability of an object to perform a function (*arthakriyāsamartha*), is the true mark of the real:

This particular alone constitutes an object [of perception]; others [viz., universals and the like] are concealed [from the purview of perception]. This [particular] is referred to in terms of cause and effect and is what we mean by [the term] "particular." As we have said, only an entity that has causal efficacy is deemed a real object [of perception]. And it is [this specific particular which we] referred to as an individual object.[43]

42. Note that for someone like Dharmakīrti, the "phenomena" under discussion are not simply internal noematic content, but infinitesimal particles that can, in principle, be perceptually apprehended. See PV III, 194. Arguably, at the (sub)atomic level of swarming infinitesimal particles the internal/external distinction no longer applies.

43. Dharmakīrti, PVSV *ad* PV III, 171cd–172: *ato viśeṣa eva/sa evārthas tasya vyāvṛttayo 'pare/tat kāryakāraṇaṃ coktaṃ tat svalakṣaṇam iṣyate//tattyāgāptiphalāḥ sarvāḥ*

Indeed, as has been argued, I think convincingly, Dignāga, Dharmakīrti, and their successors do not use the concepts of "particular" and "universal" in their original Abhidharmic sense. While examining its meaning and use by Vasubandhu in his earlier Abhidharma works, John Dunne, for instance, notes, "a *svalakṣaṇa* is a way of characterizing an object in terms of a property that is peculiar to the type of entity in question" such that attending to the particular "one understands it to have 'the characteristic of being disturbed [by contact, etc.]' (*rūpaṇālakṣaṇa*)."[44] Thus used, *svalakṣaṇa* indicates "a defining characteristic of a single type of entity (*dharma*) in the Abhidharma typology,"[45] rather than an external referent (viz., a unique particular).

But even if the Buddhist epistemologist shifts the focus of perception from unique particulars (tokens) to phenomenal types, the "uniqueness" of the perceived *as perceived* stems from its mode of presentation (even though for the Buddhist the ultimately real has no spatial or temporal extension). But the manner in which an object presents its own form is also reflective of its mode of apprehension. On the Abhidharma account, the unique and irreducible elements within its complex taxonomy are always related to conceptually cognate terms such as "unique particular" (*svalakṣaṇa*) and "intrinsic nature" (*svabhāva*). These terms are cognitive equivalents of what is generally designated as a "bearer" (*dharma*).[46] Examples of such unique particulars in the Abhidharma ontology are feelings and thoughts, although the focus is less on the kind of entities that there are and more on how they are disclosed. As Vasubandhu states: "The body is examined in relation to its particular and universal characteristics. Feelings and thoughts are dharmas; the nature of these [feelings and thoughts] is their particular characteristic."[47] It is here, I maintain, that a phenomenological reading of the apprehension of particulars serves better to capture the Buddhist epistemological account of perception. Thoughts and feeling are momentary and discrete, if recurrent, and reflect the dynamics of the psycho-physical aggregates that are constitutive of human experience. Ultimately, however, they are reflective of our condition of embodiment to which perceptual awareness provides constant and unmediated cognitive access.

As Merleau-Ponty tells us: "In perception we do not think the object and we do not think ourselves thinking it, we are given over to the object and we

---

puruṣāṇāṃ pravṛttayaḥ/yad arthakriyākāri tat eva vastv iti uktaṃ/sa ca viśeṣa eva. Cf. Dunne (2004: 84) and Dreyfus (1997: 67, 479).

44. Dunne (2004: 83–84).

45. Dunne (2004: 82).

46. See AKBh *ad* AK I, 1cd: "[They are called] *dharmas* because they 'bear' particulars." (*svalakṣanasdhāraṇād dharmaḥ*). Cf. Cox (1995: 12).

47. AK VI, 14cd: *kāyaṃ svasāmānyalakṣaṇābhyāṃ parīkṣate/vedanāṃ cittaṃ dharmāś ca/svabhāva evaiṣāṃ svalakṣaṇam*.

merge into this body which is better informed than we are about the world, and about the motives we have and the means at our disposal."[48] Perception does not provide a descriptive image of reality, an internal map of what is externally available, but a normative account of how the world must be for my experience of it to be practically efficacious or, in Merleau-Ponty's terminology, to have maximal grip on it. The Buddhist would most certainly agree with Merleau-Ponty when he claims that "every perception takes places in an atmosphere of generality," even though "when seen from the inside, expresses a given situation: I can see blue because I am *sensitive* to colors."[49]

Whether such unique particulars are regarded as real and unitary entities, existing over and above their intentional apprehension, or as constitutive of the phenomenal content and character of experience, thus also as qualitative aspects of experience,[50] cannot be settled on the basis of conceptual analysis alone. Granted commitment to a type of phenomenalism, the Buddhist takes perceptual awareness in its varied forms to be perfectly suited to disclose both the external domain of empirical phenomena and the internal domain of reflection. And, while conceptual entities are outside the realm of phenomenal experience (abstract concepts are phenomenally inert), the perceptual object *as perceived* or, in phenomenological terms, the noematic content, is *not*, despite the fact that it is only by means of its unique defining characteristics that we intend a particular as such. What is thus intended is an object given under a specific phenomenal or qualitative aspect[51] that is to be understood as perceiver-dependent phenomenal content. Perception, when closely attended to, discloses an array of phenomenal experiences of hardness, softness, roughness, luminance, weight, etc. But when these qualitative experiences are fused together into something like a distinct spatio-temporal object,[52] we no longer move within the horizon of perceptual awareness, but are instead caught in the operations of thought.

So, how do we apprehend these particulars as unitary wholes given that their constitutive elements are never dissociated at once? For some

48. Merleau-Ponty (2002: 238).

49. Merleau-Ponty (2002: 250).

50. For a comprehensive taxonomy of qualia, see Harman (1990) and Ramachandran and Hirstein (1997). A classical reductionist view of qualia is found in Levine (1983). Addressing the question of whether qualitative experiences can be naturalized, McIntyre (1999: 429) argues that only by taking a non-phenomenological stand can qualia be reduced to external representations.

51. I understand phenomenal qualia to have epistemic valence and be causally efficacious, though I take the efficacy of our perceptions to be covariant with the sensory input. Cf. Wright (2008: 35, 343), who borrows the notion of covariance from Palmer's (1999) view that vision science reveals a structural isomorphism between sensory input and phenomenal experience.

52. Even though the object is apprehended as a cluster of phenomenal properties, for someone like Vasubandhu conditioned things are real insofar as they are causally effective. See AKBh *ad* AK II, 55cd.

Abhidharma philosophers (viz., the Vaibhāṣikas), all aggregated entities comprise the four elements, but the physical aspect of any given aggregated entity depends on additional causal and conditional factors: for instance, under certain circumstances something solid may become liquid, like heat causing the melting of a block of ice into water. For others (viz., the Sautrāntikas), physical qualities are present only as mere potentialities. In a block of ice, the fire element is only potentially present, for without this potentiality, ice cannot melt and become water. The primary property of any given substance thus depends on the preponderance of any one element (viz., earth, water, etc.) with which that property is associated. The same principle of preponderance applies to all natural kinds. In the case of aggregated entities such as trees and cows, it is no longer the principle of preponderance that applies but rather that of being a product of certain causes and conditions. A cow is not a mere collection of elements with a certain predominant property like solidity, heat, or capacity to produce milk. It is also not a conceptually constructed entity like a forest, or a car, that is analytically reducible to its primitive parts.

If particulars designate the phenomenal aspects of objects *as experienced objects*, then what is given in perception are partless wholes, rather than differentiated structural elements. The question, then, is whether this Abhidharma analysis tells us something about the nature of the particular itself or, perhaps, about the epistemic function of perception itself: surely, this question is a crucial one for any epistemological project, foundationalist or otherwise. Pursuing a similar sort of question, Dan Arnold has recently concluded that it is Dignāga's intuition about particulars that is served by his account of perception, rather than the other way round.[53] In other words, the account of perception Dignāga advances ultimately aims to justify the existence of particulars as uniquely qualified entities. For this reason, Dignāga is, to a certain degree, constrained to adopt precisely the sort of definition of perception that justifies his understanding of the particular.

Dignāga's understanding and definition of the particular is the logical conclusion of a long tradition of speculation about the irreducible elements of existence. Now, are these "particulars" in the sense of "irreducible phenomenal aspects of experience," or in the sense of "ontologically primitive categories"? Arnold interprets Dignāga as departing from Vasubandhu's view that these are particulars as types rather than things, "types of which there can be, presumably, an infinite number of tokens."[54] Arnold proposes that we understand the particulars as *properties* of phenomenal objects, because such an understanding reflects the common usage of the term in Abhidharma texts. Whether or not we treat particulars as types, it is obvious

53. Arnold (2005a: 22).
54. Arnold (2005a: 18).

that Vasubandhu's Abhidharma project seems concerned with more than sorting through an elaborate taxonomy of ontological primitives—the sole purpose of which is to provide a causal account of what is taken to exist only conventionally.

Although the Buddhist epistemologist does take the phenomenally given "particular" to correspond to an object that is perceived, there is an apparent wavering between an externalist account of evidence and an internalist account of reasons. We may interpret this wavering, clearly an attitude that Śāntarakṣita and Kamalaśīka adopt from Dharmakīrti, as testimony that a resolution to the question of how mind and world arise and are co-constituted in each instance of awareness is yet to be reached. In chapter 9 we will venture a speculative account of what such a resolution might look like if we rework the Buddhist epistemological account of the relation between mind and body in the context of contemporary debates about emergence in cognitive science. For now, let me simply reiterate that, regardless of whether the 'data' of perception (at least under certain conditions of warrantability) is to be taken as real and unassailable, such 'data' cannot be ascertained as being observer independent. Rather, what is given emerges fully in perception along with an intentional act of consciousness. Consciousness may be characterized thus as "awareness of an object,"[55] as inherently intentional, essentially as consciousness *of* something in the Husserlian sense. This consciousness is essentially an object-oriented consciousness in the same manner in which "hardness" or "resistance" is an inherent property of the experience of what we generically designate as "earth." Thus, Arnold's suggestion that "*svalakṣaṇas* in virtue of which *dharmas* qualify as such are, in fact, universals or abstractions"[56] effectively collapses the difference between the particular that *acts as* support for the perceptual cognition and the particular *as perceived*.

But, whereas Vasubandhu's analysis of types includes both "substantial" properties and "conceptual" designations, Dignāga's understanding of the particular as found, *inter alia*, in the *Collection* is purely phenomenological: the particular is a sort of uniquely characterized phenomenon accessible only through a perceptual cognition, and serving as the latter's noematic content (viz., the perceived as such). For Dignāga, then, the particular is not simply internal, uniquely characterized sense-data but veridical, nonconceptual content. What makes it veridical is the fact that it is intersubjectively available and pragmatically effective. Indeed, the causal efficacy of objects informs both Dignāga and Dharmakīrti's arguments that what should generally be termed "perception" consists in a series of distinct cognitive events

55. For the sake of consistency and also because consciousness and perceptual awareness are not interchangeable for the Buddhists, I translate *vijñāna* as "consciousness" and *vijñapti* as "awareness."

56. Arnold (2005a: 26).

that are causally related. On this model, contact between sense and object gives rise to a perceptual event, which re-presents (in the sense of *making present*) the specific characteristics of the object. The relationship between the perceptual aspect and the empirical object is one of similarity. Thus, whereas the object causally determines its perceptual aspect, the manner of its appearance (its phenomenal character)[57] is determined by factors that are intrinsic to cognition itself.

As Dharmakīrti states: "Except for a cause, there is nothing else that [could constitute an entity's] being an apprehended object. Among the [causes of awareness], that [cause] in the image of which awareness [arises] is called the apprehended object of that [awareness]."[58] Note, however, that although both Dignāga and Dharmakīrti appear to adopt an empirical standpoint regarding the status of external objects, their analysis of perception reflects an internalist perspective that ultimately denies the reality of external objects.

Now, let us continue our discussion with the idea that the reliability of perception must be intrinsically ascertained. It seems to me that when the Buddhist defends the idea that certain perceptions must be regarded as intrinsically ascertained the primary concern is avoiding the problem of infinite regress. As Śāntarakṣita reminds us, "there can be no infinite regress if validity depends [upon an external cause]. Hence, certainty about self-validity only ensues when there is an apprehension of effective action."[59] Indeed, what is characteristic of perceptual cognitions is precisely the fact that they reflect the causal power of the apprehended phenomena. For the Buddhist, thus, I know that I am perceiving fire, for instance, when I apprehend something as capable of fulfilling a certain purpose or function: burning and radiating heat.[60] An opponent, in this case a Mīmāṃsaka realist, would be curious, of course, to find out exactly what kinds of specific conditions must be in place in order to differentiate between succeeding cognitions.

---

57. Dharmakīrti distinguishes between four types of perceptual appearances (*pratyakṣābhāsa*), three of those pertain to conceptual cognitions and one to nonconceptual factors pertaining to perturbations at the basis (*āśrayopaplava*) (the basis here refers to the sensory systems). See PV III, 288.

58. PVin I, 34: *hetubhāvād ṛte na anyā grāhyāta nāma kācana. tatra buddhir yadākāra tasyās tadgrāhyam ucyate*. Whether or not Dharmakīrti retains the causal model of perception in the case of internal objects is a subject of some dispute. See Dreyfus (1997: 336) and Dunne (2004: 84) for a discussion of this issue.

59. TS 2958: *ucyate—vastusaṃvādaḥ prāmāṇyamabhidhīyate/tasya cārthakriyābhyāsajñānādanyanna lakṣaṇam//arthakriyāvabhāsaṃ ca jñānaṃ saṃvedyate sphuṭam*.

60. The criterion of efficacy for the entity capable of producing an effect is its spatiotemporal restriction (*deśakālapratiniyama*). Following Vasubandhu, the efficacy (*sāmarthya*) of fire in cooking is established precisely on the basis of radiating heat, and its effects (warmth, cooked meats, etc.) are always spatiotemporally restricted. See AKBh 130, 27 *ad* III, 19d and AKV *ad* III, 284. Cf. Yoshimizu (2007).

The answer comes in the form of a unique type of Buddhist pragmatism: the condition of validity is defined by the formal similarity of cognition with the real entity—a similarity whose warrant is none other than the continuous cognition of practical efficacy.

But "practical efficacy," we are told, does not come in leaps and bounds. Each perception always manifests its practical efficacy with certainty, even in the case of perceptual illusions, which is precisely why no subsequent cognition of practical efficacy is ever needed. For Śāntarakṣita only cognitions causally anchored in reality count as knowledge events—a typical case of reiterating Dharmakīrti's position that only cognitions that are in conformity with their respective objects are epistemically warranted. Isn't it true, says the Buddhist, that it is only when one wants to attain a certain goal that the reliability of cognitions becomes a matter of concern? How else would one get thinking about epistemic warrants? I take it that here we have a typical case of reducing the epistemic impulse to various personal and interpersonal dispositions that are part of the structure of being. Presumably, on Dharmakīrti's suggestion, if one were not concerned with actions and their results, one would not be particularly bothered with issues of reliability and efficacy. It is only because successful action depends on having veridical cognitions (that conform with the object) that an individual is driven to pursue epistemic inquiries.

While it may be true that Indian epistemological theories did not draw a distinction between the causal question and the questions of justification, there are good reasons to believe that the absence of such a distinction simply reflects the pragmatic concerns of Indian philosophers, rather than a failure to address the normative question—of why might we be justified in believing something—on its own. If, indeed, Indian epistemologies treat as warranted only that cognition which "corresponds to its object" and "is produced in the right way,"[61] their explanations of the nature and scope of epistemic dispositions must perforce be anchored in the sensorimotor contingencies of phenomenal experience.

7.3 FOUNDATIONALISM AND ITS MALCONTENTS

Recall our previous observation that the reflexivity of perception is mainly geared to address the problem of infinite regress. In effect, the notion that only direct modes of perception that are also self-intimating are epistemically warranted addresses two main issues: (i) the fallacy of infinite regress, where cognition always depends upon another cognition for the ascertainment of its epistemic status, and (ii) the practical efficacy of perceptual cognitions,

61. Mohanty (2000: 149).

since, unlike conception, perception constitutes a direct introduction to an object. It is the first of these issues—the construal of perception as intrinsically ascertained—that has forced upon the epistemological program of Dignāga and Dharmakīrti the label of empiricist foundationalism.

Let us return to Tillemans's view that Buddhist epistemology is best described as a type of foundationalism about empirical beliefs. This view was first sketched in a study of the dispute between the Svātantrika and Prasaṅgika Mādhyamikas on the existence of self-validating cognitions.[62] Recently, however, Tillemans has argued cogently—and at some length—that the Buddhist, like his Western counterpart, not only asserts the givenness of particulars, but does so regardless of whether he or she operates with an externalist or an internalist perspective. Particulars are the sort of things available only as objects of perception.

Here, it might be helpful to recall that both Dignāga and Dharmakīrti treat particulars as external objects that provide a basis for the phenomenal content of awareness, regardless of whether they operate from the perspective of external realism or phenomenalism. Thus Tillemans: "Particulars are the sort of thing *naturally suited to be present to non-inferential awareness*, and hence can be considered as a type of given."[63] But whereas the Buddhist may extend the meaning of "particular" to include the referent of the phenomenal content of awareness, ultimately particulars cannot be thought of apart from the causal and cognitive chains of elements and events that are constitutive of the interdependent web of existence.

Tillemans again: "Not surprisingly, in the Yogācāra-Svātantrika system of Śāntarakṣita and Kamalaśīla, appearances (*pratibhāsa*) to perception end up being the customary-truth counterparts to the particulars of the Buddhist logician's Yogācāra ontology."[64] To illustrate his interpretation of the apparitional nature of empirical objects, which is supposedly to confirm their adherence to a putatively idealist Yogācāra ontology, Tillemans quotes Kamalaśīla as advocating the notion that images appearing in consciousness *erroneously* lack intrinsic natures, despite being restricted to a specific time and place:

> [Objection:] But if all entities lack their own intrinsic natures, then why isn't it contradictory that they appear as having intrinsic natures, such as possessing the quality of [being] blue, flat, etc., that is, as restricted in space, time, and so forth? [Response:] No, it is not [contradictory], because [these images] do appear even though they are deceptive, just like the forms that appear to erroneous consciousness.[65]

---

62. Tillemans (1990).
63. Tillemans (2003: 98).
64. Tillemans (2003: 98).
65. *Sarvadharmaniḥsvabhāvasiddhi* 313a8–313b3: *gal te dngos po thams cad rang bzbin med pa nyid yin na/'o na ni de'i tshe dde dagyul dang dus la sogs pa nges par sngon po dang/phya le ba la sogs pa'i ngo bor snang ba ji ltar mi 'gal zhe na ma in te/'khrul ba'i rnam*

The idea that particulars are restricted in time and space is discussed extensively by Dharmakīrti throughout his work.[66] A closer look at Dharmakīrti's account of how particulars are apprehended in perception yields a different result: despite their uniqueness, particulars are not pure representational aspects and can become an object of empirical awareness.[67] So: what Dharmakīrti means by the "unique particular" are phenomena within the reach of empirical consciousness; in other words, entities determined by their spatio-temporal location and formal appearance. Thus, for Dharmakīrti, conceptual entities, unlike the particulars disclosed by perception, are necessarily *unreal*, precisely because they lack spatio-temporal determination. The contrast with perceptual objects is now obvious: these, unlike concepts, are positioned outside the arbitrary realm of thought.

Tillemans's position only becomes more problematic if we factor in the well-known observation that a necessary condition for inference is the presence of "appearing objects." It is these objects appearing to perceptual consciousness that provide "the actual subject of debate." Foundationalism, at least on Tillemans's reading of the Buddhist epistemological program, obtains only if these appearing objects are a kind of sense data. But from a phenomenological standpoint, perceiving is constitutive of a mode of engaging the world such that it manifests its (i.e., the world's) horizon structure. Perception is thus foundational for knowledge only to the extent that it provides an implicit basis for these "appearing objects," that is, only to the extent that these objects are appearing for someone (for it is impossible to talk about appearing objects in the absence of a subject of experience).

Now, this phenomenological (thus descriptive) account of perception also captures, I think, what Dreyfus has in mind when he points out that, for the Buddhist epistemologist, perception and inference "are distinguished not only on the basis of their modes of apprehension but mostly on the basis of their objects."[68] In other words, perception apprehends real individuals by virtue of its constitution (its cognitive architecture and organization: seeing only occurs in organisms endowed with a visual system), whereas inference can only apprehend what are essentially conceptual constructs. This copresence of perception and object *as perceived* explains why only perception can be said to be providing a direct causal-cognitive link to reality, with the caveat that "reality" here stands not for some objective, mind independent realm of entities, but for the occurring events in which perceiver and object perceived are phenomenologically disclosed.

---

par shes pa la snang ba'i gzugs bzhin du brdzun pa yang snang ba'i phyir ro. Translation, slightly altered, *per* Tillemans (2003: 116f. n.13).

66. See PVSV *ad* PV I, 35 and HB XXVI, 12–13.
67. For a discussion of this issue, see Dreyfus (1997: 69).
68. Dreyfus (1996: 224).

I take Dreyfus to be reiterating here—in no uncertain terms—Dignāga's position that perception and conception operate with different objects. For as Dignāga declares, "there is no object of cognition other than the unique particular and the universal, because perception has as its object the unique particular and inference the universal."[69] Conception, on Dignāga's view, is a secondary- rather than higher-order cognition, so understood because of the chasm between the world *as experienced* and its conceptual apprehension. There is, however, more to this story: contrary to the empiricist thesis—that knowledge is reducible to experience—perception in and of itself does not provide knowledge of relations and concepts. Indeed, propositional knowledge requires the participation of perceptual judgments and perceptual judgments, we all know, require memory. How do perceptual judgments become knowledge? They do so by means of apperception, which bridges the memory gap and retrieves previously learned concepts. In addition, apperception is "indubitable": we may well be mistaken about the object of experience but we can never be mistaken about the object of experience *as experienced*, about our awareness of any experience whatsoever.

Capitalizing on this seemingly unbridgeable gap for the Buddhist (between the indeterminate perception of particulars and the sphere of conception), one might argue that something like a Nyāya-Kantian understanding of perception, as always involving the participation of conception, further undermines the Buddhist intuition about the cognitive function of perception. Such a view, for instance, is advanced by Monima Chadha, whose thesis is that recognition, which is required in order to form perceptual judgments, is possible only when perceptual awareness attends to universal features: "the very notion of experience or perceptual cognition is that of cognizing or (recognizing) the particular datum as an instantiation of a property or a universal."[70]

While not directly addressing the question of epistemic foundationalism, Chadha's arguments are relevant for another reason: they raise the hermeneutically interesting question, which we have partially addressed in chapter 4,

69. See PS, I, 1 and PSV *loc. cit.*: (*mngon sum dang ni rjes su dpag, tsad ma'o mtsan nyid gnyis gzhal bya, de la rab sbyor phyir tsad ma, gzhan ni yod pa ma yin no*). Text and translation (slightly altered) per Hattori (1968: 24, 176). On this passage, I follow the suggestions of Herzberger (1986: 14) and van Bijlert (1989: 15) that translating *hi* in *na hi svasāmānyalakṣaṇabhyām* as "for" or "because," and not as "only" (as Hattori does), avoids the unwarranted consequence (untenable, I think, considering Dignāga's doctrine of *apoha*) that there is a complete and unbridgeable gap between the perceptual and the conceptual.

70. Chadha (2001: 205). Chadha's main argument is that the Kantian model of perception provides a satisfactory explanation of why the intuition of a late Naiyāyika like Gaṅgeśa, namely, that "seeing" is best understood as "*seeing* a particular *as a* property-instance" should, in fact, be extended to all instances of perceptual cognition.

of what interpretive model best serves to translate, in this case, the Buddhist and Nyāya epistemological programs and, conversely, to what extent these programs anticipate, or complement, similar philosophical programs in the West. In a defense of the Buddhist epistemological position Mark Siderits is right, I think, to point out that—epistemic considerations apart—a Naiyāyika, a Sautrāntika-Yogācāra Buddhist like Dignāga and Dharmakīrti, and someone like Kant, work with rather different notions of the "given."[71] For the Naiyāyika the category of the "given" (the object of perceptual awareness) includes both particulars (entities such as red roses) and the universals by which they are qualified (such as *redness* and *rosehood*). The Nyāya claim is that particulars are always cognized as such, that is, as individuals bearing a relation of inherence to a universal. For the Buddhist, perception can only apprehend a unique particular as phenomenally given (that is, as part of the structure of awareness), whereas, for someone like Kant, the "given" is simply the phenomenal appearance of objects as seen by the individual through the lens of space, time, and the categories.

Thus, enlisting Kant's support to claim that we never perceive particulars as such and that categories structure our awareness of what we take to be phenomenally (as opposed to metaphysically) real, confronts Chadha with all sorts of unwarranted assumptions about the scope of the Kantian epistemological project, on the one hand, and about what we take to be phenomenally real, on the other. There is, moreover, an important way in which both the Buddhist and the Naiyāyika agree that indeterminate perception stands for an awareness of the particular alone, whose causal and pragmatic link to perceptual cognition is undisputed. A dispute only arises when the Buddhist and the Naiyāyika consider whether this causal-pragmatic model also applies to perceptual judgments. Note though that for the Naiyāyikas indeterminate perception only apprehends unrelated entities (e.g., roses, red color, rosehood, etc.) and that this apprehension is not epistemically warranted because it occurs prior to our modal judgments.

Obviously, the Kantian model of apperception is a statement about the anti-foundationalist role of perception. Tillemans, too, calls into question the Kantian model of the role of apperception in cognition, indicating that Dignāga and Dharmakīrti advocate a thesis that is exactly contrary to Kantian anti-foundationalism: intuitions (or, for the Buddhist, perceptions) are not blind without concepts. Perceptions are indeed cognitive, even if only rudimentarily so. Tillemans takes the Buddhist to be "saying pretty much the opposite: it is concepts that are blind, while sense intuition does see, albeit unintelligently."[72]

---

71. Siderits (2004b: 368–372).
72. Tillemans (2003: 103).

Tillemans's contention is that insofar as Dharmakīrti and his successors regard any cognition that conforms to its object as warranted (that is, as a *pramāṇa tout court*) they are empiricists of a foundationalist bent:

> The fact is, however, that people of an empiricist bent have consecrated considerable energy and ingenuity to doing epistemology this way and have thought perceptual awareness is not just one of the many animal functions necessary for cognition to occur, but is itself a type of cognition of a certain kind of thing. I think that Dharmakīrti is one of these empiricists, and I think that Śāntarakṣita and Kamalaśīla are too.[73]

To buttress his claim that Dharmakīrti, as well as Śāntarakṣita and Kamalaśīla, are full-fledged empiricists, Tillemans interprets their commitment to reflexivity—namely that each cognitive episode is accompanied by self-awareness (*svasaṃvedana*),[74]—to mean that in the direct apprehension of an object, perceptual cognition and self-awareness are fused into one dual-property cognition.

Tillemans favorably cites Robert Brandom's interpretation of the "Myth of the Given" as proposing the view that direct perception is always accompanied by a special sort of awareness that can discern objects and their properties without the aid of concepts:

> The "Myth of the Given" is the idea that there can be a kind of *awareness* that has two properties. First, it is or entails having a certain sort of *knowledge*... that the one whose state it is possesses simply in virtue of being in that state. Second, it entails that the capacity to have that sort of awareness... does not presuppose the acquisition of any *concepts*—that one can be aware in that sense independently of and antecedently to grasping or mastering the use of any concepts (paradigmatically through language learning).[75]

Now: it is not, I think, too much of a stretch to understand how the Buddhist epistemologist can lay claim that such dual property awareness can be epistemically warranted without thereby succumbing to a putative "Myth of the Given." She could simply claim that the (nonconceptual, but not bare) contents of awareness are intentionally constituted: that is, they reveal a world that cannot be thought apart from its immediate apprehension (a world that is disclosed and in turn discloses how actions and intentions are pre-theoretically realized). It seems to me that the Buddhist's reaction

73. Tillemans (2003: 102–103).

74. Self-awareness, as Tillemans rightly notes, is crucial to the Buddhist epistemologists, but is strongly rejected by Mādhyamika philosophers such as Candrakīrti.

75. Sellars (1997: 121–122) as quoted in Tillemans (2003: 120).

to the realist's (chiefly the Naiyāyika and the Mīṃāṃsaka) claim that in perception one apprehends real objects endowed with both individuality and generality, works against the sort of foundationalism advocated by twentieth-century sense datum theorists. This point is made quite clearly by Matilal in his own attempt to position the classical debate between the Naiyāyikas, the Mīmāṃsakas, and the Buddhists in a modern philosophical context:

> There is . . . one important difference between the nature of the given according to the Buddhist and that which is current among the modern Western phenomenalists. The given, which the Buddhist would call *svalakṣaṇa*, has no structure. It is a structureless unitary whole. But a Russellian datum would probably have the structure "*x* is *Q*" or "*x* resembles *y*." This is what Wilfred Sellars has called the structure of "primordial awareness" required by all abstractionists or foundationalists.[76]

It is this structureless unitary whole that the Buddhist phenomenological account of perception ultimately discloses. The Buddhist epistemologist, thus, can secure an empirical foundation for his or her insights, without losing sight of the intersubjective basis of experience.

Rather, I think, the Buddhist epistemologist seems to come out not only on the side of phenomenologists but also of philosophers like Quine, who championed the cause of naturalizing epistemology. To be sure, Quine's understanding of naturalism as empirical psychology differs significantly from Husserl's, who essentially sees it as the intersubjective basis of experience. It also differs from Merleau-Ponty's conception of naturalism, confined as it is to the Gestalt psychology he critically adopts in his rejection of (reductive) behaviorism. Like Husserl's, the Buddhist epistemologist's naturalism is circumscribed to a certain conception of human agency that attributes to it the marks of intentional (or purposive) activity. In the case of perception, this purposive activity takes the form of direct apprehension of particulars. Thus, when Dharmakīrti reacts against certain definitions of perception that attribute to it the capacity to apprehend generalities, he is essentially saying that indirect perception is not veridical. Without an awareness that lacks the determination of (perceptual) judgments, one could not claim to perceive at all, but rather to be constantly superimposing upon the stream of sensory experience whatever one imagines to be the case. In this latter sense, the Buddhist appears to be saying that *ordinary, untutored perception, as conceived by the realist, does not count as an epistemic warrant, and that an effective epistemology can neither rely on the testimony of common sense*

76. Matilal (1986: 321). Matilal makes this observation in the context of his discussion of Kumārila's analysis of the phenomenology of perception. For Kumārila, as for the Naiyāyikas, perception marks the gradual progression from a stage of indetermination to a stage where the object is clearly apprehended both as a particular and as the locus of a universal.

nor on any inferential processes thereof. For the Buddhist, a trained perception (*abhyāsavat pratyakṣa*) is a perception that does not err, and thus one that holds the key to successful epistemic practices. While not exactly an invitation to disciplined observation, Quine's often quoted plea for naturalism rests on the assumption that we stand a better chance of knowing how we arrive at our picture of the world if we let (empirical) psychology explore the nature and function of cognition:

> But why all this creative reconstruction, all this make-believe? The stimulation of his sensory receptors is all the evidence anybody has had to go on, ultimately, in arriving at his picture of the world. Why not just see how this construction really proceeds? Why not settle for psychology? Such a surrender of the epistemological burden to psychology is a move that was disallowed in earlier times as circular reasoning. If the epistemologist's goal is validation of the grounds of empirical science, he defeats his purpose by using psychology or other empirical science in the validation. However, such scruples against circularity have little point once we have stopped dreaming of deducing science from observation.[77]

Unlike Quine's appeal to what is essentially a third-person psychological perspective on the mechanisms that underpin perception and belief formation, the Buddhist epistemologist relies on the complex introspective psychology of the Yogācāra tradition. Like Quine, the Buddhist is also concerned with the causal processes of belief formation. But there is a difference in motivation between Quine's project of naturalizing epistemology—that is, making philosophy more receptive to the findings of natural sciences and withdrawing the claim that epistemology, construed as a metatheoretical discourse, is foundational for all knowledge—and the Buddhist's pragmatic-phenomenological approach to epistemology: the Buddhist wants to understand the mechanisms and function of belief formation (or, of the invariable concomitance (*avinābhāva*) between conscious apprehension and bodily behavior), and seeks knowledge only insofar as he or she intends to reach a certain goal, whether simple ones such as object recognition (e.g., whether or not the variegated colors of a butterfly's wings are perceived by a single instance of perception), or more metaphysically challenging ones (e.g., the ontological status of constructed phenomena like sound).

Thus, to doubt the trustworthiness of ordinary sense experience is to call into question, on naturalist rather than skeptical grounds, the foundationalist's claim that ordinary experience is a trustworthy source of knowledge. For someone like Quine, epistemology can benefit from being placed in a psychological setting because it solves the "enigma" of a priori reasoning.

77. Quine (1969: 74).

Indeed, a cursory review of some of the empirical data would suffice as proof that the embodied cognition thesis is a more accurate working hypothesis for how we come to form beliefs and be justified in holding them. Take several examples from vision science: first, light irradiates the retina in two-dimensions, yet we see the world three-dimensionally; second, color sensitivity is only available in a small central region of the visual field, yet it does not seem as though there is a difference in our experience of color saturation between the central and peripheral regions of the visual field;[78] third, there is a discrepancy between the seeming richness and presence of the visual world and the rather poor and fragmentary data processed by the visual system;[79] finally, we ordinarily see the world as complete, dynamic, and uniformly detailed, when, in fact, it is constructed out of momentary retinal images within a certain threshold of awareness.[80] These examples suggest that there is more to perception than the transparency claimed for it by the (naïve) realist. Furthermore, perceiving is not simply knowing *what* object appears as endowed with *which* specific characteristics. Rather, on the pragmatic-phenomenological model sketched here, perceiving is learning the "rules" of sensorimotor contingency, that is, the non-propositional form of *knowing how*, which governs how changing the orientation of our sensory apprehension transforms the character of the perceived world.[81]

For the Buddhists, whose approach to knowledge is both pragmatic and broadly empirical, the return to naturalism in epistemology should be regarded as a welcome move. Indeed, the very idea of epistemology as establishing the number and nature of reliable sources of belief formation, reflects a project that is essentially non-foundationalist because it does not understand knowledge in terms of dependency relations between basic, non-inferential, beliefs and beliefs that inherit their epistemic status from these basic beliefs. It is also a project that understands the difference between veridical and non-veridical states of cognitive awareness in causal terms rather than in terms of the justification of these basic beliefs.[82] The Buddhist's own interest in grounding epistemology in the psychological analysis of cognition, it seems, echoes both the Husserlian phenomenological project, as well as the shift of focus in contemporary philosophy of mind toward working in close collaboration with the sciences of cognition. I should make clear at this point that the phenomenalist reading of Buddhist epistemology outlined above does not address the importance of

78. For a discussion of the philosophical implications of research in color constancy, see Thompson (1995b: 97–98), Hilbert (2005), Thompson (2005), and Bradley (2008).
79. See O'Regan (1992: 484–485).
80. See Blackmore et al. (1995: 1075–1076).
81. See Rowlands (2002: 172).
82. Cf. Siderits (1995: 2).

Sautrāntika and Yogācāra psychologies in informing the Buddhist epistemological account of how cognition actually operates, partly because Dignāga, Dharmakīrti, and their successors seldom expand on the psychological views that underpin their theories.

7.4 NATURALISM AND ITS DISCONTENTS

It is by now a received view among philosophers that cognitive science has radically changed the scope of traditional epistemology and its normative assumptions. Significant advances in the empirical study of consciousness and cognition have called into question both the premise and the viability of a priori modes of inquiry. The naturalism turn in contemporary epistemology, therefore, is almost entirely informed by a growing body of scientific data pointing to the fact that ordinary everyday experience does not constitute a reliable source of knowledge. In a minimal sense, naturalism represents an invitation to consider the empirical evidence from cognitive psychology in settling questions about how we actually form beliefs.

We have already noted that Quine's influential analysis of the failure of traditional epistemology to answer the challenge of skepticism opened epistemology to input from the sciences of cognition. But the program of naturalizing epistemology is not without its critics. Jaegwon Kim, for instance, has argued on more than one occasion that Quine's proposal effectively amounts to abandoning justification and, with it, "the entire framework of normative epistemology."[83] Kim's trenchant criticism of the naturalism thesis follows four simple steps (adopted, with some modification, by most critics of naturalistic epistemology): first, set out the agenda of Western epistemology (as inherited from Descartes); second, explain the strategy of this epistemological agenda as the (a priori) exercise of rationality itself; third, show that naturalism strips epistemology of its knowledge claims; and finally, introduce under the notion of supervenience the claim that normative epistemology is not susceptible to "psychologistic" reduction.

Following Kim's example, Laurence BonJour argues, "skepticism about the very possibility of a priori justification appears to undermine the rational cogency of reasoning and argumentation."[84] Indeed, for BonJour to claim that there is no a priori justification—as Quine does—obscures the fact that this claim itself needs to be justified, something that cannot be plausibly accomplished a posteriori. Besides, BonJour regards this claim as slightly odd, if not downright suspicious, coming from someone so dedicated to rebuilding epistemology on a strong empiricist basis. The main point of

83. Kim (1988: 48).
84. BonJour (1998: 62).

contention in BonJour's rejection of the naturalistic paradigm is the skeptical conclusion it inevitably upholds: that all our beliefs are based on observational "sentences" and that we have no way of determining whether they are, indeed, true. What BonJour takes issue with is not so much Quine's view that the Humean condition is the human condition, but rather his rejection of normative epistemic priority.

For Quine skeptical doubts are quintessentially scientific doubts, for it is science and its empiricist program that reveal illusions (e.g., rainbows, afterimages, double images) for what they are: phenomena that do not fall into the strict category of genuine physical bodies and, as such, cast doubt on the very possibility of epistemic certainty. BonJour sees skepticism about normative epistemology as a purely philosophical move, one that challenges "the adequacy of our reasons for accepting our beliefs,"[85] not the evidential basis of this acceptance (as may be the case with an appeal to illusions).

But the main reason for rejecting the naturalist paradigm, claims BonJour, is that it makes differentiating between the degrees of veracity of different classes of belief irrelevant. Just as naturalized epistemology has nothing to say about the justification of our scientific or even our common sense beliefs about the world, so too it has nothing to say about why we are justified in holding a particular set of religious beliefs, something that any Buddhist philosopher presumably would take issue with. While it may give us a descriptive account of how we come to hold such beliefs (allegedly its main concern) it cannot tell us whether we have any reasons to prefer one set of beliefs over another.

Despite these criticisms, Quine has helped inaugurate a movement in epistemology that strong advocates of naturalism such as Hilary Kornblith call "replacement naturalism," which now exists side by side with other, more moderate, forms of naturalism.[86] The majority of philosophers, however, favor a weaker form of naturalism that allows for evaluative questions about rationality, justification, and knowledge to be pursued in a traditional manner. Advocates of this later approach agree that the sciences of cognition have much to contribute in resolving epistemological problems.[87]

85. BonJour (1998: 87).

86. See Kornblith (1997, 1999). For arguments against rationality as a foundational principle for traditional epistemology, see Stich (1984, 1990).

87. For a critique of the notion of justified belief in epistemology, see Goldman (1993). Goldman was also among the first authors to argue for the mutual relevance of epistemology and cognitive science (1992a). In a more recent review of the internalist vs. externalist debate in naturalized epistemology, Goldman (2002: 3–23) also mounts an extensive critique of recent attempts to play the a priori against the radical empiricism that naturalism appears to endorse.

Traditional analytic epistemology is foundationalist and normative.[88] It has inherited from Descartes its two criteria for establishing certainty: the conditions for accepting or rejecting beliefs and the conditions under which acceptable beliefs count as knowledge. Note that the criteria for determining which beliefs are justified were not initially established on naturalistic grounds. Having a "good reason" or being "beyond reasonable doubt" was sufficient as a truth condition for a given belief. Justification, thus understood, also explains why traditional (Western) epistemology is a normative discipline: it does not simply tell us why we are justified in believing something but also that it is *reasonable* and *permissible* to do so. If epistemology is essentially a normative discipline, the story goes, it is because its foundation lies on a bedrock of indubitable beliefs, usually about common sense experience and the immediate accessibility of our mental states.

Now, unlike the traditional Cartesian epistemologist, but like his Naiyāyika opponent, the Buddhist epistemologist shares with Quine and other proponents of naturalism the view that causation, not justification, is the determining factor in deciding which cognitive events count as instances of knowledge. For Quine, causality is understood in terms of the stimulatory conditions and situations that generate propositional content. The first problem, in that case, is explaining how the cognitive equivalence of sentences is possible, given the difference between universal sentences and sentences expressing particular states of affairs. The second problem is the fact that even equivalent universal sentences of the type "Socrates is a man" (or "Devadatta is a human being") are not always prompted by the same stimulations. For Quine, it is an individual's disposition to treat sentences as cognitively equivalent, even if they are occasioned by different circumstances, that informs his causal account of cognition. On the other hand, for someone like Dignāga, who follows the Ābhidharmikas' account of perception, there is an understanding that the perceptual aspect, while causally related to the stimulus, represents more than is available at the sensory level: it apprehends particulars as uniquely qualified phenomena, such that words and sentences can never truly designate, other than by a process of exclusion of all other possibilities (as accounted for by the theory of semantic exclusion). What Quine calls "occasion sentences" (that is, sentences whose truth value changes as the occasion changes), might correspond to what Dignāga calls "verbal utterances" (*vacana*) of the sort that connect a word with a thing.[89]

---

88. I follow Kim (1988), whose detailed account of the Cartesian legacy in epistemology clearly spells out the divisions between the causal and normative questions.

89. As Hayes notes in his examination of Dignāga's semantic theory, "the conclusion towards which Dignāga argues is the fact that underlying the truth of the sentence 'Devadatta is a human being' is no more than the fact that, by whatever conventions there may be that govern the use of symbols in a given language, the equivalent in that language to the word 'human being' is applicable to the individual Devadatta" (1988: 205).

Keep in mind, however, that the Buddhist, unlike Quine, generally warns against relying on our ordinary language intuitions.

For the Buddhist, the question of reliability of cognitions is set out in pragmatic terms: all cognitions, even impulsive and habitual ones, have their source in preceding cognitions, so that the successful accomplishment of any human goal is wholly dependent on having correct knowledge (in this case, both knowledge of the causal order of events, as well as metacognitive knowledge). Operating with the premise that all cognitive events are intentional (that is, they are about some object of their own (*saviṣayaka*)), Indian epistemological theories seek to identify the specific causal order in which intentions translate into actual cognitive events. For the Buddhist epistemologist who follows Dignāga's account of cognition, the intentional act and the resulting apprehension of an object are not differentiated, so that a reliable cognition (i.e., a *pramāṇa*) and its ensuing apprehension (*pramāṇaphala*) are in fact identical. Since the Buddhist epistemologist does not differentiate between a source of knowledge and its result, that is, knowledge itself (*pramā*), for a cognitive event to count as an instance of knowledge, cognition must have the capacity to effect some sort of determination, the result of which is connection or conformity (*arthasārūpya*) with a particular object. It is for this reason that Dharmakīrti rejects the cognitive instrumentality of the senses. Take the eye, or rather the visual system, as an example: as a uniform source, it is nonetheless the cause of many varied cognitions. It apprehends both blue and yellow, both distant and proximal objects. Given this sort of evidence, differentiation, argues the Buddhist, cannot be a function of the operation of the senses. What, then, causes this differentiation to occur? How does the apprehension of a patch of color, result in the cognition "this is blue"? The Naiyāyika direct realist answers this question by pointing to the objects themselves. Although we know by means of the instrumentality of some cognition—the Naiyāyika, unlike the Buddhist, does distinguish between sources of knowledge and their results—the object itself must be as much a cause for the arising of a cognitive event as is the sense itself (and, of course, contact between the two). So differentiation for the Naiyāyika is accounted for by the specific mode of presentation of the object.

Such an account, of course, begs the question: how do we know that it is a difference in the object that causes the difference in cognition (rather than the other way round)? How, that is, do we apprehend differences in the empirical domain, if not by means of the operations of some cognitive modality? We have no way of knowing how the object is in itself. Addressing precisely this issue, Dignāga's commentator, Jinendrabuddhi notes:

> Even though we may grant the existence of external objects, an object of cognition is apprehended [as such] only be means of its being reflexively present; therefore, only that cognition [which apprehends an object reflexively] counts as a result. Indeed, there is no experience of an object as it is in itself, for if that were the case it

would be ascertained on the basis of its natural constitution, which would have the unwarranted consequence that the cognitions of multiple individuals would have the same phenomenal aspect. [For an individual] cognitions intend varied phenomenal aspects. Indeed, even in relation to a single object, many cognitions are apprehended, on account of differences in the perceivers, as being phenomenally qualified by varying [degrees of] vividness, and so on; for a single entity is not itself characterized by multiple aspects, [or] else its multiplicity would follow.[90]

What we have here is a case of two typical assertions: first, a claim that object apprehension necessitates consciousness; I have varying cognitive states to the extent that I am reflexively aware. Non-conscious cognitive processing does not count as a source of knowledge. I cannot lay any claim to having veridical cognitions except when I am reflexively aware that cognizing is occurring. While ordinarily cognition is a constant and ongoing process, a cognitive event becomes epistemically warranted only when accompanied by self-awareness (and only in specific circumstances that preclude the possibility of error). Secondly, for Jinendrabuddhi to say that an object is apprehended as such on account of its natural constitution is equivalent to claiming that the phenomenal content of experience would be uniform regardless of individual perspectives (an unwarranted outcome, since individuals occupy unique points of view and are subject to multiple and shifting dispositions). Similarly, although singular, an object is apprehended as having multiple aspects, on the basis of differences that are inherent in the object itself, but also as a result of its collective or intersubjective disclosure. In other words, cognition is inherently aspectual, since to cognize is to bring forth the ubiquitous phenomenon of perspectival variation. In Hume's now famous dictum, "no man who reflects ever doubted that the existences which we consider when we say *this house* and *that tree* are nothing but perceptions in the mind."[91]

7.5 BEYOND REPRESENTATION: AN ENACTIVE PERCEPTION THEORY

I would like to suggest, therefore, that mere surface resemblances between the sense datum theorist and various other brands of modern naïve empiricism, on the one hand, and the Buddhist epistemological project, on the other, might,

90. PSṬ *ad* PS I, 9a, in Steinkellner, Krasser, and Lasic (2005: 68.12–69.3): *bhavatu nāma bāhyhārthah, tathāpi yathāsamvedanam eva viṣayo niściyata iti tadevaphalaṃ yuktam/na hi yathāsvabhāvamanubhavo 'rthasya, yato yathāsau vyavasthitasvarupastathā sakyeta niścetum, sarvajñānānam eka ākāratvaprasaṅgāt/anekākārastu vijñaptayaḥ/ tathā hi ekasmin eva vastuni pratipattrbhedena patūmandatādibhir ākārairanugatāni vijñānānyupalabhyante/na ca ekam vastvanekākāram, anekatvaprasaṅgāt.* Cf. Arnold (2009: 144).

91. Hume (1999: 118).

indeed, suggest that the Buddhists operate with a foundationalist stance; however, this intuition is misguided. To say about an instance of perceptual awareness that it discloses some truth and, as such, provides a basis for valid reasoning is already equivalent to "placing it within the logical space of reasons," to use Sellars's expression. From afar, Dignāga and Dharmakīrti may well appear guilty of according perception this grounding status. When looked at more closely, however, their account of the role of perception as a sort of anchorage into the given does not appear to support a foundationalist reading.

Indeed, it should be possible to offer an anti-foundationalist reading of the Buddhist epistemological project if we abandon the requirement that perceptual awareness provide a justification for basic empirical beliefs. After all, self-awareness and various types of cognitive conditioning are central to the Buddhist epistemological program. For the Buddhists seeing (and any other type of perceptual knowing) is already conditioned by past experience and operates as a function of the enactive and intentional aspects of consciousness.[92] I do think, however, that we can move beyond the argument that memory and self-awareness are precisely the conditioning factors necessary for a perceptual event to become cognitive.

Following the return to naturalism in epistemology, as well as significant recent developments in cognitive science, it is debatable whether anti-psychologism is still tenable as a philosophical attitude. Any reservation that defining philosophy too narrowly as "naturalism" would make the broader questions of Buddhist (and Indian) philosophy—the ultimate goal of human life or the idea of emancipation from suffering—irrelevant may be abandoned. In what is arguably his most significant and mature work—*Perception, An Essay on Classical Indian Theories of Knowledge* (1986)—Matilal saw the empirical study of cognition as having only marginal philosophical import: "'What do we perceive *directly*?' is, to be sure, not a scientific question. For it is not a question that is generally answered by observation and experiment. It is a philosophical question. Its answer requires conceptual analysis and philosophical argument."[93] Although he conceded that philosophers could not ignore the experimental data, Matilal resisted the naturalist move in epistemology. Such resistance may be legitimate if a historical reconstruction of classical philosophical arguments is our primary concern, but it is less profitable if we seek to evaluate their premises on the basis of our expanded understanding of cognition provided by the sciences of the mind.

---

92. A somewhat similar view is expressed by McClintock (2003: 129) when she writes that "even though Buddhist pramāṇa theorists understand perception... as a kind of direct and full-blown encounter with the real... there are good grounds for caution in referring to the contents of perception as the given, since perceptual awareness alone seems unable to ground or justify basic beliefs."

93. Matilal (1986: 224).

Quine's "naturalistic" conception of knowledge began with an analogy meant to illustrate the scope of his proposal: just as mathematics may reduce to logic and set theory, so too our knowledge of natural kinds may reduce to sense experience. This analogy assumes an implicit bifurcation of knowledge into the conceptual and the empirical. The problem, as we now know, is that mathematics mostly reduces to set theory, whose axioms, as Gödel has demonstrated, have less certainty than logical principles. Similarly, our common sense experience lacks the certainty that a foundationalist epistemology would claim for it: basic, naïve beliefs about sense experience are less certain than phenomenological descriptions and doctrinal positions about what it is that we actually perceive. But phenomenological descriptions and the doctrinal positions that ensue grow from sustained reflection on our specific modes of being in the world. We have also learned that experience cannot be fully translated into phenomenologically neutral terms. Should we, then, abandon epistemology altogether, as the late Wittgenstein suggested? Is the view that there are real epistemological problems simply a delusion that philosophers must be cured of? Wittgenstein surely thought so, and so have Mādhyamika philosophers from Nāgārjuna to Candrakīrti and beyond. But Quine (much like Dignāga and Dharmakīrti) is quite categorical on this point: epistemology is an effective discipline and brings about real results. So epistemology continues, though in a new setting: that of cognitive science. This is a new epistemology, one that is contained in sciences of cognition rather than containing them.

Quine's explanation of this mutual containment strategy hinges on the fact that what should count as observation can now be settled in terms of our understanding of the structure and dynamics of our perceptual systems. As we no longer need to justify our knowledge of the external world through rational reconstruction, awareness can finally be understood in causal terms. It is out of the co-occurrence of pre-reflective perceptual experience and an awareness of perceiver and object perceived that questions about the cognitive status of perception are born. The phenomenological tradition warns that to move all too quickly from this pre-reflective awareness to an analysis of the content of experience may result in object properties being determined as in principle observer-independent. On the other hand, recent advances in perception research seem to suggest that object properties are in fact the result of information processing of sensory input in the visual and somato-sensory cortex. The information at the level of retinal receptors is quite different from what "we actually see." In vision science, it is now acknowledged that most of the actual processing is in fact unconscious, with the visual awareness arising farther away on the pathways of sensory information processing.[94]

94. For a discussion of the dynamics of visual awareness and its underlying neurophysiological correlates, see Palmer (1999: chs. 10–13, and 616ff.).

Let me clarify the standpoint of my proposal. By setting the Buddhist epistemological project in a modern cognitive scientific setting, my intention is not to neutralize its arguments by showing that these are, after all, pre-modern thinkers whose ideas reflect the cultural concerns of their historical time and place and thus have little to offer contemporary philosophers. As our foregoing analysis has shown, in the tradition of reflection initiated by Dignāga and Dharmakīrti, arguments are already called to bear on the insights of Abhidharma psychology. It is for this reason that the Buddhist epistemological enterprise ought to be, at least in principle, receptive to new findings in cognitive science. Conversely, cognitive science stands to benefit from a tradition of philosophical inquiry with a rich history of first-person phenomenological reflection, if the interdisciplinary study of the practice of mindfulness meditation is any indication to this effect.[95]

While Buddhist meditative traditions may be regarded as supplying effective methods for a phenomenological exploration of the constituent elements of experience, they cannot be divorced from the practice of epistemological inquiry that has evolved to bear on the results of such experience. Take, for instance, Dharmakīrti's resemblance theory, which admits that our categorizing practices follow primarily our aims and expectations, but only within the constraints imposed by the essential qualities of things.[96] What that means is that, say, in cognizing a tree, it is not only my mental disposition and my knowledge of flowing plants that play a role in my apprehension of the given entity but also the specific causal-cognitive chains by means of which the respective entity (or rather its aspect) enters the horizon of my cognitive awareness as a unique particular. In other words, I apprehend something as a redwood, a live oak, or a willow, not because each of these presumed *tokens* of the same *type* tree bear any structural similarity, but because they are all excluded by the force of their natural constitution from serving as a causal basis for the apprehension of that which is other than this specific instance of redwood, live oak, and so on.[97] If historically, Dharmakīrti's resemblance theory may be seen as providing a middle ground between the extremes of nominalism and realism,[98] within the broader research program of naturalist epistemology, it may be seen as doing work that is similar to that of cognitive psychological theories on the role of prototypes in concept

95. For a detailed survey of the recent literature on the topic of neuroscientific research on various types of mindfulness meditation, see Shear and Jevning (1999), and Lutz, Dunne, and Davidson (2007).

96. See, for example, HB I, 6.

97. For an illuminating discussion of this aspect of *apoha* theory with respect to Dharmakīrti, see Dunne (2011).

98. As noted, in detail, by Dreyfus (1997: 133ff.).

formation.[99] Indeed, one of the surprising findings of studies in concept acquisition is the fact that judgments of similarity violate the logical principles of symmetry and reversibility. Furthermore, Dharmakīrti's resemblance theory also suggests some interesting correspondences to recent research on the role of imagery in behavioral and cognitive simulation.[100]

Naturalizing Buddhist epistemology, then, amounts to more than simply placing it in a modern psychological setting. Rather, it also means examining the presuppositions of Abhidharma psychology that inform it in a modern setting, while recognizing its contribution to expanding our knowledge of the phenomenology of first-person experience. This expanded knowledge can contribute—along with the Husserlian phenomenological tradition—to a widening of our conception of nature currently at work in the sciences of cognition, one that includes consciousness and intentionality. Indeed, as David Woodruff Smith (following Husserl) observes, our encounter with, and categorization of, our cognitive activities is prior to our theorizing in domains such as physics and neuroscience.[101] An expanded conception of nature would allow for material and formal categories to interweave, thus acknowledging the ontological complexity of our world of experience. On such an expanded understanding of nature, a cognitive activity such as perception is an intentional event that can be categorized materially under "event" and formally under "intentionality." So, following the practical efficacy model of cognition, a perception has a subjective aspect (that is, it is self-revealing), carries intentional content, such as the perceptual object as intended, and, if veridical, is directed toward an actual object of experience.

Central to Buddhist epistemology, from the time of Dignāga, has been the view that in order to secure an epistemic status for perception one must have nondeceptive experiences. Consequently, even natural occurrences of misperception have been regarded as threatening the foundational role of perception for knowledge. Whether this insight, which the Buddhist tradition had sought to defend mainly on phenomenological grounds, does find empirical support, can now be settled beyond speculative arguments. So,

---

99. Cf. Rosch (1978: 28ff.; 1999). Rosch (1999: 65) identifies a number of criteria that play an important role in concept acquisition, among them: *learning* (good examples provide an early basis for naturalistic acquisition of concepts in both children and adults), *speed of processing* (more representative concepts are learned better than those less representative of their class), *expectation* (priming plays an important role in retaining unfamiliar concepts), *inference* (we infer from more representative to less representative examples of token in any given category), and *judgment of similarity* ("less good examples of categories are judged more similar to good examples than vice versa").

100. As examined at length in Neisser (1978), Kosslyn (1994), Barsalou (1999), Thomas (1999), and Hesslow (2002).

101. Smith (1999: 83).

let me finally conclude with some references to modern research on the interface between perception and imagery, which explores both the ways in which imagery appears to interfere with and to alter the contents of perception (and the possibility of accessing a nonconceptual but cognitive type of awareness). Reviewing some of the neuroscientific data relating to the cognitive functions of imagery, Hesslow notes that "imagining perceiving something is essentially the same as actually perceiving it, only the perceptual activity is generated by the brain itself rather than by external stimuli."[102] The most interesting fact is that the same is true also for simulations of action, which activate areas in the brain in a manner similar to the actual performance of a physical action. Simulation using imagery appears thus to "elicit perceptual activity that resembles the activity *that would have occurred* if the action had actually been performed."[103]

To the extent that these cognitive scientific uses of imagery capture the sense of Dignāga's use of *kalpanā* (usually translated as "conception" or "conceptual construction"), it is possible to argue that indirect perception is such that its contents are functionally indistinguishable from those of conceptual and imagistic thought. In other words, indirect perception is not free from the activity of imagery: it both apprehends and construes the object of perception. On the other hand, direct perception, as a cognition that lacks conceptual determination meets the Buddhist epistemological demand for providing access to the perceived as such. Evidence for direct perception has come mainly from experiments in ecological perception, which cite such factors as the persisting layout of the environment (the size of objects at ground level is covariant with the size of objects that are constitutive of the ground) and the fact that objects appear to perceptual awareness not as the locus of various qualities but as affordances for different types of activities: a chair affords sitting, though this affordance is neither a property of the chair, nor of the person that sits or intends to sit on it, but a precondition of its apprehension.[104] For the Buddhist epistemologist direct perception affords

102. Hesslow (2002: 242).

103. Hesslow (2002: 242). See also Pessoa, Thompson, and Noë (1998), Kaski (2002), and Thompson (2007a). It turns out that there exist associative mechanisms that enable both behavioral and perceptual activity in the sensory areas of the brain. However, most researchers are still cautious about drawing any extravagant conclusions from these hypotheses, such as that images and representations are real mental entities, even though the recent discovery that subcortical areas of the brain appear to be actively involved in cognitive processing does call for a reexamination of the causal role of consciousness in relation to mental imagery.

104. See, especially, Gibson (1979: chs. 9 and 10). See also Vicente and Burns (1996). Gibson's theory of affordance, and its recent reworking in active theories of perception, is meant to "rescue us from the philosophical muddle of assuming fixed classes of objects, each defined by its common feature and then given a name" (1979: 134). The theory of affordances is meant to capture our pragmatic encounter with

precisely the kind of immediate acquaintance with particulars as conducive to various pragmatic ends. It is perceptual judgments that imagery interferes with, thus generating the illusion that entities are primarily characterized by their possession of intrinsic properties.

There is another angle from which the problem of the "Myth of the Given" does not quite capture the intent of the Buddhist epistemological enterprise: that of the *content* of the perceptual event. If we take the "Given" to refer to noematic content (that is, to the perceived as such), rather than to some presumably independent sense datum, then what is given in perception is also constitutive of its mode of apprehension: for example, sound is constitutive of auditory and verbal experience; shape and color, of visual experience. What is given in perception is a phenomenal aspect, notwithstanding the causal chain of events that traces that aspect to some occurring entity. We may, thus, interpret these phenomenal aspects neither as some kind of internal representations of external reality nor as purely imagistic or conceptual aspects of cognition. Rather, following proponents of the embodied cognition thesis, such as George Lakoff and Mark Johnson, we may interpret them—in terms of embodiment—as image schemas or Gestalt structures of experience: cognitive and thus part of the intentional act, yet indirectly connected to the external world.[105] These Gestalt structures of experience may not explain how impressions traveling across the sensory pathways can emerge as an intentional object, but they do provide a more accurate account of our perceptual modes of knowing that avoid the pitfalls of empiricist foundationalism. On this account of phenomenologically embodied experience, the manner in which impressions select and group across these sensory pathways, drawing the contour of a unique particular, depends as much on the functioning of the perceptual systems and the propensity of the mind toward grasping after aggregated objects as upon the phenomenal properties of the apprehended entity.

At the level of pure sensations, however, only the embodied forms of intentionality, as pure presence to the world, are given; determined "selves"

---

things, the fact that we can perceive their uses without identifying their properties or assigning them to specific classes.

105. Lakoff (1987: 284–290). More recently, Lakoff and Johnson (1999: 36, 102) have argued that these basic cognitive images or "image schemas," which are reflective of our "phenomenological embodiment," are the means by which we apprehend the world nonconceptually through the body. As the means by which we orient ourselves in the environment and act out our purposeful actions, our apprehension of what is phenomenally given in any situation "depends on our embodied understanding of the situation." Likewise, Gallagher (2005: 41–64) differentiates between "body-image" and "body schema," and understands the latter as a structure that integrates body and environment in ways that go beyond the distinction between an objective body and the phenomenal body as internally represented. See *infra* chapter 8.1 for a detailed discussion.

and "entities" are yet to emerge from the perceptual stream. Once more, Merleau-Ponty provides a vivid account of what it might be like to be fully immersed in the perceptual experience: "If I wanted to render precisely the perceptual experience, I ought to say that *one* perceives in me, and not that I perceive. Every sensation carries within it the germ of a dream of depersonalization such as we experience ... when we really try to live at the level of sensation."[106]

As we saw in the previous chapter, in his own attempt to explain the causes of perceptual illusions, Kamalaśīla claims that one conjures and grasps after things—such as a circle of fire caused by the rapid rotation of a fire brand—that, in fact, do not exist: For his part, Kamalaśīla uses this example to argue that in some sense all ordinary, untutored, perceptions are like that—generating the illusion of aggregated objects having enduring, substantive, natures.[107] These untutored perceptions are, in fact, typical of what the Husserlian phenomenologist calls the "natural attitude." The problem lies not in perception, whose mechanisms are generally not alterable at will, but *in the awareness that attends to it*. For it is the latter that, when devoid of any conceptual content, gives perceptual experience the directness that the Buddhist claims for it. Untutored perception is determined, for it already appears laden with judgment. By contrast, direct perception is an intentional cognitive act, at least in the sense that, given the inherently intentional nature of consciousness, to perceive is to directly apprehend whatever appears in awareness without allowing the surge of conceptualization to interfere. It is this process of direct apprehension that informs the Buddhist epistemologist's descriptive account of the phenomenology of perception.

The causal model of perception adopted by the Buddhist epistemologists thus rests on two sets of premises: first, what is apprehended in perception is merely the effect of a causal chain reaching back to the co-presence of sense, object, and empirical consciousness; second, real objects (or for the Buddhist unique particulars) are capable of producing real effects, even when additional circumstances cause a cognitive discrepancy between the object and its perceptual representation, as in the case of perceptual illusions. In the final analysis, the Buddhist argues that, given immediate acquaintance with our own mental states, the nonconceptual noema of a pure act of intending is truly the only warranted type of perception. The only indubitable cognitions we have, whatever the status of the particulars they intend, are those nonconceptual, non-inferential cognitions that define direct, non-mediated perception.

106. Merleau-Ponty (2002: 250).
107. See TS 1253–55 and TSP *loc. cit.*

Whether we do ultimately interpret phenomenology as anti-foundationalist or not, I hope that I have convincingly demonstrated that something like a phenomenological attitude more aptly describes the philosophical program of the Buddhist epistemologists. I have not argued that current debates about foundationalism in epistemology are not relevant as interpretive tools, only that considerable philosophical insights can be gained from exploring the Buddhist epistemological program through the intentionally wide-angled lens of the Western phenomenological tradition. In the next chapter we turn to one of the most important aspects of the Buddhist account of perception: its defense of the notion that perception in inherently constituted by an intentional relation that pertains at once to its content and to its mode of disclosure.

CHAPTER 8

Perception, Self-Awareness, and Intentionality

The Buddhist epistemological analysis of "self-awareness" or "self-cognition" (*svasaṃvedana, saṃvitti*)[1] underscores a conception of consciousness that takes into account not only its phenomenal content but also its phenomenal character. I have already explained[2] that the Buddhist epistemological account of reflexivity—conceived as a pre-reflective form of self-awareness—closely resembles that of the Husserlian phenomenologist. It is now time to examine in some detail the extent to which recent work at the intersection of phenomenology and philosophy of mind, particularly in the areas of perception and intentionality, could be profitably used in unpacking the implications of the Buddhist defense of reflexive awareness. But I am also concerned with reflexivity more generally, and the ways in which the theoretical model of embodied and enactive cognition can provide an explanatory framework for the Buddhist epistemological account of perception.

Just as newcomers to philosophy of mind often find it hard to concede that pain is a mental state, so too newcomers to phenomenology tend to resist the notion that intentionality, as Brentano puts it, is the mark of the mental.[3] On the naïve view, pain is located in the body and defined by its qualitative aspect, though one may refer to anxiety or distress as states of mental pain. However, as one attends to the experience of pain, one learns

1. My discussion of self-awareness (*svasaṃvedana*) in this chapter builds on several seminal contributions to this topic, especially Williams (1998), Garfield (2006), Dreyfus (2007), Arnold (2005b, 2009, 2010), MacKenzie (2007), Kellner (2010, 2011), and Chadha (2011).

2. See *supra* chapter 4.

3. Brentano's formulation captures specifically what he calls the "intentional inexistence of the object," such that mental phenomena are by definition those phenomena which contain "an object intentionally within themselves" (Brentano 1981: 68).

to recognize that pain is an event in consciousness, and that its qualitative aspect is complemented by an awareness of what pain discloses: a minimally cognitive state of bodily damage or mental distress. A similar perspective on the mental basis of sensory experience is also at work in the Buddhist Abhidharma. Here too we come across systematic efforts to identify sensations, volitions, desire, and so on, as mental states.

Vasubandhu, for instance, uses an interesting analogy meant to illustrate the relation between mind and mental constituents: just as it may be difficult to discriminate between the flavors of different plants, which we know by means of one sense only, taste, so too it may difficult to discriminate between sensation, volition, desire, and so on in a single instance of cognitive awareness, despite the fact that their constitutive elements are always present.[4] Do I sense a slight drop in temperature or am I wishing the room were warmer? Do I judge that my talk might be too long or am I simply hoping to finish on time? Indeed, it takes a well-developed capacity for reflection to be able to discriminate between a mental event and its constitutive elements. We may ordinarily talk about sensation having a somatic aspect but, as Vasubandhu reminds us, all sensation (just like all judgment and desire) is in the mind.[5]

It is in large measure following Vasubandhu that Dignāga advances the notion that self-awareness is constitutive of perception. In doing so, Dignāga simply extends his commitment to the reflexivity thesis without which, he claims, we are unable to account adequately for the phenomenal character of conscious experience. By singling out self-awareness as a constitutive aspect of perception, Dignāga seeks to account for the specific mode of presentation of all mental states insofar as they arise bearing an intentional relation. Indeed, by stating that each cognitive event arises in the form of a relation between apprehending subject and apprehended object, Dignāga in effect posits the aspectual nature of intentional reference. In what follows I will argue that the dual-aspect account of mental states is primarily aimed at explaining the nature of intentional reference.

8.1 REFLEXIVITY AND THE ASPECTUAL NATURE OF INTENTIONAL REFERENCE

Dignāga, and all those who follow the tradition of epistemic inquiry that he helped to initiate, including Śāntarakṣita and Kamalaśīla, makes an important and somewhat radical claim: a reliable source of cognition is to be taken, *pace* the received tradition of Indian epistemological thinking, not as an instrument that makes knowledge (or the acquisition thereof) possible, but

4. See AKBh *ad* AK II, 24.
5. See AKBh *ad* AK II, 25.

rather as the result (that is, as knowledge itself). For Dignāga, therefore, "a source of knowledge is effective only as a result, because of being comprehended along with its action."[6] Thus, the cognition that arises having the aspect of its object, while appearing to comprise the action of cognizing, in fact is nothing but the result of cognitive activity.

For instance, in apprehending an object, say a lotus flower, all that a cognizer can be certain of is the internal aspect of that cognitive event, or, in Husserl's terms, "the intended object just as it is intended."[7] For Dignāga, thus, "that which appears in cognition is the known object, the reliable cognition and its result, are [respectively] the subjective aspect of [cognition] and the cognition [itself]."[8] Dignāga's understanding of what counts as a reliable cognition in this context comes, I think, significantly close to something like Husserl's notion of noematic content (the "perceived as such"), which the method of phenomenological reduction is supposed ultimately to reveal. For Dignāga, just as for Husserl, perception is ultimately constituted by intentional content: perceiving is an intentional (that is, object-directed) and self-revealing (*svaprakaśa*) cognition.

More specifically, Dignāga understands cognition as having a double aspect: that of a subjective appearance (*svābhāsa*) and that of an objective appearance (*viṣayābhāsa*). The subjective aspect (*grāhakākāra*) is just that individual's self-awareness as cognizing agent, while the objective aspect (*grāhyākāra*) captures the intentional aspect of cognition or its object-directedness. In this regard, I find myself in complete agreement with Jonardon Ganeri who claims, I think rightly, that the problem of self-awareness (or, as he calls it, "knowledge intimation") for the Buddhist epistemologists cannot be properly addressed without taking into account the intentionality of perception. Indeed, the double aspect theory of mental states serves as the only nonproblematic way by means of which "one can distinguish between thoughts and thoughts about thoughts, the intentional object of the latter being the subjective aspect of the former."[9] In effect, by claiming that self-awareness is the only truly occurrent ground for knowledge, Dignāga (and following him Dharmakīrti as well as Śāntarakṣita) does nothing more than advance a phenomenological account of cognition.[10]

Following Dignāga's example, the Buddhist epistemologists accept the reality of reflexive awareness in the classical Yogācāra sense of self-luminosity, and they support their arguments with such examples as the lamp that

6. PS I, 8: *savyāpārapratītatvāt pramāṇaṃ phalam eva sat*. Cf. Hattori (1968: 97).
7. Husserl (1983: 312): "*vermeinten Gegenständlichen, so wie es vermeint ist.*"
8. PS I, 10: *yad ābhāsaṃ prameyaṃ tat pramāṇaphalate punaḥ. grāhakākārasaṃvittī trayaṃ nātaḥ pṛthak kṛtam*. Translation, slightly altered, *per* Hattori (1968: 29).
9. Ganeri (1999b: 474).
10. For an alternative (idealist) view, which takes *svasaṃvitti* to function in much the same way as the unity of apperception does for Kant, see Arnold (2005b).

illuminates itself while simultaneously revealing other objects. This notion that consciousness is inherently reflexive is, however, strongly opposed by Mādhyamika thinkers like Candrakīrti and Śāntideva (fl. eighth century), and also by the Naiyāyikas, all of whom claim that consciousness cannot be thought of as reflexive, even on a conventional level, for that would imply that consciousness is self-validating.[11] Candrakīrti takes issue in particular with the characteristically Yogācāra view that the object of cognition is not extrinsic to cognition but is an aspect of cognition itself. It suffices to mention that the Buddhist epistemologists, who adopt an ontological position that most closely aligns with that of the Sautrāntikas (for whom external objects are real only insofar as they provide a basis for cognitive activity) take consciousness to be inherently reflexive and describe it not with the aid of mirror metaphors—that is, consciousness as a mirror reflecting back the nature of perceived phenomena—but rather with plastic metaphors in which consciousness is said to assume the form of whatever object it cognizes.

We know that the Buddhist epistemologists adopt the dual-aspect theory of cognition from Vasubandhu. But the adoption of this theory also reflects their commitment to an internalist epistemology. Furthermore, unlike their Brahmanical opponents, the Buddhist epistemologists are also committed to the view that the sources of knowledge (in this case, perception and inference) are not different from the ensuing cognitions. Instead of understanding cognition in terms of a relation between perception and its object, the Buddhist epistemologists offer us an account of cognition as constituted by its intentional content, that is, by the object *as perceived* (or *as conceived*). This view is motivated, at least in part, by the radical and essential separation of sensation from conception.[12]

What does it mean for cognitive awareness to be self-revealing? One perfectly acceptable way to answer this question is to say that self-awareness accompanies (by virtue of arising together with) each perceptual event. And perception, specifically any type of perception lacking conceptual elaboration (*kalpanāpoḍha*), is associated with knowledge of particulars. It is precisely this aspect of the Buddhist epistemologist's theory of perception that is the main target of criticism by Mādhyamika philosophers like Candrakīrti. An axiomatic principle of all Madhyamaka philosophy, following Nāgārjuna, is that all things, including all cognitive episodes, by virtue of being the product of cause and conditions, lack inherent existence (*svabhāva*) and are thus empty (*śūnya*).[13] That is, nothing truly exists on its own, and no entity

11. See, for example, MAV VI, 74–75.
12. This view is known as "the separation between the two sources of cognition" (*pramāṇa-vyavasthā*).
13. See, for example, MMK III, 6–9; IV, 1–8.

or mental state has its characteristics intrinsically. Candrakīrti's critique of reflexive awareness, then, targets this notion that there is a class of cognitive events that are essentially self-characterizing: they reveal their own content without recourse to an additional instance of cognitive awareness, an object, or the positing of a subject of experience. More to the point, Candrakīrti rejects the notion that reflexive awareness has this unique property of giving access to the pure datum of experience.[14]

It is precisely with the intention of answering critics like Candrakīrti that Śāntarakṣita identifies the character of cognition as being contrary to insentient objects: "Cognitive awareness arises as something that is excluded from all insentient objects. This reflexive awareness of that cognition is none other than its non-insentience."[15] In effect, Śāntarakṣita simply follows Dharmakīrti's critique of the physicalist claim that consciousness arises from the four material elements. Indeed, as Dharmakīrti maintains, if the four elements, or a special transformation thereof, are the ultimate basis of consciousness, then consciousness ought to arise whenever and wherever the elements occur, which is to say at anytime and everywhere.[16] Furthermore, even if consciousness were said to arise at a particular point in time and only in regions of space occupied by (or configured as) bodies, it cannot arise from something that is not sentient. Attempting to further clarify the issue of the causal basis of consciousness, Dharmottara invokes the intentional character of cognition by explaining that what sets apart the occasioning of a cognitive event is that it accomplishes more that the causal process by which it arises allows—that is, it accomplishes its goal by revealing the object as the pragmatic outcome of cognition.[17] Dharmottara contrasts the intentional character of cognitive awareness with merely causal accounts of generation, such as is the case with seeds and sprouts: "Sprouts are not established [as the result] though their production is invariably concomitant with [causes like] seeds. Thus, even though a cognition arises as establishing a given object, it has the function of causing it to arrive at [its object] necessarily, by means of which its goal is accomplished."[18] Elsewhere, Dharmottara explains that the relation between cognition and object cognized is unlike that of elements in a causal chain, which exist as the relation between producer and produced.

---

14. See MAV VI, 72–78. As Tillemans (1990: 49 n. 109) observes, Candrakīrti does not seem to want to concede that there is a difference between "seeing" and "seeing as," and rests his criticism of reflexivity on the notion that all seeing is in effect seeing as.

15. TS 2000: *kriyākārakabhāvena na svasaṃvittir asya tu/ekasya-anaṃśarūpasya trairūpyānupapattitaḥ.*

16. See PV II, 35 and PVĀ *loc. cit.* Cf. Franco (1997: 171–172).

17. See NBṬ[d] *ad* NB I, 1, 4.1.

18. NBṬ[d] *ad* NB I, 19, 14.21: *bījādyavinābhāvino 'py aṅkurāder aprāpakatvāt/tasmad prāpyād arthād utpattāv apy asya jñānasyāsti kaścidavaśyakartavyaḥ prāpakavyāpāro, yena kṛtenārthaḥ prāpito bhavati.*

Rather, it is like the relation between an establishing factor and what it has established (*vyavasthāpravyavasthāpakabhāva*), that is, between reflexive awareness and the intentional object as intended.[19]

For the Buddhist epistemologists, then, consciousness (as reflexive awareness) is not just another phenomenon in the chain of dependently arising phenomena: rather, it is that medium which has the unique capacity of disclosing itself in the process of revealing the other. As Dharmakīrti declares, "if ascertaining were not [itself] directly perceived, the perception of objects would not be established."[20] Indeed, as Paul Williams has argued, the Buddhist epistemologist's assertion of the unity of consciousness as reflexive awareness goes against the sort of reductive explanation of cognition that discriminates between agent, act, and object, or cognizer, cognizing, and cognizable.[21] As such, it parallels Aristotle's view of reflexivity as found in *De Anima*[22] and, more recently, the views of Brentano, Husserl, and Sartre, all of whom have argued at length that to talk about consciousness as lacking self-awareness effectively amounts to altogether denying the very possibility of consciousness.

Indeed, as Brentano notes, "every consciousness upon whatever object it is primarily directed, is constantly directed upon itself."[23] For Brentano, just as for the Buddhist epistemologists, the apprehension of an event and awareness of this apprehension constitute one dual-aspect cognition. Thus Brentano: "every mental act, no matter how simple, has a double object."[24] Such mental acts are thus constituted by the act of perceiving something and the act in which the respective perception is experienced. In seeing a blue sky, I am not merely aware of the object, in this case an expanse of blue, but also of its mode of presentation, of the fact that the blue sky is for me to see. The reflexive form of consciousness that accompanies the act of seeing

---

19. See NBṬ^{d} *ad* NB I, 19, 15.3.

20. PVin I, 55: *dmigs pa mngon sum ma yin na//don mthong rab tu 'grub mi 'gyur.*

21. Williams (1998: 234–235) makes precisely such a point. Taking a radically opposite stance on the possibility of reflexive awareness, Garfield has argued that a commitment to reflexivity in effect amounts to abandoning "the publicity and conventional character of the concepts through which we know ourselves" and hence to saddling "ourselves with an insuperable problem of other minds, and an insuperable problem about how we ever develop those concepts in the first place" (Garfield 2006: 223). However, the "public" and "conventional" character of concepts presupposes an intentional identification and application of those concepts, and that in turn necessitates reflexivity, which applies to consciousness as a whole: indeed, one recognizes and learns to apply publicly available concepts because one is capable of discerning them as such, that is, as categories that extend the intentional arc of conscious awareness.

22. See *De Anima* III, 2 (425b11–17). Aristotle's reflexive view of consciousness rests on the regress argument. For an insightful commentary on Aristotle's reflexive approach to consciousness, see Caston (2002).

23. Brentano (1982: 25).

24. Brentano (1982: 153–154).

is disclosed in the individual perspective from which seeing takes place (with all its qualitative aspects). There is something it is like to be seeing just like there is something it is like to be hearing. The reflexivity of conscious awareness is apparent in the primary and secondary objects of any intentional act. As Brentano claims: "The simplest act, for example, the act of hearing, has as its primary object the sound, and for its secondary object, itself, the mental phenomenon in which the sound is heard."[25] For Husserl, who follows the Brentanian model up to a point, the self-manifestation of consciousness that accompanies each cognitive event is understood not only in intentional terms but also in terms of embodiment, temporality, attention, and intersubjectivity. Nonetheless, Husserl clearly identifies the implicit reflexivity of conscious apprehension: "whenever I take myself or something else as an object, I am always necessarily unthematically cogiven as a functioning I."[26] This tacit (or pre-thetic) self-awareness that intentional acts possess precedes reflection rather than being a product of it. Husserl, again: "When I say 'I,' I grasp myself in a simple reflection. But this self-experience (*Selbsterfahrung*) is like every experience (*Erfahrung*), and in particular every perception, a mere directing myself toward something that was already there for me, that was already conscious, but not thematically experienced, not noticed."[27] Even though Husserl often takes this self-awareness to be an internal or *innermost* sort of perception, this should not be understood in introspective terms.[28] Introspective thought is deliberate and effortful, whereas implicit self-awareness is nondeliberate and effortless. One can choose to introspect one's mental states or to attend to the contents of perceptual awareness. Implicit self-awareness is, however, ongoing and cannot be voluntarily halted: one cannot stop being implicitly self-aware of the act of perceiving or introspecting. Rather reflection presupposes self-awareness: when I reflect on my experience of the blue sky, I thematically attend to what is already there. But I can only consciously reflect on my experience if there

25. Brentano (1981: 153–154). The "mental act" in question may not imply activity, but rather the specific nature (and character) of the mental event in question. Cf. Janzen (2008: 105 n. 7).

26. Husserl (1973a: 431). For a discussion of this passage, see Zahavi (2003: 162).

27. Husserl (1973b: 492–493). Cf. Zahavi (2003: 162). The notion that Husserl does not offer an account of pre-reflective self-awareness or that he understands self-awareness in reflective terms only (or as a kind of internal perception akin to introspection), has been advanced by those interpreters who mainly rely on the works that were published during his lifetime. See, for instance, Tugendhat (1979: 15), Frank (1986: 53ff.), and Gloy (1998: 203). But, as Zahavi (1999, 2003) clearly demonstrates, in the posthumously published works, one does comes across a detailed account of pre-reflective self-awareness that is embedded in Husserl's treatment of other central topics (intentionality, spatiality, embodiment, etc.).

28. Such is the case with Searle's (1992: 141ff.) rejection of reflexivity, which he understands in terms of introspective attentiveness. See also White (1987) for a similar view.

is an implicit self-awareness already in place guiding my reflection. Thus, I can attend to the content of my perception, but when I try and attend to the act of perceiving itself, the implicit self-awareness shifts from the content of perception to the perceiving act itself (hence, the elusive character of self-awareness). Self-awareness is thus constitutive of the phenomenal character of conscious states. Without self-awareness it becomes impossible to discern how an experience acquires its phenomenal content, that is, how it comes to be about something at all.

Like Brentano and Husserl before him, Sartre too takes the view that self-awareness is a constitutive aspect of conscious mental states. But unlike Brentano, he takes conscious states to be a given of experience. Such states acquire an objective or a subjective aspect only when reflected upon. It is largely this Sartrean reinterpretation of self-awareness that is followed by contemporary defenders of the reflexivity thesis of consciousness.[29] According to Zahavi, to conceive of self-awareness in subject-object terms is akin to understanding conscious states as the sort of (mental) events individuals stand in a particular relation to.[30] But self-awareness is not something that only arises when we turn our gaze within, so to speak, when we scrutinize our experience. As will be argued shortly, we already possess an internal body-schema that serves as the basis for our implicit sense of agency. In other words, self-awareness is not the result of catching myself in the mirror, using the first-person pronoun, or reminiscing one's life story. Rather self-awareness is intrinsic to consciousness; it is what confers upon conscious experience its unique *reflexive* character, which tells a person that the experience is hers, that it occurs in her mental stream.[31] Thus, what makes an experience conscious is its phenomenal character, but also, and more significantly, the fact that this phenomenal character arises bound up with a sense of inner awareness of itself. Phenomenal character and self-awareness are intimately linked. Is phenomenal character, then, simply the result of manifest conscious awareness or does it have to be explained in terms of perceptual experience assuming the aspect of its intentional object? In other words, is self-awareness present in the direct apprehension of a given object, but

---

29. See, for instance, Zahavi (1999), Kriegel (2003b, 2009), and Janzen (2008). Note that higher-order approaches to consciousness such as one finds, for instance, in Rosenthal (1986, 2004), Gennaro (1996, 2002), and Lycan (1996) also give support to the reflexivity thesis, though as Jenzen (2008: ch. 6) has conclusively demonstrated, it is possible to defend the reflexivity thesis on a Brentanian "one-state" model of conscious awareness.

30. See Zahavi (1999, 2004a, 2005).

31. Cf. Flanagan (1992: 194), for whom the phenomenal character of consciousness consists specifically in the experience being an instance of self-awareness. Likewise, Kriegel (2003a, 2003b) defines a mental state as conscious just in case it involves implicit self-awareness.

not present in its absence, assuming it is possible to have pure, contentless experiences?

We have already seen that in certain meditative states—as the Buddhist epistemologist claims—cognitive awareness displays something like a phenomenal type of intentionality.[32] Are we dealing here, then, with attempts to work out the implications of a deep phenomenology of non-ordinary experience for a theory of perception? Is the reflexivity thesis simply the result of an unreflective subjectivity that sees itself (or its structure) in everything that it apprehends? Finally, should the dual aspect theory of mental states be taken as a statement about the nature of cognition? The central thesis of this book is predicated on a positive answer to the first question. A satisfactory answer the second question demands that we distinguish between "unreflective" and "pre-reflective" self-awareness and resist the uncharitable tendency to attribute to the Buddhist epistemologist a dogmatic commitment to any putatively implicit reflexivity thesis. Finally, the Buddhist epistemologist's guiding phenomenological insight is that correct perception amounts to an implicit (reflexive, but pre-thetic) knowing of the sort that is not mediated by any notion of subjectivity. Of course, it is highly improbable that the Buddhist epistemologist's analysis of experience is meant to reveal the merely aspectual (*ākāramātra*) nature of phenomena, without any sort of commitment to the distinction between appearance and reality.

The phenomenological account of self-cognition advanced here is also, at least in part, conceived in response to a generally doxographical tendency to examine the ideas of the Buddhist epistemologists in terms of their allegiance to the presumably idealist ontology of the Yogācāras. Dan Arnold, for instance, has built a strong case for interpreting the Buddhist epistemological account of self-cognition as advancing something more like a "full-blown metaphysical idealism" rather than "simply a representationalist epistemology,"[33] given the essentially internalist account of cognition we find in his works. Arnold's interpretation rests on the premise that self-cognition, which he renders (following Kant) as "apperception" is to be understood as endorsing the view that mental events are all that we can directly know. Such a view would, indeed, be deeply problematic: if apperception is the only accredited source of knowledge it becomes difficult to account for the difference between the particular aspects of the phenomenal content of

32. See *supra* pp. 170–171.

33. See Arnold (2005a: 88) and also Arnold (2005a: 35). In his very extensive and philosophically interesting discussion of the concept of self-awareness (*svasaṃvitti*), Arnold takes into account Dignāga's position, its refutation by Candrakīrti, and later reworkings of it by Śāntarașita, Dharmottara, and Mokṣākaragupta. I am concerned less with the historical underpinnings of this debate and more with Arnold's reading of self-awareness as doing the same kind of work that the notion of "apperception" does for Kant.

experience. So Arnold asks, "How, that is, does 'whatever appears as the content' of the cognition (*yad ābhāsaṃ prameyam*) relate at once to the 'cognition itself' (*saṃvitti*) and its 'subjective aspect' (*grāhakākāra*)?"[34] The problem with Dignāga's account of self-awareness, claims Arnold, is the assumption that all cognitions (at least, all veridical ones) are perspectival, the immediate and unwarranted consequence of which is that one dispenses with the need to explain the subject-object relation. Even though the Buddhist (unlike his Naiyāyika opponent) is primarily concerned with cognitive aspects (*ākāra*) and not with ontologically distinct substances, the question of how a subjectively phenomenal aspect can meaningfully tell us something about what objectively appears remains presumably unanswered. Does, then, Dignāga operate with something like the cognitive model of the sense datum theorist (or, alternatively, that of the cognitivist), and is he, therefore, guilty of creating an unbridgeable gap between the purely perceptual (hence, nonconceptual) aspects of cognition and the purely discursive modes which seek to explain it?

I want to claim that it is possible to read Dignāga, and to a certain extent Dharmakīrti as well as Śāntarakṣita and Kamalaśīla, as advancing something like a phenomenological account of cognition of the sort we find particularly in Husserl and, to an even larger extent, in the embodied account of cognition advanced by Merleau-Ponty. Read through the lens of a specifically embodied account of cognition, the Buddhist epistemologist's understanding of the intentional aspect of perceptual cognitions would be less problematic, and also less amenable to the sort of transcendental interpretation of self-awareness that Arnold proposes. I will argue (i) that Dignāga's understanding of self-awareness as a dual-aspect cognition rests on a careful analysis of the phenomenology of first-person experience; (ii) that it is possible to read Dignāga's use of cognitive aspects (*ākāra*) as something analogous to Merleau-Ponty's notion of body-schema; and (iii) that Buddhist epistemologists in general take the position that aspectual cognitions are inherently intentional.

Let me first clarify my suggestion that the Buddhist epistemologist's understanding of "cognitive aspects" is best captured by the notion of "body-schema." The phenomenological method opens access to an investigation of the intentional relation itself and does not assimilate the body to some kind of instrumental object as reductive models of embodied cognition do. From a phenomenological perspective, then, "body-schema" and "body-image," although often used interchangeably in the literature, effectively intend different sorts of objects. Shaun Gallagher, for instance, identifies at least three distinctive features that set apart the notions of "body-schema" and "body-image." First, the body-image has an "intentional status" in that it is either "a conscious

34. Arnold (2005a: 89).

representation of the body or a set of beliefs about the body."[35] By contrast, the body-schema, while having an effect on consciousness itself, operates at the pre-conscious level. Second, whereas the body-image captures the sense of a body that is owned (or at least one whose experiences are owned), the body-schema functions at the subpersonal level. Finally, the body-image "involves an abstract... or articulated representation of the body insofar as conscious awareness typically attends to only one part... of the body at a time," whereas the body-schema functions in a "holistic way."[36] The Buddhist epistemologist's understanding of cognitive aspects as structuring elements of experience—without which no object (whether internal or external) is apprehended as such—suggest a pre-reflective, embodied, and holistic function.

An axiomatic principle of existentialist phenomenology in general (and of Merleau-Ponty's phenomenology in particular) is that we simply cannot conceptually articulate the particular ways of our being-in-the-world. The limits of categorization—understood in relation to particular domains rather than in terms of conceivability—is one of the reasons why phenomenological accounts of cognition seek to go beyond the traditional opposition between the "conceptual" intentionality of belief and the "nonconceptual" intentionality of sense-experience to the habitual matrix of experience which neither "posits" nor "represents" its objects. As Charles Siewert notes in a reworked version of Merleau-Ponty's account of sensorimotor intentionality, however odd it might sound, it is possible to think of non-positional consciousness as being intentional without at the same time thinking of it as *representational.* Siewert claims, rightly in my view, that the phenomenal character of some of our experiences "differs in ways we have reason to think cannot be specified by attributing distinct representational content to the experiences."[37]

It was Husserl who first noted, while exploring the experiential background of perception, that things in our perceptual field appear even before they are "seized upon." For instance, as I sit at my desk leafing through an *editio princeps* of Dante's *Divina Comedia* I am surrounded by a whole range of objects (books, papers, letters, pens, frames, memorabilia, etc.) which are *perceptually* present only as a "field of intuition." They are appearing even before they are properly perceived or seized upon in attentive perceiving. Thus Husserl: "Every perception of a physical thing has, in this manner, a halo of *background-intuitions* (or background seeings...), and that is also a '*mental process of consciousness*' or, more briefly, 'consciousness... of' all that which lies in the objective 'background' seen along with it."[38] When Husserl

35. Gallagher (1995: 228). Gallagher expands on the implication of this distinction between the body-image and body-schema, while drawing from recent findings about cross-modal communication in some of his more recent work (2005: 40–64).
36. Gallagher (1995: 229).
37. Siewert (2005: 276).
38. Husserl (1983: 70).

singles out the role that background intuitions play in informing the phenomenal character of experience, he is also making an important claim about differences in the horizon of perceptual experience: less attended surroundings look phenomenally rather different than whatever it is that we direct our attention to.[39] This difference is not easily verbalized, for, in trying to "find out" what the surrounding areas look like one would have inevitably shifted the attention. The resulting verbal report, therefore, is no longer about the initial surroundings but about whatever has now come into focus. On Siewert's reading of this shift in attention, "the effort to specify the character of the less attentive experience by attributing content to it invites a redirection of attention that risks *assimilating* the prior experience *to*—and not *distinguishing* it *from*—a more attentive experience that differs from it in phenomenal character."[40] What does resisting this assimilation (of the prior, essentially undefined and unrepresented experience) to the new experience that is fully attended to reveal that the resulting verbal report cannot? As Siewert puts it, it reveals "a difference in character between the inattentive experience of the visually apparent surroundings of what you are looking at and the attentive experience of what you are looking at."[41] Attentiveness differs from inattentive experiences mainly in the way in which it effects the indexicality of perceptual content. We cannot make sense of our perceptual acts without attributing indexical content to our thoughts. But appealing to thoughts alone is not the only way to explain the salient difference between perception and action.[42] Indeed, there is significant difference between perception and conception in terms of their indexical content. In whatever terms one may understand thoughts to operate, it is always the case that deploying concepts in ways that are not explicitly indexical will invariably have no reference to relations between the individual and the content of his or her experience. The same is not the case with perception—as an experience that is essentially nonconceptual in terms of its content—for here an individual's relation to the content of his or her experience is always internal to the content of that experience.[43]

39. Mangan (1993, 2001) and Kriegel (2009) have reworked Husserl's notion of "background intuition" into what they call "inner" and "outer peripheral awareness." As Kriegel observes, peripheral awareness of ongoing experience is precisely what "makes detailed information about the experience much more available to the subject than it would otherwise be" (Kriegel: 2009: 259).

40. Siewert (2005: 277).

41. Siewert (2005: 278).

42. For an account of why an agent's actions can only be offered a rationally intelligible explanation if the indexicality of thought is assumed, see Peacocke (1986).

43. This account of the relation between the indexical features of conceptual and nonconceptual content follows Bermúdez and Macpherson (1998). Bermúdez and Macpherson challenge the view, advanced by Gareth Evans (1982) that nonconceptual content derived from perception counts as a source of reliable knowledge only if the perceptual experience provides input to conceptual reasoning.

How might we profitably employ these insights about the intentional (and indexical) character of perceptual experience for the purpose of explicating the Buddhist epistemologist's account of self-cognition (*svasaṃvitti*)? First, let me briefly review Dignāga's position. As noted above, Dignāga claims that the difference between cognition and its result is in fact merely apparent: "we do not admit, as the realists do, that the resulting cognition (*pramāṇaphala*) differs from the accredited sources of cognition (*pramāṇa*)."[44] It is only because "the resulting cognition arises bearing in itself the form of the cognized object" that it is regarded as comprising the cognitive act itself and is thus called a reliable cognition. For Dignāga, this resulting cognition, whose content bears formal resemblance to the apprehended object, is effectively the self-cognition itself in its twofold appearance, as subject and object. Furthermore, Dignāga tells us that what we ordinarily take to be the object of cognition is but the form or the phenomenal character of experience itself. This account of cognition raises an important question: how do we know that cognition has this two-aspectual character? Dignāga's answer is quite categorical: because object-cognition without self-cognition and self-cognition without object-cognition would otherwise be indistinguishable.[45]

I take Dignāga to be offering here something like a phenomenological account of embodied self-awareness: we sense not only the properties of the objects with which we come into contact but also perceive ourselves as the locus of qualitative experience (which explains why sensing is both transitive and intransitive). The intentionality of self-awareness, then, may be understood as something like the immediate sense of embodied agency that is characteristic of epistemic feelings such as doubt, certainty, curiosity, etc.

Recall that Arnold interprets Dignāga's use of "self-cognition" as advancing something like a full blown metaphysical idealism. His interpretation is based on an overtly Kantian understanding of the unity of apperception, which takes the faculty of apperception to be the highest form of understanding comprising logic and transcendental philosophy, if not "understanding itself."[46] Citing favorably Pippin's reading of Kant's use of apperception "as a logical condition," in the sense that "all consciousness, including what Kant is calling experience, *is* a species of self-consciousness,"[47] Arnold seems to imply that Dignāga holds precisely such a view. At stake is Dignāga's notion of self-awareness as a dual-aspect cognition, which Arnold (following Pippin) regards as vulnerable to "the iteration problem":

44. PSV *ad* PV I, 8cd: *'di la phyi rol pa rnams kyi bzhin du tsad ma*. Translation *per* Hattori (1968: 28).
45. See PSV *ad* PS I, 11ab.
46. Kant (1998: B134).
47. Pippin (1989: 20).

That is, if it is thought that any act of consciousness must, in order to count as such, be accompanied by a further act of consciousness, then the latter—again, if it is to count as such—must in turn be accompanied by a yet further act... [T]his could serve just as well as a concise statement of the characteristically Mādhyamika argument against Dignāga's idea of *svasaṃvitti*.[48]

As we saw above, the problem with this mentalist conception of consciousness is that it takes for granted the apparent structures of perceptual experience. Rationalist traditions in epistemology (of the sort that Arnold draws upon) still carry through, it seems, the old legacy of distinguishing between transparent consciousness and opaque sensation. Even Husserl, whose phenomenological reduction was primarily conceived as a method for suspending belief in a natural world and examining not the objects that we ordinarily intend, but intentionality itself, remains committed, as Taylor Carman has argued, to "the sort of intellectualism that in effect renders embodied consciousness metaphysically unintelligible."[49]

Echoing Merleau-Ponty's view that the intentional gap between mind and world can only be bridged in our understanding of bodily skills (and not through cognitive attitudes, as Husserl thought), Carman captures rather well the *non-positional* consciousness characteristic of our embodied condition. Thus, having a body does not consist in "having abstract thoughts about a body or concrete sensations localizable in a body, since embodiment is what makes possible the very ascription of thoughts and sensations to subjects."[50] Now, Husserl is most certainly not an empiricist, nor does he subscribe to anything like a sense datum theory. For him sensations, while not the immediate and original objects of awareness, are, however, the basic constitutive material of consciousness.[51] But Husserl does not see bare sensations as having any intentional character. For that we must turn to Merleau-Ponty, who finds the key to our understanding of sensorimotor intentionality in the notion of body-schema, which he describes as an "inter-sensory or sensorimotor unity of the body...that is not confined to contents actually and fortuitously associated in the course of our experience... [but rather] is anterior to them and makes their association possible."[52]

Note that something like an analogous notion of schematic bodily representation can be traced at least as far back as Kant's *Critique of Pure Reason*. Thus Kant's "transcendental schema," which is supposed to provide a solution to the problem of bridging the gap between concepts and pure intuitions, is precisely the ground on which sensible concepts are anchored, not

48. Arnold (2005a: 82).
49. Carman (1999: 215).
50. Carman (1999: 206).
51. See Husserl (1989: 292) for an account of the sensory basis of subjectivity.
52. Merleau-Ponty (2002: 114).

as internal representations but as the specific rules and procedures that govern the faculty of imagination. For Kant, "it is not images of objects but schemata that ground our pure sensible concepts" even as he admits that how sensible objects appear to us by means of these schemata, as well as their operations, "is a hidden art in the depths of the human soul."[53] This much Kant does concede: that images are the product of the empirical faculty of productive imagination, whereas schema is a product of pure imagination itself. Unlike Kant, however, Merleau-Ponty does not understand the conception of schema as explicit formal rules for negotiating the application of categories to experience. Rather, the schema for Merleau-Ponty operates as "habit" or "coping skills"—the perceptual background that conditions how we actually experience and respond to the environment we inhabit. This embodied account of perceptual agency goes well beyond Husserl's attempt to explain intentionality by appeal to various hypothetical inferences and associations between kinesthetic and outward-directed sensations. Rather, as Carman clearly illustrates, our sense of embodiment "is nothing like an object-directed awareness focused on any of its distinct parts, as for example when we locate tactile sensations on our skin or in our joints... [instead it] is bound up... with a primitive understanding of the body as a global and abiding horizon of perceptual experience."[54]

This double apprehension of the body as the locus of particular sensations and at the same time as the horizon of perceptual experience comes very close, I think, to the Buddhist epistemologist's understanding of self-awareness. Take the example of my two hands touching each other: whereas Husserl would see it as an interaction between a kinesthetic sense of voluntary movement and a passive sensation,[55] Merleau-Ponty, much like Dignāga, interprets the phenomenon as a dual-aspect perception that shifts from an embodied sense of agency (effectively the result of past habituation) to being the locus or "bearer of sensations." It is only at the level of pure sensation, however, that one can directly experience the inadequacy of the overtly mentalist notion that the body is a quasi-objective thing one identifies with by means of localized subjective sensations. This account of direct perceptual awareness, again, takes us back to Merleau-Ponty's notion that pure sensations carry within them a "germ of depersonalization."

53. Kant (1998: A141).

54. Carman (1999: 221).

55. As Husserl writes, describing the reflexive nature of tactile experience: "The hand lies on the table. I experience the table as solid, cold, smooth. Moving it over the table I experience it and its determinations as a thing. At the same time, however, I can always pay attention to the hand and find on it tactile sensations, sensations of smoothness and coldness" (Husserl 1989: 153). See also Welton (1999: 47), who finds in Husserl's account of the lived-body a prefiguration of an active perception theory: "To say that the lived-body reflexively senses itself... means that the lived-body moves itself in the ongoing course of perception."

8.2 PHENOMENAL OBJECTS AND THE COGNITIVE SUBCONSCIOUS

How are we, then, to understand Dignāga and Dharmakīrti's innovative synthesis of epistemology (viz., *pramāṇa* theory) and Abhidharma psychology? Why is it that, despite Nāgārjuna and Candrakīrti's critiques of epistemology[56] and Wittgenstein's invitation to abandon the illusions of the knowledge project, epistemology goes on? For the Buddhist epistemologists, the answer lies not simply in the need for establishing certainty—specifically, certainty about Buddhist metaphysical principles and the effectiveness of the Buddhist path—but also in the pragmatic concerns that are at the heart of any epistemology: what must I know in order to achieve a given goal?

As we saw in the previous chapter, the Buddhist epistemological program initiated by Dignāga rests on the notion that the two categories of particular and universal need to be translated back to their specific knowledge source—particulars to perception and universals to inferential reasoning—in order for them to become operationally effective. The Buddhist epistemologist, thus, appears to be claiming that all objects of cognition cannot be properly understood in isolation from their mode of givenness, that is, if separated from the types of cognitive events in which they are instantiated. This claim, of course, is consistent with Vasubandhu's Abhidharma account, which states that perception (for instance) opens us to a world of characteristically unique phenomenal properties: shapes, shades, textures—a vast array of sensory experiences each having its distinctive qualitative aspect. That we apparently come to apprehend this fragmentary and discontinuous sensory content either as enduring external objects or as universals is due to the constructive aspects of conception.

However, as we discussed earlier, Dignāga is not entirely faithful to Vasubandhu's account of particulars.[57] Whereas Vasubandhu understands particulars as types, Dignāga, it seems, thinks of them as tokens. For instance, visual perception apprehends entities whose specific characteristics are visible types: shape, color, size, etc. For Vasubandhu, these are all particular characteristics in the sense that they all have the quality of being visible

56. Siderits (1980, 1981) seems to have been the first to suggest that the Prāsaṅgika interpretation of Madhyamaka advanced by Candrakīrti amounts not simply to a critique of epistemology but effectively to *no epistemology*. For an in-depth look at the question of whether the Prāsaṅgika does use reasons and arguments to establish various philosophical positions, see Huntington (2007) and Garfield (2008). For various arguments in support of the view that Candrakīrti, despite his rejection of intrinsic natures (*svabhāva*), does accept the epistemic efficacy of the sources of cognition (*pramāṇas*), see Thakchöe (2011).

57. See *supra* chapter 7.2.

(*rūpāyatana*).[58] With Dignāga, the particular comes to designate an utterly unique and ultimately real entity. The properties of being visible, round, or having a color in the blue spectrum, are no longer regarded as types (of which, presumably, there can be numerous tokens).[59] The specific shades of blue and bloomlike shape by which something is apprehended as a blue lotus become for Dignāga an instance of uniquely characterized phenomena.

Reflecting on the type-token distinction while tracing the semantic shifts of the notion of particular from Vasubandhu to Dignāga, Dharmakīrti, and Śāntarakṣita is helpful for another reason: it shows that the Buddhist epistemologists are much more careful to work out the implications for Buddhist philosophy of the debate among the Sanskrit grammarians regarding the generation of meaning from verbal content.[60] For the Buddhist epistemologist, the debate about the nature of word-meaning relations is important for at least two reasons. First, it explains why he excludes from his definition of perception the possibility that word-meaning relations could be perceptually apprehended. Instead, the Buddhist epistemologist claims that verbal expressions are primarily associated with conceptual cognitions because they require the deployment of categories such as genus and species, as well as reasoning and deliberation, all of which are by definition outside the domain of sensory experience. Secondly, it explains why the notion that universals can be perceptually apprehended as relations of inherence is to be rejected: in perception we do not apprehend whole objects, but only their "perceptible" parts, and perception does not involve any inferential component.[61] For the Buddhist epistemologist, the debate over the nature of perceptual objects is primarily centered on his or her analysis of the manner in which various classes of names are attributed to phenomena as directly experienced. It is in *direct experience* that one encounters a total separation of perception from conception, which is why the Buddhist epistemologists restrict the domain of the former to inexpressible particularities (viz., phenomenal qualia) and of the latter to universal properties (viz., genera). Of course, Dignāga's use of particulars and universals in this manner is not new. Vasubandhu writes:

> One examines the body in its proper and general characteristics, as well as sensation, mind and constitutive elements of existence. [Their] own being is their proper characteristic. But the general characteristic is the non-eternity of produced [things], the

58. See AKBh *ad* AK II, 10cd.
59. We may also reconstruct this understanding of the particular in terms of what Ganeri (2001: 99)—following Stout (1921) and Williams (1953)—calls "thin" properties of tropes: not blueness as such but the blue of, say, blue irises.
60. See *supra* chapter 4.2 and 4.3.
61. The question of whether a perceptual appearance (*pratyakṣābhāsa*) is inferential in nature is treated at length by the Naiyāyikas. See NS II, 1.30–32 and NSB, NV, and NVTṬ *loc. cit.* For a detailed discussion of this issue, see Matilal (1986: 255–291).

fact that [everything that is] connected with the [four] afflictions is suffering, and the fact that all things are empty and not the self.[62]

Note that while a specific characteristic may be expressed in terms of a phenomenal feature as apprehended, such as a unique shade or shape, it is also structureless and momentary in nature. Perception, thus, enables us to apprehend the specific particularities of objects as aggregated entities, but at the same time reveals their momentariness. Inference, which relies on the testimony of direct experience, extends this awareness to entities as classes of objects or as universals. Dignāga, as it is well known, follows Vasubandhu in his explicit association of perception with particulars. For Vasubandhu, direct perception in its dual aspect, as apprehension of external objects and as awareness of internal states such as feelings and emotions, also lacks any association with conception.

Now, by limiting the sphere of perception to indeterminate content only, the Buddhist epistemologist parts with the received view (chiefly that of Nyāya) that indirect perception is the sort of cognition naturally suited to connect objects and universals. Following Dignāga, the Buddhist epistemologist sees this connection as being the function of inferential rather than perceptual cognitions, a view that accords with the Abhidharma account of cognitive dynamics. On this account, cognition results from a maturation of the flow of discrete elements of consciousness. This flow of consciousness—called "mind-continuum" (*citta-santāna*) by the Sautrāntikas and "receptacle consciousness" (*ālaya-vijñāna*) by the Yogācāras—is ultimately seen as reflecting the dynamics of three types of action: volitional (*cetayitvā karman*), vocal (*vākkarman*), and mental (*manaskarman*). Vasubandhu again: "It is through the force of its seeds supported on the material organs that the mind posterior to absorption comes into existence. In fact, the seeds which give rise to the mind and to mental states rest according to circumstance on [one] of the two following series: the mental series or the series of the material organs."[63] It is this mind continuum that effectively supports all cognitive activity and generates the sense of continuity that comes with self-awareness. In its indeterminate aspect, this mind continuum is nothing but the repository of a direct and nonconstructed form of cognitive awareness. For Vasubandhu, as for all Ābhidharmikas, apprehending subject and apprehended phenomena are emergent properties of the threefold transformation of consciousness. The main point of this theory of cognitive emergence, then, is to take into account the role that residual forces of past cognitive events

62. AKBh *ad* AK VI, 14ab: *kāyaṃ svasāmānyalakṣaṇābhyāṃ parīkṣate/vedanāṃ cittaṃ dharmāś ca/svabhāva evaiṣāṃ svalakṣaṇam/sāmānyalakṣaṇaṃ tu anityatā saṃskṛtānāṃ duḥkhatā sāsravāṇāṃ śūnyatā'anātmate sarvadharmāṇāṃ.*

63. KSP III, 2, 23. Translation *per* Lamotte (1936: 58).

have in "seeding" this receptacle consciousness. On this model, it is the dynamics of the residual forces of past cognitions that generates the intentional forms of apprehension that subsequent cognitions depend upon.

Exploring possible parallels between this Buddhist account of cognitive dynamics and cognitive science models of cognition, William Waldron has argued that the notion of a "cognitive unconscious" as the structuring principle of experience provides a compelling account of the sort of coupling of world and its conscious apprehension that the phenomenology of perception exhibits.[64] It is possible, I think, to take the notion of a "cognitive unconscious" as indicating one way (the other being Husserl's eidetic phenomenology) in which the Cartesian dilemmas of a thinking subject seeking the justification of his or her beliefs can be overcome. Indeed, the psychological account of cognitive maturation put forth in works such as the *Saṃdhinirmocana Sūtra* ("Examination of the Profound Meaning") suggests an intimate link between "the substratum of the material sense-faculties along with their supports" and "that which consists of the predispositions toward conceptual proliferation in terms of conventional usage of images, names, and conceptualizations."[65] As Waldron rightly points out, this model of the underlying structures of cognitive awareness, is explained in an encyclopedic work such as the *Yogācārabhūmi* ("Examination of the Stages of Yoga") as the result of a threefold process of causal coupling in which a residual cognitive awareness arises together with the sensory systems, and the habitual tendencies generated by past linguistic experience such as conceptualization and naming. Waldron nicely sums up the explanatory gap that any theory of consciousness must confront: "we live... in a world whose predominant structuring influences—linguistic and physiological structures built up over time through extended organism-environment interaction—we cannot fully discern."[66]

Whether the Buddhist Yogācāra model of cognitive dynamics can bridge this gap is less relevant to our analysis of the constitutive elements of phenomenal content than its implicit epistemic claim: namely, that cognition, in the mode of linguistic and symbolic representation, is habitual and driven by the power of the predispositions inherent in ordinary language propositions.[67] In other words, ordinary language propositions, which purport to describe the world of common sense experience, subtly condition the very way we commonly conceive the world. Consequently, instead of an awareness of

64. Waldron (2002) borrows the notion of the "cognitive unconscious" from Lakoff and Johnson (1999), which Waldron claims, I think convincingly, is structurally similar to the Yogācāra notion of receptacle consciousness (*ālaya-vijñāna*).

65. Waldron (2002: 39) quotes this passage following its reconstruction and translation in Schmithausen (1987: 357 n. 511).

66. Waldron (2002: 40).

67. See *Mahāyāna-saṃgraha*, I, 58, and discussion in Waldron (2002: 40).

the mutual co-determination of self-cognition and cognition of object, which Dignāga's dual-aspect model of cognition exemplifies, we ordinarily experience a world of external objects standing over against an apparent self.

Recall that the Buddhist epistemological project goes beyond causal accounts of cognition to questions of reliability and pragmatic efficacy. Its "spartan" epistemology, which reduces the sources of knowledge to perception and inferential reasoning alone, cannot be understood, therefore, apart from the Abhidharma cognitive psychological account that informs it. It is for this reason that Arnold's decidedly Kantian understanding of self-cognition leaves our broader discussion of the scope of the Buddhist epistemological enterprise vulnerable to precisely the sort of criticism he thus advances: that the tradition of epistemic inquiry initiated by Dignāga and Dharmakīrti with its "foundationalist emphasis on constitutively caused perceptions... adduce[s] not *reasons*, but only causes."[68] I have addressed the question of whether the Buddhist epistemological enterprise is properly characterized as a type of foundationalism in the previous chapter. While arguing that the justification of knowledge based on basic empirical beliefs—which is the primary concern of foundationalism—falls outside the scope of the Buddhist epistemological enterprise, I claimed that it should be possible to offer an anti-foundationalist reading of the Buddhist epistemological project if we abandon the requirement that perceptual awareness provide a justification for basic empirical beliefs.

Granting Dignāga's discrimination between sensory experience and self-awareness, we might conclude that self-awareness is simply a special mode of nonconceptual awareness.[69] It is this nonconceptual awareness that provides direct access to the content of experience, which, although nonconceptual, is *meaningfully* given. Without self-awareness providing an intentional horizon for all other cognitive events, cognition would happen in the dark. Cognition requires perspectival apprehension and that, in turn, necessitates consciousness.

---

68. Arnold (2005a: 51).

69. The first attempt to interpret "self-awareness" (*svasaṃvedana*) as an aspect of mental perception is found in Hattori (1968: 27). Similar interpretations have been proposed by Nagatomi (1979) and Franco (1993). Franco's account is also a critique of Wayman's (1991) view that Dignāga did indeed treat self-awareness as a different type of perception. Yao (2004) has reopened this debate by adducing some further evidence to support Dignāga's endorsement of self-awareness as a type of perception. Yao bases his claim primarily on the Chinese translations of *Nyāyamukha* by Xuanzang (600–664) and Yijing (635–713), as well as on Kuiji's (632–682) commentaries on Dignāga's principal works, all of which seem to indicate, in no ambiguous terminology, that Dignāga treats self-awareness as a distinct form of perception. For Yao mental perception (*manasa-pratyakṣa*) and the mental faculty of cognitive awareness (*mano-vijñāna*) are to be clearly differentiated, the first being just an aspect of the latter. Likewise, self-awareness and yogic perception too are taken to be just different states of this mental cognitive awareness. See also Tillemans (1989), Steinkellner (1978, 1982, 1999), and Dunne (2006) for discussions of this issue.

Thus, Dignāga does not merely systematize into a system of epistemic warrants what has traditionally been known as empirical awareness and self-awareness: he goes a step further and assigns to each cognitive modality a specific epistemic role—perception does the job of apprehending particulars as uniquely characterized phenomena, but only if operating in a nonconstructive mode. If accounting for the sense of intimation that accompanies each cognitive event is the goal, it is to the phenomenology of perception that one must turn for answers. Essentially, perception appears in its dual aspect as awareness of something coupled with self-awareness. It is the implicitly reflexive aspect of this cognition, that is, its (the cognition's) capacity to disclose its bearer (and the pragmatic consequences thereof) that ultimately counts as a result. I am being disclosed to myself as a knower to the extent that I grasp myself as the locus of a cognitive event that has pragmatic consequences. On this account, self-awareness is precisely the type of cognition in which there is awareness that perceiving (or thinking) is taking place without there being any engagement in it. Husserl, likewise, clearly distinguishes this ongoing pre-reflective self-awareness from its thematic noticing in reflective engagement with it:

> For this [viz., subjectivity] is not merely a continuously streaming lived-experience (*Erleben*), rather when it streams there is always simultaneously consciousness of this streaming. This consciousness is self-perceiving. Only exceptionally it is thematic noticing performed by the I. To that exception belongs the reflection, possible at any time. This perception, which makes all experiencing conscious, is the so-called internal consciousness or internal perception.[70]

Such is the case, also, with feelings and memories. Insofar as the Buddhist epistemological project seeks to frame the definition of perception by looking outward at the phenomena of experience, rather than inward at our intuition about them, it seems to be also operating on naturalist grounds. Following Kornblith, I take it that the naturalist is concerned with the empirical investigation of phenomena, and that one of the benefits of empirical approaches to cognition is that it can "reveal possibilities which we would not, and sometimes could not, have imagined before."[71]

8.3 THE INTENTIONAL STRUCTURE OF AWARENESS

I have argued that, in conceiving of self-awareness as constitutive of perception, the Buddhist epistemologist shares a common ground with

70. Husserl (1966: 320). For discussion of this and related key passages from Husserl's posthumous works on self-awareness, see Zahavi (2003: 160).
71. Kornblith (2002: 16).

phenomenologists in the tradition of Husserl and Merleau-Ponty, who contend that perception is best understood as bearing intentional content. The notion that the primacy of perception for Dignāga, Dharmakīrti, and their successors implies that perception is intentionally constituted is, however, controversial. Georges Dreyfus, for instance, claims that bare sensations such as pains and aches are non-intentional, and that perceptions, at least for Dharmakīrti, "do not identify [*sic*] their objects" because they are non-conceptual (and it takes conception to grasp an object as such, that is, as the bearer of specific characteristics and/or identity relations).[72] Taking a different line of argumentation, Arnold thinks the self-intimating aspect of perceptual experience, as defined by Dignāga, cannot explain the subject-object relation or how the subjective aspect can be phenomenologically about something, in this case about the objective aspect.[73] Finally, for Birgit Kellner the self-aware aspect of perception does not reflect the intentional character and content of mental states but simply provides "access" to the mental domain.[74]

For my own part I am not at all convinced that Dignāga, Dharmakīrti, and their successors can be interpreted unambiguously to claim that perception lacks intentionality. Apart from the fact that such a position denies that perceptual experiences are inherently indexical, which is incontrovertibly the hallmark of the Buddhist epistemological project, it also goes against what I take to be certain salient features of first-person phenomenology. In the Buddhist epistemological context, as shall become clear below, the account of intentionality is articulated mainly in terms of the structure of perceptual experience, which does not reveal an object *simpliciter* but rather the object as perceived under a specific aspect that also discloses the perceiver's vantage point. Similarly, on a phenomenological account of intentionality, to perceive an object (or to have a perceptual experience) is to apprehend an intentional relation: the question is not whether the object intended in perception (that is, the one the perception is *of*) is a real object but whether perception is characterized by a certain orientation or directedness toward its content (regardless of whether this content is constituted as an imagined or real entity). Indeed, the central feature of intentionality is that it reveals the co-constitutive nature of perception and that which is perceived. For instance, visual perception, which is characterized by its relation to elements within one's surroundings, also discloses one's location within these surroundings: I am seeing the smoke on the hill *from afar*.

Simply put, one cannot first identify *perceiving* subject and object *as perceived*, and subsequently establish a relationship between the two, for the

72. Dreyfus (2007: 106).
73. Arnold (2005b: 89).
74. Kellner (2010: 227).

relata only make sense in reference to each other. As a distinctive feature of consciousness, intentionality thus discloses a world as the domain of experience rather than a relationship between mind and a discrete, "external" world. This world, as experienced, which Husserl calls the life-world (*Lebenswelt*) is what the Buddhist canonical literature refers to as the "phenomenal world of experience" (*lokasaṃjñā*).[75]

In the transient world of sensory awareness, as we saw in chapter 3, cognitive modalities (and the entities they disclose) are present only as aggregated phenomena of experience. Indeed, *what* appears in perception and *how* it appears is always already constituted by the dynamic structures of our cognitive architecture. I perceive color because I am sensitive to light. The world as perceived is brought into existence through cognitive activity and goes out of existence with the cessation of cognitive activity. This is not an "objective world" that exists over and above its intersubjective apprehension, for such a world, devoid of any reference to subjective experience, is not within the purview of empirical awareness. For the Buddhist, empirical awareness is an awareness of a specific domain (of visibles, tangibles, audibles) as disclosed by a specific mode of cognitive awareness (visual awareness, auditory awareness, and so on). The Buddhist thus appears to advocate the view that what we mean by world (*loka*) is the diversity and manifoldness of perceptual phenomena that finds its ultimate source in the activity of the conscious mind. The notion of a world *as experienced*, however, does not imply that the elements of existence and/or experience (*dharmas*) are not real in an empirically tractable sense, only that their reality cannot be ascertained independently of any reference to their mode of givenness. From a first-person perspective, the body—as an aggregate of such elements of existence and/or experience—is both the medium of contact with the world and the world with which it comes in contact.

Such a view, as we saw earlier, parallels Husserl's account of the paradoxical nature of the body in its twofold appearance: first, as a biological entity connected to the continuum of life and second as a medium for the expression of life.[76] This intuition about the dual nature of embodied awareness (as locus of lived experience) discloses a world of lived experience whose boundaries are not fixed but constantly shifting in relation to the desires, actions,

75. See *supra* chapter 3.2.

76. Husserl (1970a: 107–108) distinguishes between the physical body (*Körper*) and the living body (*Leib*), noting that one's own body is never alien to oneself. We do not simply find the living body within our perceptual field; rather, the living body itself extends to this perceptual field that also allows one to encounter objects, and to think of one's body also as a physical body. The living body, as Husserl makes quite clear, is essentially disclosed kinesthetically through such actions as lifting, carrying, pushing, and so on. See also *supra* chapter 3.1.

and attitudes of an agent.[77] The world or, better still, the environment that I inhabit is not just a structured domain of causally nested objects and relations but also a meaningful world of experience. The question that both Buddhist philosophers and phenomenologists must address is whether intentional experiences—of the sort that disclose a world as pre-reflectively but meaningfully given—presuppose that consciousness itself, as the disclosing medium, is a knowable object. My claim is that the Buddhist epistemologists (and some of the Abhidharma traditions they draw from, in particular those of the Sautrāntikas and the Yogācāras) answer this question in the negative: consciousness is not diachronically (or inferentially) known by a subsequent instance of cognitive awareness but rather is inherently self-aware, even if only minimally so. Although we may intend a previous moment of conscious awareness in introspection, this retrospective apprehension of consciousness as an object cannot be its essential feature.[78] If that were so, we would be confronted with the well-known problem of infinite regress. The Buddhist epistemologists are thus concerned, in true phenomenological fashion, not with how things, including mental states, are judged to be (without any reference to their mode of presentation) but with how things show up to us, with the phenomena of experience just as they appear to us before we set out to reflect and theorize about them.

For the purpose of the present analysis, I am less concerned with achieving a historically accurate reconstruction of the semantic evolution of the notion of self-awareness (*svasaṃvitti, svasaṃvedana*) as gleaned from the works of the Buddhist epistemologists,[79] than with working out a consistent account of the role that perception and intentionality play in the Buddhist epistemological context. The Buddhist epistemologists share with the Abhidharma the view that the defining characteristic of consciousness is its discrete apprehension of objects.[80] Even though the Abhidharma traditions distinguish between mind (*citta*) and mental constituents (*caitta*), they do not regard the latter as attending to different objects. The same object is consciously apprehended by a particular mode of apprehension such as, say, visual awareness, and at the same time disclosed as an event in the mental stream (for instance, as a sensed patch of color). At least in the context of Indian Buddhist Abhidharma, the general assumption is that all cognitions are inherently intentional: they are necessarily about an object of their own. But this Abhidharmic understanding of intentionality requires that

77. See especially, Husserl (1970a: ch. III, A).
78. For an illuminating take on this issue, see Siewert (2012).
79. The reader is directed to consult the comprehensive historical survey of the notion of self-cognition (*svasaṃvedana*) in Yao (2005: 97–118), who finds its source in one particular Abhidharma school, that of the Sautrāntikas. See also Arnold (2009) for a detailed survey of the evolution of the term in later epistemological works.
80. See AK I, 16a.

there be particular types or modes of cognitive awareness that are uniquely constituted as such, that is, as always being directed to, or being about, something.

In keeping with the Buddhist metaphysical commitment to the momentary nature of all phenomena, this "something" is but a temporal instance in the stream of psychophysical events that arises together with a moment of cognitive awareness. This account, however, poses a problem: how can (presumably noncognitive or subpersonal) factors contributing to the arising of cognitive awareness in turn become a subject of reflective inquiry? That is, to use an example, how can a visual experience of reflected light and an apparent surface give rise to a metacognitive awareness of blue? Many of those who find appealing the idea that conscious awareness is the hallmark of the mental, consider it improbable that there should be mental events, such as bare sensations, that are noncognitive until they are attended to in a subsequent moment of awareness.[81] Indeed, the notion of "self-awareness" (*svasaṃvedana*) is meant to capture both the *character* and the *content* of mental events. First, there is the intentional aspect of experience, the "what it is like" character of perceiving a sunset, remembering a childhood experience, or imagining an object such as Escher's impossible staircase. Second, there is the intentional object of experience, that of which the experience is an experience *of* (the sunset, the childhood experience, or Escher's impossible staircase). Every state of cognitive awareness, according to Dignāga, Dharmakīrti, and their successors, has this dual-aspect: that of a self-apprehensive intentional act (*grāhakākāra*) and that of a world-directed intentional object (*grāhyākāra*). The subjective aspect is constitutive of an implicit openness to what is given, while the objective aspect is characterized by what it thus intends: a mental state or an object of some kind. According to this account, even the subjective aspect can become the object of an intentional act when it is reflected upon. Given their commitment to reflexivity, the Buddhist epistemologists must therefore reject the notion that cognitive states such as sensations, volitions, and desires lack intentional content. So it may be worth investigating how a Buddhist epistemologist should understand the intentionality of perception.

Let me begin by illustrating what I mean by the notion that perception is intentionally constituted. In taking the intentionality of perception as

81. Of course, for theorists who reject the unity of consciousness (Dennett 1993; O'Brien and Opie 1998; Rosenthal 2003), there is no singular phenomenon of consciousness but rather a plurality of such phenomena as "phenomenal consciousness," "access consciousness," "monitoring consciousness," and "self-consciousness." Critics of this disunified view of consciousness point to a somewhat misleading assumption: namely, that these so-called different phenomena underscore the subjective character of consciousness, which can be explored apart from its qualitative character. See, for example, Kriegel (2009) and Bayne (2010).

fundamental, phenomenology describes our perceptual encounter with the world in the most concrete sense possible. There is thus a unique way in which perception intends an object or a particular state of affairs: it gives us the object as immediately experienced and without any mediation.[82] The perceptual experience is also fulfilling (or, in Dharmakīrtian terms, pragmatically efficacious (*arthakriyā*)) for, unlike imagination or desire, it actually attains the object: as I stroll down Fifth Avenue the Empire State Building looms larger and towers higher than I have imagined it to be from seeing it in pictures or in movies. It is relatively easy to see why that is the case. My direct encounter with the Empire State Building happens within a certain horizon of background intuitions about size and height based on foreground-background relations, conditions of luminescence, and personal expectations. Seen under a low-hanging cloud cover obscuring the upper floors, it might well appear even higher (high enough to warrant the "sky-scraper" appellation). Thus, what sets apart the intentionality of perception from that of thinking or imagination is its directness: indeed, for Husserl all indirect modes of cognizing are forms of representation (*Vergegenwärtigung*) that ultimately derive from an original presentation (*Gegenwärtigung*).[83]

Note that phenomenologists do not use the concept of representation in the same way as Locke, Hume, and most contemporary analytic philosophers of mind do, that is, in reference to a specific medium such as ideas, mental imagery, or propositional content (which acts as intermediary between the perceived object and its internal apprehension). Indeed, as Shaun Gallagher and Dan Zahavi have recently argued, phenomenologists tend to dismiss representational theories of perception as both empirically false and conceptually nonsensical.[84] To claim that perception generates an internal image of some external reality that resembles it in some way is to assume that there is a direct way of knowing that the representation corresponds to the object. But I can only know that *x* resembles *y* if there is a way to access *y* without the mediation of *x*. But if there is such a way *z* of accessing *y*, then how do I know that *z* correctly discloses that *y* is accurately depicting *x*, if not by some subsequent cognition. Barring infinite regress, there is no way of knowing that *x* is a resemblance of *y*. What is problematic about representational theories of perception is that they presuppose that which they seek to explain: the representational medium.

Phenomenology, thus, operates with a nonrepresentational theory of perception. On this phenomenological account of perception, as Merleau-Ponty has clearly demonstrated, there are no such things as self-evident sensations that together constitute the representational content of

82. Husserl (2003: 107).
83. Husserl (2001: 216).
84. Gallagher and Zahavi (2008: 91).

perception.[85] Rather, perceiving is an integral experience, which involves at once the perceived something, the field of perception, the perceiver, as well as his or her disposition, interests, and orientation. Taking his inspiration from Merleau-Ponty, Alva Noë has recently proposed—against certain tendencies toward pure phenomenology present in Husserl's earlier work—that we regard perceptual experience as essentially amounting to an "involvement with or entanglement with situations and things."[86] Aware of the kinesthetic nature of embodied experience, Husserl too insisted that movement is not necessarily something that we perceive but something that perceptual intentionality must presuppose, for to perceive is to understand how we cope with the environment we inhabit.[87]

Now, let's consider once more Dignāga's account of perception as worked out in his major work, the *Collection*. Notwithstanding the critical and polemical aspect of this work, here Dignāga advances what I take to be essentially a phenomenological account of cognition. First, Dignāga singles out perception and inferential reasoning as the only two reliable sources of knowledge, and claims that perception apprehends unique particulars whereas inferential reasoning apprehends only generalities. But he also insists on the primacy of perception, and offers an ingenious way of translating logical arguments back to their perceptual source, the intricate (and controversial) aspects of which have already been addressed above.[88] For now, all I want to suggest is that in taking the individual properties of a perceptual event as providing a basis for conceptual meaning, Dignāga, much like Husserl, seems to be claiming that all cognitive differences (and/or similarities) find their ultimate source in experiential differences (and/or similarities). In seeing a cow, I do not perceive a generic entity (a token of a type) characterized by dewlap and so on, but a unique cow, from a specific viewpoint, in particular circumstances, and with a specific disposition or interest, say, of feeding it, milking it, or simply petting it. My meaningful deployment of the concept of "cow," then, can be said to be rooted in specific perceptual experiences: a farm stay in Transylvania, a ranch visit in Joseph, Oregon, or, as was the case with my first trip to India, simply stepping out of the Bombay International Airport.

It is primarily this notion that there is no distinction between what seeing seems (or feels) like and what one *thinks* seeing amounts to that Dignāga challenges, particularly in response to realist definitions of perception such as those advanced by Nyāya. It is thus that Dignāga takes self-awareness to be the mode of presentation of all perceptual experiences. He does not

85. Merleau-Ponty (1962: 5).
86. Noë (2007: 235).
87. Husserl (1962: 196ff.).
88. See chapter 4. For a comprehensive recent treatment of the semantic theory of exclusion (*apoha*), see Siderits, Tillemans, and Chakrabarti (2011), and contributions therein.

merely offer a unified account of what had traditionally been known as empirical awareness and self-awareness; rather he advances descriptive expositions of the characteristics of these cognitive modalities: perception is thus capable of apprehending unique particulars only if freed from conceptual elaborations. Naïve realist assumptions about how the mind interacts with the world cannot capture the sense of intimation that accompanies each cognitive event; only a phenomenological approach to perception can. For Dignāga, who adopts the Abhidharma analysis of consciousness and cognition, perception is dually constituted as an awareness of something coupled with self-awareness. As he explains:

> Every cognition comes about with a double appearance, namely that of itself [i.e. as awareness of itself] and that of the object. The awareness of itself as [possessing] this double appearance is the result [of the intentional act]—because the determination of the object [to be cognized] conforms to it. When a cognition intending its [own] object itself becomes an object of apprehension, then one apprehends it as either desirable or undesirable in conformity with self-awareness. When, on the other hand, the object to be apprehended is an external entity, then the source of knowledge is simply the cognition taking on the [intentional] aspect of the object. In this second instance, the source of knowledge refers simply to cognition as intending the object, thus ignoring the character of cognition as self-awareness, even though it is self-awareness that brings it forth [as such]. Why? Because the object as perceived [viz. the external object] is apprehended only by means of this [intentional aspect]. Thus, in whatever way the object may be apprehended, for instance as something white or nonwhite, it is an object in that form [viz., as intended] that is thus perceived.[89]

Dignāga appears to be making here two important claims. First, all cognitions are self-intimating: regardless of whether an object is present or not, and of whether the present object is real or imagined, cognition arises having this dual appearance. Second, Dignāga tells us that the determination of the object, that is, how the object appears in cognition, conforms in effect to how it is intended: for example, as something desirable or undesirable. It should be possible therefore to interpret Dignāga's descriptive account of cognition as providing support for the dual-aspect nature of intentional acts. On the one hand, intentional experiences span a whole range of cognitive modalities: perceiving, remembering, judging, etc. On the other, each intentional

89. PS I, 9ad and PSV *loc. cit.*: *dvyābhāsaṃ hi jñānam utpadyate svābhāsaṃ viṣayābhāsaṃ ca. tasyobhayābhāsasya yat svasaṃvedanaṃ tat phalam. kiṃkāraṇam. tadrūpo hy arthaniścayaḥ yadā hi saviṣayaṃ jñānam arthaḥ, tadā svasaṃvedanānurūpaṃ artham pratipadyata iṣṭam aniṣṭam vā. yadā tu bāhya evārthah prameyaḥ, tadā viṣayābhāsataivāsya pramāṇam tadā hi jñānasvasamvedyam api svarūpam anapekṣyārthābhāsataivāsya pramāṇam. yasmāt so 'rthah tena mīyate yathā yathā hy arthākāro jñāne pratibhāti śubhāśubhāditvena, tattadrūpah sa viṣayaḥ pramīyate*. Cf. Kellner (2010: 207–210).

experience is also about a specific object, whether it be something concrete, like a pot, or something imagined, like a unicorn or, to use a stock example in the Sanskrit philosophical literature, "a city in the sky" (*gandharva-nagara*).[90]

8.4 AN EPISTEMOLOGICAL CONUNDRUM: EXPLAINING THE SUBJECT-OBJECT RELATION

What role does self-awareness, then, play for Dignāga? Given his allegiance to Yogācāra epistemology, Dignāga interprets self-awareness as playing the role of an intentional self-revealing aspect of cognition. As far as the object is concerned, cognition operates simply by revealing its intentional aspect or its object-directedness. As I briefly noted above, in taking Dignāga to be operating with an internalist account of cognition (especially in his *Ālambanaparīkṣā* ("Examination of the Object")), Arnold thinks the Buddhist epistemological account of self-cognition is best characterized as advancing a full-blown idealism, on account of the possibility of interpreting Dignāga's account of self-cognition in Kantian terms. However, read through the perspective of a phenomenological account of intentionality such as the one I am proposing here, the Buddhist epistemologist's understanding of the intentional aspect of perceptual cognition is less susceptible to transcendental interpretation. Indeed, Arnold himself seems to have revised his view in his subsequent interpretation of self-awareness as a bridging concept between the internal domain of first-person awareness and the external world of objects—one which guarantees that such objects do not have their conditions of intelligibility outside the bounds of awareness.[91] I will return to this point below.

Pursuing a different line of argumentation, Kellner rejects the interpretation of Dignāga's account of self-awareness as the only truly occurring source of knowledge. Nonetheless she regards self-awareness as a resulting type of cognition presumably because it provides "access" to the subjective aspect of object apprehension, regardless of whether we are talking about intentional objects or mental constituents.[92] Kellner is in general agreement with Williams that there appears to be a marked distinction between Dignāga's understanding of the role of self-awareness in intentional terms and Śāntarakṣita's

90. *Contra* philosophers whose conception of intentionality is limited to object directedness, the phenomenologist, following Husserl, does not take intentionality to be contingent on the presence for the intentional act of a given object. That mental states are intentionally constituted even in the absence of intentional objects becomes obvious, however, only after the operation of *époche*.

91. See Arnold (2010: 362).

92. Kellner (2010: 226 and *passim*).

account of self-awareness in terms of reflexivity or luminosity.[93] She argues, however, that Williams's notion that intentional states cannot be apprehending their objects or objective aspects unless they are also inherently reflexive goes a step too far. Her rationale is that Dignāga's rather laconic treatment of self-awareness contains no proof as such that mental states are intentionally constituted, that is, that they are about an object of their own. Furthermore, she claims that the proof of self-awareness, at least in Dignāga's case, has nothing to do with the intentional aspect and everything to do with memory, presumably because Dignāga frames his proof of self-awareness in terms of access to experiences that can be recalled precisely because one is aware of having had them.[94] Kellner thus seems to imply that Dignāga's understanding of self-awareness is to be taken as lacking intentionality, something that, I claim, goes against basic first-person phenomenology.

But self-awareness is not a contentless experience: "what it is like"—to use Thomas Nagel's well-worn formula for conscious experience—is not a generic type of awareness, for it is only realized in concrete modes such as perceiving, desiring, judging, and so on. Even assuming that Dignāga has in mind a nonobjectifying or intransitive type of experience when he describes self-awareness, something akin to the Yogācāra notion of consciousness-only (*cittamātra*), or perhaps a type of primitive and pre-reflective self-awareness, of the sort that phenomenologists like Zahavi define as implicit and nonconceptual,[95] it is still the case that this is an intentional experience. If self-awareness were not implicitly intentional, it could not be a necessary condition for genuine aboutness. Even assuming, on metaphysical rather than phenomenological grounds, that there could be non-intentional modes of awareness, these could not serve as the basis for intentional experience. Being pre-thematically present to oneself (that is, being present in a way that does not entail the perceptual or conceptual apprehension of an object) does not mean that, as phenomenologists like Michel Henry have argued, there is no internal distance.[96] Self-awareness has a horizon structure that discloses the dual aspect nature of mental states: self-awareness and object-awareness are interdependent and inherently intentional.[97]

---

93. See Williams (1998: 4). For Śāntarakṣita's account of self-awareness as luminosity, see, *inter alia*, TS 2020–2021.

94. For an illuminating discussion of the memory argument for self-awareness, see Williams (1998: 9–10), Yao (2005: 115–117), and Thompson (2011: 161–168). Thompson, in particular, offers an interesting reformulation of the memory argument in non-egological terms, thus eliminating appeal to higher-order theories of reflective cognition for explaining how the subjective side of experience (the fact that I remember myself perceiving the object) is recalled.

95. See Zahavi (1999: 33).

96. See, for instance, Henry (1963).

97. For more on this account of the intentional structure of awareness in the context of debates about the psychological and psychopathological underpinnings of first-person experience, see Parnas (2000: 119–121).

In this regard, it may be worth considering the so-called existentialist phenomenology that Heidegger develops in *Being and Time*. Heidegger's groundbreaking work helped shift the scope of phenomenology from Husserlian descriptions of the contents of bracketed experience to an analysis of existence in its concrete, ontological sense. Whereas Husserl saw intentional experiences as immanent in the subject, Heidegger claims that the only way phenomenology can escape the language of immanence is for it to describe intentionality as always already "world-constituted." Indeed, for Heidegger this "intentionality" must belong to the ontological constitution of Dasein (his term for the human condition, usually translated as "being there"), for Dasein only exists such that it is "always already with other beings."[98] Thus, Heidegger's major contribution to understanding the intentionality of perception is to have disclosed the particular ways of our *being-in-the-world*. As he shows in his analysis of human experience, Dasein always already finds itself in the world, in one mood (*Stimmung*) or another, and never simply there, as bare existence.

Of course, there may be limitations to this Heideggerian perspective on intentionality as world-constituted. There is a long-standing debate in the Buddhist literature on meditative attainments about the nature and indeed possibility of mental states of pure non-mentation, in which there is complete cessation of all cognitive activity (*nirodha-samāpatti*). Unfortunately, these accounts are not accompanied by any positive descriptions and are thus phenomenologically opaque.[99] Mention must be made, however, that even the Buddhist epistemologists rest their proof of self-awareness on the experience of states of pure luminosity that presumably transcend the subject-object dichotomy. From the point of view of self-illumination theorists such as Śāntarakṣita, ultimately the phenomenal character of cognition and its phenomenal content, its subjective and its qualitative character, are indistinguishable.[100]

98. Heidegger (1986: 157).

99. In his extensive study of this debate, Griffiths (1986: 5–6) claims, rightly in my view, that "a purely phenomenological approach" in which a state of non-mentation is described "in terms that attempt to capture the way it appears to the experiencing subject" is unlikely "to be of much use for the analysis of the attainment of cessation since the central point about this altered state is that it permits no experience while it endures." Drawing from the recent literature on meditation, Fasching (2008: 464) argues that certain non-ideational meditative states aim at a temporary inhibition of that aspect of self-awareness that induces identification with the contents of what one experiences, and thus at recovering the very ground of conscious experience. While I agree with Fasching that "consciousness is precisely what meditation is all about" (2008: 465), the claim that meditation techniques are capable of halting the intentional aspect of conscious experience seems to reflect a metaphysical commitment to pure consciousness that is stated without argument.

100. See especially, TS 2000 (*kriyākārakabhāvena na svasaṃvittir asya tu/ekasyānaṃ śarūpasya trairūpyānupapattitaḥ*) and TSP *loc. cit.* See also MĀ 17. Incidentally, a

Let me turn now, if only briefly, to a passage from Dharmakīrti's *Commentary*, which raises the issues of whether self-awareness is a constitutive aspect of all mental states, not just of perception:

> Various [feelings] such as pleasure, pain, desire, etc. are nothing but cognitions, inasmuch as [they] arise differently in accordance with the differences of [their] basis (sense faculty), object-support (*ālambana*, i.e., external object) and repeated practice. They are perceived [by themselves]. And apart from them, no other [factor] that cognizes them becomes manifest. If one knows [these feelings] by other [cognitions], another [person] would also experience these [feelings, e.g., pleasure and pain].[101]

In this passage, Dharmakīrti claims that various feelings and moods are intrinsically self-revealing insofar as they occur in specific modes of apprehension (vision or hearing), intend particular kinds of objects, and result from past habituations (a view similar to that put forward by Vasubandhu[102]). Dharmakīrti's argument is that such feelings are inherently cognitive, that is, they do not require a second (or higher) order thought in order to become known. This quality is taken as proof that self-awareness is a defining characteristic of all experience, not just of a narrow range of states of metacognitive awareness. Now, Dreyfus understands Dharmakīrti, I think correctly, to be advancing the notion that self-awareness is neither introspective nor reflective, but rather simply a non-thetic awareness of mental states.[103] This self-awareness is really nothing over and above a mode of apprehension in which a subjective aspect beholds an objective aspect. Dreyfus claims to be drawing support for such a non-thetic, pre-reflective view of self-awareness from Zahavi's work,[104] though that view of self-awareness can ultimately be traced to Sartre.[105]

While self-intimation is an essential characteristic of a cognitive event, Dreyfus claims that it is not sufficient for intentionality and does not guarantee its status as a source of knowledge (that is, as a *pramāṇa*). Veridical perceptions—the kind that is free of any conceptual determination—are necessary in order to provide a pragmatic anchorage for cognition. But Dreyfus takes

similar view of the dual aspect nature of phenomenal consciousness is defended in Kriegel (2009).

101. PV III (*Pratyakṣa*), 448–449: *āśrayālambanābhyāsabhedād bhinnapravṛttayaḥ/ sukhaduḥkhaabhilāṣādibhedā buddhaya eva tāḥ//pratyakṣās tadviviktaṃ ca na anyat kiṃ cid vibhāvyate/at tajjñānam paro apy enāṃ bhuñjīta anyena vid yadi//.*

102. See, especially, AK II, 34b2–d1.

103. Dreyfus (2007: 102).

104. See, especially, Zahavi (1999, 2005).

105. Sartre's view is that all conscious experience is in some sense implicitly self-given. He writes, "It is not reflection which reveals the consciousness reflected-on to itself. Quite the contrary, it is the non-reflective consciousness which renders the reflection possible; there is a pre-reflective *cogito* which is the condition of the Cartesian *cogito*" (Sartre 2003: 9–10). Note that Zahavi cites this passage in Zahavi (2011a: 56), and endorses Sartre's view of consciousness.

Dharmakīrti to be claiming that bare sensations are noncognitive, and that they become cognitive only when integrated in a conceptual schema (which, given his generally nominalist stance, Dharmakīrti presumably cannot avoid). This interpretation, however, goes against both Dharmakīrti's claim that raw feelings like pleasure and pain are self-revealing and against a basic phenomenological description of experience. Pain appears as a mode of conscious apprehension not because it corresponds to a given notion of painfulness, but because it discloses to us the state of our being. Self-awareness is key to this phenomenological appraisal of pain.[106] I am not merely conscious of pain; rather, *I am* in pain, and the pain is of a particular kind: throbbing, stinging, or burning. It is part of the very nature of sensory experiences such as pains and pleasures that there is something it is like to be in them and for them to have the specific qualitative aspects that they do.

Drawing on the long-standing debate in phenomenology regarding the status of what Husserl called *noema* or the *object-as-intended*, Georges Dreyfus comes in on the side of those, like Hubert Dreyfus and Dagfinn Føllesdal, who take the *noema* as referring to an ideal sense that mediates the intentional relation between the cognitive state and its object. Given the importance of the so-called theory of cognitive aspects (*ākāravāda*) for the Buddhist epistemologists, Georges Dreyfus interprets Dharmakīrti as advancing the view that direct experience only supplies the raw sense data, which is apprehended as such only by means of an aspectual cognition, that is, by a cognition representing or taking the form of whatever it cognizes. Georges Dreyfus does concede that perception, especially in certain meditative states, might have something like "phenomenal intentionality."[107] But he understands intentionality as a "function" that perception has, namely that of "delivering impressions." To say about a perceptual state that it is intentionally constituted is to mark its orientation and mode of disclosure. To the extent that the notion of "function" can be used at all in an analysis of intentionality, it is only in order to capture the two facets of experience.[108]

106. For an illuminating defense of the view that qualitative experiences such as pains have a representational or intentional aspect, see Perrett (2003). Note that Perrett, who distinguishes between weak and strong intentionalism, does not think that the intentionality of consciousness entails the self-awareness thesis, namely that consciousness is always implicitly self-conscious. In this chapter, I defend the opposite view: that the self-illumination thesis in fact is compatible with the intentionality thesis.

107. Dreyfus (2007: 109).

108. Indeed, "function" is a dispositional notion the purpose of which is to explain what something is for (as in, for instance, perception is *for* accessing sense data). But the Buddhist understands perception primarily as a specific type of awareness, and awareness is something that *is* and makes *manifest*. To perceive a blue sky amounts to more than simply having a certain disposition toward something (say, certain sensory impressions). Rather it is also the case that perceiving is a kind of self-revealing experience, without which dispositions would be intractable. Cf. Kriegel (2009: 253 n. 32 and chs. 2 and 4).

Colin McGinn, in fact, makes this point quite clear when he argues that intentionality is not a contingent aspect of conscious experience, but rather its essential character: "what the experience is like is a function of what it is of, and what it is of is a function of what it is like."[109]

I have already explained—when considering the role of intentional aspects for cognition—why representational theories of knowledge are problematic. Basically, if intentional experiences are always about something, then, as Gallagher and Zahavi have argued, they cannot "achieve a reference to the world by virtue of some intermediate representational entity."[110] The *noema* or the *object-as-intended*, that is, as perceived, desired, or judged, cannot be understood on this alternative interpretation as a concept, sign, or as propositional content. If that were the case, then perceiving, desiring, and judging would lack intentionality until such moment when the object *as perceived* or *as desired* was attended to in conceptual analysis.[111] But to perceive is already to open up to a horizon of experience that presents (or, rather, re-presents) objects in their immediate mode of givenness. And while the mode of givenness of the object may be constitutive of experience, its properties are not fixed by the object alone but also in some sense determined by the intentional stance: in seeing a white lotus on a clear lake, my visual experience is not simply constituted by the properties of the object (i.e., whiteness, bloomingness, etc.) but also by the phenomenal character of my awareness. I can only experience the white lotus in a specific mode of first-person givenness that is only available to conscious subjectivity.[112]

Now, Dharmakīrti in effect seems to be making precisely such a point in a passage of the *Pramāṇaviniścaya* ("Settling on the Sources of Reliable Cognition"), in which he requires that all cognitions be intrinsically reflexive:

> Awaiting the end [of a series] of apprehensions, a person does not comprehend any object, because of the non-establishment of all [cognitions] when there is non-establishment of one [i.e., of the first-personally known one]. And since there is no end to the arising of apprehensions, the whole world would be blind and deaf. If there is [to be] any termination [to the series of cognition], that [cognition must] intrinsically apprehend itself and the aspect of an object simultaneously.[113]

---

109. McGinn (1991: 29–30).

110. Gallagher and Zahavi (2008: 127 n. 7).

111. See Zahavi (2005: 121).

112. Note that while the Buddhist epistemologists admit that phenomenal character is an intrinsic aspect of conscious experience, they reject the notion that such character discloses something like a minimal phenomenal self. Rather, the Buddhist epistemologists put forward a self-illuminationist nonself theory (cf. Siderits, Thompson, and Zahavi, 2011: 12). For an insightful account of how evidence for the phenomenal character of consciousness could be reconciled with a nonself view, see Krueger (2011).

113. PVin 41–42: *tan na tāvad ayaṃ puruṣaḥ kañcid arthaṃ pratyety upalambhaniṣṭhāṃ pratīkṣamāṇaḥ, ekāsiddhau sarvāsiddheḥ. na côpalambhānām*

If, as Dharmakīrti seems to be arguing here, we were to reject the reflexivity thesis, then we would be confronted with the absurd situation of there being an interminable series of cognitions that are noncognitive until an instance of self-awareness first occurs. Arnold does interpret Dharmakīrti in this context as advancing the notion that self-awareness must be an integral aspect of the mode of presentation of all cognitions in order to avoid the idea that we could somehow be "non-cognitively acquainted with the world."[114] But, if I read him correctly, he still insists that Dharmakīrti's defense of the reflexivity thesis commits him to a type of epistemic idealism that is presumably threatened by transcendental arguments about the structure of experience. His interpretation rests on an overtly Kantian approach to the role of apperception for cognition. Basically, Arnold claims that Dharmakīrti (like Dignāga before him) understands self-awareness to function in much the same way that the transcendental unity of apperception does for Kant (who, arguably, treats all forms of consciousness as a species of self-consciousness).[115]

But Dharmakīrti adopts a thesis that is exactly contrary to Kantian anti-foundationalism: intuitions (or, in this case, perceptions) are not blind without concepts. Perceptions are indeed cognitive, even though only as pre-reflective modes of experience. Most importantly, perceptions are intentionally constituted in the wider sense in which phenomenologists understand intentionality to operate: not merely as object-directedness, but as openness to what is present within the structure of awareness itself. The self-aware aspect of perception that captures its intentional constitutiveness is a non-positional (thus non-reflective) but conscious experience. To use one of Sartre's well-known examples of such an instance of perceptual self-awareness: "When I run after a streetcar, when I look at the time, when I am absorbed in contemplating a portrait, there is no I. There is consciousness-of-the-streetcar-having-to-be-overtaken, etc., and non-positional consciousness of consciousness."[116]

That self-awareness must be an integral aspect of the mode of presentation of all cognitive events does not mean that self-awareness is transcendentally constituted as a form of radical subjectivity. Rather, it simply means that the subject of experience can also become an intentional object of experience when it is reflectively apprehended, when, as in Sartre's example, I attend not simply to the portrait but also to my experience of contemplating the portrait. The intentional object and the intentional act, however, lack reference to a presumably transcendental subject or self. My reason for belaboring this

---

utpattiniṣṭhety andhamūkaṃ jagat syāt. kvacin niṣṭhāyāṃ sa svayam ātmānaṃ viṣayākāraṃ ca yugapad upalabhata iti... tat siddhaḥ sahopalambhaniyamaḥ, ekavyāpāre kramāyogāt, tasyāviśeṣāt.

114. Arnold (2010: 362).
115. See Pippin (1989: 20).
116. Sartre (1991: 48–49).

distinction rests precisely on a phenomenological understanding of intentionality. Even such apparently non-intentional experiences as moods are not without reference to the world, for a cognition's self-referentiality is always embedded within a wider horizon of experience that also affects the way the world appears to us. Rather than being simply attendant phenomena, moods act as radical modes of disclosure: happiness is likely to disclose a world that is brimming with significance and potentiality.

Regarding the issue of whether the Buddhist epistemologists recognize that cognition must be intentionally constituted in order to be counted as a source of knowledge, Arnold identifies Dharmottara as making the clearest statement to this effect (that is, as arguing that only "intentional (*prāpaka*) cognition" is a sources of knowledge).[117] But Arnold seems to imply that the intentionality of perception is to be understood (in this particular case) in terms of perceptual "judgments" concerning empirical objects.

As mental states or states of cognitive awareness, perceptions, desires, and judgments are characterized as such by the objects they intend and cannot be understood independently of these intentional objects. But the intentional object is neither just the empirical correlate of experience nor just the mental aspect; rather it is the object *as intended*, the pain *as felt* or the state of affairs *as judged*. It does not mean, however, that there is no difference between the *object as intended* and the *object that is intended*, though, of course, the nature of this distinction is subject to debate.[118]

Whereas most philosophers agree that mental states such as beliefs and desires have intentional content, the claim that states of perceptual awareness are also intentional is controversial. Perceptions, in particular a broad class of bodily sensations and moods, are regarded as lacking intentionality. For instance, in articulating the position of those who deny the intentionality of perception, David Rosenthal makes a distinction between two types of mental states: thoughts and desires, usually classed under the rubric of propositional attitudes, and sensations and sense impressions, which are said to lack intentional content and instead be characterized by qualitative properties or qualia.[119] The basic intuition behind this distinction is that sensations are not *about* a specific object but *characterized by* a specific qualitative feel. However, as critics of this distinction have noted,[120] it does not take much reflection to realize that qualia are conscious mental states and as

117. See Arnold (2010: 343).

118. Note that on a more traditional interpretation, philosophical phenomenology calls into question the very notion that we can make a distinction between how things are in and of themselves and how they are perceived.

119. Rosenthal (1994: 349).

120. See Crane (2003: 35). Note that in Crane (2009), he does endorse the view that indirect perception possesses some kind of representational content, but just not of the truth-conditional sort.

such share certain features with propositional attitudes, and vice versa, that propositional or intentional content in turn displays qualitative features: I can suddenly become aware that I need to remind one of my colleagues to proctor my finals, and at the same time experience what it is like to have that sudden realization.

It is for this reason, I think, that phenomenology, as a descriptive method for the analysis of experience, is inescapable. In disclosing to us the primacy of experience, phenomenology also invites a suspension and bracketing of theoretical assumptions about experience. Most important, it invites us to go beyond traditional positions in metaphysics concerning the relation between mind and world, and thus to move beyond the externalist/internalist divide and its variants. It offers as an alternative an account of experience that requires a completely new vocabulary for its expression, one capable of capturing the specific ways of our *being-in-the-world*, a world that is inseparable from its mode of apprehension.

It is precisely to the extent that we go beyond the interplay between sense and object and seek to account for the structure of the intentional act that we operate within the phenomenological attitude. The anti-foundationalism that drives most debates in epistemology testifies to this oversight, lacking, as it mostly does, an account of intentional consciousness. Until recently, most discussions in analytic epistemology either neglected intentionality or reduced it to analyses of perceptual content.[121] While phenomenological analyses of intentionality have shifted the attention in most analytic epistemology away from reductive explanations of experiential content,[122] much remains to be done.

Among the most influential reductive accounts of experience is Daniel Dennett's eliminativist theory of consciousness, which he first put forward in his *Consciousness Explained*. The aspect of this theory that interests us here is the notion that our intuitions about the features of our perceptual experience are unfounded and therefore our judgments about the intentional aspects of consciousness must be fallible.[123] On this generic eliminativist view there are no such things as raw subjective qualities or seemings (the experiential or "what it is like" character of cognitive awareness) but only judgments about, and internal representations of, such experiences. In short,

121. For instance, Drummond claims that such reductive treatments "reduce the immediate object of our experience from the object itself to the perceptual content, thus subjectifying the objective content, and they conceive this content as a psychic content" (Drummond 1991: 49). See also Drummond (2006) for a robust phenomenological response to reductive analyses of experiential content that argue against the presumption that the objects of experience could be examined as though they belonged to a world that is pre-consciously given.

122. See Strawson (2005).

123. See Dennett (1991: 66ff.). Several aspects of this theory are reprised in Dennett (2001, 2002).

Dennett is not willing to grant the phenomenologist access to the phenomenon as such but only to a judgment about it.[124] Indeed, for Dennett, there is no difference between what we apprehend perceptually and our reflection on the contents of such perceptual experiences.[125] Dennett has been known to challenge those who take seriously the phenomenal character of experience to provide evidence (presumably of the functional or behavioral kind) for the postulation of such experience.[126] But as Chalmers has persuasively argued, to ask for such "evidence" is essentially to miss the point: "Conscious experience is not 'postulated' to explain other phenomena in turn; rather, it is a phenomenon to be explained in its own right. And if it turns out that it cannot be explained in terms of more basic entities, then it must be taken as irreducible, just as happens with categories such as space and time."[127]

As Chalmers quite aptly notes, physicists (and other hard scientists) have yet to come forward with "independent" evidence for the fundamental categories of space and time. The Buddhist who takes reflexivity to be an irreducible aspect of conscious experience would most certainly concur with Chalmers when he states that the relevant evidence for (the categories of) space and time is "spatiotemporal through and through, just as the evidence for experience is experiential through and through."[128]

But we cannot begin to make sense of our perceptual experiences if we empty them of any intentional content: what makes perception instrumental for knowledge is precisely its intentional character, the fact that what we perceive is disclosed in an intentional setting of objects and meaning. The perception of an object devoid of any reference to its mode of presentation (that is, to the *object-as-perceived*), much like an abstract quale, has no basis in experience. How do we, then, come to conceive of perception as being essentially transparent, providing a direct access to the sense data? Once again, Merleau-Ponty captures the problematic nature of naïve, common sense approaches to perception: we assume that perception is shot-through with conceptuality "because instead of attending to the experience of perceptions, we overlook it in favor of the object perceived."[129] In other words, we commit what psychologists call the "experience error"—the tendency to assume that the properties that belong to the thing itself are present in our consciousness about them—or, in Merleau-Ponty's terms, "we make percep-

124. Critics have claimed that Dennett's eliminativist theory of consciousness rests on an implausible reduction of the phenomenal content of experience to cognitive judgment, with the result that how things seem to us is reduced to an account of how we think they seem (see, especially, Carman 2005: 76; 2007: 100ff.).

125. Dennett's denial of any perceptual content other than representational structure misunderstands the very nature of perceptual experience.

126. See Dennett (1996: 5).

127. Chalmers (2010: 33).

128. Chalmers (2010: 33).

129. Merleau-Ponty (1962: 4).

tion out of things perceived."[130] What we have here is an attempt to reduce the content of experience to a set of self-evident assumptions about it.

Since all discussion of perception and its mode of presentation takes place within the horizon of consciousness, it is consciousness that ultimately provides the evidential ground for all modes of inquiry. For the Buddhist, as we have argued above, consciousness—in its dual-aspect mode of presentation—is not just another event in the chain of dependently arisen phenomena, but its *disclosing medium*. Insofar as phenomenology is concerned with analyzing the structure of experience (and with overcoming traditional positions in metaphysics about the ontological status of mental and physical objects), it can also help us to understand that self-awareness is intentionally constituted. This is precisely the point I take Dignāga to be making when he claims that *we apprehend a cognition intending its own object as having a particular quality* (desirable or undesirable) only to the extent that *that apprehension is in conformity with self-awareness*. When we understand the intentional character of self-awareness in a phenomenologically rich fashion, perceiving a color or feeling a pain appear not only as aspects of what-it-is-like-to-be-in a certain kind of state, but also as intentional states, for perception ultimately marks an intentional orientation in a world that cannot be thought of apart from experience.

130. Merleau-Ponty (2002: 5).

CHAPTER 9

In Defense of Epistemological Optimism

In the preceding I have examined the central arguments of the Buddhist epistemology of perception by tracing their historical development and exploring their wider philosophical significance. I have argued that Buddhist epistemology appears to operate on naturalist grounds, and that, although framed by the broader dialogical-disputational concerns of the Sanskritic philosophical tradition, it is firmly anchored in the phenomenological accounts of consciousness and cognition developed in the Abhidharma traditions. A peculiar characteristic of the mode of inquiry devised by the Buddhist epistemologists (which, after Dharmakīrti, becomes normative for all Buddhist philosophers concerned with knowledge and its means of acquisition) is an appeal to descriptive accounts of our cognitive architecture in settling epistemological disputes: specifically, to the notion that perception and that which is perceived are essentially constituted by intentional content.[1] While my analysis has been anchored on a close reading and interpretation of the relevant textual materials, I have adopted a broadly constructive approach by engaging with contemporary debates in phenomenology and analytic philosophy of mind.

A great deal of our discussion has focused on a critical analysis of the three-way debate about the content and character of perceptual knowledge between our main protagonists: the Naiyāyikas, the Mīmāṃsakas, and the Buddhist epistemologists. While emphasizing Śāntarakṣita and Kamalaśīla's indebtedness to Dharmakīrti, I have also noted their unique contributions

1. Crane (2001), for instance, proposes that we observe a difference between "things" and "objects." Unlike things, which are ostensibly identified and defined by their spatio-temporal location and properties, objects are "intentional" or "intentionally constituted." We customarily talk about "the *object* of experience" but not about "the *thing* of experience," which suggests that being an object is essentially being an intentional object of some kind; it is not being a thing.

to furthering the scope of the Buddhist epistemological project. Indeed, as it has been conclusively demonstrated, near contemporaries of Śāntarakṣita and Kamalaśīla such as Vinītadeva, Jinendrabuddhi, and Dharmottara share at least some of their views, even as these views show significant differences from each other.[2]

Exegetical considerations apart, some of the controversial issues in Dharmakīrti's system, issues whose clarification would arguably have only a minimal impact on our assessment of the scope of the Buddhist epistemological enterprise, have been deliberately skirted. Fortunately, the ambiguities that characterize some of Dharmakīrti's positions, which are a hallmark of his style (and, some may say, of his genius), are less prevalent in his commentators, and to an even lesser degree in Śāntarakṣita and Kamalaśīla's philosophical undertakings in the *Compendium* and its *Commentary*. This striving for clarity, then, should provide sufficient justification for treating their views separately, even if some of their arguments originate in the works of Dharmakīrti. Indeed, the issue of whether a consensus about key aspects of Dharmakīrti's thought is reached in the scholarly community should not act (at least in principle) as a deterrent to examining on their own the views of Buddhist thinkers who carried forth his legacy of critical inquiry.[3]

Arguably, Śāntarakṣita and Kamalaśīla's contributions to furthering the scope of the Buddhist epistemological enterprise reflect both their attitudes toward a received tradition and their attempt to consolidate that tradition, whether as innovators or simply as interpreters. Of course, one always feels compelled to return to the originator of an idea in order to properly trace its history and assess its impact on future generations. This privileging of origins is just as true of Indian and Buddhist philosophy as it is of Western philosophy.[4] No amount of exegetical work on Plato or Kant would ever suffice to replace their original works, although we may choose to study a neo-Platonist like Plotinus or a neo-Kantian like Cassirer on their own.

Thus, in concluding our assessment of the Buddhist epistemological contribution to the analysis of perception we should ask ourselves the following questions: is perception foundational to knowledge, and if so, in what sense? What makes the operations of conception so different that they are regarded as operating outside—and in some way having a distorting effect on—the domain of sense experience? How does the Buddhist

2. Cf. Krasser (1992) and Funayama (1999).

3. For instance, Dunne (2004: 9ff.) claims that in order to properly appreciate Śāntarakṣita's views on topics such the *apoha* theory, one must be able to identify his philosophical innovations, which in turn requires that the views of his predecessors be also unambiguously ascribed.

4. Indeed, the deconstructive project of poststructuralist philosophers like Derrida is conceived primarily as an attempt to resist a privileging of origins and their presumed authenticity.

epistemological tradition negotiate the difference between phenomenal content and intentional act, between what is apprehended and the sources or modes of apprehension?

The issues raised by these questions have been addressed at various stages in this book: first, there is the phenomenological perspective of the Abhidharma traditions, which postulate that the senses open up to specific domains of experience rather than act as cognitive instruments for apprehending objects in the empirical domain. On this phenomenological understanding of perception, the Buddhist epistemologists claim that only a cognition in which the mental tendency toward conceptual proliferation is bracketed counts as a true instance of perception (and, as such, is epistemically warranted). Secondly, there is the view that the domains of language and discursive thought are coextensive, a view held by Sanskrit grammarians such as Bhartṛhari and also present, albeit in a less articulated form, in Vasubandhu. Lastly, we have the "fluid" ontology of the Buddhist epistemologists who appear to accept the reality of external objects as unique particulars, although only provisionally, while at the same time denying that they exist other than as perceived, thus subscribing to what I have identified as a version of process externalism.[5]

9.1 A MOVING HORIZON

In outlining a strategy for naturalizing Buddhist epistemology, I have argued that a philosophical approach to Buddhist thought that sees its concerns as in many ways continuous with current topical debates in phenomenology and analytic epistemology can contribute novel ways of conceptualizing enduring philosophical problems and new perspectives on core areas in the philosophy of perception. Indeed, some of the most interesting and insightful work in Indian and Buddhist thought has been done by those committed to constructive engagements with trends in contemporary philosophy. This is not the proper place to examine the merits (and possible limitations) of these approaches (or the significance of their contributions to advancing our understanding of Indian and Buddhist philosophy). As Matilal reminds us, anyone engaged in the study of a philosopher from a different cultural and

5. As Williams notes in relation to the position of the Sautrāntikas,—who, while admitting the existence of external objects, postulate that external objects act merely as a cause for the appearance of their image in consciousness—"we know from the history of Western philosophy that once an 'objective aspect' (perception? sense-datum?) has been introduced between the perceptual object and its cognition some form of idealism becomes a strong temptation" (Williams 1998: 6). As I noted above (see §2.5 and §4.4), this idealist "temptation" is easily averted if we take perception to be a form of embodied action.

linguistic horizon than one's own is inevitably bound to the method of comparative philosophy:

I believe that anyone who wants to explain and translate systematically from Indian philosophical writings into a European language will, knowingly or unknowingly, be using the method of "comparative philosophy." In other words, he cannot help but compare and contrast Indian philosophical concepts with those of Western philosophy, whether or not he is conscious of so doing. Otherwise, any discourse on Indian philosophy in a Western language would, in my opinion, be impossible.[6]

In his appraisal of Matilal's contribution to this discourse of comparative philosophy, Mohanty recalls that, despite certain misgivings about superficial comparisons that merely tag theories from different philosophical cultures that bear certain resemblances, Matilal's impetus for a comparative approach to philosophy was motivated by the mutually enhancing value that such an undertaking would have for philosophy in general:

Indian philosophy could contribute to the formation of a global philosophy, not in the sense of a philosophical theory acceptable to all (for that would not be philosophical), not in the sense of a common project to which all different traditions can contribute, but as a common discourse in which they can participate.[7]

This sentiment is also echoed by Garfield who, while taking a critical stance on the comparative approach (which favors the adoption of Western ideas and methodology in the translation and interpretation of non-Western thought), goes one step further by suggesting that one also adopt non-Western standards of philosophical analysis and doxography in reading some Western texts. Sharing in Matilal and Mohanty's optimism, Garfield envisions a time when the comparative method would have given way to a plurality of discourses operating within a philosophical arena of global proportions:

Comparative philosophy, when pursued properly, can still be genuinely revelatory to all parties to the dialogue and can assist in bringing together the resources of all traditions in preparation for a future in which such comparative exercises will be passé and a plurality of traditions, each conscious of its own history and of the histories of those with which it comes into contact, can interact through collective activity.[8]

Despite the promise that such a global philosophical discourse holds for those engaged in the more immediate task of translating and interpreting

6. Matilal (1971: 13).
7. Mohanty (1992c: 401).
8. Garfield (2002: 154).

the thought of classical Indian and Buddhist philosophers, the fact remains that modern Western philosophy itself is in a process of constant transformation. Thus, whatever models the philosophical perspectives of Kant, Husserl, Sellars, Merleau-Ponty, or Quine may provide to those engaged in interpreting the thought of classical Indian and Buddhist authors (or vice versa), those models are bound to be superseded in time. Mohanty gives a good summation of the dilemmas facing the modern interpreter of classical Indian and Buddhist philosophy:

> Stcherbatsky, for example, interpreted Buddhism using the jargon of the prevailing neo-Kantianism of the late nineteenth century. Analytical philosophy itself has undergone great transformations. What do we do, then, to ensure that interpretations of Indian philosophy, in the light of any current trend, will last? Now to this I will give the following response on behalf of Matilal. For one thing, one can only do something best, and one can only interpret, as Gadamer insisted, from one's own present historical situation and not *sub specie aeternitatis*. There is no guarantee that one's interpretations will outlast time and history.[9]

The difficulties inherent in any effort to ensure that the study of Indian and Buddhist philosophy remains relevant to contemporary debates, as Mohanty clearly indicates, should be obvious to anyone committed to doing philosophy in a cross-cultural mode, and not simply because one is often confronted with the dilemma of incommensurability. Comparative philosophy developed in response to the findings of early nineteenth-century orientalists,[10] who argued that systematic philosophical reflection was neither a Greek invention nor confined to the West. The initial response to these findings—coming, as it did, from the influential figure of Hegel—was mixed: indeed, Hegel regarded Oriental philosophy more as a preliminary abstract to proper philosophical inquiry, which for him began with the Greeks.[11] Less impervious to the German Romantic fascination with origins and with the Orient, Schopenhauer adopts a more discerning and sympathetic stance: his critique of the principle of individuation may at least in part be a response to his readings from the Upaniṣads.[12] But it is Nietzsche, arguably, who gives comparative philosophy its first impetus through his creative appropriation of

9. Mohanty (1997: 12ff.).

10. The first systematic attempt to develop a comparative method, however, is more recent. It is associated with Paul Masson-Oursel's *La Philosophie comparée* (1923), a work that offers a positive and anti-ethnocentric platform for comparative philosophy. Masson-Oursel appears to have borrowed the term "comparative philosophy" from the Bengali philosopher Brajendranath Seal (1864–1938), who uses it in his *The Positive Sciences of the Ancient Hindus* (1915).

11. See Hegel (1940) and discussion in Halbfass (1988: 84–99).

12. See Schopenhauer (1969: §54), Droit (2004: 168ff.), and Berger (2004: 113–114).

Vedantic and especially Buddhist ideas. Whether Nietzsche's philosophy of the *Übermensch*[13] and of overcoming has any true association with Buddhist ideas is less significant than the perceived affinity between his thought and core Buddhist doctrines.[14] The exploration of such perceived affinities and the promise of establishing a truly intercultural philosophical dialogue, have been from the beginning the goals of comparative philosophy. Even though a philosophical discourse that knows no cultural and linguistic barriers may seem like a utopian dream (if not altogether impossible in the absence of a universal language), there is no denying that intercultural dialogue and reflection can often provide (and act as) a corrective lens for our own philosophical intuitions.[15] The most important aspect of an intercultural philosophical discourse is not, however, the recognition of the extraordinary diversity of positions (or -isms: realism, naturalism, idealism, antirealism, etc.) within each philosophical tradition and culture. Rather, it is the promise that such recognition holds for enhancing, refining, and expanding the range of philosophical arguments and possibilities, the ultimate (and obvious) aim of which is to become better philosophers.[16]

Recognizing that any work of interpretation is contingent upon the theoretical and cultural presuppositions that inform one's own historical situatedness as an interpreter need not mean that the interpretation bears no direct relation to the author's original insight. For those laboring to understand how the thought of an author from a different culture or epoch can contribute to contemporary philosophical debates, it is not simply a matter of acquiring the right methodological tool set for doing comparative philosophy but also of cultivating the right attitude toward the enterprise of doing philosophy in a global context. While attempting a reading of Western idealism as reflected in the works of Berkeley, Kant, and Schopenhauer through the lens provided by Vasubandhu's doctrine of the three natures (*trisvabhāva*), Garfield sums up his comparative exercise—which, *inter alia*, finds that Schopenhauer, unlike Berkeley and Kant, shares with Vasubandhu the view that "the distinction between duality and non-duality marks the distinction between appearance and reality"—by stating that a comparative philosophy "done right" is one that "sheds light from one tradition upon another."[17] The

13. For an innovative interpretation of the *Übermensch* as an "ecstatic moment in the experience of the free spirit," see Hough (1997). Hough's model goes beyond conventional accounts that view the *Übermensch* as a higher type of human being.

14. See Mistry (1981: 161) for an in-depth study that finds strong affinities between one of Nietzsche's core ideas, that of Eternal Recurrence, and the Buddhist confidence in the possibility of overcoming the limitations of conditioned and impermanent phenomena (even as it postulates the impermanence of all things).

15. See Garfield and Edelglass (2011: 6) for a programmatic statement on the value of a globally aware philosophical discourse.

16. Cf. Deutsch and Bontekoe (1997: xiii).

17. Garfield (2002: 168).

real issue, as I see it, is not that of "shedding light" or shedding it in the right direction, for that is easily accomplished by strict adherence to the protocols of the comparative enterprise. Rather, the main issue concerns the attitude that is brought to bear upon such an enterprise. It is not enough to notice surprising relationships between two distinct traditions or to find ways of conceptualizing various aspects of our own tradition in ways not previously anticipated (and certainly, not merely as a historian or "curator of dead traditions"[18]). Philosophy, whether in the East or in the West, is an ongoing and live enterprise, undergoing constant revision and spawning new ideas, even as (and when) it finds its anchor in historical debates and modes of reasoning. It is for this reason that I have sought to align and make continuous the concerns of the Buddhist epistemologists with those of their contemporary Western counterparts, mindful that the global context in which these concerns find their articulation is marked by a constantly shifting horizon structure.

9.2 EMBODIED CONSCIOUSNESS: BEYOND "SEEING" AND "SEEING AS"

It has been my intention in this book to argue that the naturalist paradigm can indeed reveal interesting new ways of thinking about the problems raised by the Buddhist epistemologists. The naturalist paradigm in epistemology (and to a lesser extent in phenomenology[19]) at least as framed by its proponents, is primarily concerned with one of the two concepts of mainstream epistemology: that of knowledge or true belief (the other being justification). Those pursuing a naturalist agenda operate on the assumption that the sciences of cognition, having turned their focus toward investigating the mind, are best suited for answering questions about belief formation, while the problem of justification can still be pursued in a traditional manner. But the sciences of cognition, like all other sciences, rely on observation, and observation leads to the old philosophical problem of the difference between "seeing" and "seeing as." While working out the implications of this difference for naturalized epistemology, Jerry Fodor quite aptly notes that notwithstanding the constraints applied to the meaning of "observe" in experimental science, the "uses of 'observe' and its cognates have pretty clearly come unstuck from 'seeing as' or, indeed, from *anything* that's

18. Garfield (2002: 168).

19. A thorough attempt at naturalizing phenomenology, the stated aim of which is an integration of phenomenology into the explanatory framework of cognitive science such that its properties are made continuous with the properties of natural science, is found in Petitot et al. (1999) and contributions therein. For a critique of attempts to naturalize phenomenology, see Zahavi (2004b) and Aikin (2006).

psychological."[20] Consequently, the empiricist claim that observation in some way is a type of seeing is unsupported. Letting psychology settle what an observation is or just letting the observations be the data is, therefore, legitimate. But as Fodor claims—rightly, in my view—"it's sheer Empiricist dogmatism to take it for granted that you can do both at once. In fact, there is no good reason to suppose that the psychological notion of perception—or, indeed, *any* psychological notion—will reconstruct the epistemological notion of a datum."[21] Indeed, neither empiricism nor conceptualism can reconstruct the epistemological notion of the given. It is only in the mode of phenomenological reflection that seeing reveals an intentional relation that does not detach it from seeing as: our perceptual judgments are rooted in pre-predicative types of awareness that are nonconceptual but not bare. As Husserl reminds us, all modes of *representation* (e.g., memory, imagination) are rooted in presentation, in an intuitive experience of the given.[22]

For the Buddhist epistemologists, this distinction between seeing and seeing as is instrumental in discriminating conception-free from conception-laden cognitive states and, indeed, for claiming that only the former warrant the proper label of veridical perception. Although most of the examples provided by Śāntarakṣita and Kamalaśīla to mark this distinction are drawn from ordinary experience (for instance, being able to attend to perceptual input while thinking of something else), the ultimate proof for this decoupling comes from the testimony of yogic perception. This yogic decoupling of conception from perceptual awareness raises a philosophically interesting issue: what role does insight into the structure of our cognitive architecture play in settling epistemological disputes? For the Buddhist epistemologist questions about the structure of our cognitive architecture (and about the ultimate basis of cognitive activity) lead to questions about causation, intentionality, and the nature of experience itself. Human experience, argues the Buddhist, is best captured by the model of the causal relations that obtain between the sensory systems (including the mind and its mental constituents) and their domains of activity.

In the West the problem of what constitutes a basis or, more specifically, an object of cognition has been framed (at least since Descartes) in terms of relations between the subjective and empirical poles of experience. The attempt to locate that base in either the mental or the physical domain is ultimately what marks the fundamental difference between rationalist and empiricist positions. With Husserl—who, as we saw in the second chapter, conceived of phenomenology as a middle ground between rationalism and empiricism—questions about the basis of cognition became questions about

20. Fodor (1991: 200).
21. Fodor (1991: 200).
22. See Husserl (1970b: II, 260).

the intentional structure of experience. Eventually, those same questions came to revolve around the problematic nature of embodiment itself: that is, how does having a specific type of body condition conscious experience? But the question of embodiment has become a contested issue in contemporary philosophy, pitting dualists (whether substance and property dualists) against epiphenomenalists, and both camps denying the claims of supervenientists and panpsychists, who want to attribute to consciousness causal powers either by allowing it to play a functional role or by asserting the ubiquity and physical reality of experience itself.[23] Regardless of what position we may adopt on the ontological status of consciousness, the difficult problem of adequately specifying the criteria under which cognitive events can be identified as correlates of brain states still remains. Chalmers, for instance, has identified at least five questions underlying the project of finding the neural correlates of consciousness. These questions pertain to both consciousness and the brain either in separation or taken together: "(1) What do we mean by 'consciousness'? (2) What do we mean by 'neural correlate of consciousness'? (3) How can we find a neural correlate(s) of consciousness? (4) What will a neural correlate of consciousness explain? (5) Is consciousness reducible to its neural correlate(s)?"[24] In his analysis, Chalmers observes that a perfect isomorphism between consciousness phenomena and neural phenomena cannot be established, and that it is the content of experience rather than its mere occurrence that is hard to account for. Moreover, groups and families of neurons may appear to correlate with more than one aspect of conscious experience. The situation is further complicated by the need to take into account the background of experience on which conscious events take place.

Chalmers's proposal, to the extent that he advances one, is for identifying "a minimal neural representational system N such that representation of a content in N is sufficient, under conditions C, for representation of that content in consciousness."[25] This proposal is not, however, unproblematic. As Noë and Thompson have argued, such a model presupposes that correlations between the content of neural systems and that of conscious states in some sense "match," a problematic notion given that we are dealing here we

23. Note that, unlike the supervenience thesis—which states that mental properties supervene on physical properties such that there are no mental differences without physical differences—panpsychist models, such as recently advanced by Strawson (1994, 2006), propose that experience cannot be taken to emerge from a wholly nonmental, nonexperiential substrate. For Strawson, a commitment to physicalism entails (rather than undermines) panpsychism: that is, the realistic physicalist (as opposed to, say, the reductive physicalist) cannot "deny the existence of the phenomenon whose existence is more certain than the existence of anything else" (2006: 3).

24. Chalmers (2000: 17).

25. Chalmers (2000: 31).

two different types of content.[26] Indeed, from a phenomenological perspective, conscious experience is not simply reducible to the content of a particular state of cognitive awareness. Rather, as Thompson argues, "experience is intentional (world-presenting), holistic (constituted by interrelated perceptions, intentions, emotions, and actions), and intransitively self-aware (has a nonreflective subjective character)."[27] Insofar as correlations between conscious episodes and brain states can be established, they pertain to the phenomenal structure of consciousness and its temporal dimension, rather than its content. Representational models of conscious mental content cannot account for the factors that precede or provide pre-conscious background for the arising of a given cognitive event. In an account that is reminiscent of the Yogācāra notion of receptacle consciousness (*ālaya-vijñāna*), Thompson appeals to Searle's theory of a unified field of experience[28] to describe conscious events as "modulations" of this pre-existing ongoing experiential domain: the visual recognition of a face, for instance, "is not a constituent of some aggregate conscious state, but rather a modification within the field of a *basal* or *background consciousness*" (emphasis mine).[29]

The upshot of these debates about how best to bridge experience and the underlying dynamic neural activities that correlate with it is that no explanatory model for the place of consciousness in nature can ignore its constitutive aspects that phenomenology alone can disclose. These constitutive aspects, though quite different from the structures and patterns unraveled by empirical science, are not, however, entirely dissimilar from them. The neurophenomenological program (conceived as a method for bridging science and experience) has adduced compelling evidence, against Husserl's view that the unity of consciousness finds no analogue in the physical domain, that the formal structure of the temporal aspects of consciousness *does* have "an analogue in the dynamic structure of neural processes."[30] As I noted in the introduction to this book,[31] the enactive model of cognition has the advantage of being non-reductionist because it takes into account different types of analysis (phenomenological, biological, and dynamic). But if the methodology of phenomenological naturalism is to offer more than a parallelism of explanations,

26. See especially Noë and Thompson (2004a, 2004b). Noë and Thompson have dubbed this model the "matching content doctrine," arguing that it is in effect a category mistake to confuse the two sorts of contents.

27. Thompson (2007a: 350). Thompson points to the neurophenomenological program initiated by Varela, which takes into account not just the content of a given mental state but also bodily activity and coping skills, which together constitute the embodied dynamicism that alone can capture the full spectrum of conscious experience.

28. See Searle (2000a: 574).

29. Thompson (2007b: 351).

30. Thompson (2007b: 356).

31. See chapter 1 (n. 9).

in which first-person accounts of experience correlate (and/or are isomorphic) with the accounts provided by natural science, then it must, as a matter of necessity, be more intrepid. This is precisely the thrust of Merleau-Ponty's approach,[32] which insists both on the notion that the phenomenology of lived experience can be informed by the life sciences, and also on the role that phenomenology itself can have in expanding our conception of nature to include also the intentional. Indeed, the phenomenological tradition agrees that our encounter with, and categorization of, the elements of experience is prior to our theorizing in domains such as physics and neuroscience.[33]

An expanded conception of nature such as phenomenology provides allows for material and formal categories to interweave, thus acknowledging (rather than minimizing) the ontological complexity of our world of experience. Note, however, that the causal account of cognition that phenomenological naturalism advances is descriptive rather than reductive. Thompson offers a clear and programmatic statement of how phenomenology can augment the explanatory frameworks of natural science:

> Phenomenology provides a way of observing and describing natural phenomena that brings out or makes manifest their properly phenomenological features—selfhood, purposiveness, normativity, subjectivity, intentionality, temporality, and so on—which otherwise would remain invisible to science. Put another way, phenomenology offers a way of seeing the inner life of biological systems. That the autopoietic form of an organism realizes a kind of purposive selfhood normatively related to the world, that the dynamic form of neural activity realizes a special structure of temporality—these insights become available only if we bring the resources of phenomenology to bear on biological phenomena.[34]

This fusion of phenomenology and biology is not, however, without its critics.[35] Apart from the difficulties inherent in any attempt to close the explanatory gap, whether from the direction of experience or from that of neuroscience, phenomenological naturalism (and naturalized epistemology in general) is also confronted with what Ricoeur quite aptly terms "semantic amalgamation": confusing the discourse of the mental with the discourse of the brain (and its underlying processes). This semantic amalgamation has

---

32. See Merleau-Ponty (1963). For an elaboration of this account, see Roy et al. (1999) and Zahavi (2004b).

33. This aspect of the phenomenological approach to experience has begun to take root among analytic philosophers of mind. As Fodor (2008: 10) puts it in his reworking of the language of thought model of cognition, "abilities are prior to theories" and "competence is prior to content."

34. Thompson (2007b: 358–359).

35. See, for instance, Bruzina (2004), Dennett (2011), Foglia and Grush (2011), Hutto (2011), Newen (2011), Siewert (2011b), and Van Gulick (2011), Wheeler (2011), and Zahavi (2011b).

a simple diagnostic: it results from the "tendency to slip from a dualism of discourses to a dualism of substances," which itself "is encouraged by the fact that each field of study tends to define itself in terms of what may be called a final referent."[36] This referent, which is the mind for philosophers and the brain for neuroscientists, is also in some way defined "as the field itself is defined." Ricoeur warns us about the risks of collapsing these two referents:

> Prohibiting this elision of the semantic and the ontological has the consequence that, on the phenomenological plane... the term *mental* is not equivalent to the term *immaterial* in the sense of something noncorporeal. Quite the opposite. Mental experience implies the corporeal, but in a sense that is irreducible to the objective bodies studied by the natural sciences.[37]

I draw attention to this semantic amalgamation partly as a criticism of the usual "the brain thinks" or the "amygdala knows fear" modes of discourse currently in use in neuroscientific literature, and partly to emphasize the discursive nature of knowledge representation in which both phenomenological and neuroscientific accounts of cognition find their expression. Furthermore, the notion that cognitive events imply the corporeal can be construed to mean not only that the body provides a support for cognition but also that the body itself (or its sensory systems) is disclosed by cognition. Drawing from the works of Husserl, and especially Merleau-Ponty, the phenomenological response to the problematic nature of embodiment has focused on the enactive model of cognition. On this model, the body is the medium where lived experience takes place and, as such, is part of the continuum of life.

In the Buddhist context, the problem of embodiment finds expression mainly in discussions concerning karma and rebirth. For the Buddhist epistemologists, thus, the problem of embodiment is framed by the dispute over the relationship between cognition and the body. This issue is addressed in detail, for instance, in Dharmakīrti's anti-reductionist stance in his dispute with the Cārvāka philosopher Kambalāśvatara,[38] and by Śāntarakṣita and Kamalaśīla in their own refutation of Lokāyata physicalism. Dharmakīrti defends a thesis that is somewhat contrary to modern views of biological determinism:[39] "[Nor are the senses, or the body together with the senses, the cause of cognition, for] even when every single one of the senses is

36. Changeux and Ricoeur (1998: 14).
37. Changeux and Ricoeur (1998: 14–15).
38. See Franco (1997: 5) for his identification of the opponent in Dharmakīrti's dispute with the Cārvākas in the PV II, 34–131.
39. Arnold (2008b: 1088) dubs Dharmakīrti's arguments in the so-called proof of rebirth as "vitalist" insofar as his understanding of bodily awareness presupposes the presence "of some kind of intrinsically 'sentient' force or principle." As I argued above (chapter 3), consciousness acquires for the Buddhist the character of a dynamic principle of sentience akin to something like a "life force." Cf. Kapstein (2001: 107).

impaired, the mental cognition is not impaired. But when [the mental cognition] is impaired, their (i.e., the senses') impairment is observed."[40] The gist of Dharmakīrti's argument here is that sensory impairment should not adversely impact self-awareness, but only the apprehension of the contents of experience in the domain that corresponds to the impaired sensory modality. Astigmatism, color blindness, blindsight, and other similar forms of impairment simply diminish the capacity for experiencing phenomena in the visual field; they do not impair the mental capacity of self-awareness. The reverse, however, is not true, since loss of conscious awareness renders the senses useless. Dharmakīrti's position on the causal relation between cognition and its basis corresponds roughly to what modern cognitive psychology calls *agnosia*, a state in which one is unable to recognize (and interpret) objects, faces, sounds, smells, and so on despite the fact that the primary sensory pathways are intact.[41] Metaphysically, we may identify this position as a version of property dualism, since it is clear that we are dealing here with one reality, the causal nexus of phenomena, the elements of which display two different sets of properties: formal and intentional.

Central to this account is a consideration of the so-called causal principle of "similar kind(s)" (*sajāti*), which demands that phenomena arise not in an arbitrary manner, but thorough homogeneous causal chains. In our review of the Abhidharma analysis of consciousness and cognition, we saw that visual awareness is said to arise from factors that are associated with the sense modality (in this case vision) rather than the object (viz., entities with reflectance properties), an insight that is also borne out by recent empirical research. But the deeper point here is the implication that causal accounts of cognition have for the view that intentionality is an essential dimension of consciousness (and constitutive of its modes of apprehension). The causal account ensures that cognitive awareness (or phenomenal consciousness) is described in terms that can explain its pragmatic efficacy. At the same time, it guarantees that the effects of karmic processes (of actions and their results) are not overlooked in any account of consciousness and its operations. Body, feeling, perception, and the other aggregates are constitutive of lived experience: cognition must also be explained in terms of gender and somatic type, affective and perceptual saliencies, and dispositions. But for all these causal factors—which provide a largely unconscious and embodied structuring of experience—to become reasons for acting in a reflective fashion, one needs a specific kind of awareness that is irreducibly reflexive.

---

40. PV I, 41: *pratyekamupaghāte'pi nendriyāṇāṃ manomateḥ/ upaghāto'sti bhaṅge'syāstwṣāṃ bhaṅgaś ca dṛśyate*. For other translations and discussions of this stanza, see Vetter (1964: 22), Hayes (1993: 120), and Franco (1997: 186).

41. For a detailed discussion of agnosia, with specific focus on the visual sense, see Farah (2004).

Ostensibly, the Buddhist epistemologist's justification for taking reflexivity as the condition of the possibility for warranted states of cognitive awareness is simply an extension of his or her theoretical commitment to the self-luminosity of mental states (and, indirectly, to the doctrine of momentariness). One place where this theory comes into particularly sharp focus is Śāntarakṣita and Kamalaśīla's debate with the Cārvāka physicalists. The Cārvāka's objection to any presumed continuity of awareness is framed by some easily recognizable arguments. First, if (as the Buddhist claims) an individual is nothing but a bundle of aggregates that are in turn reducible to more basic material substrata (viz., atoms), then conscious awareness must be an emergent property.[42] Just like fermented acids (*śukta*) and spirits (*surā*), consciousness too must be regarded as nothing more than a product of the type of material organization that is constitutive of biological organisms.[43] Second, since consciousness takes the form of an apprehension of objects (that is, since it is inherently intentional), and apprehension only occurs in specific modes of cognizing such as perceiving, imagining, or remembering, consciousness cannot be present either when the sensory systems are not yet developed (as in the embryonic stage) or when they are not responsive (as in a state of comatose).[44] Finally, the physicalist argues for what seems like an obvious point: different types of bodies (for instance, those of humans and nonhuman animals), and different tokens of the same human body, manifest different types of consciousness. Assuming otherwise would be akin to postulating that consciousness can apprehend that which is contrary (*viruddha*)—a problematic position (for the Buddhist) given our lack of direct access to the minds of others (and to the interior life of nonhuman animals).

This last argument, about the factors on which cognition depends (*jñāna-āśraya*), is particularly interesting for its appeal to the principle of positive and negative covariance (*anvaya vyatireka*). This principle turns on the notion that consciousness can only become manifest in one specific cognitive chain. As such, it can only be associated with (or take residence in) the one body

---

42. See Ganeri (2011) for a detailed study of the concept of "emergence" in classical Indian philosophy with special reference to Cārvāka physicalism. Ganeri not only identifies possible Indian influences on the "emergence" of British emergentism but also showcases interesting parallels between modern accounts of supervenience (principally those advanced by Kim and Shoemaker), and classical Indian accounts proposed by Cārvākas like Bhāvivikta and Udbhaṭa. The Indian emergentist account of mind introduces, *inter alia*, the notion of an "assistive" (*upakāraka*) cause, which is conceived as having the function of supplementing the material causation (*upādāna-kāraṇa*) associated with the organization of physical elements.

43. See TS 1857–1858. This choice of metaphors reflects a deeply ironic and ambivalent position on consciousness (seen here as a state of either euphoria or deluded intoxication).

44. See TS 1864–1867.

that serves as its basis. In other words, the sameness of the chain of cognitive events—which forms the basis for personal identity throughout an individual's lifetime—is only invariably concomitant with residing in the same body, and not with residing in different bodies. This argument is thus meant to confront the Buddhist with a dilemma: either accept the physicalist position or be left with the unwarranted view that persons undergo rebirth in a cycle with neither beginning nor end (*anādinidhana*).[45]

Śāntarakṣita and Kamalaśīla's rebuttal of the Cārvāka version of reductive physicalism is complex and far-ranging, and its systematic study in the context of current debates in philosophy of mind about emergence and supervenience still awaits treatment.[46] For now, our concern is simply with how the Buddhist can answer the physicalist's challenge without undermining the explanatory function of a causal account of consciousness, which must take into account all the elements in the chain. In a long and very detailed analysis of the explanatory role of material causation, Kamalaśīla identifies an important difference between the order of the causal domain and the domain of cognition:

> Whenever an effect is dependent on a collection of causes and conditions it does not arise when even one of these conditions is absent, for it would not be dependent upon them, if it did. It could be said, "All the atoms insofar as they occur in [its] proximity are the cause of cognition." In that case a difference should be observable between the effect produced by a non-deficient cause and that produced by a deficient cause, as the two are different. Otherwise, a distinction in the [capacity of the] cause [to bring about different effects depending on its fitness] would be futile. In effect, when a cause that has been perfect in all its aspects becomes defective in some respect, it does not occasion a difference in the mind and that which is mental (*mano-mati*), on account of the fact that preceding auditory and other kinds of impression continue intact [in the mental stream].[47]

What we learn here is that, regardless of whether we assume the arising of a cognitive event to be dependent upon the proximity of all its underlying causal factors (perceptual, volitional, etc.) or their atomic totality, the possibility of error rules out a tight causal-cognitive coupling. Human cognition

45. See TS 1870 and TSP *loc. cit.*

46. Ganeri (2011), as we already noted above, identifies in the Cārvāka physicalist theory that consciousness resides in the body (which serves as causal support for its manifestation) a form of proto-emergentism.

47. TSP *ad* TS 1886: *na hi sāmagrīpratibaddhaṃ kāryamanyatarābhāve bhavati; tat pratibaddha svabhāvatvahāniprasaṅgat/atha yathā sanidhānam sarve 'pi caitanyasya hetavaḥ? evam tarhi vikalāvikalāṅgadehajanitayorviśeṣena bhavitavyam; kāranabhedat, anyathā kāryasya bhedo nirhetukaḥ syāt. na vā 'vikalāṅgasya sataḥ paścād vikalāṅgatāyām upajātāyām kaścin manomaterviśeṣo asti; śrutādisamskārasya tadānīmapyavikalasya eva anuvṛtteḥ.*

is not merely an involuntary process, as Kamalaśīla (unwittingly) assumes to be the case with animal cognition, but also a reflexive one. As such cognition is characterized by its capacity to refer back to (and be affected by) the impressions of past cognitions while at the same time attending to the object at hand. It is this attentive capacity (*manaskāra*) that makes a certain dimension of human cognition not merely the effect of causal chains in the physical domain but also a cause in its own right in the domain of cognition. That the attentive or self-aware aspect of cognition could remain constant with respect to a given object of experience (say, a column of smoke), despite it being prompted by a deficient cause (in this case, a dust column), is taken as proof that consciousness can be neither entirely grounded in, nor explainable in terms of, physical elements and processes. The Buddhist does not deny that cognitive states are made manifest (*abhivyajyate*) when the body is present, only that their manifestation is not to be understood in strictly physical causal terms. For this reason, instead of following the conventional translation of *upādāna-kāraṇa* as "material cause," a more suitable rendering that captures the phenomenological perspective of the Buddhist would be "appropriating cause" or "acquiring cause." Thus a case could be made that the elements, in their particular dynamic grouping as bodies, "acquire" the emergent property of thinking or consciousness only when the latter, in the form of attentiveness, is directed toward this causal chain. Indeed, Kamalaśīla's gloss on the relationship between cause and effect (*kārya-kāraṇa*)[48] seems to suggest precisely this reading of causation in the psychophysical or phenophysical domain: something which causes emergent properties such as consciousness to become manifest.

This understanding of the relationship between the "autonomy" of cognition and material causation suggest a different approach to the largely reductive and eliminative model of the physicalist. Not only is a minimal sense of non-reflective self-awareness or attentiveness covariant with the body and its sensory systems, it is also assistive in the emergence of cognition in its manifold aspects. In the case of perception, its importance is obvious in the fact that by themselves, object, sense, and additional contributing factors (ambient light or scale and proximity to the visible range, in the case of vision) do not give rise to a percept. In other words, it is only insofar as we take intentionality to be an essential dimension of consciousness that we can talk about cognition having one aspect of another. Should we, then, understand this Buddhist perspective on the relation between mind and body as yet another account of downward causation? Appeal to the specific character of consciousness, which can be explained neither in terms of the physical characteristics of elements such as atoms and bodies nor in terms of their formal properties, would seem to suggest so.

48. See TSP *ad* TS 1864–1867.

But here I want to propose a more interesting alternative, one that deserves further consideration. As proponents of the embodied and enactive approach to cognition suggest, whether we approach the problem of embodiment from first-, second-, or third-person perspectives, the theoretical framework of a descriptive phenomenology is inescapable. It is indisputable that much of the discussion on supervenience in analytic philosophy of mind, certainly the work of Jaegwon Kim, Brian McLaughlin, and others, can supply useful conceptual tools for illuminating the causal account of cognition at work in the Indian and Buddhist epistemologies. But in order to avoid faux pas and the gridlock between eliminativists, property and substance dualists, and panpsychists (to name but a few of the more dominant positions), it is important that one also take into account crucial work in the philosophy of biology (and neurobiology), particularly the work done by Humberto Maturana and Francisco Varela on autopoiesis,[49] as well as Varela's work on neurophenomenology,[50] and more recent work by Thompson, Gallagher, Noë, and others on embodied and enactive cognition. What is significant about these contributions is that they provide interesting ways of explaining causation in living organisms (that is, mainly in terms of the dynamics of autopoietic systems) that do not dispense with the notion of agency or reduce intentional behavior to accounts of biological and neurobiological processes: causation works (in biological organisms) because there is autopoietic emergence and an adaptive selection—indeed, an autopoietic system is more coherent and self-determined than a dissipative one.

Instead of Kim's concept of "downward causation,"[51] Maturana and Varela's autopoietic model invites us to think of mental causation not as a top-down or downward acting on the elements but rather, to use Searle's account of "volitional consciousness" and its relation to neurobiology, simply as "a system of causation."[52] The problem with classical philosophical debates about emergence and downward causation is a certain fixation on mereology and the causal power of elements. Complex systems theory and autopoietic models of emergence (specially those sensitive to the phenomenology of living systems) usually move beyond substance-property analyses of supervenience to an account of whole-part influence. So, instead of substance-property relations, one investigates symbiotic relations of interconnectedness within the

49. See Maturana and Varela (1980), for the first systematic development of the model of autopoiesis and cognition. See also Thompson and Varela (2001), and Thompson (2007b: ch. 5, and 356ff.) for a more recent treatment of the intersections between phenomenology and biology.

50. Varela (1996) defines neurophenomenology largely as a working hypothesis for how descriptive accounts of the structure of experience can be related to their counterparts in cognitive science through a system of reciprocal constraints.

51. As developed at length in Kim (1993).

52. Searle (2000b: 7).

organism and between the organism and its environment, since living systems are to be understood not only in terms of their structure but also their organization and environmental embeddedness. Furthermore, the elements that make up the body are treated as a "structuring" cause for the emergence of mental activities. In a philosophically insightful investigation of Buddhist and enactivist approaches to the emergence of a sense of self, Matthew MacKenzie explains why the rigorously reductionist Abhidharma account of agency needs to be revised if we are to explain in a satisfactory way the dynamic interactions between perception and action, mind and world:

> [T]he fundamental problem for reductionism is the centrality of the first-person perspective. A living sentient being is not a mere aggregate or bundle of components and cannot fully be understood from a purely external, third-person perspective. The living organism displays the interiority of its own immanent purposiveness and its needful and precarious relations to its (enacted) milieu. The stream of experience becomes self-referential, given to itself, through the recursive structure of time-consciousness. The embodied being is pre-reflectively aware of itself in and through its active, striving body.[53]

This focus on embodied cognition as the locus of lived experience, and on the phenomenology of the present moment, has been adopted and adapted from Husserl's account of time-consciousness and the life-world. It should come as no surprise, therefore, that Yogācāra psychology and the Husserlian phenomenological tradition operate on a common ground: the primacy of the moment.[54] Indeed, the Yogācāra analysis of consciousness, much like Husserl's examination of the structures of experience, converges on the intentional act: it seems as though a thought, a cognitive event, is only of an object (as though thoughts and perceptions were transparent with regard to their objects); it is, in effect, also an extension within the intentional arc of experience. This intentional arc reaches beyond the tight connection between apprehending subject and apprehended phenomena to that ground of being which the phenomenologist understands as *being-in-the-world* and the Buddhist as the arising of phenomena in a mutually interdependent web of causes and conditions.[55]

A phenomenological reading of the Buddhist epistemological project places greater emphasis on the fact that its arguments find their ultimate support in the Sautrāntika and Yogācāra psychologies. The methodological

53. MacKenzie (2010: 97).
54. See Lusthaus (2002: 25) for a useful discussion that draws out some common aspects of the two accounts.
55. For discussion of the intentional arc and its role in framing a phenomenological account of self-awareness as the fundamental nature of consciousness, see Dreyfus (1982) and Zahavi (2002).

approach of these two Abhidharma schools, much like Husserl's phenomenological method,[56] consists in bracketing common assumptions about the ontological status of external objects in favor of an analysis of the contents of experience itself.

It has been my intention in this book to emphasize the Buddhist epistemologist's insistence on differentiating between a pre-reflective (but cognitively non-bare) awareness characteristic of direct perception, and the inferential processes that are a characteristic of conceptual elaborations. This co-occurrence of a pre-reflective direct perception and of an awareness of its subjective and objective aspects (the *grāhya-* and *grāhakākāra*) is instrumental for understanding the cognitive status of perception. I argued that the Naiyāyikas, like many analytic epistemologists who espouse some version of direct realism, move all too quickly over this pre-reflective awareness to a direct analysis of the perceived objects, with the result that object properties are determined in principle as being observer-independent. Such is the case, as we saw in the chapter 8, with Dennett's view that things appear to us the way we *think* they appear, and also with the Nyāya commitment to realism about universals. Drawing from recent research on visual perception, I argued that object properties are in fact the result of information processing of sensory input in the visual and somato-sensory cortex. The information at the level of retinal receptors, however, is quite different from what "we actually see." In vision science, it is now acknowledged that most of the actual processing is in fact unconscious, with the visual awareness arising farther away on the pathways of sensory information processing.[57]

For the Buddhist epistemologist, the object *that* is perceived and the object *as* perceived share a direct causal-cognitive link. Insofar as the perceived is disclosed in a complex setting of objects and meaning, of phenomenal content and phenomenal character, cognition is said to arise taking "the form of the object" (*artharūpa*). But it is also determined by its specific mode of apprehension: visual, auditory, tactile, etc. There is thus a resemblance (*sādṛśya*) between the object and its re-presentation in cognition, insofar as the former is constituted as the intentional content of the latter. It is this aspectual nature of intentional reference that underpins the phenomenalist stance of the Buddhist epistemologist.[58]

---

56. It may be noted here that Husserl conceived his phenomenological method largely as an alternative to introspectionism, and to its alleged failure to adequately distinguish between the mere reportability of internal mental states and their epistemic status. See Vermersch (1999) for a historical survey of introspectionism, which also explores the potential usefulness of its methodologies in contemporary consciousness studies.

57. See, for example, Palmer (1999: 616).

58. Dharmakīrti discusses the causal mechanism of perception at several places in the *Commentary*. See e.g., PV III, 109; 247–248; and 333–341. See also TS 1999,

Naturalized epistemology regards epistemic inquiry as part of the larger project of investigating the underlying processes of cognition, as well as its functional and embodied aspects. To take a phenomenologically naturalist approach to Buddhist epistemology, then, is to refrain from divorcing epistemic questions from questions about the source (and underlying processes) of cognition and, indeed, from an analysis of the content and character of experience in its immediate mode of givenness. In the Buddhist context, epistemological questions are framed by preoccupations with identifying and defining reliable sources of knowledge. Unlike their Nyāya and Mīmāṃsā opponents, the Buddhists give knowledge a pragmatic definition: *what counts as knowledge is what ensures successful action*. For Śāntarakṣita and Kamalaśīla, whose epistemological deliberations rely on the Abhidharmic accounts of consciousness and cognition, the world of phenomenal experience is dynamic rather than static. As such, each cognitive event is to be viewed as a constantly new introduction to an object. On this account of what cognition entails, object coherence is attributed to a combination of at least four factors: (i) memory traces, (ii) the constructive aspects of conceptual thought, (iii) the apprehension of aggregated versus organic wholes, and (iv) the fact that perception of single particles is not possible without reference to the proximity of (other) similar or dissimilar particles, the context in which they are apprehended, and the habitual tendencies of our cognitive capacities (in this case, of conception).[59] The Buddhist epistemologist, much like Husserl, thus appears to link object coherence to perceptual constancy, even if ultimately each cognitive episode is treated as a constantly renewed encounter with its object.

If close regard for the complex processes underlying cognition is any indication, then the Buddhist epistemologists appear already to operate on

---

2004–2006 and TSP *loc. cit.*, for an extensive discussion of the epistemological function of cognitive aspects (*ākāra*).

59. Śāntarakṣita and Kamalaśīla derive their account of object constancy from Dharmakīrti, whose analysis of object recognition rests on a complex theory of features that are intrinsic to the cognitive process. See e.g., PV III, 194–196: *sañcataḥ samusāyaḥ sa sāmānyaṃ tatra cākṣadhīḥ/sāmānyabuddhiś cāvaśyaṃ vikalpenānūbadyate//arthāntarābhisambandhājjāyante ye'ṇavo'pare/uktāste sañcitāste hi nimittaṃ jñānajanmanaḥ//aṇūnāṃ sa viśeṣaś ca nāntareṇāparānaṇun/tadekāniyamājjñāmamuktaṃ sāmānyagocaram*. "That which is aggregated is a collection, and as such it is a universal. That [aggregated thing] can be perceived. In addition, the apprehension of a universal is associated with conceptuality. On account of their relation with other things momentary particles, which are different from [particles] at previous moments, arise [such that they are discernible]. Thus, they are said to be an 'aggregate', and they are said to be a condition for the arising of awareness. Furthermore, the distinctive quality of particles does not emerge in the absence of proximal particles. Thus, [inferential] cognition is said to have a universal [as it object], on account of the fact that it does not have a relation to a single particle." Cf. Dunne (2004: 396).

naturalist grounds—this, however, is not the naturalism of modern science. Rather, naturalist explanations in the Buddhist context pertain simply to the notion that arguments are not to be divorced from the psychological accounts of cognition that inform them. On the one hand, there is the aggregated view of self as a complex of physical and mental constituents and, on the other, the causal principle of dependent arising, generally understood to imply that things come into existence due to the cooperation of multiple causes and conditions, including, but not limited to, mental factors such as attachment and grasping. This aggregated view of personal identity is at the center of all discussions about the nature of agency and cognition. While the generic Buddhist viewpoint is that there is no such thing as a self, the lesson of Buddhist epistemology is that an adequate account of the role and function of cognition cannot dispense with a minimal sense of agency. This cognizing agent is not merely another way of referring to the embodied and dynamic functioning of the five aggregates, but a recognition of irreducible character of conscious experience.

The five aggregates, then, provide a dynamic model of psychological continuity, underlying which is a nexus of karmic tendencies, whose operational function is to cause either the continuation of similar factors (*niṣyanda*) or the maturation of transitional factors (*vipāka*). A generic way to explain the difference between similar and transitional karmic factors is to conceive of the difference between auspicious and inauspicious or intentional and unintentional cognitive events usually employed with reference to practices conducive to the accumulation of merit. Transitional factors are thus instrumental in the emergence of new properties. Take the example of moral cultivation: pursuing compassionate aims leads to a reversal of egocentric impulses, giving rise to feelings of empathy.[60] Furthermore, from a Yogācāra perspective the principle of causality must, at least in part, be psychologically and/or phenomenologically anchored: developments at the level of cause (*hetu pariṇāma*) and at the level of effect (*phala pariṇāma*) in effect are reduced to a more fundamental transformation at the level of the repository consciousness, understood here as the largely subconscious cognitive mechanisms from which thoughts and experiences arise.[61]

---

60. The role of empathy as an essential condition for a phenomenologically sensitive epistemological naturalism has received considerable support in recent treatments of intersubjectivity as a new methodological approach in cognitive science. See Thompson (2000), Depraz (1995), Depraz, Varela, and Vermersch (2000), and Gallagher and Meltzoff (1996).

61. Cf. Waldron (1995). The receptacle consciousness has been taken sometimes to stand for an enduring form of consciousness, from which all other consciousnesses (those of the five senses, the mental, and the reflexive) evolve. This view, which is found in classical texts such as the *Saṃdhinirmocana* and *Laṅkāvatāra sūtras* ("Examination of the Profound Meaning" and "Descent into Laṅkā" scriptures, respectively), and reiterated in Vasubandhu's works, bears some similarity to the self

A central argument of this book is that an enduring solution to various epistemological disputes cannot be had without taking into account the structure our cognitive architecture. To the extent that Śāntarakṣita and Kamalaśīla pay close attention to the analyses of consciousness and cognition developed in the Abhidharmic traditions, theirs is an epistemology sensitive to naturalism. But Śāntarakṣita and Kamalaśīla are also representatives of what later scholars, for taxonomic reasons, call the Madhyamaka-Yogācāra synthesis (or the Yogācāra-Svātantrika-Madhyamaka)—an attempt to bring together within a unified discourse the perspectives of the two dominant schools of Madhyamaka and Yogācāra, while at the same time incorporating the fundamental epistemological insights of Dignāga and Dharmakīrti.[62] At least in the *Compendium* and its *Commentary*, Śāntarakṣita and Kamalaśīla do appear to emulate the example of Dignāga and Dharmakīrti in that their intentions are best characterized as expressing a need to establish core Buddhist principles on a sound epistemological foundation. Their stand is a polemic one: challenge the views of the Brahmanical critics that principles such as that of momentariness and dependent arising are fanciful ideas based on nothing more than Buddhist scriptural sources. Recall that in the *Compendium* and its *Commentary*, Śāntarakṣita and Kamalaśīla are not merely summarizing debates between Buddhists and their Brahmanical opponents; they also offer their unique insights on issues such as the analysis of external objects, the perception of variegated things, and the structure of awareness.

Dignāga's pivotal role in shifting Buddhist attitudes toward the role of positive argumentation answered a pressing need: if core Buddhist principles such as that of dependent arising are to appeal to an educated philosophical audience (regardless of doctrinal affiliation or metaphysical proclivities), then one must be prepared to argue for them on both rational and empirical grounds. My brief discussion of Dignāga's definition of perception, and Dharmakīrti's emendations to that definition, outlined the scope of the

of the Vedantic philosophers, which is considered to be an objectless and contentless consciousness. Western translators have been quick to show its parallels to psychoanalytic concepts such as that of the subconscious. Thus, Kochumutton (1982: 135) calls it the "individual unconscious," while Anacker (1984: 61ff.) compares it with Jung's collective unconscious, which also includes the archetypes. Lusthaus (2002: 4–9), however, takes a critical stand against metaphysical interpretations, arguing that later traditions in fact abandoned the term in favor of more neutral concepts such as that of the "mind continuum" (*cittasantāna*).

62. On this important doctrinal distinction, see Dreyfus and McClintock (2003), and contributions therein. Tillemans (2003: 96) nicely sums up Śāntarakṣita and Kamalaśīla's indebtedness to Dignāga and Dharmakīrti: "In the case of the two eighth century Indian Svātantrikas . . . Śāntarakṣita and Kamalaśīla, they had a massive and clear debt to the logicians, Dignāga and Dharmakīrti, and were avowed adherents of the Buddhist logic school. Indeed their Svātantrika philosophy is largely an attempt to resituate the metaphysics, epistemology, and logic of Dharmakīrti by placing them, intact, on the level of customary truth."

Buddhist epistemology of perception and singled out its key points. In my cursory survey of the debates surrounding the definitions of perception, I also briefly discussed the Nyāya and Mīṃāmsa contributions to that debate. In addition, I noted that Dharmakīrti's attempt to address the opponents' criticism, particularly in regards to Dignāga's problematic stance on the source of perceptual illusions, had not received unanimous support among his successors, and that Kamalaśīla had adopted a conciliatory position on this matter (retaining Dharmakīrti's solution while not completely disregarding Dignāga's original intention of grounding any kind of cognitive error, including perceptual illusions, in the mind).

I also noted that some of the problems that Śāntarakṣita and Kamalaśīla address in the *Compendium* and its *Commentary*—concerning the proper basis for distinguishing between perceptual awareness and its contents—appear almost seamlessly to integrate with those that concern modern philosophers. Indeed, it seems as though Buddhist philosophers are just as preoccupied with charting out the phenomenology of first-person experience as Western phenomenologists. As I concluded in the last chapter, the Buddhist epistemologist—much like Husserl with regard to his description of the intentional character of experience—adopts a characteristically reflexivist view and takes empirical consciousness to be essentially disclosing both subject and object, both intentional act and intentional object. This is also one of the points where Buddhist and Brahmanical accounts of perception significantly differ. Whereas most Brahmanical philosophers regard the senses as faculties of an internal agent, the Buddhists adopt a strongly phenomenalist stance that ultimately aims to capture the specific ways in which the domains of sensory activity and their causal and conditioning factors dovetail with the intentionality of perception.

This account of intentionality as disclosing two types of phenomena—the external domain of activity and the internal domain of representation—provides the basis for Dignāga's definition of perception as a conception-free cognition. While this definition has proved problematic and has been the target of both Brahmanical and Buddhist critics, it has received strong support from Dharmakīrti, whose position on this issue is adopted with little modification by Śāntarakṣita and Kamalaśīla. Not all critics of the Buddhist definition of perception oppose the notion that, at least in its initial stages, a percept may lack determination. As we noted, Kumārila does admit direct nonconceptual perception as a necessary, albeit preliminary, step of the perceptual process (which also includes perceptual judgments). For their part, the Naiyāyikas, following Uddyotakara, understand perception as being always in some way determined (*savikalpa*). This is true at least of the old school of Nyāya. Following Gaṅgeśa's introduction of the notion of pre-predicative perception, the Naiyāyikas would eventually concede that a proper account of perception must include indeterminate awareness.[63] This concession has to do, at least in part, with an axiomatic principle of Nyāya epistemology: namely, that perceptual awareness, though always comprising an inferential component, is to be thought as formless.[64] The Naiyāyika thus subscribes to the view that every entity that is apprehended in perception possesses both generality (*jāti*) and individuality (*vyakti*), with the exception of the extreme universal (*parasāmānya*) and the extreme individual (*antyaviśeṣa*). But this notion that in perception one apprehends the object as a whole, and not merely its perceptible parts, runs counter to the fundamental Buddhist intuition about the composite and momentary nature of phenomena: wholeness, claims the Buddhist, is a conceptual construct superimposed upon a constantly changing domain of discrete mental and physical events.[65]

9.3 EPISTEMIC AUTHORITY WITHOUT MANIFEST TRUTH

An epistemology that relies on the notion that perception (specifically, a direct mode of cognitive awareness) grasps things as they truly are (that is, as momentary and discrete), and is thus implicitly cognitive even in the absence of perceptual judgments, reflects a genuine optimism about the possibility of knowledge. As Roger Jackson quite aptly puts it, on the traditional Buddhist account of perception:

> the very first moment of cognition of an object is unmediated and pure, the subject to *a posteriori* conceptual construction. It is what might be called an "optimistic" epistemology, since it allows that direct cognition of ultimates *is* possible for beings. A "pessimistic" epistemology (e.g. that of Kant or Wittgenstein) would maintain that although the mind is capable of forming useful approximate representations, its cognitions never are unmediated by conceptions.[66]

63. For a clear philosophical treatment of the notion of pre-predicative awareness, see Bhattacharyya (1993). See also Phillips (1995: 122ff.), Mohanty (1992b: 174), and Chakrabarti (2000).

64. Whether Gaṅgeśa's introduction of pre-predicative perception represents progress for the Nyāya is, however, a contested issue. Arindam Chakrabarti (2000) has offered several reasons why Nyāya could very well do without what he calls "immaculate perception" (though his critique relies on an externalist account of perceptual functioning, which assumes that object properties can be determined as being largely observer-independent).

65. Misunderstanding the difference between what is merely perceptually apprehended and what is discriminated and brought under a concept *can* result in a failure to fully grasp the implications of the principle of dependent arising. One might reasonably conclude that in the TS/P, Śāntarakṣita and Kamalaśīla are not merely concerned with refuting rival doctrines but also, and perhaps more importantly, with clearing unfounded assumptions among the Buddhists themselves.

66. Jackson (1993: 416 n. 3). See also Jackson (1990) and the contributions in Forman (1990) for further discussions on the issue of "optimistic epistemology."

We may trace this optimism—as the example of Śāntarakṣita's defense of the Buddhist principle of dependent arising demonstrates—to a steadfast confidence in the efficacy of the Buddha's path, whose methods and practices are taken to be effective in the removal of both afflictive proclivities and cognitive obscurations (which the Buddhist regards as adventitious rather than endemic to the human condition). Such optimism affects not only the epistemological but also the ontological stance that underpins the Buddhist metaphysical picture: all phenomena are momentary, interdependent, and a constant cause of concern for the unenlightened, whose only comforting thoughts are his or her (false) beliefs in the endurance and permanence of things. Sharing in this optimism about the possibility of apprehending things as they truly are, Śāntarakṣita expresses confidence in the Buddha for having revealed dependent arising, a tested and testable principle, as the ultimate causal law governing the realms of phenomena. This gesture of unconcealment, by means of which the Buddha points at the real and at the same time provides an effective method of its realization, is indeed a testimony to the optimism that characterizes the Buddhist quest for truth (an optimism that Buddhists share with most of their Brahmanical opponents even as they pursue it by different means). Unlike the pessimist, who does not think that philosophical truths, however they may be conceived, have the possibility utterly to alter the human condition, the optimist appeals to the transformative and edifying nature of non-ordinary experience. In Jackson's words again:

> The disagreement between the optimistic and pessimistic views is derived in part from the differing kinds of evidence used to support each: pessimists rely on observations of "ordinary" psychological states, while optimists rely on observations gleaned from meditative states that are not commonly accessible, but which are, nevertheless, regarded by the optimists as more normative (if not ordinary) than other, more accessible states.[67]

The question remains: if meditative states manifest a different, more normative kind of evidence, how can we ensure that such evidence becomes intersubjectively available and open to the sort of critical scrutiny that alone can guard against the dogmatism implicit in any attitude of absolute certainty?

In what is perhaps the first clear articulation of the difference between epistemological optimism and epistemological pessimism, Karl Popper set out to identify those early modern philosophers, principally Bacon and Descartes, who were most responsible for advancing a doctrine of manifest truth. Inspired by the birth of modern science and technology, the doctrine of manifest truth (in both its empiricist and rationalist orientations) is linked

67. Jackson (1993: 417 n. 5).

with what might properly be termed the liberation of the individual from the premodern mindset and its dependence on scriptural authority. By adopting a critical attitude toward traditional concepts of philosophy, religion, and science, epistemological optimism is essentially antiauthoritarian at its core. But Popper also warns that epistemological optimism itself is not immune to ideology: "One can see that an attitude of tolerance which is based upon an optimistic faith in the victory of truth may easily be shaken. For it is liable to turn into a conspiracy theory which would be hard to reconcile with an attitude of tolerance."[68] For Popper, epistemological optimism carries in its wake the risk of absolutism—of assuming that something like an absolute (or ultimate) truth manifests itself within the historical process. Thus, the epistemological optimist needs to be reminded, in Nietzsche's terms, that knowledge, though not subject to individual whims and arbitrariness, is ultimately a human—all too human—affair.[69] Popper's response to epistemological optimism comes in the form of his well-known falsificationist methodology: philosophers must, as a rule, be willing to falsify their theses or else they become susceptible to selectively adopting preconceived worldviews. For Popper, science offers the best guard against the dogmatism of absolute certainty, for scientific theories in general represent nothing more than generalizations on the basis of currently known and testable facts. Can first-person, disciplined explorations of experience offer the same sort of critical safeguards one has come to associate with experimental science? In other words, can the Buddhist (or the phenomenologist) advance a model of epistemic authority without at the same time embracing the doctrine of manifest truth?

It is important to keep in mind that, in appealing to the testimony of nonordinary states of cognitive awareness, the Buddhist epistemologists do not necessarily deny that individuals occupy a specific point of view or that their cognitive abilities rest on (and are thus realized by) their embodied condition. If Śāntarakṣita and Kamalaśīla's defense of the principle of dependent arising is any indication, the Buddhist epistemologists argue for an enactive and pragmatically efficacious account of cognition, on the grounds that insight into the order of the causal domain reveals natural efficacy (*bhāvaśakti*) rather than indetermination as the ground of being.

Some have interpreted this epistemological optimism as stemming from a commitment to foundationalism, precisely to the type of direct (perceptual) access to "sense data" that is susceptible to Sellars's criticism of the "Myth of the Given."[70] I have argued, on the contrary, that the Buddhist

68. Popper (2002: 10).
69. Popper (2002: 21).
70. See, especially, Tillemans (2003), McClintock (2003), and Arnold (2005a, 2005b).

epistemologists build upon a phenomenological analysis of embodied experience. I surmise, therefore, that understanding bare awareness as in some sense noncognitive masks an undisclosed commitment to a "Myth of the Mental." I have also noted that, on a minimalist reading, it may be possible to interpret Buddhist epistemologists as claiming that perceptual disclosure of what is phenomenally given (or the givenness of experience itself), if at all possible, must be rudimentary. The limitations of ordinary states of cognitive awareness notwithstanding, what seems to motivate the Buddhist epistemological enterprise are the findings of extraordinary perceivers: it is possible, allegedly, to unravel not just the direct and indirect types of cognitive awareness but, more importantly, the intrinsic and extrinsic modes of ascertainment. Neither Dignāga nor Dharmakīrti deal with the question of whether cognition is intrinsically or extrinsically ascertained. This question is explicitly treated only in the commentarial literature, with Śākyabuddhi and Dharmottara among the first to address this issue. It is Kamalaśīla, however, who provides perhaps the most detailed classification of cognitions on the basis of their mode of ascertainment. Kamalaśīla not only contends that certain types of cognitive awareness, such as yogic perception and trained perception,[71] are intrinsically ascertained but also that it is possible to effect something like the phenomenologist's *epoché* and examine not just the objects of cognition but the intentional acts themselves. Of course, the phenomenological epistemology that Śāntarakṣita and Kamalaśīla advance in the *Compendium* and its *Commentary* is markedly different from the realist epistemology of the Naiyāyikas or that of modern-day empiricists in that its fundamental insights are grounded on what are claimed to be inerrant modes of observation.

In his concluding remarks to the *Examination of Perception*, Kamalaśīla offers a critical summary of the debate over what is and what is not apprehended in perception that I think identifies what could well be one of the most important issues confronting the perception theorist: can genuine epistemic authority ever be achieved given our irredeemably perspectival outlook and singular mode of being in the world? At stake is the Naiyāyika's contention that removing any trace of discrimination from perception not only creates a wide and virtually unbridgeable gap between perception and conception but also renders perception ineffective. If someone were to have only indeterminate perceptions, that person would arguably be incapable either of directing his or her actions toward an object, or refrain from acting on it: for, in order

71. Note that in the notion of "trained perception" (*abhyāsavat pratyakṣa*) "*abhyāsa*" denotes an effort to achieve through repeated training a state of pure cognitive awareness. Trained perception thus captures both states such as the stabilized introspective equipoise of yogic perception and the coping skills of expert apprehension, whether it is the expert meditator's capacity to maintain a state of open awareness or the elite cricket batsman's striking visual attentiveness.

to do so, one must first be able to discriminate and form judgments. One's actions would otherwise be uniform irrespective of any differences among the objects of experience.

Kamalaśīla's solution to this conundrum is to emphasize once again the difference between ordinary, common sense notions of what one takes to be the case and a methodical, disciplined, and direct apprehension of what is (or at least seems to be) the case:

> The nature of things cannot be determined at will, for a definition [of how things are] cannot be produced [at will]. It is necessary that things are approached according to their own nature, and that the definition of a thing embodies the specific aspect of that thing alone toward which one's intention is directed. For instance, one [ostensibly] identifies "roughness" to be a characteristic of ploughed earth.[72]

If such a direct apprehension of the nature of things were not possible, then one could neither differentiate perceptions from other types of cognitive apprehension nor distinguish between an object and its mode of givenness. This trust in the possibility of getting to the things themselves is, indeed, an expression of genuine epistemological optimism, even if such optimism does not ultimately stem from the testimony of ordinary experience. That such testimony alone is not sufficient to justify Śāntarakṣita and Kamalaśīla's epistemological optimism is amply indicated by their readiness to defend their views on rational grounds.

The phenomenological naturalism advanced in this book, then, may be regarded simply as an account of why mental states must be understood as intentionally constituted, and how such intentional content, in turn, becomes causally relevant to explaining how acting toward some end is successfully accomplished. If such an account can be given, then even philosophers of a more rationalist bent (such as the Buddhist epistemologists)—who believe that reasons are causes (or at least are causally relevant for action), but who are, at the same time, deeply committed to defending a strictly Abhidharmic metaphysical picture of reality—can feel at ease. Of course, critics of this line of inquiry would say that the reductionist models of cognitive science and that of Abhidharma philosophy, which informs the metaphysical commitments of the Buddhist epistemologists, are incompatible: after all, Śāntarakṣita and Kamalaśīla do not entirely forgo the Sanskritic philosophical tradition of understanding causality in terms of the tripartite action-object-agent model. Alternatively, some critics might invoke the causal closure of physical events.

72. TSP *ad* TS 1358–1360: *na hi svecchayā vastunāṃ svabhāvavyavasthānaṃ kartuṃ labhyam, yenānyathāpraṇīyeta lakṣaṇam; api tu yathāvasthitam eva vastusvarūpamanūdya prasiddhasvabhāvama prasiddhasvabhāva viśeṣapratitipādayiṣayā lakṣaṇaṃ praṇayanti tadvidaḥ. lakṣaṇaṃ pranayanti tadvidhaḥ, yathā prithavyaḥ khaṭasvam.*

Indeed, many philosophers argue that mental events should be understood as causing actions,[73] not physical effects, since intentional acts are not the sort of things studied by the natural sciences.

The first objection can be easily answered, either by showing that the reductionist model of cognition at work in the Abhidharma is open to revision, or by pointing to embodied and enactive models of cognition in order to show that not all cognitive science is eliminativist. The second objection is a little more difficult to answer, in part because it implies that mental events cannot be explained in terms of physical causes. But if mental events cause actions, and actions exhibit physical properties (I intend to raise my arm, and my arm thus displays behavioral properties), then mental events are either physical events of a different type (a position known as token physicalism) or simply supervene on physical events. Critics of the supervenience thesis often invoke the casual closure of the physical domain[74] as evidence for the epiphenomenal character of mental states. Since a satisfactory answer to this objection could well fill an entire monograph, I will simply point out, for now, that even philosophers with naturalist leanings (the present author included) find the epiphenomenalist stance odd and unattractive.[75] Indeed, it is rather peculiar to think that cognitive events, which arise as a result of the tight causal coupling between perception, reflection, and action, should themselves be causally inert. Furthermore, arguments that invoke the causal closure of the physical domain need to be empirically grounded, or else they cannot provide a strong basis for refuting positions that argue for some version of dualist emergentism. Lastly, causation in the mental domain rests on principles of intelligibility (that is, on principles which state that it is perfectly intelligible that mental intentions have a causal role in initiating behavior) rather than on principles of mechanism (that is, on principles which explain how causality is actually realized).

If the dominant direction in the Buddhist epistemological account of cognition points toward a naturalistic explanation of perception, intentionality and reference, then we would do well to open up our investigation of this tradition's causal account of knowledge to input from the sciences of cognition. This book represents a first step in that direction. The following concern might linger: if Buddhist epistemology is naturalized, does it not somehow

73. This is specifically the case with Davidson (1963).

74. Such is the case, for instance, with Peacocke (1979: 134ff.) and Papineau (1998: 375). However, even philosophers who advocate for such closure, like Jonathan Lowe (2008), content that there is still room for a "genuine and autonomous causal role for mental states in the genesis of intended physical behavior" (Lowe 2008: 41). For more on the significance of causal explanation in the mental domain, see also Lowe (2008: 58ff.).

75. Some philosophers have gone as far as to argue that a full-blown epiphenomenalism is actually incoherent (see Lowe 2008: 89ff.).

cease to be Buddhist? To anyone who fears what an affirmative answer might spell out for Buddhist theories of knowledge, I have this much to say: true or false friend, naturalism is here to stay, and if our reception of, and engagement with, this venerable tradition of epistemological inquiry is to remain relevant to contemporary philosophical debates, then we must, at the very least, seek its acquaintance.

BIBLIOGRAPHY

Achinstein, Peter. 2001. *The Book of Evidence*. Oxford: Oxford University Press.

Aikin, Scott F. 2006. "Pragmatism, Naturalism, and Phenomenology." *Human Studies* 29: 317–340.

Albahari, Miri. 2006. *Analytical Buddhism: The Two-Tiered Illusion of Self*. Houndmills, Basingstoke, Hampshire: Palgrave Macmillan.

Almeder, Robert. 1998. *Harmless Naturalism: The Limits of Science and the Nature of Philosophy*. Chicago and LaSalle, Ill.: Open Court.

Amaladass, Adand S. J. 1984. *Philosophical Implications of Dhvani: Experience of Symbol Language in Indian Aesthetics*. De Nobili Research Library. Vienna: Institut für Indologie der Universität Wien.

Anacker, Steven. 1984. *Seven Works of Vasubandhu: The Buddhist Psychological Doctor*. Delhi: Motilal Banarsidass.

Andersen, Dines, and Helmer Smith, eds. [1913] 1990. *Suttanipāta*. London: Pali Text Society.

Armstrong, David M. 1973. *Belief, Truth, and Knowledge*. Cambridge: Cambridge University Press.

Arnold, Dan. 2005a. *Buddhists, Brahmins, and Belief*. New York: Columbia University Press.

______. 2005b. "Is Svasaṃvitti Transcendental? A Tentative Reconstruction Following Śāntarakṣita." *Asian Philosophy* 15 (1): 77–111.

______. 2006. "On Semantics and *Saṃketa*: Thoughts on a Neglected Problem with Buddhist *Apoha* Theory." *Journal of Indian Philosophy* 34: 415–478.

______. 2008a. "Buddhist Idealism, Epistemic and Otherwise: Thoughts on the Alternating Perspectives of Dharmakīrti." *Sophia* 47 (1): 3–28.

______. 2008b. "Dharmakīrti's Dualism: Critical Reflections on a Buddhist Proof of Rebirth." *Philosophy Compass* 3 (5): 1079–1096.

______. 2008c. "Transcendental Arguments and Practical Reason in Indian Philosophy." *Argumentation* 22: 135–147.

______. 2009. "*Svasaṃvitti* as Methodological Solipsism: 'Narrow Content' and the Problem of Intentionality in Buddhist Philosophy of Mind." In *Pointing at the Moon: Buddhism, Logic, Analytic Philosophy*, edited by Mario D'Amato, Jay L. Garfield, and Tom J. F. Tillemans, 135–159. New York: Oxford University Press.

______. 2010. "Self-Awareness (*Svasaṃvitti*) and Related Doctrines of Buddhists Following Dignāga: Philosophical Characterizations of Some of the Main Issues." *Journal of Indian Philosophy* 38: 323–378.

Ballard, Dana. H. 2002. "Our Perception of the World Has to Be an Illusion." *Journal of Consciousness Studies* 9 (5–6): 54–71.

Bandyopadhyay, Nandita. 1979. "The Buddhist Theory of Relation between *Pramā* and *Pramāṇa*." *Journal of Indian Philosophy* 7 (1): 41–78.

———. 1988. "The Concept of Contradiction in Indian Philosophy." *Journal of Indian Philosophy* 16 (3): 225–246.

Barlingay, Surendra S. 1975. *A Modern Introduction to India Logic*. Delhi: National Publishing House.

Barsalou, Lawrence. W. 1999. "Perceptual Symbol Systems." *Behavioral and Brain Sciences* 22: 577–660.

———. 2005. "Situated Conceptualization." In *Handbook of Categorization in Cognitive Science*, edited by H. Cohen and C. Lefebvre, 619–650. St. Louis: Elsevier.

———. 2009. "Simulation, Situated Conceptualization, and Prediction." *Philosophical Transactions of the Royal Society of London: Biological Sciences* 364: 1281–1289.

Bayne, Tim. 2010. *The Unity of Consciousness*. Oxford: Oxford University Press.

Bealer, George. 1998. "Intuition and the Autonomy of Philosophy." In *Rethinking Intuition: The Psychology of Intuition and Its Role in Philosophical Inquiry*, edited by M. De Paul and W. Ramsey, 201–239. Lanham, Md.: Rowman and Littlefield.

Bell, John. 2001. "Pragmatic Reasoning: Pragmatic Semantics and Semantic Pragmatics." In *Modeling and Using Context*, Vol. 2116: 45–58. London: Springer-Verlag.

Berger, Douglas L. 2004. *"The Veil of Maya": Schopenhauer's System and Early Indian Thought*. Binghamton, N.Y.: Global Academic Publishing.

Bermúdez, José L. 1995. "Ecological Perception and the Notion of a Nonconceptual Point of View." In *The Body and the Self*, edited by José L. Bermúdez, Anthony Marcel, and Naomi Eilan, 153–174. Cambridge, Mass.: MIT Press.

———. 1998. *The Paradox of Self-Consciousness*. Cambridge, Mass.: MIT Press.

———. 2000. "Naturalized Sense Data." *Philosophy and Phenomenal Research* 61 (9): 353–374.

Bermúdez, José L., and Fiona Macpherson. 1998. "Nonconceptual Content and the Nature of Perceptual Experience." *Electronic Journal of Analytic Philosophy* 6.

Bhaduri, Sadananda. 1947. *Studies in Nyāya-Vaiśeṣika Metaphysics*. Poona: Bhandarkar Oriental Research Institute.

Bhate, Saroja, and Johannes Bronkhorst. 1993. *Bhartṛhari, Philosopher and Grammarian*. Bern: Peter Lang AG (reprint Delhi: Motilal Banarsidass, 1994).

Bhattacharya, Kamaleshwar. 1973. *L'Ātman-Brahman dans le bouddhisme ancien*. Paris: École Française d'Extrême Orient.

Bhattacharya, Vidhushekhara. 1943. *The Āgamaśāstra of Gauḍapāda*. Delhi: Motilal Banarsidass (reprint 1989).

Bhattacharyya, B. 1926. "Forword." In *Tattvasaṃgraha of Śāntarakṣita with the Commentary of Kamalaśīla*, edited by E. Krishnamacharya, i–cxvii. Baroda: Gaekwad Oriental Series.

Bhattacharyya, Sibajiban. 1993. *Gaṅgeśa's Theory of Indeterminate Perception*. New Delhi: Indian Council of Philosophical Research.

Bhikkhu, Pāsādika. 1989. *Kanonische Zitate im Abhidharmakośabhāṣya des Vasubandhu*. Göttingen: Vandenhoeck and Ruprecht.

Biardeau, Madelaine. 1957. "La Définition dans la pensée indienne." *Journal Asiatique* 245: 371–384.

———. 1964. *Théorie de la connaissance et philosophie de la parole*. Paris: Mouton.

Bijalwan, C. D. 1977. *Indian Theories of Knowledge*. New Delhi: Heritage Publishers.

Bilimoria, Purushottama. 1985. "*Jñāna* and *Pramā*." *Journal of Indian Philosophy* 13 (1): 73–102.

———. 1988. *Śābdapramāṇa, Word and Knowledge: A Doctrine in Mīmāṃsā-Nyāya Philosophy*. Dordrecht, Boston: Kluwer Academic Publishers.

Bilimoria, Purushottama, and Jitendranath N. Mohanty, eds. 1997. *Relativism, Suffering and Beyond.* Oxford: Oxford University Press.

Binsted, G., K. Brownell, Z. Vorontsova, M. Heath, and D. Saucier. 2007. "Visuomotor System Uses Target Features Unavailable to Conscious Awareness." *Proceedings of the National Academy of Sciences* 104 (31): 12669–12672.

Blackmore, S. J., G. Brelstaff, K. Nelson, and T. Troscianko. 1995. "Is the Richness of our Visual World an Illusion? Trans-saccadic Memory for Complex Scenes." *Perception* 24: 1075–1081.

Block, Ned. 1981. "Psychologism and Behaviorism." *Philosophical Review* 90 (1): 5–43.

______. 1995. "On a Confusion about the Function of Consciousness." *Behavioral and Brain Sciences* 18: 227–247.

Blumenthal, James. 2004. *The Ornament of the Middle Way: A Study of the Madhyamaka Thought of Śāntarakṣita.* Ithaca, N.Y.: Snow Lion Publications.

Bodhi, Bhikkhu. 2000. *The Connected Discourses of the Buddha: A New Translation of the Samyutta Nikāya.* Boston: Wisdom Publications.

BonJour, Laurence. 1994. "Against Naturalized Epistemology." *Midwest Studies in Philosophy* 19: 283–300.

______. 1998. *In Defence of Pure Reason.* Cambridge: Cambridge University Press.

Bradley, Peter. 2008. "Constancy, Categories and Bayes: A New Approach to Representational Theories of Color Constancy." *Philosophical Psychology* 21 (5): 601 -627.

Bramão, Inês, Alexandra Reis, Karl Magnus Petersson, and Luís Faísca. 2011. "The Role of Color Information on Object Recognition: A Review and Meta-analysis." *Acta Psychologica* 138: 244–253.

Breet, Jan A. de 1992. "The Concept *Upāyakauśalya* in the *Aṣtasāhasrikā Prajñāpāramitā.*" *Wiener Zeitschrift für die Kunde Südasiens* 36: 203–216.

Brentano, Franz. 1924. *Psychologie vom empirischen Standpunkt.* 2d ed. Edited by Oskar Kraus. Leipzig: Meiner.

______. 1981. *Psychology from an Empirical Standpoint.* Translated by A. C. Rancurello. D. B. Terrell, and L. McAlister. London: Routledge, 1973. (2d ed., introduction by Peter Simons, 1995).

______. 1982. *Descriptive Psychology.* Translated by Benito Müller. London: Routledge.

Bridgeman, Bruce. 2002. "The Grand Illusion and Petit Illusions: Interactions of Perception and Sensory Coding." *Journal of Consciousness Studies* 9 (5–6): 29–34.

Bronkhorst, Johannes. 1993. *The Two Traditions of Meditations in Ancient India.* Delhi: Motilal Banarsidass.

Bruzina, R. 2004. "Phenomenology and Cognitive Science: Moving Beyond the Paradigms." *Phenomenology and the Cognitive Sciences* 20: 43–48.

Buswell, Robert E., and Robert E. Gimello, eds. 1992. *Paths to Liberations: The Mārga and Its Transformations in Buddhist Thought.* Honolulu: University of Hawaii Press.

Butzenberger, Klaus. 1996. "On Doubting What There is Not: The Doctrine of Doubt and the Reference of Terms in Indian Grammar, Logic and Philosophy of Language." *Journal of Indian Philosophy* 24: 363–406.

Cabezón, José I. 1990. "The Canonization of Philosophy and the Rhetoric of Siddhānta in Tibetan Buddhism." In *Buddha Nature: A Festschrift in Honour of Minoru Kiyota*, edited by Paul Griffiths and John. P. Keenan, 7–26. San Francisco: Buddhist Books International.

———. 1994. *Buddhism and Language: A Study of Indo-Tibetan Scholasticism*. Albany, N.Y.: State University of New York Press.

———. 1995. "Buddhist Studies as a Discipline and the Role of Theory." *Journal of the International Association of Buddhist Studies* 18: 231–268.

Cardona, George. 1967–68. "Anvaya and vyatireka in Indian grammar." *Adyar Library Bulletin* 31–32: 313–352.

Carey, D., M. Harvey, and D. Milner. 1996. "Visuomotor Sensitivity for Shape and Orientation in a Patient with Visual Form Agnosia." *Neuropsychologia* 34: 830–849.

Carman, Taylor. 1999. "The Body in Husserl and Merleau-Ponty." *Philosophical Topics* 27 (2): 205–226.

———. 2005. "On the Inescapability of Phenomenology." In *Phenomenology and Philosophy of Mind*, edited by David W. Smith and Amie L. Thomasson, 67–89. Oxford: Oxford University Press.

———. 2007. "Dennett on Seeming." *Phenomenology and the Cognitive Sciences* 6: 99–106.

Caston, V. 2002. "Aristotle on Consciousness." *Mind* 111: 751–815.

Chadha, Monima. 2001. "Perceptual Cognition: A Nyāya-Kantian Approach." *Philosophy East and West* 51 (2): 197–209.

———. 2011. "Self-awareness: Eliminating the Myth of the 'Invisible Subject'," *Philosophy East and West* 61 (3): 453–467.

Chakrabarti, Arindam. 2000. "Against Immaculate Perception: Seven Reasons for Eliminating *Nirvikalpaka* Perception from Nyāya." *Philosophy East and West* 50 (1): 1–8.

Chakrabarti, Arindam, and Mark Siderits. 2011. "Introduction." In *Apoha: Buddhist Nominalism and Human Cognition*, edited by Mark Siderits, Arindam Chakrabarti, and Tom Tillemans, 1–49. New York: Columbia University Press.

Chakrabarti, Kishor. K. 1975. "The Nyāya-Vaiśeṣika Theory of Universals." *Journal of Indian Philosophy* 3: 363–382.

———. 1995. *Definition and Induction: A Historical and Comparative Study*. Honolulu: University of Hawaii Press.

———. 1999. *Classical Indian Philosophy of Mind: The Nyāya Dualist Tradition*. New York: State University of New York Press.

Chalmers, D. 1995. "Facing up to the Problem of Consciousness." *Journal of Consciousness Studies* 2 (3): 200–219.

———. 1996. *The Conscious Mind: In Search of a Fundamental Theory*. New York: Oxford University Press.

———. 2000. "What is a Neural Correlate of Consciousness." In *Neural Correlates of Consciousness*, edited by Thomas Metzinger, 17–39. Cambridge, Mass.: MIT Press.

———. 2006. "Phenomenal Concepts and the Explanatory Gap." In *Phenomenal Concepts and Phenomenal Knowledge: New Essays on Consciousness and Physicalism*, edited by Torin Alter and Sven Walter, 167–194. Oxford: Oxford University Press.

———. 2010. *The Character of Consciousness*. New York: Oxford University Press.

———. 2011. "Verbal Disputes." *Philosophical Review* 120 (4): 515–566.

Chalmers, Robert. 1994. *The Majjhima-Nikāya*. Vol. III. Oxford: Pali Text Society.

Changeux, Jean-Pierre, and Paul Ricoeur. 1998. *Ce qui nous fait penser: La Nature et la régle*. Paris: Edition Odiles Jacob.

Chatterjee, D. C. 1933. "*Hetucakranirṇaya*." *Indian Historical Quarterly* 9: 266–272.

Chatterjee, Satischandra C. 1950. *The Nyāya Theory of Knowledge*. Calcutta: University of Calcutta.
Chi, R. S. Y. 1969. *Buddhist Formal Logic: A Study of Dignāga's Hetucakra and K'uei -chi's Great Commentary on the Nyāyapraveśa*. London: Luzac.
Chinchore, Mangala R. 1989. *Dharmakīrti's Theory of the Hetu-Centricity of Anumāṇa*. Delhi: Motilal Banarsidass.
______. 1991. "Post-Udayana Nyāya Reactions to Dharmakīrti's Vādanyāya—An Evaluation." In *Studies in the Buddhist Epistemological Tradition: Proceedings of the Second International Dharmakīrti Conference*, Vienna, June 11–16, 1989, edited by Ernst Steinkellner, 3–18. Vienna: Verlag der Österreichischen Akademie der Wissenschaften.
Chinn, Ewing Y. 1994. "The Anti-abstractionism of Dignāga and Berkeley." *Philosophy East and West* 44 (1): 55–77.
Christensen, Carleton. 2008. *Self and World: From Analytic Philosophy to Phenomenology*. Berlin and New York: Walter de Gruyter.
Chu, Junjie. 2004. "A Study of *Sataimira* in Dignāga's Definition of Pseudo-Perception (PS 1.7cd–8ab)." *Wiener Zeitschrift für die Kunde Südasiens* 48: 113–149.
Churchland, Patricia S. 1986. *Neurophilosophy: Toward a Unified Science of the Mind-Brain*. Cambridge, Mass.: MIT Press.
Churchland, Paul. 2002. *Brain-Wise: Studies in Neurophilosophy*. Cambridge, Mass.: MIT Press.
Clark, Andy. 1997. *Being There: Putting Brain, Body, and World Together Again*. Cambridge, Mass.: MIT Press.
______. 2002. "Is Seeing All It Seems? Action, Reason and the Grand Illusion." *Journal of Consciousness Studies* 9 (5–6): 181–202.
Clark, Andy, and David Chalmers. 1998. "The Extended Mind." *Analysis* 58: 10–23.
Cohen, Jonahan. 2010. "Color Relationalism and Color Phenomenology." In *Perceiving the World*, edited by Bence Nanay, 13–32. Oxford: Oxford University Press.
Collins, Steven. 1982. *Selfless Persons: Imagery and Thought in Theravāda Buddhism*. Cambridge: Cambridge University Press.
Conze, Edward. 1962. *Buddhist Thought in India*. London: George Allen & Unwin.
______. 1963. "Buddhist Philosophy and Its European Parallels." *Philosophy East and West* 13 (1): 9–23.
______. 1967. *Thirty Years of Buddhist Studies*. Oxford: Bruno Cassirer.
Coseru, Christian. 2009a. "Buddhist 'Foundationalism' and the Phenomenology of Perception." *Philosophy East and West* 59 (4): 409–439.
______. 2009b. "Mind in Indian Buddhist Philosophy." *The Stanford Encyclopedia of Philosophy* (Winter 2009 Edition), edited by Edward N. Zalta. http://plato.stanford.edu/entries/mind-indian-buddhism/.
______. 2009c. "Naturalism and Intentionality: A Buddhist Epistemological Approach." *Asian Philosophy* 19 (3): 239–264.
______. 2015 "Taking the Intentionality of Perception Seriously: Why Phenomenology is Inescapable." *Philosophy East and West* 63 (5): 227–248.
Cousins, Lance S. 1973. "Buddhist Jhāna: Its Nature and Attainment According to Pāli Sources." *Religion* 3 (2): 115–131.
Cox, Collett. 1995. *Disputed Dharmas: Early Buddhist Theories on Existence*. Tokyo: International Institute of Buddhist Studies.
Crane, Tim. 2001. "Intentional Objects." *Ratio* 14: 336–349.
______. 2003. "The Intentional Structure of Consciousness." In *Consciousness: New Philosophical Perspectives*, edited by Q. Smith and A. Jokic, 33–56. Oxford: Oxford University Press.

———. 2009. "Is Perception a Propositional Attitude?" *Philosophical Quarterly* 59: 452–469.
Dainton, Barry. 2000. *Stream of Consciousness: Unity and Continuity in Conscious Experience*. London: Routledge.
D'Amato, Mario. 2003. "The Semiotics of Signlessness: A Buddhist Doctrine of Signs." *Semiotica* 147 (1/4): 185–207.
D'Amato, M., Jay L. Garfield, and Tom J. F Tillemans, eds. 2009. *Pointing at the Moon: Buddhism, Logic, Analytic Philosophy*. New York: Oxford University Press.
Davidson, Donald. 1963. "Actions, Reasons, and Causes." *Journal of Philosophy* 60: 685–700.
Davidson, Richard J., and Anne Harrington. 2001. *Visions of Compassion: Western Scientists and Tibetan Buddhists Examine Human Nature*. Oxford: Oxford University Press.
Davidson, Ronald M. 1999. "Masquerading as *Pramāṇa*: Esoteric Buddhism and Epistemological Nomenclature." In *Dharmakīrti's Thought and Its Impact on Indian and Tibetan Philosophy: Proceedings of the Third International Dharmakīrti Conference, Hiroshima, November 4–6, 1997*, edited by Shoryu Katsura, 25–36. Vienna: Verlag der Österreichischen Akademie der Wissenschaften.
De Jong, J. W., ed. 1977. *Nāgārjuna's Mūlamadhyamakakārikā Prajñā Nāma*. Revised by Christian Lindtner, 2004. Chennai: Adyar Library.
Demiéville, Paul. 1947. "Le Miroir spirituel." *Sinologica* 1 (2): 112–137.
———. 1952. *Le Concile de Lhasa: Une controverse sur le quiétisme entres les bouddhistes de l'Inde et de la Chine au VIIIe siecle de l'ere chrétienne*. Paris: Presses Universitaires de France.
Dennett, Daniel. 1991. *Consciousness Explained*. Boston: Little, Brown & Co.
———. 1993: "The Message Is: There Is No Medium." *Philosophy and Phenomenological Research* 53: 919–931.
———. 1996. "Facing Backward on the Problem of Consciousness." *Journal of Consciousness Studies* 3: 4–6.
———. 2001. "Surprise, Surprise." *Behavioral and Brain Sciences* 24: 982.
———. 2002. "How Could I Be Wrong? How Wrong Could I Be?" In *Is the Visual World a Grand Illusion*, edited by Alva Noë, 13–16. Special issues of the *Journal of Consciousness Studies* 9 (5–6) . Thorverton: Imprint Academic.
———. 2011. "Shall We Tango? No, but Thanks for Asking." *Journal of Consciousness Studies* 18 (5–6): 23–34.
Depraz, Natalie. 1995. *Transcendence et incarnation: Le Statut de l'intersubjectivité comme altérité à soi chez Husserl*. Paris: Librarie Philosophique J. Vrin.
Depraz, Natalie, Francisco J. Varela, and Pierre Vermersch. 2000. "The Gesture of Awareness: An Account of its Structural dynamics." In *Investigating Phenomenal Consciousness*, edited by Max Velmans, 121–138. Amsterdam: John Benjamins Publishing Company.
———. 2003. *On Becoming Aware: A Pragmatics of Experiencing*. Amsterdam: John Benjamins Publishing Company.
Derrida, Jacques. 1972. *Marges: De la Philosophie*. Paris: Les éditions de Minuit.
Descartes, Rene. 1972. *Treatise of Man*. Cambridge, Mass.: Harvard University Press.
De Silva, Padmasiri. 2005. *An Introduction to Buddhist Psychology*. 4th ed. London: Palgrave Macmillan.
Deutsch, Eliot, and Ron Bontekoe. 1997. "Preface." In *A Companion to World Philosophies*, edited by E. Deutsch and R. Bontekoe, xii–xvi. Oxford: Blackwell.

Dhammajoti, K. L. 2007. "Ākāra and Direct Perception." *Pacific World Journal* 3 (9): 245–272.

Dhruva, A. B. 1930. *The Nyāyapraveśa*. Part I. Sanskrit Text with Commentaries. Baroda: Reprint as *Nyāyapraveśa of Diṅnāga with Commentaries of Haribhradra Suri and Parsavadeva*. Delhi: Sri Satguru.

Dokic, Jérôme, and Elizabeth Pacherie. 2007. "Too Much Ado about Belief." *Phenomenology and the Cognitive Sciences* 6: 185–200.

Dravid, N. S. 1996. "The Nyāya-Vaiśeṣika Explanation of Illusion." *Journal of Indian Philosophy* 24: 37–48.

Dravid, R. R. 1972. *The Problem of Universals in Indian Philosophy*. Delhi: Motilal Banarsidass.

Dretske, Fred. 1995. *Naturalizing the Mind*. Cambridge, Mass.: MIT Press.

Dreyfus, Georges. 1991. "Dharmakīrti's Definition of *Pramāṇa* and Its Interpreters." In *Studies in the Buddhist Epistemological Tradition: Proceedings of the Second International Dharmakīrti Conference*, Vienna, June 11–16, 1989, edited by Ernst Steinkellner, 19–38. Vienna: Verlag der Österreichischen Akademie der Wissenschaften.

______. 1995. "Is Dharmakīrti a Pragmatist?" *Asian Studies/Études Asiatiques* 49: 671–691.

______. 1996. "Can the Fool Lead the Blind? Perception and the Given in Dharmakīrti's Thought." *Journal of Indian Philosophy* 24: 209–229.

______. 1997. *Recognizing Reality: Dharmakīrti's Philosophy and Its Tibetan Interpretations*. Albany: State University of New York Press.

______. 2007. "Is Perception Intentional? A Preliminary Exploration of Intentionality in Dharmakīrti." In *Pramāṇakirtiḥ: Papers Dedicated to Ernst Steinkellner on the Occasion of his 70th Birthday*, edited by Birgit Kellner, Helmut Krasser, Horst Lasic, Michael T. Much, and Helmut Tauscher, 95–114. Vienna: Arbeitskreis für Tibetische und Buddhistische Studies.

______. 2008. "What Is Debate for? The Rationality of Tibetan Debates and the Role of Humor." *Argumentation* 22: 43–58.

______. 2011. "Apoha as a Naturalized Account of Concept Formation." In *Apoha: Buddhist Nominalism and Human Cognition*, edited by Mark Siderits, Tom J. F. Tillemans, and A. Chakrabarti, 207–227. New York: Columbia University Press.

Dreyfus, Georges, and Sara McClintock, eds. 2003. *Svātantrika-Prasaṅgika Distinction: What Difference Does It Make?* Boston: Wisdom Publications.

Dreyfus, Hubert L. 1972. "The Perceptual Noema: Gurwitsch's Crucial Contribution." In *Life-World and Consciousness*, edited by L. Embree, 135–170. Evanston, Ill.: Northwestern University Press.

______. 1979. *What Computers Still Can't Do: A Critique of Artificial Intelligence*. New York: Harper and Row.

______. 1988. "Husserl's Epiphenomenology." In *Perspectives on Mind*, edited by H. R. Otto and J. A. Tuedio, 85–104. Dordrecht: D. Reidel Publishing Company.

______. 1993. "Heidegger's Critique of Husserl's (and Searle's) Account of Intentionality." *Social Research* 60 (1): 17–38.

______. 2006. "How Philosophers Can Profit from the Phenomenology of Everyday Expertise." Presidential Address, American Philosophical Association, Eastern Division Meeting, Washington, D.C.

Dreyfus, Hubert, and H. Hall, eds. 1982. *Husserl, Intentionality and Cognitive Science*. Cambridge, Mass.: MIT Press.

Dreyfus, Hubert, and Sean Kelly. 2007. "Heterophenomenology: Heavy-Handed Sleigh-of-Hand." *Phenomenology and the Cognitive Sciences* 6: 45–55.

Droit, Roger-Pol. 1997. *Le Culte du néant: Les Philosophes et le Bouddha*. Paris: Éditions du Seuil.

———. 2004. *L'Oubli de l'Inde: Une amnésie philosophique*. 2d ed. Paris: Éditions du Seuil.

Drummond, John. 1991. "Phenomenology and the Foundationalism Debate." *Reason Papers* 16 (Fall): 45–71.

———. 2003. "The Structure of Intentionality." In *The New Husserl: A Critical Reader*, edited by D. Welton, 65–92. Bloomington and Indianopolis: Indiana University Press.

———. 2006. "Phenomenology: Neither Auto- nor Hetero- Be." *Phenomenology and the Cognitive Sciences* 6 (1–2): 57–74.

Duerlinger, James. 2003. *Indian Buddhist Theories of Persons: Vasubandhu's "Refuration of the Theory of Self."* Abingdon, Oxon: RoutledgeCurzon.

Dunne, John. 2004. *Foundations of Dharmakīrti's Philosophy*. Sommerville, Mass.: Wisdom Publications.

———. 2006. "Realizing the Unreal: Dharmakīrti's Theory of Yogic Perception." *Journal of Indian Philosophy* 34: 497–519.

———. 2011. "Key Features of Dharmakirti's Apoha Theory." In *Apoha: Buddhist Nominalism and Human Cognition*, edited by Mark Siderits, Tom Tillemans, and Arindam Chakrabarti, 84–108. New York: Columbia University Press.

Dupuy, Jean-Pierre. 1999. "Philosophy and Cognition: Historical Roots." In *Naturalizing Phenomenology: Issues in Contemporary Phenomenology and Cognitive Science*, edited by Jean Petitot, Francisco J. Varela, Bernard Pachoud, and Jean-Michel Roy, 539–558. Stanford, Calif.: Stanford University Press.

Edelglass, William, and Jay L. Garfield, eds. 2009. *Buddhist Philosophy: Essential Readings*. Oxford, New York: Oxford University Press.

Edelman, Shimon. 1998. "Representation Is Representation of Similarities." *Behavioral and Brain Sciences* 21: 449–498.

Edgerton, F. 1953. *Buddhist Hybrid Sanskrit Grammar and Dictionary*. Vol. II, *Dictionary*. New Haven: Yale University Press.

Ellis, Ralph D. 1995. *Questioning Consciousness: The Interplay of Imagery, Cognition, and Emotion in the Human Brain*. Amsterdam: John Benjamins.

Eltschinger, Vincent. 2001. *Dharmakīrti sur les mantras et la perception du suprasensible*. Vienna: Wiener Studien zur Tibetologie und Buddhismuskunde.

———. 2008. "Pierre Hadot et les 'exercises spirituels': Quel modèle pour la philosophie bouddhique tardive?" *Asiatische Studies/Etudes Asiatique* 62: 485–544.

———. 2009. "On the Career and the Cognition of *Yogins*." In *Yogic Perception, Meditation and Altered States of Consciousness*, edited by Eli Franco, 169–214. Vienna: Verlag der Österreichischen Akademie der Wissenschaften.

Embree, L., E. A. Behnke, D. Carr, J. Claude Evans, J. Huertas-Jourda, J. J. Kockelmans, W. R. McKenna, I. Algis Mickunas, J. N. Mohanty, T. M. Seebohm, and R. M Zaner. 1997. *Encyclopedia of Phenomenology*. Boston, Dordrecht: Kluwer Academic Publishers.

Evans, G. 1982. *The Varieties of Reference*. Edited by J. McDowell. Oxford: Clarendon Press.

Faddegon, B. 1918. *The Vaiçeṣika-System, Described with the Help of the Oldest Texts*. Verhandelingen der Koninklijke Akademie van Wetenschappen te Amsterdam, Afdeeling Letterkunde, Nieuwe Reeks XVIII 2. Amsterdam: Johannes Müller.

Fahle, Manfred, and Tomaso Poggio. 2002. *Perceptual Learning*. Cambridge, Mass.: MIT Press.
Farah, Martha J. 2004. *Visual Agnosia: Disorders of Object Recognition and What They Tell Us about Normal Vision*. 2d ed. Cambridge, Mass.: MIT Press.
Fasching, Wolfgang. 2008. "Consciousness, Self-Consciousness, and Meditation." *Phenomenology and the Cognitive Sciences* 7: 463–483.
______. 2011. "'I am of the Nature of Seeing': Phenomenological Reflections on the Indian Notion of Witness-Consciousness." In *In Self, No Self: Perspectives from Analytical, Phenomenological, and Indian Traditions*, edited by Mark Siderits, Evan Thompson, and Dan Zahavi, 193–216. Oxford: Oxford University Press.
Faure, Bernard. 1993. *Chan Insights and Oversights: An Epistemological Critique of the Chan Tradition*. Princeton, N.J.: Princeton University Press.
Feer, L. 1975–2006. *Saṃyutta Nikāya*. Pali Text Society, London: Oxford University Press.
Fenner, Peter G. 1983. "Candrakīrti's Refutation of Buddhist Idealism." *Philosophy East and West* 33 (3): 251–261.
Filliozat, Pierre-Sylvain. 1975. *Le Mahābhāṣya de Patañjali*. Vols. I–V. Pondichéry: Institute Française d'Indologie.
Flanagan, Owen. 1992. *Consciousness Reconsidered*. Cambridge, Mass.: MIT Press.
______. 2002. *The Problem of the Soul*. New York: Basic Books.
______. 2011. *The Bodhisattva's Brain: Buddhism Naturalized*. Cambridge, Mass.: MIT Press.
Flew, Anthony. 1971. *An Introduction to Western Philosophy: Ideas and Arguments from Plato to Sartre*. London: Thames & Hudson.
Fodor, Jerry A. 1975. *The Language of Thought*. Cambridge, Mass.: Harvard University Press.
______. 1987. *Psychosemantics*. Cambridge, Mass.: MIT Press.
______. 1991. "The Dogma that Didn't Bark (A Fragment of a Naturalized Epistemology)." *Mind* 100: 201–220.
______. 2001. *The Mind Doesn't Work That Way*. Cambridge, Mass.: MIT Press.
______. 2008. *LOT 2: The Language of Thought Revisited*. Oxford: Oxford University Press.
Fodor, Jerry A., and Zenon Pylyshyn. 1981. "How Direct is Visual Perception? Some Reflections on Gibson's Ecological Approach." *Cognition* 9: 139–196.
Foglia, Lucia, and Rick Grush. 2011. "The Limitations of a Purely Enactive (Non-Representational) Account of Imagery." *Journal of Consciousness Studies* 18 (5–6): 35–43.
Foley, Richard. 1994. "Quine and Naturalized Epistemology." *Midwest Studies in Philosophy* 19 (1): 243–260.
Føllesdal, Dagfinn. 1969. "Husserl's Notion of Noema." *Journal of Philosophy* 66: 680–687.
Forman, Robert K. C., ed. 1990. *The Problem of Pure Consciousness*. Oxford: Oxford University Press.
Franco, Eli. 1984. "On the Interpretation of *Pramāṇasamuccaya(vṛtti)* I, 3d." *Journal of Indian Philosophy* 12: 389–400.
______. 1986. "Once Again on Dharmakīrti's Deviation from Dignāga on *Pratyakṣābhāsa*." *Journal of Indian Philosophy* 14: 79–97.
______. 1993. "Did Dignāga Accept Four Types of Perception?" *Journal of Indian Philosophy* 21: 295–299.

———. 1994. *Perception, Knowledge, and Disbelief: A Study of Jayarāśi's Scepticism.* Delhi: Matilal Banarsidass.

———. 1997. *Dharmakīrti on Compassion and Rebirth.* Vienna: Wiener Studien zur Tibetologie und Buddhismuskunde.

———. 1999. "Two Circles or Parallel Lines?" In *Dharmakīrti's Thought and Its Impact on Indian and Tibetan Philosophy: Proceedings of the Third International Dharmakīrti Conference, Hiroshima, November 4–6, 1997,* edited by Shoryu Katsura, 63–72. Vienna: Verlag der Österreichischen Akademie der Wissenschaften.

———. 2009. "Meditation and Metaphysics: On their Mutual Relationship in South Asian Buddhism." In *Yogic Perception, Meditation and Altered States of Consciousness,* edited by Eli Franco, 93–132. Vienna: Verlag der Österreichischen Akademie der Wissenschaften.

Frank, Manfred. 1986. *Die Unhintergebarkeit von Individualität.* Frankfurt am Main: Suhrkamp.

Frauwallner, Erich. 1934. "Dharmakīrtis *Sambandhaparīkṣā*: Text und Übersetzung." *Wirner Zeitschrift für die Kunde des Morgenlandes* 41: 281–304.

———.1951. *On the Date of the Buddhist Master of the Law Vasubandhu.* Rome: Istituto Italiano per il Medio ed Estremo Oriente.

———. 1958. *Die Philosophie des Buddhismus.* Edited by Walter Ruben. Berlin: Akademie-Verlag. Revised edition 1969.

———. 1959. "Dignāga, sein Werk und seine Entwicklung." *Wiener Zeitschrift für die Kunde des Süd- und Ost-Asiens* 3: 83–164.

———. 1961. "Landmarks in the History of Indian Logic." *Wiener Zeitschrift für die Kunde des Süd- und Ost-Asiens* 5: 125–148.

———. 1968. *Materialien zur ältesten Erkenntnislehre der Karmamīmāṃsā.* Vienna: Österreichische Akademie der Wissenschaften.

———. 1995. *Studies in Abhidharma Literature and the Origins of the Buddhist Philosophical Systems.* Albany: State University of New York Press.

Frege, Gottlob. 1960. "On Sense and Reference." Translated by M. Black from "Über Sinn und Bedeutung," *Zeitschrift für Philosophie und philosophische Kritik.* In *Translations from the Philosophical Writings of Gottlob Frege,* edited by P. Geach and M. Black, 56–78. Oxford: Basil Blackwell.

Fumerton, Richard. 1994. "Skepticism and Naturalistic Epistemology." *Midwest Studies in Philosophy* 19 (1): 321–340.

Funayama, Toru. 1992. "A Study of kalpanāpoḍha: A Translation of the *Tattvasaṃgraha* vv. 1212–1263 by Śāntarakṣita and the *Tattvasaṃgrahapañjikā* by Kamalaśīla on the Definition of Direct Perception." *Zinbun* 27: 33–128.

———. 1995. "Arcaṭa, Śāntarakṣita, Jinendrabuddhi, and Kamalaśīla on the Aim of a Treatise." *Wiener Zeitschrift für die Kunde Südasiens* 39: 181–201.

———. 1999. "Kamalaśīla's Interpretation of 'Non-Erroneous' in the Definition of Direct Perception and Related Problems." In *Dharmakīrti's Thought and Its Impact on Indian and Tibetan Philosophy: Proceedings of the Third International Dharmakīrti Conference, Hiroshima, November 4–6, 1997,* edited by Shoryu Katsura, 73–100. Vienna: Verlag der Österreichischen Akademie der Wissenschaften.

———. 2000. "Two Notes on Dharmapāla and Dharmakīrti." *Zinbun* 35: 1–11.

Gadamer, Hans-Georg, 1975. *Wahrheit und Methode: Grundzüge einer philosophischen Hermeneutik.* 5th ed. Tübingen: J. C. B. Mohr. Translated as *Truth and Method.* By G. Barden and J. Cumming. New York: Seabury.

———. 1976. *Philosophical Hermeneutics.* Translated by David E. Linge. Berkeley: University of California Press.

Gallagher, Shaun. 1995. "Body Schema and Intentionality." In *The Body and the Self*, edited by José L. Bermúdez, 225–244. Cambridge, Mass.: MIT Press.

______. 2005. *How the Body Shapes the Mind*. New York: Oxford University Press.

Gallagher, Shaun, and Andrew Meltzoff. 1996. "The Earliest Sense of Self and Others: Merleau-Ponty and Recent Developmental Studies." *Philosophical Psychology* 9 (2): 213–236.

Gallagher, Shaun, and Dan Zahavi. 2008. *The Phenomenological Mind: An Introduction to Philosophy of Mind and Cognitive Science*. London and New York: Routledge.

Ganeri, Jonardon. 1990. "Dharmakīrti on Inference and Properties." *Journal of Indian Philosophy* 18: 237–247.

______. 1999a. *Semantic Powers: Meaning and the Means of Knowing in Classical Indian Philosophy*. Oxford: Clarendon Press.

______. 1999b. "Self-Intimation, Memory and Personal Identity." *Journal of Indian Philosophy* 27: 469–483.

______. 2001. *Philosophy in Classical India*. London, New York: Routledge.

______. 2007. *The Concealed Art of the Soul: Theories of Self and Practices of Truth in Indian Ethics and Epistemology*. Oxford: Oxford University Press.

______. 2011a. "Emergentism, Ancient and Modern." *Mind* 121 (479): 1–33.

______. 2011b. *The Lost Age of Reason: Philosophy in Early Modern India 1450–1700*. Oxford: Oxford University Press.

______. 2012. *The Self: Naturalism, Consciousness, and the First-Person Stance*. Oxford: Oxford University Press.

Gangopadhyaya, Mrinal Kanti. 1971. *Vinītadeva's Nyāyabinduṭīkā. Sanskrit Original Reconstructed from the Extant Tibetan Version with English Translation and Annotations*. Calcutta: Indian Studies, Past and Present.

______. 1982. *Nyāyasūtra with Vātsyāyana's Commentary*. Calcutta: Indian Studies.

Ganguli, H. M. 1963. *Philosophy of Logical Construction: An Examination of Logical Atomism and Logical Positivism in the Light of the Philosophies of Bhartṛhari, Dharmakīrti and Prajñākaragupta*. Calcutta: Sanskrit Pustak Bhandarkar.

Garbe, Richard. 1888. *The Sāṃkhya Sūtra Vṛtti or Aniruddha's Commentary and the Original Parts of Vedāntin Mahādeva's Commentary to the Sāṃkhya Sūtras*. Calcutta: Baptist Mission Press.

Garfield, Jay L. 1990. "Epoché and Śūnyata: Scepticism East and West." *Philosophy East and West* 40 (3): 285–307.

______. 1995. *The Fundamental Wisdom of the Middle Way: Nāgārjuna's Mūlamadhyamakakārikā*. New York, Oxford: Oxford University Press.

______. 2002. *Empty Words: Buddhist Philosophy and Cross-Cultural Interpretation*. Oxford: Oxford University Press.

______. 2006. "The Conventional Status of Reflexive Awareness: What's at Stake in a Tibetan Debate?" *Philosophy East and West* 56 (2): 201–228.

______. 2008. "Turning a Madhyamaka Trick: Reply to Huntington," *Journal of Indian Philosophy* 36 (4): 507–527.

______. 2012. "Ask Not What Buddhism can do for Cognitive Science; Ask what Cognitive Science can do for Buddhism." *Tibet Review* 47 (1): 15–30.

Garfield, Jay L., and William Edelglass. 2011. "Introducton." In *The Oxford Handbook of World Philosophy*, edited by Jay L. Garfield and William Edelglass, 3–8. New York: Oxford University Press.

Garfield, Jay L., and Graham Priest. 2003. "Nāgārjuna and the Limits of Thought." *Philosophy East and West* 53 (1): 1–21.

———. 2009. "Mountains are Just Mountains." In *Pointing at the Moon: Buddhism, Logic, Analytic Philosophy*, edited by Mario D'Amato, Jay L. Garfield, and Tom J. F. Tillemans, 71–82. New York: Oxford University Press.

Garzilli, Enrica. 1996. *Translating, Translations, Translators from India to the West*. Cambridge, Mass.: Harvard University Press.

Gennaro, R. 1996. *Consciousness and Self-Consciousness: A Defense of the Higher-order Thought Theory of Consciousness*. Amsterdam: John Benjamins Publishing Company.

———. 2002. "Jean-Paul Sartre and the HOT Theory of Consciousness." *Canadian Journal of Philosophy* 32: 293–330.

Gethin, Rupert M. L. 1998. *The Foundations of Buddhism*. Oxford: Oxford University Press.

———. 2001. *The Buddhist Path to Awakening*. 2d ed. Oxford: OneWorld.

Gibson, J. J. 1979. *The Ecological Approach to Visual Perception*. Dallas, Tex.: Houghton Mifflin.

Giles, J. 1993. "The No-Self Theory: Hume, Buddhism and Personal Identity." *Philosophy East and West* 43 (2): 175–200.

Gloy, Karen. 1998. *Bewusstseinstheorien: Zur Problematik und Problemgeschichte des Bewusstseins und Selbstbewusstseins*. Freiburg: Alber.

Gnoli, Raniero, ed. 1960. *The Pramāṇavārttikam of Dharmakīrti: The First Chapter with the Autocommentary*. Rome: Serie Orientale Roma 23.

Goldman, Alvin I. 1967. "A Causal Theory of Knowing." *Journal of Philosophy* 64: 357–372.

———. 1992a. *Liaisons: Philosophy Meets the Social and Cognitive Sciences*. Cambridge, Mass.: MIT Press.

———. 1992b. "Empathy, Mind, and Morals." *Proceedings and Addresses of the American Philosophical Association* 66 (3): 17–41.

———. 1993. "Epistemic Folkways and Scientific Epistemology." *Philosophical Issues* 3: 271–285.

———. 2002. *Pathways to Knowledge: Private and Public*. Oxford: Oxford University Press.

———. 2009. "Internalism, Externalism, and the Architecture of Justification." *Journal of Philosophy* 106 (6): 1–30.

Goldstone, R., and L. W. Barsalou. 1998. "Reuniting Perception and Conception." *Cognition* 65: 231–262.

Gombrich, Richard. 1990. "Recovering the Buddha Message." In *The Buddhist Forum*, edited by Tadeusz Skorupski, Vol. 1: 5–20. London: SOAS.

Gómez, Luis O. 1987. "Purifying Gold: The Metaphor of Effort and Intuition in Buddhist Thought and Practice." In *Sudden and Gradual: Approaches to Enlightenment in Chinese Thought*, edited by Peter N. Gregory, 67–165. Honolulu: University of Hawaii Press.

———. 1995. "Unspoken Paradigms: Meanderings through the Metaphors of a Field." *Journal of the International Association of Buddhist Studies* 18 (2): 183–230.

Gregory, Peter N., ed. 1987. *Sudden and Gradual Approaches to Enlightenment in Chinese Buddhism*. Honolulu: University of Hawaii Press.

Griffiths, Paul J. 1986. *On Being Mindless: Buddhist Meditation and the Mind-Body Problem*. LaSalle, Ill.: Open Court.

———. 1999. "What do Buddhists Hope for from Antitheistic Argument?" *Faith and Philosophy* 16 (4): 506–523.

Grzegorczyk, A. 1999. "Is Antipsychologism Still Tenable?" In *Alfred Tarski and the Vienna Circle: Austro-Polish Connections in Logical Empiricism*, edited by J. Wolenski and E. Köhler, 109–114. New York: Cambridge University Press.

Gudmunsen, Chris. 1977. *Wittgenstein and Buddhism*. London: Macmillan.

Gurwitsch, A. 1967. "Husserl's Theory of the Intentionality of Consciousness in Historical Perspective." In *Phenomenology and Existentialism*, edited by Edward N. Lee and Maurice Mandelbaum, 25–57. Baltimore: Johns Hopkins Press.

Gyatso, Janet, ed. 1992. *In the Mirror of Memory: Reflections on Mindfulness and Remembrance in Indian and Tibetan Buddhism*. Albany: State University of New York Press.

Haack, Susan. 1975. "The Relevance of Psychology to Epistemology." *Metaphilosophy* 6 (2): 161–176.

Hacker, Paul. 1958. "Ānvīkṣikī." *Wiener Zeitschrift für die Kunde des Süd- und Ost-Asiens* 2: 54–83.

Hadot, Pierre. 1995. *Philosophy as a Way of Life*. Oxford: Blackwell.

Haidt, J., S. Koller, and M. Dias. 1993. "Affect, Culture, and Morality, or Is It Wrong to Eat Your Dog?" *Journal of Personality and Social Psychology* 65: 613–628.

Halbfass, Wilhelm. 1988. *India and Europe: An Essay in Philosophical Understanding*. Albany: State University of New York Press.

______. 1991. *Tradition and Reflection: Explorations in Indian Thought*. Albany: State University of New York Press.

______. 1992. *On Being and What There Is: Classical Vaiśeṣika and the History of Indian Ontology*. Albany, N.Y.: State University of New York Press.

Hardcastle, V. J. 1995. *Locating Consciousness*. Amsterdam and Philadelphia: John Benjamins.

Hardy, E. 1976–1979. *The Aṅguttara-Nikāya*. Vols. III–V. The Pali Text Society. London: Luzac.

Harman, G. 1990. "The Intrinsic Quality of Experience." In *Philosophical Perspectives 4*, edited by J. Tomberlin, 31–52. Northridge, Calif.: Ridgeview Publishing Company.

Harvey, Peter. 1995. *The Selfless Mind: Personality, Consciousness and Nirvāṇa in Early Buddhism*. Richmond, Surrey: Curzon Press.

Hattori, Masaki. 1965. "*Pratyakṣābhāsa*: Dignāga's View and Dharmakīrti's Interpretation." *Indogaku Shironshū* 6 (7): 122–128.

______. 1968. *Dignāga, On Perception*. Cambridge, Mass.: Harvard University Press.

______. 1977. "The Sautrāntika Background of the *Apoha* Theory." In *Buddhist Thought and Asian Civilization: Essays in Honor of Herbert V. Guenther on his Sixtieth Birthday*, edited by Leslie S. Kawamura and Keith Scott, 47–58. Emeryville, Calif.: Dharma Press.

______. 1980. "*Apoha* and *Pratibhā*." In *Sanskrit and Indian Studies. Festschrift in Honour of Daniel H. H. Ingalls*, edited by M. Nagatomi, B. K. Matilal, and E. Dimock, 61–73. Dordrecht and Boston: D. Reidel Publishing Company.

______. 1993. "Kamalaśīla's Interpretation of Some Verses in the *Vākyakāṇḍa* of Bhartṛhari's *Vākyapadīya*." In *Bhartṛhari, Philosopher and Grammarian*, edited by S. Bhate and J. Bronkhorst, 135–140. Bern: Peter Lang AG.

Hayes, Richard. 1980. "Dignāga's Views on Reasoning (*Svārtānumāna*)." *Journal of Indian Philosophy* 8: 219–277.

______. 1984. "The Question of Doctrinalism in the Buddhist Epistemologists." *Journal of the American Academy of Religion* 52 (4): 645–670.

———. 1987. "On the Reinterpretation of Dharmakīrti's *svabhāvahetu*." *Journal of Indian Philosophy* 15 (4): 319–332.

———. 1988. *Dignāga on the Interpretation of Signs*. Dordrecht: Kluver Academic Publishers.

———. 1993. "Dharmakīrti on *Punarbhava*." In *Studies in Original Buddhism and Mahāyāna Buddhism*, edited by Egaku Maeda, 111–130. Kyōto: Nagata Bunshodo.

———. 1994. "Nāgārjuna's Appeal." *Journal of Indian Philosophy* 22 (4): 299–378.

———. 1995. "Did Buddhism Anticipate Pragmatism?" *Journal of the Faculty of Religious Studies McGill University* 23: 75–88.

———. 1997. "Whose Experience Validates What for Dharmakīrti." In *Relativism, Suffering, and Beyond*, edited by P. Bilimoria and J. N. Mohanty, 105–118. Oxford: Oxford University Press.

Hayes, R., and B. Gillon. 2008. "Dharmakīrti on the Role of Causation in Inference as Presented in *Pramāṇavārttika Svopajñavṛtti* 11–38." *Journal of Indian Philosophy* 36: 335–404.

Hegel, Georg W. F. 1940. *Vorlesungen über die Geschichte der Philosophie*. Edited by J. Hoffmeister. Hamburg: Felix Meiner.

———. 1985. *Introduction to the Lectures on the History of Philosophy*. Translated by T. M. Knox and A. V. Miller. Oxford: Oxford University Press.

Heidegger, Martin. 1986. *Sein und Zeit*. Tübingen: Max Niemeyer.

———. 1996. *Being and Time*. Translated J. Stambauch. Albany: State University of New York Press.

Henry, Michel. 1963. *L'Essence de la manifestation*. Paris: Presses Universitaires de France.

Herzberger, Radhika. 1986. *Bhartṛhari and the Buddhists: An Essay in the Development of Fifth and Sixth Century Indian Thought*. Dordrecht, Boston: D. Reidel Publishing Company.

Hesslow, G. 2002. "Conscious Thought as Simulations of Behavior and Perception." *Trends in Cognitive Science* 6 (6): 242–247.

Hilbert, David R. 2005. "Color Constancy and the Complexity of Color." *Philosophical Topics* 33 (1): 141–158.

Hill, Claire O. 2009. "Husserl and Phenomenology, Experience and Essence." *Analecta Husserliana*, ed. A.-T. Tymieniecka 103 (2): 9–22.

Hirsch, Eric. D. 1976. *The Aims of Interpretation*. Chicago: University of Chicago Press.

———. 1984. "Meaning and Significance Reinterpreted," *Critical Inquiry* 11: 202–215.

Ho, Chien-Hsing. 1996. "How Not to Avoid Speaking: A Free Exposition of Dignāga's Apoha Doctrine." *Journal of Indian Philosophy* 24: 541–562.

Honderich, Ted, ed. 1995. *The Oxford Companion to Philosophy*. Oxford: Oxford University Press.

Horgan, Terence E. 1982. "Supervenience and Microphysics." *Pacific Philosophical Quarterly* 63: 29–43.

———.1984. "Supervenience and Cosmic Hermeneutics." *Southern Journal of Philosophy Supplement* 22 (S1): 19–38.

———.1994. "Naturalism and Intentionality." *Philosophical Studies* 76 (2/3): 301–326.

Horgan, Terence E., and John L. Tienson. 2002. "The Intentionality of Phenomenology and the Phenomenology of Intentionality." In *Philosophy of Mind: Classical and*

Contemporary Readings, edited by David J. Chalmers, 520–533. New York: Oxford University Press.

Horner, Isaline B. 1936. *The Early Buddhist Theory of Man Perfected: A Study of the Arahan Concept and of the Implications of the Aim to Perfection in Religious Life*. London: Routledge & Kegan Paul.

Houben, Jan E. M. 1995. *The Saṃbandha-samuddeśa (Chapter on Relation) and Bhartṛhari's Philosophy of Language*. Groningen: Egbert Forstern.

______. 2002. "The Brahmin Intellectual: History, Ritual and "Time out of Time." *Journal of Indian Philosophy* 30: 463–479.

Hough, Sheridan L. 1997. *Nietzsche's Noontide Friend: The Self as Metaphoric Double*. University Park: Penn State Press.

Hugon, Pascale. 2011. "Is Dharmakīrti Grabbing the Rabbit by the Horns? A Reassessment of the Scope of *Prameya* in Dharmakīrtian Epistemology." *Journal of Indian Philosophy* 39 (4/5): 367–389.

Hulin, M. 1978. *Le Principe de l'ego dans la pensée indienne classique: La Notion d'ahaṃ kāra*. Publication de l'Institut de Civilisation Indienne. Paris: Diffusion E. de Boccard.

Hume, David. 1999. *An Inquiry Concerning Human Understanding*. New York: Oxford University Press.

______. 2000. *A Treatise of Human Nature*. Edited D. F. Norton. Oxford: Oxford University Press.

Huntington, C. 2007. "The Nature of the Mādhyamika Trick." *Journal of Indian Philosophy* 35: 103–131.

Hurley, S. L. 1998. *Consciousness in Action*. Cambridge, Mass.: Harvard University Press.

Husserl, Edmund. 1950. *Cartesianische Meditationen und Pariser Vorträge*. Edited by S. Strasser. The Hague: Martinus Nijhoff.

______. 1952. *Ideen zu einer reinen Phänomenologie und phänomenologischen Philosophie: Erstes Buch*. Edited by Karl Schuhmann. The Hague: Martinus Nijhoff.

______. 1954. *Die Krisis der europäischen Wissenschaften und die transzendentale Phänomenologie: Eine Einleitung in die phänomenologische Philosophie*. Edited by W. Biemel. The Hague: Martinus Nijhoff.

______. 1962. *Phäenomenologische Psychologie*, Husserliana IX. The Hague: Martinus Nijhoff; *Phenomenological Psychology: Lectures, Summer Semester, 1925*, trans. by J. Scanlon. The Hague: Martinus Nijhoff, 1977.

______. 1966. *Analysen zur passiven Synthesis: Aus Vorlesungs und Forschungs manuskripten 1918–1926*, edited by Margot Fleischer. Husserliana, Vol. II. The Hague: Martinus Nijhoff.

______. 1969. *Formal and Transcendental Logic*. Translated by D. Cairns. The Hague: Martinus Nijhoff.

______. 1970a. *The Crisis of European Sciences and Transcendental Phenomenology*. Translated by David Carr. Evanston, Ill.: Northwestern University Press.

______. 1970b. *Logical Investigations*. Vol. I. Translated by J. N. Findlay. London: Routledge: and Kegan Paul.

______. 1973a. *Experience and Judgment*. Translated by S. Churchill. Evanston, Ill.: Northwestern University Press.

______. 1973b. *Zur Phänomenologie der Intersubjectivität, Zweiter Teil: 1921–1928*. Edited by Iso Kern. Husserliana, Vol. XIV. The Hague: Martinus Nijhoff.

______. 1977. *Cartesian Meditations: An Introduction to Phenomenology*. Translated by D. Cairns. Dordrecht: Kluwer Academic Publishers.

———. 1978. *Formal and Transcedental Logic*. Translated by D. Cairns. The Hague: Martinus Nijhoff.

———. 1983. *Ideas Pertaining to a Pure Phenomenology and to a Phenomenological Philosophy*. Vol. I. Translated by Frank Kersten. Dordrecht: Kluwer Academic Publishers.

———. 1989. *Ideas Pertaining to a Pure Phenomenology and to a Phenomenological Philosophy*. Vol. II. Translated by R. Rojcewicz and A. Schuwer. Dordrecht: Kluwer Academic Publishers.

———. 2001. *Logical Investigations*. Vol. II. Translated by J. N. Findlay. London: Routledge.

———. 2003. *Transzendentaler Idealismus: Texte aus dem Nachlass (1908–1921)*. Husserliana, Vol. XXXIII. Dordrecht: Kluwer Academic Publishers.

———. 2006. *Phantasy, Image Consciousness, and Memory (1898–1925)*. Translated by J. B. Brough. Berlin, Heidelberg, New York: Springer.

Hutchins, E. 1995. *Cognition in the Wild*. Cambridge, Mass.: MIT Press.

Hutto, Daniel D. 2011. "Philosophy of Mind's New Lease on Life: Autopoietic Enactivism Meets Teleosemiotics." *Journal of Consciousness Studies* 18 (5–6): 44–64.

Ichigo, M., ed. 1985. *Madhyamakālaṃkāra of Śāntarakṣita with his own Commentary or Vṛtti and with the Subcommentary or Pañjikā of Kamalaśīla*. Kyoto: Buneido.

———. 1989. "Śāntarakṣita's *Madhyamakālamkāra*." In *Studies in the Literature of the Great Vehicle: Three Mahāyāna Buddhist Texts*, edited by Luis Gómez and Jonathan Silk, 185–188. Ann Arbor: University of Michigan.

Inami, M. 1999. "On the Determination of Causality." In *Dharmakīrti's Thought and Its Impact on Indian and Tibetan Philosophy: Proceedings of the Third International Dharmakīrti Conference, Hiroshima, November 4–6, 1997*, edited by Shoryu Katsura, 131–154. Vienna: Verlag der Österreichischen Akademie der Wissenschaften.

Ingalls, Daniel H. H. 1954. "The Comparison of Indian and Western Philosophy." *Journal of Oriental Research* 22: 1–11.

Ingalls, Daniel H. H., Jeffrey M. Masson, and M. P. Patwardhan. 1990. *The Dhvanyāloka of Ānandavardhana with the Locana of Abhinavagupta*. Cambridge, Mass.: Harvard University Press.

Iwata, T. 1991. "On the Classification of Three Kinds of Reason in *Pramāṇaviniścaya* III—Reduction of Reasons to *svabhāvahetu* and *kāryahetu*." In *Studies in the Buddhist Epistemological Tradition: Proceedings of the Second International Dharmakīrti Conference*, Vienna, June 11–16, 1989, edited by Ernst Steinkellner, 85–96. Vienna: Verlag der Österreichischen Akademie der Wissenschaften.

Iyengar, H. R. R. 1950. "Bhartṛhari and Diṅnāga." *Journal of the Bombay Royal Asiatic Society* 26: 147–149.

Iyengar, H. R. Rangaswamy, ed. 1952. *Tarkabhāṣā and Vādashtāna of Mokṣākaragupta and Jitāripāda*. Mysore: Government Oriental Library.

Jack, A. I., and A. Roepstorff. 2002. "Introspection and Cognitive Brain Mapping: From Stimulus-Response to Script-Report." *Trends in Cognitive Science* 6 (8): 333–339.

Jackson, David P. 1987. *The Entrance Gate for the Wise: Sa-Skya Paṇḍita on Indian and Tibetan Traditions of Pramāṇa and Philosophyical Debate*. Vienna: Wiener Studien zur Tibetologie und Buddhismuskunde.

Jackson, Roger R. 1988. "The Buddha as *Pramāṇabhūta:* Epithets and Arguments in the Buddhist 'Logical' Tradition." *Journal of Indian Philosophy* 16: 335–365.

______. 1989. "Matching Concepts: Deconstructive and Foundationalist Tendencies in Buddhist Thought." *Journal of the American Academy of Religion* 57 (3): 561–589.

______. 1990. "Luminous Mind among the Logicians: An Analysis of *Pramāṇavārttika* II: 205–11." In *Buddha Nature: A Festschrift in Honour of Minoru Kiyota*, edited by Paul J. Griffiths and J. P. Keenan, 95–123. Las Vegas: Buddhist Books International.

______. 1993. *Is Enlightenment Possible? Dharmakīrti and rGyal tshab rje on Knowledge, Rebirth, No-Self and Liberation*. Ithaca, N.Y.: Snow Lion.

Jain, Padmanabh S., ed. 1977. *Abhidharmadīpa with Vibhāṣāprabhāvṛtti: Critically Edited with Notes and Introduction*. Patna, Kashi Prasad Jayaswal Research Institute.

Jambuvijaya, Muni. 1961. *Vaiśeṣikasūtra of Kaṇāda: With the Commentary of Candrānanda*. Baroda: Gaekwad Oriental Series 136.

______. 1966. *Dvādaśāraṃ Nayacakram of Ācārya Śrī Mallavādi Kṣamāśramaṇa with the Commentary Nyāyāgamānusāriṇī of śrī Siṃhasūri Gaṇi Vādi Kṣamāśramaṇa* Part I (1–4 Aras) Bhavnagar.

James, William. 1907. *Pragmatism*. Cambridge, Mass.: Harvard University Press.

Janzen, Greg. 2008. *The Reflexive Nature of Consciousness*. Amsterdam and Philadelphia: John Benjamins Publishing Company.

Jayatilleke, K. N. 1963. *Early Buddhist Theory of Knowledge*. London: George Allen and Unwin.

Jetly, J. 1971. *Praśastapādabhāṣyam with the Commentary Kiraṇāvalī of Udayanāchārya*. Gaekwad Oriental Research Institute 154. Baroda: Oriental Institute.

Jhā, Gaṇgānātha. tr. 1915. *Nyāya-Sūtras of Gautama with with Vātsyāyana's Bhāṣya and Uddyotakara's Vārttika*. Allahabad: Belvedere Stream Printing Works.

______. 1937–1939. *The Tattvasaṃgraha of Shāntarakṣita With the Commentary of Kamalaśīla*. Vols. I–II. Baroda: Gaekwad Oriental Series (reprint Delhi: Motilal Banarsidass, 1986).

Kajiyama, Y. 1965. "Controversy between the Sākāra- and Nirākāra-vādins of the Yogācāra School—Some Materials." *Journal of Indian and Buddhist Studies* 14 (1): 418–429 (reprinted in Kajiyama 1989: 389–400).

______. 1989. *Studies in Buddhist Philosophy: Selected Papers*. Edited by K. Mimaki et al. Kyoto: Rinsen & Co., Ltd.

______. 1998. *An Introduction to Buddhist Philosophy: An Annotated Translation of the Tarkabhāṣā of Mokṣākaragupta*. Vienna: Arbeitskreis für Tibetische und Buddhistische Studien, Universität Wien.

Kalupahana, David J. 1986. *Nāgājuna: The Philosophy of the Middle Way*. Albany, N.Y.: State University of New York Press.

______. 1987. *The Principles of Buddhist Psychology*. Albany, N.Y.: State University of New York Press.

Kant, Immanuel. 1998. *Critique of Pure Reason*. Translated by P. Guyer and A. W. Wood. Cambridge: Cambridge University Press.

Kapstein, Matthew. 2001. *Reason's Traces: Identity and Interpretation in Indian and Tibetan Buddhist Thought*. Somerville, Mass.: Wisdom.

Kaski, D. 2002. "Revision: Is the Visual Perception a Requisite for Visual Imagery?" *Perception* 31: 717–731.

Katsura, Shōryū. 1979. "The Apoha Theory of Dignāga." *Journal of Indian and Buddhist Studies* 28 (1): 16–20.

______. 1983. "Diṅnāga on Trairūpya." *Journal of Indian and Buddhist Studies* 32 (1): 544–538.

———. 1984. "Dharmakīrti's Theory of Truth." *Journal of Indian Philosophy* 12: 215–235.

———. 1991. "Dignāga and Dharmakīrti on Apoha." In *Studies in the Buddhist Epistemological Tradition: Proceedings of the Second International Dharmakīrti Conference*, Vienna, June 11–16, 1989, edited by Ernst Steinkellner, 129–146. Vienna: Verlag der Österreichischen Akademie der Wissenschaften.

———. 1993. "On Perceptual Judgment." In *Studies in Buddhism in Honour of Professor A. K. Warder*, edited by W. K. Wagle and F. Watanabe, 66–75. Toronto: University of Toronto.

———. 2004. "The Role of *Dṛṣṭanta* in Dignāga's Logic." In *The Role of the Example (Dṛṣṭanta) in Classical Indian Logic*, Vol. 58 of *Wiener Studien zur Tibetologie und Buddhismuskunde*, edited by S. Katsura, and E. Steinkellner, 135–173. Arbeitskreis für tibetische und buddhistische Studien Universität Wien.

———. 2007. "How Did Buddhists Prove Something? The Nature of Buddhist Logic." *Pacific World* 3 (9): 63–84.

Katz, J. 1998. *Realistic Rationalism*. Cambridge, Mass.: MIT Press.

Keijzer, F., and M. Schouten. 2007. "Embedded Cognition and Mental Causation: Setting Empirical Bounds on Metaphysics." *Synthese* 158: 109–125.

Keira, R. 2004. *Mādhyamika and Epistemology: A Study of Kamalaśīla's Method for Proving the Voidness of All Dharmas*. Vienna: Wiener Studien zur Tibetologie und Buddhismuskunde.

Kellner, Birgit. 1997. *Nichts bleibt nichts. Die buddhistische Kritik an Kumārilas abhāvapramāṇa. Übersetzung und Interpretation von Śāntarakṣita Tattvasaṃgraha vv. 1647–1690 mit Kamalaśīlas Panjīkā*. Vienna: Wiener Studien zur Tibetologie und Buddhismuskunde.

———. 1999. "Levels of (Im)perceptibility: Dharmottara's Views on the *Dṛśya* in *Dṛśyānupalabdhi*." In *Dharmakīrti's Thought and Its Impact on Indian and Tibetan Philosophy: Proceedings of the Third International Dharmakīrti Conference, Hiroshima, November 4–6, 1997*, edited by Shoryu Katsura, 193–208. Vienna: Verlag der Österreichischen Akademie der Wissenschaften.

———. 2010. "Self-Awareness (*Svasaṃvedana*) in Dignāga's *Pramāṇasamuccaya* and *-vṛtti*: A Close Reading." *Journal of Indian Philosophy* 38: 203–231.

———. 2011. "Self-awareness (*Svasaṃvedana*) and Infinite Regresses: A Comparison of Arguments by Dignāga and Dharmakīrti." *Journal of Indian Philosophy* 39 (4–5): 411–426.

Kelly, J. 1993. "Meaning and the Limits of Analysis: Bhartṛhari and the Buddhists, and Post-structuralism." In *Bhartṛhari, Philosopher and Grammarian*, edited by S. Bhate and J. Bronkhorst, 171–194. Bern: Peter Lang AG (reprint Delhi: Motilal Banarsidass, 1994).

Kelly, Sean. 2010. "The Normative Nature of Perceptual Experience." In *Perceiving the World*, edited by Bence Nanay, 146–159. Oxford: Oxford University Press.

Kielhorn, F. 1962–1972. *Vyākaraṇa-Mahābhāṣya*. 3d ed. Edited by K.V. Abhyankar. Poona: Bhandarkar Oriental Research Institute.

Kim, J. 1984. "Concepts of Supervenience." *Philosophy and Phenomenological Research* 45: 153–176.

———. 1988. "What is 'Naturalized Epistemology'?" In *Philosophical Perspectives II: Epistemology*, edited by J. E. Tomberlin, 381–406. Atascadero, Calif.: Ridgeview Publishing Company.

______. 1993. *Supervenience and Mind*. Cambridge: Cambridge University Press.

Kitagawa, H. 1965. "A Study of a Short Treatise Ascribed to Dignāga." *Sino-Indian Studies* 5: 3–4.

Klein, A. 1986. *Knowledge and Liberation: Tibetan Buddhist Epistemology in Support of Transformative Religious Experience*. Ithaca, N.Y.: Snow Lion.

______. 1991. *Knowing, Naming and Negation: A Sourcebook on Tibetan Sautrāntika*. Ithaca, N.Y.: Snow Lion.

Knobe, Joshua, and Shaun Nichols, eds. 2008. *Experimental Philosophy*. New York: Oxford University Press.

Kochumutton, Thomas A. 1982. *A Buddhist Doctrine of Experience: A New Translation of the Works of Vasubandhu the Yogācārin*. Delhi: Motilal Banarsidass.

Konkle, Talia, and Aude Oliva. 2006. "Normative Representation of Objects: Evidence for an Ecological Bias in Object Perception and Memory." *Proceedings of the 29th Annual Meeting of the Cognitive Science Society*. 407–412.

Kornblith, Hillary, ed. 1997. *Epistemology Naturalized*. Cambridge, Mass.: MIT Press.

______. 1999. "In Defense of Naturalized Epistemology." In *The Blackwell Guide to Epistemology*, edited by J. Greco and E. Sosa, 158–169. Oxford: Blackwell.

______. ed. 2001. *Epistemology: Internalism and Externalism*. Oxford: Blackwell.

______. 2002. *Knowledge and Its Place in Nature*. Oxford: Oxford University Press.

Kosslyn, Stephen. 1980. *Image and Mind*. Cambridge, Mass.: Harvard University Press.

______. 1994. *Image and Brain: The Resolution of the Imagery Debate*. Cambridge, Mass.: MIT Press.

Krasser, Helmut. 1991. *Dharmottaras kurze Untersuchung der Gültigkeit einer Erkenntnis. Laghupramāṇyaparīkṣā*. Vols. I–II. Vienna: Verlag der Österreichischen Akademie der Wissenschaften.

______. 1992. "On the Relationship between Dharmottara, Śāntarakṣita and Kamalaśīla." In *Tibetan Studies: Proceedings of the 5th Seminar of the International Association of Tibetan Studies*, 151–158. Narita.

______. 1995. "Dharmottara's Theory of Knowledge in his *Laghupramāṇyaparīkṣā*." *Journal of Indian Philosophy* 23: 247–271.

______. 2001. "On Dharmakīrti's Understanding of *Pramāṇabhūta* and His Definition of *Pramāṇa*." *Wiener Zeitschrift für die Kunde Südasiens* 45: 173–199.

______. 2003. "On the Ascertainment of Validity in the Buddhist Epistemological Tradition." *Journal of Indian Philosophy* 31: 161–184.

Krasser, Helmut, and Ernst Steinkellner. 1989. *Dharmottaras Exkursus zur Definition gültiger Erkenntnis im Pramāṇaviniścaya: Materialien zur Definition gültiger Erkenntnis in der Tradition Dharmakīrtis I. Tibetischer Text, Sanskritmaterialen und Übersetzung*. Beiträge zur Kultur- und Geistesgeschichte Asiens 2. Vienna: Verlag der Österreichischen Akademie der Wissenschaften.

Kriegel, U. 2003a. "Consciousness as Sensory Quality and as Implicit Self-Awareness." *Phenomenology and the Cognitive Sciences* 2: 1–26.

______. 2003b. "Consciousness as Intransitive Self-Consciousness: Two Views and an Argument." *Canadian Journal of Philosophy* 33: 103–132.

______. 2004. "Consciosness and Self-Consciousness." *The Monist* 87: 182–205.

______. 2009. *Subjective Consciousness: A Self-Representational Theory*. New York: Oxford University Press.

______. 2011. *The Sources of Intentionality*. New York: Oxford University Press.

Krishnamacharya, Embar, ed. 1926. *Tattvasaṃgraha of Śāntarakṣita with the Commentary of Kamalaśīla*. Vols. I–II. Baroda: Gaekwad Oriental Series.

Krueger, J. W. 2011. "The Who and the How of Experience." In *Self, No Self: Perspectives from Analytical, Phenomenological, and Indian Traditions*, edited by M. Siderits, E. Thompson, and D. Zahavi, 27–78. Oxford: Oxford University Press.

Kumari, Kamala. 1987. *Notion of Truth is Buddhism and Pragmatism*. Delhi: Capital Publishing House.

Kunjunni Raja, K. 1963. *Indian Theories of Meaning*. Madras: The Adyar Library.

Kusch, M. 2007. "Psychologism." *The Stanford Encyclopedia of Philosophy* (Winter 2009 Edition), Edward N. Zalta (ed.), URL = http://plato.stanford.edu/archives/win2009/entries/psychologism/.

Laine, Joy. 1998. "Udayana's Refutation of the Buddhist Thesis of Momentariness in the *Ātmatattvaviveka*." *Journal of Indian Philosophy* 26 (1): 51–97.

Lakoff, George. 1987. *Women, Fire, and Dangerous Things: What Categories Reveal about the Mind*. Chicago: University of Chicago Press.

Lakoff, George, and M. Johnson. 1980. *Metaphors We Live By*. Chicago: University of Chicago Press.

———. 1999. *Philosophy in the Flesh: The Embodied Mind and Its Challenge to Western Thought*. New York: Basic Books.

Lamotte, Étienne. 1936. *Karmasiddhiprakaraṇa: Le Traité de l'acte de Vasubandhu*. Bruxelles: Mélanges Chinois et Bouddhique.

———. 1938. *La Somme du Grand Véhicule d'Asaṅga (Mahāyānasaṃgraha)*. Vols. I–II. Louvain-la-Neuve: Université de Louvain.

Larson, Jerry, and Eliot Deutsch. 1989. *Interpreting Across Boundaries: New Essays in Comparative Philosophy*. Delhi: Motilal Banarsidass.

Lasic, H. 1999. "Dharmakīrti and His Successors on the Determination of Causality." In *Dharmakīrti's Thought and Its Impact on Indian and Tibetan Philosophy: Proceedings of the Third International Dharmakīrti Conference, Hiroshima, November 4–6, 1997*, edited by Shoryu Katsura, 233–242. Vienna: Verlag der Österreichischen Akademie der Wissenschaften Katsura.

Laurence, Stephen, and Eric Margolis. 1999. "Concepts and Cognitive Science." In *Concepts: Core Readings*, edited by E. Margolis and S. Laurence, 3–81. Cambridge, Mass.: MIT Press.

———. 2003. "Concepts and Conceptual Analysis." *Philosophy and Phenomenological Research* 67 (2): 253–282.

———. 2007. "The Ontology of Concepts—Abstract Objects or Mental Representations." *Noûs* 41 (4): 561–593.

La Vallée Poussin, Louis de. 1903–13/1970. *Mūlamadhyamakakārikās (Madhyamikasūtras) de Nāgārjuna: Avec la Prasannapadā, Commentaire de Candrakīrti*. St Petersburgh: Bibliotheca Buddhica IV.

———. 1912. *Madhyamakāvatāra* par Candrakīrti. St Petersburgh: Bibliotheca Buddhica IX.

———. 1923–31/1984. *L'Abhidharmakośa de Vasubandhu*. Paris: Paul Greuthner.

Lévi, Sylvain. 1925. *Vijñaptimātratāsiddhi. Deux traités de Vasubandhu: Viṃśatikā et Triṃśikā*. Paris: Bibliothèque de l'École des Hautes Études.

Levine, Joseph. 1983. "Materialism and Qualia: The Explanatory Gap." *Pacific Philosophical Quarterly* 64: 354–361.

Lindtner, Christian. 1980. "Apropos Dharmakīrti—Two New Works and a New Date." *Acta Orientalia* 41: 27–37.

———. 1984. "Marginalia to Dharmakīrti's Pramāṇaviniścaya I–II." *Wiener Zeitschrift für die Kunde Südasiens* 28: 149–175.

———. 1993. "Linking up Bhartṛhari and the Bauddhas." In *Bhartṛhari, Philosopher and Grammarian*, edited by S. Bhate and J. Bronkhorst, 195–214. Bern: Peter Lang AG (reprint Delhi: Motilal Banarsidass, 1994).

———. 1997. "Cittamātra in Indian Mahāyāna until Kamalaśīla." *Wiener Zeitschrift für die Kunde des Süd- und Ost-Asiens* 41: 159–206.

Locke, John. 1964. *An Essay Concerning Human Understanding*. London: Collins.

Lopez, Donald S., ed. 1988. *Buddhist Hermeneutics*. Kuroda Institute.

Lowe, E. J. 1995. "There Are No Easy Problems of Consciousness." *Journal of Consciousness Studies* 2 (3): 266–271.

———. 2008. *Personal Agency: The Metaphysics of Mind and Action*. Oxford: Oxford University Press.

Lusthaus, Dan. 2002. *Buddhist Phenomenology: A Philosophical Investigation of Yogācāra Buddhism and the Chéng wei-shih lun*. London: Routledge Curzon.

Lutz, Antoine, John Dunne, and Richard Davidson. 2007. "Meditation and the Neuroscience of Cognition." In *The Cambridge Handbook of Consciousness*, edited by P. Zelazo, M. Moscovitch, and E. Thompson, 499–554. Cambridge: Cambridge University Press.

Lycan, W. 1996. *Consciousness and Experience*. Cambridge, Mass.: MIT Press.

———. 2006. "Representational Theories of Consciousness." *The Stanford Encyclopedia of Philosophy* (Fall 2008 Edition), Edward N. Zalta (ed.), URL = http://plato.stanford.edu/archives/fall2008/entries/consciousness-representational/.

Mack, Arien, and Irvin Rock. 1998. *Inattentional Blindness*. Cambridge, Mass.: MIT Press.

MacKenzie, Matthew. 2007. "The Illumination of Consciousness: Approaches to Self-Awareness in the Indian and Western Traditions," *Philosophy East and West* 57 (1): 40–62.

———. 2010. "Enacting the Self: Buddhist and Enactivist Approaches to the Emergence of the Self." *Phenomenology and the Cognitive Sciences* 9: 75–99.

Macpherson, F., and J. L. Bermúdez. 1998. "Nonconceptual Content and the Nature of Perceptual Experience." *Electronic Journal of Analytic Philosophy* 6.

Magliola, Robert. 1984. *Derrida on the Mend*. West Lafayette, Ind.: Purdue University Press.

Malvania, D. D., ed. 1955. *Nyāyabindu of Dharmakīrti with the Nyāyabinduṭīkā of Dharmottara and Durvekamiśra's Dharmottarapradīpa*. Patna: Kashi Prasad Jayaswal Research Institute.

Mangan, Bruce. 1993. "Taking Phenomenology Seriously: The 'Fringe' and its Implications for Cognitive Research." *Consciousness and Cognition* 2: 89–108.

———. 2001. "Sensation's Ghost: The Non-Sensory 'Fringe' of Consciousness." *Psyche* 7 (18). http://www.theassc.org/files/assc/2509.pdf (accessed May 20, 2011).

Mapelli, Daniela, and Marlene Behrmann. 1997. "The Role of Color in Object Recognition: Evidence from Visual Agnosia." *Neurocase* 3: 237–247.

Marcel, A. J. 2003. "Introspective Report." *Journal of Consciousness Studies* 10 (9/10): 167–186.

Margolis, Eric, and Stephen Laurence, eds. 1999. *Concepts: Core Readings*. Cambridge, Mass.: MIT Press.

———. 2007. *Creations of the Mind: Theories of Artifacts and their Representation*. Oxford: Oxford University Press.

Matilal, Bimal K. 1971. *Epistemology, Logic and Grammar in Indian Philosophical Analysis*. The Hague: Mouton.

———. 1985. *Logic, Language, and Reality: Indian Philosophy and Contemporary Issues*. Delhi: Motilal Banarsidass.

———. 1986. *Perception: An Essay on Classical Indian Theories of Knowledge*. Oxford: Oxford University Press.

———. 1988. "Śābdabodha and the Problem of Knowledge-Representation in Sanskrit." *Journal of Indian Philosophy* 16: 107–122.

———. 1990. *The Word and the World: India's Contribution to the Study of Language*. Delhi: Oxford University Press.

———. 1991. "Dharmakīrti and the Universally Negative Inference." In *Studies in the Buddhist Epistemological Tradition: Proceedings of the Second International Dharmakīrti Conference*, Vienna, June 11–16, 1989, edited by Ernst Steinkellner, 161–168. Vienna: Verlag der Österreichischen Akademie der Wissenschaften.

———. 1998. *The Character of Logic in India*. Edited by J. Ganeri and H. Tiwari. Oxford: Oxford University Press.

———. 2002a. *Philosophy, Culture, Religion: The Collected Essays of Bimal Krishna Matilal*. Edited by J. Ganeri. Oxford, Delhi: Oxford University Press.

———. 2002b. "*Pramāna* as Evidence." Reprinted as "On the Concept of Philosophy in India," in *Mind, Language and World*, chap. 24. Delhi: Oxford University Press.

Matilal, Bimal K., and Arindam Chakrabarti, eds. 1994. *Knowing from Words: Western and Indian Philosophical Analysis of Understanding and Testimony*. Dordrecht, Boston: Kluwer Academic Publishers.

Matilal, Bimal K., and R. D. Evans, eds. 1986. *Buddhist Logic and Epistemology: Studies in the Buddhist Analysis of Inference and Language*. Dordrecht, Boston: Kluwer Academic Publishers.

Matilal, Bimal K., and J. L. Shaw, eds. 1985. *Analytical Philosophy in Comparative Perspective*. Dordrecht: D. Reidel Publishing Company.

Maturana, Humberto, and Francisco J. Varela. 1980. *Autopoiesis and Cognition: The Realization of the Living*. Dordecht: D. Reidel Publishing Co.

Maund, B. 1995. *Colors: Their Nature and Representation*. Cambridge: Cambridge University Press.

May, Jacques. 1959. *Prasannapadā Madhyamakavrtti: Douze chapitre traduits du sanskrit et du tibétain*. Paris: Adrien-Mainsonneuve.

———. 1971. "La Philosophie bouddhique idéaliste." *Asiatische Studien / Études Asiatiques* 25: 265–323.

McClintock, Sara. 2003. "The Role of the 'Given' in the Classification of Śāntarakṣita and Kamalaśīla as Svātantrika-Mādhyamikas." In *Svātantrika-Prasaṅgika Distinction: What Difference Does It Make?* edited by Georges Dreyfus and Sara McClintock, 125–172. Boston: Wisdom Publications.

———. 2008. "Rhetoric and the Reception Theory of Rationality in the Work of Two Buddhist Philosophers." *Argumentation* 22: 27–41.

———. 2010. *Omniscience and the Rhetoric of Reason: Śāntarakṣita and Kamalaśīla on Rationality, Argumentation, and Religious Authority*. Somerville, Mass.: Wisdom.

McDermott, A. C. S. 1970. "Empty Subject Terms in Late Buddhist Logic." *Journal of Indian Philosophy* 1: 22–29.

McDowell, John. 1994. *Mind and World*. Cambridge, Mass.: Harvard University Press.

McGinn, Colin. 1991. *The Problem of Consciousness*. Oxford: Blackwell.

McIntyre, R. 1986. "Husserl and the Representational Theory of Mind." *Topoi* 5: 101–113.

______. 1999. "Naturalizing Phenomenology? Dretske on Qualia." In *Naturalizing Phenomenology*, edited by J. Petitot, F. J. Varela, B. Pachoud, and J. M. Roy, 429–439. Stanford, Calif.: Stanford University Press.

McLaughlin, Brian. 2003. "The Place of Color in Nature." In *Colour Perception: Mind and the Physical World*, edited by R. Mausfeld and D. Heyer, 475–502. New York: Oxford University Press.

McRae, John. R. 1986. *The Northern School and the Formation of Early Ch'an Buddhism*. Honolulu: University of Hawaii Press.

______.1987. "Shen-hui and the Teaching of Sudden Enlightenment in Early Ch'an Buddhism." In *Sudden and Gradual: Approaches to Enlightenment in Chinese Thought*, edited by Peter N. Gregory, 227–278. Honolulu: University of Hawaii Press.

Meiland, J. 1976. "Psychologism in Logic: Husserl's Critique." *Inquiry* 19: 325–339.

Meindersma, T. E. 1991. "A Brief Reference to *Apoha* Theory in the Section on *Paralokasiddhi* in *Pramāṇavārttika*." In *Studies in the Buddhist Epistemological Tradition: Proceedings of the Second International Dharmakīrti Conference*, Vienna, June 11–16, 1989, edited by Ernst Steinkellner, 169–174. Vienna: Verlag der Österreichischen Akademie der Wissenschaften.

Merikle, P. M., and M. Daneman. 1996. "Memory for Unconsciously Perceived Events: Evidence from Anesthetized Patients." *Consciousness and Cognition* 5: 525–541.

Merikle, P. M., and S. Joordens. 1997. "Measuring Unconscious Influences." In *Scientific Approaches to Consciousness*, edited by J. D. Cohen and J. W. Schooler, 109–123. Mahwah, N.J.: Erlbaum.

______. 1998. " Psychological Investigations of Unconscious Perception." *Journal of Consciousness Studies* 5: 5–18.

Merleau-Ponty, Maurice. 1945. *Phénoménologie de la perception*. Paris: Gallimard.

______. 1962. *Phenomenology of Perception*. Translated by C. Smith. London: Routledge.

______. 1963. *The Structure of Behavior*. Translated by A. Fischer. Pittsburgh, Penn.: Dusquene University Press.

______. 1968. *The Visible and the Invisible*. Translated by A. Lingis. Evanston, Ill.: Northwestern University Press.

Mikogami, E. 1979. "Some Remarks on the Concept of Arthakriyā." *Journal of Indian Philosophy* 7: 79–94.

Milner, D., and M. Goodale. 1995. *The Visual Brain in Action*. Oxford: Oxford University Press.

Mimaki, K. 1976. *La Réfutation bouddhique de la permanence des choses (sthirasiddhidūṣaṇa) et la preuve de la momentané*. Paris: Publication de l'Institut de Civilisation Indienne.

Mistry, F. 1981. *Nietzsche and Buddhism: Prolegomenon to a Comparative Study*. Berlin, New York: de Gruyter.

Miyasaka, Y. E. 1971–1972. "*Pramāṇa-vārttika-kārikā* (Sanskrit and Tibetan) Chapter 2, 3, 4." *Acta Indologica* 2: 1–206.

Mohanty, Jitendra Nath. 1972. *The Concept of Intentionality*. St Louis, Mo.: Warren Green.

______. 1980. "Understanding Some Ontological Differences in Indian Philosophy." *Journal of Indian Philosophy* 8 (3): 205–217.

______. 1985. "Psychologism in Indian Logical Theory." In *Analytical Philosophy in Comparative Perspective*, edited by Bimal K. Matilal and J. L. Shaw, 203–212. Dordrecht: D. Reidel Publishing Company.

———. 1986. "Levels of Understanding Intentionality." *The Monist* 69 (4): 505–520.
———. 1992a. "Indian Epistemology." In *A Companion to Epistemology*, edited by Jonathan Dancy, Ernst Sosa, and Matthias Steup, 434–438. Oxford: Wiley-Blackwell.
———. 1992b. *Reason and Tradition in Indian Thought*. Oxford: Clarendon Press.
———. 1992c. "On Matilal's Understanding of Indian Philosophy." *Philosophy East and West* 42 (2): 397–406.
———. 2000. *Classical Indian Philosophy*. Lanham, Md.: Rowman and Littlefield.
———. 2002. *Explorations in Philosophy: Western Philosophy*. Essays by J. N. Mohanty. Edited by B. Gupta. New Delhi: Oxford University Press.
Mookerjee, Satkari. 1935. *The Buddhist Philosophy of Universal Flux: An Exposition of the Philosophy of Critical Realism as Expounded by the School of Dignāga*. Calcutta: University of Calcutta.
Moriyama, S. 1984. "The Yogācāra-Madhyamika Refutation of the Position of the Satyākāra and Alīkākāra-vādins of the Yogācāra School—A Translation of Portions of Haribhadra's *Abhisamayālaṃkārāloka Prajñāpāramitāvyākhyā*." In *Bukkyō Daigaku Daigakuin Kenkyū Kiyō (Memoirs of the Postgraduate Research Institute*, Bukkyō University) Part I (Mar. 1984): 1–58; Part II (Oct. 1984): 1–35; Part III (Dec. 1984): 1–28.
Morris, Charles. 1971. *Writings on the General Theory of Signs*. The Hague: Mouton.
Morris, Richard. 1989–1995. *The Aṅguttara-Nikāya*. Vols. I–II. The Pali Text Society. London: Luzac.
Much, M. T. 1991. *Dharmakīrti's Vādanyāyaḥ*. Vols. I–II. Vienna: Verlag der Österreichische Akademie der Wissenschaften.
Mukhopadhyay, P. K. 1984. *Indian Realism*. Calcutta: K. P. Bagchi.
Murti, T. R. V. 1960. *The Central Philosophy of Buddhism: A Study of the Mādhyamika System*. London: George Allen & Unwin.
Nagasaki, H. 1991. "Perception in Pre-Dignāga Buddhist Texts." In *Studies in the Buddhist Epistemological Tradition: Proceedings of the Second International Dharmakīrti Conference*, Vienna, June 11–16, 1989, edited by Ernst Steinkellner, 221–226. Vienna: Verlag der Österreichischen Akademie der Wissenschaften.
Nagatomi, M. 1957. "A Study of Dharmakīrti's Pramāṇavārttika: An English Translation and Annotation of the Pramāṇavārttika Book I." Ph.D. dissertation, Harvard University.
———. 1959. "The Framework of the Pramāṇavārttika, Book One." *Journal of the American Oriental Society* 79: 262–266.
———. 1967–68. "Arthakriyā" in Dr. V. Raghavan Felicitation Volume. Madras: Adyar Library 31–32; 52–72.
———. 1979. "*Mānasa-pratyakṣa*. A Conundrum in the Buddhist Pramāṇa System." In *Sanskrit and Indian Studies: Essays in Honour of Daniel H.H. Ingalls*, edited by M. Nagatomi, B. K. Matilal, J. M. Masson, and E. Dimock, 243–260. Dordrecht: Reidel.
Nagel, T. 1974. "What Is It Like to be a Bat?" *Philosophical Review* 83 (4): 435–450.
———. 1986. *The View from Nowhere*. Oxford: Oxford University Press.
Namai, Ch. M. 1991. "Two Aspects of Paralokasādhana in Dharmakīrtian Tradition." In *Studies in the Buddhist Epistemological Tradition: Proceedings of the Second International Dharmakīrti Conference*, Vienna, June 11–16, 1989, edited by Ernst Steinkellner, 227–242. Vienna: Verlag der Österreichischen Akademie der Wissenschaften.

Ñāṇamoli, Bhikkhu, trans. 1975. *The Path of Purification: Visuddhimagga by Buddhaghoṣa*. Kandy: Buddhist Publication Society. 3d ed. 1991.

______. 1985. *The Magic of the Mind: An Exposition of the Kālakārāma Sutta*. Kandy: Buddhist Publication Society.

______. 1986. *Concept and Reality in Early Buddhist Thought: An Essay on Papañca and Papañca-sañña-saṅkha*. Kandy: Buddhist Publication Society.

______. 1995. *The Middle Length Discourse of the Buddha: A New Translation of the Majjhima Nikāya*. Boston: Wisdom Publications.

Nanay, Bence. 2010. "Philosophy of Perception—The New Wave." In *Perceiving the World*, edited by Bence Nanay, 3–12. Oxford: Oxford University Press.

Neisser, U. 1978. "Anticipations, Images and Introspection." *Cognition* 6: 167–174.

Newen, Albert. 2011. "Merits and Limits of a Philosophy of Autopoiesis." *Journal of Consciousness Studies* 18 (5–6): 65–82.

Newmann, Hanns-Peter. 2004. "Knowledge between Science, Historicism and Ideology: The Problem of the Historiography of the History of Philosophy." Paper delivered at *Philosophy: Problems, Aims, and Responsibility: A Conference to Mark the 10th Anniversary of the Death of Karl Popper*, University of Warwick. 1–9.

Nichols, Shaun, Stephen Stich, and Jonathan Weinberg. 2001. "Metaskepticism: Meditations in Ethno-Epistemology." In *The Skeptics*, edited by S. Luper, 227–247. Burlington, Vt.: Ashgate.

Nisbett, R. E., and L. D. Ross. 1980. *Human Inference: Strategies and Shortcomings of Social Judgment*. Englewood Cliffs, N.J.: Prentice-Hall.

Nisbett, R., K. Peng, I. Choi, and A Norenzayan. 2001. "Culture and Systems of Thought: Holistic vs. Analytic Cognition." *Psychological Review* 108 (2): 291–310.

Noë, A. ed. 2002a. "Is the Visual World a Grand Illusion." *Journal of Consciousness Studies* 9 (5/6): 1–12.

______. 2002b. "On What We See" *Pacific Philosophical Quarterly* 83 (1): 57–80.

______. 2002c. "Is Perspectival Self-Consciousness Nonconceptual?" *Philosophical Quarterly* 52 (207): 185–194.

______. 2004. *Action in Perception*. Cambridge, Mass.: MIT Press.

______. 2007. "The Critique of Pure Phenomenology." *Phenomenology and the Cognitive Sciences* 6 (1–2): 231–245.

Noë, A., and J. K. O'Regan. 2002. "On the Brain-Basis of Visual Consciousness: A Sensorimotor Account." In Noë and Thompson (2002): 567–598.

Noë, A., and E. Thompson, eds. 2002. *Vision and Mind: Selected Readings in the Philosophy of Perception*. Cambridge, Mass.: MIT Press.

______. 2004a. "Are There Neural Correlates of Consciousness?" *Journal of Consciousness Studies* 11: 3–28.

______. 2004b. "Sorting Out the Neural Basis of Consciousness. Authors' Reply to Commentators." *Journal of Consciousness Studies* 11: 87–98.

Nyanaponika Thera. 1965. *Abhidharma Studies: Buddhist Explorations of Consciousness and Time*. Kandy: Buddhist Publication Society. Reprint 1998.

Oberhammer, Gerhard. 1963. "Ein Beitrag zu den Vāda-Traditionen Indiens." *Wiener Zeitschrift für die Kunde Süd- und Ostasiens* 7: 63–103.

Obermiller, E. 1931. "The Sublime Science of the Great Vehicle to Salvation, being a Manual of Buddhist Monism: The Work of Ārya Maitreya with a Commentary by Āryāsaṅga." *Acta Orientalia* 9: 81–306.

O'Brien, Gerald, and John Opie. 1998. "The Disunity of Consciousness." *Australasian Journal of Philosophy* 76: 378–95.

Oetke, Claus. 1988. *"Ich" und das Ich: Analytische Untersuchungen zur buddhistisch-brahmanischen Ātmankontroverse*. Stuttgart: Franz Steiner Verlag.

———. 1991. "Svabhāvapratibandha and the Types of Reasons in Dharmakīrti's Theory of Inference." In *Studies in the Buddhist Epistemological Tradition: Proceedings of the Second International Dharmakīrti Conference*, Vienna, June 11–16, 1989, edited by Ernst Steinkellner, 243–268.Vienna: Verlag der Österreichischen Akademie der Wissenschaften.

———. 1993. *Bemerkungen zur Buddhistischen Doktrin der Momentanheit des Seinden: Dharmakīrti's Sattvānumāna*. Wiener Studien zur Tibetologie und Buddhismuskunde 29 Vienna: Universität Wien.

———. 1994. *Studies on the Doctrine of Trairūpya*. Vienna: Wiener Studien zur Tibetologie und Buddhismuskunde.

Ogawa, H. 1999. "Bhartṛhari on Representations (*buddhyākāra*)." In *Dharmakīrti's Thought and Its Impact on Indian and Tibetan Philosophy: Proceedings of the Third International Dharmakīrti Conference, Hiroshima, November 4–6, 1997*, edited by Shoryu Katsura, 267–286. Vienna: Verlag der Österreichischen Akademie der Wissenschaften.

Omae, F. 1999. "Dharmakīrti as a Varṇavādin." In *Dharmakīrti's Thought and Its Impact on Indian and Tibetan Philosophy: Proceedings of the Third International Dharmakīrti Conference, Hiroshima, November 4–6, 1997*, edited by Shoryu Katsura, 295–300. Vienna: Verlag der Österreichischen Akademie der Wissenschaften Katsura.

Ono, M. 1999. "Dharmakīrti on *asādhāraṇānaikāntika*." In *Dharmakīrti's Thought and Its Impact on Indian and Tibetan Philosophy: Proceedings of the Third International Dharmakīrti Conference, Hiroshima, November 4–6, 1997*, edited by Shoryu Katsura, 301–316. Vienna: Verlag der Österreichischen Akademie der Wissenschaften.

O'Regan, J. K. 1992. "Solving 'Real' Mysteries of Visual Perception: The World as an Outside Memory." *Canadian Journal of Psychology* 46 (3): 461–499.

O'Regan, J. K., and Alva Noë. 2001. "A Sensorimotor Account of Vision and Visual Consciousness." *Behavioral and Brain Sciences* 24 (5): 939–973.

———. 2002. "What It Is Like to See: A Sensorimotor Theory of Perceptual Experience." *Synthese* 29: 79–103.

Palmer, S. 1999. *Vision: From Photons to Phenomenology*. Cambridge, Mass.: MIT Press.

Pandeya, Ram Chandra, ed. 1989. *The Pramāṇavārttikam of Ācārya Dharmakīrti with the Commentaries "Svopajñavṛtti" of the Author and "Pramāṇavārttikavṛtti" of Manorathanandin*. Delhi: Motilal Banarsidass.

Papineau, D. 1993. *Philosophical Naturalism*. Oxford: Blackwell.

———. 1998. "Mind the Gap." In *Philosophical Perspectives, 12: Language, Mind and Ontology*, edited by E. Tomberlin, 373–388. Oxford: Blackwell.

———. 2007. "Naturalism." The Stanford Encyclopedia of Philosophy (Spring 2009 Edition), Edward N. Zalta (ed.), URL = http://plato.stanford.edu/archives/spr2009/entries/naturalism/.

Parnas J. 2000. "The Self and Intentionality in the Pre-psychotic Stages of Schizophrenia: A Phenomenological Study." In *Exploring the Self: Psychopathological and Philosophical Perspectives on Self-awareness*, edited by D. Zahavi, 115–147. Philadelphia: J Benjamins Publishing Company.

Patil, Parimal. 2009. *Against a Hindu God: Buddhist Philosophy of Religion in India*. New York: Columbia University Press.

Peacocke, Christopher. 1979. "Deviant Causal Chains." *Midwest Studies in Philosophy* 4 (1): 123–155.

______. 1986. "Analogue Content." *Aristotelian Society* Supplementary Volume 60: 1–17.

______. 1992. *A Study of Concepts*. Cambridge, Mass.: MIT Press.

Pelletier, F. J., R. Elio, and P. Hanson. 2008. "Is Logic all in our Heads? From Naturalism to Psychologism." *Studia Logica* 86: 1–65.

Perdue, D. E. 1992. *Debate in Tibetan Buddhism*. Ithaca, N.Y.: Snow Lion Publications.

Perelman, C., and Olbrechts-Tyteca, L. 1969. *The New Rhetoric: A Treatise on Argumentation*. Translated by J. Wilkinson and P. Weaver. Notre Dame, Ind.: University of Notre Dame Press.

Perrett, Roy. 2003. "Intentionality and Self-Awareness." *Ratio* 16 (3): 222–235.

Perry, J. 2001. *Possibility, Consciousness and Conceivability*. Cambridge, Mass.: MIT Press, Bradford Books.

Pessoa, L., Thompson, E., and Noë, A. 1998. "Finding Out about Filling In: A Guide to Perceptual Completion for Visual Science and the Philosophy of Perception." *Brain and Behavioral Sciences* 21 (1998): 723–780.

Petitot, J., F. J. Varela, B. Pachoud, and J. Roy. 1999. *Naturalizing Phenomenology: Issues in Contemporary Phenomenology and Cognitive Science*. Stanford, Calif.: Stanford University Press.

Phillips, S. 1995. *Classical Indian Metaphysics: Refutations of Realism and the Emergence of "New Logic."* Chicago: Open Court.

Pickering, J., ed. 1997. *The Authority of Experience: Essays on Buddhism and Psychology*. Richmond, Surrey: Curzon Press.

Pieris, Aloysius, S.J. 1997. "*Cakkhu-viññana* Which is *Dassanamatta*: Visual Perception or Non-Perceptual Vision?" In *Recent Researches in Buddhist Studies: Essays in Honour of Professor Y. Karunadasa*, edited by A. Tilakaratne and K. Abhayawansa, 540–566. Colombo.

Pietersma, H. 2000. *Phenomenological Epistemology*. Oxford: Oxford University Press.

Pind, O. 1991. "Dignāga on *śabdasāmanya* and *śabdaviśeṣa*." In *Studies in the Buddhist Epistemological Tradition: Proceedings of the Second International Dharmakīrti Conference*, Vienna, June 11–16, 1989, edited by Ernst Steinkellner, 269–280. Vienna: Verlag der Österreichischen Akademie der Wissenschaften.

______. 2009. *Dignāga's Philosophy of Language: Dignāga on Anyāpoha*. Vienna: Dissertationsgebiet lt. Studienblatt: Tibetologie und Buddhismuskunde.

Pippin, R. B. 1989. *Hegel's Idealism: The Satisfactions of Self-Consciousness*. Cambridge: Cambridge University Press.

Plantinga, Alvin. 1986. "Epistemic Justification." *Noûs* 20: 3–18.

______. 1993. *Warrant: The Current Debate*. New York: Oxford University Press.

Pollock, S. 1989. "Mīmāṃsa and the Problem of History in Traditional India." *Journal of the American Oriental Society* 109 (4): 603–610.

Popper, Karl R. 2002. *The Poverty of Historicism*. London and New York (first published 1957).

Potter, Karl H. 1963. *Presuppositions of India's Philosophies*. Englewood Cliffs, N.J.: Prentice-Hall. Reprint Delhi: Motilal Banarsidass (1991).

______. 1968–69. "*Astitva, Jñeyatva, Abhideyatva*." *Wiener Zeitschrift für die Kunde Südasiens* 12–13: 275–289.

______. 1984. "Does Indian Epistemology Concern Justified True Belief." *Journal of Indian Philosophy* 12: 307–327.

———. ed. 1977. *Indian Metaphysics and Epistemology: The Tradition of Nyāya-Vaiśeṣika up to Gaṅgeśa*. Encyclopedia of Indian Philosophies. Vol. II. Delhi: Motilal Banarsidass.

Powers, John. 1993. *Hermeneutics and Tradition in the Saṃdhinirmocana-sūtra*. Leiden, New York: E. J. Brill.

———. 1994. "Empiricism and Pragmatism in the Thought of Dharmakīrti," *American Journal of Philosophy and Theology* 59–86.

Pradhan, Prahlad. 1967. *Commentary on the Compendium of Superior Knowledge (Abhidharmakośabhāṣyam)*. Patna: Kashi Prasad Jayaswal Research Institute (revised 2d. ed. A. Haldar, 1975).

Prasad, R. 2002. *Dharmakīrti's Theory of Inference: Revaluation and Reconstruction*. Oxford: Oxford University Press.

Pylyshyn, Z. 1981. "The Imagery Debate: Analogue Media Versus Tacit Knowledge." *Psychological Review* 88: 16–45.

———. 1999. "Is Vision Continuous with Cognition? The Case for Cognitive Impenetrability of Visual Perception." *Behavioral and Brain Sciences* 22: 341–423.

Quine, W. V. O. 1948. "On What There Is." *Review of Metaphysics* 2: 21–38 (reprinted in *From a Logical Point of View*, rev. 2d ed. Cambridge: Harvard University Press, 1980).

———. 1969. "Epistemology Naturalized." In *Ontological Relativity and Other Essays*. New York: Columbia University Press, 69–90.

———. 1978. "Facts of the Matter." *Southwestern Journal of Philosophy* 9 (2): 155–169.

———. 1981. *Theories and Things*. Cambridge, Mass.: Harvard University Press.

Rahula, W. 1971. *Le Compendium de la Super-Doctrine (Philosophie) (Abhidharmasamuccaya) d'Asaṅga*. Paris: Ecole Française d'Extrême-Orient.

Ramachandran, V. S., and W. Hirstein. 1997. "Three Laws of Qualia: Neurology of Consciousness." *Journal of Consciousness Studies* 4: 429–457.

Randle, H. N. 1930. *Indian Logic in the Early Schools*. Oxford: Oxford University Press.

Rani, V. 1982. *The Buddhist Philosophy as Presented in the Mīmāṃsāślokavārttika*. Delhi: Parimal Publications.

Rau, W. 1977. *Bhartṛhari's Vākyapadīya: Die Mūlakārikās*. Abhandlung für die Kunde des Morgenlandes 42, 4. Wiesbaden: Deutsche Morgenländische Gesellschaft.

Rhys Davids, C. A. F. 1904. *The Vibhaṅga. Being the Second Book of the Abhidhamma Piṭaka*. Pāli Text Society. London: Oxford University Press.

———. 1924. *Buddhist Psychology: An Inquiry into the Analysis and Theory of Mind in Pali Literature*. 2d ed. London: Luzac and Co.

Rhys Davids, T. W., and Joseph E. Carpenter. 1995. *Dīgha Nikāya*. Pāli Text Society. London: Oxford University Press.

Ricoeur, P. 1969. *Le Conflit des interprétations: Essais d'herméneutique*. Paris: Editions du Seuil.

Robinson, R. 1957. "Some Logical Aspects of Nāgārjuna's System." *Philosophy East and West* 6 (4): 291–308.

———. 1972. "Did Nāgārjuna Really Refute all Philosophical Views?" *Philosophy East and West* 22 (3): 325–331.

Rorty, R. 1980. *Philosophy and the Mirror of Nature*. Princeton: Princeton University Press.

Rosch, E. 1978. "Principles of Categorization." In *Cognition and Categorization*, edited by Eleanor Rosch and Barbara B. Lloyd, 27–48. Hillsdale, N.J.: Lawrence Erlbaum.

______. 1999. "Reclaiming Concepts." In *Reclaiming Cognition: The Primacy of Action, Intention and Emotion*, edited by R. Nunez and W. J. Freeman. Special issue of the *Journal of Consciousness Studies* 6 (11–12): 61–77.

Rosch, E., and C. B. Mervis. 1975. "Family Resemblances: Studies in the Internal Structure of Categories." *Cognitive Psychology* 7: 573–605.

Rosenthal, D. 1986. "Two Concepts of Consciousness." *Philosophical Studies* 49: 329–359.

______. 1994. "Identity Theories." In *A Companion to the Philosophy of Mind*, edited by S. Guttenplan, 348–355. Oxford: Blackwell.

______. 2002. "Persons, Minds, and Consciousness." In *The Philosophy of Marjorie Grene*, Library of Living Philosophers, Vol. XXIX, edited by Randall E. Auxier and Lewis Edwin Hahn, 199–220. La Salle, Ill.: Open Court.

______. 2003. "Unity of Consciousness and the Self." *Proceedings of the Aristotelian Society* 103 (3): 325–352.

______. 2004. "Being Conscious of Ourselves." *The Monist* 87: 159–181.

Rowlands, M. 2002. "Two Dogmas of Consciousness." *Journal of Consciousness Studies* 9 (5–6): 158–180.

Roy, J.-M. 1999. "Saving Intentional Phenomena: Intentionality, Representation, and Symbol." In *Naturalizing Phenomenology*, edited by J. Petitot, F. J. Varela, B. Pachoud, and J. M. Roy, 111–147. Stanford, Calif.: Stanford University Press.

Roy, J.-M., J. Petitot, B. Pachoud, and F. J. Varela. 1999. "Beyond the Gap: An Introduction to Naturalizing Phenomenology." In *Naturalizing Phenomenology*, edited by J. Petitot, F. J. Varela, B. Pachoud, and J. M. Roy, 1–80. Stanford, Calif.: Stanford University Press.

Ruegg, David Seyfort. 1981. "On the Thesis and Assertion in the Madhyamaka/dBu ma." In *Contributions on Tibetan and Buddhist Philosophy and Religion: Proceedings of the Csoma de Körös Symposium*, edited by Ernst Steinkellner and Helmut Tauscher. Vol II. Vienna: Universität Wien.

______. 1982. "Toward a Chronology of the Madhyamaka School." In *Indology and Buddhist Studies*, edited by L. A. Hercus et al., 505–530. Canberra: Australian National University.

______. 1989a. *Buddha-Nature, Mind and the Problem of Gradualism in a Comparative Perspective: On the Transmission and Reception of Buddhism in India and Tibet.* London: University of London.

______. 1989b. "The Buddhist Notion of an 'Immanent Absolute' (*tathāgatagarbha*) as a Problem in Hermeneutics." In *The Buddhist Heritage, Buddhica Britannica Series Continua I*, edited by T. Skorupski, 229–245. Tring, England: Institute of Buddhist Studies.

______. 1990. "On the Authorship of Some of the Works Ascribed to Bhāvaviveka/Bhavya." In *Panels of the VIIth World Sanskrit Conference*, Vol. II, *Earlier Buddhism and Madhyamaka*, edited by D. Seyfort Ruegg and L. Schmithausen, 59–71. Leiden: Brill.

______. 1992. "Some Reflections on Translating Buddhist Philosophical Texts from Sanskrit." *Asiatische Studien/Études Asiatiques* (Études bouddhiques offertes à Jacques May) 46 (1): 367–391.

______. 1994a. "La Notion du voyant et du 'connaisseur suprême' et la question de l'autorité épistémique." *Wiener Zeitschrift für die Kunde Südasiens* 38: 403–419.

______. 1994b. "*Pramāṇabhūta, Pramāṇa(bhūta)-Puruṣa, Pratyakṣadharman* as Epithets of the *ṛṣi, āchārya* and *tathāgata* in Grammatical, Epistemlogical and Madhyamaka Texts." *Bulletin of the School of African and Oriental Studies* 57: 303–320.

______. 1995. "Some Reflections on the Place of Philosophy in the Study of Buddhism." *Journal of the International Association of Buddhist Studies* 18 (2): 145–182.

______. 2004. "The Indian and the Indic in Tibetan Cultural History, and Tsoṅg khan pa's Achievement as a Scholar and a Thinker: An Essay on the Concepts of Buddhism in Tibet and Tibetan Buddhism." *Journal of Indian Philosophy* 32: 321–343.

Rupert, Robert D. 2008. "Causal Theories of Mental Content." *Philosophy Compass* 3 (2): 353–380.

Sanghavi, S. 1949. *Hetubinduṭīkā of Bhaṭṭa Arcaṭa: With the Subcommentary Āloka of Durveka Miśra*. Baroda, India: Oriental Institute.

Sāṅkṛ tyāyana, R., ed. 1938–1940. "Dharmakīrti's Pramāṇ avārttika with Commentary by Manorathanandin," Appendix to the *Journal of the Bhandarkar Oriental Research Institute* 24–26.

______. ed. 1953. *Pramāṇavārttikabhāṣya or Vārttikālaṃkāra of Prajñakaragupta*. Patna: Kashi Prasad Jayaswal Research Institute.

Sarathchandra, E. R. 1958. *Buddhist Psychology of Perception*. Colombo: University of Colombo, 2d ed. Dehiwala: Buddhist Cultural Centre 1994.

Sartre, Jean-Paul. 1991. *The Transcendence of the Ego: An Existentialist Theory of Consciousness*. Translated by F. Williams and R. Kirkpatrick. New York: Hill and Wang.

______. 2003. *Being and Nothingness: An Essay on Phenomenological Ontology*. Translated by Hazel Barnes. London: Routledge.

Schmithausen, L. 1967. "Sautrāntika-Voraussetzungen in Viṃśatikā und Triṃśikā." *Wiener Zeitschrift für die Kunde des Süd- und Ost-Asiens* 11: 109–136.

______. 1972. "The Definition of *Pratyakṣam* in the *Abhidharmasamuccayaḥ*, First Chapter." *Wiener Zeitschrift für die Kunde Südasiens* 16: 199–206.

______. 1973. "Spirituelle Praxis und Philosophical Theorie im Buddhismus." *Zeitschrift fur Missionswissenschaft und Religionswissenschaft* 57 (3): 161–186.

______. 1987. *Ālavijñāna: On the Origin and the Early Development of a Central Concept of Yogācāra Philosophy*. Tokyo: International Institute for Buddhist Studies.

Schopenhauer. A. 1969. *The World as Will and Representation*. Vols. I–II. New York: Dover Publications.

Schwitzgebel, E. 2002. "A Phenomenal, Dispositional Account of Belief." *Nous* 36: 249–275.

______. 2011. *Perplexities of Consciousness*. Cambridge, Mass.: MIT Press.

Searle, John R. 1992. *The Rediscovery of the Mind*. Cambridge, Mass.: MIT Press.

______. 2000a. "Consciousness." *Annual Review of Neuroscience* 23: 557–578.

______. 2000b. "Consciousness, Free Action, and the Brain." *Journal of Consciousness Studies* 7 (10): 3–22.

Sellars, W. 1997. *Empiricism and the Philosophy of Mind*. (1st ed. 1956) Cambridge, Mass.: Harvard University Press.

Shah, N. J. 1967. *Akalaṅka's Criticism of Dharmakīrti's Philosophy: A Study*. Ahmedabad: L. D. Institute of Indology.

Shanks, David R., and M. F. St. John. 1994. "Characteristics of Dissociable Human Learning Systems." *Behavioral and Brain Sciences* 17: 367–447.

Sharma, Ram Karan, and Bhagawan Dash, eds., trans. 1976. *Agniveśa's Caraka Saṃhita: Text with English Translation and Critical Exposition Based on Cakrapaṇi Datta's Ayurveda Dīpika*. Vārāṇasī: Chowkhamba Sanskrit Series.

Shastri, P., ed. 1940. *Dhvanyāloka with Abhinava's Locana*. Kashi Sanskrit Series, Vārāṇasī: Chowkhamba Sanskrit Series.

Shastri, Swami Dwarikadas, ed. 1968. *Tattvasaṃgraha of Āchārya Shāntarakṣita with the Commentary "Pañjikā" of Shrī Kamalaśīla*. Vols. I–II. Vārāṇasī: Bauddha Bhāratī Series.

______. ed. 1970–1973. *Abhidharmakośa* and *Bhāṣya of Āchārya Vasubandhu with Sphuṭārtha Commentary of Āchārya Yaśomitra*. Vārāṇasī: Bauddha Bhāratī Series.

______. ed. 1978. *Ślokavārttika of Śrī Kumārila Bhaṭṭa with the Commentary Nyāyaratnākara of Śrī Pārthasārathi Miśra*. Vārāṇasī: Tārā Publications.

Shaw, J. L. 1974. "Empty Terms: The Nyāya and the Buddhists." *Journal of Indian Philosophy* 2: 332–343.

______. 1978. "Negation and the Buddhist Theory of Meaning." *Journal of Indian Philosophy* 6 (1): 59–77.

Shear, J. 1997. *Explaining Consciousness: The "Hard Problem."* Cambridge, Mass.: MIT Press.

______. 1999. "Experiential Clarification of the Problem of Self." In *Models of The Self*, edited by S. Gallagher and J. Shear, 407–420. Thorverton: Imprint Academic.

Shear, J., and R. Jevning. 1999. "Pure Consciousness: Scientific Exploration of Meditation Techniques." *Journal of Consciousness Studies* 6 (2–3): 189–209.

Shim, M. 2005. "The Duality of Non-conceptual Content in Husserl's Phenomenology of Perception." *Phenomenology and the Cognitive Sciences* 4 (2): 209–229.

Shukla, B. N., ed. 1984. *Buddhaghosācariya's Visuddhimaggo with Paramatthamañjūsā-ṭīkā of Bhadantāchārya Dhammapāla*. rev. ed. Rewatadhamma, Vols. I–III. Vārāṇasī: Varanaseya Sanskrit Vishwavidyalaya Press.

Siderits, Mark. 1980. "The Madhyamaka Critique of Epistemology I." *Journal of Indian Philosophy* 8: 307–335.

______. 1981. "The Madhyamaka Critique of Epistemology II." *Journal of Indian Philosophy* 9: 121–160.

______. 1985. "Word Meaning, Sentence Meaning, and Apoha." *Journal of Indian Philosophy* 13: 133–151.

______. 1986. "The Sense-Reference Distinction in Indian Philosophy of Language." *Synthese* 69: 81–106.

______. 1997. "Buddhist Reductionism." *Philosophy East and West* 47 (4): 455–478.

______. 1999. "Apohavāda, Nominalism and Resemblance Theories." In *Dharmakīrti's Thought and Its Impact on Indian and Tibetan Philosophy: Proceedings of the Third International Dharmakīrti Conference, Hiroshima, November 4–6, 1997*, edited by Shoryu Katsura, 341–348. Vienna: Verlag der Österreichischen Akademie der Wissenschaften.

______. 2003. *Personal Identity and Buddhist Philosophy*. Aldershot: Ashgate.

______. 2004a. "Causation and Emptiness in Early Madhyamaka." *Journal of Indian Philosophy* 32: 393–409.

______. 2004b. "Perceiving Particulars: A Buddhist Defense." *Philosophy East and West* 54: 367–382.

______. 2008. "Contradiction in Buddhist Argumentation." *Argumentation* 22: 125–133.

Siderits, Mark, Evan Thompson, and Dan Zahavi, eds. 2011. *Self, No Self: Perspectives from Analytical, Phenomenological, and Indian Traditions*. Oxford: Oxford University Press.

Siderits, Mark, Tom J. F. Tillemans, and A. Chakrabarti, eds. 2011. *Apoha: Buddhist Nominalism and Human Cognition*. New York: Columbia University Press.

Siewert, Charles. 1998. *The Significance of Consciousness*. Princeton: Princeton University Press.

———. 2005. "Attention and Sensorimotor Intentionality." In *Phenomenology and Philosophy of Mind*, edited by David W. Smith and A. L. Thomasson, 270–294. Oxford: Oxford University Press.

———. 2007. "In favor of (plain) phenomenology." *Phenomenology and the Cognitive Sciences* 6: 201–220.

———. 2011. "Embodied Consciousness and the Explanatory Gap." *Journal of Consciousness Studies* 18 (5–6): 117–138.

———. 2012. "On the Phenomenology of Introspection." In *Introspection and Consciousness*, edited by D. Smithes and D. Stoljar, 236–267. Oxford: Oxford University Press.

Singh, A. 1984. *The Heart of Buddhist Thought: the Philosophy of Dignāga and Dharmakīrti*. Delhi: Munishram Manoharlal Publishers.

Singh, B. N. 1985. *Bauddha-Tarkabhāṣā of Mokṣākaragupta*. Vārāṇasī: Banaras Hindu University.

Sinha, J. 1958. *Indian Psychology: Cognition*. Calcutta: Sinha Publishing House.

———. 1961. *Indian Psychology: Emotion and Will*. Calcutta: Sinha Publishing House.

———. 1969. *Indian Epistemology of Perception*. Calcutta: Sinha Publishing House.

Skorupski, T. and U. Pagel, eds. 1994. *The Buddhist Forum*. Vol. III. London: School of Oriental and African Studies.

Sloman, S. A. 1996. "The Empirical Case for Two Systems of Reasoning." *Psychological Bulletin* 119: 3–22.

Smith, Barry. 1995. "Common Sense." In *The Cambridge Companion to Husserl*, edited by B. Smith and D. W. Smith, 394–437. Cambridge: Cambridge University Press.

Smith, David W. 1995. "Mind and Body." In *The Cambridge Companion to Husserl*, edited by B. Smith and D. W. Smith, 323–393. Cambridge: Cambridge University Press.

———. 1999. "Intentionality Naturalized?" In *Naturalizing Phenomenology*, edited by J. Petitot, F. J. Varela, B. Pachoud, and J. M. Roy, 83–110. Stanford, Calif.: Stanford University Press.

Smith, David W., and R. McIntyre. 1982. *Husserl and Intentionality*. Dordrecht: D. Reidel.

Smith, David W., and Amie L. Thomasson. eds. 2005. *Phenomenology and Philosophy of Mind*. Oxford: Oxford University Press.

Smith, Quentin, and Aleksandar Jokic. 2003. *Consciousness: New Philosophical Perspectives*. New York: Oxford University Press.

Soames, S. 2007. "The Quine, Carnap Debate on Ontology and Analyticity." *Soochow Journal of Philosophical Studies*, 16: 17–32.

Solso, Robert, L. 1994. *Cognition and the Visual Arts*. Cambridge, Mass.: MIT Press.

Sprung, M. 1979. *Lucid Exposition of the Middle Way: The Essential Chapters from the Prasannapadā of Candrakīrti*. London: Routledge.

Staal, J. F. 1961. "The Theory of Definition in Indian Logic." *Journal of the American Oriental Society* 33: 122–126

Stanley, Jason. 2005. *Knowledge and Practical Interests*. Oxford: Oxford University Press.

Stcherbatsky, T. 1927. *The Conception of Buddhist Nirvāṇa*. Leningrad: Academy of Sciences.

______. 1930. *Buddhist Logic*. Vols. I–II. Delhi: Motilal Banarsidass.

______. 1989. *The Conception of Buddhist Nirvāṇa*. Delhi: Motilal Banarsidass.

Steinkellner, Ernst. 1967. *Dharmakirti's Hetubindu*. Vols. I–II. Vienna: Verlag Der Österreichischen Akademie der Wisenschaften.

______. 1971. "Wirklichkeit und Begriff bei Dharmakīrti." *Wiener Zeitschrift für die Kunde Südasiens* 15: 179–211.

______. 1973. "On the Interpretation of the *Svabhāvahetuḥ*." *Wiener Zeitschrift für die Kunde Südasiens* 18: 117–129.

______. 1978. "Yogische Erkenntnis als Problem in Buddhismus." In *Transzendenzerfahrung: Vollzugshorizont des Heils: Das Problem in indischer und christlicher Tradition*, edited by G. Oberhammer, 121–134. Vienna: De Nobili Research Library.

______. 1979. *Dharmakīrti's Pramāṇaviniścaya. 2 Kapitel: Teil 2: Übersetzung und Anmerkungen*. Vienna: Verlag Der Österreichischen Akademie der Wisenschaften.

______. 1982. "The Spiritual Place of the Epistemological Tradition in Buddhism." *Nanto Bukkyo* 49: 1–18.

______. 1983. "*Tshad ma'i skyes bu*—Meaning and Historical Significance of the Term." In *Proceedings of the Csoma de Körös Symposium Velm-Wien*, Vol. II, edited by Ernst Steinkellner and Helmut Tauscher, 275–284. Vienna: Universität Wien.

______. 1991a. "The Logic of the svabhāvahetu in Dharmakīrti's Vādanyāya." In *Studies in the Buddhist Epistemological Tradition: Proceedings of the Second International Dharmakīrti Conference*, Vienna, June 11–16, 1989, edited by Ernst Steinkellner, 311–324. Vienna: Verlag der Österreichischen Akademie der Wissenschaften.

______. 1991b. ed. *Studies in the Buddhist Epistemological Tradition: Proceedings of the Second International Dharmakīrti Conference*, Vienna, June 11–16, 1989. Vienna: Verlag der Österreichischen Akademie der Wissenschaften.

______. 1992. "Early Tibetan ideas on the ascertainment of validity (*nges byed kyi tshad ma*)." In *Tibetan Studies. Proceedings of the 5th Seminar of the International Association of Tibetan Studies, Narita 1989*, edited by Ihara Shōren and Yamagucchi Zuihō, 257–273. Narita: Naritasan Shinshoji.

______. 1993. "Buddhist Logic: The Search for Certainty." In *Buddhist Spirituality: Indian, Southeast Asian, Tibetan, and Early Chinese*, edited by Takeuchi Yoshinori, 171–187. New York: Crossroad.

______. 1994. "Śākyabuddhi's Commentary on *Pramāṇavārttika* I 3 and its *Vṛtti*." *Wiener Zeitschrift für die Kunde Südasiens* 38: 379–387.

______. 1997. "Kumārila, Īśvarasena, and Dharmakīrti in Dialogue: A New Interpretation of Pramāṇ avārttika I 33." In *Bauddhavidyāsudhākāraḥ: Studies in Honour of Hanz Bechert on the Occasion of His 65th Birthday*, edited by P. Kieffer-Pülz and J.-Uwe Hartmann, 625–646. Swistal-Odendorf.

______. 1999. "Yogic Cognition, Tantric Goal, and Other Methodological Applications of Dharmakīrti's *kāryānumana* Theorem." In *Dharmakīrti's Thought and Its Impact on Indian and Tibetan Philosophy: Proceedings of the Third International Dharmakīrti Conference, Hiroshima, November 4–6, 1997*, edited by

Shoryu Katsura, 349–362. Vienna: Verlag der Österreichischen Akademie der Wissenschaften.

———. 2003. "Once More on Circles." *Journal of Indian Philosophy* 31: 323–341.

———. 2005. Dignāga's *Pramāṇasamuccaya*, Chapter 1. A hypothetical reconstruction with the help of the two Tibetan translations on the basis of the hitherto known Sanskrit fragments and the linguistic materials gained from Jinendrabuddhi's *ṭīkā*. URL: http://ikga.oeaw.ac.at/Mat/dignaga_PS_1.pdf (last accessed May 10, 2011).

Steinkellner, Ernst, and M. T. Much. 1995. *Texte der erkenntnistheoretischen Schule des Buddhismus*. Systematische Übersicht über die buddhistische Sanskrit-Literatur II. Göttingen: Vandenhoeck and Ruprecht.

Steinkellner, E., H. Krasser, and H. Lasic. 2005. *Jinendrabuddhi's Viśālāmalavatī Pramāṇasamuccayaṭīkā: Chapter I*. Vienna: Austrian Academy of Science.

Stich, S. 1984. "Relativism, Rationality, and the Limits of Intentional Description." *Pacific Philosophical Quarterly* 65: 211–235.

———. 1990. *The Fragmentation of Reason*. Cambridge, Mass.: MIT Press.

Stoljar, Daniel. 2005. "Physicalism and Phenomenal Concepts." *Mind and Language* 20 (5): 469–494.

———. 2010. *Physicalism*. New York: Routledge.

Stout, G. F. 1921. "The Nature of Universals and Propositions." *Proceedings of the British Academy* 10: 157–172.

Strawson, Galen. 1994. *Mental Reality*. Cambridge, Mass.: MIT Press.

———. 1998. "Reply to Arindam Chakrabarti." In *The Philosophy of P. F. Strawson*, edited by L. E. Hahn, 324–329. Chicago: Open Court.

———. 2005. "Intentionality and Experience: Terminological Preliminaries." In *Phenomenology and Philosophy of Mind*, edited by David W. Smith and A. L. Thomasson, 41–66. Oxford: Oxford University Press.

———. 2006. "Realistic Monism: Why Physicalism Entails Panpsychism." *Journal of Consciousness Studies* 13 (10–11): 3–31.

Taber, J. 1989. "The Theory of the Sentence in Pūrva Mīmāṃsā and Western Philosophy." *Journal of Indian Philosophy* 17: 407–430.

———. 2001. "Much Ado About Nothing: Kumarīla, Śāntarakṣita, and Dharmakīrti on the Cognition of Non-being." *Journal of the American Oriental Society* 121/1: 72–88.

———. 2003. "Dharmakīrti Against Physicalism." *Journal of Indian Philosophy* 31: 479–502.

———. 2005. *A Hindu Critique of Buddhist Epistemology: Kumārila on Perception*. London and New York: Routledge Curzon.

Tachikawa, M. 1971. "A Sixth-century Manual of Indian Logic: A Translation of Nyāyapraveśa." *Journal of Indian Philosophy* 1: 111–145.

Tanaka, J., D. Weiskopf, and P. Williams. 2001. "The Role of Color in High-Level Vision." *Trends in Cognitive Sciences* 5: 211–215.

Tani, T. 1991. "Logic and Time-ness in Dharmakīrti's Philosophy—Hypothetical Negative Reasoning (*prasaṅga*) and Momentary Existence (*kṣaṇikatva*)." In *Studies in the Buddhist Epistemological Tradition: Proceedings of the Second International Dharmakīrti Conference*, Vienna, June 11–16, 1989, edited by Ernst Steinkellner, 325–402. Vienna: Verlag der Österreichischen Akademie der Wissenschaften.

Tarānātha, T., T. Amarendramohan, and T. Hemantakumar, eds. 1985. *Nyāyadarśanam: With Vātsyāyana's Bhāṣya, Uddyotakara's Vārttika, Vācaspati Miśra's Tātparyaṭīkā and Viśvanātha's Vṛtti*. Delhi: Munshiram Manhoharlal Publishers.

Tatia, Nathman. 1976. *Abhidharmasamuccaya-bhāṣyaṃ*. Patna: K. P. Jayaswal Research Institute.
Thakchöe, Sonam. 2011. "Prāsaṅgika Epistemology in Context." In *Moonshadows: Conventional Truth in Buddhist Philosophy*, The Cowherds, 39–55. New York: Oxford University Press.
Thakur, Anantalal, ed. 1987. *Jñānaśrīmitranibandhāvali: Buddhist Philosophical Works of Jñānaśrīmitra*. Patna: Kashi Prasad Jayaswal Research Institute.
Thomas, N. J. T. 1999. "Are Theories of Imagery Theories of Imagination? An Active Perception Approach to Conscious Mental Content." *Cognitive Science* 23: 207–245.
Thomasson, Amie. L. 2008. "Phenomenal Consciousness and the Phenomenal World." *The Monist* 91 (2): 191–214.
Thompson, Brad J. 2005. "Color Constancy and Russellian Representationalism." *Australasian Journal of Philosophy* 84 (1): 75–94.
Thompson, Evan. 1991. "Is Internal Realism a Philosophy of Scheme and Content." *Metaphilosophy* 22 (3): 212–230.
______. 1995a. "Colour Vision, Evolution, and Perceptual Content." *Synthese* 104: 1–32.
______. 1995b. *Color Vision: A Study in Cognitive Science and Philosophy of Perception*. London: Routledge.
______. 2000. "Empathy and Consciousness." *Journal of Consciousness Studies* 8 (5–7): 1–32.
______. 2005. "Sensorimotor Subjectivity and the Enactive Approach to Experience." *Phenomenology and the Cognitive Sciences* 4: 407–427.
______. 2007a. *Mind in Life: Biology, Phenomenology, and the Sciences of Mind*. Cambridge, Mass.: Harvard University Press.
______. 2007b. "Look Again: Phenomenology and Mental Imagery." *Phenomenology and the Cognitive Sciences* 6: 137–170.
______. 2011. "Self-No-Self: Memory and Reflexive Awareness." In Siderits et al. (2011): 157–175.
Thompson, Evan, and Francisco J. Varela. 2001. "Radical Embodiment: Natural Dynamics and Consciousness." *Trends in Cognitive Science* 5: 418–425.
Thompson, Evan, A. Noë, and L. Pessoa. 1999. "Perceptual Completion: A Case Study in Phenomenology and Cognitive Science." In *Naturalizing Phenomenology*, edited by J. Petitot, F. J. Varela, B. Pachoud, and J. M. Roy, 161–195. Stanford, Calif.: Stanford University Press.
Thurman, Robert A. F. 1980. "Philosophical Nonegocentrism in Wittgenstein and Chandrakīrti in Their Treatment of the Private Language Problem." *Philosophy East and West* 30 (3): 321–337.
Tillemans, Tom J. F. 1984. "Sur le *parārthānumāna* en logique bouddhique." *Asiatische Studien / Études Asiatiques*, 37 (2): 73–99.
______. 1989. "Indian and Tibetan Mādhyamikas on *Mānasapratyakṣa*." *Tibet Journal* 14 (1): 70–85.
______. 1990. *Materials for the Study of Āryadeva, Dharmapāla and Candrakīrti*. Vienna: Arbeitskreis für Tibetische und Buddhistische Studien.
______. 1991. "More on *Parārthānumāna*, Theses and Syllogisms." *Asiatische Studien / Études Asiatiques* 45 (1): 133–148.
______. 1992. "La Logique bouddhique est-elle une logique non-classique ou déviante? Remarques su le tétralemmem (*catuḥkoṭi*)." In *Les Cahiers de Philosophie* 14, Lille, edited by J.-L. Solère, 183–198. In Tillemans (1999): 187–205.

———. 1993. *Persons of Authority: The sTon pa tshad ma'i skye bur sgrub pa'i gtam of A lag sha Ngag dbang bstan dar: A Tibetan Work on the Central Religious Questions of Buddhist Epistemology*. Stuttgart: Franz Steiner Verlag.

———. 1995. "Remarks on Philology." *Journal of the International Association of Buddhist Studies* 18 (2): 269–278.

———. 1996. "What Would It Be Like to be Selfless? Hīnayānist Versions, Mahāyānist Versions and Derek Parfit." *Études Asiatiques / Asiatische Studien* 50 (4): 835–852.

———. 1997. "Où va la philologie bouddhique?" *Études et Lettres: Revue de la Faculté des lettres de l'Université de Lausanne* 4: 3–18.

———. 1999. *Scripture, Logic, Language: Essays on Dharmakīrti and his Tibetan Successors*. Somerville: Wisdom Publications.

———. 2000. *Dharmakīrti's Pramāṇavārttika: An Annotated Translation of the Fourth Chapter (Parārthānumāna)*. Vienna: Österreichischen Akademie der Wissenschaften.

———. 2003. "Metaphysics for Mādhyamikas." In *Svātantrika-Prasaṅgika Distinction: What Difference Does It Make?* edited by Georges Dreyfus and Sara McClintock, 93–124. Boston: Wisdom Publications.

———. 2008a. "Introduction: Buddhist Argumentation." *Argumentation* 22: 1–14.

———. 2008b. "Reason, Irrationality and Akrasia (weakness of the will) in Buddhism: Reflections upon 'Śāntideva's Arguments with Himself'." *Argumentation* 22: 149–163.

Tola, F., and C. Dragonetti. 1982. "Dignāga's *Ālambanaparīkṣāvṛtti*." *Journal of Indian Philosophy* 10: 105–134.

Trenchner, Vilhelm. 1993–2004. *Majjhima-Nikāya*. Vols. I–II. Oxford: Pali Text Society.

Tucci, G. 1928. "Buddhist Logic Before Dignāga." *Journal of the Royal Asiatic Society* 7: 377–390.

———. 1929. *Pre-Dignāga Buddhist Texts on Logic from Chinese Sources*. Baroda: Oriental Institute.

———. 1930. *The Nyāyamukha of Dignāga*. Materialen zur Kunde des Buddhismus 15. Heidelberg.

———. 1956. *Minor Buddhist Texts*. Rome: Instituto Italiano per Medio el Extremo Oriente.

Tuck, A. 1990. *Comparative Philosophy and the Philosophy of Scholarship*. New York: Oxford University Press.

Tugendhat, Ernst. 1979. *Selbstbewusstsein und Selbstbestimmung*. Frankfurt am Main: Suhrkamp.

Tye, Michael. 1995. *Ten Problems of Consciousness*. Cambridge, Mass.: MIT Press.

———. 2000. *Consciousness, Color, and Content*. Cambridge, Mass.: MIT Press.

van Bijlert, V. 1989. *Epistemology and Spiritual Authority*. Vienna: Wiener Studien zur Tibetologie und Buddhismuskunde.

van der Kuijp, Leonard W. J. 1979. "Introductory Notes to *Pramāṇavārttika* Based on Tibetan Sources." *Tibet Journal* 4 (2): 6–28.

———. 1987. "An Early Tibetan View of the Soteriology of Buddhist Epistemology." *Journal of Indian Philosophy* 15: 57–70.

———. 1998. Review of J. I. Cabézon, *Buddhism and Language*. *Journal of the American Oriental Society* 118 (4): 563–567.

———. 1999. "Remarks on the 'Person of Authority' in the Dga' ldan pa / Dge lugs pa School of Tibetian Buddhism." *Journal of the American Oriental Society* 119 (4): 646–672.

Van Gulick, Robert. 2011. "Life, Holism and Emergence: Converging Themes." *Journal of Consciousness Studies* 18 (5–6): 139–147.

Varela, Francisco J. 1996. "Neurophenomenology: A Methodological Remedy for the Hard Problem." *Journal of Consciousness Studies* 3: 330–350.

______. 1997. "The Naturalization of Phenomenology as the Transcendence of Nature: Searching for Generative Mutual Constraints." *Alter* 5: 365–381.

______. 1999. "The Specious Present: The Neurophenomenology of Time Consciousness." In *Naturalizing Phenomenology*, edited by J. Petitot, F. J. Varela, B. Pachoud, and J. M. Roy, 266–314. Stanford, Calif.: Stanford University Press.

Varela, F. J., and J. Shear. Eds. 1999. *The View from Within: First-Person Approaches to the Study of Consciousness*. Thorverton, UK: Imprint Academic.

Varela, F. J., E. Thompson, and E. Rosch. 1991. *The Embodied Mind: Cognitive Science and Human Experience*. Cambridge, Mass.: MIT Press.

Velmans, M. 2000. *Understanding Consciousness*. London: Routledge.

Vermersch, P. 1999. "Introspection as Practice." In *The View from Within: First-Person Approaches to the Study of Consciousness*, a special issue of *Journal of Consciousness Studies*, edited by F. Varela and J. Shear, 6 (2–3): 17–42.

Vetter, T. 1964. *Erkenntnisprobleme bei Dharmakīrti*. Veröffentlichungen der Kommission für Sprachen und Kulturen Süd und Ostasiens Vienna: Österreichische Akademie der Wissenschaften.

______. 1966. *Dharmakīrti's Pramāṇaviniścaya, I. Kapitel: Pratyakṣam*. Vienna: Verlag Der Österreichischen Akademie der Wisenschaften.

______. 1990. *Der Buddha und Seine Lerhe in Dharmakīrtis Pramāṇavārttika*. Vienna: Wiener Studien zur Tibetologie und Buddhismuskunde.

Vicente, K. J., and C. M. Burns. 1996. "Evidence for Direct Perception from Cognition in the Wild." *Ecological Psychology* 6 (3): 269–280.

Vidyābhuṣaṇa, Satish Chandra. 1921. *A History of Indian Logic*. Delhi: Motilal Banarsidass, reprint 1971.

Waldron, William. S. 1995. "How Innovative is the *ālayavijñāna*? The *ālayavijñāna* in the Context of Canonical and Abhidharma *Vijñāna* Theory." *Journal of Indian Philosophy* 23: 9–51.

______. 2002. "Buddhist Steps to an Ecology of Mind: Thinking about 'Thoughts Without a Thinker'." *The Eastern Buddhist* 34 (1): 1–52.

______. 2003. *The Buddhist Unconscious: The Ālaya-vijñāna in the Context of Indian Buddhist Thought*. London: Routledge Curzon.

Warder, A. K. 1970. *Indian Buddhism*. Delhi: Motilal Banarsidass.

Watson, R. A. 1995. *Representational Ideas: From Plato to Patricia Churchland*. Dordrecht: Kluwer Academic Publishers.

Wayman, Alex. K. 1958. "The Rules of Debate According to Asaṅga." *Journal of the American Oriental Society* 78: 1.

______. 1965. "The Yogācāra Idealism." *Philosophy East and West* 15: 65–74.

______. 1991. "Dharmakīrti and the Yogācāra Theory of Bīja." In *Studies in the Buddhist Epistemological Tradition: Proceedings of the Second International Dharmakīrti Conference*, Vienna, June 11–16, 1989, edited by Ernst Steinkellner, 419–430. Vienna: Verlag der Österreichischen Akademie der Wissenschaften.

______. 1999a. "Does the Buddhist 'Momentary' Theory Preclude Anything Permanent." In *Dharmakīrti's Thought and Its Impact on Indian and Tibetan Philosophy: Proceedings of the Third International Dharmakīrti Conference, Hiroshima, November 4–6, 1997*, edited by Shoryu Katsura, 433–440. Vienna: Verlag der Österreichischen Akademie der Wissenschaften.

———. 1999b. *A Millennium of Buddhist Logic*. Delhi: Motilal Banarsidass.
Weberman, D. 2000. "A New Defense of Gadamers' Hermeneutic." *Philosophy and Phenomenological Research* 60 (1): 45–65.
Weiskrantz, L. 1998. *Blindsight: A Case Study and Implications*. Oxford: Oxford University Press (2d ed. of 1986 edition).
Weinberg, Jonathan M., Shaun Nichols and Stephen Stich. 2001. "Normativity and Epistemic Intuitions." *Philosophical Topics*, 29 (1–2): 429–460.
Welton, Donn. 1999. "Soft, Smooth Hands: Husserl's Phenomenology of the Lived Body." In *The Body*, edited by D. Welton, 38–56. Oxford: Blackwell.
———. 2003. "World as Horizon." In *The New Husserl: A Critical Reader*, edited by D. Welton, 223–232. Bloomington and Indianopolis: Indiana University Press.
Westerhoff, Jan. 2009. *Nāgārjuna's Madhyamaka: A Philosophical Introduction*. New York: Oxford University Press.
———. 2010. *Twelve Examples of Illusion*. Oxford: Oxford University Press.
Wheeler, M. 2011. "Mind in Life or Life in Mind? Making Sense of Deep Continuity." *Journal of Consciousness Studies* 18 (5–6): 148–168.
White, S. 1987. "What is Like to Be a Homunculus." *Pacific Philosophical Quarterly* 68: 148–174.
Willemen, C., B. Dessein, and C. Cox. 1998. *Sarvāstivāda Buddhist Scholasticism*. Leiden, New York: Brill.
Williams, D. C. 1953. "On the Elements of Being." *Review of Metaphysics* 7: 171–193.
Williams, P. 1998. *The Reflexive Nature of Awareness*. London: Curzon Press.
Wood, T. 1991. *Mind Only: A Philosophical and Doctrinal Analysis of the Vijñānavāda*. Honolulu: University of Hawaii Press.
Wright, E. ed. 2008. *The Case for Qualia*. Cambridge, Mass.: MIT Press.
Yaita, H. 1999. "Yogācārabhūmi and Dharmakīrti on Perception." In *Dharmakīrti's Thought and Its Impact on Indian and Tibetan Philosophy: Proceedings of the Third International Dharmakīrti Conference, Hiroshima, November 4–6, 1997*, edited by Shoryu Katsura, 441–448. Vienna: Verlag der Österreichischen Akademie der Wissenschaften.
Yamaguchi, S., and H. Meyer. 1929. "Dignāga, Examen de l'objet de la connaissance (*Ālambanaparīkṣa*), textes tibétain et chinois et traduction des stances et du commentaire, éclaircissements et notes d'après le commentair tibétain de Vinītadeva." *Journal Asiatique* 1–65.
Yao, Zhihua. 2004. "Dignāga and the Four Types of Perception." *Journal of Indian Philosophy* 32: 57–74.
———. 2005. *The Buddhist Theory of Self-Cognition*. London: Rutledge.
Yoshimizu, C. 2007. "Causal Efficacy and Spatiotemporal Restriction: An Analytical Study of the Sautrāntika Philosophy." In *Pramāṇakirtiḥ: Papers Dedicated to Ernst Steinkellner on the Occasion of his 70th Birthday*, edited by Birgit Kellner, Helmut Krasser, Horst Lasic, Michael T. Much, and Helmut Tauscher, 1049–1078. Vienna: Arbeitskreis für Tibetische und Buddhistische Studies.
Zahavi, Dan. 1999. *Self-Awareness and Alterity: A Phenomenological Investigation*. Evanston, Ill.: Northwestern University Press.
———. 2002. "First-Person Thoughts and Embodied Self-Awareness: Some Reflections on the Relation between Recent Analytical Philosophy and Phenomenology." *Phenomenology and the Cognitive Sciences* 1: 7–26.
———. 2003. "Inner Time-Consciousness and Pre-reflective Self-Awareness." In *The New Husserl: A Critical Reader*, edited by Donn Welton, 157–180. Bloomington and Indianapolis: Indiana University Press.

———. 2004a. "Husserl's Noema and the Internalism-Externalism Debate." *Inquiry* 47: 42–66.
———. 2004b. "Phenomenology and the Project of Naturalization." *Phenomenology and the Cognitive Sciences* 3: 331–347.
———. 2005–2008. *Subjectivity and Selfhood: Investigating the First-Person Perspective*. Cambridge, Mass.: MIT Press.
———. 2009. "Is the Self a Social Construct?" *Inquiry* 52 (6): 551–573.
———. 2011a. "The Experiential Self: Objections and Clarifications." In *Self, No Self: Perspectives from Analytical, Phenomenological, and Indian Traditions*, edited by Mark Siderits, Evan Thompson, and Dan Zahavi, 56–78. Oxford: Oxford University Press.
———. 2011b. "Mutual Enlightenment and Transcendental Thought." *Journal of Consciousness Studies* 18 (5–6): 169–175.
Zeki, S. 1993. *A Vision of the Brain*. Oxford: Blackwell.
Zeki, S., and A. Bartels. 1999. "Toward a Theory of Visual Consciousness." *Consciousness and Cognition* 8: 225–259.

INDEX

Abhidharma 51–52, 54, 57–59, 62–63, 66, 68–69, 71–75, 78–79, 82–83, 85, 87, 97, 108, 111, 138, 144, 150–151, 154, 169, 177, 194, 199–200, 206–208, 210–211, 229–230, 236, 250, 252, 254, 258, 262, 274, 276, 286, 291–292, 301–302
  defining traits 51–52, 57–59
  as reductionism 7, 51–52,
  as phenomenological psychology 6, 8, 68, 87, 108, 111
  see also Buddhaghosa; Sautrāntika; Stiramathi; Vaibhāṣika; Vasubandhu; Yogācāra
Abhinavagupta 48–49
Achinstein, Peter 6
active perception, theory of 142, 249
Advaita Vedānta 18, 103, 136
affordance 231–232
agency 58, 62, 117, 158, 219, 242, 247, 249, 290–291, 294, 296
agnosia, visual form 116, 286
Aikin, Scott F. 280
Albahari, Miri 60
Almeder, Robert 52
Amaladass, Anand S. J. 48
apperception (*saṃjñā*) 36, 64, 69, 74, 81, 131
Aristotle 26, 42, 240
Armstrong, David M. 51, 142
Arnold, Dan 6, 19–20, 32, 41, 107–108, 113, 210–211, 226, 235, 237, 243–244, 247–248, 254, 256, 258, 263, 269–270, 285, 299
Asaṅga 58, 69, 101–102
ascertainment (*prāmāṇya*) 93, 98, 129, 138, 187, 195–197, 213, 300
  extrinsic 133, 138, 196–197, 199, 238, 300
  intrinsic 20, 138, 195–197, 212, 214, 300
aspects (*ākāra*)
  phenomenal 232
  emergence of 137
  objective 64, 170, 237, 256, 259, 266, 276, 292
  subjective 64, 69, 74, 170, 230, 237, 242, 244, 256, 259, 263, 266, 292
  theory of 12, 66, 97, 102–103
  under which phenomena appear 243
  see also dual aspect cognition; body-schema; body-image
astigmatism 199, 286
atomism
  conceptual 28–29
  tenet of Abhidharma ontology 79, 207
attention 4–5, 23, 36, 50–51, 53, 70–75, 84, 122, 124, 139, 151, 169, 177, 181, 187, 204–205, 241, 246, 249, 271, 285, 295
  role in perception 70, 73, 74
  see also attentive capacity; inattentional blindness
attentive capacity (*manasikāra*) 46–47, 73, 76, 241, 246, 289, 300
Austin, J. L. 162
autonomy 24, 169, 289
autopoiesis 284, 290

background intuitions
  Husserl's concept of 117, 245–246, 260

Bacon, Francis 298
Bandyopadhyay, Nandita 42
Barsalou, Lawrence 168–169, 230
Bartels, A. 174
basis (*āśraya*)
  on which cognition depends 287
  perturbations at 212
  transformation of 46
Bayne, Tim 9, 259
Behrmann, Marlene 186
Bermúdez, José 202, 246
Bhāmaha 124
Bhartṛhari, 87, 108, 119–120, 124, 148–150, 152–153, 155, 159, 167, 182, 276
Bhattacharyya, B. 109, 125
Bhattacharyya, Kamaleswar 60
Bhattacharyya, Sibajiban 18, 297
Bhattacharyya, Vidhushekhara 65
Bhāsarvajña 88
Bhāvivikta 125, 163, 287
Biardeau, Madelaine 139, 147, 149
Bilimoria, Purushottama 18, 120
binding, perceptual 174
Binsted, G. 116
Blackmore, Susan 221
blindsight 116, 286
Block, Ned 118, 210
Blumenthal, James 15
body
  as the basis for action 150
  as instrument of sensory activity 66
  as medium for the expression of life (*Lieb*) 67, 257
  image 232, 244–245
  mistaken for the self 61
  physical (*Köper*) 67, 257
  relation to cognition (Dharmakīrti) 56
  schema 242, 244–245, 248
  see also embodied cognition; embodiment
BonJour, Laurence 52, 222–223
Bontekoe, Ron 279
Bradley, Peter 221
Bramão, Inês 186
Brentano, Franz 9, 41, 235, 240–242
Bruzina, R. 284
Buddhaghosa 69
Burns, C. M. 231
Buswell, Robert 21
Cabezón, José 23, 26
Candrakīrti 2, 20, 41, 218, 228, 238–239, 243, 250
Cardona, George 112
Carey, D. 116
Carman, Taylor 10, 67, 248–249, 272
Carnap, Rudolf 180
Cartesianism
  and belief justification 10, 253
  legacy of 54, 224
  view of the *cogito* 5, 185, 194, 266
  and the given 204
Cārvāka 21, 56, 285, 287
Caston, V. 240
causal account
  of cognition 3, 156, 224, 254, 284, 286, 290
  of consciousness 288
  of generation 239
  of knowledge 3, 23, 32, 302
  of perception 194
  of reference 147
  see also causation
causal closure 301–302
causal totality (*hetusāmagrī*) 113–115, 117, 142
causation
  and mind 294, 302
  and naturalism 224
  chain of 65, 73
  contrast with justification 95
  Quine's account of 224
  pluralist account of 138
  proleptic 46
  relation to cognition 56
  and reasoning 114–115, 301
  models of 287–290
  tripartite model of 301–302
Chadha, Monima 216–217, 235
Chakrabarti, Arindam 27, 33, 261, 297
Chakrabarti, Kishor 18, 119
Chalmers, David 9, 30, 55, 118, 147, 167, 272, 282
Changeux, Jean-Pierre 285
Chatterjee, Satischandra 20
Chinchore, Mangala 89
Christensen, Carleton 19
Chu, Junjie 92, 188
Churchland, Paul 55
Churchland, Patricia 55
Clark, Andy 4, 118

cloudy vision (*timira*) 183, 188
cognitive activity
  and mind continuum 152, 252
  categorization of 230
  result of 237–238
  basis of 238, 281
  as bringing forth a world 257
  complete cessation of 265
cognitive awareness (*vijñāna*) 5, 63, 69, 71, 74, 78, 81–82, 211, 252–254, 283
cognitive dynamics 84, 252–253
cognitive error (*bhrānti-jñāna*) 91–92, 101, 121–122, 154, 182, 185, 187–188, 190, 296
  Dignāga's account of 92, 101
  five kinds of 121–122
  Kamalaśīla's interpretation of 173, 174, 177
  caused by 183–188
  as deception 95, 102, 185–186, 188
cognitive events (*jñeya-vṛtta*)
  characteristics 90–91, 173, 225, 239
  epistemology as a theory of 109–111
  relation to self-awareness 148, 200, 254, 269
  relation to knowledge 224
  and the transformation of consciousness 252
  correlation with brain states 282
  as concomitant with the body 285, 288
cognitive science 3–4, 27, 29, 51–54, 186, 2–4, 211, 222–223, 227–230, 253, 280, 290, 294, 301–302
coherentism 36, 42, 72, 203–204, 290
Collins, Steven 57, 60–61, 68–69
color qualia 80, 200
colorblind 185, 189
comatose 287
common sense 65, 142, 147, 190, 219, 223–224, 228, 253, 272, 301
conceivability 30, 147, 245
concepts
  classical theory of 27
  naturalized account of 29–30, 230
  nominalist theory of 11
  perception-based theories of 168
  phenomenal 30, 160, 164–167, 181
  primitive 147
  prototype theory of 28
conceptual atomism 28–29
conceptual construction (*kalpanā*) 29, 101, 105, 143, 145, 182, 184, 200, 231, 297
conceptualism 157, 201, 281
consciousness
  Abhidharma theory of 68–84
  and causal explanation 71
  and continuity of awareness 252, 287
  and no-self view 68
  as sentience 5, 68, 71, 285
  as luminosity 2, 264–265, 287
  non-positional 245, 248, 269
  one level theories of 67
  pre-reflective 266, 269, 289
  pure 62, 265
  temporal dimension of 41, 241, 283, 284
  unity of 240, 259, 283, 294
Conze, Edward 35, 45
coping skills 80, 111, 249, 283, 300
covariance, positive and negative 287
Cox, Collett 1, 208
Crane, Tim 176, 270, 274
cross-modal, cognition 173, 245

D'Amato, Mario 19, 33, 130–131
Dasein 22, 265
Davidson, Donald 302
Davidson, Richard 44, 229
De Silva, Padmasiri 60, 64
definition, concept of (*lakṣaṇa*) 48, 130–131, 139, 146–147
delusion, mental
  contrast with perceptual illusion 186–187
  Dignāga's treatment of 199
  Kamalaśīla's treatment of 183, 186–187
Demiéville, Paul 67
Dennett, Daniel 55, 259, 271–272, 292
dependent arising (*pratītya-samutpāda*) 13–14, 62, 70, 97, 125–126, 131, 134–136, 138–139, 142, 144, 192, 199, 294–295, 297–299
Depraz, Natalie 44, 294
Derrida, Jacques 22, 30, 275
Descartes, René 4, 10–11, 35, 59, 222, 224, 281, 298

Deutsch, Eliot 279
Devendrabuddhi 25, 101, 109, 196–197
Dharmakīrti, 1–2, 4, 6–10, 12, 14, 20, 24–27, 29–32, 34–35, 39, 42–47, 56–59, 68, 74, 85, 87, 89–90, 92, 94, 96, 99–102, 105–106, 108–110, 112–115, 117–118, 121–125, 127–128, 135, 137–140, 142, 145, 149, 152, 155–156, 159, 161, 167, 170–173, 177, 182–185, 188–189, 193, 196, 199, 206–208, 211–215, 217–219, 222, 225, 227–230, 233, 237, 239–240, 244, 250–251, 254, 256, 259, 266–269, 274–275, 285–286, 292–293, 295–296, 300
  argument from analogy for other minds 56, 285
  on identity and causal generation 112–114, 129, 159
  on perception as involving error 182–190
Dharmaśri 57
Dharmottara 30–31, 59, 101, 109, 128, 190, 196, 239, 243, 270, 275, 300
Dias, M 5
Dignāga 1–2, 6–10, 20, 24, 31–32, 34–36, 41, 43, 45, 47, 57–59, 68, 74, 85, 87, 90–92, 94, 99–101, 105–113, 115, 119, 122–124, 127, 137, 140, 142–143, 146, 149, 153, 155, 157–163, 165–167, 170–171, 178, 182–183, 185, 188–189, 193, 196, 199–200, 206, 208, 210–212, 214, 216–217, 222, 224–225, 227–231, 236–237, 243–244, 247–252, 254–256, 259, 261–264, 269, 273, 295–296, 300
  definition of perception 100–101, 140, 178, 182
  inductive method of reasoning 34–35, 111–112
  on perception as inerrant 101, 183, 185
  on the dual aspect view of cognition 244–247, 254, 262
direct realism 142, 144, 292
disjunctivism 105
downward causation 289–290
Dretske, Fred 3
Dreyfus, Georges 6, 14, 20, 26, 27, 43, 100, 106–107, 171–172, 208, 212, 215–216, 229, 235, 243, 256, 266–267, 295
Dreyfus, Hubert 4, 201–202, 267, 291
Drummond, John 104, 204–206, 271
dual-aspect cognition 2, 64, 83, 240, 244, 247
dualism
  property 282, 286, 290
  substance 79, 137, 244, 282, 285, 290
  trope 251
Duerlinger, James 78
Dunne, John 14, 25, 43–46, 90, 95, 100–102, 106, 108–109, 118, 121, 159, 196–197, 208, 212, 229, 254, 275, 293
dynamic systems theory 4

ecological, approach to perception 115, 202, 231
Edelglass, William 18, 279
eliminativism 3, 52, 55, 118, 271–272, 302
Elio, Renée 14
Ellis, Ralph 54
Eltschinger, Vincent 38, 46, 121
embodied cognition 4, 117, 194–195, 221, 232, 244, 248, 280, 291
embodiment
  and consciousness 248
  condition of 207–208, 249
  of the sources of knowledge (Buddha) 44–45
  thesis 195, 232, 282
  phenomenological 232
  see also enactive cognition
Embree, L. 9
emergent properties 55, 80, 142, 158, 252, 287, 289
emergentism 287–288, 302
empirical
  awareness 2, 64–67, 69, 78, 84, 94–95, 100, 139, 165, 189, 192, 206, 215, 255, 257, 262
  consciousness 57, 65, 67, 70, 72, 74–76, 215, 233, 296
empiricism 23, 41, 56, 94, 110, 192, 223, 226, 281
emptiness 24, 203

enactive, cognition 3–4, 16, 43, 46, 117, 226–227, 235, 283, 285, 290, 299, 302
entailment, a priori 41, 42
epiphenomenalism 282, 302
epistemic authority 297, 299–300
epistemic gap
  between perception and conception 105, 155, 216, 300
  between concepts and pure intuitions 248
Evans, Gareth 181, 246
exclusion, semantic theory of (*apoha*) 13–14, 18, 29, 31, 50, 87, 105–107, 113, 155–156, 159, 163, 216, 229, 261, 275
experience error 272
explanatory gap
  problem of 29, 253, 284
  between phenomenology and natural science 115
  between mind and world 248
externalism 10, 11, 117–118, 137, 211, 214, 223, 271, 276, 297

Farah, Martha 286
Fasching, Wolfgang 265
Faure, Bernard 22–23, 30
Filliozat, Pierre-Sylvain 44
Flanagan, Owen 37, 55, 242
Flew, Anthony 19
Fodor, Jerry 3, 11, 29, 161, 202, 280–281, 284
Foglia, Lucia 284
Foley, Richard 52
Føllesdal, Dagfinn 202–203, 267
Forman, Robert 297
foundationalism 9, 15, 94, 191–193, 195–197, 204–205, 213–217, 219, 232, 234, 254, 269, 271, 299
Franco, Eli 40, 44–45, 56, 102, 121, 156, 160–161, 239, 254, 285–286
Frank, Manfred 241
Frauwallner, Erich 1–2, 7–8, 57, 87, 119
Frege, Gottlob 14, 41, 118, 205
Fumerton, Richard 52
Funayama, Toru 8, 102, 109, 122, 145, 156, 173, 185, 188, 190, 275
fusion of horizons 7, 35

Gadamer, Hans-Georg 7, 35–36, 109, 278
Gallagher, Shaun 4, 104, 232, 244–245, 260, 268, 290, 294
Ganeri, Jonardon 3, 6, 18–19, 119, 237, 251, 287–288
Gaṅgeśa 216
Ganguli, H. M. 119
Garfield, Jay 18–19, 33, 37–38, 51, 111, 235, 240, 250, 277, 279–280
Gauḍapāda 65
Gautama, Akṣapāda 88, 91, 99, 124
Gestalt 202, 219, 232
Gethin, Rupert 72–73
Ghoṣaka 57
Gibson, J. J. 115, 202, 231
Giles, J. 61
Gillon, Brendan 113, 115, 117
Gimello, Robert 21
givenness, mode of
  of objects 75, 141, 165, 214, 250, 257, 268
  of mental content 78, 141,
  of perception 167, 193
  of phenomenal character 176, 293
  of experience 199, 300–301
  first-personal 268
Gloy, Karen 241
Goldman, Alvin 3, 5, 52, 223
Goldstone, Robert 168–169
Gombrich, Richard 72
Gómez, Luis O. 23, 25, 47
Goodale, Melvyn 116
Griffiths, Paul J. 135, 265
Grush, Rick 284
Grzegorczyk, Andrzej 118
Gudmunsen, Chris 23, 110
Gurwitsch, Aron 202

Haack, Susan 118
Hacker, Paul 20
Hadot, Pierre 21
Haidt, Jonathan 5
Halbfass, Wilhelm 19–20, 95–96, 278
Hanson, Philip 14
Hardcastle, V. G. 55
Harman, G. 209
Harvey, Peter 60, 69, 116
Hattori, Masaaki 8, 58, 87, 91–92, 101–102, 119, 153, 155–156, 200, 216, 237, 247, 254

Hayes, Richard 8, 31, 36–37, 45, 87, 98, 107, 111–113, 115, 117, 119, 153, 159, 224, 286
Hegel, Georg W. F. 278
Heidegger, Martin 22, 265
Henry, Michel 50, 264
Herzberger, Radhika 31, 87, 112, 119, 149, 153, 155, 216
Hesslow, G. 230–231
higher order
  theories of consciousness 67
  cognitive processes 90, 101, 116, 178, 189, 199, 202
Hilbert, David 221
Hill, Claire 41, 256
Hirsch, Eric 35
Hirstein, William 54, 209
Ho, Chien-Hsing 47, 153
Honderich, Ted 19
Horgan, Terence 55
Horner, Isaline 60
Houben, Jan 24, 119, 149–150
Hough, Sheridan 5, 279
Hugon, Pascale 5
Hulin, Michel 60
Hume, David 1, 61, 226, 260
Huntington, C. W. 111, 250
Husserl, Edmund 4, 9–10, 12, 35, 41–42, 51–52, 54, 66–67, 104, 171, 193, 201–203, 205, 219, 230, 237, 240–242, 244–246, 248–249, 253, 255–258, 260–261, 263, 265, 267, 278, 281, 283, 285, 291–292, 292, 296
  on imagination 54
  on intentionality 265, 291, 296
  on logical reasoning 41
  on perception 10, 189, 193, 201, 233, 245
  on the life-world 4, 52, 67, 257
  on the perceived as such (noema) 202–203, 237
  on pre-reflective self-awareness 104, 241, 255
  on the reflexive nature of feeling 249
Hutchins, Edwin 4
Hutto, Daniel 284

illusion 60, 64–65, 140, 174–178, 183–184, 187, 190, 232–233
imagery 53–54, 64, 111, 164, 202, 230–232, 260
imagination 54, 59, 65, 83, 102, 111, 152, 157, 198, 249, 260, 281
impaired cognition 84, 86, 102, 183, 188–189, 285–286
inattentional blindness 73
indexicality 29–30, 61, 147, 153, 164, 246–247, 256
individuation, principle of 70, 278
inherence (*samavāya*) 95, 126, 137, 139, 142, 158, 161–163, 217, 251
intentional
  act 13, 51, 104, 111, 150, 200, 205, 211, 225, 232, 241, 259, 262–263, 269, 271, 276, 291, 296, 300, 302
  character of cognition 94, 97, 170, 239, 248, 256, 272, 296
  content 9–10, 107, 115, 176, 198, 201, 205, 230, 237–238, 256, 259, 270–272, 274, 292, 301
  object 103, 106, 166, 205, 232, 237, 240, 242, 259, 269–270, 274, 296
  reference 236, 292
  relation 9, 90, 104, 171, 234, 236, 244, 256, 267, 281
  states 6, 71, 264, 273
  structure of awareness 255, 264, 282
intentionality
  Abhidharma account of 151, 258
  and action 130–131
  constitutive features of 9, 51, 218, 256–257, 263–270, 296, 301
  and aspectual cognition 103–104
  sensorimotor 116, 245, 248
  in meditative states 171–172, 267
  naturalized 205–206,
  and embodiment 233
  and self-awareness 247, 264–267
  of perception 143, 193, 213, 237, 259–260, 265, 270, 296
internalism 10–11, 137, 211–212, 214, 223, 238, 243, 263, 271
intersubjective, basis of experience 66, 211, 219, 226, 241, 257, 294
introspection 70, 77, 90–91, 170, 185, 187, 220, 241, 258, 266, 300

Jackson, Roger 44–45, 47, 297–298
Jaina 89, 136–137

James, William 98, 202
Janzen, Greg 55, 241–242
Jayanta Bhaṭṭa 88
Jayarāśi, 40
Jevning, Ron 229
Jinendrabuddhi 31, 59, 101, 109, 143, 185, 188–189, 225–226, 275
Johnson, Mark 4, 232, 253
Jokic, Aleksandar 19

Kajiyama, Yuichi 97, 103
Kalupahana, David 60, 110
Kamalaśīla 2, 8–12, 14–15, 25, 30, 35, 39–40, 43, 46–50, 52, 57–58, 85–86, 97–98, 100–106, 108–109, 122–146, 148, 150–159, 161–164, 166–167, 170, 172–179, 182–192, 197, 214, 218, 233, 236, 244, 274–275, 281, 285, 287–289, 293, 295–297, 299–301
  argument against meditation entailing unconsciousness 47
  on the aims of a treatise 127–133
  on the definition of perception 145–147
  on simultaneity of cognition 174–177
  on the difference between perceptual illusion and mental delusion 187–189
Kambalāśvatara 285
Kant, Immanuel 14, 35, 118, 201, 217, 237, 243, 247–249, 269, 275, 278–279, 297
Kapstein, Matthew 35, 61, 132, 285
Kaski, D. 231
Katsura, Shoryu 34, 87, 100, 107–108, 112, 121, 153
Katyāyana 148–149, 153
Kātyāyanīputra 57
Keijzer, Fred 117
Keira, Ryusei 127
Kellner, Birgit 43, 156, 235, 256, 262–264
Kelly, Sean 53
Kelly, John 87
Kierkegaard, Søren 22
Kim, Jaegwon 52, 55, 222, 224, 287, 290
Knobe, Joshua 169
Koller, S. 5
Konkle, Talia 53
Kornblith, Hillary 10, 52, 223, 255
Kosslyn, Stephen 53, 230
Krasser, Helmut 44, 102, 109, 188, 197, 226, 275
Kriegel, Uriah 9, 55, 205, 242, 246, 259, 265, 267
Kripke, Saul 28
Krueger, J. W. 268
Kuiji, 254
Kumārila Bhaṭṭa 57, 92–93, 109, 124–125, 138, 140, 144–145, 163, 219, 296
Kunjunni Raja, K. 120

Laine, Joy 89
Lakoff, George 4, 232, 253
Lamotte, Étienne 69, 102, 151, 252
Laurence, Stephen 11, 27–29, 222
life world (*Lebenswelt*) 4, 52, 67, 257
  experience of 67, 257, 284–286, 291
Levine, Joseph 209
Lindtner, Christian 8, 87
Locke, John 10–11, 104, 260
Lokāyata 138, 152, 285
Lowe, E. J. 302
Lusthaus, Dan 291, 295
Lutz, Antoine 44, 229

Mack, Arien 73
MacKenzie, Matthew 235, 291
Macpherson, Fiona 246
Madhyamaka 15, 18, 20, 89, 103, 127, 238, 250, 295
  see also Nāgārjuna; Candrakīrti
Magliola, Robert 111
Mallāvadin 119
Mangan, Bruce 246
Mapelli, Daniela 186
Margolis, Eric 11, 27–29
form (*rūpa*) 65, 79–81, 168
Mathurānātha 90
Matilal, Bimal Krishna 25, 26, 28, 38, 39, 40, 62, 107, 114, 119, 120, 131, 132, 139, 150, 159, 162, 167, 186, 188, 218, 239, 247, 271, 296, 297, 298
Maturana, Humberto 290
Maund, B. 186

McClintock, Sara 8, 15, 20, 42–43, 46, 49, 97, 126–127, 134–135, 227, 295, 299
McDermott, A. C. S. 94
McDowell, John 201
McGinn, Colin 55, 267–268
McIntyre, Ronald 104, 209
McLaughlin, Brian 186, 290
meditative states 44–46, 73, 171–172, 229, 243, 265, 267, 298
Meltzoff, Andrew 294
memory
  argument 264
  episodic 111
  long-term 169, 186
  role in object recognition 186
  and perception 216
mental constituents (*caitta*), 69, 76, 81, 83, 236, 258, 263, 281, 294
Merleau-Ponty, Maurice 9–10, 53, 67, 201, 208–209, 219, 233, 244–245, 248–249, 256, 261, 272–273, 278, 284–285
  on body-schema 248
  on habit 249
  on maximal grip 53, 209
  on perception 208, 233, 249, 256, 260, 272
  on the lived-world 67
  on the character of experience 201
Mervis, C. B. 28
metaphysical idealism 32, 243, 247
Mikogami, Esho 100
Milner, David 116
Mīmāṃsā 20, 22, 24, 59, 87–88, 93, 119, 124, 131, 136, 138, 159, 293
mind (*manas*)
  Abhidharma account of 68–70
  cognitive architecture of 14, 27, 66, 90, 98, 115, 215, 257, 274, 281, 295
mind-body problem 32, 54–55
mindfulness, foundations of 73
Mistry, Freny 279
Mohanty, Jitendra Nath 1, 4, 6, 8, 14, 18, 33, 100, 103, 119, 213, 277–278, 297
Mokṣākaragupta 243
momentariness 13, 89, 97, 110, 113, 135–136, 141, 162, 176, 199, 207, 287, 295
Moore, George E. 12
Moriyama, Seitetsu 97
Morris, Charles 131
Much, Michael 28, 109, 119
Murti, T. R. V. 110
'Myth of the Given' 196, 204, 218, 232, 299
'Myth of the Mental' 201, 300

Nāgārjuna, 21, 35, 40, 45, 65, 87, 110, 125–127, 228, 238, 250
Nagatomi, Masatoshi 45, 100, 254
Nanay, Bence 53
natural kinds 161–162, 201, 210, 228
naturalism 1, 3, 7, 17, 50–52, 54, 219–224, 227, 279, 283–284, 294–295, 301, 303
naturalized epistemology 7, 23, 204, 223, 280, 284, 293
Neisser, Ulric 230
neural correlates of consciousness 282–284
neurophenomenology 283, 290
Newen, Albert 284
Nichols, Shaun 5, 169
Nietzsche, Friedrich 278–279, 299
Nisbett, Richard 5
no-self
  doctrine 58, 60–62, 130
  and agent causation 130
Noë, Alva 4, 54, 175, 231, 261, 282–283, 290
noema 104, 202–203, 233, 267–268
noematic content 102, 202–203, 207, 209, 211, 232, 237
non-deceptive cognition (*avisaṃvādaka*) 182, 187, 190
non-ordinary, cognition 47, 192, 243, 298
non-perception (*anupalabdhi*) 89, 156–157, 169, 179
non-conceptual cognition 9–10, 13, 47, 81, 111, 143, 166, 171, 184–185, 189, 201–204, 211–212, 218, 231, 233, 244–246, 254, 256, 264, 281, 296
  and ecological perception 202
  and meditative absorption 47
  and self-awareness 254
  as noematic content 203

as not bare 202
as perception 13, 189, 204
McDowell's rejection of 201
nonerroneous (*abhrānta*) cognition 83, 101–102, 133, 140, 145, 182–185, 187–191, 199
Nyāya 6, 13, 20, 27, 51, 59, 75, 87–91, 95–96, 99–101, 103, 110, 118, 131, 136–137, 139, 141, 147, 154, 156–157, 159, 165, 194, 199, 216–217, 252, 261, 292–293, 296–297
see also Gautama; Jayanta; Udayana; Uddyotakara; Vācaspati; Vātsyāyana

Obermiller, E. 58
O'Brien, Gerald 259
O'Regan, Kevin 175, 221
object coherence 293
objectivism 7
Oetke, Claus 34, 61, 112, 159
Oliva, Aude 53
Opie, John 259
other minds, problem of 240, 287

Palmer, Stephen 209, 228, 292
panpsychism 55, 282, 290
Papineau, David 3, 167, 302
Parnas, J. 264
Patañjali 44, 131, 149
Patil, Parimal 8, 19, 89, 107, 135
Peacocke, Christopher 181, 246, 302
Pelletier, Francis 14
perceptual
awareness 1, 84, 93, 101, 114, 116–117, 154, 164, 170–171, 177, 183, 185, 187, 195, 198–201, 208–209, 211, 216–218, 227, 231, 241, 249, 254, 270, 296–297
constancy 195, 293
judgment 63, 90, 96, 144, 168, 171, 183, 193–194, 216–217, 232, 281, 296–297
Perdue, Dan 47
personal identity
problem of 10, 61, 288, 294
see also no-self; self-awareness; continuity of awareness
perspectival
character of empirical awareness 2, 84, 90, 193, 226, 244, 254, 300
see also aspect
pervsion (*vyāpti*) 33, 152, 157, 165
Pessoa, Luiz 175, 231
Petitot, Jean 19, 51, 280
phenomenal
character of experience 12, 46, 66, 69, 97, 103, 165, 175–176, 185, 209, 212, 235–236, 242, 245–247, 265, 268, 272, 292–292, 296
consciousness 9, 259, 265, 286
concepts 30, 160, 164–167, 180–181
content 12, 102, 137, 165, 181, 209, 214, 226, 235, 242–243, 253, 265, 272, 276, 292
intentionality 205, 267
qualia 209, 251
self (minimal) 268
see also 'what it is like'
phenomenal concept strategy 29
phenomenological naturalism 3, 17, 50–52, 54, 283–284, 301
see also naturalized epistemology
phenomenological reduction (*epoché*), 44, 66, 171, 202, 204–205, 222, 237, 248, 272, 300
phenomenological tradition 55, 228, 230, 234, 284, 291
phenomenology of perception 8–9, 79, 87, 178, 192, 194, 202, 219, 233, 253, 255
Phillips, Stephen 119, 297
physicalism 30, 62, 79, 186, 282, 287–288, 302
non-reductive 79
reductive 30, 55, 287–289
and panpsychism 282
token 302
see also Cārvāka; Lokāyata
Pind, Ole 8, 87, 105, 153, 182
Pippin, Robert 247, 269
Plantinga, Alvin 5
Pollock, Sheldon 24
Popper, Karl 298–299
Potter, Karl 21, 95
Powers, John 6, 59, 98, 110, 136, 282
pragmatic efficacy (*arthakriyā*) 4, 189, 199, 254, 286

Praśastapāda 89, 95
presence 12, 19–20, 33, 65, 72, 74–75, 84, 86, 107, 114, 149, 172, 177, 179, 192–193, 215, 221, 233, 263, 285
presentation (*pratibhāsa*, *Gegenwärtigung*)
  cognition's mode of 11, 15, 66, 70, 102–103, 176, 199, 236, 240, 258, 260–261, 269, 272–273, 281
  continuous 75
  see also givenness
Priest, Graham 111
principle of clarity/vividness (*spaṣṭa*) 53, 102, 139–140, 172, 176–177, 185
Prinz, Jesse 169
process externalism 117–118, 276
pseudo-perception 183, 185
psychological continuity 294
psychologism 14, 100, 118, 205, 227
Putnam, Hilary 28
Pylyshyn, Zenon 53, 202

qualia 80, 103 200, 203, 206, 209, 235–236, 250–251, 270
Quine, W. V. O. 14, 23, 52, 179–180, 219–220, 222–225, 228, 278

Ratnakīrti 89, 135
realism 43, 68, 96, 106, 118, 142, 144, 154, 214, 229, 279, 292
receptacle consciousness (*ālayavijñāna*), 60, 69, 137, 151, 252–253, 283, 294
recognition (*pratyabhijñāna*) 6, 12–13, 33, 53, 174–175, 185–186, 199, 216, 220, 279, 283, 293
reductionism
  Abhidharma 7
  Buddhist epistemologist's response to 240
  Dharmakīrti on 32
  Hume on 61
  mereological 137, 290
  phenomenological response to 205, 271
  see also phenomenological naturalism
reflexive awareness 2, 15, 32, 235–236, 237, 239–240, 242
reliable cognition (*pramāṇa*) 3, 5, 45–46, 51, 97–98, 135, 193, 195, 225, 237, 247, 268
  as source of knowledge 5, 12–13, 49, 51, 53, 86, 88, 92–94, 111, 113, 117, 119, 121, 129, 184, 190–191, 196–197, 220, 222, 225–226, 237, 243, 262–263, 266, 270
representation 11, 30, 53, 76, 102, 104, 149–150, 169, 175, 202, 205, 226, 233, 244–245, 248, 253, 260, 281–282, 285, 296
representationalism 10–12, 96, 142
resemblance (*sādṛśya*) 11–12, 30, 64, 95–96, 104, 106, 137, 229–230, 247, 260, 292
  relations 11, 96, 106
  theories 229–230
residual impressions (*vāsanā*) 82, 84, 137, 151–152
Rhys Davids, T. W. 60
Ricoeur, Paul 25, 284–285
Rock, Irvin 73
Rorty, Richard 204
Rosch, Eleanor 28, 194–195, 230
Rosenthal, David 242, 259, 270
Ross, Lee 5
Rowlands, Mark 221
Ruegg, David S. 5–6, 36, 44, 47–48, 89

Śākyabuddhi, 25, 101, 109, 138, 196, 300
Sāṃkhya, 59, 75–76, 79, 103, 136
Śāntarakṣita, 2, 8–12, 14–15, 25, 30, 35, 39–40, 43, 46–50, 52, 57–58, 60, 85, 97, 99–106, 108–109, 122–127, 130, 132–135, 137–142, 144–145, 148, 150–158, 160–161, 163–164, 167, 170, 172–173, 178–180, 182–187, 191–192, 212–214, 218, 236–237, 239, 243–244, 251–252, 263–265, 274–275, 281, 285, 287–288, 293, 295–301
  argument for color qualia 164
  definition of perception 145
  on representationalism 104
  on dependent arising 126, 134–135
  on the connection between language and conceptual thought 151–153
Sarathchandra, E. R. 72

Sartre, Jean-Paul 240, 242, 266, 269
Sarvāstivāda 57–58, 96, 181
Sautrāntika 7, 39, 44, 57, 68, 71, 74, 80, 103, 108, 125, 151, 154, 181, 184, 199, 207, 217, 222, 291
Schmithausen, Lambert 253
Schopenhauer, Arthur 278–279
Schouten, Maurice 117
Schwitzgebel, Eric 8–9
Searle, John 176, 241, 283, 290
self
 as witness, 25, 60, 63, 96
 sense of 60–61, 237, 291
self-awareness (*svasaṃvedana*)
 and memory 227
 as constitutive of perception 9, 236–238, 241
 pre-reflective 27, 52, 82, 228, 235, 241, 243, 245, 255, 258, 264, 266, 281 291–292, 296–297
 see also reflexivity; introspection; phenomenal character
Sellars, Wilfrid 9, 108, 142, 195, 197–198, 201, 204, 218–219, 227, 278, 299
sensation (*vedanā*) 42, 53, 57, 59, 63, 65, 67, 72, 80–82, 174, 201–202, 233, 236, 238, 248–249, 251
 pure 201, 249
 see also sense experience; sense data
sense data 9, 12, 194, 215, 267, 272, 299
sense experience 10, 64, 69, 147, 194, 220, 224, 228, 253, 275
sensorimotor
 contingencies of perception 116, 213, 221
 aspect of cognition 121
 aspect of visual perception 175–176
 see also sensorimotor intentionality
Shanks, David 169
Shaw, J. L. 94
Shear, Jonathan 229
Shim, Michael 203–204
Siderits, Mark 6, 19–20, 27, 33, 37, 41, 52, 87, 153, 156, 217, 221, 250, 261, 268
Siewert, Charles 9–10, 245–246, 258, 284
Sinha, J. 58, 76
Sloman, Steven 169
Smith, David W. 104, 115, 230
Smith, Quentin 19
Solso, Robert 183
St. John, M. F. 169
Staal, J. F. 139, 147
Stanley, Jason 24
Stcherbatsky, Theodore 30–31, 33, 45, 102, 110, 278
Steinkellner, Ernst 8, 31–32, 44–46, 99–101, 159, 197, 226, 254
Stich, Steven 5, 52, 223
Stoljar, Daniel 29, 79
Stout, George F. 251
Strawson, Peter 41
Strawson, Galen 6, 205, 271, 282
stream of consciousness 78
structure of awareness 1–2, 217, 255, 264, 269, 295
subject-object relation,
 account of 82, 90, 195, 198, 244
subjectivity 40, 243, 248, 255, 268–269, 284
supervenience 52, 55, 79, 118, 222, 282, 287–288, 290, 302

Taber, John 56, 93, 156
Tanaka, James 186
Thakchöe, Sonam 250
Thomas, Nagel 230
Thomasson, Amie 19, 67
Thompson, Evan 4, 10, 52, 54, 175, 194–195, 221, 231, 264, 268, 282–284, 290, 294
Thurman, Robert 110
Tillemans, Tom 6, 19–20, 23, 31–33, 40, 44, 58, 61, 97, 110–111, 135, 196, 199, 214–215, 217–218, 239, 254, 261, 295, 299
time-consciousness 291
trained perception 196, 220, 300
trope 43
Tucci, Giuseppe 87, 99
Tuck, Andrew 23, 35
Tugendhat, Ernst 241

Udayana 89
Udbhaṭa Bhaṭṭa 287
Uddyotakara 57, 88, 92, 95, 109, 112, 124–125, 136, 144, 146–147, 163, 165, 168, 296

universals
as word particulars 164, 167, 179
and the classical theory of concepts 27
empirical approach to 27–29
and Buddhist nominalism 96–107, 154
Nyāya perspective on 144
problem of 26–77
Upaniṣads 59–60, 62, 64–65, 99, 278

Vācaspati 31
Vaibhāṣika 57, 77, 79, 103, 138, 182, 210
Vājapyāyana 148
van Bijlert, V. 33, 44–45, 155, 216
van der Kuijp, Leonard 26, 31, 44
van Gulick, Robert 284
Varela, Francisco 4, 44, 194–195, 283, 290, 294
Vasubandhu 7, 31, 35, 43, 57–60, 69, 76–81, 83–84, 90, 95, 99, 108, 112, 143, 150–151, 206–212, 236, 238, 250–252, 276, 279, 294
Vātsyāyana 88, 92, 95, 144, 146, 193–194
Velmans, Max 11, 55
verbal dispute 147, 167
Vermersch, Pierre 44, 292, 294
Vetter, F. T. 44–45, 286
Vicente, K. J. 231
Vinītadeva 31, 59, 109, 190, 275
visual awareness 80, 116, 175, 228, 257–258, 286, 292
Vyāḍi 148
volition (*cetanā*) 10, 78, 81, 150–151, 236

Waldron, William 253, 294
Warder, A. K. 60, 110
Weberman, David 7
Weinberg, Jonathan 5
Weiskopf, Daniel 186
Weiskrantz, Lawrence 116
Welton, Donn 42, 249
Westerhoff, Jan 127
'what it is like'-ness 69, 165, 167, 200, 259, 264, 268, 271
see also phenomenal character of experience
Wheeler, Michael 284
White, S 241
Williams, Paul 186, 235, 240, 251, 263–264, 276
Wittgenstein, Ludwig 35, 228, 250, 297
Wood, Thomas 127, 203
Wright, E. 209

Xuanzang 254

Yao, Zinhua 2, 68, 121, 254, 258, 264
Yijing 254
Yogācāra 7, 39, 43–44, 51, 57–58, 64, 68–69, 71, 74, 89, 96–97, 103, 108, 125, 127, 137, 151, 154, 184, 207, 214, 217, 220, 222, 237–238, 253, 263–264, 283, 291, 294–295
yogic perception 46, 92–94, 121, 139, 170, 197, 254, 281, 300
Yoshimizu, Chizuko 212

Zahavi, Dan 10, 104, 202, 241–242, 255, 260, 264, 266, 268, 280, 284, 291
Zeki, Semir 174

www.ingramcontent.com/pod-product-compliance
Ingram Content Group UK Ltd.
Pitfield, Milton Keynes, MK11 3LW, UK
UKHW042005230426
12048UKWH00009B/570

9 780190 253110